# Odilo Globocnik

# Odilo Globocnik

## THE DEVIL'S ACCOMPLICE

MAX WILLIAMS

FONTHILL

*Fonthill Media Language Policy*

Fonthill Media publishes in the international English language market. One language edition is published worldwide. As there are minor differences in spelling and presentation, especially with regard to American English and British English, a policy is necessary to define which form of English to use. The Fonthill Policy is to use the form of English native to the author. Max Williams was born and educated in the United Kingdom; therefore, British English has been adopted in this publication.

Fonthill Media Limited
Fonthill Media LLC
www.fonthillmedia.com
office@fonthillmedia.com

First published in the United Kingdom and the United States of America 2020

British Library Cataloguing in Publication Data:
A catalogue record for this book is available from the British Library



ISBN 978-1-78155-795-2



Typeset in Minion Pro 11pt on 14pt
Printed and bound in England

# CONTENTS

# FOREWORD

THIS PROJECT WAS launched with the intention of delivering an illustrated biography of the man I consider, outside of the Nazi hierarchy, as the most culpable in the planned and almost successfully executed attempt to annihilate the Jews of Europe. I was soon to discover several interesting facets to the history of this unsavoury character. Not only did he play a leading role in the process of murdering the Jews, he was also the arch highwayman in the plunder of their possessions. Additionally, he was responsible for the compulsory uprooting of thousands of Polish non-Jewish citizens, the destruction of their communities, and the trafficking of enforced slave labourers. Often justifiably vilified for his crooked dealings as Gauleiter of Vienna, his function as asset stripper of the Polish Jews is overshadowed by his unquestionable major role in their physical destruction. The ultimate crime of mass murder far outweighs the less significant, but nevertheless considerable, offences of robbery and people trafficking, for obvious reasons. Odilo Globocnik was guilty of them all.

What was his motivation for genocide? Was it anti-Semitism? Was it corruption? Or was it sourced to his desire to provide new territories to enable the Germanic people to expand? The latter explanation may be traced to the need to please his mentor, Heinrich Himmler, whose own implausible ideas of race were allied to that of his own demigod, Adolf Hitler. Globocnik's corruptive behaviour may have been the result of his inability to correctly manage and record his financial dealings. He arrogantly did not genuinely see the need to show from where funds were obtained, or where they were going. This lends itself to malpractice, and although possibly not originally intended, Globocnik took advantage by enriching his own coffers along the way.

It appears that he stole from the Jews to sincerely supplement the business enterprises of the SS, an organisation to which he owed a debt of gratitude in saving his career. And if he personally benefitted economically along the way, who would complain? The system he introduced provided others in lesser roles to supplement their SS salaries, but the vast majority of the wealth plundered by his operations in Poland did find its way into the vaults of the SS in Berlin. Was this the driving force behind the plunder operation which evolved into a murder campaign? What better way of dealing with the victims of one's robbery than to get rid of them altogether?

Emphasis has always been placed upon Globocnik's acts of murder, rather than his resettlement policies. These did not always involve the Jews. Many thousands of Poles were victimised and displaced by the policies introduced by the Nazis during the Second World War. Villages and towns were decimated of their Polish inhabitants, replaced by ethnic Volksdeutsche and even Jews prior to their 'deportation further east'. This is a subject ripe for further research and a consequent book in its own right.

Where Globocnik differs from many of the conventional Nazi gangsters, is the unalterable fact that he was not just a 'desk murderer'. He actually participated in some of the actions carried out in his regions of authority. Not only was he part-responsible for the murder of a Jewish jeweller in a bomb outrage during 1933, but evidence suggests that he did personally supervise the shooting of Jews on at least one occasion. These were 'honours' not experienced by Hitler, Himmler, Heydrich, or Eichmann, as far as we know. Himmler and Eichmann were witnesses to murder, but did not actually participate. Globocnik also actively took part in anti-partisan activities in north-east Italy and Slovenia, some of which attract the justifiable label of 'ethnic cleansing' operations. He was also a junior officer in a SS unit that fought in the Polish campaign in 1939, which gained a reputation for its uncompromising brutality towards the local Polish populace.

Globocnik proved to be an extremely complicated character. His claim to fame is marred by the fact of overwhelming secrecy surrounding a crime of such magnitude that nearly all traces of it were expunged by its perpetrators in an effort to destroy any evidence and avoid retribution. In many cases, they were successful—very little documentary evidence exists. Even obtaining images of pertinent and important figures proved impossible in some cases, such as that of Georg Wippern, despite every effort. Even the tangible evidence of the installations used was destroyed. Perpetrator witnesses were understandably biased towards saving their own necks—when that opportunity appeared forlorn, some took their own lives, almost certainly not out of a feeling of guilt. The captured majority of those who survived must be considered somewhat unreliable. However, their tales, when laced together, provide an overall picture of events.

Very few survivors lived to tell their stories. Those that did, relate tales so harrowing that one is left bewildered by the ability of man's inhumanity to man.

Some survivors were of an advanced age, and it was not uncommon to hear variations of the same events from different people. Some witnesses may have been prone to exaggeration. Generally speaking, most provided similar stories of brutality and a total lack of compassion by the masters for their victims.

The common thread throughout the disturbing events depicted in this study is that a large proportion of those committing the most serious crimes of murder, robbery, kidnapping, and displacement were not German. They were Austrians and Ukrainians, or from one of the Baltic states.

The subject matter and events of this book are so far-reaching that several volumes could be researched and the results would provide ample material for additional publication. For example, Christian Wirth is a subject literally crying out for an academic biography, and I am aware that Lublin historian Michael Tregenza is negotiating with a prospective publisher for an English language account of his life.

Any illustrated book is limited by page numbers, and I hope that I have chosen the correct features to represent Globocnik's life. Globocnik's influence on modern-day Europe should not be underestimated. He was solely responsible for the wholesale movement of entire populations. Homes and families were wrecked, many beyond repair. Whole communities disappeared forever, and surviving descendants were robbed of their futures. Globocnik not only appropriated their assets, but also robbed them of their futures and aspirations; literally, he stole their lives. In these circumstances, it is all the more remarkable that the name Odilo Globocnik is rarely one of the first that slips off the lips of the man in the street when the subject of the Holocaust is discussed. Possibly, this book may help to redress that omission.

Time is the greatest arbitrator of justice, and as it advances through all our lives, we and those who come after us must never forget or repeat the mistakes and the brutality of deeds that man is capable of inflicting upon his fellow human beings. This book should serve as a reminder of the millions, of all nations and religions, who paid with their lives during the greatest catastrophe of the twentieth century; of the numerous mistakes, and the heinous exploits carried out in the name of political policy or simple hatred. Many became victims as they were in the wrong place at the wrong time.

Max Williams
2020

# ACKNOWLEDGEMENTS

No work of this nature would be possible without the assistance of others. Sadly, as age advances on all of us, I find that my list of surviving friends and associates in the field of historical research is diminishing. We have lost some true giants, never to be replaced. For my generation, the Second World War and its immediate aftermath is in living memory. In a few years, the only records of this never-to-be-repeated tragedy of mankind will be the written word, or images captured by the cameras and newsreels.

First and foremost, I must record my sincere thanks to several individuals who provided help and guidance far in excess of that reasonably expected.

In Lublin, Mike Tregenza not only acted as my guide, but provided much valuable information in the form of both advice and copies of documentation. Without his valuable help, this work would never have got off the ground. He is the undisputed tsar of historians for the Nazi occupation period in Lublin, and the recognised expert on the history of Aktion Reinhardt, especially the death camp at Bełżec and Christian Wirth. His contribution to this study is immeasurable. He provided copies of unpublished manuscripts that proved to be of such value that words of gratitude are insufficient. Much of what I write on Christian Wirth emanates from Mike's exhaustive research on the man, which he kindly allowed me to use. His lecture paper on the disappearance of Lorenz Hackenholt was also extensively utilised. To him, I extend my grateful sincere thanks.

Joseph Poprzeczny of Perth, Western Australia, is a global authority on the enforced resettlement of Slavic peoples by the German authorities in the Second World War. Without asking, he offered and then shipped his entire Globocnik archive from Australia to me in the UK. Joe provided answers to my numerous questions, especially concerning Globocnik's failed love affair with Irmgard

Rickheim, with whom Joe enjoyed a lengthy post-war friendship. My thanks to him will never be sufficient for the assistance he provided.

Another historian of the highest calibre, Maurice Williams of Canada, provided indispensable help. His knowledge of Friedrich Rainer and Austrian Nazism is unsurpassed. He also gave an additional valuable insight into Irmgard Rickheim's post-war activities, having met her in her adopted new home in the USA.

Michal Sika, currently settled in Vienna, worked tirelessly to obtain information from both the Vienna archives and the Austrian author and university lecturer, Dr Johannes Sachslehner. I will always be grateful for his tenacity and hard work.

Stephen Tyas of St Albans, England, provided information and copies from his own archive. Steve is always my port-of-call when I have any question relating to material from the State Archives of the United Kingdom in Kew. His knowledge of the British post-war interrogations of Nazis is immense, and he is extremely willing to share it.

My old friend in the USA, Kurt Gamer, obtained information from the US National Archives at College Park, Maryland, on my behalf. To him, I send my grateful appreciation.

A special mention must be made of the assistance provided by Gerhard Raiss in Eschborn. He went to great efforts to decipher Globocnik's handwriting. Not only did Globocnik write in Sütterlin German, but his handwriting style was almost impossible to read. Gerhard spent hours examining examples of his unusual character composition and execution, in order to arrive at a workable version to translate. Not an easy task. I extend my earnest appreciation and admiration.

In addition, I must register my sincere thanks to the following, all of whom provided help and guidance over the years in the form of their company on field trips, or providing images, documents, or advice:

Carol Amis
Eric-Jan Bakker +
Andrey Bespalov
Wolfram Böttger
Ray Brandon
Katrin Bruennlein
Michael Butler +
Darko Cafuta
Tommaso Chiussi
Herbert Dunkl
Michael Eckert
Stuart Emmett
Peter Etherington
Stefano di Giusto
Jerzy Kowalski +
Erwin Lerner +
Steven 'Eddy' Marz +
Lucio Mircovich
Michael D. Miller
Phil Nix +
Robin O'Neil
John Pickett +
Dr Johannes Sachslehner
Ian Sayer
Kerstin Seemann
Uwe Seltmann
Antun Sontaki
James Townsend +
Mark Yerger +

Added to this list are the contributors who wished to remain anonymous, or those I have simply and regretfully overlooked. Thank you, one and all.

# INTRODUCTION

The concept of Lebensraum (living space in the East for the Germanic people) comprises policies and practices of settler colonialism which proliferated in Germany from the 1890s to the 1940s.[1] The so-called 'September Programme' laid out the territorial policy goals of the Second Germanic Reich in the First World War. Part of this was territorial expansion to the east. In his book *Mein Kampf*, Adolf Hitler dedicated an entire chapter to the concept of Lebensraum. He declared that new territory should be obtained that German people could colonise and that the new land should provide the means to feed them:

> ... we National Socialists consciously draw a line beneath the foreign policy tendency of our pre-War period. We take up where we broke off six hundred years ago. We stop the endless German movement to the south and west, and turn our gaze toward the land in the East. At long last, we break off the colonial and commercial policy of the pre-War period and shift to the soil policy of the future.[2]

Lebensraum became an ideological principle of the Nazi programme, and the geopolitics of Lebensraum developed into the ultimate foreign policy goal of the National Socialist German Workers' Party (NSDAP). This policy justified subsequent German Third Reich territorial expansion into Central and Eastern Europe. To achieve this goal, the indigenous population would have to make way for the new German settlers. The methodology was driven by three possibilities—enforced deportation, enslavement, and death. Those affected were the Jews, the Poles, Ukrainians, Czechs, Russians, and other Slavic nations, all considered racially inferior by the Aryan master race.

Hitler declared before the Reichstag on 6 October 1939:

> At a moment when Germany is struggling to consolidate her own living space, which only consists of a few hundred thousand square kilometres, insolent journalists in countries which rule over 40,000,000 square kilometres state Germany is aspiring to world domination!...
>
> As the most important task, however, to establish a new order of ethnographic conditions, that is to say, resettlement of nationalities in such a manner that the process ultimately results in the obtaining of better dividing lines than is the case at present. In this sense, however, it is not a case of the problem being restricted to this particular sphere, but of a task with far wider implications for the east and south of Europe are to a large extent filled with splinters of the German nationality, whose existence they cannot maintain....
>
> In their very existence lie the reason and cause for continual international disturbances. In this age of the principle of nationalities and of racial ideals, it is utopian to believe that members of a highly developed people can be assimilated without trouble. It is therefore essential for a far-sighted ordering of the life of Europe that a resettlement should be undertaken here so as to remove at least part of the material for European conflict. Germany and the Union of Soviet Republics have come to an agreement to support each other in this matter.[3]

He added, to Wilhelm Keitel on 20 October, that the war was a difficult racial struggle and that the role of the General Government was to 'purify the Reich territory from Jews and Pollacks'.[4] The first steps towards this objective were the invasion and subsequent occupation of Poland in the autumn of 1939. By the time the resultant war was well under way, Jews, Poles, and Gypsies were commonly referred to as 'Untermenschen' ('subhumans').

Australian journalist and historian Joseph Poprzeczny contends that Hitler had no intention of the oft-voiced aim of world domination or of even waging war in the West, and this argument has some basis. Poprzeczny opines that Hitler fought two 'intended' campaigns—those in Poland and the USSR. His other military campaigns in Western Europe, the Balkans, and North Africa were unintentional and were driven by circumstances. Hitler's sole aim, Poprzeczny convincingly argues, was territorial expansion towards the East in order to provide living space for the German Aryan nation.[5] His undisputed racial policies in the occupied conquered lands were a natural progression. By 1942, the hierarchy of the NSDAP still nurtured visions of the East being permanently settled by an ethnic German population.

The historical emphasis of the Nazi war against the Jewish race always takes centre stage, and less attention appears to be paid to other genocidal actions carried out in occupied Europe. This may be attributed to the unwillingness of Jews to let the matter be consigned to the history books. They have been represented in the international arena since the late 1940s by the State of Israel and the World

Jewish Congress. Other non-Jewish victims were, until recent years, constrained politically as being integrated by, or satellite states of, the Soviet Union. Crimes against other ethnic groups are now gaining prominence. In particular, the Poles have complained that discourse about the war focuses too narrowly on Jewish victims. Recognising the criticism, the current German Foreign Minister Heiko Maas called for a change in the German 'culture of remembrance', in relation to the Second World War, to include non-Jewish Polish victims of Nazi crimes. Speaking at an international conference held in Berlin, entitled 'A century of Germany's Poland policy: Tradition—the betrayal of all civilized values—understanding—partnership', Maas recognised Germany's responsibility for causing the suffering and murder of non-Jewish groups alongside the Jews, as well as admitting that Germans have been under-informed about the non-Jewish victims. He declared: 'The unspeakable crimes that Germans committed against, and in, Poland during ... six years are, to this day, a source of shame for us'. He added: '... we also have to admit that even now we do not pay enough attention in Germany to the crimes against Poles'. As examples, he noted Germany did not know enough about 'the almost complete destruction of entire Polish villages in order to create "Lebensraum" for German settlers' and the 'almost complete destruction' of Warsaw after the Warsaw Uprising in 1944, in addition to the 'attempts to take Polish children away from their parents and integrate them into German families'.[6]

According to Polish researchers, 3 million Poles—in addition to the 3 million Polish Jews—were killed by the Nazis. German historian Professor Stephan Lehnstaedt uses the term 'genocidal violence' in relation to Germany's treatment of Polish citizens at the beginning of the war. Lehnstaedt says that from the first day of the war, 1 September 1939, the SS was given full authority to eradicate the Polish intelligentsia. He added that by the spring of 1940, at least 60,000 Polish citizens had been killed. According to Lehnstaedt's research, at the beginning of the occupation, the murderous German agenda was focused on the Polish nation and the Catholic Church, not the Jews. He emphasised that Germans today are unaware that Polish Jews were not the only victims of the Nazis, but that Poles, Ukrainians, Lithuanians, and Belarusians living in Poland had also been victims.[7]

The death in Prague of SS-Obergruppenführer und General der Polizei Reinhard Heydrich, on 4 June 1942, did not have any major effect on the SS policy towards the Jews of Europe. For some months, the German war machine had been utilised as a cover for the execution of a verbal order to exterminate the Jewish race. This instruction, issued by Adolf Hitler certainly no later than December 1941 to his faithful SS disciple, Heinrich Himmler, had resulted in the acceleration of the murders of men, women, and children who had been absorbed by the advancing Teutonic military steamroller.[8]

The plain language of murder was forbidden; it was rarely uttered, and was never committed to the written word. The terms 'evacuation' and 'deportation' began to hold new meaning, and the phrase 'special handling' was introduced to signify killing.

For a year before his death, the special action killing squads—Einsatzgruppen—of Heydrich's Police and SD had been laying waste large numbers of Jewish communities, political commissars, intelligentsia, and prisoners of war, in the western USSR. What remained of the Jews of Poland, after a similar murderous campaign, were herded together into Jewish enclaves. The largest of these ghettos were centred in the cities of occupied Poland, the largest section of which was now termed the 'General Government'. To each large city, Himmler had appointed a new official to control the Police and SS administration of the immediate area. The SS-und Polizei Führer (SSPF) was subordinate to a Höhere SS-und Polizei Führer (HSSPF) who had command of all SS and Police in his military district (Wehrkreis).

Following the lightning defeat of Poland in 1939, Hitler replaced the military administration with a more permanent, civilian authority:

**Decree of the Führer and Reich Chancellor concerning the administration of the occupied Polish territories, 12 October, 1939**

In order to restore and maintain public order and public life in the occupied Polish territories, I order:

**Section I**

The territories occupied by German troops shall be subjected to the authority of the Governor General of the occupied Polish territories, except in so far as they are incorporated within the German Reich.

**Section II**

1. I appoint Reich Minister Dr. Hans Frank as Governor General of the occupied Polish territories.
2. As Deputy Governor General, I appoint Reich Minister Dr. Seyss-Inquart.

**Section III**

1. The Governor General shall be directly responsible to me.
2. All branches of the administration shall be directed by the Governor General.

**Section IV**

The laws at present in force shall remain in force, except so far as they are in conflict with the taking over of the administration by the German Reich.

**Section V**

1. The Cabinet Council for Reich Defence, the Commissioner for the Four Year Plan, and the Governor General may legislate by decree.
2. The decrees shall be promulgated in the Verordnungsblatt für die Besetzten Polonischen Gebiete.

**Section VI**

The chairman of the Cabinet Council for Reich and Commissioner for the Four Year Plan, and also the Supreme Reich Authorities, may make the arrangements required for the planning of German life and the German economic sphere with respect to the territories subject to the authority of the Governor General.

**Section VII**

1. The cost of administration shall be borne by the occupied territory.
2. The Governor General shall draft a budget. The budget shall require the approval of the Reich Minister of Finance.

**Section VIII**

1. The Central Authority for the occupied Polish territories shall be the Reich Minister of the Interior.
2. The administrative decrees required for the implementing of the present decree shall be issued by the Reich Minister of the Interior.

**Section IX**

1. The present decree shall come into force as soon as, and to the extent to which I withdraw the order given to the Commander-in-Chief of the Army for the exercise of military administration.
2. Authority for the exercise of executive power shall be the subject of special provisions.

[Signed] **Adolf Hitler**
Führer und Reichskanzler
Berlin, 12 October, 1939[9]

The General Governor delegated administrative powers to local Governors:

Warschau: Dr Ludwig Fischer: 26 October 1939–17 January 1945
Krakau: Otto Wächter: 26 October 1939–22 January 1942
Dr Richard Wendler: 31 January 1942–26 May 1943
Ludwig Losacker: 26 May–10 October 1943
Dr Kurt Burgsdorff: 23 November 1943–18 January 1945

| | |
|---|---|
| Lublin: | Friedrich Schmidt: 26 October 1939–1 February 1940[10] |
| | Ernst Zörner: 1 February 1940–10 April 1943 |
| | Dr Ludwig Fischer (Kommissar): 10 April 1943–27 May 1943 |
| | Dr Richard Wendler: 27 May 1943–22 July 1944 |
| Lemberg: | Dr Karl Lasch: 1 August 1941–24 January 1942 |
| | Otto Wächter: February 1942–July 1944 |
| Radom: | Dr Karl Lasch: 28 December 1939–1 August 1941 |
| | Ernst Kundt: 1 August 1941–January 1945 |

Otto Wächter, Friedrich Schmidt, and Richard Wendler were also SS men.[11, 12]

The HSSPF in the General Government was based in Krakow where the seat of government was situated at the Wawel Castle. SS-Obergruppenführer und General der Polizei Friedrich-Wilhelm Krüger answered directly to the Reichsführer-SS in Berlin. This situation created friction with the Governor General, Dr Hans Frank. The two Nazi tsars were constantly at loggerheads. Frank persistently complained to Hitler and Himmler that Krüger ignored his directions. Krüger did not recognise Frank's authority when dealing with security and racial matters, both of which he considered were the domain of the Reichsführer-SS. Krüger also suspected—with justification—that Frank was corrupt.

The largest and most significant Jewish community in the world had been based in Poland for centuries. The focus of Jewish culture was in Poland, mainly as a result of a long period of legal religious tolerance and social autonomy. From the establishment of the Kingdom of Poland in 1025, through to the early years of the Polish–Lithuanian Commonwealth created in 1569, Poland proved to be the most tolerant country in Europe for ethnic and religious minorities. It was known as *paradisus judaeorum* (Latin—'Paradise of the Jews') and it became a refuge for oppressed and exorcised European Jewish communities, developing into the domicile for the world's largest Jewish community of the time. About three-quarters of the worlds Jews lived in Poland by the middle of the sixteenth century. The protestant reformation and the catholic counter-reformation contributed to the destabilisation of the Commonwealth, and Poland's traditional tolerance began to wane from the seventeenth century onwards. After the Partitions of Poland in 1795, and the destruction of Poland as a sovereign state, Polish Jews were subject to the laws of the partitioning powers—the increasingly anti-Semitic Russian Empire, the Austro-Hungarian Empire, and Prussia. As Poland regained independence in the aftermath of the First World War, it was the centre of the European Jewish world with a Jewish community of over 3 million. Anti-Semitism, although prevalent in Europe for many years, began to grow throughout the continent in those years, from both the political establishment and the general population.

One-fifth of the Polish population perished during the Second World War. Half of them were 3 million Polish Jews murdered in the Holocaust—90 per cent of all Polish Jews. Although the Holocaust was largely carried out in the German-occupied territories of Poland and the Soviet Union, there was little collaboration with the Germans by the citizens of Poland. Collaboration by individual Poles has been pronounced as less than in other occupied countries. Post-war statistics of the Israeli War Crimes Commission indicate that less than 0.1 per cent of Poles collaborated with the Germans.[13] Examples of Polish responses to German atrocities varied broadly—from actively risking arrest and execution (sometimes of an entire family) in order to save Jewish lives, through passive refusal to inform on them; to indifference, blackmail, and, in some extreme cases, participation in individual murder and slaughters, such as the Jedwabne pogrom, where approximately 350 Jews were murdered by Polish locals.[14] Grouped by nationality, Poles represent the largest number of people who rescued Jews during the Holocaust.

Hitler declared his intention to destroy the European Jews in speeches and in open conversation prior to the war. In his monotonous bestseller, *Mein Kampf*, he also declared his objective of seizing 'living space in the east' for the Germanic people. As early as 1919, Hitler declared in a letter his support for rational and scientific anti-Semitism.[15] He also called for the Jews to be irrevocably removed from German life, although it is clear he meant by territorial means or by segregation. The notion of systematic murder was still a long way off.

Anyone could be forgiven for thinking the rantings of the failed artist from Austria was political claptrap, but on 30 January 1933, that failed artist was legally appointed by President Paul von Hindenburg as the chancellor of Germany. Approximately 565,000 Jews inherited a leader who hated them. On 22 March 1933, the first concentration camp under the Nazi regime at Dachau opened its gates with the transfer of approximately 200 prisoners from Stadelheim and Landsberg Prisons. A wave of arrests by the Himmler dominated Bavarian Police had placed a great strain on the prisons, and Adolf Wagner suggested congregating a number of them in a fenced enclosure. Himmler declared Dachau to be the first concentration camp for political prisoners.[16]

By April 1933, a boycott of Jewish shops and businesses was in force, and on 11 April 1933, a Nazi decree declared that a non-Aryan was anyone descended from non-Aryan stock, especially Jewish ancestry. One parent or grandparent defined the descendant as non-Aryan, especially if the parent or grandparent was of the Jewish faith. In July 1933, a law was enacted that provided the courts with the power to forcibly sterilise anyone found by a 'Hereditary Health Court' to have genetic defects.

The year 1933 came to an end with the prohibition of Jews from the arts, from owning land, or editing newspapers. The Nazis had also introduced a law that allowed beggars, alcoholics, and the habitually unemployed to be sent to a concentration camp.

The new year provided no relaxation on anti-Jewish policies. The German Labour Front banned Jews, and on 17 May 1934, they lost the possibility of national health insurance. On 22 July 1934, Jews were barred from the legal profession, and on 21 May 1935, they were prohibited from serving in the military.

The Nuremberg Race Laws were introduced on 15 September 1935:[17]

Law for the Protection of German Blood and German Honour
Moved by the understanding that purity of German blood is the essential condition for the continued existence of the German people, and inspired by the inflexible determination to ensure the existence of the German nation for all time, the Reichstag has unanimously adopted the following law, which is promulgated herewith:

**Article 1**

1. Marriages between Jews and subjects of the state of German or related blood are forbidden. Marriages nevertheless concluded are invalid, even if concluded abroad to circumvent this law.
2. Annulment proceedings can be initiated only by the state prosecutor.

**Article 2**

Extramarital relations between Jews and subjects of the state of German or related blood are forbidden.

**Article 3**

Jews may not employ in their households female subjects of the state of German or related blood who are under 45 years old.

**Article 4**

Jews are forbidden to fly the Reich or national flag or display Reich colours. They are, on the other hand, permitted to display the Jewish colours. The exercise of this right is protected by the State. Exercise of this right is protected by the state.

**Article 5**

1. Any person who violates the prohibition under Article 1 will be punished with prison with hard labour.
2. A male who violates the prohibition under Article 2 will be punished with prison or prison with hard labour.
3. Any person violating the provisions under Articles 3 or 4 will be punished with prison with hard labour for up to one year and a fine, or with one or the other of these penalties.

**Article 6**

The Reich Minister of the Interior, in co-ordination with the Deputy of the Führer and the Reich Minister of Justice, will issue the legal and administrative regulations required to implement and complete this law.

**Article 7**

The law takes effect on the day following promulgation, except for Article 3, which goes into force on 1 January 1936.

**Reich Citizenship Law**

The Reichstag has unanimously enacted the following law, which is promulgated herewith:

**Article 1**

1. A subject of the state is a person who enjoys the protection of the German Reich and who in consequence has specific obligations toward it.
2. The status of subject of the state is acquired in accordance with the provisions of the Reich and the Reich Citizenship Law.

**Article 2**

1. A Reich citizen is a subject of the state who is of German or related blood, and proves by his conduct that he is willing and fit to faithfully serve the German people and Reich.
2. Reich citizenship is acquired through the granting of a Reich citizenship certificate.
3. The Reich citizen is the sole bearer of full political rights in accordance with the law.

**Article 3**

The Reich Minister of the Interior, in co-ordination with the Deputy of the Führer, will issue the legal and administrative orders required to implement and complete this law.[18]

On 17 June 1936, Heinrich Himmler was appointed chief of the German Police in the Reich Ministry of the Interior. He immediately delegated Kurt Daluege to command all Gendarmerie and Ordnungspolizei—basically, the ordinary uniformed police. Reinhard Heydrich gained control of the rest—Security Police (Gestapo), SD, Criminal Investigation Police, Frontier Police, and the Counter-Espionage Police. Importantly, Theodor Eicke retained control of the concentration camps administration.

Anti-Jewish rhetoric gained momentum. Alfred Rosenberg, a rabid anti-Semite, is credited with several noteworthy quotes: 'Anti-Semitism is the unifying element of the reconstruction of Germany', quoted in *Famous Trials: Cases that Made History* (page 104), by Frank McLynn in 1995; 'Germany will regard the Jewish question as solved only after the very last Jew has left the Greater German living space.... Europe will have its Jewish question solved only after the very last Jew has left the continent', quoted in *World Politics in Our Time* (page 375) by David C. Jordan in 1970; and 'We let 50,000 Jewish intellectuals get across the border. Just as I wanted Lebensraum for Germany, I thought Jews should have a Lebensraum for themselves—outside of Germany', 15 December 1945, quoted in *Nuremberg Diary* (page 72) by G. M. Gilbert in 1995.

The year 1937 witnessed Jews being gradually squeezed further out of everyday German life a little more. They were disqualified from being accountants and dentists, and prohibited from teaching Germans. They lost all rights to tax reductions and refunds, and were no longer entitled to child allowances. Anti-Semitic exhibitions appeared in Germany, the first being 'the Eternal Jew' exhibition in Munich.

The Austrian Anschluss in March 1938 extended the anti-Jewish policies outside the German borders for the first time and increased the number of Jews within the Greater Reich by approximately 200,000. Most lived in and around Vienna. Heydrich appointed Adolf Eichmann to the newly created office for Jewish emigration in Vienna. The first concentration camp outside Germany opened soon after at a village near Linz called Mauthausen.

Gradually, the Jews were ordered to register their wealth, property, and their business interests. The Nazi authorities gained the knowledge of just how much the Jews were worth. The next step was to prohibit the transfer of this wealth by the withdrawal of permission to trade or provide specific commercial services. The Nazis wanted the Jews gone, but they wanted their assets to remain.

In July 1938, the US government convened a conference at Evian, France, in order to discuss the emigration of the Jews from the persecution of Hitler's Greater Reich. Delegates from thirty-two League of Nation member countries were invited, but agreement could not be reached as no country would agree to accept them.

On 25 July 1938, Jewish doctors were forbidden to practice medicine, and on 17 August, Jewish women were ordered to include the name 'Sarah' on all personal legal documents. Men did not escape—the name 'Israel' was to be added to similar documents. This regulation applied to passports, which soon appeared with a large letter 'J' in red ink stamped on them.

Heydrich ordered the arrest of approximately 17,000 Jews of Polish descent on 28 October 1938. They were shunted to the Polish border, where they were earmarked for expulsion. The Polish government refused to accept them and they were left there confused and without means of support, unable to return to their homes. In desperation, a son of one couple entered the German embassy in Paris on 7 November and fatally shot Third Secretary Ernst vom Rath. In response to Herschel Grynszpan's extreme, but desperate action, Dr Josef Goebbels unleashed the wrath of the Nazis on the innocent Jews of the Greater Reich.

During the night of 9–10 November 1938, Nazi thugs attacked Jewish homes, schools, businesses, and places of worship. Reichskristallnacht marked a turning point in the persecution of the Jews. The policy changed from economic and social expulsion from German life, to one of physical assault. Hermann Göring was in favour of expropriating Jewish assets and thought the wanton destruction of property simply pointless. He complained to Heydrich: 'I'd rather you had done in two hundred Jews than destroy so many valuable assets!'

At a meeting called by Göring on 12 November to discuss the events of Kristallnacht, Göring declared:

> Gentlemen! Today's meeting is of a decisive nature. I have received a letter written on the Führer's orders by the Stabsleiter of the Führer's deputy, Bormann, requesting that the Jewish question be now, once and for all, co-ordinated and solved one way or another. And yesterday once again did the Führer request by phone for me to take co-ordinated action in the matter. Since the problem is mainly an economic one, it is from the economic angle that it shall have to be tackled. Naturally a number of legal measures shall have to be taken which fall into the sphere of the Minister for Justice and into that of the Minister of the Interior; and certain propaganda measures shall be taken care of by the office of the Minister for Propaganda. The Minister for Finance and the Minister of Economic Affairs shall take care of the problems falling into their respective resorts. In the meeting, in which we first talked about this question and came to the decision to aryanize German economy, to take the Jew out of it, and put him in our debit ledger, was one in which, to our shame, we only made pretty plans, which were executed very slowly. We then had demonstrations, eight here in Berlin, we told the people that something decisive would be done, but again nothing happened. We have had this affair in Paris now, more demonstrations followed and this time something decisive must be done! Because, Gentlemen, I have had enough of these demonstrations! They don't harm the Jew, but me who is the last authority for co-ordinating the German economy. If today, a Jewish shop is destroyed, if goods are thrown into the street, the insurance company will pay for the damages, which the Jew does not even have; and furthermore, consumer goods belonging to the people, are destroyed. If in future, demonstrations, which are necessary, occur, then, I pray, that they be directed, so as not to hurt us. Because it is insane to clean out and burn a Jewish warehouse, then have a German insurance company make good the loss. And the goods, which I need desperately, whole bales of clothing and what not, are being burned and I miss them everywhere. I may as well burn the raw materials before they arrive. The people of course, do not understand that. Therefore, we must make laws which will show the

> people once and for all, that something is being done. I should appreciate it very much if, for once, our propaganda would make it clear that it is unfortunately not the Jew who has to suffer in all this, but the German insurance companies. I am not going to tolerate a situation in which the Insurance companies are the ones who suffer.
>
> Under the authority invested in me, I shall issue a decree, and I am, of course, requesting the support of the competent government agencies, so that everything shall be processed through the right channels, and the insurance companies will not be the ones who suffer. It may be, though, that these insurance companies may have insurance in foreign countries—if that is the case, foreign bills of exchange would be available which I would not want to lose. That shall have to be checked. For that reason, I have asked Herr Hilgard of the insurance companies to attend, since he is best qualified to tell us to what extent the insurance companies are protected against damage, by having taken out insurance with other companies. I would not want to miss this under any circumstances. I should not want to leave any doubt, Gentlemen, as to the aim of todays meeting. We have not come together merely to talk again, but to make decisions, and I implore the competent agencies to take all measures for the elimination of the Jew from German economy and to submit them to me, as far as it is necessary....
>
> Now the foreign Jews. There we'll have to make distinctions between the Jews who have always been foreigners and who shall have to be treated according to the laws we arranged with their respective countries. We shall try to induce them through slight and then through stronger pressure, and through clear manoeuvring, to let themselves be pushed out voluntarily. But regarding those Jews who were Germans, have always lived in Germany, and have acquired foreign citizenship during the last year, only because they wanted to play safe. I ask you not to give them consideration. We'll finish with these. Or have you any misgivings?[19]

As a mark of irony, Göring therefore ordered that the Jews themselves be fined 1 billion Reichsmarks in order to pay for the damages. In one simple move, he created the policy of 'atonement', which would have repercussions on the Jews in the approaching Holocaust. On 14 December 1938, Göring was officially placed in charge of resolving the Jewish Question.

One of his first actions was to direct Heydrich to accelerate the emigration of the Jews. The official policy was still geographical. On 21 February 1939, the Jews were forced to surrender all gold and silver items. The *St Louis*, a Hamburg-America transatlantic liner, sailed from Hamburg bound for Cuba on 13 May 1939. Aboard were 937 passengers, the vast majority of which were Jews who had applied for US visas and already had transit visas or landing certificates issued by the Cuban Immigration Office. They were unaware that the director of that office was under investigation for corruption and consequently all authorities to land in Cuba issued by him were now revoked.

On arrival in Havana on 27 May, the Cuban immigration authority allowed just twenty-eight passengers to land—one passenger had died at sea. Accompanied by much political discussion, the *St Louis* was eventually ordered to sail from Cuban waters, still carrying its human cargo. The White House flatly refused entry into the USA. Without hope of friendly reception, the *St Louis* was forced to return to Europe on 6 June. However, Britain took 288 passengers, the Netherlands accepted 181, Belgium accepted 214, and France provided temporary shelter for 224. Those in Britain survived the war, apart from one air raid casualty. Of the 620 passengers who returned to the continent, eighty-seven managed to emigrate before Hitler invaded, leaving 532 trapped after Hitler conquered Western Europe. A total 254 fell victim to the Holocaust.

The invasion of Poland on 1 September 1939 sounded the death knell for the Jews of Europe. Poland itself was a country of 3.35 million Jews, the largest in Europe. Heydrich's Einsatzgruppen and the SS-Selbstschutz units were released from their lairs to set about the unsuspecting Polish population. The Polish intelligentsia, mentally ill, disabled patients, and Jews fell victim to the advancing hordes.

The start of the war in Poland also provided Hitler with suitable cover for a policy of euthanasia. It was time to rid Germany of its 'useless mouths' to feed. The Master Race had no room for mentally ill or those disabled souls with no chance of recovery. In October 1939, he seized upon the opportunity to ratchet up his policy of creating the Master Race. On a page of personal headed stationery, he signed an authority for Dr Karl Brandt and Reichsleiter Philipp Bouhler to administer legal euthanasia:

> Berlin, 1. September 1939
>
> Reichsleiter Bouhler and Dr Brandt, M.D. are charged with the responsibility of enlarging the authority of certain physicians to be designated by name in such a manner that persons who, according to human judgment, are incurable can, upon a most careful diagnosis of their condition of sickness, be accorded a mercy death.
>
> [signed] Adolf Hitler[20]

The authority was backdated to 1 September 1939, the day of the Polish invasion. Despite the official opposition to the programme by the church, many victims were inmates of church asylums and they were murdered with the full knowledge of church authorities.

According to the post-war testimonies of Dr Karl Brandt and the former head of the Reich Chancellery, Hans Heinrich Lammers, Hitler favoured the killing of incurables, but he realised that public opinion would not support it. In 1935,

Hitler informed Gerhard Wagner (the Reich doctors' leader) that 'mercy killing' could not be carried out in peacetime. He was provided with an opportunity when petitioned by the parents of Gerhard Kretschmar, a severely disabled child, born in February 1939.[21] Both parents wanted the doctors to mercy kill their son, but were told it was illegal. Hitler sent Dr Brandt to investigate, and on 25 July 1939, the child was dead.

Reichsleiter SS-Obergruppenführer Philipp Bouhler was chief of the Führer's chancellery. On his staff were Viktor Brack and Werner Blankenburg. These two men took the lead on euthanasia. Their names will recur throughout this study. Bouhler was, in effect, the titular head of the euthanasia programme, but he must bear responsibility for his office. Brack had direct responsibility and Blankenburg was more 'hands on'. In fact, it is alleged that Blankenburg was the official who dictated the wording of Hitler's authority to a secretary for typing.

On 21 September 1939, Heydrich instructed his Einsatzkommandos in Poland to gather Jews into ghettos near rail connections in preparation for the future 'final goal'. His directive included the establishment of Jewish councils to implement Nazi decrees.

By the end of September, Poland had been divided up between the Germans and the Soviets (the USSR invaded eastern Poland on 17 September). In excess of 2 million Jews resided in the German sphere; in the Soviet sphere, 1.3 million. Their time was limited.

The year 1939 came to an end with the introduction of an identification measure—all Polish Jews, over the age of ten years, must wear a yellow star. In Berlin, Heydrich and Heinrich Müller agreed that their Jewish expert, Adolf Eichmann, was the ideal candidate to take over the desk dealing with Jewish affairs and evacuations—Gestapo section IV B4. Dieter Wisliceny later described Eichmann in the following terms:

> Eichmann was very cynical in his attitude toward the Jewish question. He gave no indication of any human feeling toward these people. He was not immoral; he was amoral and completely ice-cold in his attitude...[22]

The rabid anti-Semite Julius Streicher published this proclamation in his newspaper, *Der Stürmer*, in January 1940: 'The time is near when a machine will go into motion which is going to prepare a grave for the world's criminal—Judah—from which there will be no resurrection'.[23]

A relatively small number of Reich Jews were included in the deportations to the region near Lublin from late 1939 and early 1940. A strategy for resettlement, known as the Nisko Project, was co-ordinated by Eichmann and resulted in approximately 78,000 Jews, mainly from Bohemia-Moravia, Austria, and Germany, arriving in what was termed the 'Lublin reservation'.[24] The plan was short-lived and was soon abandoned through force of circumstances. The next territorial solution to the Jewish problem was the Madagascar Plan, formulated by Franz Rademacher, head of the Jewish Office in the Foreign Ministry. Presented in July 1940 by Eichmann, it proposed sending all European Jews to the island of Madagascar under a police and SS authority. Rademacher's proposal was for an autonomous state under German supervision, and stated:

> That part of the island not required for military purposes will be placed under the administration of a German Police Governor who will be under the administration of the Reichsführer-SS. Apart from this, the Jews will have their own administration in this territory—their own mayors, police, postal and railroad administration, etc.[25]

The Rademacher–Eichmann plan failed to get past Heydrich's scrutiny, and it was eventually abandoned through force of circumstances and in favour of a more radical solution.

The segregation of the Jews in Poland, herded into walled enclosures, was not the first time Jews had been singled out and forced to live in a specific area. Venice had practised segregating its Jews in the sixteenth century. The word 'ghetto' is derived from the Italian word '*borghetto*', the diminutive of the word '*borgo*' ('little town'). The Nazi-created ghettos in Poland were Jewish 'waiting rooms'. They provided areas in the towns and cities of occupied Poland where the Nazis could ship their unwanted Jews and 'store' them until a decision could be made what to do with them. In many cases, the lack of food and everyday services resulted in a sharp increase in the death rate, and this was viewed as a bonus by the German authorities.

The largest ghetto in Warsaw, eventually holding between 350,000 and 400,000 people, was created on 12 October 1940. It was sealed off on 15 November 1940. The Lodz ghetto—Litzmannstadt—in the Wartheland, was the second largest, holding 164,000 people in May 1940. Over 1,000 ghettos were established, of varying sizes.

Dr Hans Frank was forced to accept thousands of unwanted Jews. In 1941, he stated: 'I ask nothing of the Jews except that they should disappear'. *Der Stürmer* screamed anti-Semitic phrases, increasingly threatening. One declared: 'Now judgement has begun and it will reach its conclusion only when knowledge of the Jews has been erased from the earth'.[26]

Operation Barbarossa burst on to the world stage on 22 June 1941, as Hitler's armies advanced across the Russo-German frontiers. This expanded the Jewish population under German rule by a possible additional 3 million. Hitler and Himmler realised that a more radical solution to the Jewish question had to be found. That summer, Himmler summoned Rudolf Höss from Auschwitz and declared: 'The Führer has ordered the Final Solution of the Jewish question. We—the SS—have to carry out this order.... I have chosen Auschwitz for this purpose.'[27]

On 23 October 1941, Jews were forbidden to emigrate from the Reich. The geographical solution appears to have been superseded by a more extreme resolution. In early November 1941, construction on a new camp at Bełżec, south-east of Lublin, had begun, and on 8 December 1941, a manor house at Chełmno, near Lodz, became operational as a killing centre. The victims were loaded into sealed vans and then driven to a clearing in the forest about 4 km away. *En route*, the exhaust fumes were fed into the airtight rear compartment, killing its occupants. During its two major operational phases, Chełmno took the lives of a minimum 160,000 people, a large number of whom came from the Lodz ghetto.

In the General Government, Dr Frank was keen to deal with 'his' Jews. First, he targeted the Jews of Krakow, declaring on 12 April 1940:

> If the authority of the National Socialist Reich is to be upheld, then it is unacceptable that representatives of the Reich should be obliged to meet Jews when they enter or leave the house, and are in this way liable to infection with epidemics. I therefore intend to clear the city of Krakow, the seat of the Governor-General of the General Government, of Jews, as far as at all possible, by 1 November, 1940. There will be a major operation to move the Jews, on the grounds that it is absolutely intolerable that thousands upon thousands of Jews should go slinking around and occupy apartments in the city which the Führer has granted the great honour of becoming the seat of a high Reich Authority...[28]

On 16 December 1941, he further declared at a cabinet meeting:

> Let me tell you quite frankly: in one way or another we will have to finish with the Jews. The Führer once expressed it as follows: should Jewry once again succeed in inciting a world war, the bloodletting could not be limited to the peoples they drove to war but the Jews themselves would be done for in Europe. If the Jewish tribe survives the war in Europe while we sacrifice our blood for the preservation of Europe, this war will be but a partial success. Basically, I must presume, therefore, that the Jews will disappear. To that end I have started negotiations to expel them to the east. In any case, there will be a great Jewish migration. But what is to become of the Jews? Do you think that they will be settled in villages in the conquered eastern territories? In Berlin, we have been told not to complicate matters: since neither these territories, nor our own, have any use for them, we should liquidate them ourselves! Gentlemen, I must ask you to remain unmoved by pleas for pity. We must annihilate the Jews wherever we encounter them and wherever possible, in order to maintain the overall mastery of the Reich here.... For us the Jews are also exceptionally damaging because

> they are being such gluttons. There are an estimated 2.5 million Jews in the General Government, perhaps. 3.5 million. These 3.5 million Jews, we cannot shoot them, nor can we poison them. Even so, we can take steps which in some way or other will pave the way for their destruction, notably in connection with the grand measures to be discussed in the Reich. The General Government must become just as 'Judenfrei' [free of Jews] as the Reich![29]

In a speech to German soldiers the same month, he declared:

> This war would be only a partial success if the whole lot of Jewry survived it, while we shed our best blood to save Europe. My attitude toward the Jews will therefore be based solely on the expectation that they must disappear. They must be done away with. Gentlemen, I must ask you to rid yourself of all feeling of pity. We must annihilate the Jews wherever we find them and wherever it is possible.[30]

The SS already had its own plans. Himmler had received orders direct from Hitler and was already preparing to take the lead on the destruction of the European Jews. Frank's General Government provided the greatest source to quench Himmler's thirst for 'sub-human material'. The greatest concentration of Jews already at his disposal was in the General Government. Heydrich's murder squads were already cutting a swathe through the ranks of Jews in the western USSR. Himmler looked to his SS and Police commanders in the General Government. He involved Friedrich-Wilhelm Krüger in his plans for the Polish Jews, but Krüger was constantly upsetting Dr Frank. Krüger was a SS man first, and he did not consider Frank as his boss. Frank ruled his region as a king and deemed all, including the SS, as his subordinates. He therefore believed that he had the right to make the decisions concerning 'his' Jews. It would be a while before the realisation that Himmler was much better equipped to deal with the Jewish question in the General Government dawned on Dr Frank.

Reichsmarschall Hermann Göring had not helped matters in July 1941, when, as the supreme head of the Four-Year Plan, he had tasked Heydrich with the solution of the Jewish problem.[31] This placed the national policy towards the Jews squarely in the realm of the SS. In response, Heydrich clearly set out his vision of that policy at the Wannsee Conference on 20 January 1942. Both Frank and Krüger sent representatives to that meeting in the form of State Secretary Josef Bühler and the Krakow SD and Security Police supremo, SS-Oberführer Dr Eberhard Schöngarth.[32] The Himmler-Heydrich partnership required the co-operation of the pertinent government ministries to avoid any future obstruction, and it used the conference to rubber stamp the policy already decided.

Aktion Reinhardt was already underway as the gathered state secretaries and SS personnel sipped their coffees and brandies on the shores of the Wannsee in the dining room of the former Minoux villa. Not in the true sense of the operation, but preliminary steps had already been taken and proverbial wheels set in motion. In a recently discovered letter in Poland, dated 6 June 1942, the word 'Reinhardt' appeared for the first time in the context of an operation.[33] The letter was addressed to the 'SS-und Polizeiführer Reinhardt' at Chopinstrasse 27 in Lublin. A warehouse was situated at this address, which was used for the sorting of items seized from the deportees to camps located at Bełżec and Sobibor. Both were operational by the time of Heydrich's death. Suffice to say at this stage that the name Auschwitz is the most persistent of camps mentioned by the majority of laymen when questioned about the Holocaust. Auschwitz has long been viewed as the central symbol of the Holocaust, and the Reinhardt death camps have received relatively less attention for many years. While Auschwitz had a reasonable number of survivors to reconstruct the history, very few survived the camps of Aktion Reinhardt to convey their experiences. When asked about the role of Lublin in the Nazi genocide programme, most people look puzzled. Why Lublin?

The Reichsführer-SS and chief of the German Police in the Reich Ministry of the Interior, to give Heinrich Himmler his correct title, was a sycophant of his Führer, Adolf Hitler. By the outbreak of war, he wielded incredible power in the structure of the Third Reich. He was a devoted follower of his leader, and he interpreted Hitler's vision of a master Aryan race without any doubts of its defects. Himmler himself could not be described as a typical Aryan type. His physical appearance was reminiscent of that of an archetypal school master. Surprisingly, he commanded unquestionable obedience from the majority of his senior SS lieutenants.

Himmler had a habit of appointing SS officers he knew personally to important posts. When he needed a suitable candidate to control the SS and Police in Lublin, and also to manage a special task in 'deepest, darkest' Poland, he had a particular man in mind. SS-Oberführer Odilo Globocnik, the former NSDAP Gauleiter of Vienna, was a SS officer with a certain reputation. He had fallen foul of Hermann Göring and also the Catholic Church in Vienna, and he was destined to follow an unremarkable career following his enforced removal as Gauleiter. Himmler had other plans. He offered the post of SSPF Lublin to Globocnik who readily accepted.

This appointment triggered a chain of events that catapulted the former Gauleiter into the forefront of the Jewish question. His name would henceforth be linked inexorably with the evacuation of the Jews and eventually their ultimate murder. He ranks among the most prolific killers of Jews and Poles, and yet his name is largely unknown when competing with the likes of Himmler, Heydrich, and Eichmann in the fate of the Jews in occupied Europe. He was an exponent of mass suffocation by carbon monoxide poisoning, as opposed to the more efficient hydrogen cyanide employed at Auschwitz-Birkenau. Yet he succeeded in devastating the Jewish communities in the Polish General Government. He had similar plans for the

Jewish populace of the western USSR. Had the tide of war not turned against Hitler, Globocnik would surely be counted as the single greatest mass murderer in history.

'Globus', as Himmler liked to call Globocnik, was quick to prove that Himmler's opinion of him was correct.[34] He did not accept criticism lightly and often brushed aside rational objections to his ideas with a sweep of his arm. His determination to push through his plans, no matter how sometimes unsustainable, gained him enemies. Undaunted, he would press on, convinced of his infallibility in his efforts to improve his standing in the eyes of Hitler and Himmler. He followed orders to the letter, and if he was unsure of their meaning, he would seek clarification. He demanded strict compliance from his staff, and he usually received it. One of his secretaries, Wilhelmine 'Mimi' Trsek, described him as a 'pleasant boss'.[35] He has been pronounced variously as a 'professional killer' and a 'bloodhound' by post-war authors, in contradiction to the recollections of some of his staff. He supposedly retired to his bedroom after returning from a visit to a camp and stayed there for several days. Allegedly, the visit made a deep impression. He was certainly possessed of a burning ambition and was prone to exaggeration.

He cannot be described as popular among his contemporaries, and, likewise, he did not make friends easily, although he was renowned for throwing lavish parties during his Lublin years. He reserved his judgement of others for his select inner circle, famously declaring, 'Thank God that sow has gone to the butcher' on receipt of the news of Heydrich's demise.[36]

Gauleiter Friedrich Rainer held a special place in Globocnik's inner circle. The two young men worked closely together in their political development, and the relationship evolved into a close friendship which lasted for many years. They complemented each other perfectly—Rainer the more intelligent, capable, and principled; Globocnik driven by personal ambition and an opportunist. Rainer was articulate and a good public speaker. Globocnik, on the other hand, was something of a 'rough diamond' and an ineffective orator. Rainer overlooked his friend's shortcomings and rescued him on several occasions.

For an unknown reason, Himmler also came to his salvation and saw in him just the right man for what he had in mind. Had the Reichsführer not provided Globocnik with an escape from oblivion, he would now be a mere footnote in history.

Globocnik was emphatically a man to be trusted. Not with one's life savings, but to carry out any task he was ordered to do. Himmler chose well. Lublin was earmarked for a unique status in the General Government, and Globocnik was well equipped to ensure Himmler's special task was executed.

# 1

# EARLY DAYS

ODILO LOTHAR LUDOVICUS Globocnik entered this world at Via Guilia 34 in Trieste on Thursday 21 April 1904. The six-storey apartment building still exists to this day and is fronted by a kebab shop. Badly in need of a high-pressure clean at the time of this author's visit in 2007, the non-descript building frontage above the ground floor is typical of late nineteenth-century architecture with a single window balcony on the second floor. The front entrance provides access to numbers 30–36 Via Guilia.

Throughout history, the sovereignty of the town of Trieste has been likened to a ping-pong ball—one minute the subject of one kingdom, the next the subject of another. As the end of the nineteenth century rolled into the twentieth century, Trieste was part of the Austro-Hungarian Empire. It is situated on the northern coastline of the Adriatic Sea, in 1904 only a few miles from the Italian frontier. Its geographic position was of utmost importance to the Habsburg monarchy, providing the empire with a thriving seaport, sitting on the gulf of the same name. This section of coastline was often referred to as the 'Austrian Riviera'. It was considered as the coastal gateway to the Balkan Peninsula. The warm climate, Venetian architecture, and coffee houses were popular with artists, authors, and philosophers, such as James Joyce, Sigmund Freud, Italo Svevo, Dragotin Kette, and Scipio Slataper.

The unreliable Austrian population census of 1910 showed a population of approximately 230,000. Italian was the dominant language, with over 51 per cent of the residents being of Italian descent. Around 25 per cent spoke Slovenian. A small German enclave of around 5 per cent spoke its mother tongue, the remainder consisting of various nationalities and consequential languages. The Globocnik family spoke German at home at the insistence of Globocnik senior, but the young Odilo subsequently learnt fluent Italian at school.

The politicians of the town administration were mainly members of the Italian Liberal National Party, which supported the Italian claim on the sovereignty of Trieste and drew its support from the Italian majority, which lived in the town centre. Included in this number were many Freemasons. In direct opposition to the Italian viewpoint were the Slovenes, who lived mainly in the suburbs of the town and the surrounding villages. The Social Democrats represented the working class, made up of seafarers, dock workers, shipyard employees, and quarrymen. There was also a thriving Jewish community. Regardless of the diametrical opposition of the various political parties, Trieste was not a hotbed of politics. According to historical researcher Ales Brecelj, the first Austrian parliamentary elections that allowed all males of voting age to vote in 1907, only 28,440 Triestans out of 39,821 registered voters actually bothered to exercise their right. It would be true to say that, before the First World War, Trieste relied upon its Italian influence culturally, but financially, it was dependent upon Vienna.

Globocnik's father, Franz Globocnik, was born on 8 February 1870 in Tržič (also known as Neumarktl) near the Austro-Slovene border.[1] Although inside Slovenia, the area was predominantly Austrian. His own father, Franz Johann Globotschnigg (born in 1825), was a professor at the high school in Laibach (today, Ljubljana). He was married to Josefine Stegnar and was descended from a line of physicians. Franz Johann Globotschnigg's father, Rochus Globotschnigg, practiced medicine in Tržič (as did his father, Josef Globotschnigg) and had used his skills during the war against Napoleon I in 1809. The family used the Austrian family name of Globotschnigg (also, Globotschnitsch) until the mid-nineteenth century, when they adopted the more Slovenic version, Globocnik, as a result of an entry in a register by a local priest. The family name is Slovenian in origin, meaning 'from the lower valley'.

The female lineage on the paternal side appears to have been largely ignored, as if the women of the Globotschnigg clan never existed. The same applies to Odilo Globocnik's maternal pedigree. Doubt still exists today over the Globocnik maternal ancestry origins. Odilo's mother, Anna Globocnik, has been variously described as of Hungarian, Slav, or German descent.

Anna Petschinka was born in Werschetz (today, Vrsac in Serbia) on 24 July 1870. The area was known as the Banat and was in the Hungarian part of the Hapsburg Empire. Her father, Wilhelm Petschinka, was a judicial military advisor, and therefore the family was considered middle class. He was killed at the age of forty-nine after being trampled and crushed between two wagons. His wife, Theresia Hagel, died from kidney failure aged fifty-four. The family name, Petschinka, was also of Slovenian origin.

Franz Globocnik was a cavalry officer in the Austro-Hungarian Army, and when the time came for his discharge as an Oberleutnant, he was unable to afford to buy out his commission and, therefore, he was placed on the reserve list of officers. He found employment with the postal service in Trieste.

Franz and Anna were married in the Catholic Church in Slavina, not far from the small town of Postojna, on 24 October 1898.[2] This region is approximately 30 km east of Trieste. Why this particular location was chosen is unclear.

By the time their first child was born, they were living at Via della Caserma 9 (today, Via Trente Ottobre) in Trieste. Hildegardis arrived in late January 1900, but she died of athrepsia (marasmus—severe malnourishment) on 20 April at just three months of age. Her death and funeral are recorded in the records of the Church Sant' Antonio Taumaturgo. A second child was born 8 August 1901. Lydia Matilde Milena was baptised at Sant' Antonio Taumaturgo on 8 September 1901, with Stefan Brann and Teresa Petschinka acting as godparents.[3] Brann was a friend of Franz Globocnik from the postal service, and Teresa appears to be a relative of Anna Globocnik.

The Globocnik family moved to Via Guilia 34 before the arrival of a baby boy on 21 April 1904. He was delivered in a home birth by midwife Eugenia Tyrichter, who performed a similar role at the births of both Lydia and Henrica. Odilo Lothar Ludovicus was baptised in the catholic faith on 19 July 1904 at the Church of San Vivanni Decollato. The godparents were Ludovicus Hullerl and his wife, Elisa, both close family friends and possibly relatives. There is no record of the name Odilo being used by the family prior to this occasion. An ancient duke of the Bavarian aristocratic family Agilolfinger was named Odilo in the eighth century. The name derives from 'Odhil', meaning 'manor' or 'property'. Lothar was a common Germanic name and Ludovicus was almost certainly influenced by that of his godfather. It appears that the family may have lived at Scorcola 300 (today via dei Cordaroli) from the end of 1904 until 1907. A fourth child, Henrica Maria, was born on 21 August 1909 at Via Molin Grande. She was known as Erika and was baptised on 23 October 1909 at Sant' Antonio Taumaturgo on 23 October 1909, with Maria Pratiwa acting as godmother. Why the family returned to this church is not clear, but by 1913, the family home was confirmed at Via Molin Grande 42 on the fourth floor (today, Via Guglielmo Marconi 36).

From 1910, Odilo attended the local elementary school in Trieste, and he achieved good grades. Franz Globocnik was appointed as a senior post official, the IX Class of state officials, on 26 August 1913, in the Post Direction of Trieste. His salary was 2,800 Kronen per year, plus an activity allowance of 960 Kronen per year. By the outbreak of the First World War, Odilo's father had decided upon a military career for his son.

Franz Globocnik himself was recalled to military service, but he was not suitable for frontline active duty as a result of a stomach condition. He served behind the line at Landschütz (today, Bernolakavo) near Pressburg (today, Bratislava). One advantage of this posting is that his family were able to move nearby. He was promoted to Hauptmann on 1 November 1917. Franz was discharged from the army with the cavalry rank of Rittmeister and died of tuberculosis on 1 December 1919 in Klein Sankt Paul, once again an employee of the postal service.

The date that the family moved from Trieste to Austria is in dispute. Little is known of the family history between 1915 and 1923. Police registration records in Klagenfurt indicate the family was there in 1923 and the Trieste Police records of that year confirm the departure. Various researchers have suggested 1915, 1918, and 1923 as the removal date, but it is likely that the family left Trieste in 1915 and headed for Austria, via Cseklész in Slovakia (then part of Hungary).[4] Correspondence from both Anna and Franz Globocnik show the family was resident in Getriedegasse, Klagenfurt, from late 1918. The municipal clerks of Trieste were informed that the family was no longer in the city from 1915. Where they settled in those intermediate years is open to conjecture, but several sources indicate Odilo attended the elementary school in Landschütz—Cseklész (now Bernolákovo) in 1915. This was the location of his father's military posting. It may well be that the German-speaking Globocnik family felt more secure in an eventual move further inland, away from a return to a town with an Italian-speaking majority, so close to the frontier with the enemy Italian Kingdom. It makes sense that family events of 1915 signalled the initial move.

In order to prepare for a place at a military cadet institution in the Habsburg Empire, boys from all walks of life could apply to attend a military secondary school. All applicants had to have completed an elementary primary education and be in possession of a qualifying report. They also had to sit and pass an entrance examination. Pupils of the military lower secondary schools, who had reached fourteen years of age and had completed the fourth year with sufficient success, were transferred to the first year of an infantry cadet school. The Militär-Unterrealschule at St Pölten was originally founded in 1856. From 1875, it was designated as a military lower secondary school. The school's sole aim was to prepare its students for one of the military academies. One of the students in 1885 was the famous poet Rainer Maria Rilke. His time at the school was not happy. Today, the site is occupied by the Federal School Centre, since the original building was destroyed in 1945.

With the outbreak of war, the Globocnik family declared their allegiance to Austria. On Monday 13 December 1915, Odilo Globocnik entered the Militär-Unterrealschule at St Pölten. As the son of an officer, Odilo's school fees were subsidised by the Ministry of Defence. The family had to pay the meagre sum of 28 Kronen per year towards his tuition fees. During his period there, his class reports reflect a conscientious student with an obvious flair for military life. He was described in various reports as 'very talented and very diligent'. Also, 'very decent with pleasing manners … exemplary adaptation'. He was 'serious, willing, reliable, cheerful, ambitious and kind'. For 'special skills', it is noted that Odilo Globocnik was a violinist.[5] For the school year 1916–1917, Globocnik came eighth in a class of forty-nine. The outcome of the war decided his future, and with the defeat of Austria, his ambitions for a military career, for the time being, came to an abrupt conclusion. His family adopted the theory that the Austro-German alliance had been 'stabbed in the back' and the seeds of anti-Semitism had been sown.

The Globocniks formally became Austrian citizens at the end of 1918. The exact date of Odilo's departure from the military school, as a fourth year student, is unknown, but was sometime in late 1918 or early 1919. Initially, he attended the Realschule in Klagenfurt for five months.[6] From 1919, Odilo enrolled in the Higher State Technical School for Mechanical Engineering at Lastenstrasse in Klagenfurt, studying constructional engineering. The school originated from the mid-nineteenth century and was extended in 1911 when converted to a state vocational school. The school was damaged during air raids in the Second World War. Globocnik joined the nationalistic and anti-Semite student movements, 'Markomannia' and 'Teutonia'. As in all German and Austrian schools after the Second World War, the students and teachers were forced to watch the film *Death Mills* about the evils of National Socialism. They responded by chanting Nazi slogans out loud. While a student there, Globocnik was threatened with expulsion at a meeting of teachers on 30 April 1921, probably as a result of his political agitation. However, he completed the course and graduated on 11 July 1923 with distinction.

By 1923, the Globocniks were firmly established in Klagenfurt. The death of Franz Globocnik left the family struggling financially, and Odilo, now the only male, took odd jobs to make ends meet, including one as a baggage porter at the railway station.[7] Anna Globocnik was awarded a monthly pension of 160 Kronen per month. She began a lengthy dispute with the Post Directorate, claiming that the grade of her late husband entitled her to a higher pension. The family home was a rented apartment at Getreidegasse 3, on the first floor. Globocnik lived in this small apartment with his mother and two sisters. Lydia later married a photographer, Karl Pommerhanz, and had a daughter, Henrika 'Henny' Maria. They moved to St Martin in the west of Klagenfurt. Anna Globocnik and her daughter, Erika, would move to an apartment at Bahnhofstrasse 65 in 1939.[8] Not far away from Getreidegasse was the location of the Café Lerch at Wiener Gasse 10, at the junction with Heuplatz.

The Café Lerch became a famous jazz venue in post-Second World War years, but during the interwar period, it was a café restaurant named after its owner. His son, Ernst, was born on 19 November 1914, and would learn the restaurant and hotel trade working as a waiter in Switzerland, France, and Hungary during the early 1930s. By the late 1920s, the café was regularly frequented by the young men of Klagenfurt for political discussion with their beverages. It became a political hotbed of intrigue as the extreme right-wing Germanic nationalist cause began to emerge as the most influential among the café clientele. Today, the building still exists, albeit with major alterations. During the 1960s, under the ownership of Ernst Lerch, it was famed as the Tanzcafé Lerch and was a regular venue for popular music artist Udo Jürgens. Remodelled as a fast-food outlet, it transformed into a Wienerwald chicken restaurant, before becoming a branch of the McDonald's chain.

Around 1922, Globocnik made the acquaintance of Emil Michner, a retired Austrian Oberstleutnant and campaigner for Austrian sovereignty over Carinthia. Two former college friends, the sons of an officer acquaintance of Michner, introduced Globocnik to him in the Café Lerch on the occasion of a dance evening. Michner's two daughters, Grete and Herta, accompanied their father. The hard-up Globocnik had fashioned a suit out of his late father's former uniform, but his efforts failed to disguise the original tailoring, much to the amusement of the two girls. Michner's officer friend was indignant at their immature behaviour, and he invited the embarrassed Globocnik to join them at their table.

Even as a teenager, Globocnik was an above-average dancer. He organised dances and was popular with the ladies as a dance partner. He was described as an introvert, but good hearted.[9] One took a particular shine to the young man, with a certain amount of encouragement from her father. In 1922, Margarete 'Grete' Michner was fifteen years old, born in Maria Saal, not far from Klagenfurt.[10] Obviously smitten by the older Globocnik, she listened to his unpolished and somewhat monotonous opinions on politics. Her father was an Austrian nationalist who took the impressionable Globocnik under his wing. He genuinely liked the young man, and when the couple announced their engagement in 1923, possibly under some pressure by Michner, he welcomed Globocnik into his family as a father would a long-lost son. It would seem, however, that not all older women found Globocnik as pleasing. His future mother-in-law, Else Michner, remained unconvinced as to his motives with her daughter. Her opinion was that he was dull and over-eager.[11]

The young Globocnik displayed early signs of his organisational skills while arranging dance evenings at the café. His ambition also played a part in his selection of dance partners. Those women who could provide something of use to the aspiring youth found themselves being whisked around the dance floor.

Around this time, Globocnik started to become politically active. His Lebenslauf in his SS file, written in his own hand, states that he had already participated in the skirmishes with Slovenian supporters and that he had been awarded the Cross of Carinthia.[12] However, Pucher points out that a surviving list of recipients of this award does not include the name Globocnik.[13] According to Globocnik, he was involved with local paramilitaries in clashes and acts of sabotage around Grafenstein and Bleiburg, during the plebiscite campaign in the period immediately after war.

By reason of his age, had he taken part in the skirmishes, it is most likely he had been a runner or messenger. He strongly advocated Austrian sovereignty over Carinthia in opposition to the claims of Yugoslavia.

In 1922, Globocnik joined the Austrian NSDAP and the fledgling SA.[14] The Café Lerch was a meeting point for like-minded young men, and it may have been for this very reason that Globocnik began to frequent the establishment. His face at the café began to appear frequently and soon became almost a permanent fixture. Emil Michner's nationalist right-wing beliefs certainly reinforced and encouraged his future son-in-law's views, as they did subsequently those of a new young friend, Paul Gasser. Globocnik not only preached National Socialist policies, he actively helped organise local SA units. This was a period of revolutionary politics, and across the border in southern Germany, Adolf Hitler was leading the German NSDAP towards the doomed Putsch of November 1923.

Globocnik became acquainted with staunch Carinthian anti-Slovene protagonists, such as the rabid anti-Slovene Alois Maier-Kaibitsch, born in Leoben on 20 May 1891. Both Rainer and Globocnik respected and praised Maier-Kaibitsch, and later described him in glowing terms: '... a willing helper at all times ... a valuable political adviser, as the most important secret employee and nationally valuable force'.[15]

Maier-Kaibitsch was appointed in 1936 to the National Council of the Fatherland Front and was also the National Political Advisor for the mixed language area of the Carinthian Gauleitung. After the Anschluss, he became a member of the Carinthian State Government and was appointed to the Ribbentrop Bureau. He evolved into the central figure for National Socialist Slovene policy, but this position became superfluous after the invasion of Yugoslavia in 1941. However, Maier-Kaibitsch had already overseen the forcible evacuation of around 2,500 Slovenians from Carinthia as the prelude to his plans for the enforced relocation of over 100,000 inhabitants. Former SS-Standartenführer Maier-Kaibitsch was sentenced to life imprisonment in 1947. He declared: 'I am not to blame. If it had been up to me, nothing would have been taken away, but something would have been given to everyone else'.[16] He died on 26 November 1958, having been released on medical grounds in 1956.

Michner was well acquainted with the Kommerzialrat Engineer Adolf Wolf, a director of KÄWAG (Kärntner Wasserkraftwerke AG).[17] This company was a hydroelectric construction firm in Carinthia. Michner was able to promote his future son-in-law as a candidate for employment with KÄWAG, since Globocnik had graduated on 11 July 1923. Wolf was impressed enough to offer Globocnik a post with the company, and he started work soon after, eventually working his way up to site manager. His work often took him away from Klagenfurt during the week, but he was able to return home at weekends. It was during this time working away from Klagenfurt that he almost certainly met and befriended the aforementioned builder, Paul Gasser (18 November 1904 to 21 October 1941).

By 1927, he had decided to improve his qualifications, and encouraged by his friend, Paul Gasser, already a master builder, he attended evening classes for the building trade. As the Roaring Twenties began to falter and the economic crash of 1929 brought about the closure of numerous businesses in Austria, Gasser was offered a position in Istanbul. He moved his entire family to Turkey, but he maintained contact with his friend, Globocnik.

Aided once more by his prospective father-in-law in 1930, Globocnik took employment with Robert Rapatz, a construction company in Klagenfurt. Although lacking the necessary qualifications as a building site manager, he nevertheless worked as such at various sites around Klagenfurt. His new positions allowed him to rekindle his relationships with old friends and he began to actively participate in politics once more.

The economic situation in Austria promoted the rise of far-right political parties. Among them was the NSDAP. The agricultural community in Carinthia was hit hard by the financial crash. In former times, the farmers had a good income, but the financial crisis resulted in the majority going into heavy debt. The Nazis seized upon this opportunity and cleverly used propaganda to attract the rural population. In February 1930, the Nazis boasted 820 members in Carinthia; by the end of 1931, their ranks had swelled to 3,600 members, and by the end of 1932, this number had increased to 6,060. The day that the Nazi Party was banned—19 June 1933—it numbered 10,450 illegals.[18] The authorities were in fear of open revolt by the farmers.

Globocnik became a regular visitor to the Café Lerch once again. His interest in politics intensified to such a degree that he joined the German NSDAP on 1 March 1931, and was allocated membership number 442 939. He worked tirelessly for the party, distributing propaganda leaflets. This did not go unnoticed by the local party hierarchy, and he soon graduated towards a more senior role. He was appointed as the Gau Operational Propaganda Leader under Gau Operational Cell Leader Erwin Seftschnigg.

At 7.45 a.m. on 30 August 1931, Globocnik was arrested for trying to communicate with fellow party members incarcerated in the Klagenfurt police cells. After a police interrogation, he was released without charge. That same year, Globocnik became acquainted with a young Klagenfurt lawyer, Dr Friedrich Rainer. The two men met in the office of local party leader, Hubert Klausner, and they formed an alliance that would last until one of them died.[19] Rainer was an above-average intellectual who could hold his own in academic company; Globocnik was more 'hands on'. He was frequently incompetent and was more suited to the working classes. However, they struck up a relationship that began as political colleagues, but developed into mutual admiration and friendship.

Around this time, Globocnik's interest in politics usurped his construction career as the more important element of his life. His time with KÄWAG had sharpened his organisational skills, but his financial acumen remained poor. His 'rough edges' manifested in a willingness to participate in the clandestine elements of political agitation. He was not averse to the use of explosives to sabotage the opposition cause, and he was convicted for the secretion of explosives on his employer's industrial lot for which he served a jail term. On one occasion, he escorted Bishop Adam Hefter of Gurk around the construction site of a seminary in Klagenfurt where he had hidden packages of explosives. The bishop also unwittingly delivered unopened packages containing explosives to illegal Nazis as a favour to Globocnik, believing they contained food.[20]

What is certain is that Globocnik's face appeared on police posters. The surviving police files indicate that he received several terms of imprisonment for illegal political activities:

1. 17 September 1933, six weeks: arrested while driving his car in the company of Karl Glasmug, Otto Drumbl, and Robert Tusch. They were in possession of leaflets of the NSDAP. Emil Michner intervened with Landeshauptmann Hülgerth, an old wartime comrade, and Globocnik was released. He was also allowed to sit the construction examination for his certificate as a master builder.
2. 13 November 1933: arrested as a suspect for bomb atrocities in the Klagenfurt area. He was given 28 days in prison and handed over to the Area Court of Klagenfurt, but was released after eight days when the prosecution dropped all charges.
3. Following an anonymous tip off, on 11 December 1934, the police searched the Krumpendorf house of a young female former nurse named Maria Bauer. She was once employed at the State Mental Hospital in Klagenfurt. Now she worked at an underground Nazi press in Klagenfurt and performed secretarial duties for Globocnik. Incriminating material was found in her house and she was arrested. Globocnik's passport was also discovered, which indicated several trips abroad since February that year. He was arrested the following day and both he and Bauer were handed over to the Regional Court in Klagenfurt, suspected of High Treason. Both denied knowledge of people listed in the incriminating documents and Globocnik declared he had surrendered his passport to a friend in February 1934 in order to return it to the General Consulate in Trieste. He had no knowledge of it after that. A further search of Emil Michner's villa in Krumpendorf on 10 January 1935 uncovered 2,300 Schillings and 350 Lira in a sealed package labelled 'my savings'. Michner stated it belonged to his daughter, Margarete, but she denied it and declared she had received the package from Erika Globocnik at the insistence of Anna Globocnik. Globocnik's mother, Michner, and his daughter were arrested for questioning, but Erika was supposedly skiing and could not be traced. A Klagenfurt civil servant who extended

Globocnik's passport was also arrested and more incriminating evidence was discovered. The 'Globocnik circle' had been discovered and penetrated. Hubert Klausner was arrested on 17 January 1935 and stated he knew Globocnik and his family, but only superficially. Globocnik was found guilty of high treason and sentenced to six months in prison. Upon release, he immediately returned to his old ways.

4. On 22 August 1935, Globocnik registered his address as an 'insurance broker' at Wiedner Hauptstrasse 59/2/7, Vienna, and it was here he was arrested a week later after evidence of treason was discovered during the arrest of his co-conspirator, Friedrich Rainer. He was accused of receiving funds under the name of 'Schlagg', from Emil Klauer, for NSDAP propaganda purposes in Klagenfurt. He was given another six-month sentence for high treason, but was released seventy days early under the terms of a general amnesty for political prisoners.

The files also indicate that a warrant for high treason was also issued. This carried a possible eighteen-month prison term.[21]

Globocnik was suspected of being heavily involved in the murder of a Jewish jeweller. Norbert Samuel Futterweit owned a shop at Meidlinger Hauptstrasse 19 in Vienna. In April 1933, stink bombs were thrown into his shop and anti-Semitic posters were pasted on the windows. At 10.30 a.m. on 12 June 1933, a package making a buzzing sound was tossed into the jewellery shop by unemployed waiter Josef Kreil. A shop assistant and a customer called Herr Futterweit, who picked up the package and carried it to the door to throw it out into the street. The package exploded, killing Futterweit and injuring an innocent passer-by, sixty-three-year-old decorator Johann Hodik. Hodik died from his injuries the following day. The attack was believed to have been planned by SS man Max Grillmayer with the co-operation of Globocnik, who escaped to Germany.[22] In Krems, on 19 June 1933, SA men threw grenades at servicemen and sportsmen. The result was a complete ban on the NSDAP and all of its related organisations in Austria.

While still in Istanbul, Paul Gasser joined the NSDAP on 1 May 1933. He returned to Carinthia and settled in Wolfsberg on 31 March 1934. Along with his brother, Herbert Gasser (1910–1971), Paul Gasser became very active in the NSDAP. The two Gasser brothers were the sons of the mayor of Wolfsberg, Gregor Gasser. Herbert Gasser played a role in the failed July Putsch and Paul went to Vienna and then Lublin with his friend, Globocnik. Another important contact was Ernst Ploetz, who had inherited the farming journal '*Unterkärtner Nachrichten*'. He also joined the SS in 1933 and was a good friend of Hitler Youth activist, Franz Novak, one of his employees in the journal print shop.[23] Around this time, Globocnik became acquainted with another Wolfsberg resident. The barber, Karl Tiefenthal, was known by his Nazi underground codename 'Heart'. Tiefenthal followed Globocnik to Lublin in 1940.[24] Among a number of female followers was the young poet Ingeborg Teuffenbach.[25] She became renowned for her poems to the Führer and soon became a close friend of Globocnik. When she married Heinz Capra in November 1937, Globocnik acted as a witness.

In June 1934, Ernst Lerch, the son of the Café Lerch owner, returned to Klagenfurt from Paris where he had been learning his trade at the Hotel Royal in Versailles since September 1932. He had spent much of his free time at the Deutscher Klub, where he was heavily influenced by fanatical National Socialists. Prior to that, he worked in Budapest for two weeks in August 1932 and in St Moritz for two months from July 1931 until September 1931. He had also been in Laibach, Venedig, and Triest.[26] Lerch joined the NSDAP on 1 December 1932 (membership number 1 327 396). On his return to Carinthia, he managed to be appointed as head of the local Sicherheitsdienst (SD)—part of SD-Oberabschnitt 'Österreich'—having joined the SS on 1 March 1934, with membership number 309 700. He also saw service with the Arbeitsdienst from 1 July to 1 November 1934.[27]

Lerch struck up a friendship with the older Globocnik and the two began to associate with other high-profile Nazi sympathisers such as the lawyer Ernst Kaltenbrunner. The young Lerch was not averse to helping Globocnik with his acts of sabotage. They even invented codenames—their group was the 'Kohlmaier family'; Lerch was 'Luise'; and Globocnik 'Herr König', a pseudonym he would use again in 1945. Although Globocnik was ten years Lerch's senior, the two conspirators grew very close and Globocnik even stood as Lerch's best man when he married Gertrude Fercher on 15 August 1938. By this time, Globocnik was already NSDAP Gauleiter of Vienna.

# 2

# CITY OF MUSIC

Globocnik was not involved in the attempted seizure of power and the assassination of Austrian Chancellor Engelbert Dollfuss in July 1934. He did, however, assist some insurgents to escape the Austrian authorities, first by hiding them at the Michner villa and then assisting them across the border into Yugoslavia, from where they escaped to Germany. Globocnik lived for part of the time at the Michner villa at Lannerweg 25 (formerly Messinerweg) in Krumpendorf, a village settled on the north shoreline of the Wörthersee.[1] He was employed officially by the Michners as their gardener. A German national by the name of Graefe also allowed Globocnik the use of his villa for clandestine meetings. The Villa Oblasser was empty for most of the year. Set back from the road in a cul-de-sac, it overlooked Römerweg, just over the road from the Michner villa and was therefore ideal for Globocnik's purpose. He collected membership funds there, aided by Maria Bauer.

From January 1933, Globocnik shared the Carinthian Deputy Gauleiter position with his friend, Friedrich Rainer. This role in a relatively minor political party in Austria was not as important as it later became. His duties consisted mainly of propaganda dissemination. He was also responsible for the communications and intelligence service of the NSDAP in Carinthia. Globocnik's heavy involvement with the NSDAP and his political activities were frowned upon by his employers, and he consequently lost his job with Robert Rapatz in January 1934 when it was discovered he had hidden explosives in a warehouse of the firm. Rapatz himself was arrested as a suspect, but was released when he was able to prove he knew nothing of the explosives.[2] Globocnik then began a lengthy period of unemployment.

Globocnik joined the SS on 1 September 1934 and was allocated membership number 292 776. The period following the failed Vienna coup saw several unsuccessful minor attempts to seize power by force, instigated by various paramilitary groups. Members of the SA were forced to flee Austria or were detained by the authorities. This opened up opportunities for Globocnik and his friend, Rainer, who took advantage of the situation and they rapidly rose in seniority within the local NSDAP. Among the numbers who absconded were Ploetz and Novak. They had participated in the fighting, Novak's rifle butt being pierced by enemy rounds. Ploetz ended up in Leipzig as a student of economics and philosophy, and Novak entered one of the several Austrian Legion camps where he was ideologically moulded for his future role on Eichmann's staff.

Globocnik based his subversive and spying operation in Budapest, and then in Maribor and Munich. He travelled extensively between the cities. Records show that he flew from Venice airport to Munich on at least twelve occasions in a three-year period. He also travelled by train out of Vienna to Munich and back. Ernst Lerch and Reinhold von Mohrenschildt were his main contacts in Austria.

Viewed by some NSDAP members as somewhat of an upstart, even Klausner considered Globocnik unreliable, but described him as having a 'boyish freshness with a farmer's cunning'.[3] Globocnik struggled with written German grammar. A report submitted by him in German had to be rewritten by an embarrassed Rainer as it was almost unreadable. Globocnik denied he was the author, but Rainer suspected otherwise.[4]

By the time Globocnik joined the SS, he had made the acquaintance of the von Mohrenschildt family in Klagenfurt. They were an aristocratic family, originally from Estonia. They were vehemently anti-Communist. The Carinthian cousin, Erich von Mohrenschildt (1879–1943), was married to Valerie and they had three children—Ebba (born 1911; married 1. Natter, 2. Skreiner), Hilde (born 1913; married Hansemann), and Reinhold (8 November 1915, Leifling to 2 November 1990, Klagenfurt).[5] Erich von Mohrenschildt was a successful owner of several bus companies in partnership with a Herr Kaposi, and was a wealthy backer of the Austrian Nazis. He purchased Schloss Freudenberg at Pischeldorf and the adjoining farmlands, intended for his son, Reinhold, but he maintained a Klagenfurt town house at Pernhartgasse 3. This town house evolved into a command base for the Carinthian Nazis.

Rieger describes Reinhold von Mohrenschildt as an 'aloof youngster'.[6] He funded the Krumpendorf branch of the Hitler Youth. Despite the eleven-year age gap, he became a close friend of Globocnik and subsequently acted as a kind of unofficial private secretary. In these early days of their friendship, von Mohrenschildt was keen to help his friend with propaganda work. In 1934, he went to Vienna to study economics and diplomacy, but he continued with his work for the Nazis. Globocnik often stayed at his apartment when in the capital. From 1936, Globocnik charged von Mohrenschildt with the building of a Viennese

SD unit. The young aristocrat followed Globocnik to Poland where he helped administer the resettlement programme. His sister, Ebba, acted as a sort of hostess and housekeeper for Globocnik in Lublin, and eventually married a SS officer on the staff of Globocnik in Lublin.[7] Later in the war, Reinhold von Mohrenschildt maintained an office at Gasometergasse 8 in Klagenfurt, and the Liaison Office for the HSSPF Operationszone Adriatisches Küstenland (Globocnik) was situated next door at Gasometergasse 6.

The group around Globocnik and Rainer contrasted the policies of the Austrian leader of the Nazis, Hauptmann Josef Leopold (1889–1941). Leopold was in favour of an independent Nazi Austria, while Globocnik and Rainer favoured an Austria as part of a German Reich with Hitler at its head. Hitler was keen for the two young Nazis to develop a relationship with the more conservative Arthur Seyss-Inquart. In 1935, at a meeting in Villach chaired by Hubert Klausner, Rainer, and Globocnik discussed the elevation of Klausner to the position of Landesleiter, but Klausner refused. This meeting highlighted the increased stature of the two young leaders within the Austrian Nazi Party. Post-war, SS-Obersturmführer and Kriminalkommissar Adolf Hertz commented: 'Klausner wasn't much good. Rainer was the brains of the party. I've always hated Globocnik. He was a brutal swine; a typical SS man'.[8]

On 16 July 1936, postponed from 10 July for 'communication problems', Globocnik and Rainer were received at the Berghof by Hitler, in the presence of Bormann and Goebbels. Expecting a warm welcome and praise, they were astonished when he rebuked them. The real reason for the delayed reception became obvious. Hitler had met Edmund Glaise-Horstenau—Schuschnigg's representative—on 10 July, and an agreement was reached. Schuschnigg would integrate the nationalist opposition elements in his government. Hitler then explained his position to the incredulous two young Nazis:

> My foreign political actions do not tolerate this burden with Austria. Continuously, I receive complaints about Paris and London and I have to extend the friendly relations with Italy, and I need time to enlarge the Deutsche Wehrmacht.... I need two more years to make politics. Until then the Party in Austria has to keep discipline. The Party has to obey, to make politics with all means, and to stick to the facts.[9]

Globocnik and Rainer pledged their loyalty and undertook to carry out the Führer's wishes. They returned across the border during the night of 16–17 July, arriving at 4 a.m. in Grossgmain. They realised that, if they failed, they could both end up as 'guests' in a concentration camp. They called an immediate meeting of the senior NSDAP representatives of the region to explain their instructions. Agreement was reached to comply with Hitler's instructions, and Globocnik was tasked with the organisation of the new policy.

Josef Leopold was released from the internment camp at Wöllersdorf on 23 July 1936, and he immediately convened a meeting of party activists in Carinthia, in his apartment in Krems on 31 July. Globocnik and Rainer informed Leopold of Hitler's instructions and confirmed their loyalty to Leopold as their leader. Leopold proposed them as his 'special cabinet' with him at its head and they all agreed. However, after only two weeks, Leopold was uncomfortable with the new policy and he mistrusted the two men from Klagenfurt. He feared that they could form an opposition alliance with the Styrian Gauleiter, Walter Rafelsberger, and that they could go behind his back and make direct contact with Berlin, usurping his authority. Leopold decided to marginalise Globocnik and Rainer, but he realised that he had to be patient and cunning.

Meanwhile, the nationalist opposition selected a new leader—the lawyer Arthur Seyss-Inquart. Rainer formed a good relationship with Seyss-Inquart, but Globocnik and the lawyer had an uneasy rapport. The catholic and conventional Seyss-Inquart was unsure how to deal with the young activist, and Globocnik disliked the hesitant Seyss-Inquart, who was not even a member of the NSDAP. Seyss-Inquart was disliked by Leopold even more. Things came to a head in August 1937 when Leopold excluded Globocnik from the party and declared Seyss-Inquart and his followers as 'traitors, scoundrels and riff-raff'. Even Rainer was ostracised and ordered not to contact his friend. This proved Leopold's downfall as Hitler and Himmler supported Globocnik, Rainer, and Seyss-Inquart.

Globocnik fell afoul of the law once again in the spring of 1937. On 8 March, he instructed Karoline Thaler to receive a large sum of money from a lawyer, Dr Heinrich Gmoser. The money was for the NS-Hilfswerk—NSDAP Aid Organisation. Thaler handed over the cash in Klagenfurts Bahnhofstrasse, and Globocnik promptly disappeared with it. He was being observed by the police. A warrant for his arrest for high treason was issued, and it was executed at 12.10 p.m. on 14 July 1937. At 5 p.m. the same day, a call was received from the State Secretary for security, Michael Skubl, ordering Globocnik's immediate release. By now, the young Carinthian had important influence.[10]

The relationship between Globocnik and Margarete Michner was still one of intended marriage, but the former had lost interest in his fiancée. She was still keen, but Globocnik had now found that she was no longer as useful to his ambitions. Her father had also been all but replaced by Heinrich Himmler as Globocnik's mentor. Things had rapidly moved on since the days of local influence required in Klagenfurt. Globocnik was now playing to a larger audience on a bigger stage.

Arthur Seyss-Inquart was born in Stannern on 22 July 1892. He studied law at the University of Vienna and qualified as a lawyer during the last months of the First World War. He became involved with politics and his first association with the Nazi Party was in 1931. By 1937, he was an Austrian state councillor and was an established politician. Although initially not a full member of the NSDAP, he quickly realised its potential and lent his support to Hitler's policies. He held covert meetings with Globocnik in a rear room at the Hotel Regina in Vienna. The two men collaborated, but never became friends.

The pace of events began to accelerate. By 25 January 1938, Globocnik was registered as a 'builder', living at Köstergasse 11/2/22 in the Mariahilf district of Vienna. Around this time, Rainer and Seyss-Inquart were in talks at Garmisch-Partenkirchen with Franz von Papen, the German ambassador in Vienna. Hitler then invited Austrian Chancellor Kurt Schuschnigg to talks in Germany at his mountain retreat, the Berghof, at the Obersalzberg. On 4 February 1938, Schuschnigg accepted the invitation.

At Globocnik's suggestion, Hitler bullied and threatened the Austrian chancellor and his minister for foreign affairs, Guido Schmidt. They were pressurised into an agreement that became known as 'the Berchtesgaden Agreement'. Seyss-Inquart would be appointed as minister of the interior and security, and the Austrian Nazis would be allowed complete freedom of political activities. Hitler then summoned Leopold to Berlin and summarily dismissed him from all his posts.

On 9 March 1938, Schuschnigg travelled by train to Innsbruck where he wanted to announce a plebiscite to decide the fate of Austria. This would clearly scupper Hitler's plans. The Nazi secretary of Minister Guido Zernatto, a close friend of the chancellor, passed on the information to the Nazis. Rainer, Klausner, Globocnik, and Dr Hugo Jury decided to consult with Interior Minister Seyss-Inquart who confirmed the news. They decided to inform Hitler, and Rainer telephoned State Secretary Wilhelm Keppler. Hitler was angered and Keppler was ordered to go to Vienna immediately. Globocnik reported personally to Hitler in Berlin, where Hitler directed him to remain and await further instructions.

The following day, Hitler informed Globocnik to advise Seyss-Inquart that a messenger would soon arrive from Berlin with clear instructions. He also passed on a written instruction, which lifted his hitherto ban on all aggressive actions against the Schuschnigg Government by the Austrian Nazis—the gloves were off. Globocnik flew to Aspern Airport in Vienna where he was met by Rainer, and the two men drove to the Hotel Regina at the renamed Dollfussplatz (today, Rooseveltplatz).

At the hotel, a rapidly convened meeting of the important members of the Nazi movement in Austria discussed the strategy. Dr Ernst Kaltenbrunner, the Austrian SS leader, was not at the meeting but arrived soon after. Globocnik took the lead and decided to keep the Führer's written authority to re-engage in aggressive tactics from the more reluctant Seyss-Inquart. The Carinthian was concerned over the hesitancy shown by Seyss-Inquart. Furthermore, he had worries about the interior minister's favour towards the Catholic movement, which rivalled the Nazis in their quest for dominance. Finally, Rainer declared the three possible outcomes:

1. The withdrawal of the planned plebiscite and the organization of major demonstrations.
2. A demand for the resignation of the Chancellor which would nullify the need for demonstrations.
3. Should Schuschnigg decide to stand firm and fight, all Party leaders must take whatever action is necessary on their own initiative in order to gain power.

Elsewhere, by 11 March 1938, the German 8th Army prepared for invasion under the as-yet unsigned Case 'Otto'. The goal of this operation was to seize power with the will and agreement of the Austrian people. A 'peaceful' invasion.

At 10 a.m., Schuschnigg received his Interior Minister Seyss-Inquart and Minister without Portfolio Edmund Glaise-Horstenau, both by now committed Nazi puppets. Seyss-Inquart concealed the intention to request 'help' from Hitler, but advised Schuschnigg of Hitler's ultimatum—call off the plebiscite by 2 p.m.

Seitezergasse 1, in the Viennese city centre, was the office of Walther Pembaur, the leader of the Volkspolitischen Referat. Here the Carinthian Circle awaited further news. Seyss-Inquart and Glaise-Horstenau arrived at approximately noon and informed their comrades of the current situation. Seyss-Inquart also penned a letter to Schuschnigg, reiterating the ultimatum and threatening to resign as interior minister if the plebiscite was not cancelled. In Berlin, Hitler signed 'Directive no. 1 of Case Otto' at exactly 1 p.m.

Schuschnigg desperately tried to seek out an alternative, both home and abroad. One by one, the foreign governments refused to support him, and at 2.45 p.m., his defiance collapsed and he cancelled the plebiscite. The news was received immediately in Berlin, but Hitler, encouraged by Hermann Göring, issued a further ultimatum at 3.05 p.m.—Schuschnigg and his cabinet must resign, and Seyss-Inquart must be appointed chancellor.

At 3.30 p.m., Globocnik and Kajetan Mühlmann met Glaise-Horstenau at the Federal Chancellery.[11] Glaise-Horstenau confirmed that Schuschnigg was finished and so, Globocnik advised Seyss-Inquart of the latest update and demanded the use of SA and SS units to assist the police with security measures. Soon after, Schuschnigg announced his and his government's resignation. President Wilhelm Miklas refused to appoint Seyss-Inquart as chancellor and offered the post to State Secretary Michael Skubl, who declined.[12] Miklas was therefore forced to decide between Seyss-Inquart as chancellor or immediate invasion by Germany.

Göring telephoned at 3.55 p.m. and demanded to know if Schuschnigg had resigned and if Seyss-Inquart had been appointed. The hesitant Seyss-Inquart delayed in telling him and promised an answer by 5.30 p.m. Meanwhile, Schuschnigg and his diplomats once again appealed to the western powers for help, without success.

Impatient with the pace of events, Globocnik and Rainer drove to the German Embassy in Vienna and there Globocnik telephoned Göring at 5 p.m. He updated the German Reichstag president with the current situation, but he lied when Göring asked him if Seyss-Inquart had been appointed as chancellor.[13] Impatiently, Göring demanded the new cabinet be formed by 7.30 p.m. at the latest, and the two men discussed the names acceptable to Hitler. Included was a brother-in-law of Göring, Dr Franz Hueber.

Göring then reported the facts to Hitler, who postponed the invasion in the mistaken belief that Seyss-Inquart was already chancellor. Göring then made several calls to Vienna, including one to his brother-in-law, Franz Hueber. Hitler chose Hueber as his preferred choice for Austrian foreign minister. Göring also spoke to Seyss-Inquart and it soon became clear that Globocnik had lied to him. He was beside himself with rage, and Globocnik had created an enemy with a long memory. Göring insisted that President Miklas should appoint Seyss-Inquart as chancellor immediately. Failing that, Germany would invade Austria that very night.

On arrival at the government building again, Rainer and Globocnik met once more with Glaise-Horstenau and Seyss-Inquart. The latter refused to present Göring's ultimatum to President Miklas, but the president heard the news from Generalleutnant Muff. Once more, Miklas refused to be cajoled into an appointment by threats, even after meeting Wilhelm Keppler, Hitler's representative.

Rainer and Globocnik were then in favour of 'drastic measures' to take power, but Keppler dissuaded them. In the meantime, Skubl spread the rumour that the Germans had already invaded. This also failed to move the president.

At 8 p.m., Schuschnigg announced his resignation on the radio. In an emotionally charged broadcast, he stated that the Bundespräsident had instructed him to inform the Austrian people that 'we yield to force.'[14] At 8.18 p.m., Seyss-Inquart, still unnamed as chancellor, appealed on the radio for calm and to maintain law and order.

In Berlin, at 8.45 p.m., Hitler ordered Directive No. 2 of Case Otto—the German Wehrmacht would peaceably occupy Austria at dawn on 12 March 1938. Keppler was ordered to present the wording of a telegram, requesting Hitler's assistance, to Seyss-Inquart for his despatch in Vienna.

Hitler remained concerned over the reaction of Italy to the day's events. At 10 p.m., he was relieved to hear from Prince Philipp of Hessen, his representative in Rome, that Mussolini had accepted the Austro-German situation with friendly ease and had no intention to complain. Hitler was pleased with this response and henceforth viewed *Il Duce* as a friendly ally.

Everywhere in Vienna, there was much rejoicing and singing of the Horst Wessel song. The majority of Viennese appear to have accepted German domination with open arms. Klausner, Rainer, and Edmund Veesenmayer (Keppler's adjutant) all sat in the government building preparing a list of ministers. At 10 p.m., the government building was occupied by a contingent of SS men from Standarte 89 under the leadership of the former athlete Felix Rinner.

At 11 p.m., President Miklas asked Seyss-Inquart to take over the affairs of government, but failed to appoint him as Bundeskanzler. This was made possible by Paragraph 84 of the Constitution of May 1934, which required the signature of the president for all decisions by the government. Although this was only a partial victory, the Nazis had a foot in government.

Seyss-Inquart then pressed President Miklas to appoint him legally as chancellor. Just before midnight, the president relented, but on three conditions: the spilling of blood must be avoided; peace and the rule of law must be maintained; and war must be avoided. It was already too late to avoid the German invasion, but Seyss-Inquart still had hopes of preventing it. Globocnik said to him: '... I seized power for you, but I refrained from telling you because you would have dissuaded me from taking any action'.[15]

At 1.08 a.m. on 12 March 1938, from a balcony of the government building, Hubert Klausner made the official announcement of victory: 'I am deeply moved to announce at this solemn hour that Austria is free. Austria is National Socialist!...'

Globocnik and Rainer also appeared on the balcony to the cheering of the crowd below. A location for photographs of the new government was then chosen. It happened to be the room of the chancellor's secretary, Franz Krisch—the same room in which Engelbert Dollfuss had bled to death nearly four years previously.[16]

Klausner, Rainer, Globocnik, Veesenmayer, Kaltenbrunner, and Skubl drove in three cars to Aspern Airfield to greet Reichsführer-SS Himmler on his arrival. His Ju 52 landed just after 4.30 a.m. and Himmler's party disembarked. It included Reinhard Heydrich, Kurt Daluege, and August Meyszner, a former Austrian police officer.[17] Rainer and Globocnik gave up their seats in the car to accommodate the visitors and were left at the airport as the convoy headed to the city centre. Only after waiting for an hour or two were they able to obtain a taxi back to town.

The German 8th Army crossed the frontier into Austria at 8 a.m. on 12 March 1938, and the Republic of Austria ceased to exist. The shouts of 'Ein Volk! Ein Reich! Ein Führer!' echoed around the streets of Vienna and soon spread to far flung outposts of the newly created Greater German Reich.[18] The western powers issued a note of protest. Dr Josef Goebbels's radio address 12 March 1938 (on behalf of Hitler):

> Germans!
> For years we have witnessed the fate of our fellow Germans in Austria with deep distress. An eternal historical bond, severed only by the events of the year 1866, but forged anew in the World War, has from time immemorial destined Austria to take its

place in the German national community and share its fate. The suffering which was imposed on this country, first from outside and then from within, we experienced as our own, and we know that the misfortunes of the Reich caused millions of German Austrians similar anxiety and concern!

When the German nation regained the proud self-confidence of a great People, thanks to the triumph of the ideals of National Socialism, in Austria a new period of suffering and most bitter adversity began. A regime with no legal mandate was attempting by means of the most brutal terror and physical mistreatment as well as punitive and destructive economic measures, to maintain an existence which was rejected by the vast majority of the Austrian People. Thus, we as a great people saw how a numerically small minority, which had simply been able to seize the necessary instruments of power, was suppressing more than six million people with whom we share a common origin. Their political disenfranchisement and the deprivation of their freedom was accompanied by an economic decline which was a shocking contrast to the blossoming of new life in Germany.

Who could blame these unfortunate fellow Germans if they looked toward the Reich with longing eyes? To that Germany with which their forefathers had been united for so many centuries, with which they had once fought shoulder to shoulder in the most terrible of all wars, whose culture was their culture and to which they themselves had contributed their most cherished values in so many areas. To suppress these longings was to condemn hundreds of thousands of people to the most profound spiritual distress. Whereas years ago this suffering was still borne patiently, as the prestige of the Reich steadily increased, the determination to end this oppression became stronger and stronger.

Germans! In recent years, I have tried to warn the former rulers in Austria not to continue on this path. Only a maniac could believe that suppression and terror can deprive human beings of their love of their own People. European history proves that this causes nothing but more intense fanaticism. This fanaticism then forces the suppressor to employ ever more cruel and violent methods, which in turn only increase the revulsion and hatred felt by the victims of this violence. I also tried to convince those in power that in the long run it is impossible, because it is unworthy, for a great nation to be forced constantly to watch as a People of the same nationality are persecuted and incarcerated merely because of their origin, or their allegiance to a People, or their dedication to an idea. Germany alone has had to accept more than 40,000 refugees, 10,000 others have been in jails, prison cells and holding camps in this small land. Hundreds of thousands have been made beggars, reduced to misery and poverty. In the long run, no nation in the world could tolerate such conditions on its borders without itself deserving same disrespect.

In 1936, I tried to find some way which could offer the prospect of alleviating the tragic fate of this German brother nation, and in this way perhaps achieve genuine reconciliation. The Agreement of July 11 was signed only to be breached a moment later. The vast majority remained deprived of their rights. Their humiliating position as a pariah in this state was in no way changed. Anyone who openly supported the ideal of one German nation continued to be persecuted, no matter whether he was a National Socialist street labourer or an old meritorious army commander who had fought in the World War.

I tried a second time to reach an understanding. I attempted to explain to the representative of this regime, who without any legitimate mandate of his own stood before me in my capacity as the elected leader of the German People, I tried to explain to him that in the long run this situation would become intolerable, since the growing outrage of the Austrian People could not be suppressed forever by the increasing use of force, and that from a certain point in time the Reich would find it impossible to continue to stand idly by and silently observe such outrageous treatment.

Today, when even the solution to colonial problems must take into consideration the right of inferior nations to self-determination, it is intolerable that six and a half million members of an old and great civilized People are in practical terms deprived of these rights by the nature of the governing regime. Hence in a new agreement I wanted all Germans in this country to be granted the same rights and be subject to the same obligations. This agreement was to fulfil the terms of the Treaty of July 11 1936.

A few weeks later it unfortunately became obvious that the men of the Austrian government in power at that time had no intention of complying with the terms of this agreement. However, in order to acquire an alibi for their continued failure to grant equal rights to the Austrian Germans, a plebiscite was devised which was intended to finally deprive the majority in this country of its rights! The modalities of this procedure were to be unique. A country which has not had an election for many years, which lacks all the documentation required to compile voters' lists, announces a vote which is to take place within just three and a half days.

There are no electoral lists. There are no voters' cards. There is no scrutiny of the eligibility to vote. There is no obligation to preserve secret ballot. There is no guarantee that the voting will be conducted with impartiality. There is no method of ensuring fair counting of the votes, and so on. If these are the methods to give a regime legality, then we National Socialists in the German Reich were utter fools for 15 years! We went through a hundred election campaigns and took great pains to gain the approval of the German People!

When the late Reichspräsident finally called upon me to form the government, I was the leader of the party which had by far the strongest support in the Reich. Since then I have repeatedly sought to have the legality of my existence and my actions confirmed by the German People, and it was confirmed. If the methods Herr Schuschnigg wanted to use were the right ones, then the plebiscite we once held in the Saar can only have been a device to harass a People whose return to the Reich we

> wanted to make more difficult. We, however, do not subscribe to that view. I believe we can all be proud that it was in this very plebiscite in the Saar that we received such an indisputable vote of confidence from the German People.
>
> The German People of Austria themselves finally rose up in protest against this unprecedented attempt at election fraud. If, however, it was again the intention of the regime to simply crush the protest movement with brute force, the result could only be a new civil war. The German Reich will, however, henceforth not permit Germans to be persecuted in this territory because of their membership in our nation or because they profess certain views. It wants peace and order.
>
> I have therefore decided to offer the millions of Germans in Austria the assistance of the Reich. Since this morning soldiers of the German armed forces have been crossing all of the German–Austrian borders. Armoured units, infantry divisions and SS units on the ground and the German Luftwaffe in the skies, summoned by the new National Socialist Government in Vienna, will ensure that the Austrian People are within the very near future finally given the opportunity to determine for themselves their future, and thus their fate, through a genuine plebiscite. And these units are supported by the will and determination of the entire German nation.
>
> I myself, as Führer and Chancellor of the German People, will be happy once again to be able to enter the country which is also my homeland as a German and a free citizen. The world, however, shall see for itself that for the German People in Austria these days are filled with hours of blissful joy and deep emotion. They regard their brothers who have come to their aid as saviours who have rescued them from great distress! Long live the National Socialist German Reich! Long live National Socialist German Austria!
>
> The Führer, Adolf Hitler.[19]

The new master crossed the frontier into his homeland at Braunau-am-Inn on 12 March. He headed for Linz where he was received by Seyss-Inquart at about 7.30 p.m. From the town hall balcony, Seyss-Inquart declared Article 88 of the 1919 International Treaty of St Germain to be null and void. This article stated that the independence of Austria was unalterable unless the Council of the League of Nations agreed to a modification. Hitler's reply, his first public speech in Austria, stated that it was the will of the German-speaking people that his own homeland be returned to the German Reich. The enthusiastic crowd met these words with applause and cheering. The following day, Hitler drove to Leonding to visit his parents' grave.

By 13 March 1938, Hitler announced to the world the incorporation of Austria to the German Reich. In an interview with G. Ward-Price for the London *Daily Mail*, Hitler was asked: 'Will the developments of today have any effect on the

Anglo-German conversations that are beginning?' He replied: 'On our side, none at all, and I hope none on the British side. What harm have we done to any foreign country? Whose interests have we hurt by falling in with the will of the overwhelming majority of the Austrian people to become Germans? I cannot understand the Anglo-French note of protest. These people here are Germans…'[20]

Hitler entered Vienna on 14 March. His first night in Vienna was described by Pierre J. Huss of the International News Service:

> He took over the royal suite, a high-ceilinged affair of three main rooms done up in much red drapery and furniture of white and gold. The bathroom was modernised, but not much else. The Imperial Hotel definitely had been coasting along on its reputation and made no attempt to rival the up-to-date Bristol and Grand across the way. But Hitler had his reason for coming to the Imperial, and that night he gathered a small circle of intimates around him and talked to them until the small hours of Vienna and his days there. He had [Julius] Schaub, the personal adjutant, pull the glossy boots off his feet and occasionally bring him a glass of warm milk. Then he reclined in loose comfort on the sofa and delved into reminiscences, waxing excited enough to sit up straight and rumple his hair when telling of some of the hard times he had seen in that city.
>
> 'Even as a boy I knew inside of me that I could never reconcile myself to living for very long in a small Austrian village like Braunau,' he told the listeners around him, who were served all the food and drinks they wanted but did not smoke. 'My father wanted me to enter government service but even in those days I had a horror of the Beamte [official] who carries his letters from house to house day by day or who sits for a fixed number of hours behind a desk and fills out the same papers until he can retire on pension. I left home when I was seventeen years old to escape this fearful future and came to Vienna to create my own life….'
>
> 'In the old days the Viennese used to have a sentimental way of saying: "And when I die, I want to go to Heaven and have a little hole among the stars to see my Vienna, my fair Vienna." I didn't feel very much that way. The Hapsburgs and the spendthrifts may have looked at Vienna as a playground and paradise, but to me it was a city going to decay in its own grandeur. Only the Jews made money, and only those with Jewish friends or those willing to do the work for Jews made a decent living. I, and a lot of others like me, practically starved, and some went begging.'
>
> 'I used to walk past the Imperial Hotel of nights when there was nothing else to do and I hadn't even enough money to buy a book. I'd watch the automobiles and the coaches drive up to the entrance and be received with a deep bow by the white-moustached porter out in front, who never talked to me if I came near him. I could see the glittering lights and chandeliers in the lobby but I knew it was impossible for me to set foot inside. One night, after a bad blizzard which piled up several feet

of snow, I had a chance to make some money for food by shovelling snow. Ironically enough, the five or six of us in my group were sent to clean the street and sidewalk in front of the Imperial Hotel.'

'That was the night the Hapsburgs were entertaining. Old Josef [Kaiser Franz Josef] was still alive but he didn't appear. I saw Karl and Zita step out of their imperial coach and grandly walk into this hotel over the red carpet. We poor devils shovelled the snow away on all sides and took our hats off every time the aristocrats arrived. They didn't even look at us, although I still smell the perfume that came to our noses. We were about as important to them, or for that matter to Vienna, as the snow that kept coming down all night, and this hotel did not even have the decency to send out a cup of hot coffee to us. We were kept there most of the night, and each time the wind blew hard it covered the red carpet with snow. Then I'd take a broom and brush it off, glancing at the same time into the brilliantly lit interior, which fascinated me. I heard the music and it made me wish to cry. It made me pretty angry, too, and feel the injustice of life. I resolved that night that someday I would come back to the Imperial Hotel and walk over the red carpet into that glittering interior where the Hapsburgs danced. I didn't know how or when, but I have waited for this day and tonight I am here.'

'I shall have this hotel listed as our party hotel and I shall come here each time I am in Vienna. I shall have it renovated and modernized, but the name shall remain the same. And a red carpet shall be on the sidewalk every time I come so that I can walk over it into the hotel the same as those aristocrats did back in the days when I shovelled snow. I have never forgotten the resolution I made. Providence fulfilled my wish.'[21]

On 15 March, Hitler delivered a speech to a vast crowd on the Heldenplatz:

Germans! Men and Women!
Within a few short days a radical change has taken place in the German Volksgemeinschaft, whose dimensions we might see today, yet whose significance can only be fully appreciated by coming generations. In the past few years, the rulers of the regime which has now been banished often spoke of the special 'mission' which, in their eyes, this country was destined to fulfil. A leader of the legitimists outlined it quite accurately in a memorandum.

Accordingly, the so-called self-sufficiency of this land of Austria, founded in the peace treaties and contingent upon the mercy of foreign countries, was to perform the function of preventing the formation of a genuinely great German Reich and hence block the path of the German Volk to the future.

I hereby declare for this Land its new mission. It corresponds to the precept which once summoned the German settlers of the Altreich to come here. The oldest Ostmark of the German Volk shall from now on constitute the youngest bulwark of the German nation and hence of the German Reich. For centuries, the storms of the East broke on the borders of the Old Mark in the turbulent times of the past. For centuries into the future, it shall now become an iron guarantor of the security and freedom of the German Reich, and hence a safeguard for the happiness and peace of our Great Volk. I know the old Ostmark of the German Reich will do justice to its new task just as it once performed and mastered the old.

I am speaking on behalf of millions of people in this magnificent German Land, on behalf of those in Styria, in Upper and Lower Austria, in Carinthia, in Salzburg, in Tirol, and above all on behalf of the city of Vienna, when I assure the sixty-eight million other German Volksgenossen in our vast Reich listening this very minute: this land is German; it has understood its mission, it will fulfil this mission, and it shall never be outdone by anyone as far as loyalty to the great German Volksgemeinschaft is concerned. It will now be our task to devote our labour, diligence, shared dedication, and joint strength to solving the great social, cultural and economic problems; yet first and foremost to make Austria ever grow and expand to become a fortress of National Socialist willpower.

I cannot conclude this address to you without calling to mind those men who, together with me, have made it possible to bring about this great change—with God's help—in such a short time. I may thank the National Socialist members of the government, with the new Reichsstatthalter Seyss-Inquart at their fore. I may thank the innumerable party functionaries; I may thank above all the countless anonymous idealists, the fighters of our formations who have proven in the long years of persecution that the German, when put under pressure, only becomes tougher.

These years of suffering have served but to strengthen me in my conviction of the value of the German Austrian being within the framework of our great Volksgemeinschaft. At the same time, however, the splendid order and discipline of this tremendous event is proof of the power of the idea inspiring these people. Hence in this hour, I can report to the German Volk that the greatest orders of my life have been carried out.

As the Führer and Chancellor of the German nation and the Reich, I now report to history that my homeland has joined the German Reich.[22]

In a plebiscite on 10 April 1938, 99.73 per cent of those Austrians who voted, were in favour of being absorbed into the German Reich.

# 3

# GAULEITER

THE SHORT-LIVED FEDERAL government of Seyss-Inquart looked like this: chancellor and minister of defence—Arthur Seyss-Inquart; vice-chancellor—Edmund Glaise-Horstenau; foreign minister—Wilhelm Wolf; justice minister—Franz Hueber; education minister—Oswald Menghin; minister for social administration—Dr Hugo Jury; minister of finance—Rudolf Neumayer; minister for agriculture and forestry—Anton Reinthaller; minister for trade and transport—Hans Fischböck; State Secretary of security—Michael Skubl; public affairs secretary—Dr Ernst Kaltenbrunner; special advisor to the chancellor for political affairs—Hubert Klausner; and secretary of state in the federal chancellery—Friedrich Wimmer (from 13 March).

On Sunday 13 March 1938, Seyss-Inquart submitted a bill for the reunification of Austria with the German Reich to the cabinet for its approval. This was duly received and then it was forwarded to President Miklas for his signature. He refused on the grounds that his terms of office oath permitted him only to carry out his duties for an independent Austria. Miklas then resigned and the duties of federal president transferred automatically under the constitution to the chancellor. Seyss-Inquart was therefore in a position to ratify the law himself and Austria was legally incorporated into the Third Reich. The Seyss-Inquart cabinet continued as a state government within the Reich, with Seyss-Inquart as governor. This ceased on 1 May 1939 with the introduction of the Ostmark Law, and the Austrian State Government was dissolved.

Although appointed as a State Secretary in the meaningless Ministry for Political Affairs, effectively, Globocnik—and Rainer—had been left out in the cold. There was no government appointment for either, and they were both at risk of disappearing into obscurity. A new important face then appeared on the block—Josef Bürckel, the Gauleiter for the Saarland, was appointed by Hitler to reorganise the Austrian NSDAP.

Himmler did not waste any time. On 13 March, he replaced Seyss-Inquart's choice of Michael Skubl as security supremo, with Dr Ernst Kaltenbrunner. Skubl was arrested by the Gestapo on 24 May 1938 and was exiled to Kassel in Germany, unable to return to Vienna until 1946. August Meyszner, the inspector for Ordnungspolizei in Austria, did not see eye to eye with his boss, Kaltenbrunner, and the two men clashed. In the chaos of the time, Kurt Daluege was forced to intervene and Meyszner was eventually transferred.

Despite all his efforts over the previous ten years as a diehard Nazi, Globocnik found himself in the political wilderness. He had gained the SS rank of Untersturmführer, effective from 9 November 1937, and he was promoted direct to SS-Standartenführer on 23 May 1938, with retrospective effect from 12 March 1938.[1] However, at this stage in his life, he did not envisage a career in the SS. The jobs that he was allocated were largely temporary, such as the office for the organisation of the plebiscite. He was assigned as a member for Austria in the German Reichstag from 10 April 1938.[2]

Globocnik set up temporary headquarters at the Hotel Kaiserhof, Frankenbergergasse 10, in Vienna. He considered returning permanently to Klagenfurt with his fiancée and even borrowed money from her father to rent an office at Bahnhofstrasse 65/2/12. He registered for the plebiscite at the Hotel Kaiserhof and declared Grete as his wife, an indication that the intended marriage was going ahead.

Prior to the plebiscite, Globocnik approached his new mentor, Heinrich Himmler, and discussed with him and his lieutenant, Reinhard Heydrich, an idea that he, Globocnik, was unhappy he had been overlooked and that he should be considered for the post of Gauleiter in Vienna.[3] As part of his campaign, he visited the office of Rudolf Hess and met Helmut Friedrichs, the Deputy Führer's department head. Friedrichs was a supporter of Globocnik's rival, Christian Opdenhoff, one of Bürckel's minions. Tactically astute, Globocnik was at pains to point out that his nomination for Gauleiter had been as a result of encouragement from Himmler and Heydrich. In turn, Opdenhoff suggested Klausner as Gauleiter in Vienna—Bürckel's choice—but Klausner declined, wishing to return to Carinthia. Klausner proposed Globocnik. Next, Opdenhoff suggested August Eigruber as the new Vienna supremo and attempted to push '… Pg. Globotschnigg [*sic.*] … in the centre of the Party'.[4]

The final decision rested with Hitler, and two weeks later, he made his decision. The influence of Himmler and Heydrich proved too strong for Bürckel and Opdenhoff. Globocnik was appointed as Gauleiter for Vienna on 23 May 1938 in the presence of Hess and Bürckel.

The policies intended for a Globocnik administered Vienna soon became all too evident. He proposed a radical 'brown revolution', expunging all but pro-Nazi ideals. His enthusiasm for the task ahead could not be criticised. He appeared all over the city in a concerted effort to promote himself as the 'people's man'. On 11 June, he was photographed in the morning with Seyss-Inquart outside the State Opera House, collecting funds for the German School Society Südmark. The same afternoon, Reichsminister Dr Goebbels arrived at Aspern Airport where he was received by Globocnik and Seyss-Inquart. The party then moved on to the city hall where Globocnik delivered a rousing speech before 2,200 political leaders. He set out his vision for the future of Vienna: the old values of the city must be smashed, to make way for the new city to rise once again as the Reich cultural city under National Socialist leadership. Unknown to Globocnik, Hitler was already nursing plans to replace Vienna as the cultural centre of the Reich with his old beloved city of Linz.

In the evening of 12 June 1938, Globocnik accompanied Goebbels, Seyss-Inquart, Bürckel, and the new NSDAP mayor of Vienna, Hermann Neubacher, to a performance of *Der Rosenkavalier*, by Strauss, at the Vienna State Opera.[5] Gauleiter Globocnik had little interest in, or knowledge of, opera, but he knew how to impress the Reichsminister who had the most influence over the Führer. The performance was followed by a reception at the city hall where Neubacher thanked Goebbels for relocating the Reich Theatre Festival Week to Vienna.

The following day, at the Vienna State Opera, the Vienna Philharmonic Orchestra presented Handel's Concerto Grosso in D minor, Op. 3, No. 5 under the direction of Karl Böhm. The audience consisted of invited high dignitaries of the NSDAP. Following the opening address by Ludwig Körner, the president of the Reich Theatre Chamber, Dr Goebbels delivered an important speech to the expectant crowd. He announced the formation of a German People's National Theatre and attacked Jewish influence in the arts. The oration was received with tumultuous applause, and the orchestra played the final movement of Schubert's Symphony No. 7. After thanking the 'First Artist of the Reich', Adolf Hitler, the audience rounded off the evening with a resounding 'Sieg Heil!'

A shrewd Globocnik appeared at 4.30 a.m. on 15 June at the historic Naschmarkt, Vienna's famous fruit and vegetable outdoor market. He took the opportunity to speak with the stall holders, market workers, suppliers, and the shoppers about their problems. Making promises to rectify their problems before he left after a few hours, he cleverly endeared himself to that section of the workers. The cameras were not far away.

While gaining the support of the working class, his policies against the Jews were tightened. Michael Skubl's replacement as police president of Vienna was Otto Steinhäusl. One of his first actions against the Jews of Vienna was their prohibition from the parks of the 1st and 9th districts of the city. Jewish children were also to be excluded from all secondary and commercial schools. The hand of Globocnik can be detected moving in the direction of subsequent, more drastic, and final measures.

A junior SS officer in one of Heydrich's departments in Berlin was soon to set up the Zentralestelle für jüdische Auswanderung in Wien (the Central Office for Jewish Emigration in Vienna). Created in August 1938, this office under Adolf Eichmann and his subordinate, Alois Brunner, administered and assisted the legal emigration of Austrian Jews. It also oversaw the seizure of Jewish property and goods, including the building in which it was housed.

The Palais Albert Rothschild at Heugasse 26—today Prinz Eugen Strasse 20–22—was designed and built between 1876 and 1884 by French architect Gabriel-Hippolyte Destailleur, for the Jewish banking Rothschild family. The Rothschild family owned the most valuable art collection in Austria. After the Anschluss, Baron Albert Rothschild fled to England but was forced to sign away his Austrian assets to save his brother, an inmate of Dachau concentration camp. The building at Heugasse 26 was quickly occupied by the SD. After the emigration policy was halted by Himmler, the SS occupants moved out and a postal and communications office was set up in the auspicious surroundings. The building was slightly damaged during the war and was left unoccupied until it was demolished in 1954.

By the end of October 1938, around 50,000 Jews had fled Austria. Not satisfied with this trend, anti-Jewish demonstrations were organised for 5 and 6 October. Jews were openly attacked in the streets, and their houses and shops were damaged. One of the causes of the heightened anti-Jewish measures was the exhibition 'The Eternal Jew', opened by Globocnik in the Nordwestbahnhalle on 2 August 1938. But not all anti-Jewish measures had proved popular—a directive that Jewish doctors were prohibited from practising from 30 September caused chaos when, the following winter, an influenza epidemic ravaged the city. The now defunct surgeries of Jewish doctors were inundated with callers, many of whom had gleefully driven out the previous resident general practitioners.

Elsewhere, on 18 June, Globocnik held a meeting of all senior directors of major firms in Vienna, at which he encouraged them to be more resourceful and to deplete any lavish lifestyle they were following. The following day, the city held a midsummer festival at the Jesuitenwiese meadow in the Prater amusement park, where 300,000 people attended. The usual trio of Seyss-Inquart, Globocnik, and Bürckel were joined by Neubacher and his deputy, Johannes Blaschke. The guest of honour once more was Dr Goebbels, whose speech railed against the democrats of Paris and London. The evening was rounded off with a bonfire and the singing of Nazi songs. Mayor Neubacher promised that the festival would henceforth be an annual event.

During the Hitler Youth propaganda week, 20–27 June 1938, Globocnik encouraged all boys and girls of Vienna to register for the NSDAP youth organisations to become 'fighters for Greater Germany and Adolf Hitler'.[6]

On 30 June, Globocnik spoke at a mass meeting of Viennese operations managers and their senior staff in the Concert House. He promoted the first German Workers'

Front (DAF) holiday to Hamburg and declared that 306,000 Viennese were members of the DAF. He attacked the Jews again and declared that he was responsible for the 'social peace', and if that was to be maintained, he would remove the Jews from the workplace. Here we see another indication of Globocnik's gradual slide towards more radical methods to eliminate the Jews from society. His speech was met with spontaneous and enthusiastic applause.

On 27 July 1938, Globocnik and six others, including old comrades Klausner and Rainer, were officially sworn in as Gauleiter in the ornate Wappensaal of Klagenfurt town hall.[7] At the end of the same month, a NSDAP ceremony and parade in the city marked the fourth anniversary of the failed July Putsch. Rows of Brownshirts marched through the city streets, and a special ceremony was held at the site of the execution of Otto Planetta and Franz Holzweber to commemorate the thirteen executed Putschists.[8] A large stone tablet was inserted in the wall of the chancellery, under the window of the room where Dollfuss was shot and bled to death. Globocnik was a prominent participant at the anniversary parade which proved to be his only real success as Gauleiter.

From July, his old ally and friend, Paul Gasser, joined him in the Gauleitung as his personal advisor. Globocnik's obvious popularity with the city's population, albeit mainly before select audiences, belied his appeal to certain high profile NSDAP officials. Göring had not forgotten Globocnik's lie over the telephone, and soon he would be joined by another strong adversary in the form of NSDAP treasurer Franz Xaver Schwarz.

The attitude of the new Gauleiter towards accounting for Gau expenditure and income can only be described as slapdash. This was sure to gain the attention of the correct Schwarz. Globocnik acquired a new limousine for the use of the Gauleiter on official business. Globocnik recorded the car as a private purchase, but, in truth, it was confiscated from its Jewish owner. This 'oversight' was brought to Schwarz's attention, resulting in an overreaction from Globocnik. Not satisfied with his explanation, and bemused by the upstart Gauleiter's attitude, Schwarz complained to Bürckel. Globocnik was forced to apologise, but not before Schwarz directed Reichsamtsleiter Ludwig Meiler to open a confidential file on the Gauleiter from Vienna.

It soon became obvious that Globocnik's idea of administering his Gau differed from the accepted methods adopted by other Gauleiter. Meiler reported to his boss that he had instructed Party member Globocnik on the correct procedures and that he should not have a 'hands-on' attitude to all financial dealings. He was satisfied that Gauleiter Globocnik would keep correct records and accounts for all transactions.

Both Schwarz and Meiler were soon proved wrong. Ignoring the sound advice from Munich, Globocnik next turned his attention to ways of increasing funds for the Party in Vienna. He liquidated the Vaterländische Front and seized its assets without keeping any books. Taken aback, Meiler reported in September that Globocnik had apparently misappropriated the sum of 1.5 million Austrian schillings. No receipts or invoices existed. This episode instigated an enquiry that lasted for ten months without resolution. Unknown to Munich, Globocnik had set up two private secret accounts, which he used for transactions he wished to remain out of the public eye.

The erstwhile Carinthian building engineer had elaborate plans in the sphere of publishing. His dream was to become a sort of small time press baron—a position from which he could deliver his political message to the masses. Ambition was never his weak trait. He saw the struggling publishing house of Adolf Luser as his entrance ticket. Adolf Luser Verlag published a magazine, *Der getreue Eckart*, well known to Austrian Nazis for its true Aryan stance. Although the firm was having financial problems, Globocnik overlooked this and planned to amalgamate it with the former Jewish fashion publishing house Societät-Graphik. As negotiator, Globocnik appointed the Nazi editor of *Der Türner*, Karl Bauer. The price—300,000 Reichsmark. With an additional loan, the total cost of the transaction eventually amounted to 666,333 Reichsmark. Bauer was the nominal owner, but the real power behind the throne was yielded by the Carinthian trio—Globocnik, Rainer, and Klausner. Globocnik appointed author Bruno Brehm as editor.

All transactions of this nature required the prior approval of the NSDAP treasurer, Reichsleiter Franz Xaver Schwarz. True to form, Globocnik ignored protocol and bulldozed on, without reference to his superior. Schwarz would never forgive the Carinthian upstart for this slight and a powerful enemy now loomed over the unsuspecting young Gauleiter of Vienna.

Globocnik obliged by giving his enemy additional ammunition to fire at him. The building of the former Vaterländische Front was put up for sale at the reduced price of 630,000 Reichsmark. Schwarz's auditors managed to prevent this sale by Globocnik and the building eventually sold for a more realistic 1.2 million Reichsmark. Schwarz was becoming angrier with the 'cowboy' antics of the Vienna Gauleitung. Next, the ageing Schwarz discovered that Globocnik had purchased a building at Johannesgasse 4 in Vienna, intended to house the Union for the Reorganisation and Improvement of Greater Vienna. No prior authority had been sought from Munich. Schwarz also discovered that Globocnik had issued unsecured loans to Rainer and a Hitler Youth official, amounting to 33,000 Reichsmark.

By the end of August 1938, after only three months in office, the Vienna Gau was fast approaching bankruptcy. Schwarz could take no more. The die was cast and Schwarz began to take steps to remove the unreliable Carinthian from office.

On 8 October 1938, sections of the Nazis turned their vitriolic anger towards the Catholics. Young brownshirt extremists entered the Archbishop's Palace and smashed windows and furniture. The curate, Johannes Krawarik, was hurled from a window and lay for hours in the courtyard with a fractured neck. Globocnik distanced himself and the Viennese Nazi Party from the rioting.

Back in Berlin, Hermann Göring had joined the ranks of Globocnik enemies. He had not forgiven Globocnik for his lie and his memory was long. Bürckel approached him with an appeal to 'give the Carinthian one more chance', but Göring and Schwarz were too powerful and determined. Klausner was suggested as a possible replacement. Globocnik, himself, appeared unconcerned by the machinations going on behind his back. Despite a personal request by Bürckel to 'do something positive', Globocnik approached Rudolf Hess for support. It was a bad move. Hess did not possess the necessary attributes or influence to outgun such strong opposition. However, the Gauleiter crisis was soon overshadowed by events.

The annual celebrations in Munich to mark the anniversary of the November 1923 Putsch attracted the party faithful and all senior party members. Globocnik was no exception. He travelled to Munich on 8 November 1938, despite the stirrings of moves to remove him. This particular meeting was overshadowed by the murder in Paris of Ernst vom Rath, by the young Jew, Herschel Grynszpan, and the subsequent anti-Jewish pogrom. Globocnik was in touch with the Vienna Gauleitung office by telephone and passed on instructions for the anti-Jewish action. On his return to the Austrian capital, he was satisfied with the results—4,000 of the 5,000 Jewish shops were closed; approximately 2,000 apartments had been seized; and Jewish stock had been seized and handed over to Aryan shops.

In some areas of the city, the SA hoodlums had sunk to new areas of depravity. Not satisfied with the straightforward arrest of Jewish women, some were compelled to perform for their persecutors. Naked and sexual acts, aimed at acute embarrassment and shame, were forced upon them. When some party members complained that these thugs had overstepped the mark, Globocnik replied: 'What do you want me to do? Jail myself?'[9]

In a clear indication of his corrupt nature, Globocnik gave authority to certain party members to enter Jewish shops, businesses, and homes in order to remove anything that took their fancy. Any Jew who resisted would be arrested. The Gauleiter held the view that Aryans had a right of ownership over Untermenschen (subhumans).

Another embarrassing incident arose when it became evident that Globocnik had been paid for telephone communications with the Reich Chancellery during the days leading up to the Anschluss. He could not account for the money he had received from a Hilfswerk account overseen by Hanns Albin Rauter, an old comrade from Carinthia.[10] Rauter's auditors discovered the payments were 'for political purposes'.

Globocnik's shortcomings were now renowned; Dr Goebbels recorded a diary entry on 25 November 1938: 'Maul reports on Vienna. Much confusion there. One cannot achieve much with this town. Everybody fights all the time, and Globocnik is neither smart nor capable enough to handle it'.[11] Berndt Rieger's description of Globocnik as 'an incompetent blunderer' just about sums up the opinion held by the majority of senior NSDAP members.[12]

In December 1938, Globocnik received Heinrich Himmler in Vienna. The two men got along very well and Himmler pledged his support, but it was not enough and came too late. Even Seyss-Inquart joined the ranks of anti-Globocnik agitators. The situation came to a head with the introduction of new taxes on 1 January 1939. Some workers rioted in Vienna and Globocnik was at a loss of how to deal with them. His old enthusiasm of the previous summer had gone. Although he attended a nationwide Gauleiter meeting on 13 January 1938 in Berlin, he must already have realised his term as Vienna supremo was at an end. On 30 January 1939, Hitler was also convinced and announced Globocnik's resignation as Gauleiter of Vienna. Coincidentally, this was the day that Hitler prophesied the extermination of the Jewish race in a speech before the Reichstag.

Of all the high-profile Nazis in Austria, only Klausner voiced his concern that such a loyal party member should lose his post in such a way. On 12 February 1939, Klausner was found dead in his Vienna apartment, the victim of a stroke. His funeral was attended by Hitler and Hess, with all the usual cronies in evidence.

Meanwhile, the disgraced, now former Gauleiter Globocnik decided to take four weeks' leave, but not in Vienna. He gave up the tenancy on his apartment in Köstlergasse, the police residency registration certificate being noted 'Departed, destination not known'.

Himmler never believed that Globocnik's record of poor financial dealings were ever motivated by personal gain. Not monetary gain anyway. There may be some substance to his belief that his young Carinthian protégé was prompted by promotion and not greed. The usually astute Reichsführer-SS opined that Globocnik was just useless at bookkeeping. Others would argue, with good reason, that the former Vienna Gauleiter had committed grand larceny. Whatever the truth, Globocnik was favoured by Himmler, who may well already have had a particular posting in mind for the former Gauleiter, even at this early stage.

Somewhat puzzled and depressed by the obvious end of his political career, Globocnik looked to the SS for his future. He had held the rank of SS-Untersturmführer from 9 November 1937 and had received promotion to SS-Standartenführer, with effect from 12 March 1938. His position as Gauleiter dictated a higher SS rank, and Himmler duly obliged by promotion to SS-Oberführer on 28 September 1938, backdated to 25 July 1938.[13]

From 1 February 1939, he was transferred from Staff SS-Oberabschnitt Donau to the Personal Staff RFSS. After his vacation, Globocnik and Paul Gasser reported to SS-Standarte 'Der Führer' for military training. The attachment lasted from 1 March to 3 June 1939. The performance report by his superiors recorded that Globocnik was enthusiastic, mentally active, and that he showed a distinct understanding of military procedures. His physical abilities were satisfactory and he was considered an above-average student in combat tactics. He held the SS-Verfügungstruppe rank of SS-Rottenführer der Reserve from 3 June 1939, but he was soon promoted to SS-Unterscharführer d. Res. in mid-1939.

While still on service duty with the SS-Verfügungstruppe, he confidentially informed a concerned future father-in-law that he had been promised an important role, but could not divulge its details. Globocnik also reiterated his intention to marry Grete Michner—music to Emil Michner's ears.

Himmler arranged for his protégé to take further leave on completion of his military service attachment, but first Globocnik underwent a thorough medical examination on 5 June. This was conducted by Dr Hans Kutschera von Aichbergen at the Wilhelmine Hospital in Vienna. The findings were satisfactory: cardio vascular levels were normal; resting blood pressure was 120/70, rising to 130/70 during exercise, and falling to 115/70 after three minutes; lung capacity was 4,400 cubic centimetres; his recorded height was 176 centimetres; and there was no sign of illness or infirmity, other than a nervous sleeplessness. His pulse rate was 82 at rest, 104 during exertion, 88 after 30 seconds of rest, and 80 one minute later. Dr Kutschera noted that his heartrate and breathing were normal, and the restoration of his breathing and pulse rate were excellent. He mentioned a low broadening in the X-ray images, but indicated that this was insignificant.[14] On 5 July 1939, both Globocnik and Gasser were attached to 1 Battalion SS-Standarte 'Germania' in Hamburg-Langenhorn. Himmler's order, dated 24 June 1939, was that both men should gain military experience and train towards gaining the leadership of first a platoon, and then a company.[15]

On 19 August, SS-Standarte 'Germania' was mobilised and transferred to the east, under Generaloberst Wilhelm List's 14th Army command, part of Army Group South.[16] Globocnik was awarded the SS-Totenkopfring on 23 August 1939. In the first days of the war, the former Gauleiter informed the SS Personnel Office that he was now entitled to use the title 'Engineer' and also had been awarded the Sudeten Medal.[17] His final SS-VT promotion to SS-Untersturmführer d. Res. occurred on 1 November 1939, with backdated effect from 30 January 1939.

Next to no information exists concerning Globocnik's battle experiences during the Polish campaign. He certainly experienced being under fire. His postal address during this period was Feldpost 32999, and he was constantly on the move with his unit. Consequently, on 10 October 1939, he had to apologise to Himmler for not replying sooner to an earlier communication: 'Since 19 August I have been on the move as I have been participating in the Polish campaign … the letter has only reached me today…'[18]

# 4

# THE NEW MAN IN TOWN

PRESENT-DAY LUBLIN IS the ninth largest city in Poland. It is the capital of Lublin Province and is located 106 miles to the south-east of Warsaw by road. It is the largest Polish city east of the Vistula River, and is twinned with Lancaster in the UK, Erie (Penn.) and Lublin (Wisconsin) in the USA, and Delmenhorst and Münster in Germany. The picturesque and historical Old Town has been preserved and has been designated as one of Poland's official national historic monuments. The cobbled streets and unique ambiance have been described as 'Little Krakow'. The historic architecture is home to many venues supporting art galleries, cafés, and clubs.

The city's foundations can be traced back to a complex of settlements developed on the future modern site of Lublin and in its environs in the sixth and seventh centuries. Remains of communes dating back to the sixth century were discovered in the centre of today's Lublin on Czwartek Hill. The oldest historical document mentioning Lublin dates from 1198, so the name must have come into general use some time earlier.

The location of Lublin at the eastern borders of the Polish lands gave it military significance. During the first half of the thirteenth century, the town was the target of devastating attacks by Ruthenians, Lithuanians, and Mongols. During the rule of Prince Boleslaw V, the town was founded between 1258 and 1279. It was ruled by the Kingdom of Galicia-Volhynia between 1289 and 1302. In 1341, Casimir III built a castle and surrounded the town with masonry walls in recognition of the strategic location of the site. A stone church from the period still exists to this day on Castle Hill.

The Polish–Lithuanian Union of Krewo in 1385 contributed to the development of the town. It began to thrive as a centre of trade and commerce as a result of its strategic location on the road between Vilnius and Krakow. In the sixteenth century, the Polish–Lithuanian Commonwealth was a real union between the Crown

Kingdom of Poland and the Grand Duchy of Lithuania. In 1578, Lublin was selected as the seat of the Crown Tribunal, the highest appeal court in the Commonwealth. By then, Lublin had witnessed the early stages of Reformation. The city became a global centre for Arianism, and it was frequented by many outstanding poets and writers of the age, competing with Warsaw, Krakow, Poznan, and Lviv as a centre of culture and education. Lublin remained a royal city in the Crown Kingdom of Poland until the partitions at the end of the eighteenth century.

From 1795, Lublin was part of the Austrian Empire until 1809 when it was ruled by the Duchy of Warsaw. From 1815, it came under Russian rule. Developments at the start of the nineteenth century saw the construction of new streets, squares, and public buildings. In 1877, a railway link to Warsaw and Kovel was established and a new railway station was erected. This contributed to the industrial development of the city. The population increased from 28,900 in 1873 to 50,150 in 1897. This included 24,000 Jews.

By 1915, the city was occupied by the armies of Germany and the Habsburg Empire. In 1918, the first independent Polish government operated from Lublin for a short period and the Catholic University of Lublin was founded. During the interwar period, the city population grew and important industrial enterprises were established, including the first aviation factory in Poland. By 1921, Catholics made up 58.9 per cent of the population and Jews 39.5 per cent. This changed to 63.7 per cent and 34.7 per cent respectively by 1931.

The history of the Jews in Lublin stretches back to the fourteenth century. There is an unconfirmed record of Casimir III allowing a settlement of Jews in the area known as Piaski. In 1523, King Sigismund I declared the Jews had an important role to play in the economy of the city. The oldest preserved tombstone in the old cemetery—that of Yaakov Kopelman haLevi—dates from 1541. In 1655, Russian troops set fire to the Jewish quarter and approximately 2,000 Jews were killed by Cossacks. The Tatar invasion of Lublin in 1672 resulted in the complete destruction of the Jewish quarter. The same area suffered from another fire in 1702. Another calamity struck the Jewish population in 1829 when an outbreak of cholera decimated its numbers. The twentieth century witnessed the opening of Jewish schools, the establishment of Jewish societies and unions, and the opening of a Jewish public library in 1917. By 1939, Lublin population had grown to 122,000 citizens, with nearly 43,000 of them following the Jewish faith.

The city experienced heavy bombing by the Luftwaffe on 9 September 1939, followed by further raids on 13 and 17 September. The area around Krakowskie Przedmieście was badly damaged. German troops of Army Group South first entered Lublin on 18 September 1939. They immediately set about persecuting the Jewish inhabitants and Polish intelligentsia. Mass arrests were carried out, but there was worse to come.

Odilo Globocnik's political career was at an end. The auditors of NSDAP treasurer Franz Xaver Schwarz were determined not to be easily put off the scent for blood. The questions regarding the former Gauleiter's financial dealings still required answering. Globocnik himself either thought the auditors would give up now he was no longer in office, or that he had acted correctly. In any case, he ignored the repeated requests from Munich about providing a statement in answer to the questions. He was now fighting as a SS-Unterscharführer der Reserve for Führer and Fatherland in southern Poland with SS Regiment 'Germania', a motorised infantry unit. The matter was not settled until 1941, when Globocnik finally apologised to Schwarz for his lack of respect.

Heinrich Himmler ultimately settled Globocnik's future when, on 1 November 1939, he announced that the former Gauleiter in Vienna had been appointed as the SS and Police Leader (SSPF) in Lublin. SS-Oberführer Globocnik arrived in his new domain on Monday 6 November 1939. Apparently, his appointment came as a surprise in Berlin. Kurt Daluege had expected SA-Obergruppenführer Karl-Siegmund Litzmann to be the new Lublin police supremo.[1] Globocnik was also promoted to SS-Brigadeführer on 18 November 1939, with an effective date from 9 November 1939.[2]

The Reichsführer-SS was acutely aware of the vulnerability of his authority where local political leaders sought to gain the upper hand in the introduction and administration of Nazi policies. To ensure his will was carried out, he introduced trusted local SS leaders and designated them Höhere SS–und Polizeiführer (Higher SS and Police Leaders—HSSPF). They were responsible for all SS and police matters in their region—aligned with the local military area or Wehrkreis—and they answered directly to the Reichsführer-SS. These responsibilities included security, other than military. For ease, they were usually based in the same location as the local SS-Oberabschnitt headquarters, as the role of HSSPF and SS-Oberabschnitt commander were carried out by the same man. Throughout each SS designated region, several SS–und Polizeiführer (SS and Police Leaders—SSPF) were created in major towns and cities. These were subordinate to the HSSPF, but wielded similar power in their own regions.

By the nature of their roles and responsibilities, the HSSPF were often at odds with the local political leaders—Reichsstatthalter and Gauleiter. This created problems where SS and Police policy differed from political policy. Often, personalities clashed, and nowhere was this more evident than the General Government. The HSSPF in the General Government was SS-Obergruppenführer Friedrich-Wilhelm Krüger. He was a favourite of Himmler and a dyed-in-the-wool Nazi. His SS loyalty was not in question. During the Ernst Röhm years, Krüger held Obergruppenführer rank in the Sturmabteilung (SA). He was in charge of SA training. Krüger was also an early member of the SS. He recognised that the SA was becoming a thorn in the side of Hitler with the army generals, and he acted as Himmler's 'eyes and ears' in the SA leadership. After the events of 30 June 1934, Krüger's role became evident, and he was never forgiven by certain senior SA leaders. He left the SA and concentrated on his SS career, receiving just reward from his master.

Krüger and Hans Frank fell out early in their relationship. Often, the SS man introduced policies at odds with the Governor General or ignored his directions. When reprimanded by Frank, Krüger just referred him to Himmler. Frank constantly complained to the Reichsführer-SS about his man in Krakow, but the matter remained unresolved until 1943 when Himmler finally relented and replaced Krüger with Wilhelm Koppe. Krüger was transferred, at his own request, to active duty with the Waffen-SS and was a successful combat leader, winning the Knights Cross of the Iron Cross. He committed suicide in May 1945.

Globocnik became the police and security overlord of 26,000 square kilometres, boasting a population of 2.5 million. The civil administration was administered by Friedrich Schmidt as representative of the Governor General. Although Schmidt also held the SS rank of Brigadeführer, his promotion to that rank taking effect on the same day as that of Globocnik, he was Frank's man. As far as Globocnik was concerned, he considered that his fall from grace had only been temporary. He was back.

However, it could so easily have been a different story. In the original agreement between Germany and the USSR, Lublin had been in the Russian sphere of influence, and Lithuania in the German. At the last minute, Hitler requested the change. Globocnik may easily have been the SS overlord in Lithuania but for Hitler's change of mind.

The 122,000 inhabitants of Lublin city were hopeful that the initial brutality shown by their new masters was temporary. They were given hope when schools were reopened and surgical procedures at the Catholic University Hospital were allowed to proceed once more. The theatres and cinemas reopened, and the printing presses of the newspaper *Ekspress Lubelski* were once again allowed to roll. Their hopes were soon dashed after the arrival of the new SSPF.

No sooner had Globocnik set up his new office headquarters at Ostlandstrasse 8–10 (today ul. Wieniawska, on the corner with Czysta) than further mass arrests followed. The Gestapo prison in the old castle received new inmates, consisting of judges, lawyers, teachers, engineers, university professors, and priests. Many never saw the light of day as free men again until the end of the war, some never again. The university was closed down on 17 November and the buildings were used initially as a barracks, and then a military hospital. Some sixty students were also arrested. Bishops Marian Fulman and Wladyslaw Goral faced trial with other priests on 27 November 1939, charged with secreting forbidden weapons and the distribution of illegal pamphlets. Sentenced to death, it took an intervention by the Vatican and the Governor General to commute the sentences to life in prison. Fulman survived Sachsenhausen concentration camp, but Goral died in suspicious circumstances in the same camp in 1945.

November 1939 also saw the arrival in Lublin of Globocnik's old compatriot from his Klagenfurt days, Reinhold von Mohrenschildt. Von Mohrenschildt set up an office in the newly named Julius Schreck barracks, situated in the former Stefan Batory College, Powiatowa 11 (then Bronislaw Pierackiego 11, today Spokojna 1). This three-storey building would soon be the location of the headquarters of Aktion Reinhardt. Today, it is an educational institute once more, the Collegium Iuridicum of the John Paul II Catholic University of Lublin, belonging to the Faculty of Law, Canon Law, and Administration of the Catholic University of Lublin, acquired from the Medical Faculty. The building dates from 1910–1911.

Globocnik realised that he would achieve more, be able to deflect objections to the policies he was about to introduce, and feel more at ease personally if he surrounded himself with his own inner circle. Von Mohrenschildt was an integral part of that circle. His sister, Ebba, who had been involved in the undercover illegal activities in pre-Anschluss Austria, soon arrived in Lublin to take care of Globocnik's household. Her husband, Ernst Natter, was on Globocnik's staff. The ever-present Paul Gasser accompanied his friend, and even Globocnik's own sister, Erika von Gayl, now a teacher, volunteered at a Lublin school. Lublin was where von Mohrenschildt would subsequently meet his future wife, Margarete Kauffmann, when she worked as a typist for SS-Standartenführer Ludolf Jakob von Alvensleben.

One of Globocnik's first initiatives was to create the Lubliner Selbstschutz, a type of self-defence unit. In mid-November 1939, he ordered SS-Standartenführer Walter Gunst to recruit young men from the rural community. They were mostly farmers, or farm labourers, who were prepared to take action against Poles and Jews alike by the use of force. The SSPF would have overall command. By 23 November, five companies were standing by in Janów Lubelski. Each company consisted of between 100 and 150 uniformed men, and they soon became the scourge of the district.

Their primary aim was to seize Jewish inhabitants and their property. Their methods were similar to those of the Einsatzgruppen—first, surrounding villages and rounding up the inhabitants. Jewish men were seized and transported to two small temporary camps on Kochmalna, to the south of Lublin City. Jewish work battalions were forced to search Jewish houses and business premises and seize goods of value that were then stored at the Selbstschutz headquarters situated at Chopin Strasse 27 (now number 29 ul. Chopina). This depot was destined later to become the main storage and sorting facility for goods stolen under the umbrella of Aktion Reinhardt.

At first, the Selbstschutz men acted with the co-operation of the local civilian authorities, but soon Jews were attacked and robbed in the street. Gunst and his adjutant profited from the illegal seizures to such an extent that they were transferred in early 1940. The corrupt Gunst moved to Warsaw and was replaced by SS-Standartenführer Ludolf von Alvensleben. By April 1940, Friedrich Schmidt's replacement as head of the civil administration, Emil Zörner, complained bitterly to Globocnik about the lack of discipline and corrupt behaviour of the Selbstschutz units. The relationship between Zörner and Globocnik never recovered and the two men were at odds for the entire period they were together in Lublin.

In January 1940, the German authorities in Lublin established a Judenrat—Jewish Council. The first announcement of the creation of new Jewish institutions in the territories of occupied Poland was a telegram of Reinhard Heydrich, head of the Reich Main Security Office (RSHA), directed on 21 September 1939 to the Einsatzgruppen commanders. The order involved the creation of senior councils—Jüdische Ältestenräte—at each Jewish community, which could include no more than twenty-four men. The members were to be generally respected persons. The elderly councils were obliged to implement orders issued by the German authorities in a timely and punitive manner. These actions included an order to conduct a census of the Jewish population, as well as to provide care for refugees and displaced persons.[3] Despite the recommendations issued by Heydrich in many localities, no senior councils were established, but for a time, the Jewish Religious Communities (ŻGW) were allowed to function, which in response to new challenges expanded their administrative structure.

On 28 November 1939, Hans Frank had issued a regulation that constituted the legal basis for the creation of the Judenrat, subordinating them to the civil administration. In towns where there were less than 10,000 Jews, the council had to number twelve members, and in larger cities, twenty-four councillors. The composition of the Jewish Council was chosen by the existing members of the ŻGW, usually from among its own group, and then candidates were submitted for approval to the local starost, who had the right to make personnel changes.[4] In the Governor General's order, the council's tasks were defined as follows:

> The Jewish Council is obliged to accept the orders of the German authorities by the chairman or his deputy. He is responsible for conscientiously carrying out these services to the full extent. Jews and Jewesses should be obedient to the orders issued by him for the execution of German ordinances.[5]

The majority of members were the existing members of the Jewish community. The task of the Judenrat was, on the one hand, to ensure the influx of forced labourers, responding to threats resulting from the progressive pauperization process and the deteriorating sanitary and hygienic situation, and on the other, the role of the conduit, through which the regulations and guidelines of the German authorities reached the ghetto. Above all, it was to follow the orders of the authorities (a particularly tragic role was given to the Judenrat during the liquidation of the Lublin ghetto in Podzamcze, when it was involved in the process of displacement of the Jewish population).

The Jewish Council usually included people known for social, charitable, religious, and political activities. Until the outbreak of the war, many of them fulfilled the role of city councillor. An important factor was their knowledge of the German language, which was supposed to help facilitate direct contact with Germans. The regulation allowed the creation of the Judenrat until 31 December 1939, but in many places the deadline was exceeded.

After the Germans entered Lublin in mid-September 1939, the Jewish community was represented by the Jewish Religious Community Board for the following few months. On 7 January 1940, the WŻGW prepared a list of candidates who would form the Jewish Council. On 24 January, the Starost Grodski accepted it without any changes, establishing the composition of the Judenrat.

The first Judenrat meeting was held on 25 January 1940. The chairman selected was engineer Henryk Bekker; the vice-chairman was Dr Marek Alten. Only a few days later, the second vice-chairman, Salomon Kestenberg, was appointed. The executive body was the Presidium, which included the chairman, two vice-chairmen, and councillors Szlomo Halberstadt and Maurycy Schlaf.[6]

For almost a year, the Lublin Judenrat functioned in the composition established in January 1940. The first major change took place in November 1940, when Councillor Aron Bach died as a result of being beaten by the Germans. His replacement was Dr Josef Siegfried, whose candidacy was approved by Starost Grodzki.[7]

Globocnik's intention was to employ the Judenrat to obtain valuables from the Jews who were to be displaced. He also wanted a Jewish workforce to dig and construct anti-tank ditches along the border with territory held by the USSR between the River San and the River Bug. In order to do so, he needed the Judenrat to carry out his 'dirty work' on his behalf to recruit the manpower. He required thousands of labourers, and to supplement those recruited by the Judenrat, he ordered numerous raids on the Jewish population to 'press-gang' potential workers.

He established a labour camp on the open ground site of the former Academic Sports Organisation of Lublin, at Lindenstrasse 7 (today, ul. Lipowa) and populated it with Jewish workers and Jewish Polish prisoners of war. The site today, between Marii Curie-Sklodowskiej and a large cemetery, is occupied by a modern shopping plaza. At first, the camp housed about 1,000 inmates, but the numbers soon grew.

At a General Government district meeting in February 1940, Globocnik displayed his willingness to accept mass deaths in the Jewish population. He declared that the Jews should be self-supporting, and if this failed, he was willing to let them starve.[8]

Other labour camps were erected at Lipsko, Cieszanów, Bełżec, and Plazkow. Thousands of forced labourers were involved in the construction of the border defences. The working conditions were appalling, with sanitary and hygiene low on the priority list. Security was provided by Selbstschutz guards, whose brutality was by now legendary.

All this activity was sourced to the Führer decree of 7 October 1939—Die Festigung deutschen Volkstums (the Consolidation of German Nationhood)—in which Hitler declared:

> The consequences of Versailles in Europe are eliminated. Thus, the Greater German Reich has the possibility to take in and settle German people, who had to live abroad, in their space, and to arrange the settlement of the ethnic groups within its boundaries of interest so that better dividing lines between them can be achieved.

In other words, rooted in his original phrase, quoted in *Mein Kampf*, of 'living space' in the East.

On the same day, Hitler appointed Heinrich Himmler as Reich Commissioner for the Consolidation of German Nationhood. Hitler outlined his role and responsibilities:

> The Reichsführer-SS is responsible, according to my guidelines, for:
>
> 1. The repatriation of Reich and ethnic Germans abroad, which are to be considered for the final homecoming in the Reich;
> 2. The elimination of the harmful influence of such non-national sections of the population, which represent a danger to the Reich and the German national community;
> 3. The design of new German settlement areas by resettlement, in particular by settling the Reich and ethnic Germans returning from abroad.
>
> The Reichsführer-SS is authorized to make all general arrangements and administrative measures necessary for the performance of these obligations.…
>
> In occupied former Polish territories, the head of administration Ober-Ost carries out the tasks entrusted to the Reichsführer-SS according to his general instructions. The head of administration Ober-Ost and the subordinate heads of administration of the military districts are responsible for the implementation. Their measures are to be adapted to the needs of the military leadership. Persons who are provided with special assignments for carrying out these tasks are not subject to the Wehrmacht jurisdiction.
>
> Moreover, in the territory of the German Reich, the Reichsführer-SS uses the existing authorities and institutions of the Reich, the Lander and the municipalities, as well as the other public bodies and the existing settlement companies to carry out his mission.[9]

This gave the power-hungry Himmler *carte blanche* to flex his muscles and carry out his racial policies in the occupied territories. The Office of the Reich Commissioner for Consolidation of German Nationhood (RKFDV) was created in mid-October 1939. As his delegated representative, Himmler nominated SS-Oberführer Ulrich Greifelt at its head. Greifelt was an old school German with corresponding values. Highly thought of by Himmler, he eventually attained the rank of SS-Obergruppenführer, but the two men often fell out over Himmler's methods. In December 1942, Greifelt suffered a heart attack following one such disagreement with his boss. He died in Landsberg Prison in 1949. In February 1942, whilst serving on Himmler's staff, Greifelt wrote a directive for dealing with children. According to what this laid out, the former Polish government had been responsible for seizing ethnic German children and placing them in orphanages, and it was the duty of the Nazis to reclaim these children. He continued that those who 'looked' German should be selected from orphanages, taken for medical examination at the SS-Rasse- und Siedlungshauptamt (SS Race and Settlement Central Office), before undergoing extensive psychological study. Those that were found to be of desirable racial stock were to be sent to German boarding schools and subsequently made available for adoption by the families of SS members, with their Polish origin to be concealed from any prospective parents.[10]

The newly created department had the following organizational structure at the end of 1939:

1. Planning questions.
2. Manpower control, distribution of settlers to new areas.
3. Compensation claims.
4. Procurement and management of financial resources.
5. Central soil office, confiscation and redistribution of land.
6. Settlement office.

The head of the Department of Planning and Soil was Konrad Meyer-Hetling.[11] This was mainly responsible for the preparation of the General Plan Ost.[12] A sub-division of the Planning and Soil Department was the Spacial Planning and Planning Department, founded on 3 May 1940, and responsible for the (Polish) cities. Its head was Josef Umlauf.[13, 14]

On 5 May 1940, Himmler visited his protégé in Lublin for the first time with Krüger and Karl Wolff.[15] He arrived from a visit to Lodz and stayed overnight with Globocnik. During his visit, the host provided a working lunch at the SS casino on the corner of today's ul. Wieniawska and Jerzego de Tramecourta. Part of the original building still existed in 2014, but has since been demolished.[16] On the agenda was the plan for the Lublin Reservation. They continued the tour and discussions the following day, before Himmler flew to Berlin in the evening.[17]

At the beginning of the year, the owner of a house situated at 8A-8B ul. Lubomelska (today the house is actually located behind ul. Lubomelska in a small side street called Boczna Lubomelska, at number 4–6) was summoned to appear at the office of the SSPF. The house owner, Gustaw Haberlau, was given an ultimatum: the SS needed his house and he must agree to rent it to them, initially for two years. They presented him with a rental agreement already filled in, with a monthly rental of 120 Zloty. All it required was his signature. Sensibly, Haberlau signed on the dotted line. The arrangement for rent collection involved a cousin of Haberlau from Oswiecim, who was fluent in German, visiting the villa once a month and collecting the sum due from an adjutant of Globocnik. The tenant was never seen by the cousin.

The original building was designed and built in the early 1930s by architect Tadeusz Witkowski, who gained inspiration from trips to Italy. The original design was of two separate dwellings in a single building. One half was owned and occupied from 1937 by the owner of the largest pharmacy in Lublin, situated at 29 Krakowski Przedmiescie—the location of the Hotel Europa—Gustaw Haberlau, and the other was occupied by his son-in-law and daughter, Witold and Irena Łobarzewski. Witold was also a pharmacist, and his son, Jerzy, still owns and lives in the villa. The original projected cost of the building was 30,000 PLN, but it ended up costing almost double that figure. This caused a certain amount of friction between the pharmacists and Witkowski as the final reckoning was a huge figure—a teacher's salary in those days was an average of 200 Zloty. Witkowski explained that the additional cost was caused by the design and erection of the characteristic pillars of the structure running vertically through two floors.

Unfortunately for the pharmacists, the villa was situated within the 'German district' of Lublin. Poles were not allowed, unless on business. The house was of the appropriate size and in a secluded location—not surrounded then by many other buildings—required for the new SSPF. It was also within a short walking distance of his offices and the main SS facilities.

The building required some renovations to satisfy the needs of the SSPF. Two rooms on the ground floor were knocked into one by removal of a dividing wall. The result was a large room, 10 metres by 12 metres, which Globocnik used as his parlour where he entertained guests. In the only known contemporary photo, it looks smaller. A large desk was decorated with swastika decorations. On the wall hung a customary portrait of Hitler. Globocnik's bedroom was upstairs on the first floor. Above the recessed bed and on the heavy triple door wooden wardrobe, swastika marquetry was added. The internal white doors were veneered with darker brown wood and a Greek-style swastika frieze was added above each doorframe. The heating and plumbing system was renovated and the radiators timber enclosed. They are still in good working order today. Large grey carpets were laid throughout the house.

Upon entering the villa, one was found to be in a large hallway with a huge conference table. A record player stood to one side, with a collection of records of Richard Wagner's work. There was also a grand piano. Globocnik's sitting room was used for entertaining. On the first floor there was a breakfast room, Globocnik's bedroom, and another smaller private room, subsequently occupied by Globocnik's lover, Irmgard Rickheim. This floor remained as two accommodations, separated by the original dividing wall. Anna Globocnik occupied the other half, which only had separate access from the floor below and not from her son's half.

'Mimi' Trsek described it as such:

> He lived close by the staff building in a house which was actually a combination of two, with the wall removed downstairs in order to combine them. On the ground floor, an orderly sat in an office by the telephone. Towards the back, there was a large meeting room that doubled as Globocnik's dining room. On the first floor, Globocnik lived in a small apartment where he had his work desk. His mother lived on the other side. The first floors weren't connected.[18]

Globocnik ordered a 20-metre long, covered nine-pin bowling alley added to the ground floor for recreation. It was built by Jews. On one side, it had windows open to the garden and it extended over the neighbour's property, but this house had also been acquired by the SS. The bowling alley no longer exists and is now occupied by a car parking space. A cultivated area of the garden, measuring 6 by 15 metres, was paved over by Globocnik to enable him to sit outside in the summer months.[19]

Globocnik employed two Polish servant girls and a handyman. One of the girls spoke fluent German and could have been Volksdeutsche. The household was completed by a SS orderly who acted as Globocnik's valet and whose duty it was to awaken the boss each morning at the appointed time.

The new tenant moved into his acquired quarters in the spring of 1940. His mother, Anna, his sister, Erika, and her little daughter also arrived in Lublin. His niece, Henny, the daughter of his sister, Lydia, also joined them. Erika von Gayl, taught at a Lublin school, no doubt employment easily obtained for the sister of the police chief. Another Globocnik acquaintance from his early Carinthian days, Ebba von Mohrenschildt, arrived to keep house for the SS-Brigadeführer at ul. Lubomelska.

The villa was the scene of numerous parties thrown by the entertainment loving tenant. Lublin was ideally situated as a stopover for senior German officers and officials headed for the East. The champagne flowed freely, and at some point during the war, forty bottles a day were being consumed. Guests were first treated to one of the latest films from Berlin in the main hall where a screen was lowered. Afterwards, the party got into full swing. Only when the Reichsführer-SS visited was the atmosphere more sombre. Himmler first stayed overnight in the Globocnik residence prior to the arrival of Irmgard. The house experienced a thorough search beforehand to ensure no explosive devices had been planted. Local historian Michael Tregenza contends that, subsequently, Globocnik arranged for his boss to stay overnight at a local house.

Often, Globocnik utilised the villa as an office. The hallway also served as a conference room where monthly staff meetings were held, again accompanied by free-flowing champagne. Within these confines, in the atmosphere of champagne fuelled discussions, the fate of thousands was deliberated and decided.
The ordinance declared:

> … the average daily consumption in this house consisted of about two dozen eggs, 1.5 to 2kgs of butter, a large quantity of roasted coffee, and a sea of various brands of champagne, wine and spirits. Alcohol stocks reached 2000 bottles. It was drunk almost every evening. The average consumption of champagne was about forty bottles each evening.[20]

Irmgard Rickheim stated post-war that her former lover and fiancée, Globocnik, regularly took pills for vigour or to relax his mood.

The house was not returned to the owners following Globocnik's departure from Lublin as it was still located within the German area. Even after the German Army withdrew from the city, Haberlau and his daughter's family did not regain occupation of the building. The house was occupied by Polish cinematographers as part of the Polish Army formed in the USSR. The very first post-war Polish films were created in the basement of the villa. Ironically, the subject was Nazi crimes committed in the concentration camps. The famous propaganda documentary *Majdanek: European Cemeteries* was developed in the Globocnik villa. It was premiered in Lublin on 26 November 1944. The film company eventually moved to Lodz and vacated the villa, but the pharmacy family was still unable to regain occupation. The building then became the location of an officer's casino.

Finally, Witold Łobarzewski hit upon the idea of turning the house into a drug factory. Medication was desperately needed in post-war Poland and the pharmacist convinced the authorities to agree to his idea. Polfa Lublin, the manufacturer of medical equipment and materials, was born. The Pharmaceutical Factory Orfa became Lubelskie Zaklady Farmaceutyczne 'Polfa' when it became a state-owned enterprise in 1974. In 1950, the pharmacy at Krakowskie Przedmieście was forcibly taken over by the Polish State, and Haberlau and Łobarzewski lost control.

The building today is still owned and occupied by the son of Witold Łobarzewski. Jerzy Łobarzewski, now a professor, has made extensive alterations. The ground floor is occupied by a coffee company. The fireplace in Globocnik's sitting room has been removed and all evidence of the Globocnik era, but the wood panelling, the heating radiators with original timber housing, and the bedroom furnishing fixtures, was either stolen by the Germans or Soviets. The original built-in bed remains, but with a different mattress. When asked if he minded who had slept in his bed previously, Professor Łobarzewski replied: 'I did not think about it. Anyway, Globocnik and his crimes were not immediately well known after the war. When I became interested in Globocnik's activities, it did not change much. For me, this is primarily a family home'.[21]

The offices of the SSPF Lublin were situated further south along Ostlandstrasse at number 8–10 (present-day ul. Wieniawska). The building still exists, but it is totally occupied from the first floor up by residential apartments. Opposite stands a rather sorry looking detached house, badly in need of repair and decoration at the time of the author's visit. This is where the infamous Christian Wirth, inspector of Aktion Reinhardt death camps, resided in Lublin. All the major SS and Aktion Reinhardt locations in Lublin are within walking distance of each other within the city centre.

Globocnik's arrival in Lublin coincided with the termination of his relationship with Grete Michner. The long-suffering fiancée had patiently waited for her *beau* to conclude his promise of marriage, made at a time when the young Globocnik had craved social status and stability in order to raise his profile. The Michner family expected an announcement soon after Globocnik's appointment as Gauleiter of Vienna. This had been the pinnacle of his success. Emil Michner had treated Globocnik as he would a son, lavishing him with praise and gifts of financial support.

Globocnik's disastrous few months as Gauleiter highlighted his inability to organise and manage the administration of local government. His financial dealings were at best inept, and at worst dishonest. Regardless of his future son-in-law's failures, Michner still expected his daughter to tie the knot. Globocnik, on the other hand, had different ideas. His few months experience at the front with SS-Germania had changed him. No longer was he the political dreamer of pre-Anschluss days. He now considered himself a soldier—a bastion against racial infection. His new mentor, Heinrich Himmler, led the way towards purifying the Germanic race and clearing away the obstacles on the land intended to support this new master race. Globocnik recognised that the SS order now provided his pathway to the top. His ambitions could be realised by following and obeying his new guru. Himmler had shown faith in him when all others abandoned him. It was now his turn to repay the debt.

Grete's own view of their situation did not vary a great deal from that of her fiancée. The pair had become disenchanted with the idea of marriage together. Globocnik had become bored. Status in Carinthia no longer held the attraction it once had. He was now the feudal lord of a major city in occupied Poland and he wielded power over life and death for thousands. For her part, Grete's body clock was ticking away. She wanted to settle down and raise a family, and she was no longer content to play the waiting game. It is possible that she had also become bored with their relationship.

Globocnik informed his fiancée on 7 November 1939 that he considered their agreement as no longer valid. By way of compensating her family, he naïvely offered the sum of 10,000 Reichsmark for 'expenses incurred'. Furious, on 8 November 1939, Emil Michner wrote to Deputy Führer Rudolf Hess:

> My Deputy Führer!
> The undersigned, retired Lieutenant-Colonel Emil Michner, Party member and recipient of 13 March 1938 medal, took part in the World War against Serbia and Italy in the first line, was disabled in the war with a 40% reduction in his work ability, but has nevertheless since continued battling for Carinthian freedom in the first line. My daughter, Grete Michner, made the acquaintance of Party comrade Odilo Globocnik in 1923. Globocnik was then unemployed and I secured him employment with the Carinthian Water Power Utility. Then came the time of struggle against the system, in which Globocnik admirably participated. My daughter demonstrated her great love and dedication for her fiancé and their National Socialist ideals, for which Globocnik was fighting! She accompanied him on the most dangerous recruiting missions, concealed him and other wanted Nazis in our house and did not cease even when she—and I, her father—were incarcerated....
>
> During this time, Globocnik repeatedly confirmed that he desired a matrimonial union with my daughter....
>
> His visits became more and more infrequent. As the months passed, the setting of a wedding date was postponed with explanations of decreasing credibility....
>
> He never visited again and did not respond to letters. This was the moment to get to the heart of the matter. In March, I went to Vienna and took him to task. He gave me his word of honour that as soon as he could secure a new post, he would get married right away. This gentlemen's agreement was broken when Globocnik sent my daughter a letter of compensation yesterday, in which he offered 10,000 Reichsmark as 'recompense'. The reason I am bringing this unbelievable behaviour of my Party comrade to your attention, my Deputy Führer, is my conviction that the terms of the officers' corps apply in their entirety to the Party as well.
> Heil Hitler! Heil my Deputy Führer![22]

This letter indicates the old-fashioned values of Michner's generation. In his world, an officer and a gentleman's word was his bond. He had no reason to suspect that Globocnik's generation was beginning to think otherwise. Although Austro-German culture still maintained an element of honour, Michner had not reckoned on the pedantic Heinrich Himmler and his ideals. The fact that he was a decorated world war veteran held little or no value to the mind of the Reichsführer-SS when assessing brides for his beloved SS order. Michner had also miscalculated the interest level of either Hitler or Hess in such matters. As long as either party had no tainted blood, they had little interest. Hess delegated a member of his staff to deal with the affair. Michner's letter was duly brought to the attention of Globocnik.

On 31 December 1931, Himmler had issued the 'SS Marriage Directive':

1. The SS is a band of German men of strictly Nordic descent chosen according to certain principles.
2. In accordance with National Socialist ideology and in the realisation that the future of our people rests upon the preservation of the race through selection and the healthy inheritance of good blood, I hereby institute the Marriage Certificate for all unmarried members of the SS, effective 1 January 1932.
3. The desired aim is to create a hereditary healthy clan of strictly Nordic German variety.
4. The Marriage Certificate will be awarded or denied solely on the basis of racial health and heredity.
5. Every SS man who intends to get married must procure for this purpose the Marriage Certificate of the Reichsführer-SS.
6. SS members who marry despite having been denied Marriage Certificates will be stricken from the SS; they will be given the choice of withdrawing.
7. Working out the details of marriage petitions is the task of the Race Office of the SS.
8. The Race Office of the SS in in charge of the Clan Book of the SS, in which the families of SS members will be entered after being awarded the marriage certificate or after acquiescing to the petition to enter into marriage.
9. The Reichsführer-SS, the leader of the Race Office, and the specialists of his office are duty bound to secrecy on their word of honour.
10. The SS believes that, with this command, it has taken a step of great significance. Derision, scorn and incomprehension do not move us. The future belongs to us!

Reichsführer H. Himmler[23]

Not only did Himmler control the service status and behaviour of his SS cohorts, he also manipulated and influenced their private lives. Globocnik referred his engagement problem to his mentor. The two men obviously discussed the situation, and it appears that Himmler may have been the instigator of the engagement break-up. A Carinthian girl was no longer suitable as the partner of a SS General who would spearhead Himmler's racial plans in Eastern Europe. Globocnik wrote to Himmler:

> Reichsführer!
>
> Since I do not know whether I will be able to see you before I leave, I decided to report to you the following:
>
> The answer to my engagement termination was an awful letter by her father, which I do not think I should take too seriously. Otherwise, this may result in a never-ending conflict. The fact that he notified the Führer's office [*sic.*] is significant. I have no idea what the letter means. Nothing pleasant, in any case. I ask you, Reichsführer, to advise me, since you know all the particulars.[24]

This memorandum clearly indicates that Himmler had a previous input. By 17 November, Globocnik was satisfied that he had the support of the Reichsführer-SS and this was borne out on 22 November when Himmler wrote to Martin Bormann offering to 'gladly take charge of the matter'. Unknown to the naïve Emil Michner, Himmler had no intention of allowing a marriage union between his 'Globus' and the young woman from Krumpendorf. Himmler had already approached Friedrich Rainer to 'handle the Michner case'.

Rainer had displayed excellent qualities during the period of the Anschluss and his record as Gauleiter of Salzburg since then was exemplary. Added to this, he was an old comrade of Globocnik who knew both parties well. For Emil Michner and his unfortunate daughter, Rainer did not possess an unbiased opinion on the matter, for he too had encouraged his old friend to terminate the engagement. On 24 November 1939, he wrote to Himmler:

> I have known Globocnik since 1933. Klausner told me [in 1934] that Globocnik had a girlfriend who was Lieutenant-Colonel Michner's daughter and that the Michner family was trying to secure him as a husband for the daughter. Friends of Globocnik told me at the time that the active party in these marriage plans was the Michner family.
>
> Globocnik has always had the habit of including personal relations and friends in his staff of underground fighters. Upon his arrest in 1934, the police arrested his mother, his sister, his fiancée Grete and the Lieutenant-Colonel along with him.
>
> Globocnik confided in me in 1936 … that as a political refugee he was unsuitable for marriage and couldn't expect his girl to wait for him any longer. I already had the impression then that the relationship, although seemingly intact on the outside, was no longer a happy one inside, and that only his decency prevented him from making a clean break. I then recommended that he choose either of the following solutions:
>
> 1. If he truly loved her, then get married … regardless of financial considerations.
> 2. If he did not love her, then finish it in a clear and clean break.

> … Everybody, including Miss Michner and her family, clearly saw that Globocnik struggled. The Michner family, however, showed no understanding for his turmoil. On the contrary, they doggedly insisted on a wedding … my advice to comrade Globocnik … was that he should terminate the relationship … he disregarded my advice, however. It was of my own accord, therefore, that I notified the Reichsführer-SS about the case in November 1938.…
>
> I have no idea whether Globocnik ever gave Lieutenant-Colonel Michner his word of honour. He never told me anything about it.… When the Reichsführer named him for the Lublin post, I repeated that the time had come to resolve his private matter in the proper fashion. Globocnik then told me that within the last year he had come to realise that he no longer loved the girl and consequently should not marry her. A mutually acquainted family then proposed a painless and proper way for the dissolution of the relationship. His bride, however, responded that she would insist on him fulfilling his word of honour. She wanted to carry his name and desired to bear his children. Before his transfer to the east, Globocnik finally decided to tell his bride that he wanted to break off, and reported this to the Reichsführer-SS.
>
> In my view, party comrade Globocnik's only fault lies in the belated realisation of his own feelings and that he didn't take this step earlier.…
>
> … regarding his word of honour. Considering the state he was in during March 1939, I doubt that he actually gave it. I can imagine, however, that Lieutenant-Colonel Michner demanded it from him in an extortionist manner, by threatening scandal if he refused to comply.… I am of the opinion that the promise of marriage in this case would have never resulted in a conjugal union fitting for a SS officer.
>
> Heil Hitler! Rainer.[25]

The contradictory letter indicates that Globocnik had second thoughts about his intended marriage at least two years before the Anschluss. Whether Rainer brought the matter to the attention of the Reichsführer with Globocnik's consent is a matter of conjecture. Rainer's last sentence was certainly designed to gain support from Himmler, knowing how fastidious the boss was over the image of his officer corps. Himmler plainly opposed the marriage and knew beforehand that Rainer was of a similar opinion. Michner was fighting a lost cause.

Himmler replied that he had 'no doubt whatsoever that Globocnik and Fräulein Michner ought not to marry, it would result in disaster for both.… If Michner thinks he can lean on Globocnik because of his word of honour, then we will get him for extortion. Globocnik treated the girl decently throughout, but not out of love, but because he is decent'.[26] Himmler also told Rainer to inform Michner that it was his and Rainer's instructions that Globocnik should end the engagement. If anyone was to blame, it was them.

On 21 December 1939, Rainer visited the Michners in Krumpendorf. Upon hearing the news first hand, Michner suggested that Anna Globocnik had influenced her son into the break. Rainer pointed out that referral to the laws of 'Volk and Race' indicated that the couple were not suited. Throughout the break-up, Grete herself seemed less concerned than her father. She had admonished her father for stirring up trouble unnecessarily and now she wished to put the matter behind her and concentrate on running a kindergarten in Klagenfurt. In the light of what we now know, a fortuitous escape!

However, the old Austrian officer was not so easy to pacify. He wanted financial compensation, not only for the slight against his daughter, but for all the help he had afforded Globocnik over the years. His claims were rebutted by Rainer on 18 January 1940 when the Gauleiter declared that 10,000 Reichsmark was the maximum amount Globocnik and the SS would pay. Michner reluctantly agreed in March 1940 to accept the offer as half the settlement. Himmler then intervened and suggested a final figure in total settlement of 15,000 RM to be paid by Globocnik to Michner. To soften the blow, Himmler agreed to reimburse Globocnik with 8,000 RM.[27]

The Michner affair finally came to an end one year later when Globocnik received a cheque from the Reichsführer-SS for 8,000 RM. By then, his economic situation had improved somewhat, following the benefits to his personal account he had gained from his various nefarious financial dealings. He wrote to Himmler, thanking him, but suggesting that the funds might be redirected to a needier cause. The Lublin police chief now had more important things to concentrate on.

# 5

# THE FIRST GRAND STRATEGY

MANY EYEBROWS WERE raised at Himmler's choice for the senior SS and Police chief for the General Government. Friedrich-Wilhelm Krüger boasted a less than spectacular record. Krüger was born in Strasbourg on 8 May 1894. His father, Alfred Krüger, was an Oberst and the Regimental Commander of Infantry Regiment 27 when he was killed in action in the vicinity of Lüttich on 6 August 1914. His mother, Helene, whose maiden name was Glünder, died in 1930. Friedrich-Wilhelm was one of three brothers and the family were evangelists. He attended the Bürgerschule in Rastatt from 1900 until 1903, and then the local Gymnasium until 1909, before enrolling in the officer cadet school in Karlsruhe. He finally transferred to the cadet academy at Berlin-Lichterfelde.

He was commissioned as a Leutnant, without Patent, with the Royal Prussian Infantry Regiment 25 'von Lützow' on 22 March 1914, and this was confirmed on 16 June 1914. Some observers would say his commission came at a very opportune moment, with the threat of war looming on the horizon. During the subsequent Great War, Krüger was wounded three times and was promoted to Oberleutnant in 1915. Apart from six months' temporary service as an orderly officer on the staff of the 208 Infantry Division in 1917, he served with the same unit throughout. He was assigned as a platoon and company commander, a machine-gun company commander, and then the regimental adjutant. With such a promising start, an exemplary combat record, which provided decorations for bravery and leadership, why did he advance no further than one higher rank?[1]

In February 1919, he served with the 1 Torpedo Boat Flotilla and then the Freikorps 'von Lützow' until May 1920, when he was discharged from military service. From 1920 until 1922, he was a clerk with a bookseller and publisher in Berlin, and then a despatch clerk with a Berlin publisher in 1923. This was followed by a term as a member of the board of a Berlin waste disposal firm from 1924 until 1928. Following a short period of unemployment, in 1929, Krüger became a self-employed businessman.

Krüger was married on 16 September 1922 to Elisabeth Rasehorn (born on 15 November 1896 in Bad Lausick; NSDAP number 1 066 106). They had two children, both boys, born on 4 May 1929 and on 13 March 1936. On an official document dated 12 March 1937, Krüger arrogantly declared his religion as 'deutschgläubig' (German believer).

He joined the NSDAP on 15 November 1929 and held party membership number 171 199, becoming a street cell leader. Until joining the Nazi Party, he had shown no particular political leaning. Krüger applied to join the SS in August 1930 and was accepted on 1 February 1931. He was issued with SS number 6 123. He held the rank of SS-Mann and was attached to the staff of SS-Abschnitt III. On 16 March 1931, he was promoted to SS-Sturmführer, but Krüger's SS career was overshadowed by his SA activities for the next four years.

Krüger joined the SA on 3 April 1931 and was assigned as SA-Sturmführer and Stabsleiter of SA-Gruppe Ost. He was promoted to SA-Oberführer on 31 July 1931. On 10 September 1931, he was appointed SA-Gruppenführer Ost, and on 1 July 1932, chief of Group Staff of the SA with special responsibilities on the staff of the supreme SA leadership.

That month, he was also elected as a Reichstag representative for Frankfurt-Oder. On 4 October 1932, he became a member of the State Board for Youth Physical Training and was subsequently made responsible for all SA training the following year. During February 1933, he attended the International Disarmament Conference in Geneva as a police and security expert advisor to the German delegation, along with Reinhard Heydrich.

Krüger was promoted to SA-Obergruppenführer on 27 June 1933. He was a Berlin District Councillor (until December 1935) and a Prussian State Councillor. He was commander of SA border units, inspector of SA Water Sports, and the representative of the Supreme SA Leadership on the Reich Defence Council. He introduced the regulations for the SA Sports Badge in March 1934.

On 25 January 1935, Krüger returned to SS duties and was immediately promoted to SS-Obergruppenführer on the RFSS staff. For one month from 1 July 1935, he was given command of SS-Oberabschnitt Mitte in Dresden. From 1 March 1936, Krüger commanded the SS Frontier Units and in July 1937, he was appointed to the People's Court. On 16 May 1938, he was assigned as Inspector of SS Mounted Units and appointed as HSSPF Ost in Berlin. He held this latter post until 9 October 1939. Krüger held a high profile in sport and training and in January 1939, he was appointed as the Reich Supreme Authority for Equestrian Sports.

Krüger felt he was over-qualified for the roles he had been allotted so far. He was impatient for a more active role and he reminded Himmler in a letter dated 14 May 1938 that he had been promised to be considered for the command of a SS-Oberabschnitt.[2] Krüger cut a rather frustrated figure, never really suited to the SS assignments to which he was posted.

Himmler felt obligated and rewarded Krüger on 4 October 1939 by appointing him as HSSPF to the military administration in Lodz. This was followed on 26 October by his appointment as HSSPF Ost, based in the newly created General Government at Krakow.

Why Krüger? Krüger's unusual position with both the SA and the SS led to mistrust of the Obergruppenführer by both organisations. The SA were suspicious, with justification, that he had relayed information to the SS prior to and during the Röhm action of June and July 1934 when numerous senior SA men were executed. He passed on details to Heydrich's office. Krüger and Heydrich held respect for each other since their joint 1933 venture in Geneva as security consultants. Other sections of the SS were never truly convinced of Krüger's total loyalty to the SS. Even Himmler insisted on him serving a period of 'probation'.

Himmler had major plans for the occupied territories of the East. Whoever was his representative in the General Government would also administer his intended resettlement and population policy associated with his role as Reich Commissioner for Strengthening the German Nation. The HSSPF would also be the manager of the Reich's policy towards the Jews and would also oversee the seizure of property and manpower, which would be utilised for the benefit of the Reich. Last, but not least, the HSSPF would be Himmler's principal agent for the implementation and maintenance of security measures.

Krüger was available and was pressing for significant duty; he had experience of frontline combat duty. As if to prove himself loyal after the questionable behaviour around the executions of 30 June 1934, he ensured his attitude towards the SS and Himmler was beyond reproach. He would follow every order to the letter in order to prove himself both loyal and worthy of the faith in which Himmler placed in him. Himmler needed a man with such qualities to deal with the powerful and intelligent Dr Hans Frank.

Krüger's role as HSSPF in Dr Frank's General Government was not an easy task. He survived an assassination attempt on his life on 14 January 1940 and he was in constant disagreement with Dr Frank while trying to implement the racial and resettlement policies of the Reichsführer-SS. Himmler informed Krüger of his intentions to use the General Government area as a pivotal constituent of his plans for resettlement and deportation, and he updated him at an early stage on the additional role of the SSPF Lublin, Odilo Globocnik.

To give him the required muscle, Krüger was elevated to the rank of general of Police on 8 April 1941. He was invited by Heydrich to the Wannsee Conference, set initially for 9 December 1941, but was unable to attend the revised date on 20 January 1942, sending along Eberhard Schöngarth as his replacement representative.

On 21 April 1942, Hitler decreed that the HSSPF would automatically be nominated as State Secretary for security measures, and Krüger assumed this role on 7 May 1942. Krüger also became deputy Reich commissioner under Governor General Dr Hans Frank and representative for the Reich Commission for the Strengthening of German Nationhood. Himmler issued orders to Krüger on 19 July 1942 that all Jews in the General Government were to be resettled by 31 December 1942. On 15 September 1942, SS-Oberabschnitt Ost was officially upgraded from its previous status and Krüger was automatically selected as Oberabschnitt commander.

The second attempt on Krüger's life nearly succeeded. At 9.45 a.m. on 20 April 1943, Krüger left his residence at the castle in Krakow to drive to his office at Weichselufer in his PKW car, registration OST31. As his vehicle turned into the Outer Ring Road, two men attempted to kill him. Krüger himself described the incident in a report to Himmler the same day:

> … 2 men of good appearance and well dressed sprang out onto the footway from a shed which stood obliquely to the street … and threw, within an interval of seconds, 2 bombs which were shaped something like a short thermos flask. I could see the first bomb exactly as it came flying towards my vehicle. It was coloured black. Both bombs exploded immediately behind my vehicle, with the result that my right wheel and tyre were damaged and the petrol tank holed.
>
> While the second bomb was thrown, I ducked and grasped my pistol. After the explosion, when I realised that I had not been wounded, I shouted to my driver to stop at once and he pulled over to the right. I turned round, meanwhile and saw the two men disappearing in the same direction, roughly into the middle of the shed.
>
> I could no longer see them exactly, since I had already gone past the corner. When I ran to the shed myself, there was no longer any sign of the two would-be assassins. Now various Germans came running up to me, both from the direction of the 'Press Centre' and from the cul-de-sac which runs near the shed. In addition, all the windows in the vicinity were damaged by the two explosions…[3]

He also reported that a discarded pistol, a British Colt, was recovered from the roadside and handed to the police. He stated that both he and his driver were unscathed and he concluded with a scant description of the culprits.

The report is dated the day of the attack and is signed by him. There followed a thorough investigation by the Security Police and SD in Krakow, which resulted in the two would-be assassins being captured. Krüger visited them in prison before they were executed. As a result, Martin Bormann ordered that an armoured car be placed at the disposal of the HSSPF. The press agency Reuters erroneously reported that Krüger, 'renowned for his cruelty in Poland', had died from bullet wounds.

On 21 June 1943, Krüger participated in a meeting of senior SS men, including Himmler—as chair—Prützmann, Kaltenbrunner, von dem Bach, Pohl, Winkelmann, Katzmann, and Knoblauch. It was decided that von dem Bach would henceforth be responsible for anti-partisan measures. There is no doubt that the question of Krüger's role in the General Government was also discussed in private, for two days later, Himmler and Dr Frank held talks at Himmler's Field HQ 'Hochwald'. As a result, Krüger was ordered to make more of an effort to reconcile his differences with Dr Frank.

The relationship between Dr Frank and his deputy, Krüger, was not amicable. The SS man viewed Frank as interfering in his area of responsibility and *vice versa*. They fell out over policy on numerous occasions with Krüger misjudging Frank's powerful position with Hitler. The situation became intolerable. Himmler had no choice, but to replace his HSSPF and Krüger was transferred on 9 November 1943 to the RFSS staff. He was replaced in Krakow by Wilhelm Koppe.

Krüger requested a combat assignment and was attached to the SS-Prinz Eugen Division until April 1944 to train for a battle command. He took over command of the 6th SS-Mountain Division 'Nord' on 20 May 1944, and transferred to the command of V SS-Mountain Corps on 26 August 1944. From 8 July 1944, he was authorised to wear the rank insignia of General der Waffen-SS, effective 20 May 1944. On 20 January 1945, Krüger was posted to the Personal Staff RFSS. From 16 February 1945, he was posted to the Führerreserve RFSS and placed at the disposal of HSSPF Warthe in East Prussia. His last assignment was as General der Ordnungstruppen and commander of a battle group of Ordnungspolizei under the orders of Army Group South, renamed Ostmark, on 1 May 1945.

Krüger was a more than competent combat commander, being recommended for the Knights Cross of the Iron Cross by an army commander and receiving the award on 20 October 1944. His strong beliefs in National Socialism convinced him that a defeated Germany was not a suitable place in which to carry on and he committed suicide on 10 May 1945 in Libau, Courland.

His record as HSSPF Ost in the General Government was generally one of failure in the eyes of his superior, Heinrich Himmler. Faced with overwhelming demands, his role as administrator of Himmler's whims and wishes, proved catastrophic for the people who lived or subsequently entered his domain. He was no fool and realised he was fighting a losing battle. In a letter to SS Personnel Chief Max von Herff on 6 April 1944, while awaiting a Waffen-SS combat command, Krüger declared that he had 'lost honour and reputation after my four years of clean struggle in the General Government.'[4] Other than his use of the word 'clean', there are not many who would disagree with him. Had he survived the war, he would certainly have climbed the scaffold steps for crimes during his tenure as HSSPF Ost.[5]

On 30 December 1939, Globocnik sent Hitler a telegraph message:

My Führer!
We are grateful for the tasks you have set us here in the East. We are going to do our utmost in our positions to be your little helpers.

May I extend this promise to you, my Führer, as a New Year greeting and with my best wishes.
Heil, my Führer!

Globocnik, SS and Police Chief Lublin.[6]

This rather sycophantic new year greeting reveals an unusual similarity between Hitler and his minion. No other newly appointed subordinate felt the need to express his assurance that he would do his job in such terms. Globocnik appears to be apologising for his failures in the past and pledging that it will not happen again.

In a sense, Poland was a 'laboratory' for the Nazi policy of Lebensraum in the East. Specifically, the Nazis planned to exploit the Polish people and the material resources of the country. All for the benefit of the German war machine. The General Government was to be bankrupted, depleting it of not only all raw materials and agricultural supplies, but also its labour force. The more fertile vacated lands of the region would provide isolated strongholds for resettled ethnic Germans. The indigenous Slavic population would be engulfed, and eventually vanish, replaced by Volksdeutscher inhabitants in a totally Germanised territory.

In order to achieve this goal, the Nazis planned to retain the productive structures of the General Government, to enable the new workforce to recommission them for the benefit of the occupiers' war machine. Initially, the plan was to replace the evacuated Poles with thousands of Jews, non-conforming sections of the Polish community, and elements of the Polish intelligentsia. All these were deemed as superfluous to requirements and were earmarked for early annihilation by one means or another. All able-bodied Poles were to be evacuated to the Reich for enforced labour. Couples were to be separated, with the intention of reducing the proliferation of their race. The Volksdeutscher communities in the General Government would be politically re-educated and refusal to comply would be a ticket to a concentration camp. Real estate owned by displaced persons was to be seized and reallocated to the incoming incumbents, including farms and landed estates. In other words, Poland was to be treated as a colony, and the Poles would be the slaves of the Greater German Reich.

War-damaged buildings were not to be rebuilt. Deputy Führer Rudolf Hess ordered on 20 November 1939:

I hear from Party members who came from the General Government that various agencies, as, for instance, the Military Economic Staff, the Reich Ministry for Labour, etc., intend to reconstruct certain industrial enterprises in Warsaw. However, in accordance with a decision by Minister Dr Frank, as approved by the Führer, Warsaw

> shall not be rebuilt, nor is it the intention of the Führer to rebuild or reconstruct any industry in the General Government.[7]

With regard to deportation and resettlement, a secret report was prepared in January 1940 that declared that the General Government was already over-populated and could absorb 1 to 1.5 million resettlers at most. The report identified those it considered necessary for deportation:

> The Polish intelligentsia who have been politically active in the past, and potential political leaders; the leading economic personalities, comprising owners of large estates, industrialists and businessmen, etc.; the peasant population, so far as it has to be removed in order to carry out by strips of German settlements the encirclement of Polish territories in the East.... In order to relieve the living space of the Poles in the General Government as well as in the liberated East, one should remove cheap labour temporarily by the hundreds of thousands, employ them for a few years in the old Reich, and thereby hamper their native biological propagation. (Their assimilation into the old Reich must be prevented.)[8]

Governor General Dr Hans Frank entered in his diary:

> The Reichsführer-SS wishes that all Jews be evacuated from the newly gained Reich territories. Up to February, approximately 1,000,000 people are to be brought in this way into the General Government. The families of good racial extraction present in the occupied Polish territory (approximately 4,000,000 people) should be transferred into the Reich, and individually housed and thereby be uprooted as a people.[9]

At a high-level meeting held on 12 February 1940, Göring reminded those present of the necessity to strengthen the war potential by any measures, and that this must be the main aim of all policies in the East. He advocated achieving the greatest possible agriculture production without any regard to the question of ownership. In other words, he considered any method legal in order to increase production.

On 17 September 1940, Göring issued an edict that was meant to standardise the programme of confiscation. Under Section 2, it introduced the compulsory sequestration of both movable and immovable property, including stores, and other intangible assets of Jews and 'persons who have fled, or who are not merely temporarily absent'. Furthermore, sequestration was authorised under Section 2 (2), if the property was required 'for the public welfare, particularly in the interests of Reich defence or the strengthening of Germanism'. By Section 9, confiscation of sequestrated property was authorised 'if the public welfare, particularly the defence of the Reich, or the strengthening of Germanism, so requires'. However, Section 1

(2) provided that property of German nationals was not subject to sequestration and confiscation. Section 13 provided that sequestration would be suspended if the owner of the property asserted that he was a German.[10] The decree clearly indicates a purpose to strip Poles, Jews, and dissident elements of their assets, of whatever description. Plainly, it was unashamedly designed to promote the Germanisation of the affected territories.

Unremarkably, questions arose as to whether the edict required that a determination be made in each case involving the property of a Pole, in order to ascertain that the property was required for the public welfare, particularly in the interests of Reich defence or the strengthening of Germanism. The unequivocal reply was that 'in any case in which the property of a Pole was involved, the strengthening of Germanism required its seizure'. On 15 April 1941, on stationery of the Reichsführer-SS, Commissioner for the Consolidation of German Nationhood, instructions were given 'for internal use on the application of the law of 17 September 1940, concerning all property of the Poles': 'The conditions permitting seizure according to section 2 (2), are always present if the property belongs to a Pole. For the Polish real estate will be needed, without exception, for the consolidation of German nationhood'.[11]

Himmler took a similar view to Göring, but he went a step further when addressing a group of SS officers at Metz about enforced deportations, and the brutal methods necessary to carry them out:

> Very frequently the member of the Waffen-SS thinks about the deportation of this people here. These thoughts came to me today when watching the very difficult work out there performed by the Security Police, supported by your men, who help them a great deal. Exactly the same thing happened in Poland in weather 40 degrees below zero, where we had to haul away thousands, ten thousand, a hundred thousand; where we had to have the toughness ... you should hear this, but also forget it again, to shoot thousands of leading Poles.[12]

In the secret decree dated 7 October 1939, signed by Hitler and countersigned by Göring, Lammers, and Keitel, Himmler was entrusted with the task of executing the Germanisation programme. Himmler's conception of his tasks under this decree were plainly stated in the foreword of the magazine publication of the *Deutsche Arbeit* issue of June–July 1942, in which he wrote: 'It is not our task to Germanize the East in the old sense, that is, to teach the people there the German language and German law, but to see to it that only people of purely German, Germanic blood live in the East'.[13]

The 1940 edition of *Der Menscheneinsatz*, a confidential publication issued by Himmler's Office for the Consolidation of German Nationhood, contained the following statement:

> The removal of foreign races from the incorporated Eastern Territories is one of the most essential goals to be accomplished in the German East. This is the chief national political task, which has to be executed in the incorporated Eastern Territories by the Reichsführer-SS, Reich Commissioner for the Consolidation of the German Nation.[14]

It is therefore hardly surprising that Globocnik began implementing policies in his district to support the above resettlement programme. He took upon himself the mantle of racial warrior with an unprecedented fervour. Ever ambitious, he realised at once the importance placed on such matters by his mentor, Heinrich Himmler.

The extent of the Nazi confiscation programme in Poland is staggering. The incomplete statistics produced by the Nazis themselves indicate that, as of 31 May 1942, a total of 693,252 estates, comprising 6,097,525 hectares, had been seized. In addition, 9,508 estates, comprising 270,446 hectares, had been confiscated by the four estate offices in Danzig-West Prussia, Poznan, Zichenau, and Silesia, alone.[15] The individual figures for other offices during this period, are not available.

Globocnik was well aware that he held a post essential to the Nazi intended policy in the East. Lublin was the centre of an area densely populated by Jews that became known as the Lublin Reservation. Himmler had chosen his representative wisely. Not only did he have experience of dealing with the Jews in an acceptable manner—to the Nazi way of thinking—but he would follow orders without question in an effort to expunge his previous misdemeanours and failures. He needed to prove his suitability for high office. The ambitious streak in Globocnik had not diminished, but now he realised that his only route to the top was by way of the SS. In climbing his career ladder of success, Globocnik was destined to transform the area, first into a corral for Jews, and then a wasteland for Jews and Poles. All in the cause of expelling local Polish Slavic and Jewish populations to provide living space for Aryan settlers. Lublin would be the capital for the greatest ever demographical alteration to the inhabitants of central Europe. To achieve this goal, Globocnik's methods developed from enforced resettlement, to slavery and genocide. Himmler granted him unique power, which he used to produce a blueprint for racial murder. Given his financial track record in Vienna, it is not surprising that, along the route, he enriched the coffers of the SS and the Reich, while not omitting his own bank balance. Outright robbery was in his DNA.

In discussions and with the agreement of Hitler and Himmler, NSDAP racial theorist Alfred Rosenberg formulated a plan in 1939 for the resettlement of displaced Jews expelled under the umbrella of a territorial solution to the problem of the Jews within the sphere of German influence. His idea was the creation of an autonomous Jewish reservation in the southern General Government, within the province of Lublin. Rosenberg first aired this idea in a speech he delivered on 7 February 1939 to foreign diplomats and members of the press. This was an alternative to the subsequent so-called 'Madagascar Plan', devised by Franz Rademacher, but developed and presented by Eichmann, which allowed for the expulsion of European Jews to the French-administered island off the south-east coast of the African continent. However, the idea had been published as early as 1931 in a pamphlet by Egon von Wingheue. Although tacitly approved by Hitler before the war, the impracticalities of the Madagascar Plan ensured that it never gained a foothold in official policy, and consequently did not get off the drawing board.

The so-called 'Lublin Reservation' was intended to be the 'dumping ground' for the Jews of Europe, without giving any thought to their welfare or needs. One neutral diplomat referred to it as 'nothing more than a huge sewer' into which thousands of human beings would pour, vulnerable to the elements and to hunger.[16] The area of the reservation was approximately 400 square miles, bordered in the west by the Rivers San and Vistula, and in the east by the Soviet demarcation line.

Himmler tasked Heinrich Müller and Adolf Eichmann of Heydrich's Reich Security Office to co-ordinate the implementation of the plan. Eichmann mentioned the plan to create a reservation for Jews in the Lublin region to European Jewish leaders at a meeting in October 1939 in Berlin. Dr Hans Frank was brought on board and he delegated responsibility to his General Government deputy, Arthur Seyss-Inquart. The everyday administration was given to the Himmler man in overall charge of the Lublin police security district, SS-Brigadeführer Odilo Globocnik. The office of the new SSPF Lublin ordered the creation of a new department, under Dr Karl Hofbauer, to plan and administer the settlement and forced labour of hundreds of thousands of Jewish arrivals in the district. Hofbauer's office would also hold responsibility for other ethnic groups intended for resettlement in the Lublin area, including Poles and Gypsies.

The first transport of 901 Jews from the Protectorate of Bohemia-Moravia, arranged by Adolf Eichmann, then head of the Central Office for Jewish Emigration in Prague, set off for Nisko on 18 October 1939, prior to the appointments of both Heydrich in Prague and Globocnik in Lublin. Nisko stood on the west bank of the River San, 87 km south-west of Lublin in a direct line. Much of the surrounding area was waterlogged marshland, similar to that around the site of Birkenau village near Auschwitz. When they arrived, the Jews were forced to set up barracks in a swampy field as a transit camp. Another 1,800 Jews from Katowice and Vienna arrived a few days later. After the preparation of further transports, Müller ordered the immediate suspension of deportations, having received fresh orders from Himmler who had just been appointed as chief co-ordinator for the resettlement of ethnic Germans to the newly occupied territories in the former Poland.[17] These territories were annexed by Germany and stood outside the General Government. They consisted mainly of a large area of Upper Silesia, the Reichsgau Wartheland, and Danzig-Westpreußen. With Hitler's approval, Himmler's focus shifted to resettling the Jews and prioritising his new role. This involved moving approximately 30,000 ethnic Germans from the Lublin district to the annexed territories, deporting Austrian and Czech Jews to the Lublin Reservation, and the General Government Jews to the eastern bank of the Vistula River.

The Führer had visualised the eviction of 300,000 Altreich Jews and all Viennese Jews to the recently created Lublin Reservation. In late October 1939, he approved Himmler's plans to expel around 550,000 Jews from the annexed territories to the Lublin Reservation, plus all Poles living in the Third Reich from the area of the Soviet partition. This brought the tally to approximately 1 million people, a figure unacceptable to Heydrich who intervened on 28 November 1939 to reduce the number to 80,000.

Upon arrival, the deportees to the reservation were deposited with whatever luggage they brought and left to their own devices. They were forced to find temporary, often primitive, accommodation in the surrounding villages. By the end of January 1940, Heydrich reported that 78,000 Jews had been deported to Lublin from the Altreich, Austria, and the Protectorate. He expected the figure to rise to 400,000 by the end of 1940. The arriving Jews were subject to the authority of the Lublin Judenrat.

The German authorities initially anticipated transports every two weeks, consisting of a minimum of 2,000 people each, but this figure proved unrealistic. The procedure of deportations varied. At the point of departure, the authorities sometimes conducted superficial medical examinations. Regardless of their state of health, they were packed into trucks or trains. Deportees were officially authorised to take a maximum of 300 RM and hand luggage. Their excess belongings, businesses, furniture, and property were subject to seizure by the authorities to dispose of as seen fit.

Some sixteen forced labour camps were established throughout the region under the supervision of Globocnik. These included Bełżec, Krychow, Trawniki, Sobibor, Nisko, Tomaszow, Zamość, Chełm, Ujazdow, Milejow, and Dorohucza. The camp at Krychow was located in a former correctional facility, a branch of the Chełm Prison, which now stood empty. It held around 1,500 men and women who were forced to build farms for the incoming German settlers, dig irrigation ditches, and draining the swampy moorland. Before arriving at Sobibor to take command, Franz Stangl described Krychow:

> The first camp I saw was about half-way between Chełm and Sobibor, a farm called Krychow [Kirchof in German]. It employed two to three hundred Jewish women, mostly German or at least German speaking. I went in there to look around. There was nothing sinister about it—they were quite free. If you like it was just a farm where the women worked under the supervision of Jewish guards. Well, I suppose you could call them Jewish police. As I say I looked around and the women seemed quite cheerful—they seemed healthy. They were just working. The guards were armed with weissen Schlagmitteln [white implements] for beating the prisoners.[18]

This description is at variance with numerous other testimonies that paint the conditions in a very different light. Bełżec subsequently gained notoriety as the first permanent death camp installation, and Sobibor was also later converted for use as a killing centre, but in these early days, they were part of the camp set-up for enforced labour.

The Lublin Reservation was dissolved by the end of April 1940, after Hermann Göring ordered its suspension on 23 March 1940, with Himmler's agreement. In total, approximately 95,000 Jews were deported to the reservation. By then, many had starved to death, or had died through over-work and disease.

The termination of the reservation plan did not result in the suspension of Jewish deportations. In Lublin, Odilo Globocnik busied himself with the immediate task of resettling ethnic Germans from the Soviet occupation areas. Two of his lieutenants from Carinthia who joined him in Lublin, Paul Gasser and Reinhold von Mohrenschildt, were members of the SS-Totenkopf Reiterregiment (Mounted). Their job was to provide security for the German settlers returning from the Soviet sphere of influence. Polish guerrilla fighters would sometimes attack the settlers after they crossed into the German sector. In December 1939, Globocnik ordered the Totenkopf cavalry to the town of Chełm, but not for protection duties.

The early wartime story of Chełm is worth relating. In 1939, Chełm had approximately 15,000 Jewish residents; nearly half the entire population. The town was occupied by German forces at the beginning of September 1939, but the Wehrmacht withdrew on 25 September in advance of the Soviet Army. The Soviet authorities established a civilian administration under a Jewish major. Under the terms of the Ribbentrop-Molotov agreement, the town was ceded back to German control on 9 October 1939. Many Jews fled with the Soviet forces for fear of reprisals by the Polish population. Those Jews who remained were robbed, humiliated, attacked, and beaten by the Germans and the Chełm Poles in revenge for their central role during the Soviet occupation.

On 1 December 1939, Jews were rounded up for the first Chełm deportation organised in the name of the SSPF in Lublin. The leader of the Jewish community was ordered to concentrate 2,000 Jewish men, between fifteen and sixty years of age, from 8 a.m. in the market square (today part of ul. Lubelska, known as Plac Doctora Edwarda Luczkowskiego) under the pretence of a work detail. By 11 a.m., the desired number had been achieved. They were surrounded by a cordon of SS men. A number were badly beaten on the spot. The crowd was then addressed by an officer who declared they must surrender all their possessions.[19] At midday, the unfortunate throng was ordered to sing. They were then marched south to Hrubieszów and Sokal. The SS escort of around sixty men were on horseback and on bicycles. At times, the column was forced to run to keep up. Anyone on the march who fell by the wayside, or could not keep pace, was immediately shot on the spot.

Many gave up and resigned themselves to their fate, some throwing themselves into a river. Bodies, hastily dug graves, and blood littered the route, a point not lost on the international press. The incident gained notoriety and is remembered as the 'Chełm Death March'.[20] Dr Frank chastised the SS officers involved, not for the brutality and murders, but for the negative publicity. Globocnik was present during Frank's dressing down of his men.

In January 1940, a security police detachment shot 440 patients in the Chełm psychiatric hospital under the umbrella of euthanasia. Although Globocnik only discovered this action after the event, he still took credit for it.

He was present in 1940 when a large number of Jews were beaten to death in the marketplace at Tarnow, before marching the remainder to the cemetery where they were shot. Franz Bertl, one of Globocnik's drivers from Klagenfurt, witnessed the action and testified in 1965:

> After the bodies plunged into the ditch, four Jews were told to undress them. Those Jews were told that they would be spared if they did their work. However, in the end they were also shot. Globocnik had walked from the marketplace to the cemetery, accompanied by visitors from Berlin. They followed the SS units in order to witness the proceedings. The visitors had gone pale; two had got sick in the marketplace and were hardly able to walk.... Globocnik never discussed with me the action I had witnessed. He slept during most of the drive.[21]

Globocnik employed three other drivers—Benedikt Farkas, Leopold Veith, and Franz Eigner, all Austrians. The men participated in engagements against Polish partisans and were recommended by Globocnik for military decorations in November 1940. Eigner denied having played a part in anything other than driving his boss:

> I came to Lublin sometime in 1940. Soon after my arrival, I drove Globocnik and two members of his staff, among them his aide, to a prison in a village, the name of which I do not remember. It was a red brick building. We went into the courtyard. I had no idea why we were there. Prisoners were taken out of their cells, six to eight at a time, to be shot by the Waffen-SS. I left immediately, unable to watch. The shooting took a long time.[22]

In the heart of Lublin metropolitan area, between the large Christian cemetery and the rear of the tenement houses on the south side of today's ul. Marii Sklodowskiej-Curie, lies a twenty-first-century covered shopping mall—Lublin Plaza. The plot of land upon which it stands was once known as 7 and 9 Lipowa Street and was occupied before the war by the Academic Sports Union. The open area of land was not only used as a sports field, but also as the location of agricultural exhibitions, and where visiting circuses would erect their big tops. It was also renowned for being the site of equestrian shows in Lublin, and on the south side there was a small wooden grandstand. Along the sides of the site were single-storey garages, storage facilities, and stables. This location was identified by Globocnik as highly suitable for the establishment of a new labour camp.

The construction of the camp commenced in early December 1939, using Jewish labour. On 4 December, the German authorities ordered males between eighteen and fifty-five years of age to assemble in the square at 12 Peowiakow Street for work registration. Those selected were used to erect the first timber barracks, observation towers, and the perimeter fence. The Jewish Labour Office reached an agreement that it would provide a daily quota of 300–400 workers. This increased to 1,000 by the end of January 1940. Initially, the construction workers were allowed to return to their homes in the evening, but by the summer, they were confined within the camp.

The first commandant appointment of the Lipowa Street camp was Hermann Dolp. A locksmith by profession, Dolp was a long-term member of the SS and had attained the rank of Standartenführer. He was an officer in the Selbtschutz unit and had experience of concentration camp service. In November 1939, while heavily inebriated, he attempted to rape a Polish girl and then threatened a German official with his pistol. He was charged before a SS court on 9 January 1940 and found guilty of conduct unbecoming a SS officer. He was reduced in rank to SS-Sturmbannführer and ordered by Himmler to refrain from alcohol consumption for a period of two years, on pain of expulsion from the SS. On 4 February 1940, Himmler transferred him to Lublin and placed him under the command of Globocnik.

The Lublin SSPF used Dolp in the excavation of a planned massive tank ditch along the eastern border area of his domain, along the demarcation line with the Soviet-occupied sector of Poland. This elaborate, and militarily useless, project entailed the digging of a ditch, some 525 km in length, with a width of 40–50 metres, and to a depth of 1.5 metres below the water table. To achieve this masterpiece, Globocnik wanted to forcibly employ 2.5 million Jews. The number was subsequently reduced to 30,000 in the summer of 1940, and when the scheme was finally abandoned in October 1940, only 13 km had been excavated in the vicinity of Bełżec labour camp. Dolp first gained notoriety by his brutal selection methods at Bełżec. Another figure involved in this ill-conceived construction undertaking, and whose name would also subsequently become synonymous with brutality, was Oscar Dirlewanger.

In the initial stages of the Lipowa Street camp, all manner of Jewish tradesmen were compelled to work at the barracks of the camp. Many lived and worked in the former garages, in addition to the newly erected barracks. These included metal workers, tailors, leather and shoe makers, carpenters, painters, builders, and carters. Later, radio engineers and car mechanics joined them. If there was no work for a particular class of tradesman, they were ordered to do menial work such as street cleaning or shovelling snow. By mid-February 1940, Jewish Polish POWs were admitted to the camp. This later evolved into the predominant use of the camp—housing Jewish POWs. Globocnik showed a particular interest in 'his' camp, often visiting unannounced, sometimes with guests.

Globocnik's outward personality to his friends and co-workers was one of a polite and party-loving individual with a friendly disposition. He was certainly capable of pulling pranks on his staff, especially fuelled with excessive alcohol. His appearance lent itself to this jovial impression—slightly overweight, with a paunch and hair displaying the first signs of thinning. He stood at 5 feet 9 inches in height. He could not be described as 'good looking', but his position as the most powerful German in Lublin exuded an air of attractiveness. He was popular with the ladies.

His first personal secretary in Lublin, until 25 March 1941 when she fractured her leg skiing, Marianne Hillmann, was an Austrian who arrived in the city in March 1940. She testified post-war that Globocnik disliked long dictation, and often used general terms rather than specifics. He spoke very quickly, and she would subsequently review his dictation, correcting mistakes and flaws in his German language. She added that he was very popular, but she was horrified by his brutality towards the Jews.[23]

Another Austrian girl among the pool of secretaries was Wilhelmine 'Mimi' Trsek, a petite attractive twenty-eight-year-old single blonde. An early party member, she had been working voluntarily as a bookkeeper for the NSDAP in her hometown of Vienna, and in December 1939, she was offered secretarial work in Lublin, following an interview by Paul Gasser. Globocnik liked the young woman and found her style more amenable to his own casual approach to office procedure. Even though he favoured working at home in his villa, he would often attend Mimi's office in Ostlandstrasse for a dictation session in preference to working with the staid Fräulein Hillmann. After Hillmann's unfortunate skiing accident forced her transfer out of Globocnik's office, he was a little relieved that she was being replaced.

Mimi Trsek and the easy going Globocnik got on well together and she endeared herself into the exalted position of his confidante. There were rumours that the two enjoyed an intimate relationship, and she certainly harboured a strong affection for her boss, remaining fiercely loyal to this day. Interviewed between 1963 and 1968, Mimi denied any knowledge of atrocities committed against the Jews. She described Globocnik as a 'kind man with a big heart … a very good person'. She found him in no way brutal and she declared he always remained calm, paying particular attention to the welfare of his family. Her impression was of a man who enjoyed company and a joke 'second to none'. She was not aware of anyone speaking ill of him.

Liked by both the Brigadeführer and his family, Mimi was often a guest at lunch where they discussed all manner of subjects, including the Jews. As far as she was concerned, the Jews were treated fairly and were doing well in Lublin, especially those in the Lipowa Street camp. She had no personal experience of the subsequent Aktion Reinhardt and declared that Globocnik kept all matters pertaining to the extermination programme a closely guarded secret, even from a number of his closest staff. She recalled that an aide, Josef Nemec, was fired by the boss for mistakenly opening personal mail. She did remember certain phraseology being used in dictation, such as 'deportation, evacuation and resettlement', but she had no idea that these ever referred to murder.[24]

Such denial for someone so close to the master of ceremonies must engender an element of doubt. The West German legal authorities at that time were keen to prosecute war criminals and their associates, and any testimony provided in criminal investigations is bound to have an element of self-preservation attached. Mimi not only denied knowledge of murderous activities by her bosses, but also denied benefitting by way of receiving gifts appropriated during such endeavours: 'I never received any jewellery, neither from Globocnik, nor from anybody else'.[25] She maintained her silence and her support for Globocnik in a recent TV interview when she declared: 'That was a job for him that he certainly didn't want; wouldn't have wanted. What would have happened had he refused it? I can't say anything more about it. And that certainly somehow affected him strongly, that's for sure'.[26]

Globocnik's insistence on working from home on a regular basis, resulted in Mimi being called there on numerous occasions for dictation. His frequent 'entertaining' of an attractive young woman in his home on the premise of dictation, certainly raised a few eyebrows.

Not all members of his staff found Globocnik so easy going. Willy Natke, his SS valet, considered him a drunken brute who insisted on being attended every waking hour. He referred to his boss as a pig who simply was not the nice guy everyone thinks. According to others, during his drinking binges, he ridiculed the Jews and forced Jewish servants to perform acts of cruelty, such as consuming a whole bottle of vodka in one go.[27] His behaviour towards the Jews was both erratic and sometimes bizarre, insisting on Lipowa Street camp inmates removing their footwear and standing for hours in bare feet, regardless of the climate. He conducted some conversations with camp inmates with them standing facing the wall so they could not look him in the eye.

Whoever he dealt with, Globocnik would ignore other options or previous agreements if they were at odds with his own agenda, or that of the SS. His manner was at times abrasive, not always adhering to the Austrian trait of courtesy and good manners. As a reflection of the manner in which he performed his financial dealings in Vienna, his administration in Lublin was erratic. In modern parlance, he might be considered as suffering from a neurosis of some description.

The aforementioned Josef Nemec was another Austrian in Globocnik's circle. He had been with him during the period of struggle, and remained by his side in the office of the Vienna Gauleiter. A former furniture company clerk, Nemec joined the NSDAP in 1932 and the SS in 1935. He also served in the SA as financial manager and adjutant of SA-Obergruppe Österreich. In Vienna under Globocnik, he was a member of the SD and a Gau inspector, and for his service to the party, he was awarded the NSDAP Golden Honour Badge. Nemec served on the Lublin staff from August 1940 until March 1942, when he left following a dispute.

Walter Huppenkothen arrived in Lublin in February 1940 as the new chief of the SD and Gestapo. The two men were immediately at odds with one another. Huppenkothen's description of their relationship is important as it indicates Globocnik's special connection with Himmler:

> I made Globocnik's personal acquaintance after my transfer to Lublin. My official relationship with him was very strained. Although he had no professional knowledge of police matters, he continually gave instructions which clashed with the relevant directives I was given, and with which I could not comply for security policy reasons. Globocnik repeatedly complained about me, and unpleasant arguments arose in which my superiors supported my department and me. Whenever I objected, he would refer to special powers and special assistance from Himmler, with whom he kept up a regular personal correspondence.[28]

Huppenkothen approached Heydrich over the Jewish policy in Lublin, but he was told in no uncertain terms to stay out of the Jewish question, inferring that Globocnik was acting on Himmler's instructions. When faced with opposition, Globocnik relied upon his 'special mission' from the Reichsführer-SS.

The manpower required for Globocnik's various schemes was acquired through a form of impressment, reminiscent of the eighteenth-century methods employed by the British Navy to increase its numbers. Albeit Globocnik did not have his men scour the bars and hangouts for likely victims. Instead, he issued edicts demanding they assemble at various locations. Once in place, they were usually surrounded by a cordon of Globocnik's militia or police, and then herded off to wherever they were required.

His special representative for the resettlement of Jews, Dr Hofbauer, issued a directive dated 15 July 1940:

> Ref: Presentation of Jewish forced labourers
>
> For the accelerated expansion of the border barrier between the Bug and San we need, in the near future, considerable quantities of Jewish forced labourers.

> I ask you to bring 3,000 men to Bełżec by Wednesday the 17.7.1940.
>
> I ask you to prepare the presentation of another 5,000 Jews for the beginning of next week.
>
> In order to complete the ditch in the time required, a total of 30,000 men must be at work by the beginning of August. Therefore, I ask you to start now everything at the employment offices so that they are in a position to provide the required forced labourers.
>
> The guarding of the transports is carried out by us.[29]

This contradicted an instruction circulated on 5 July by Max Fauendorfer, the head of the Central Labour Office in the General Government, which stated: 'The allocation of Jewish workers is to be carried out exclusively by the local employment offices.... Furthermore, the Jewish workers are entitled to pay ... if desired, they can support their families. The minimum wage must be 80% of the amount paid to a Pole for the same work'.[30]

Impatient to increase his available workforce, Globocnik arbitrarily took the matter one step further. During the night of 22–23 July 1940, he despatched a troop of SS men to seize 300 Jews on a raid. He gave no notice of his intention and the result was a strongly worded protest from the labour office, which fell upon deaf ears. The labour office representative in Lublin, Oberregierungsrat Jache, eventually reached a compromise—the Jews already seized would remain in the custody of the SS and Globocnik's office would submit a back-dated application for labour. In return, the SS would refrain from further such raids.

On 6 August 1940, a meeting in Krakow was chaired by Max Frauendorfer. Dr Hofbauer represented the SSPF Lublin. A lawyer by profession, Hofbauer was a Carinthian by birth and a former lecturer in international law. Highly qualified and a cunning adversary, Hofbauer proved himself worthy of Globocnik's trust. Agreement was reached that the SS in District Lublin could take extraordinary measures to achieve their labour quota. Even the labour representatives from Radom and Warsaw lent their support.

Two days later, Globocnik decided on further labour raids. Those Jews taken would be registered with the Labour Office and would undergo a perfunctory medical examination by SS doctors for suitability to work. On 14 August, a major raid across the whole Lublin district was carried out under the codename 'Stieglitz'. Large numbers of Jews from Cholm, Tarnograd, Hrubieszów, Biłgoraj, Tomaszow, Werbkowice, and Zamość were seized. Reserve Police Battalion 104 from Hamburg, the Gendarmerie, and a Wehrmacht unit, played major roles.

Globocnik was disappointed with the results and suspected that the Jews had been tipped off in advance. He therefore ordered that the raids should continue. On 21 August 1940, the 3rd Company of Reserve Police battalion 104 reported that it had secured 888 Jews and they were being held in Zamość. Sixty-four Jewish men were subsequently transported to Bełżec to assist with the construction of the labour camp. This location was not yet designated a killing centre.

Although murders were becoming commonplace, they were still being carried out on an ad hoc basis. On the one hand, Globocnik was desperate to fulfil quotas required for construction and excavation work at the border, on the other, he authorised the murder of Polish students, lawyers, policemen, and officials, both men and women, and all highly capable of manual labour. One such location where such crimes were committed was a valley at a village called Rury Jesuickie. Here, beginning on 29 June 1940, the SS and Security Police dug a pit to a depth of 2 metres and 17 metres in length. The unfortunate victims arrived on trucks and were shot in groups of five, blindfolded and hands tied behind them. On four more occasions, the last during the night of 15–16 August 1940, the macabre scene was re-enacted. There were no survivors.

The civil governor of Lublin District, Ernst Zörner, represented the Governor General, Dr Hans Frank. Zörner was appointed as governor on 1 February 1940, replacing Friedrich Schmidt. He had been instrumental in gaining German citizenship for Adolf Hitler. His past record and friendly relationship with Hitler did not prevent a period of a power struggle between Globocnik and Zörner, triggered by the latter's appointment. Zörner often complained to Frank that the Lublin SSPF ignored his directives and implemented his own policy, irrespective of the official occupation programme. His complaints mirrored those problems Frank himself was experiencing with SS-Obergruppenführer Krüger. Himmler finally relented and intervened in both cases in 1943, when he replaced both Krüger and Globocnik, but not before having Zörner transferred on 10 April 1943.

In the meantime, the civil administration in Lublin complained about the wild raids for manpower carried out by Globocnik's men. In the late summer of 1940, work on irrigation channels and canals was carried out by seized Jews, usually toiling for ten hours per day, up to their knees in water. There was no opportunity to dry their footwear or clothes, and the leeches played havoc with their legs and feet. Working long hours in these conditions, with poor nourishment from a diet consisting of unsweetened black coffee, bread, thin soup with little or no meat, and sparse vegetables, contributed to disease and death. Globocnik's 'Jewish policy' became clear for all to see. Zörner's administration had little or no say in his own solution to the question of the Jewish population.

Unaffected by the plight of the Jews, the German community in the General Government was looking forward to a festive Yuletide in 1940. The temperature in southern Poland fell to below freezing. The war seemed a long way off from Lublin at the last Christmas before the catastrophe that awaited millions of Germans and Russians in Eastern Europe. The suffering of the Jews had begun, but it was soon to be ratcheted up through several gears to a level previously unknown to mankind.

# 6

# THE GLOBUS CLIQUE

INITIALLY, GLOBOCNIK ORGANISED his SSPF functions into five groups: the office of the SSPF; the office for the establishment of SS and police bases in the new eastern territories; the desk for all racial and ethnic matters; the planning office for SS and police bases, Jewish 'cleansing' and scientific mission within the scope of the SS-Mannschaftshaus; and Lublin District Party matters.

In addition, an independent motor pool desk was created for all transport questions. Subsequently, upon receipt of Himmler's order to carry out Aktion Reinhardt, a further department was formed—the Hauptabteilung Einsatz Reinhardt—which replaced the now defunct office for the establishment of SS and police bases.

As of October 1943, following Globocnik's departure from Lublin, the office of the SSPF numbered 153 ordinary staff members, with an additional 297 assigned on specific tasks. A total of 450 staff. These included a core staff of adjutants, departmental chiefs of staff, secretaries, drivers, interpreters, personal aides, orderlies, historians, architects, agronomists, builders, and experts on resettlement, racial, and Jewish matters. A large proportion were Austrians.

Fifteen women were subsequently identified as having worked as secretaries and typists for Globocnik's offices in Lublin. The vast majority were younger women and an air of promiscuity was evident. Globocnik was renowned for bedding his secretaries. Marianne Hillmann, Wilhelmine 'Mimi' Trsek, Irmgard 'Irma' Rickheim, and Margarete Sticks were all known to have worked as Globocnik's personal secretaries. The secretarial pool included some wives of SS staff and other Nazi officials in Lublin. Höfle's personal secretary, a young woman called Berta Gottschall, accompanied him to Warsaw and was present throughout the liquidation of the ghetto. She had also worked for Globocnik. Höfle's other Aktion Reinhardt secretary was Hanna Fuhrmann from Dresden. According to Cichotzski, it was

Wilhelmine Trsek who took dictation and typed all the secret communications for Globocnik. All the secretarial staff remained fiercely loyal to their Lublin masters, and they refused to acknowledge or confirm any incriminating material for the rest of their lives. Two police civil servants, Köbler and Weber, also dealt with important documents, but it was Ernst Lerch who handled all secret transmissions in and out of Lublin. One of Lerch's secretaries was subsequently identified as Jutta Jaroschowitz, the wife of SS-Obersturmführer Egon Jaroschowitz. She was born in Plauen on 16 September 1920, and lived post-war in Münster.

Hildegard Neuber (*née* Schitek), born in Breslau on 1 March 1913, and Edith Böhringer, both worked for Sporrenberg after Globocnik's departure. Supposedly, Globocnik's secretary in Trieste was Louise Guyon-Witzschel, but this is incorrect. She fell into Allied captivity at the end of the war.[1]

Globocnik's 'party attitude' saw him preparing for an entertaining festive season in 1940. Among those he visited over the Christmas holidays was his Volkstums-Referent (advisor on folklore), Lothar von Seltmann, and his wife, Minni, and their children. Von Seltmann was experienced in resettlement. He had been an important participant in the return of 65,000 ethnic Wolhynen-Germans to their homeland during the winter of 1939–1940. He had arrived in Lublin in May 1940, keen to assist his new boss with his plans for resettlement. His first priority was the resettlement of ethnic Germans from the territory between the Weichsel and the Bug Rivers. After a visit, Minni was so impressed with the Lublin way of life that she decided to move permanently on 30 August 1940 from Vienna to the Polish city with her two children. The young von Seltmann family settled into a nice house built by the Jews. They later moved into a larger property at Parkstrasse 8. Globocnik held the von Seltmann couple in high regard, and when Minni fell seriously ill in February 1941 after a difficult pregnancy, he arranged for a personal nurse to attend her. Von Seltmann moved to the office of the HSSPF in Krakow in June 1942, and transferred to the Eastern Front in 1943 where he was subsequently reported missing near Murmansk.

Globocnik's old comrade from Carinthia, Paul Gasser, did not fare so well. Their strong differences over the treatment of the Jews led to a breakdown in their previously solid friendship. In the spring of 1941, Gasser applied for active service with the Wehrmacht. He was subsequently killed in action on 21 October 1941, on the Eastern Front, following the invasion of the USSR. To his credit, Globocnik retained a loyalty to his old friend and applied for guardianship of Gasser's two young sons. Wolfgang Gasser was at the time fourteen years of age and in 1944, he was called up to the Wehrmacht. He fought on the Western Front and was captured by the Americans. He later took up acting and became a famous member of the Wiener Burgtheater in Vienna. He died in 2007.

Globocnik maintained an influential inner circle of past friends on his staff. Ernst 'Ernstl' Lerch arrived in Lublin to replace the departed Paul Gasser as his closest advisor, in July 1940. Lerch now held the rank of SS-Hauptsturmführer in the SD and he was destined to create a role in Globocnik's life akin to that enjoyed by Bormann with his boss, Hitler. Globocnik genuinely liked his staff and was concerned for their welfare, ensuring they received the best treatment and the best food and drink. SS-Obersturmführer Johann Offermann considered Globocnik a drunkard, particularly partial to large quantities of cognac and champagne. He stated that his boss was a heavy smoker who drank litres of good quality coffee.

Lerch's wife, Gertrude, also from Klagenfurt, was pregnant with their first child when Lerch was transferred from the SD in Klagenfurt to Globocnik's staff in Lublin. A baby girl, Roswitha, was born on 17 October 1940. At 6 feet 3 inches, Lerch towered above his boss. He wore spectacles and had the appearance of a schoolmaster. He volunteered for his army service in December 1938 and saw active service in the Wehrmacht during the Polish campaign as a signals corporal. Described by others as very friendly and as one at ease with strangers, a trait that served him well in his previous occupation as a hotelier and waiter. He enjoyed a special relationship with Globocnik from his days in Klagenfurt. Not only did he hold the exalted position as Globocnik's confidante, he succeeded Dr Hofbauer as director of Jewish Resettlement in Lublin and served as Globocnik's chief of staff.

Ernst Lerch achieved the rank of SS-Sturmbannführer on 21 July 1942 and was transferred from the SD to the Staff HSSPF Ost the same day. Long considered by many as one of the more culpable of the perpetrators of the annihilation of European Jews, he escaped justice post-war and died of natural causes in 1997. When interrogated by the British in Wolfsberg detention centre, he conveniently forgot his service in Lublin and denied any knowledge of atrocities, declaring his first meeting with Globocnik was in 1943. He escaped in 1947 and went underground until 1950 when he deemed it 'safe' to appear before a denazification tribunal.

As the man responsible for the radio communication traffic between Lublin and Berlin, Lerch clearly had first-hand knowledge of the actions against the Jews—he was one of the few staffers kept within the loop by Globocnik as a trusted aide. He was directly incriminated in murders by a former subordinate, Hermann Worthoff, who swore under oath that Lerch had personally participated as ranking officer in the liquidation of thousands of Jews from the Majdan–Tatarski ghetto in a wooded area on the south-east outskirts of Lublin at Krepiecki in 1942:

> The officers from the stationary headquarters of Sipo and SD were very well aware that the area of the ghetto held several thousand 'clandestine' Jews which caused problems with overpopulation and lodgings. Selections were deemed the only proper remedy for the situation. The first of these, as with all the future ones, was supervised by SS-Obersturmführer Hermann Worthoff, SS-Untersturmführer Wilhelm Walter, SS-Untersturmführer Harry Sturm, SS-Untersturmführer Knitzky and Ernst Kalich.

Auxiliary units of guards from Trawniki were additionally sent to help in Majdan Tatarski. The first selection started at dawn on the 20 of April in the yard dividing the area of the ghetto from the Flugplatz work camp and was carried out in a very brutal way—many people were beaten up or shot straight away. The group selected that day consisted of 3,000 women, children and the elderly. Young and middle-aged people were chosen, too. Ida Glickstein was there as well and this is how she describes the course of the selection:

'The sunrise on Monday came with yet another horrifying surprise. The ghetto was surrounded with a double line of Germans and Ukrainians and we were all ordered out into the spacious yard stretching between the plane factory and the barbed wire fence.... The order was given at daybreak when everyone was still asleep. People started throwing clothes on in all haste, some preparing backpacks and a little bit of food, others remembering only the "ausweis" cards. Germans walked from house to house, rushing people: "Schneller, los, los!" Many were taken out into the yard in their underwear only and as a punishment for not managing to get dressed on time were destined for resettlement immediately.... After a dozen or so minutes the orders were shouted out: "Take out the J-cards". Hands flickered over the dense crowd, waving the "Js", but obviously every one of us had someone in the family without the certificate. Next to me my younger sisters were standing, no "J-cards" on them, somewhere further back in the crowd my mother was with my third sister and a 10-week-old newborn baby, orphaned by my mother's brother. And people like me were plenty! After an hour and many discussions held among themselves and the representatives of the Jewish Community, German soldiers formed a line and told the owners of the "Js" to move to the left side of the yard. So we moved on, under the hail of rubber clubs urging us on faster. And the others remained where they were, despair in their hearts. A few people made it through without the "J-card".... My mother made it by a miracle as did my sister with the newborn baby, but my other two young, talented sisters left us for ever.... The Germans hit and beat anyone they came across, often firing in the air and cursing violently. [Hermann] Worthoff [responsible for the liquidation of the ghetto] gave a speech afterwards about the end of the action. He said that the eliminated people will go back to the ghetto where they will work peacefully for the Germans. They told us to form lines of five and return to Majdan Tatarski. There were more than 3,000 people left in the yard: mothers and fathers, brothers and sisters, husbands, wives and children of those who made it back...'

The selected people were rushed to the concentration camp at Majdanek. The selection was repeated there and around 200–300 relatively healthy and strong men aged 18–45 were singled out to stay. The fear of separation from their families made many men

> remain with their wives and children who were led to death. For the next several days they were transported to the nearby Księpiecki Forest to be executed in previously prepared ditches by Lublin SiPo and SD officers. Approximately 2,700–2,800 people were murdered during this short period. Their bodies were buried in a mass grave by the Sonderkommando made up of Soviet war prisoners held in KL Lublin.[2]

Lerch remained fiercely loyal to Globocnik and was with him when captured by the British in May 1945. Described by a Waffen-SS subordinate as a competent field commander, he appeared genuinely liked and respected by men under his command. Despite this, his influence over Globocnik was considered far too great by some senior SS colleagues. During his major inspection tour in May 1943, Max von Herff, the chief of the SS Personnel Central Office, remarked:

> L[erch] belongs to the circle of Ostmärker who were groomed by SS-Gruppenführer Globocnik himself. Old, long-standing comrades-in-arms of Globocnik from the time of struggle and completely loyal to him. Too weak to act as a balancing power within the staff and, owing to the long time spent together, too personally allied with the Gruppenführer. Also … too young for the position and too long in the same place. Has to be replaced at all costs, since he has it in him for superior growth. Needs tough martial education.[3]

In May 1972, Lerch was finally brought before a court to answer charges of complicity in the murders committed in the General Government. After a few days, the case collapsed and was abandoned for lack of evidence. He died in Klagenfurt in 1997.

Another insider to be considered as a prime culprit in the genocide perpetrated by Globocnik's hangers-on was Hermann Julius Höfle. Born in Salzburg, Austria, on 19 June 1911, Höfle was a motor mechanic by profession, but also plied his trade as a taxi driver. He joined the NSDAP and the SS on 1 August 1933, having previously been a member of the Austrian Nazi Party. He joined NSDAP Ortsgruppe Schallmoos West. He was posted as commander of 1. Sturmbann of 76. SS-Standarte in Salzburg and rose to the rank of SS-Hauptsturmführer. From October to December 1939, he was acting commander of 76. SS-Standarte. He was also temporarily attached for three months to the 99. SS-Standarte in Znaim during its founding period at the time of the Sudetenland annexation. From February to March 1939, Höfle attended the SS-Führer School in Munich-Dachau.

His political beliefs were never in question. In 1935, he was sentenced to seven months' imprisonment and a further three months' conditional police detention for political activities. He served a term of imprisonment from 20 May 1935 until 1 January 1936.

He was transferred to southern Poland after the Polish campaign on 10 December 1939 and served as an area Selbstschutz commander in Neu-Sandetz. He was appointed as a director of a forced labour camp, south-east of Lublin, until 1 November 1940. His camp inmates were employed on the excavation of tank ditches on the River Bug. He was soon transferred to the staff of the SSPF Lublin as a referent and deputy staff officer.

Although not arriving on scene as a Globocnik insider in the early stages of his reign, Höfle soon established himself as a proficient organiser. Globocnik recognised his abilities and subsequently utilised them to co-ordinate Aktion Reinhardt. Effectively, Höfle developed into Globocnik's representative in all matters pertaining to the enforced movement of the Jewish population, the seizure of their properties and chattels, and their eventual physical destruction. Höfle actually took up residence in a bedsit on one of the upper floors of the Reinhardt HQ in Lublin.[4] This enabled him to maintain a constant supervision of the everyday mechanics of the operation.

Höfle's reports reflect the high regard in which he was held by his superiors. At Munich-Dachau, he was described as having a satisfactory attitude towards his work and to his appearance. His relationship to his comrades was 'good' and his behaviour, both on and off duty, was also 'good'. He also attained 'good' for his understanding of military situations. This standard was transferred over to his new role in Lublin where Globocnik was happy to endorse a similar 'good' report and to recommend his promotion to SS-Sturmbannführer, a rank he achieved on 21 July 1942.

Höfle married Berta Dühr (born 25 October 1912) in Salzburg on 29 October 1933. They set up a family home at Elisabethstrasse 10A in Salzburg, before moving to Hubert-Sattler-Gasse 13. Frau Höfle started a business at the Elisabethstrasse address, which subsequently led to a dispute with a Frau Rosa Wolf who wrote to the SS newspaper *Das Schwarze Korps* describing her version of events. Höfle's SS personal file contains a number of letters pertaining to the dispute, but it does not appear to have had a detrimental effect on his career. The Höfle couple had five children, including a set of twins born on 18 August 1941. Both twins died of diphtheria in Lublin in 1942, and there is a story that a distraught Höfle jumped into the open grave in his grief. Höfle was below average height, standing at slightly under 5 feet 7 inches, and his hair began to recede at an early age. He was awarded the War Service Cross 1st Class with Swords in 1943—no doubt for his diligent contribution to the smooth running of the operation to murder the Jews of Poland and beyond—and the Iron Cross 2nd Class in 1944.[5]

Although Höfle lived at the Aktion Reinhardt headquarters in Lublin, this did not prevent his travelling around the General Government to pass on advice and his general experience. In his post-war Israeli police interrogation, Adolf Eichmann identified Höfle as the one who demonstrated gassing equipment to him.[6] Höfle was assisted by Helmut Pohl, his liaison officer with Globocnik, and two secretaries, Hanna Furmann and Berta Gottschall. He was heavily involved in the murderous Reinhardt campaign from its inception, and was also instrumental in providing personnel to carry it out. He participated in the clearing of ghettos in the General Government and the vicious Aktion Erntefest—'Harvest Festival'—where the Germans annihilated the remaining Jews of the area in November 1943.

Höfle subsequently saw service in Albania and the Netherlands, and spent several months on the staff at Sachsenhausen concentration camp, north of Berlin before joining his old boss, Globocnik, in Trieste.

Höfle was a member of Globocnik's party captured at Mößlacher Alm and was asked to confirm the identity of Globocnik's corpse. He was held in the detention centre at Wolfsburg until October 1947, but his important role in Aktion Reinhardt was not fully recognised. He was released to return to Salzburg as a car mechanic, and it was not until the Polish justice system caught up with him in July 1948, did he successfully evade arrest. He fled to Italy under a false name and remained in hiding until 1951 when he returned to Austria, before moving to Germany. Satisfied that the search for him at lost impetus, he returned to Salzburg and lived there openly until 2 January 1961 when he was arrested. He was held in prison in Vienna, awaiting trial. Before proceedings could commence, Höfle took his own life by hanging himself on 21 August 1962.

Helmut Ortwin Pohl was Höfle's deputy. Born in Klagenfurt on 27 September 1901, he had a background in industry as a blue collar worker. He joined the NSDAP in 1930, and was an active member of the subversive element in the illegal party. He was an agent for the Carinthian SD and was arrested on several occasions. In the autumn of 1939, he was posted to Krakow and Posen with the SS-Totenkopfverbände. He took an active role in numerous expulsions and resettlement actions where he gained the experience that would stand him in good stead for his future duties. By the autumn of 1940, he was back in civilian life. In late 1941, he was recalled to Poland and posted to the staff of Globocnik who subsequently assigned him to Aktion Reinhardt, where he was responsible for the daily transports to Bełżec and Sobibor. No doubt his friend, Hermann Höfle, had recommended him. Initially, Pohl was attached to the office for the establishment of SS and Police strongpoints. He returned to civilian work in June 1942, in a reserved occupation. Globocnik's efforts to recall him to SS service in Trieste were unsuccessful. Post-war he lived in Linz, Austria.

SS-Unterscharfürer Albert Susitti was Globocnik's expert on sport. He was born in Maria Rain, near Klagenfurt, in 1910; yet another Carinthian. Active in the Nazi movement since 1929, he was a manager in a sports store in Klagenfurt. In the political illegal period, Susitti founded a sports club as a cover for Nazi activities with Friedrich Rainer. He joined the SS in March 1938, and was appointed as sports expert for 90. SS-Standarte. He was conscripted into the SS-Verfügungstruppe in late 1939, and was head-hunted by Globocnik in Lublin, where he was assigned to Höfle's staff and eventually the Aktion Reinhardt office. He was one of those whom Globocnik took with him to Trieste.

Another figure from Globocnik's Klagenfurt days was Reinhold von Mohrenschildt, a member of the SD and now attached to the staff of Werner Lorenz, the head of Volksdeutsche Mittelstelle (VOMI)—Central Office for Ethnic Germans. This department was responsible for the resettlement of ethnic Germans on the lands cleared of their indigenous population. As a senior VOMI official, von Mohrenschildt became a demographic expert on resettlement and was highly qualified for a senior position on Globocnik's staff in Lublin. His junior SS rank of Obersturmführer did not obstruct his influence over his old pal from Carinthia, and he actually moved into Globocnik's villa on Ostlandstrasse for a time.

Von Mohrenschildt was born on 8 November 1915 in Leifling, Austria, the son of Erich Ferdinand (1879–1943) and Valerie (born von Stromberg) von Mohrenschildt. His family was a Baltic aristocratic dynasty that had purchased an estate at Pischeldorf in 1938. This consisted of a working farm and a castle. Young Reinhold studied diplomacy and economics in Vienna before obtaining a temporary secretarial post with Friedrich Rainer. He was a member of the Hitler Youth from 4 April 1933 until 15 September 1933, and in the SA from 15 September 1933 until 15 July 1934. He formally joined the NSDAP and the SS on 12 March 1938. From 3 October 1938 until 31 December 1938, he undertook military training as a SS-Mann with 3. SS-VT 'Der Führer'. He gave up his religion and declared himself 'gottgläubig' (a believer in God). His medical examination report of 1940 described him as a little below 5 feet 11 inches in height and of athletic build with grey-green eyes. He was in good health.[7] From 15 July 1939, he was temporarily attached to the staff of the Gauleiter of Danzig, Albert Forster, before Globocnik summoned him to Lublin in November of that year to act as one of his adjutants for resettlement.[8]

By 8 June 1940, acting in his dual role for VOMI, von Mohrenschildt was an assistant to Seyss-Inquart in The Hague, Holland. Here he was a secretary, specialising in agricultural questions. He became engaged to Margarethe Kaufmann (born 30 March 1916) on 7 July 1940 and the couple married on 15 September 1940. Margarethe was the sister-in-law of Ludolf Jakob von Alvensleben. The union produced four offspring. Heavily involved in the resettlement of ethnic Germans from Volhynia, this stood von Mohrenschildt in good stead for his subsequent important role in the clearing and resettlement of the Zamość lands.

Following the invasion of the Soviet Union in June 1941, von Mohrenschildt transferred for a time to Riga in Latvia. If he is to be believed, he declared post-war that he saw active service in the siege of Leningrad. However, he was present in

Lublin on 28 November 1942 when Globocnik identified him as second-in-command for the cleansing action for the Zamość lands, which began on that date. This contradicted von Mohrenschildt's post-war assertion that he had left Lublin the month previously. The magnetic attraction to Klagenfurt remained throughout, however, with von Mohrenschildt maintaining an office under the guise of the RKFDV at Gassometergasse 8, Klagenfurt, an address with an appropriate name, given our knowledge of subsequent events.

Von Mohrenschildt remained a close ally of Globocnik throughout, and enjoyed the backing of his powerful friend. However, this relationship did not always satisfy von Mohrenschildt's ambitions. When Globocnik recommended a promotion for his friend in February 1942, it was refused by the HSSPF Friedrich-Wilhelm Krüger, who commented: '... von Mohrenschildt is a so-called political migratory bird'.[9]

Although there is little or no evidence of von Mohrenschildt's direct involvement in the vicious murders perpetrated under the umbrella of Aktion Reinhardt, there is little doubt that he had inside knowledge of the operation. He subsequently joined his old pal in Trieste, and as a result of his roaming brief, he was able to claim that he was not present when the crimes were committed. After the war, he was interrogated by the British and interned in Wolfsberg. He never stood trial and was only investigated. One such investigation was based upon an allegation that he, and a SD man named Patterer, crossed from Carinthia into Italy in the spring of 1944 with a contingent of SS troops, and then proceeded to beat and murder local villagers before seizing their property. This incident was allegedly repeated several weeks later. The case was never proved and no trial ensued.

Von Mohrenschildt's family remain at Pischeldorf following his death from a brain tumour on 2 November 1990. His descendants have sold off part of the estate and now run the farm as a going concern.

Himmler's 'business manager' was Oswald Pohl, a former paymaster in the German Navy. An entire SS department evolved into the SS-Wirtschafts-Verwaltungshauptamt (WVHA)—Economic and Administrative Central Office—with SS-Obergruppenführer Pohl as chief. His departmental heads in 1942 were August Frank, Georg Lörner, Hans Kammler, and Richard Glücks. Pohl's SS department was important to the story of Globocnik as it controlled not only the SS construction projects and the overall administration of the concentration camp system, but also the valuables seized by the SS. However, it did not control admissions to or releases from the camps and, as we shall see subsequently, it had negligible authority over the death camps administered under Aktion Reinhardt, which Globocnik viewed as 'his camps'. He was able to do this by reason of his special status afforded to him by the Reichsführer-SS.

Attached to the SS-WVHA from the SS-Führungshauptamt was one Georg Wippern. Born on 26 May 1909 in Neuhof-Hildesheim, Wippern was married with four children. His wife, Ilse, was born Spieß on 16 October 1914 in Goslar am Harz to a family with Catholic roots. They were married in Goslar on 8 July 1933. The Wippern family declared themselves as 'gottgläubig'. It appears from his handwritten Lebenslauf in his SSO file that he first joined the SS on 1 June 1932, but subsequently left, possibly in order to rejoin the Wehrmacht. He had served in the army (Infantry Regiment 17 as a Jäger) from 26 October 1927 until 30 November 1931. Wippern joined the NSDAP on 1 September 1932 and did military service with Infantry Regiment 15 from 1 June 1934 until 31 May 1937, attaining the rank of Feldwebel Oberzahlmeister (sergeant paymaster). He joined the SS on 1 June 1937 as a SS-Mann and was immediately promoted to SS-Obersturmführer on 7 June 1937, backdated to 1 June. Himmler agreed to his being allocated his original SS number, 118 449. He was attached to the leadership staff of the SS-Verfügungstruppe, the forerunner of the Waffen-SS.

On 12 January 1938, Wippern was transferred on attachment to SS-Regiment 'Germania' as the second administration officer. He was appointed as the first administration officer of 'Germania' on 1 April 1938. Herbert Gille wrote a satisfactory report on his abilities in December 1938. Gille described him as quiet and decent with an open character. He was sporty with an avid interest in sport. He managed funds with great skill. Wippern's efforts and skills were recognised on 30 January 1939 with promotion to SS-Hauptsturmführer. From 10 June 1939, he was attached to Abteilung 1 of the SS-Artillerie-Standarte of the SS-VT as administration chief. This evolved into the SS-VT-Division and Wippern was posted as leader of Bäckerei Kompanie. Wippern served with his unit in Poland and during the western campaign. From 30 October 1940, he transferred to the Panzerjäger Replacement Section in Arolsen as head of administration. By 1 January 1941, he was attached to SS-'Nordland' within SS-Division 'Germania', based in Vienna. He was head of administration and IVa of the regiment. He remained on the staff of the Verwaltungsamt-SS in the SS-Führungshauptamt. He was given an attachment to SS-Division 'Wiking' on 31 March 1941 by August Frank and was posted to the Replacement Unit at Dachau.

On 21 July 1941, Wippern was transferred again, this time to Lublin as Leader of the SS-Standort Administration. In layman's terms, this meant he was responsible for all the fiscal duties of the town's SS garrison. This move brought Wippern, along with his economic skills, into the realm of the SSPF Lublin who was quick to realise, and then subsequently utilise, Wippern's capable abilities, tailored to the needs of Aktion Reinhardt. Globocnik rapidly ensured his potential vault keeper was aptly rewarded, and Wippern was promoted to SS-Sturmbannführer on 30 January 1942. It is also quite possible that Globocnik was not alone in recognizing Wippern's capabilities. None other than Dr Hans Frank went out of his way to personally visit Wippern in the Reserve Hospital at Cholm after he was admitted on 26 May

1942 with double through and through gunshot wounds to his left shoulder. These may well have been received during a possible assassination attempt on the life of Globocnik, but this requires confirmation. The incident was reported, however, in the Polish press.[10]

Although Wippern became a close associate of Globocnik and an essential cog in the Reinhardt wheel, there is no significant evidence that he was directly involved in the Reinhardt murders. His role appears limited to the theft and disposal of property seized in the operation. He remained throughout nominally attached to Oswald Pohl's SS economic empire. There is little doubt that Wippern, as a close associate of Globocnik, had knowledge of what transpired inside the so-called 'terminal stations' at Bełżec, Sobibor, and Treblinka, but evidence of his involvement in anything other than robbery and disposal of stolen goods continues to evade investigators. His dubious links with Frank in Krakow requires further investigation, as does his professional relationship with the mysterious SS-Standartenführer Erich Schellin, the SS administration officer in Krakow, to whom some stolen proceeds were for a time directed before onward despatch to the Reichsbank in Berlin.

Before 1939, at ul. Chmielna 1 in Lublin—German Hopfen Gasse 1—there was a building of the girls' school for housekeeping in the old Slawinski Palace. From 1941, it housed the SS-Standortverwaltung (the SS Garrison Administration) and Wippern's office. In the course of the Aktion Reinhardt, it served as a warehouse for money and valuables plundered from the Jews sent to the death camps. The sorting of goods was performed by a Sonderkommando of Jewish prisoners, including jewellers and bank clerks deported from Bohemia. These inmates were registered in KL Lublin (Majdanek), but quartered on the grounds of the SS-Standortverwaltung. Behind the main edifice of the former school, there were barracks, where a furnace melted down the gold, silver, platinum, jewellery, and dental gold. The precious metals were sent to the Berlin Reichsbank in bullion form. In the basement, a room, 4 metres by 6 metres, was converted into a strong room for the storage of valuables. This locked room was accessible only by using two separate keys simultaneously. At the beginning of 1943, on the occasion of a visit to Lublin by Heinrich Himmler, the jewellery plundered from Jews coming from the whole Europe went on the display in the warehouse.

Wippern's office and valuables vault was located in a nineteenth-century building, standing on a high scarp over the Czechówka. It is clad in eclectic architecture, which combines the features of many historical styles. The building, mainly in the neoclassical style with its colonnaded entrance portico, is covered with a high, broken mansard roof. Initially, the palace belonged to the Chrzanowski family. In 1895, Stanisław Ślawiński, a social and political activist, and owner of estates in Antopol, Sadurki, and Czesławice, purchased it. In 1903, he was one of the founders of the Nałęczów Credit Society, and in 1906, he became involved in the construction of the People's House in Nałęczów, in which the Agricultural Society was located. During the years 1919–21, Stanisław Ślawiński was the minister of provisioning of Rzeczpospolita, and was director of the Lublin Agricultural Syndicate. In the interwar period, the palace passed into the hands of the Refugee Congregation of the Servants of Jesus, a religious order founded in 1884 in Warsaw. Its doctrine was to care for and educate young women and prepare them for the cooking profession in domestic service, in addition to other training in tailoring, and to become seamstresses. Today, it is an ophthalmic clinic.

Wippern was allocated qualified staff to assist him. His office was officially known as both Abteilung Reinhardt and Abteilung IVa. At various times, his staff in this department included SS-Unterscharführer Eicholz, SS-Unterscharführer Pflanzer, and Dorl, SS-Obersturmführer Huber, and SS-Oberscharführer Teichelmann and Rzepa. The trusted regular Berlin couriers were Erich Fettke and Philip Post, later supplemented with two other T4 couriers, Zielinsky and Rose. They were in possession of special passes signed by Himmler, which allowed them to travel unmolested with sealed luggage, not subject to searches. However, on at least two separate occasions, Fettke's important luggage was seized *en route* by unknown SS men. Despite his subsequent written reports of these intrusions, Fettke never heard any more about the incidents.

To begin with, the method of despatch was rather haphazard. No real plans had been formulated for the secure delivery of the stolen goods to Berlin, and this created enormous opportunities for anyone involved on the journey between the camps and the Reichsbank to enrich themselves. In the early days at Bełżec, the loot was stored in a cellar of a former stable behind Wirth's house. In late spring of 1942, a regular courier service to Lublin, and then onward to Berlin, was established. Two heavy, padlocked, metal chests were collected from Wirth's Kommandantur by Erich Fettke from T4. With only 'Express Delivery' labels attached, they were loaded aboard the luggage car of a regular rail passenger service at Bełżec. They travelled to Lublin, where they were forwarded on the overnight express to Berlin.

A fourth known T4 courier, Josef Kölbl, who supervised the T4 motor pool, was also used to transport the loot, by his own admission: 'My job consisted of taking locked chests to Lublin and bringing back another locked chest.... I can say with certainty that I handed over the chests to Wirth, and then took another chest from him for the return journey'.[11]

Erich Bauer confirmed the courier method: 'During the whole time of the Jewish operation in the camps, the T4 couriers took with them two chests.... The chests were, to my knowledge, continuously transported between Berlin and the camps'.[12]

The movement of plundered goods was not restricted to these courier services. The 'non-valuables', such as shoes, textiles, spectacles, etc., were sorted and disinfected, before being collected to await a large enough shipment by goods wagons to their onward destinations. Dieter Allers, the executive director of T4, also took part in the collection of valuables on at least one occasion when he arrived in Bełżec with Adolf Kaufmann, the T4 building inspector, in a lorry driven by Erich Bauer. Crates of precious stones, silver cutlery, and good quality soap were loaded onto the lorry and taken to T4 in Berlin. Others involved were SS-Oberscharführer Johannes Teichelmann and SS-Oberscharführer Ernst Brosig, both staff members of the SS-Standortverwaltung. Brosig accompanied Georg Wippern on one occasion, when he collected a sack of used banknotes.

Post-war, Wippern maintained his distance from the gassing process and declared that his involvement was purely as a bookkeeper and smelter of precious metals. He declared that his first encounter with diamonds, precious gems, and other jewellery was following a direct order from Oswald Pohl. He successfully avoided prosecution, dying in Bonn in 1993. However, his important role in Aktion Reinhardt cannot, and should not, be overlooked. Consequently, the name 'Wippern' will frequently reappear throughout this study.

Georg Wippern and his family were counted among the elite social group surrounding Globocnik. Frau Wippern wore only the best clothes and both her and her husband displayed expensive jewellery—she was very proud of a diamond encrusted ring which she had no qualms about showing off.[13]

The other figure who appeared to benefit from his position was SS-Sturmbannführer Johannes Müller, the commander of the Security Police and SD in Lublin. Müller enjoyed friendly relations with Globocnik, and apparently benefited as a result. The Müllers also collected valuable jewellery, and Frau Müller was often seen out in fashionable and exclusive clothing, including a number of fur capes.

Oswald Pohl's order in the spring of 1942 to regulate the process of storage, accounting, and transportation of goods appropriated in Aktion Reinhardt, created the new office Abteilung IVa within Wippern's SS-Standortverwaltung. Effectively, this gave Wippern unrestricted power over the goods seized. According to Wippern, this resulted in his first encounter with Christian Wirth, but this is hard to believe. Pohl sent bank trained accountants to Lublin to assist Wippern and his own accountant, Alois Rzepa, an Austrian. New strict instructions were issued in order to prevent further pilfering. The smelting of precious metals in the barrack behind Wippern's office was placed under the supervision of SS-Oberscharführer Johannes Teichelmann, who also had responsibility for foreign currency. Wippern opened a special account—Account 'G'—with the Emissionsbank on Krakowskie Przedmieście in Lublin. It appears that Globocnik, Wippern, and possibly Lerch were the signatories. No record exists of the amounts that passed through this account, or who and when withdrawals were made.

Georg Michalsen was born in Wendrin (today Wedrynia) in Upper Silesia on 13 September 1906. His family name at birth was Michalczyk. His Catholic father was a primary school teacher, and little Georg attended school in Opole from 1912 until 1920. He was then placed as an apprentice office clerk in a law firm in the same town. He found employment as an accounts clerk in an agricultural co-operative, followed by work in the building materials industry and the housing construction industry. Favouring German nationalist politics under the influence of his father, Michalsen joined the Wehrwolf Organisation in 1924.[14] In 1927, a Wehrwolf pamphlet declared:

> So turn your eyes to the east. There alone is our salvation. Shout out into the people that you want the crusade, the salvation of the 20 million. Preach the crusade from west to east. The Crusade of Heimatliebe, the völkisch brotherly love, the Arterhaltung, the space extension and the work! Preach the peoples migration to the East. Calls for the exploitation of colonization: for land acquisition in war and peace.[15]

Georg Michalsen joined the NSDAP on 1 November 1928. After 1930, he was the leader of Ortsgruppe Opeln and was the local party editor and treasurer. He also joined the SA. He transferred to the SS on 10 January 1932 and was allocated SS number 29 337 in SS-Standarte 23. By 1937, in the rank of SS-Obersturmführer, he was attached to SS-Standarte 45 in Opole as the representative for sport.

In the Polish campaign, he led a SS commando from Opole, which advanced into Czestochowa. Following the defeat of Poland, he commanded a force of about seventy SS men, which trained Selbstschutz troops and performed guard duties in Petrokau (today Piotrkow Trybunalski). He also served with Selbstschutz units in Opoczno and Rawa. His tasks included training Selbstschutz troops as auxiliary police, forced expulsion of Poles, and even murder of the indigenous population. These duties provided a solid grounding for his future role in Aktion Reinhardt. In 1940, he changed his name from the Polish-sounding Michalczyk to the more Germanic name of Michalsen. He also married in this year, a union which produced a daughter.

Initially, Michalsen was posted to the staff of the SSPF Radom, Fritz Katzmann, but he transferred to the office of the SSPF Lublin in August 1940. He then commanded Selbstschutz units overseeing the forced labourers employed with the excavation of tank ditches along the Bug River. During this time, he contracted a bad case of dysentery. He returned to Globocnik's staff in April 1941. Michalsen appears to have temporarily transferred to Riga as head of a field office following the invasion of the Soviet Union, in order to carry out similar construction work. He was allegedly present during the murders of between 12,000 and 15,000 people in the Rumbuli Forest on 30 November 1941, but subsequent post-war criminal investigations could not find any evidence that Michalsen had actually participated in the mass shootings. Michalsen stated that 'the guard [for this action] was completely inadequate'.

Once again, Michalsen returned to Globocnik's staff in early summer of 1942 and joined Aktion Reinhardt. Along with Höfle, Lerch, Claasen, and Worthoff, Michalsen attended a meeting in Warsaw on 21 July 1942 to discuss with the SSPF Warsaw, Ferdinand von Sammern-Frankenegg, plans to deport Jews from the Warsaw ghetto to the facility at Treblinka under the cover of resettlement. The Lublin contingent directed that the chairman of the Jewish Council, Adam Czerniakow, must provide 6,000 Jews daily for 'resettlement in the east'. Michalsen was Höfle's deputy for this operation and was deployed to command the railway sidings where the Warsaw Jews were loaded into freight cars bound for Treblinka. It was estimated by the post-war Hamburg judicial authorities that approximately 300,000 Warsaw Jews were deported to Treblinka during the clearing of the ghetto in this action from July to early September 1942.

Consequently, Michalsen became widely known as an expert in such matters and subsequently participated in the evacuation of several large ghetto communities, including the ghetto in Bialystok when around 30,000 inhabitants were deported to Treblinka and Auschwitz-Birkenau in August 1943. During the final clearing of the Warsaw Ghetto in April and May 1943, Michalsen arranged for the transfer of the Többens business operation to the camp at Majdanek. After the outbreak of the Second World War, Walter Többens was the managing director of a wholesale and retail trade group in Berlin, and a wholesaler in the Tomaschow district. There Jewish forced labourers had to work for his firm. In 1941, Többens relocated to the Warsaw Ghetto as a member of a production commission for production orders for the Wehrmacht to be handled through a German transfer agency. Without outside financial support, Többens became independent through corruption and set up the Többenswerke in the Warsaw Ghetto. In addition to tailoring, shoemaking, and leather production, the manufacturing facilities included, among other things, a cap and a rubber factory. Up to 25,000 Jewish forced labourers had to do compulsory labour in these production facilities under inhumane living and working conditions. Selections were made regularly and workers were often deported to the Treblinka extermination camp.

At the beginning of 1943, the HSSPF for the General Government, Friedrich-Wilhelm Krüger, was ordered by Reichsführer-SS Heinrich Himmler to have an accounts audit carried out at the Többenswerke. However, Walter Többens was able to avert the auditing and was appointed by Globocnik in early 1943 as representative for the Relocation of Jewish Operations in Warsaw. This was carried out under the supervision of Michalsen and made possible a takeover of the operation by the SS and the transfer of Jewish workers to the Majdanek Concentration Camp in Lublin. In April and May 1943, at the height of the uprising in the Warsaw Ghetto, 10,000 forced labourers, including family members of the company, transferred to the forced labour camp at Poniatowa-Majdanek. The production facilities of the Többenswerke were also relocated to Poniatowa. On 4 November 1943, about 15,000 Jews from the labour camp were shot as part of Aktion Erntefest.

Michalsen transferred to the Adriatic coast along with Globocnik, where he was given responsibility for personnel matters in the office of the HSSPF. During 1944, Michalsen was placed in command of the local SS and Police units in Fiume, Pola, and Trieste at the behest of Globocnik. He was involved in anti-partisan operations in Istria and no doubt saw active service. He escaped north with his boss and was with him when arrested at the Mößlacher Alm on 31 May 1945. He insisted he was a member of the Waffen-SS and was released in 1948. He moved to Hamburg in 1950 and worked again as an accountant. He was arrested on 24 January 1961. According to press reports, he initially stated that he had been a normal soldier during the war and had worked in administration. On 25 July 1974, Michalsen received a twelve-year prison sentence for deporting Jews from Warsaw and Bialystok to the extermination camps. As a witness in a case in Wiesbaden, Michalsen declared: 'In the whole thing with the Jews, nothing was thought of. You simply did your job and did not think about it'. He died a free man on 21 May 1993.

Among those men who can be considered as 'insiders', Josef 'Sepp' Nemec was the oldest. He was born in Vienna on 25 April 1901, but little is known of his life. He was a Viennese furniture clerk by profession and joined the NSDAP in 1932, followed by the SS in 1935. He served as financial manager and adjutant to SA-Obergruppe Österreich, in addition to running the illegal Austrian NSDAP Hilfswerk from 1936. He befriended Globocnik in Austria during the pre-Anschluss days, and may even have spent time in jail with him. His name certainly appeared in a secret memo from Himmler to Wilhelm Keppler, naming Nemec as the leader of a workers' group that reported to Klausner, Globocnik and Rainer. After Globocnik took office as Viennese Gauleiter, Nemec was appointed as Gau inspector, a fairly prestigious and senior post. He was awarded the 30 January 1939 version of the NSDAP Golden Party Badge. Following his boss's removal, Nemec also lost his position. He reappeared in Lublin after Globocnik's new appointment, and he was often seen in the company of a woman called Benes, to whom he was not married.[16] Nemec was officially listed as Globocnik's chief of staff. His stay was cut short after a disagreement with Globocnik over some personal mail. He apparently held the rank of SS-Sturmbannführer, but his name does not appear in the 1944 SS-Dienstaltesliste (seniority list). Nothing more is known of this elusive character.

That cannot be said about Hans Gustav Maubach. He was born on 19 December 1904 in Roisdorf-Bonn, the son of master painter Albert Maubach and his wife, Charlotte Paula, born Justus. He was their fourth child. He attended the local Volksschule where he underwent an unspectacular education. On 1 August 1922, Maubach enlisted in the 3. Artillery Regiment 6 in Münster and he served with this unit until his discharge on 31 December 1924 as an Ober-Kanonier. He then found temporary jobs for short periods as a merchant and also with his father. By 1930, he was unemployed. He was interested in flying, and in 1929, he joined the DLV, a German flying association. He joined the NSDAP and the SA Glider Pilots Unit in February 1932. On 1 June 1933, he joined the Hitler Youth Organisation as a section leader in HJ Oberbann Saarland. By 1935, he was the personnel leader for HJ Section 25 (Saarpfalz). On 1 October 1936, Maubach was appointed as a referent—personal aide and advisor on youth matters—in the 'Ribbentrop Bureau', responsible for German–French youth. The French connection had an influence on Maubach. He wore French suits and smoked French cigarettes. Irmgard Rickheim, a secretary in Maubach's Berlin office, stated that Maubach worked in Paris until the outbreak of war, when the need for his diplomatic skills ceased to exist. Until then, he worked tirelessly to promote Franco-German relations by way of entertaining businessmen and arranging sporting events between the youth of both nations.

Maubach cut a dashing figure; in his thirties, handsome, easy going, and well dressed, he was popular with the ladies. He married a secretary who worked eventually in the same office, on 31 March 1936. Charlotte Dierssen was born into a catholic family in Hagen on 1 August 1908. An element of doubt existed about her Aryan lineage, and this was not helped by one SS doctor describing her as 'of Oriental appearance'. There was even a later suggestion by Jewish workers in Lublin that she may have been of Jewish extraction, but her ancestry table provided for the SS-Race and Settlement Office contradicts this allegation.[17] However, the doubt produced a copious exchange of letters between Maubach, Globocnik, and the SS-RuSHA.

Maubach transferred to Lublin on 1 December 1939.[18] In his own handwriting, Maubach declares he was immediately appointed to the staff of Globocnik as a personal aide—referent, advisor—on Globocnik's own initiative, but it appears that he did not switch to Globocnik's staff from the governor's staff until the summer of 1940. Rickheim further asserts that Maubach first worked on the staff of Schmidt as the officer responsible for transport. As a result of conflicts between the civil administration and the SSPF in Lublin, Friedrich Rainer felt that Maubach could exert a calming influence and suggested his appointment in Lublin. However, Maubach appears to have been allocated quarters at Ostlandstrasse 10, right next door to the Globocnik villa. This is the house that was later occupied by Anna Globocnik, her daughter, and granddaughter. Maubach's wife subsequently joined him in Lublin and worked as a photographic cataloguer.

Maubach did not join the SS until 20 April 1941, probably at the insistence of his boss. He was immediately promoted from SS-Mann to SS-Sturmbannführer on the same day as his joining. He is listed as a 'Sonderführer' (special officer) attached to the staff of HSSPF Ost from 1 September 1941, and then attached to the SS-Hauptamt from 1 November 1941 until 23 January 1941 (certainly an error; most likely 1942). After allegedly falling out with Globocnik, Maubach transferred to the Waffen-SS and was attached to various units including the SS-Panzer-Grenadier Replacement Battalion 18.[19] Maubach insisted that Lerch and Nemec exerted too much influence over the boss, which affected Maubach's ability to carry out his duties properly. The most likely reason for the break was a minor problem with Heydrich's staff in Prague for which Globocnik blamed Maubach. There is also the suggestion that Maubach had become tired of jibes regarding his wife's ancestry. Maubach also subsequently worked on the staff of Reich Health Leader, Dr Leonardo Conti.

After the war, Maubach apparently maintained some form of contact with other Globocnik staffers. He was interviewed and made a statement on 22 February 1966 to investigators preparing a case against Georg Michalsen. He was also named as a living participant in a case against Heinrich Birmes, former SS-Oberscharführer and head of the SS-ZAL clothing factory in Lublin, during the 1970s.[20] The outcome is unknown. This author was unable to discover what became of Maubach after that. Presumably, and despite allegations that he had enriched himself with a share of the stolen proceeds of the murder campaign in Lublin, he lived out the remainder of his days in obscurity as a free man.

Maubach's replacement as head of the motor pool was SS-Untersturmführer Max Meierhofer who hailed from Salzburg. Born in Mattsee in 1909, he had previous experience as transport supremo under SS-Gruppenführer Alfred Rodenbucher, the HSSPF in Salzburg. Meierhofer was temporarily assigned to Department Iva, administering the sorting and storing warehouse for property stolen from the Jews and Poles. On Höfle's staff, he participated in the clearing and liquidation of the Warsaw Ghetto. A keen amateur photographer, he famously took a snapshot of an old woman in a wheelchair before shooting her and taking a second photo of her lying on the ground. Maierhofer joined Globocnik in Trieste.

Globocnik's personal orderly was another old confidant from Austria—SS-Rottenführer Rudolf Schleißner. He was born in Klagenfurt in 1906 and had waited tables at the Café Lerch in Klagenfurt, marrying one of the cooks. A member of the SS from 1935, he worked for Lerch's SD. Schleißner and his wife, Luise, ran a hotel on the south shore of the Wörthersee, and during the war, they employed a live-in manageress. During the later transfer to Trieste, Globocnik and his travelling group stayed at the hotel for a short stopover before resuming their journey. During his period in Lublin, Schleißner ran the 'Deutsches Haus' in the town centre.[21]

Max Cichotzski—various spellings, including Cichotski, Czichotzki, and Cichoztki—did not join Globocnik's staff until April 1942, when he was offered a post as adjutant to the SSPF. He was born in Lochowo, Bydgoszcz, in northern Poland on 25 March 1916 and spoke fluent Polish. Despite a German majority, Bydgoszcz (German Bromberg) was assigned to the new Polish State by the Treaty of Versailles, 1919. The German citizens were ordered to accept Polish nationality or leave the town immediately. Cichotzski's family elected to stay. Max attended school in Lochowo and then Bydgoszcz. His father worked in agriculture and died when Max was twenty years old. Max attended arts and crafts school and became an apprentice interior decorator. He was active in the scout movement and was drafted into the Polish military service for two years. At the outbreak of war in 1939, he failed to answer his call-up and fled to Berlin, via Danzig. There he found employment with his Uncle Otto as an interior decorator. He was never court-martialled as Poland was rapidly defeated.

His experience in the scout movement stood him in good stead when a friend, SS-Obersturmführer Horst Ranke, steered him into a position in the Foreign Office as a Reich Youth Leader. Ranke, who was from Lodz, advised him to apply for work in the Lublin area where they were seeking Polish speakers for the General Government. He followed the advice, moving to southern Poland in early 1940. In the atmosphere of war, Cichotzski always wore his HJ-Oberscharführer uniform, carrying out his duties in Lublin, Chełm, and Hrubieszów. However, he did later apply to join the ranks of the SS. His skill at speaking fluent Polish brought him to the attention of Globocnik who offered him a post as adjutant. He took up the position at Easter 1942 and remained Globocnik's personal adjutant until August 1944.

Globocnik utilised Cichotzski's language skills as an interpreter, and he also acted as a part-time driver for his boss. In 1944, he legally changed his family name to Runhof in order to ditch the Polish-sounding Cichotzski. He remained with Globocnik and became a trusted aid, taking care of personal matters for his boss. Seen by other Globocnik insiders as 'weak', Cichotzski was described by Irmgard Rickheim as 'the little adjutant'. Georg Michalsen's impression of him was one of his being 'midway between an adjutant and an orderly'. He never commanded the respect of that enjoyed by his predecessors, and he always felt that Lerch was intriguing behind his back.

He transferred to Trieste with Globocnik in September 1943 where he continued in his role as Globocnik's adjutant until he was drafted into the Waffen-SS with the 3rd Communications Regiment of the SS-Totenkopf Division. In Ljubljana, his unit was visited by Karl Wolff and Globocnik. During this visit, Wolff informed Cichotzski that Himmler had wanted him to join the Waffen-SS. After this, he saw active service on the Hungarian Front. He was captured at Saatz in Czechoslovakia and remained a prisoner of the Soviets, labouring in the mines of Upper Silesia until his release in 1947. He made his way to Munich, where he encountered Maubach who was living in Augsburg. The two former colleagues met on several occasions and Cichotzski was adamant that Maubach was on the point of emigrating to Scandinavia. He also states he met Höfle in Munich who was working first in a scrap metal yard, and then in a glass factory. Soon after, Höfle fled to Italy to avoid detection by Polish authorities.

His documentation regarding his name change was not recognised in West Germany and he reapplied in 1958. His change of name to Max Runhof became official on 19 February 1958. He remarried in the same year and a son was born on 25 April 1960.

When pressed about his knowledge of the Reinhardt extermination sites, Cichotzski denied all knowledge of what went on inside the facilities. He declared that he believed they were labour camps and he was refused permission to enter them. He even stated he was ordered to wait outside for his boss on the one occasion he drove Globocnik to a camp outside Lublin on the Cholm road—almost certainly Majdanek. According to Citchotski, only Lerch, Höfle, and possibly Nemec had authorised access to secret messages to and from Berlin. Cichotzski just delivered sealed envelopes to Lerch or Globocnik.

Cichotzski recalled Himmler visiting Lublin three times when he was Globocnik's adjutant. He was always accompanied by Werner Grothmann. He also recalled Wolff visiting three times, but not always with Himmler. Both Himmler and Wolff were interested in Globocnik's SS and Police Strongpoints and he believed that Wolff actually visited some of the sites. He remembered meetings with Wirth, Kientrupp, Wippern, Müller, Lerch, and Magill, but he stated that these were regular staff meetings held by Globocnik, and he did not personally take part as one of the inner circle prevented his attendance—probably Lerch. Lerch was most put out that he had to ask Cichotzski for permission to use Globocnik's direct telephone link to the office of the Reichsführer-SS. When Cichotzski drove Globocnik, they used a PKW Ford V8. Globocnik's escort troop on visits to Bełżec and Sobibor were police units under Kientrupp, and they were known as his 'Jagdstaffel' (literally 'Hunt Staff').

Cichotzski lived in a room in Ostlandstrasse where his boss had immediate access to his aide. Cichotzski testified that he knew Globocnik better than anyone in his opinion, based on the length of time spent in his company. He was Globocnik's travelling companion when he visited the Führer and on his visits to Berlin, Krakow, Vienna, and Warsaw. He became indispensable and insisted Globocnik was an extremely hard-working individual, contrary to popular belief. Apparently, Globocnik liked to arrange things personally and was quite knowledgeable about technical subjects in addition to policy matters. His knowledge of music, literature and the theatre was astonishing. He counted Dr Fritz Todt among his close contacts. Cichotzski also suggested that senior army commanders, such as von Manstein and Guderian, were pleased to visit Globocnik in Lublin. Surprisingly, they found his company interesting.

He pointed out that Globocnik did not relish public speaking as he realised he was not an accomplished public speaker. He made up for his shortcomings in public by successfully developing his social skills. He was a popular host and enjoyed life to the full. As a boss, Globocnik was thoughtful. He did not like to burden Cichotzski with 'difficult matters'. If Cichotzski enquired after his boss's welfare, Globocnik always told him to mind his own business and not to worry about him. Cichotzski said that Globocnik's relationship with Himmler cooled somewhat after the termination of Aktion Reinhardt. Apart from the odd 'blip', the two men enjoyed a friendly relationship. He did, however, relate an occasion when Globocnik ordered him to take his uniform, his awards, his SS sword and Totenkopfring, to Himmler at the Feldkommandostelle 'Hochwald' in East Prussia. This was during the winter months of 1942–1943 and Globocnik wore civilian clothes for two weeks until the disagreement was resolved.[22] Cichotzski's view of his former boss was at variance with others, such as the batman, Willy Natke, who stated: '[Globocnik] was a brute who would not hesitate killing his own subordinates.... I had to be at attention whenever he was awake. Therefore, I was on duty from early morning until late at night.... I saw him drunk many times...'[23]

Like Maubach, Cichotzski was listed as a participant in the Hamburg investigations of the 1970s, but his final fate requires confirmation. It is believed he died a free man in Wiesbaden *c.* 2000.

Another of Globocnik's trusted aides in Lublin was Christian Wirth. Probably the most important figure in the Aktion Reinhardt set-up, his background and role in this study is better suited to other chapters where we will episodically encounter this immoral and unpleasant individual. Suffice to say at this stage that Wirth hailed from Württemberg and was a professional police officer. In December 1941, Globocnik saw in him the ideal candidate to fill the role as commandant of a new planned facility at Bełżec. His arrival in Lublin marked a turning point in the Nazi attitude and treatment of the Jews in the General Government. Wirth's previous experience in the euthanasia programme signified a bad omen for the Jewish population and heralded a shift in policy from one of resettlement to one of extermination.

One member of Globocnik's staff on the periphery of the inner circle is worthy of closer scrutiny. Gustav Hanelt was heavily implicated in the Germanisation of the Lublin lands and was well versed in the General Plan Ost—the recolonization of Eastern Europe by the Germanic people.

He was born in Schmachthagen in Holstein on 21 September 1914, the son of Gustav Hanelt and his wife, Henny (born Groenweld). Young Gustav attended school in Steinhorst before progressing to the senior school in Bad Oldesloe. From an early age, he became politically aware and joined the NS-Schülerbund on 1 May 1929. He joined the Hitler Youth on 1 May 1931 and dreamed of becoming a SS member. This he achieved in Bad Oldesloe on 9 November 1933, and he was issued with SS number 173 980. Hanelt had by then already become a fully-fledged member of the NSDAP, having joined on 1 April 1933. He was allocated NSDAP membership number 1 637 363. Of small to medium stature—5 feet 7 inches with a shoe size of 43—Hanelt wished to study law and become a jurist. He spoke a good standard of English and subsequently studied history and anthropology at Berlin University.

Having transferred to SS-Standarte 4 in Altona, he steadily rose through the ranks. From 1 October 1935 until 3 October 1937, he was in the army. Hanelt became a member of the SS-Mannschaften—a type of SS research unit. By November 1938, he lived in digs with a family called Lange at Bundesstrasse 40 in Hamburg. On 9 November 1938, Hanelt received his Allgemeine-SS commission as a SS-Untersturmführer and was then appointed to the SS Race and Resettlement Office. In this role, he served in Königsberg and developed an expertise in resettlement. He transferred to the RFSS Personal Staff on 1 March 1939 and remained attached to this unit until transferring to the Dienstelle Heissmeyer—an educational SS unit with Hauptamt status—on 21 March 1941. By then, world events had overtaken Hanelt's career.

From 25 October 1939 until 15 October 1940, Hanelt was with the Panzer Division of Erwin Rommel in the west. He was promoted to Leutnant on 1 February 1940. Globocnik recalled him to SS service and he joined the staff in Lublin on 20 October 1940. He was promoted to SS-Obersturmführer on 30 January 1941 and to SS-Hauptsturmführer on 30 January 1942. From 1 September 1941, he became a Waffen-SS Sonderführer. Hanelt obviously pressed all the right buttons as he was awarded his SS-Totenkopfring on 28 January 1942. He transferred to the Adriatic Coastline command with Globocnik and was officially posted there from 30 January 1944. On 9 September 1944, he was ordered to report to the SS-Führungshauptamt and he was then posted to the SS Panzer Grenadier Replacement Battalion 18 on 25 October 1944. He saw active service, as he received a wound for which he was awarded a Wound Badge in Black.

Hanelt was married to Waltraut Seiffert on 31 May 1941. She was born in Kiel on 16 December 1922 and the union produced a daughter, Kirsten, on 2 December 1943. Waltraut had been an active member of the BDM and was very keen on sports, having been awarded her Bronze Sports Badge. She lived in Lublin with her husband. Gustav Hanelt headed the Research Agency for Eastern Settlement in Lublin. He was an integral cog in the machinery by which Globocnik carried out his strategy for the recolonization of the eastern lands.

As in the case of Maubach and Cichotzski, it is unclear whether Hanelt was called post-war to answer for his actions. There is no evidence of direct involvement in the policy of annihilation, but Hanelt's role in the resettlement programme certainly cries out for further investigation. The same could be said for the little known SS-Obersturmführer Bareuther, who was named as Globocnik's operational deputy for the ethnic cleansing of the Zamość Lands ordered by Globocnik on

22 November 1942. These men were so important to Globocnik that he went out of his way to ensure they would accompany him to Trieste, even though they were not considered as 'insiders'.

While mentioning Hanelt, it is impossible to ignore Dr Franz Stanglica. Born in Vienna on 27 May 1907, Stanglica was the son of a government official of the same name. After studying history at Vienna University, he received his doctorate in 1931. From 1932, he was an archivist and researcher at the Court Chamber Archives where his main interest lay in the resettlement of Austro-German people in the south-east region of the Habsburg Empire in the eighteenth century. Under the false name of Berhard Klar, Stanglica financially supported the Nazi Party. On 1 January 1937, he was appointed as a permanent archivist, but continued with part-time work for Wilhelm Grau, head of Jewish research at the Reich Institute for the History of New Germany. He came out into the open in May 1938 when he joined the NSDAP. By 1939, he was a Blockleiter in Hetzendorf. He became somewhat of an expert on the colonization of the Banat region—the location of Anna Globocnik's heritage—Batschka, and Transylvania.

In 1940, Stanglica's research revealed that a number of Austro-German communities had been founded in the area of western Galicia, around the town of Zamość. This flagged up Stanglica as an expert for Globocnik's resettlement policy and he was recruited by the SS. Stanglica was attached to the SS-Totenkopf ranks and despatched to Sachsenhausen and Auschwitz on the staff of the Concentration Camp Inspectorate. In early 1941, he was transferred to Hanelt's department in Lublin. Stanglica, by his own admission, took an active role in the 'cleansing' operations, and remarked that he had done so 'with the weapon in his hand'. It was also Stanglica who provided statistical raw data for Globocnik's anti-Jewish actions.

In partnership with Gustav Hanelt, Dr Franz Stanglica was among the most significant figures in Globocnik's staff with relation to his resettlement policies. Ingrao describes Stanglica as Globocnik's 'Jack of all trades, providing his boss with lengthy memorandums, maps, statistics, and all necessary elements of spatial planning.'[24] He was promoted to SS-Untersturmführer on 1 April 1943 on the staff of HSSPF Ost, before being temporarily attached to the staff of HSSPF Ukraine—Prützmann—until the following autumn. He then moved to Trieste, in Globocnik's footsteps. He was captured by the British in Carinthia, but transferred to American custody where he died under suspicious circumstances on 28 October 1946. Considered by many as a true fanatic, Stanglica was certainly a necessary facet of Globocnik's overall strategy of depopulation and resettlement.

Before departing from the realm of important Globocnik staffers, the spotlight must be turned upon several other Lublin figures. From time to time, their names will emerge throughout this volume, so it may be wise to mention them here, along with their known roles.

Amon Göth, of Schindler fame and yet another Austrian, was a member of Globocnik's Aktion Reinhardt staff. He was born in Vienna on 11 December 1908 to a wealthy Catholic family whose prosperity was sourced to the publishing industry. He studied agriculture before abandoning the course in favour of right-wing politics. He joined the Austrian SS in 1930, and the NSDAP the same year. In January 1933, he was appointed as adjutant of 52. SS-Standarte. He dallied with the law and was arrested several times for illegal activities. Following the failed Nazi coup of July 1934, Göth was again arrested, but he successfully escaped and fled to Munich. After a dispute with SS-Oberführer Alfred Bigler, the two men left the SS. After the Anschluss, Göth returned to Vienna and rejoined the SS. He was posted to 89. SS-Standarte and then 11. SS-Standarte.

On 5 March 1940, Göth was drafted into the army, but he did not see active service. He was posted to the staff of HSSPF Ost in about summer of 1941. There he gained a reputation as an effective administrator in the identifying and relocation of the Jewish population in the General Government. On 14 July 1941, he was promoted to SS-Untersturmführer. In the summer of 1942, Göth was attached to the Aktion Reinhardt staff in Lublin where he was responsible for isolating and despatching Jews to the Reinhardt death factories. He became expert in the art of clearing ghettos.

In February 1943, Göth was ordered to construct a new Jewish labour camp at Krakow-Plaszow, after a disagreement with Hermann Höfle. His orders then directed him to clear the Krakow Ghetto and he commanded a clearance action which began on 13 March 1943. Göth was renowned for brutality, a fact portrayed in the Spielberg film *Schindler's List*. In the film, Göth is depicted shooting camp inmates from his balcony. This did not occur in reality as the camp grounds were not in the line of vision from the actual Göth villa. However, during the construction of Plaszow, he ordered Albert Hujar to shoot architect Diana Reiter after a wall collapsed, which was being erected under her supervision. Before moving into the Red House at Plaszow, Göth lived in luxurious surroundings in Krakow. His corrupt practices and lavish lifestyle brought him to the attention of the Gestapo, and he was lucky to escape severe punishment. He lost his post and was suffering from mental illness when he was arrested by Americans in Bad Tölz. He was tried and hanged at the Montelupich Prison in Krakow on 13 September 1946, the same location for the post-war executions of Arthur Liebehenschel, Hans Aumeier, Erich Mußfeldt, Karl Möckel, Josef Kollmer, August Bogusch, Fritz Buntrock, Paul Götze, Ludwig Plagge, Josef Bühler, and Max Grabner.

Some confusion exists over two names listed on Globocnik's staff—Johann Offermann and Hans Offermann. This author believes them to be one and the same person. Both are shown as specialists in personnel and Hans is the commonly shortened version of both Johann and Johannes. It appears that only Johann

Offermann was interrogated post-war. The Johann Offermann that is of some significance to Globocnik's story was interrogated by the British, following his capture in Norway. It is from those interrogation records, now kept at the National Archives in Kew, that Offermann's biographical details are drawn.

He was born on 20 September 1907 in Kornelimünster, on the south-east periphery of Aachen. He attended the local elementary school from 1914 until 1921 when he changed to a commercial school in Aachen to study textiles. He joined the SS in July 1933 and was attached to Pioneer Sturm 4 of 58. SS-Standarte. He joined the NSDAP on 1 May 1937. From August 1934 until May 1935, Offermann was suspended from the SS for an unknown reason.

He was drafted into the Waffen-SS on 13 February 1940 and was attached to 2. Kavallerie-Regiment in Lublin, but he was discharged on medical grounds, suffering from eye and lung complaints. On 15 April 1940, he was seconded to the office of the General Governor as a member of the Allgemeine-SS. From April to July 1940, he served with the Selbstschutz, training volunteer Volksdeutsche. The Selbstschutz was dissolved in July 1940 and Offermann performed a similar role for its replacement, the Sonderdienst. This time, conscription was enforced. He was promoted to SS-Untersturmführer in August 1940. From March to August 1941, he belonged to a requisitioning unit for accommodation in the East. This was a polite term for seizure of properties for settlement in the East.

In July 1941, Offermann was recalled to Waffen-SS service as a Fachführer and joined the staff of the SSPF Lublin, subordinate to the HSSPF Ost (SS- und Polizeiwesen). Fachführer were specialists in their own field and they held various SS ranks. Many of Globocnik's staff were designated 'Fachführer'. From August 1941 to March 1942, Offermann was in the office for Settlers' Economic Community. In March 1942, he was arrested twice by the SD for selling bronze to Poles, which was obviously illegal. Offermann later insisted that he was following Globocnik's orders to rectify a 150,000 zloty deficit in Globocnik's name. He covered for Globocnik's embezzlement and was sentenced to reduction in rank to SS-Sturmann and eighteen months' imprisonment in Danzig-Matzgau, starting on 1 September 1942. This was commuted on condition Offermann proved himself in active service at the front. Globocnik may have had a hand in this, as Offermann was returned to duty with the Accommodation Requisitioning Unit. He underwent training for frontline service with 4. SS Assault Gun Section at Debica, near Krakow, but soon suffered a complete physical breakdown. He was then temporarily posted to the SS Personnel Central Office in Berlin in August 1943.

Offermann returned to Lublin in September 1943 as a SS-Untersturmführer on the staff of Jakob Sporrenberg, Globocnik's replacement as SSPF Lublin. Despite his previous record, Sporrenberg reappointed him as head of his personnel department. From December 1943 until January 1944, Offermann was the liaison officer and supplier to the contractors for the erection of fortifications along the River Bug, between Biala and Podlaska. He was promoted to SS-Obersturmführer on 30 January 1944. The remainder of his time in the General Government was spent on fortifications along the River Vistula. He transferred to Oslo in January 1945 to assist Sporrenberg with accounts.

Offermann was described in his interrogation report as 'underdeveloped for his age and lacking any initiative'. He was also considered ineffective, but willing to talk. He held no loyalty for his former bosses, Globocnik or Sporrenberg. He stood at slightly under 5 feet 9 inches, with fair hair and blue eyes. He was recorded as a former businessman who wore unusually thick lenses in his spectacles. In July 1973, it appears that he received a prison term of five years in Hamburg.

One of Globocnik's personal adjutants and a referent was Herbert Ulbrich. Born in Breslau on 15 October 1908, Ulbrich joined the local 16. SS-Standarte on 27 June 1933. He steadily rose through the ranks until promoted to SS-Untersturmführer on 12 September 1937, when he was appointed adjutant of the Standarte. He was promoted again on 20 April 1939, to SS-Obersturmführer, and to SS-Hauptsturmführer on 20 April 1941. Ulbrich was well known to Fritz Katzmann as an efficient adjutant since Katzmann commanded SS-Abschnitt VI in Breslau, and it was probably Katzmann who instigated Ulbrich's move to the General Government. Ulbrich was appointed as an adjutant to Katzmann in Radom and was placed on the staff of SS-Oberabschnitt Ost. Ulbrich is recorded as a Sonderführer and subsequently as a Fachführer in his SS file.

He later transferred to Globocnik's staff in Lublin on 16 September 1940. Globocnik obviously trusted Ulbrich implicitly and gave him power of attorney to sell land and property on his behalf, and to submit all related documentation. Ulbrich, along with a certain SS-Obersturmführer Georg Michalczyk, also had Globocnik's permission to authorise and request deletions of mortgages plus other legal rights in the land register. This simplified the process of acquiring and selling off property during resettlement actions and was open to certain transactions being conducted 'under the radar'. To suggest Ulbrich was unaware of Globocnik's unscrupulous dealings is nothing short of farcical. After Globocnik's Lublin departure to Trieste, Ulbrich stayed on and remained on the staff of Sporrenberg, but only for a few weeks. Married, with four children, he transferred to active service. At the end of the war, Ulbrich was missing. His fate is unknown.

Dr Max Horn was born on 12 May 1904 in Stuttgart. He was married on 28 September 1929 to Kläre Wehe (born 28 August 1909 in Heilbronn) and they had two children. His skills lay in fiscal administration and he also studied commercial law and economics at Leipzig and Stuttgart. In 1927, he worked for a trust company. He passed his diploma examination in tax consultancy in 1930, and by 1934, he obtained his doctorate. In 1936, he qualified as an auditor. In Hamburg in 1937,

Horn was admitted to the list of tax consultants, and from 1942 he was an auditor in the Stuttgart Chamber of Commerce and Industry. His financial qualifications and experience were impeccable.

Horn joined the NSDAP on 1 May 1933, and the SS on 1 July 1933. He was promoted to SS-Untersturmführer on 30 January 1939; to SS-Obersturmführer on 15 June 1942; and to SS-Hauptsturmführer on 9 November 1943. Initially, as a welfare advisor, he was a member of SS-Standarte 28, but he was swept up by Oswald Pohl's SS-Wirtschafts- und Verwaltungshauptamt on 15 June 1942. He saw active service with the army in Belgium and Denmark and he attained the rank of Leutnant. From 1 April 1943, Horn was attached to the staff of the HSSPF Ost in Krakow, but he had been in the General Government since the previous February, where Pohl had sent him to administer the economic concerns of Ostindustrie GmbH (OSTI). This was a company created by Pohl to direct the armaments industry in the General Government and to control the other industries created by the use of Jewish and Polish forced labour. Dr Max Horn was appointed as managing director. His partner was Odilo Globocnik.

The OSTI was dissolved after only a few months as a result of various events and Horn returned to other duties with the SS-WVHA. He was appointed as head of the SS Research Institute for Nutrition and Food in Feldberg before ending the war as the commander of a Sturm Brigade. He was captured by the Soviets and was denazified in 1950, classified as a 'follower'. He became an accountant and tax consultant, forming his own company in 1966. Well respected in his field, he published numerous articles in prestigious journals. He died on 24 October 1989 in Ulm, never having answered for his activities in the General Government.

Richard Thomalla was Globocnik's building consultant. He was born on 23 October 1903 in Annahof (today Sowin, Poland). He joined the NSDAP in 1932. In Lublin, he was a member of the Waffen-SS Zentralbauleitung and he maintained an office in Zamość. Globocnik drew on Thomalla's construction expertise for the erection of the death camps at Bełżec, Sobibor and Treblinka. Thomalla built the gas chambers at the three termination stations and tested them for efficiency before they became fully operational. He was allegedly executed by the NKVD in Jicin, Czechoslovakia, on 12 May 1945.

Konrad Rheindorf, an Englishman by birth, but of German parentage, Rheindorf was the commander of Polizeiregiment 25 in Lublin, which had responsibility for bodyguard duties. These included both Globocnik and visiting dignitaries, including Himmler. Rheindorf fell into Soviet captivity because he was hospitalised when Lublin was overrun by the Red Army. He was in a Gulag until the general amnesty of 1955.

Hermann Dolp was born in Türkheim on 12 September 1889. Although not specifically a member of Globocnik's immediate staff, he is worthy of mention here as the commander of the Lipowa Street camp in Lublin. A locksmith by profession, Dolp was an early supporter of the Nazi Party. He was a former Freikorps member and belonged to the Bund Oberland. Having participated in the Putsch of November 1923, he was a holder of the coveted Blood Order. By 1931, Dolp had reached the rank of SS-Standartenführer, but there his SS career stalled. He gained camp experience at Dachau and Sachsenhausen. During the Polish campaign, Dolp was a Selbstschutz commander in Kalisch.

In November 1939, when drunk, he was involved in the scandal described previously. As part of his punishment, Dolp was transferred to the staff of the SSPF in Lublin. There he was made responsible for the new labour camp at Lipowa Street and also to oversee the construction of defences along the border with Soviet-occupied Poland. He ruthlessly administered his duties in Lublin and hundreds of deaths occurred as a result of his methods. After 'Barbarossa', he helped with the construction of SS and Police strongholds in Minsk and Mogilev. Dolp was promoted to SS-Obersturmbannführer on 21 June 1944, as a member of 19. Waffen-SS Grenadier Division. Married with four children, he was declared missing in action at war's end.

A comprehensive list of known Globocnik staffers will be included in the illustrations, but other figures connected to Globocnik in Lublin and worthy of mention here, include his driver, Franz Eigner; the first head of the Lublin Selbstschutz, Walter Gunst; his successor, Ludolf Jakob von Alvensleben; and Willy Scheper, responsible for accommodation.

Kurt Claasen was born in Itzehoe on 9 January 1908 as Kurt Kutschera. He changed his name to Claasen in 1939 in order to drop the non-German-sounding surname. He was attached to Aktion Reinhardt as a resettlement officer and succeeded Höfle as Sporrenberg's staff officer after the former left Lublin in December 1943. He remained in this post until July 1944. In May 1945, he was reported 'missing' and was subsequently declared dead by the District Court of Cuxhaven upon application by his wife.[25]

Josef 'Sepp' Slany was born in Gleiwitz on 21 February 1904. He was attached to Höfle's command and was involved in various resettlement actions, including the liquidation of the Bialystok Ghetto. He was responsible for food procurement in Lublin. He was also listed as 'missing' and was declared deceased.

Another important figure was the Bavarian SS-Untersturmführer Johann Schwarzenbacher. He was born in Munich on 3 January 1909, and was a company commander at Trawniki where he gained a reputation for brutality. He was experienced in the art of liquidating ghettos. He transferred to Trieste in late 1943 and was killed by partisans on 2 June 1944.

SS-Obersturmführer and Leutnant der Polizei Karl Mahnke was born on 24 October 1910 in Sankt Georgenberg. Mahnke was posted to Police Regiment 25 in Lublin. He was on the transport staff of the SSPF and commanded a number of trains during evacuation procedures. He had been transferred from the Selbstschutz in Radom, and served as a consultant at the border fortification construction at Bełżec from 29 August 1940 until 21 October 1940. Following this, he was attached to the office for the installation of SS and Police Strongpoints in the new eastern territories. He was reported 'missing' in May 1945.

SS-Unterscharführer Franz Hoskowitz hailed from Bruenn. He was born on 1 October 1900 and lived post-war in Linz, Austria. On Höfle's staff in Lublin, he had responsibility for confiscated real estate. He alleged post-war that these properties were only subject to seizure following combat operations. He acted as an erstwhile interpreter and part of his duties was the procurement of construction materials. In December 1942, he left Lublin and moved to the office of the RKFDV—Reich Commissioner for the Consolidation of German Nationhood (Himmler)—in Zamość, as an office clerk. His excuses after the war could not be disproved, and consequently the intended proceedings against him were dropped.

SS-Unterscharführer Willi Franz was active during the Warsaw Ghetto clearance. He was a company commander at Trawniki. Born on 16 October 1910 in Remptendorf, he was reported 'missing' on 31 July 1944.

An assistant to Josef Oberhauser in the office of the inspector of Einsatzes Reinhardt, was Oberwachtmeister der Reserve Erich Dietze. Born in Kassel on 3 March 1909, he assisted Oberhauser and Häusler with the administration of Aktion Reinhardt. His part in the massacres of Reinhardt cannot be defined, as he was killed in action on 10 January 1943.

SS-Oberscharführer Willi Häusler was born in Breslau on 9 March 1894. He joined Wirth's staff on the Reinhardt Camps Inspectorate in the Julius Schreck Barracks, and was assigned to paying the salaries for the Reinhardt killers at Treblinka, Sobibor, and Bełżec. He stated that the salaries were paid by T4 in Berlin once every month and the money was collected by the camp commandants who would sign for its receipt. After the war, he was traced to an address in Gestemünde, Bremerhaven.

# 7

# QUEST FOR GERMANIC BLOOD

By the second year of the war, Globocnik still had not resolved his problem with the NSDAP Reich Treasurer, Reichsleiter Franz Xaver Schwarz. Although Globocnik was undisputed master of his kingdom, practically unchallenged by all, including Hitler's representative in Krakow, Schwarz was an important thorn in his side. Not one to be dissuaded lightly, Schwarz was a dogged enemy with a long memory. It had not so much been Globocnik's wrongdoings that had raised his hackles, but the nonchalant manner in which the accused had responded to the justified criticism. Schwarz was a very proud man, aware of his senior position within the NSDAP hierarchy. He felt affronted and disrespected by Globocnik. To the old party campaigner, it mattered not what task had been given to the impudent young upstart in Lublin. The SS-Brigadeführer was in his crosshairs.

The auditor of the Reich NSDAP leadership, Franz Müller, set a deadline for Globocnik to answer the unresolved allegations of fiscal mismanagement during Globocnik's tenure as Gauleiter in Vienna. Once again, Globocnik fell back on his old friendship with the Reichsführer-SS by writing to him on 3 January 1941, requesting his help in this matter. He excuses his misuse of funds by declaring that he failed to receive monies promised him and was therefore forced to utilise what funds he had. He could see no wrong in what he had done. He felt affronted by the suggestion that he had no right to use such funds and the implied dishonest use of other unaccounted assets. Globocnik politely requested another audit statement from the Reichsschatzmeister's office.

Himmler contacted Schwarz who replied immediately. Schwarz once more enumerated the flaws in Globocnik's response and pointed out that Müller had already requested Globocnik on no less than eight occasions between May and October 1940 for his statement, and had received no reply. Schwarz complained of the former Gauleiter's brusque attitude to the deadline. He added that Globocnik had been allowed a period of eight months to explain his dealings and he had failed to do so. He found the whole matter 'improper' in that Globocnik was asking to overlook the audit report.

Himmler was a little taken aback by Schwarz's abrasive reply and he submitted copies of the exchanges to Friedl Rainer with a request that he advise his friend. On 28 January 1941, Globocnik finally submitted an initial statement, but Schwarz was not satisfied. An amended statement was therefore submitted on 3 March 1941.

Meanwhile, on 20 February 1941, Himmler wrote to Schwarz again and put forward excuses for Globocnik's behaviour, citing the pressure of work in Lublin—the excavation of defence ditches and the resettlement of 35,000 Chełm-Germans during 1940. He highlighted the logistical problems involved in such monumental schemes. Himmler agreed that his protégé had acted foolishly with his financial dealings, but suggested that his actions were not improper. He stated that Globocnik would apologise for his thoughtless and incorrect behaviour towards the Reichsschatzmeister. This was what Schwarz wanted to hear, and on 18 March 1941, he granted Globocnik final discharge from his fiscal dealings as Gauleiter of Vienna. Schwarz pointed out that Globocnik had carried out certain dealings that were the actual responsibility of the Gau treasurer and not the Gauleiter. With that, Schwarz closed the door on Globocnik's questionable business transactions in Vienna. Globocnik could now fully concentrate on the important task in hand.

The start of the evacuation of Volksdeutsche from the regions of Lublin and Cholm began on 2 September 1940. They were resettled near Lodz, moving into an area previously occupied by Poles, who now found themselves forcibly transferred to the regions vacated by the Volksdeutsche.

As the crow flies, Zamość is 76 km (47 miles) south-east of Lublin. The present-day city boasts a population of around 65,000 inhabitants, in an area of 11.77 square miles. It remains part of the Lublin region, as it was during the Second World War. Founded in 1580 by Jan Zamoyski, the commander of the Polish-Lithuanian Commonwealth Army, it stood on the trade route between northern Europe and the Black Sea. It is an excellent example of late sixteenth-century Renaissance architecture. Although overrun by German forces in September 1939, Zamość was initially occupied by the Soviets under the partition of Poland agreement. On 5 October 1939, the Red Army abandoned the city, which the Germans occupied three days later.

In the autumn of 1940, in a privately owned archive in the city, records were uncovered that confirmed Dr Franz Stanglica's research findings of the foundation of Palatinate villages in the Zamość region from 1790. This was an exciting discovery for the SSPF in Lublin. He informed the race fanatic Himmler at a meeting in Krakow on 26 October 1940, and then presented his Germanisation ideas to the Reichsführer-SS. Globocnik suggested that these villages should be identified and consolidated as Germanic settlements. The young inhabitants should be returned to the Reich where they were to be educated in German culture and converted to a Germanic way of life. They could then return to their homeland where they would drive a wedge between the established Polish customs and family life, and their new culture. Globocnik also aired his idea of a search for Germanic blood as a vision for the future. He had the idea of building a German Siedlungsbrücke (settlement bridge) between the German-settled Baltic region in the north to the German districts of Transylvania in the south. By this master stroke, the Slavic Polish peoples would be encircled by German settlements, before being crushed biologically and economically.

This was a variation on Globocnik's original idea put to Himmler in August 1940, of Germanised farming communities forming battalions of soldiers in the defence of the colonised territories. Himmler found this suggestion too impractical and suggested an alternative, which formed the nucleus of establishing SS and Police strongholds in the border area.

Hans Frank had meanwhile attended a meeting at the Führerhauptquartier with Hitler, Baldur von Schirach, and Erich Koch on 2 October 1940. All had put pressure on Frank to accept expelled Jews in the General Government, but he had resisted.

At the 26 October 1940 Globocnik meeting with Himmler in Krakow, Globocnik's plans included the construction of a new SS-Mannschaftshaus in Lublin, which would serve as a central research institute. Globocnik consulted Kurt Ellersiek from the SS-Rasse- und Siedlungshauptamt (SS Race and Resettlement Central Office—RSHA). To run this institute, Globocnik subsequently identified Hanelt and Claus Walter Padel, ably assisted by Dr Franz Stanglica from Vienna. Hanelt and Stanglica in effect became responsible for the overall planning of the establishment of SS and Police Strongholds, and the resettlement of the indigenous population, including the Jews.

Jürgen Lassmann headed the architectural section. He was born in Vienna in 1914 and studied at the Technical Institute of the University of Vienna. He was an active supporter of the NSDAP from 1933 and was suspended for his political activities for one year in 1934. At the university, he ran the Hochschülerschaft (Students' Association). He joined the SS in 1937, and after the Anschluss, he recruited for the SS-Mannschaftshaus in Vienna. After graduation, he worked for the German Settlement Society. In 1940, he was conscripted into the Waffen-SS and was wounded in action. In early 1942, he transferred to the Research Centre in Lublin. Lassmann also saw service at Trawniki where he gained a reputation for cruelty. In late 1943, he transferred to Trieste.

Himmler gave his tacit approval to Globocnik's latest idea of searching for German blood, and in November 1940, Hitler Youth leaders, accompanied by Polish-speaking auxiliary policemen, began their search in the villages surrounding Zamość. They completed questionnaires and compiled a register of so-called ethnic

Germans. As part of this strategy, Operation 'Blumberg' commenced in January 1941. This consisted of volunteer leaders from the BDM (German Young Women's Federation) and girls from the NSV (National Socialist Welfare Organisation) circulating among the female villagers, giving advice on such matters as childcare and hygiene. Under the supervision of Marie-Luise Gilgenmann, a Lublin resident since October 1940, they offered courses to learn German and they established several kindergarten and schools. In support of their work, they distributed a propaganda pamphlet, *Kolonistenbriefe-Listy Kolonistow*, which extols the virtues of German settlement farming. The leaflet was sourced to Lothar von Seltmann, produced on the authority of Globocnik.

The intention of Globocnik is revealed in a subsequent report dated 15 October 1941, from the Security Police commander, Johannes Müller, to SS-Gruppenführer Otto Hofmann, the chief of the SS Race and Resettlement Office: 'The Brigadeführer intends to settle Germans all over the Lublin district, and later, referring to the Baltic countries settled by Nordic or German population, to establish through the Lublin district, liaison with Transylvania with the Germans living there'.[1] In other words, Globocnik planned to encircle the Polish population between the Warthegau and the Lublin region in order to 'ruin it economically and biologically'.[2]

The Reichsführer-SS directed that 60 per cent of family-run farmsteads in the newly acquired territories of the East must be between 20 and 115 hectares. They must also be modernised in order to increase productivity.

Himmler, meanwhile, pressed for his scheme of SS and Police bases and issued an order to that effect on 2 November 1940. In response, Globocnik identified six rural estates at Rachnow, Turow, Siemien, Wytyoczne, Sarny, and Wola Zollkiewa as suitable locations.[3] From 1 March 1941, these sites, altogether 9,000 hectares, were requisitioned as SS and Police strongholds. Gustav Hanelt reported that these farm estates were inefficient and totally unsuitable for their plans, with all facilities requiring an immediate update and reorganisation to improve hygiene, accommodation, including that for livestock, and suitability for the scheme. Soon, every building was thoroughly cleaned and tidied; every animal had a nameplate and historical record. The land itself suffered from lack of drainage and was in a poor condition. Despite his negative report, Hanelt envisaged a drastic improvement and foresaw them as 'centres of German life'.[4]

By 4 December 1940, Eichmann had identified a total of 5.8 million Jews within the German economic sphere in Europe that were liable for deportation. Their destination had yet to be determined.

Globocnik was impatient. In June 1941, he visited the village of Huszczka, one of the sites destined for Germanisation. He was dissatisfied with the progress and applied to Himmler for an increase in funding. Himmler sanctioned an advance of 5,000 RM.

The eccentric Heinrich Himmler approved of his protégé's efforts and decided that the search for German bloodlines should be extended throughout the General Government. Globocnik was not the only senior SS officer in occupied Poland with radical and efficient ethnic reorganisation on his mind.

Friedrich Katzmann was born in Langendreer, between Bochum and Dortmund, on 6 May 1906, the sixth child of Andreas-August Katzmann (born 13 December 1868), a shot-firer in a coalmine, and his wife, Anna (born Zimmermann, on 9 May 1872 in Witten). His elder brother, Heinrich Katzmann (born 21 January 1899; died 15 October 1974), was also an SS officer.

After attending elementary school in Duisburg, he trained as a carpenter and decorator. From 1927 until July 1933, he was out of work. He joined the NSDAP on 1 September 1928, but he had been a member of the SA since 1 December 1927. He transferred to the SS in Duisburg on 1 July 1930, and on 1 January 1932, he attended the first SS course at the SA Leadership School in Munich. This entitled him to wear the Tyr rune on his upper tunic sleeve. On 1 December 1932, he was promoted to SS-Sturmhauptführer and was given command of 2. Sturmbann 25. SS-Standarte in Duisburg. He gained further promotion to SS-Sturmbannführer on 3 May 1933. The following November, he failed to gain a seat in the Reichstag. From 1 December 1933 until 31 January 1934, Katzmann was the district overseer of the German Labour Front.

For five days in January 1934, Katzmann commanded the 25. SS-Standarte in Essen. The same month, he was attached to the SS-Leibstandarte 'Adolf Hitler' for training in preparation for his becoming a full-time SS leader. He was posted to SS-Oberabschnitt West with effect from 30 January 1934 and promoted to SS-Obersturmbannführer on 7 February 1934. He transferred to 75. SS-Standarte in Berlin-Tempelhof on 4 April 1934. His Oberabschnitt boss, Sepp Dietrich, described him as 'unusually ambitious … a fanatical political soldier … financially impeccable … organised … his world view is completely solid'.[5] Katzmann received further promotion on 17 August 1934, this time to SS-Standartenführer.

In February 1936, Katzmann became involved in a drunken brawl in a Berlin bar. He was accused of insulting police officers and resisting arrest. On 13 February, the Chief Public Prosecutor in Berlin directed that the charges against the SS-Standartenführer were to be dropped. In July 1937, Katzmann was appointed as an honorary member of the People's Court. He was transferred to the command of SS-Abschnitt VI in Breslau on 21 March 1938 and received promotion to SS-Oberführer on 9 November 1938. Katzmann's SS units took an active role in the anti-Jewish actions of 9–10 November 1938. Katzmann subsequently reported that they had destroyed Jewish synagogues, meeting halls, shops, and business premises, and they had seized about 600 Jewish men. A convoy to Buchenwald concentration camp had been arranged.

During the Polish campaign, Katzmann was attached to the Ordnungspolizei units under the command of Wilhelm List's 14. Army in southern Poland. He served as the SS Liaison Officer with the police units of Herbert Becker. For the month of November 1939, Katzmann was nominated as commander of police in the district of Radom. On 30 November 1939, he was appointed as the first SSPF Radom.

Radom was a medium-sized city, with a population at that time of 81,000 people, nearly 25,000 of them Jews. A further 280,000 Jews lived in the surrounding district. Katzmann immediately introduced anti-Jewish regulations and brutality became commonplace. On 30 January 1940, Katzmann was a participant at a meeting in Berlin, which discussed the evacuation of Poles and Jews from the Warthegau. On 29 and 30 March 1940, Katzmann led a disastrous operation against Polish partisans in his district. A total failure, he succeeded in losing a significant amount of equipment and weapons, and cost nine police casualties. As a result, Friedrich-Wilhelm Krüger was ordered by Hitler to take personal command of a reprisal operation on 31 March, aimed at the entire male population in the conflict area. There followed a reinforced police offensive on 1 and 2 April in which about fifty partisans were killed. Katzmann's shortcomings did not hinder his career. He was promoted to SS-Brigadeführer on 21 June 1941.

From 4 August 1941, Katzmann was appointed as SSPF Galicia, based in Lvov. He continued his anti-Jewish measures, including herding the Jews into a newly created ghetto. Katzmann's decree of 21 August 1942, concerning the creation of an enclosed Jewish residential district in the city of Lvov (German Lemberg):

> Based on the Ordinance on Restrictions of Residence in the GG from 13.9.1940 with the changes by the Second Ordinance on Restrictions of Residence in the GG from 29.4.41 and the amendment by the Third Ordinance on Restrictions of Residence as well as the Ordinance on 'Administrative Punishments' in the GG from 13.9.1940., I order in consultation with the military commander of Lemberg:
>
> §1 An enclosed Jewish residential district is created in the city/town of Lemberg. With the permission of the Chief of Police of Lemberg [address] Aryans are allowed to reside further on in this district at own risk.
>
> §2 The borders of the Jewish residential district are:
> to the south: Eisenbahndamm [embankment]
> to the east: Sommersteinstrasse
> to the north: Na Torfy, Peltew [Peliew?] brook, Pod Boiskiem Lysenki, Jordanska and its prolongation till the railway line.
>
> §3 The relocation starts at once with the publication of this decree. It has to be concluded until Monday, 7. September 1942. The accommodation of the Jews within the Jewish residential district is the duty of the Jewish council.
>
> §4 This decree has the effect of an eviction order for all persons concerned by it.

Aryans not receiving the permission to stay in the Jewish residential district and not moving out by 7. September 1942 will be removed forcefully.

§5 The Jews are allowed to take along their personal belongings into the Jewish residential district. As far as they cannot take along their movable belongings, they have to leave them behind in their previous accommodation. Especially those objects have to be left behind that are left to the use of an Aryan subtenant.

The Jews are not allowed to sell objects because of the relocation, nor to alienate them in another way, nor to destroy them or to leave them to other persons for use or safekeeping. When leaving the accommodation, movable belongings left behind have to be registered via Jewish council at the SSPF [address].

§6 Leaving and entering the Jewish residential district has to be effected exclusively through the entrance and exit gate under the railway overbridge over Peliew [Peltew?] street. For ARYANS, a permit issued by the Chief of Police of Lemberg entitles to pass. It will be issued only to persons working outside the Jewish residential district. The passage of JEWS effects due to the 'Arbeitskarte' for Jews, rubber-stamped by the SSPF.

§7 Requests by non-Jewish retail shops, workshops and administrative offices to stay on in the Jewish residential district have to be directed immediately to the SSPF in Lemberg.

§8 Violations of this decree will be prosecuted by means of the Security Police, independently of the punishment by relevant laws and ordinances.

§9 This decree becomes effective with its publication by placarding at the public placarding sites of the town of Lemberg. All other earlier regulations become invalid at the same time.

Lemberg, 21. VIII. 1942

DER GOUVERNEUR DES DISTRIKTS GALIZIEN
DER SS- UND POLIZEIFÜHRER
[signed] **Katzmann**
SS-Brigadeführer
u. Generalmajor d. Polizei

In this post, Katzman directed the physical extermination of 434,329 Jewish men, women, and children. He proudly announced on 30 June 1943 in his infamous 'Katzmann Report' that Galicia was Jew free (see appendices).

Katzmann was married in Hamborn on 29 January 1934 to Hildegard Frey, the daughter of a master tailor, born in Duisburg-Hamborn am Rhein on 29 January 1913. They had four sons and one daughter. Not blessed with good looks, Katzmann had very distinctive protruding ears. He had fair hair, with a slight tinge of pale red.

After the war, Katzmann successfully evaded arrest and prosecution, and in 1952 was believed to be living in the Middle East. He apparently made his way back to Germany under the false name of 'Bruno Albrecht' and lived in Griesheim near Darmstadt, where he worked as a salesman. It was not until he was seriously ill, without hope of recovery, at the Alice Hospital in Darmstadt that he finally confessed his true identity to a nurse who was caring for him. He died without answering for his multitude of crimes, still a convinced Nazi, on 19 September 1957. Although not on such a great scale, Fritz Katzmann ranks alongside Globocnik as one of the greatest killers of Jews.

# 8

# HEAD OFFICE IN BERLIN

TIERGARTENSTRAßE, IN CENTRAL Berlin, is today a tree-lined avenue forming the southern perimeter of the Tiergarten, a large grassed inner city park with lakes, trees, and pathways. As in the 1930s, the park is popular with Berliners who desire a relaxing Sunday stroll. Formerly known as the Grosser Tiergarten, it covers an area of 520 acres and was on the central east–west axis of the city. The main thoroughfare from east to west, the Charlottenburger Chaussee, pierced the centre of the park and was adorned by the newly repositioned Berlin Victory Column.

An exclusive residential area sprang up to the south of the park and Tiergartenstraße boasted some of the most exclusive villas in the city. Today, the site of number 4 is occupied by a concert hall, the home of the Berlin Philharmonic. Construction of the original house dates from 1820. Various alterations and changes in ownership ended with the acquisition of the property by the banker and patron of the arts, Valentin Weisbach, in 1875. From 1888 to 1890, Weisbach demolished the house and replaced it with a modernised building based on plans by the popular architect Christian Heidecke.

On 31 July 1909, Georg Liebermann, the brother of acclaimed painter Max Liebermann, acquired the house on the Tiergartenstraße and converted it into a magnificent three-storey residential building with about thirty rooms, a lift, and ballroom. Even part of the roof was glazed. Liebermann was a wealthy textile manufacturer, a city councillor, and one of the most important Jewish entrepreneurs in Berlin. Else Liebermann, Georg's wife, disliked the house so much that she rarely stayed there. Before Georg's death in 1926, the unpopular house was rented.

In 1927, the business premises of an art dealer, Hermann Ball, were located on the ground floor, and the antiques and auction house Graupe was located on the first floor. Number 4 followed a trend of the large residential homes in the road being used as business premises. Walter Benjamin, the son of an art dealer, described his visit to Tiergartenstraße 4 in an article for a radio programme for children:

> I want to tell you where exactly the most beautiful labyrinths that have ever happened to me are to be seen. This is the bookseller, Paul Graupe, who has given in his big beautiful house a whole hall for the whimsical city, forest, mountain, valley, castle and bridge labyrinths ... but clean off your boots, because it is very posh with Paul Graupe. If you then look out the window between the cityscapes, maps and plans, you find there that you have the zoo again in front of you, and with that we walked around quite labyrinthine today...[1]

From 1933 to 1934, the building housed the office of SA-Gruppe Berlin-Brandenburg under the command of SA-Gruppenführer Karl Ernst. Following his murder during the Night of Long Knives purge of the SA in June–July 1934, he was replaced by SA-Obergruppenführer Dietrich von Jagow. A Jewish pharmacy owner, Dr Georg Cohn, was listed as the tenant in 1934. By January 1935, the Auslands Organisation of the NSDAP then rented the building and the adjoining property at Tiergartenstraße 4a. A letter from the AO to the building authority of the Tiergarten district reveals that breakthroughs were made between the two buildings in four places and that the combined premises had been divided into smaller units. There is no indication of where the breakthroughs occurred and whether they were subsequently rebuilt.[2] The AO, under the direction of Gauleiter Ernst Wilhelm Bohle, occupied the buildings until its move to Fehrbelliner Platz on 20 April 1939.

In June 1936, Hans Liebermann signed total ownership of the house at number 4 over to his Aryan wife, Klara, to avoid seizure by the Nazi authorities. Being a Jew, Liebermann was in danger of incarceration in a concentration camp and loss of assets. In September 1938, he fled the country to avoid arrest. As part of Albert Speer's master plan for central Berlin, the buildings at Tiergartenstraße 4 and 4a were destined for demolition to make way for Speer's grand Soldiers' Hall and a new Army High Command building. The owners, Klara Liebermann and Eva Koebner, sold their freeholds to the army on 5 October 1940, but it does appear from property records and communications that the Army High Command had already taken possession as early as 4 April 1940 and the sale was only finalised the following October. During these compulsory sale negotiations, Viktor Brack from the office of the Reich Chancellery of the Führer (RKF) personally intervened. This was the first indication of the involvement of Reichsleiter Philipp Bouhler's department.

Brack was the senior representative of the RKF, which required premises to carry out a directive of the Führer that had serious and sensitive consequences for the

Reich leadership. Brack rented the villa for a largely secret organisation, which had the cover name 'Reich Association of Sanatoriums and Care Institutions'. Before occupation, the premises underwent extensive alterations.

Adolf Hitler had always shown a particular interest in eugenics. He was an early and enthusiastic supporter of 'racial hygiene'; society would benefit by the limiting of 'inferior' individuals to procreate while maximising the ability of 'superior' beings to do so. Those people with physical deformities, mental illness, and incurable illnesses were easy and obvious targets. As early as 1895, Adolf Jost had declared that the state had the right to demand the sacrifice of the non-productive and impaired elements of society who were draining the state of its resources, with no return in compensation. By 1920, in the post-war economic climate of a defeated Germany, Karl Binding and Alfred Hoche authored a book that extolled the practice of legally terminating 'unworthy life'. Included in their definition of 'unworthy life' were deformed children, mentally retarded, mentally ill, and incurably sick adults. The authors declared that such individuals were a drain on the health service and were economically untenable. This was music to the ears of eugenicists such as Adolf Hitler.

At the 1929 Reichsparteitag, Hitler spoke of racial selection and elimination of the weak in order to strengthen the healthy. After attaining power in 1933, Hitler did not rush into state-sponsored euthanasia. He cunningly prepared the German people by slowly drip feeding the notion into everyday life. Propaganda films, radio programmes, and magazines were produced which highlighted the negative view of the mentally ill and deformed wretches that were a burden to the nation. Gradually, the notion of elimination was encouraged, until a large section of the population either accepted the idea or would not raise a voice of complaint if legal euthanasia was carried out. The power of propaganda became evident.

Only six months after gaining power, on 14 July 1933, Hitler introduced the Law for the Prevention of Genetically Diseased Offspring. The basic provisions of the 1933 law stated:

(1) Any person suffering from a hereditary disease may be rendered incapable of procreation by means of a surgical operation (sterilisation), if the experience of medical science shows that it is highly probable that his descendants would suffer from some serious physical or mental hereditary defect.

(2) For the purposes of this law, any person will be considered as hereditarily diseased who is suffering from any one of the following diseases:

    (1) Congenital Mental Deficiency;
    (2) Schizophrenia;
    (3) Manic-Depressive Insanity;
    (4) Hereditary Epilepsy;

(5) Hereditary Chorea (Huntington's Disease);
(6) Hereditary Blindness;
(7) Hereditary Deafness;
(8) Any severe hereditary deformity.

(3) Any person suffering from severe alcoholism may be also rendered incapable of procreation.[3]

By 1939, it is estimated that 200,000–350,000 people had been legally sterilised.

On 24 November 1933, the Nazis enacted the Law against Dangerous Habitual Criminals. This allowed the indefinite imprisonment in asylums of habitual criminals deemed dangerous to German society, and also legalised castration for sex offenders.

Restrictions were also placed on marriages between two people if one suffered from mental disability, or a contagious or hereditary disease. By 1938, Hitler was being petitioned for 'mercy killing' by parents of severely disabled or deformed young children. Gerhard Kretschmar was one such child who rose to prominence. He was born on 20 February 1939, blind with only one leg and a severely deformed arm. Hitler ordered Dr Karl Brandt to investigate and directed him to inform the child's physicians that if the description provided by the boy's father was accurate, that euthanasia could be carried out by order of the Führer. Brandt confirmed that the boy was as described, and he was killed by lethal injection on 25 July 1939.

On his return to Berlin, Brandt was ordered to carry out similar acts of euthanasia in other cases. Realising that this was a matter of utmost delicacy, Brandt was ordered to secretly consult with Philipp Bouhler and discreetly organise an official programme of mercy killing. Brandt and Bouhler set up the Reich Committee for the Scientific Registering of Serious Hereditary and Congenital Illnesses in May 1939. This body issued a decree on 18 August 1939 that ordered doctors and nurses to inform it of any deformed new-born offspring. This was two weeks prior to the breakout of hostilities between Germany and Poland. This followed a conference in July 1939 that discussed the mercy killing of adult mental patients, and was attended by Professor Werner Heyde.

In early October 1939, with the nation's attention elsewhere, Hitler signed the now-famous short memorandum on his personal stationery. The document was backdated to 1 September 1939, to coincide with the start of hostilities.[4] This document gave the green light to euthanasia based on eugenics. Nazi bureaucracy swung into action. Brack's administration could not, for obvious reasons, operate from the Reich Chancellery on Voss Strasse. His department—Hauptamt II of the KdF—was designated the ultimate authority for the operation, and it initially set up a branch office in the Columbiahaus building on Potsdamer Platz. It finally moved to Tiergartenstraße 4, probably in April 1940, and it gained a new codename based upon the new permanent address—T4.

Karl Brandt was Hitler's escort doctor and followed him wherever he went in order to be immediately on hand should the Führer fall ill. He was born in Mulhouse, Alsace-Lorraine, on 8 January 1904. Trained in surgery, he came to Hitler's notice after treating Hitler's adjutant following a traffic accident. He was appointed as Hitler's escort doctor in 1934 and became a member of Hitler's inner circle. A member of the SS, Brandt rose to the rank of SS-Gruppenführer by 1944. On 16 April 1945, he was arrested by the Gestapo for defeatism—he had moved his family west from Berlin in order that they could surrender to the Western Allies. He was sentenced to death by a military court, but was released on 2 May by the order of Karl Dönitz. He was arrested by the British in Kiel on 23 May 1945. Tried at Nuremberg, he was found guilty and executed at Landsberg on 2 June 1948.

Reichsleiter Philipp 'Ango' Bouhler was born into a military family in Munich on 11 September 1899. His father, Emil Bouhler, was a colonel, and he was chief of the Bavarian War Office. Philipp joined the Bavarian Cadet Corps in 1912, and remained there until 15 July 1916, when he volunteered for active service. He was commissioned as a Leutnant on 30 July 1917, and on 8 August 1917, after being sent to the Western Front, he was buried alive and sustained serious fractures to both legs. He was still in hospital at the end of the war and remained under the care of doctors until 1920, having been invalided out of the army. In 1919, his army career plans in ruins, he turned to politics. He was a convinced anti-Semite. His beliefs led him to the NSDAP in November 1921, when he worked for the *Volkischer Beobachter* newspaper and came under the influence of Max Amann. He joined the NSDAP in July 1922. He became the NSDAP deputy chief business manager, under Amann, in late September 1922. Bouhler rejoined the party after its reformation. He joined the SS on 20 April 1933, and was immediately afforded the rank of SS-Gruppenführer. He was promoted to SS-Obergruppenführer on 30 January 1936. On 17 November 1934, he was appointed chief of the Führer's Chancellery, and he retained this post until April 1945, although his influence in party matters had by then considerably reduced. As head of the Führer's Chancellery, the euthanasia programme was placed under Bouhler's direction from 1 September 1939, but the actual operational functioning was administered by Werner Blankenburg and Viktor Brack. Bouhler was arrested by US troops at Schloss Fischorn, near Zell am See, on 10 May 1945. Seen by the Allies as a major offender with his connection to the euthanasia programme, he would certainly have trod the scaffold steps at Landsberg am Lech Prison. He cheated the hangman by committing suicide on 19 May 1945, at Zell am See.

Prior to the occupancy by the staff of the KdF, the T4 building underwent extensive internal structural alterations. The building firm Vollmann and Schmidt had the contract. One of its bricklayers was Erwin Lambert who had been involved in similar alterations to the Columbiahaus office. In 1961, Lambert recalled: '[Vollmann and

Schmidt] gave me the assignment to visit the building at Tiergartenstraße 4 in Berlin, equipped with masonry tools and start work there.... When I got there, I already met two workers unknown to me who were already busy with it to create a little order in the completely empty building'.[5]

The T4 central office operated under several cover names—the Charitable Foundation for Institutional Care; the Charitable Society for the Transportation of the Sick (Gekrat); the Reich Association for Sanatoriums and Care Institutions; and the Central Compensation Office for Sanatoriums and Nursing Homes. All were designed as camouflage for the real purpose of T4.

Although Philipp Bouhler was the titular head of T4, he had little or no actual involvement in the actual running of the programme. The director of T4 was Viktor Brack, who even had a codename himself—'Jennerwein'. Brack was born in Haaren-Aachen on 9 November 1904. He had an unspectacular upbringing in a middle-class family and achieved an average educational standard. He joined the NSDAP in 1929 and became a member of the SS. Brack supervised the SS motor training unit in Munich. In 1936, he was appointed head of Hauptamt II of the Kanzlei des Führers and held responsibility for liaison between the Wehrmacht, Reich Ministries, and the NSDAP. He also dealt with clemency petitions and complaints addressed to the Führer. On 9 November 1940, Brack was promoted to SS-Oberführer.

At the 1947 Doctors' Trial in Nuremberg, Brack testified that after 1941, when the extermination of the European Jewish population by Germany was proceeding at full capacity, Himmler ordered him to liaise with physicians from T4 to find a way to sterilise Jews capable of labour in order to utilise them for the German war effort. He suggested developing a method by which the victim could be sterilised while being unaware of the procedure. Brack reported back, suggesting a method of sterilising patients using X-Rays:

> Berlin, March 28, 1941
> To the
> Reichsführer-SS and Chief of the German Police
> Berlin SW 11
> Prinz-Albrecht-Str. 8
>
> SECRET REICH MATTER
> Dear Reichsführer!
>
> Attached I submit to you with the request for notice that
> Result of the investigations on the possibility of a
> X-ray sterilisation BEZW.—castration.

I ask for instructions as to whether and what should continue to be theoretical or practical in the matter.

Heil Hitler!
Brack

Secret Reich Matter
Report on the experiments concerning X-ray castration

The experiments in this area are completed. The following result can be said to be safe and scientifically supported.

If any persons are to be made permanently infertile, then this succeeds only with the use of such high x-ray doses that with them a castration occurs with all its consequences. The high x-ray doses destroy the internal secretion of the ovary or the testicle. Lower doses would only prevent fertility for a certain period of time. The questionable consequences are z. As the absence of the period, climacteric phenomena, change in hair, change in metabolism, etc. These disadvantages must be noted in any case.

The dosage itself can be designed in different ways, and the radiation is completely imperceptible. For men, a hereditary dose of 500–600r, for women such a 300–350 is necessary. Basically, you can get along with the strongest tension and thin filter and a short distance with an exposure time of 2 minutes for men or 3 minutes for women. However, the disadvantage must be taken into account that, since an imperceptible coverage of the remaining body parts with lead is not carried out, the rest of the body tissue is damaged and thus the so-called Röntgenkater occurs. If the intensity of the radiation is too high, then, in the following days or weeks, different burns appear individually on the skin parts reached by the rays.

A way of practical implementation would be z. For example, let the persons to be dismissed step in front of a counter where they can ask questions or fill in forms, which should be stopped for about 2–3 minutes. The official sitting behind the counter can operate the apparatus, in such a way that he operates a switch with which both tubes (since the irradiation must be from both sides) are put into operation at the same time. In a system with two tubes, therefore, about 150–200 persons could be sterilised per day, with 20 systems thus already 3000 to 4000 per day. A higher number of daily deportations is in my estimation anyway out of the question.
The cost of such a plant I can only rough estimate with RM 20,000–30,000 per tube system. However, the costs of rebuilding a building are added, as extensive backups have to be installed for the civil servants on duty.

In summary, it may therefore be said that, according to the current state of X-ray technology and research, it is readily possible to carry out a mass sterilisation by X-rays. It seems impossible, however, to carry out this measure without the persons

> concerned sooner or later being able to ascertain with certainty that they have been sterilised by X-rays.[6]

Brack suggested a practical method of implementation was to allow people to approach a counter and have them ask questions or fill out forms, which should take about two or three minutes. The official sitting behind the counter could then operate a switch on the apparatus, which both tubes— the irradiation must be carried out from both sides—would simultaneously operate. In a system with two tubes, therefore, about 150–200 people could be sterilised per day, and with twenty systems, 3,000–4,000 per day. The KdF provided Dr Horst Schumann with his X-Ray sterilisation methodology in Auschwitz.

On April 23, 1941 Werner Heyde and his supervisor Viktor Brack spoke at a meeting of the State Secretary and president of the Higher Regional Courts as the acting Reich Minister of Justice, Franz Schlegelberger, about the possible prosecution of relatives of patients for murder. They introduced the activities of the 'Reich Co-operative for State Hospitals and Nursing Homes', produced Hitler's 1939 memorandum, and submitted that Hitler had rejected the adoption of a formal law on euthanasia for foreign policy reasons.

Brack visited Globocnik in early May 1942.[7] He followed this up on 23 June 1942, with the following letter to Himmler from his office at Voss Strasse 4:

> Esteemed Reichsführer,
> A long time ago, I gave a part of my men to Brigadeführer Globocnik on instructions from Reichsleiter Bouhler to carry out his special task. Due to a renewed request from him, I have now made available more staff. On this occasion Brigadeführer Globocnik took the view that the whole action of the Jews should be carried out as quickly as possible, so that one day they would not get stuck in the middle if any difficulties that make it necessary to stop the action. You yourself, Reichsführer, have already told me that you have to work as fast as possible for reasons of camouflage. Both views, which in principle produce the same result, are in my own experience more than justified. Nevertheless, I would like to ask you, in this connection, to consider the following consideration:
>
> Among tens of millions of Jews in Europe, there are, I calculate, at least two to three million men and women who are fit enough to work. Considering the extraordinary difficulties the labour problem presents to us, I hold the view that those two to three million should be specially selected and preserved. This can, however, only be done if at the same time they are rendered incapable of reproduction. About a year ago I reported to you that representatives of mine had completed the experiments necessary for this purpose. I would like to recall these facts once more. Sterilisation, as normally performed on persons with hereditary diseases, is here out of the question,

> because it takes too long and is too expensive. Castration by X-Ray, however, is not only relatively cheap, but can also be performed on many thousands in the shortest time. I think that at this time it is already irrelevant whether the people in question become aware of having been castrated after some weeks or months, once they feel the effects. Should you, Reichsführer, decide to choose this way in the interest of the preservation of labour, then Reichsleiter Bouhler would be prepared to place all physicians and other personnel needed for this work at your disposal. Likewise, he requested me to inform you that I would have to order the apparatus so urgently needed with the greatest speed.
>
> Heil Hitler! Yours
> Viktor Brack[8]

Following the letter, Himmler ordered the procedure to be tested on prisoners in Auschwitz. The letter also alludes to a visit by Brack and Bouhler to Globocnik in September 1941, referred to by Brack in his evidence at Nuremberg. Brack denied this visit had anything to do with the Jewish extermination policy. It is feasible that a new secret euthanasia centre in the Lublin District was being planned, following the official cessation of operations in the Reich ordered by Hitler the previous month.

When Brack was transferred for active duty to the SS-Prinz Eugen Division, his KdF associate, Blankenburg, took responsibility for the task and was ordered to 'immediately take the necessary measures and contact the Kommandanturs of each concentration camp'.

A Jewish French doctor, in Auschwitz from September 1943 until the camp liberation, testified at the Doctors' Trial in Nuremberg that sterilisation of Jewish inmates was carried out at Auschwitz II—Auschwitz-Birkenau—by SS doctors. He administered medical care to nearly 100 male Polish prisoners who had been sterilised at Birkenau by surgical operations. According to the witness, members of this group were later castrated by camp doctors.

During the Doctors' Trial at Nuremberg, on 14 May 1947, Brack attempted to portray himself as an innocent bystander:

> … I can only say that I believe that in my testimony so far I have explained that I never had any intention of exterminating the Jewish people, but attempted to achieve the contrary, to protect the Jews and save them from a terrible fate. That I attempted something that was far beyond my power, my position, my ability, I must admit is true. But since, in all my life, I have always been helpful toward and never had any hatred of Jews, I can't imagine why I should have become a champion of the extermination of the Jews.[9]

Brack was convicted of murder of victims in the euthanasia programme. In March 1947, while in captivity at Regensburg Internment Camp, Bouhler's personal adjutant, Karl Freiherr Michel von Tüßling, submitted an affidavit in the defence of Brack, but he was nevertheless convicted and executed by hanging at Landsberg Prison on 2 June 1948.[10]

Brack's deputy in T4 was SA-Oberführer Werner Blankenburg—codename 'Brenner'. He was born in Caputh-Brandenburg on 19 June 1905. He worked in sales before joining the NSDAP and the SA in 1929. By 1938, he was head of Abteilung IIa in the KdF. Blankenburg is believed to have dictated the euthanasia memo to a secretary dated 1 September 1939 and subsequently signed by Hitler. Brack and Blankenburg were responsible for personnel recruitment, equipment, and the running of the killing centres.

In April 1945, Blankenburg flew to Bavaria with other members of the KdF, including Viktor Brack and Albert Bormann . After the war, Blankenburg lived under a false name, Werner Bieleke, which was the maiden name of his wife. He worked as a representative of a building society in Ludwigsburg, and later as a representative of a textile factory in Freudenstadt. Although he was sought by the judiciary from the summer of 1945 until his death, he managed to lead a life in secret and to keep in touch with his parents, who lived in a retirement home in Ulm. He also maintained contact with former T4 employees. He drowned in Stuttgart-Wangen on 28 November 1957 and was buried there under his false identity. The funeral was attended by several former T4 members, including Dietrich Allers and Erwin Lambert. Officially, he had been declared dead on 15 March 1956 by the Berlin District Court of Tempelhof-Kreuzberg at the request of his wife.

Head of Abteilung IIb was Dr Hans Hefelmann. Born on 4 October 1906 in Dresden, Hefelmann studied agricultural science. In 1931, he joined the NSDAP, and in 1932, he gained a doctorate in agricultural law. For a short time, he worked in the economy office of the deputy Führer, but transferred to the KdF in 1936, rising to head of Abteilung IIb the following year. In T4, Hefelmann was an enthusiastic administrator of child euthanasia. For the trial of T4 Medical Director, Professor Werner Heyde, in 1964, Werner Kirchert provided a statement:

> At the end of September or the beginning of October, I was ordered to Dr Hefelmann. At this meeting, Dr Hefelmann planned how to kill several hundred people at once with the beginning of the action, and how to disguise such mass elimination. He spoke of railway and omnibus accidents, etc., which could be cited as a cause of sudden death to relatives and the public. Hefelmann rejected my objections that such a procedure was almost impracticable. Obviously, Hefelmann's relentless attitude resulted from the then-frequent standpoint, 'My Führer, I am reporting!' I then gave Dr Hefelmann my decision that under these circumstances I am not prepared to participate in the action.[11]

All applicants to join the staff of T4 were interviewed personally by Brack or Blankenburg. This included non-professional staff such as the cleaners and tea ladies. No member of staff was coerced into performing a duty that they were reluctant to carry out, and no retributions were made against unwilling participants. The building was guarded against access from the street and entry was strictly restricted. The whole operation was conducted in an air of utmost secrecy. Many of the lay personnel were subsequently transferred to Aktion Reinhardt, and it is estimated that around 120 members of T4 staff were made available to Globocnik, providing the kernel of professional killers, fully trained and indoctrinated by T4.

The problem facing the bureaucrats at the KdF was selecting the best method of despatching the 'infected' into the next world. Initial murders were carried out by lethal injection, but this technique could not obviously be used in great numbers. A meeting was held at the KdF in Voss Strasse on 9 October 1939. Participants included Brack, Blankenburg, Hefelmann, and Reinhold Vorberg. Also present as the medical experts were Professors Werner Heyde and Paul Hermann Nitsche, plus Doctors Gerhard Bohne and Herbert Linden representing the Interior Ministry.[12] The Reich Criminal Police Department was represented by Kriminalrat Dr Paul Werner. It is unclear whether Bouhler and Brandt attended this meeting, as it was in the case of Professor Max de Crinis, an expert psychiatrist and a close collaborator of Reinhard Heydrich. This body then formed the nucleus of the governing body of what became T4.[13]

The agenda for this meeting was mainly to discuss the possible methods of 'disinfection' and the suitable personnel required. Very quickly, the use of a painless method, such as carbon monoxide poisoning, was discussed and agreed upon.

Carbon monoxide (CO) is a colourless, odourless, and tasteless gas that is slightly less dense than air. It is toxic to animals (and humans) that use haemoglobin as an oxygen carrier (both invertebrate and vertebrate) when encountered in concentrations above about 35 ppm, although it is also produced in normal animal metabolism in low quantities and is thought to have some normal biological functions. In the atmosphere, it is spatially variable and short lived, having a role in the formation of ground-level ozone. It was also readily available in large quantities.

The most common symptoms of carbon monoxide poisoning may resemble other types of infections and poisoning. They include headache, nausea, vomiting, dizziness, and fatigue. Sometimes, people suffering from CO exposure confuse the symptoms with food poisoning. Ingestion of large quantities of CO gas will result in loss of consciousness, closely followed by death. Victims sometimes display retinal haematoma and a cherry red hue to the skin, but this is not common and cannot be used as a general guide as to cause of death.

CO gas was available in large quantities, bottled for commercial use. It is also the main gas constituent of mechanised exhaust fumes from diesel or petrol engines. To those gathered at the KdF meeting, CO was the obvious choice. An important element was the odourless nature of CO gas. It was decided very early that patients would be duped into taking a shower and that specially constructed hermetically sealed gas chambers could be disguised as innocent shower rooms into which bottled CO gas could be channelled.

The selection process was to be carried out by assessing each case on the register. A suitably qualified medical practitioner would mark each index card with a red cross for those considered appropriate for mercy killing, or a minus sign for those to be spared. Patients for further assessment were signified by a question mark. The doctors involved were informed that their actions were perfectly legal as they had the authority of the Führer.

To test the process, the KdF approached August Becker, a junior officer in the Reichssicherheitshauptamt—Heydrich's RSHA—and a qualified chemist. Becker had distinctive red hair and was known as 'Red Becker' as a result. Shortly before Christmas 1939, Becker was summoned by telephone to report immediately to Brack at the KdF. In his interrogation on 4 April 1960, Becker stated the following:

> In May 1935, I joined the SS regiment 'Germania' in Arolsen near Kassel. At that time, I was a SS-Oberscharführer and had only to do with soldierly matters with this Reg. I remained in this regiment until 28 February 1938. Subsequently, I came by a service transfer, without my own request, to the Reich Security Main Office (RSHA), Amt VI, in Berlin. This office was located in the Bernerstrasse in Grunewald. The Amt VI was responsible for the defence, head of this office was a Dr Best. I myself was entrusted with the management of the department for compatible inks and photocopies. I remained in this office until December 1939, then I was ordered by phone to the head of service Viktor Brack in the Reich Chancellery. On the same day, I went to Brack in the Führer's Chancellery, which was then housed in the building of the Reich Chancellery. Brack received me and informed me that I would be placed under a personal assignment between him, Brack, and Reichsführer-SS Himmler. At the same time, Brack told me the purpose of this transfer. He said that a euthanasia program was about to start with the purpose of destroying all idiots and mental patients. The killing method will be performed by carbon monoxide gas. This gas has already been studied and checked by a chemist, Dr Albert Widmann at the Reich Criminal Police Office (RKPA) in Berlin, on its suitability. Brack continued to tell me—without mentioning him—that I did not need any scruples on this matter, because the killing of these people would later be legalised by the Führer with the help of a law.[14]

Becker admitted to participating in the first test gassing at Brandenburg-Havel in a former prison, now converted to an asylum. Eighteen to twenty convict inmates were herded into a fake shower room, approximately 3 metres by 5 metres in area and 3 metres in height. A gas supply pipe with small perforations ran around the inside perimeter of the room. The pipe was supplied by bottles of CO gas. An SS mechanic connected the supply and ensured it operated correctly. The sealed door had a small airtight observation window. Widmann operated the valve on the bottles and introduced the gas into the room while Becker watched through the observation port. The naked victims were unaware of what was happening and rapidly fell into a state of unconsciousness. After about five or six minutes, the room was aired until all traces of the gas had been removed. The corpses lay upon one another, strewn across the floor area. All were dead.

Brack, who was present at this first test procedure with a variety of invited guests including Dr Karl Brandt, Professors Heyde and Nitsche, Dr Irmfried Eberl, and Dr Horst Schumann, was satisfied with the result and confirmed that this part of the process was only to be carried out by medical practitioners. The bodies were then removed on specially designed stretchers and taken for incineration in the site crematorium. Henceforth, Dr Eberl carried out the procedures at Brandenburg. As a witness, a then insignificant police officer from the institute at Hartheim named Christian Wirth, was also present.[15]

Six sites in Germany and the former Austria were eventually identified as suitable locations to carry out so-called 'mercy killings'. As in the case of concentration camps, they were each accorded a coded letter:

A Grafeneck, near Munsingen.
B Brandenburg-Havel.
C Hartheim, near Linz.
D Sonnenstein, near Dresden.
Be Bernburg, near Halle.
E Hadamar, near Limburg.

A comparable killing method applied at all of the centres. At his post-war trial in Nuremberg, Viktor Brack described the simple design of the gas chambers:

> No special gas chambers were built. A room suitable in the planning of the hospital was used, a room attached to the reception ward … that was made into a gas chamber. It was sealed; it was given special doors and windows, and then a few metres of gas pipe were laid, some kind of pipe with holes in it. Outside of this room there was a bottle, a compressed bottle, with the necessary apparatus, necessary instruments, a pressure gauge, etc.[16]

Apparently, it was Reichsleiter Philipp Bouhler who suggested that the gas chamber at Brandenburg should masquerade as a shower room, a deception that was to become a common feature of killing centres throughout the Nazi empire. Wooden benches lined the walls, hiding a 3-cm perforated pipe that encircled the chamber, through which CO gas was fed from pressurised metal gas bottles in the next room. Usually in batches of about fifty at a time, the patients were told they were to enter this 'inhalation room' for therapeutic reasons or to take a communal shower. The cover name for gassing was 'disinfection'.

The facility at Grafeneck officially operated from January 1940 until December 1940 under the direction of Dr Horst Schumann. It accounted for 10,654 victims. Brandenburg operated from February 1940 until October 1940 and accounted for almost 9,000 victims under the direction of Dr Irmfried Eberl. Hartheim killed 18,269 people between May 1940 and August 1941. Dr Rudolf Lonauer oversaw the murders. Sonnenstein murdered 13,720 victims between June 1940 and September 1941. Dr Horst Schumann supervised. At Bernburg between November 1940 and July 1943, Dr Irmfried Eberl oversaw the deaths of 9,385 victims. Finally, at Hadamar, Dr Ernst Baumhard ensured that 14,500 people were administered 'mercy deaths' between January 1941 and March 1945. It is estimated that in its most active period, between January 1940 and August 1941, 70,273 people fell victim to the T4 operation. In total, over 75,000 German and Austrian people died as a result of the Nazi obsession with racial hygiene. Worse was to come.

In a survey of relatives of the victims of the programme conducted in April 1941, 80 per cent agreed with the process, 10 per cent were indifferent, and 10 per cent objected. Hitler's propaganda machine was a resounding success. The survey result sent a clear message to the mind of Adolf Hitler: if the vast majority did not object to their own relatives being terminated, why would they object to strangers—Jews, Gypsies, and Slavs—suffering the same fate?

August Becker became an integral participant in the T4 programme. His job was to supply the bottles of gas to the various institutions after obtaining them from the manufacturer, I. G. Farben Industries in Ludwigshafen, after Widmann had ordered them from his office at the Criminal Technology Institute in the RSHA. Becker was assigned by Walter Rauff in December 1941 to Einsatzgruppe A in Riga. His job was to inspect mobile gas vans and the procedures employed by Walter Stahlecker's Einsatzkommandos to kill victims by CO gas expelled from sealed vans. The victims were loaded into the sealed rear compartment, which was fed by engine exhaust fumes while the vehicle was driven. Becker was then tasked with a similar assignment with Einsatzgruppe D under Otto Ohlendorf in the southern Ukraine, before moving north to Einsatzgruppen C and B.

Rauff had been tasked by Heydrich to investigate the use of mobile gas vans to replace the shooting activities of the Einsatzgruppen, which, by the nature of their brief, had to remain on the move. Rauff consulted the RSHA motor pool chief, Friedrich Pradel. In turn, Pradel commissioned Harry Wentritt, a mechanic, to develop a suitable method. He testified on 2 February 1961:

> A flexible exhaust pipe was installed at the truck's exhaust, with a diameter of 58 to 60 millimetres (2.26 to 2.34 inches), and a hole of the same size was drilled in the van floor; a metal pipe was soldered into the hole from the outside to which the flexible exhaust pipe was fixed. When the various parts were connected, the truck engine was started and the exhaust fumes were channelled into the van, through the pipe leading from the exhaust to the hole in the van floor.[17]

Becker was concerned about the outward appearance of the vans and the effect on the men who operated them. He reported to Rauff from Kiev on 16 May 1942:

> Feldpost 32704
> B Nr. 40/42
> Reich Secret Document
> To SS-Obersturmbannführer Rauff, Berlin
> The overhauling of vans of Gruppen D and C has been completed....
>
> I ordered the vans of Einsatzgruppe D to be camouflaged as house-trailers by putting one set of window shutters on each side of the small van and two on each side of the larger vans, such as one often sees on farmhouses in the country. The vans became so well known, that not only the authorities, but also the civilian population called the van 'death van', as soon as one of these vehicles appeared. It is my opinion, the van cannot be kept secret for any length of time, not even camouflaged.
>
> The brakes of the Saurer van which I took from Taganrog to Simferopol were damaged on the way.... When I reached Stalino and Gorlovka a few days later the drivers of the vans there complained of the same trouble.... Because of the rough terrain and the indescribable road and highway conditions the caulkings and rivets loosen in the course of time. I was asked if in such cases the vans should be brought to Berlin for repair. Transportation to Berlin would be much too expensive and would demand too much fuel. In order to save these expenses, I ordered them to have smaller leaks soldered and if that should no longer be possible, to notify Berlin immediately by radio, that Pol. Nr ____ is out of order. Besides that, I ordered that during application of gas all the men were to be kept as far away from the vans as possible, so they should not suffer damage to their health by the gas which eventually would escape. I should like to take this opportunity to bring the following to your attention: several commands have had the unloading after the application of gas done by their own men. I brought to the attention of the commanders of those S.K. [Sonderkommandos] concerned the immense psychological injuries and damages to their health which that work can have for those men, even if not immediate, at least later on. The men complained to me about headaches which appeared after each unloading. Nevertheless, they don't want to change the orders, because they are afraid prisoners called for that work, could use an opportune moment to flee.

> To protect the men from these damages, I request orders be issued accordingly....
>
> The gassing is generally not carried out correctly. In order to get the *Aktion* finished as quickly as possible the driver presses down on the accelerator as far as it will go. As a result, the persons to be executed die of suffocation and do not doze off as was planned. It has proved that if my instructions are followed and the levers are properly adjusted death comes faster and the prisoners fall asleep peacefully. Distorted faces and excretions, such as were observed before, no longer occur.
>
> Today I shall continue my journey to *Gruppe* B, where I may be reached for further instructions.
>
> Signed: Dr Becker
> SS-Untersturmführer[18]

Apart from the civil servants at the head of the central agency of T4, and the medically qualified personnel, the vast majority of staff recruited for the programme were of average intelligence with an average standard of education. They did not apply to the programme, but they were specifically selected for one reason or another. They included cooks, handymen, doormen, carpenters, plumbers, drivers, nurses, and telephonists. The nucleus of the subsequently trained killers of Aktion Reinhardt were among them.

In order to deliver high numbers of patients to the killing centres, buses were hired by Gekrat from the Reich Postal Service. Approximately three buses to each centre. The drivers were all SS-Totenkopf NCOs from the concentration camp service.

By 1941, all Jewish patients were sent to the General Government for 'disinfection'. Following the Polish campaign, a brutal operation commenced against Polish mental patients. Even before the issue of the Hitler memorandum, the killing of Polish patients had begun in the incorporated territories of Danzig-West Prussia and the Warthegau, in addition to German patients in Pomerania and East Prussia. The detachments involved were the Eimann Kommando, Einsatzkommando 16, and the Selbstschutz units.

The Eimann Kommando—Volksdeutsche SS-Sturmbann E—was named after SS-Obersturmbannführer Kurt Eimann, who was from Görlitz. In autumn 1939, the Sturmbann was ordered to kill 1,400 patients from Pomerania in the wood of Piasnitz near Neustadt in West-Prussia (today, the woods close to the Piasnica River, near Wejherowo). On 22 September 1939, the Eimann Kommando began killing 2,000 Polish patients in the mental hospital at Konradstein (today Kocborowo), south of Danzig (Gdansk).

In the subsequent months, thousands of Polish mental patients were murdered, initially by shooting, but in October 1939, Dr Albert Widmann had suggested the use of bottled carbon monoxide gas as an effective lethal agent. Around the same time, gassing experiments on mental patients utilising both carbon monoxide at Brandenburg and an agent similar to Zyklon B potassium cyanide, at Fort VII Bunker 17 in Posen (today Poznan). Eimann was transferred to the SS-Standortkommandantur at Lublin on 20 November 1941.

By January 1940, Polish patients were being gassed in mobile gas vans; bottled carbon monoxide gas was introduced into a sealed compartment at the rear of the vehicle. The first of these vans was operated by a kommando headed by Herbert Lange, formerly the chief of staff of Naumann's Einsatzgruppe VI. Throughout the first months of that year, Lange's Kommando travelled around the Warthegau in a van carrying a sign—'Kaisers Kaffeegeschäft' (Kaiser's Coffee Company). The Lange's Kommando also travelled to East Prussia, where within three weeks more than 1,800 German and Polish patients were gassed. It has been estimated that a total of 7,700 sick and handicapped patients fell victim to this initial, experimental gas van killing phase. Lange's Kommando was euphemistically referred to as 'the Psychopath's Club' by Dr Hans Renfranz and his wife for its brutal and casual attitude to murder.[19]

Lange went on to greater depths of depravity as the first commander of the gassing facility at Chełmno, roughly 30 miles north of Lodz. It was set up as part of the 'ethnic cleansing' of the Wartheland and operated in two phases, the first commencing on 8 December 1941, in parallel with Aktion Reinhardt in the General Government. The second phase ran from 23 June 1944 until 17 January 1945. In between, during 1943, the facility underwent alterations.

The village of Chełmno sits on the River Ner. The extermination site was located in a vacated manor house in the village—known as the Schlosslager—and at a second site about 2.5 miles outside the village in a wooded area on the road to Kolo, north-west of the village—the Waldlager. Victims undressed at the Schlosslager and were relieved of their belongings, before being forced up a ramp and into the rear of a sealed compartment in a van. Once inside, the engine was started and exhaust gas was channelled into the sealed compartment. The van remained stationary at first, with the engine ticking over. After a few minutes, the driver then put it into gear and drove to the Waldlager, where the corpses were unloaded by a Jewish Sonderkommando. The bodies were then disposed of at the Waldlager in mass graves. A brick-constructed crematorium was later added to dispose of the bodies.

Estimates of the death toll vary from an absolute minimum of 152,000 to a maximum of 340,000. A realistic figure is close to 200,000 men, women, and children from the Wartheland, Hungary, Bohemia-Moravia, Luxemburg, and the Greater Reich. Soviet POWs were also murdered at Chełmno. It was the fifth largest murder factory operated by the Nazis. There were two makes of van—the Opel Blitz, which held between fifty and seventy victims, and the Magirus, which held up to 150 victims. The sealed compartments (also known as superstructures), built on the chassis, had floor openings—about 60 mm (2.4 inches) in diameter—with metal pipes welded below, into which the engine exhaust was directed. The exhaust system was fitted with a valve to prevent or allow the exhaust gas through the floor pipes.

Although unconnected with the T4 programme, the psychiatric hospital at Chełm Lubelski, approximately 70 miles east of Lublin, was the site of a ruthless liquidation on 12 January 1940. Some 450 patients, men, women, and children, were forced out of the building and machine-gunned as the exited the doors. Those refusing or unable to leave were thrown from the windows. Local townsfolk were forced to remove the bodies from the surrounding park and transport them to a mass grave located nearby. Some were still alive, but they were still buried. The hospital staff were driven from the building and did not return.

Another atrocity occurred at the Kobierzyn mental home in south-west Krakow. Many of the patients had died of malnutrition by the time the German authorities transferred ninety-one Jewish inmates north to Warsaw on 9 and 11 September 1941. Some were gassed, the remainder shot at the new sanatorium location in Otwock. This was the first of three phases of liquidation at the Babinski Hospital in Kobierzyn. In June 1942, 535 patients were transported to Auschwitz where they were murdered.

In the spring of 1941, Himmler became concerned at the number of prisoners in the camp system. Looking for ways of reducing the numbers, he held a meeting with Philipp Bouhler as head of the euthanasia programme. Himmler suggested that a number of excess prisoners was made up of incurably sick and mentally ill patients—those deemed unworthy of inclusion in German society. T4 appeared to hold the answer. At this time, gas chambers in camps were not fully operational and the death camps had not yet been established. Remarkably, Himmler still considered that the medical profession had a part to play in the physical destruction of camp inmates. This is reflected in the subsequently established process of rudimentary ramp selections at Auschwitz-Birkenau, which were carried out by doctors.

Bouhler agreed to Himmler's request and arranged for teams of T4 doctors to visit the camps—not to perform medical examinations, but to study the camp records in order to weed out the 'undesirables'. Complying with the cloak and dagger process applied at T4, each unfortunate person selected for termination was given a code—14f13. The figure '14' denoted the camp system, 'f' denoted a death sentence, and '13' denoted gassing.

The T4 doctors went into action. The first known selection occurred at Sachsenhausen in April 1941. One doctor's experience is recorded in a letter to his wife, sent during the 14f13 process at Buchenwald:

Weimar, 25 November 1941, 8.58 p.m.
Hotel Elephant
My dearest best little Mummy!

I have been waiting almost an hour to speak to you.… I am sitting in my room, Nr. 235 9third floor) listening to music on the radio, with freshly bathed feet and a delicious dinner (little delicacies—Bouillon, Hamburg herring salad, Swiss cheese).… Earlier I had two evening drinks with Schmalenbach and Müller in a little restaurant. At 7 p.m. we had dinner here in our hotel.…

On Thursday and Friday there is a meeting in Pirna connected with the operation at which the future will be discussed and in which Schmalenbach is to take part as the medical adjutant to Herr Brack (Jennerwein). No consultants will be there … come soon—in person.…

Loving kisses from Pa!!

Wednesday, 26 November 1941, 7 a.m.…

First there were 40 forms to finish filling out on a 1st portion Aryan, on which my two other colleagues had already worked yesterday. Of these 40, I worked on about 15.… Afterwards came the 'examination' of the pat.[ients]; that is, appearance of the individual and comparison with the entries in the files. We were not yet finished with these until noon because both my colleagues only worked in theory yesterday, so that I 're-examined' the ones who Schmalenbach (and myself, this morning) had prepared and Müller did his own. At noon we took a lunch break and ate in the officers' mess (first class! Soup, boiled beef, red cabbage, boiled potatoes, apple compote—for 1.50 Marks! No ration coupons. While being introduced to all SS leaders, I recognised the second lieutenant who was adjutant at the Hinzert camp in December 1940.…

At 1.30 p.m. began the examinations again, but Ribbentrop's speech began and we stopped to listen to it … we examined some more until around 4:00; I did 105 pat[ients], Müller 78 pat[ients], so that at the end our first instalment of 183 forms were done. The second portion followed, a total of 1200 Jews, none of whom are even examined; it's sufficient to pull from the files the reasons for arrest (often very extensive!) and transfer them to the forms. So, it's a purely theoretical job that takes us to Monday, maybe longer. Of this second portion (Jews), today we did: 17 for me; for Müller 15. 5:00 p.m. sharp, we 'threw in the towel' and went to dinner.…

The next few days will also go just as I have described today, above—with exactly the same routine and the same work. After the Jews come about 300 Aryans as third portion, who again will have to be 'examined'.…

So, my dearest Mummy, once again you get soooooo many loving kisses, and I hug you very, very tightly in joyful expectation of your coming, you leetle [*sic.*] mouse, from your faithful Pa.[20]

This is an extract of one of many letters written by Dr Friedrich Mennecke, many of which are published in 'Cleansing the Fatherland'. It provides an insight into the thoughts of one of the T4 physicians, a world far removed from the unfortunate human beings who were the subject of their professional lives.

Only three of the T4 killing centres were used for Aktion 14f13—Bernburg, Sonnenstein, and Hartheim. Between 15,000 and 20,000 people fell victim to 14f13 up to 1943.

# 9

# THE PSYCHOPATH'S CLUB

*They are not all perverts...*

Prosecutor Telford Taylor at Nuremberg

WITHOUT THE COLLABORATION of men such as Dr Mennecke, T4 would not have been possible. Friedrich Mennecke was born in Gross-Freden on 6 October 1904, the son of a stone cutter and mason. After a grammar school education, he graduated in 1923, but the family were unable to fund a university education. Mennecke took up a business apprenticeship, which proved successful, but which developed his anti-Semitic views. In 1927, he began studying medicine in Göttingen, where he passed the state medical examination in 1930 at the second attempt. He qualified as a medical doctor on 11 May 1934. He joined the NSDAP and then the SS in 1932, reaching the rank of SS-Hauptsturmführer in October 1940. Mennecke was appointed as troop physician at the start of the Second World War, but he never actively participated in the fighting. Despite this, he headed his letters at the time as 'in the field'. His military service was suddenly terminated in January 1940 by order of the KdF.

During his 'advisory service' in Aktion 14f13, Mennecke is judged to have directly contributed towards the early demise of at least 2,500 people. However, his life of comfortable hotel occupation and good food did not last. He fell out with Fritz Bernotat, the chief of hospitals in Hesse, and was soon despatched to the front as a troop physician once more in 1943. As the Red Army approached, Mennecke wrote to his wife: 'If it continues this way much longer, I will consider going to hospital with a 'heart ailment' and travelling home to the Reich on a hosp. train. I am not chickening out, but I don't want to destroy myself either'.[1]

Mennecke had often criticised men with fake ailments as shirkers. In August 1943, he was heading back to Germany, not with a heart condition, but with a thyroid complaint. He failed to attract a senior hospital position, but continued as an advisor to the T4 central agency. At a routine X-Ray examination, it was discovered that Mennecke had TB. He was arrested in April 1946. At the Eichberg Trial, he was sentenced to death, convicted by his own hand in his many letters to his wife. He died on 28 January 1947 in Butzbach Prison, but not on the scaffold. Two days after a visit from his wife, he died suddenly. The prison authorities refused to comment.

The senior medical practitioner for the Reich was Leonardo Conti. He was born on 24 August 1900 in Lugano, Switzerland, the son of a Swiss-Italian postal official. Active in the national student movement, he became embroiled in politics. Conti studied medicine from 1919 until 1923 at the universities of Berlin and Erlangen, passing his state medical examinations in November 1923. He joined the SA in Erlangen in 1923, and gained his medical doctorship at Berlin University in 1924, attaining a licence to practice medicine the following year in Munich. He worked as a voluntary physician at several Berlin children's hospitals, but he was disqualified as a result of his political views, before moving to Munich. From April 1925, he worked there as a general practitioner in the Social Hygiene Academy and as a paediatrician. Conti joined the NSDAP on 20 December 1927 and the SS on 16 November 1930. He eventually attained the rank of SS-Obergruppenführer in April 1944. He was appointed as State Secretary for Public Health and Nursing in the Reich Interior Ministry on 28 August 1939, and was the advisor on all questions of public health for the Party Chancellery. It was in this capacity that Hitler chose him to administer the euthanasia programme in September 1939. Conti was unhappy about the legality of this task and requested Lammers to obtain written legal authority from Hitler. Upset at Conti's reaction, Hitler immediately replaced him with Bouhler. Leonardo Conti was arrested by the British in Flensburg on 19 May 1945, and he was held as a witness at Nuremberg Jail. He committed suicide by hanging himself with his towel from his cell window on 6 October 1945. His suicide note read: 'I depart this life because I said under oath something untrue. I was not quite all here. I have had heaviest depressions, thoughts of death and sense of fear and visions for months, although I was never cowardly'.[2]

Gerhard Bohne was appointed as head of the T4 camouflage company, the Reich Association of Sanatoriums and Care Institutions—Reichsarbeitsgemeinschaft Heil- und Pflegeanstalten. As such, he is considered as the co-organiser of Aktion T4. On 17 October 1939, he was part of a commission that, under the leadership of Viktor Brack, converted Grafeneck Castle into the Grafeneck killing facility. At the end of 1939, Bohne and Hans Hefelmann were involved in negotiations with the Bürgermeister of Brandenburg-Havel to set up the killing centre there.

In February 1940, Bohne participated in a conference in which other T4 doctors such as Dr Mennecke participated. The conference gave approval to the euthanasia programme.

Bohne is credited with the organisational framework for the identification of the victims, the transport to the killing centres, and the recording of their death, including the estate administration. He provided the formal legal protection by a special registry office to hide the high death toll from the municipal registrar. For the transport of the patients designated for gassing, a separate pseudo-company with the name Gemeinnützige Krankentransport GmbH—Gekrat—was founded. Bohne created the partnership agreement and arranged the entry in the commercial register.

On 1 March 1940, Bohne was appointed to the Ministry of the Interior in the local Department of Health. The circumstances of his departure from T4 service are unclear. Bohne probably left in June 1940. Bohne insisted he had retired, but apparently Brack had complained of maladministration in the killing centre at Grafeneck. Dr Hefelmann is purported to have coveted his position and complained about Bohne, because he supported the inclusion of patients with dementia in the programme.

In early 1942, Bohne wrote a memorandum in which he accused the staff of Aktion T4 of food misappropriation, the misuse of motor vehicles, and 'alcoholic and sexual debauchery'. Bohne also sent a copy of the memorandum to the head of the RSHA, Reinhard Heydrich. Bohne's allegations were reviewed and proved to be partly exaggerated and partly false. With the judgment on 10 August 1943, marked as 'secret', Bohne was expelled from the NSDAP by the Supreme Party Court of the NSDAP. In December 1943, he was dismissal from the SS, justified by the violation of secrecy. Bohne had disregarded the position of Reichsleiter Philipp Bouhler and collected material behind his back in an 'inconsiderate and unrestrained manner'.

In January 1943, Bohne was drafted into the Wehrmacht. He experienced the end of the war in Italy where he was captured by the Americans. Released at the end of 1946, he returned to Cologne. In Düsseldorf , he worked as a legal employee in a law office.

In 1949, Bohne emigrated to Argentina, where he worked in an industrial company and subsequently as a legal advisor. He wrote articles for *Der Weg*, the journal of the German National Socialists in the Peron Period. In 1955, he returned to Germany and was allowed to practice law.

On 10 September 1959, Bohne was arrested. On 22 May 1962, the attorney general at the Frankfurt am Main Higher Regional Court brought charges against Bohne for the 'insidious, cruel and deliberate killing of at least 15,000 people'. On 15 March 1963, he received healthcare detention, but he fled in July 1963 to

Buenos Aires. There he lived under the false name 'Kurt Alfred Rüdinger'. On 27 February 1964, he was arrested by the Argentine Federal Police and handed over to the German police on 11 November 1966. A legal battle then commenced, with Bohne's defence team citing a grave risk of a heart attack. Proceedings were dropped on 22 July 1969. Bohne died a free man on 8 July 1981.

Bohne's replacement at T4 was Dieter Allers. He was born August Eduard Ernst Dietrich Allers on 17 May 1910 in Kiel. His father, August Allers, a lawyer, was killed in action in 1914. Dieter attended elementary school in Berlin-Charlottenburg and the middle school in Pritzwalk. He then moved to the Joachimsthalsche Gymnasium in Templin, and completed his school career in 1929 with his Abitur. He then studied law at Jena and Berlin. He passed the first state law examination in September 1933, and the second state law examination in March 1937. Allers briefly worked for the District Court in Berlin-Neukölln. In June 1937, he was recruited by the Prussian civil service and began his first job at the Police President's Office in Stettin. From June 1938, he was employed by the Liegnitz local government.

Allers was an ardent Nationalist. He joined the SA on 16 February 1932 and the NSDAP on 1 March 1932.

Allers exerted substantial influence in the murderous policies of the Third Reich from 1941 onwards. He had come to T4 by pure chance. As a young lawyer in 1939, Allers had been sent to Poland as a training sergeant in the army. In November 1940, his mother met an acquaintance in the street. It was Werner Blankenburg. She informed him of her son and Blankenburg offered to arrange for termination of his military service with a job offer at the KdF. This was a common method used by Brack and Blankenburg to recruit staff for the programme—word of mouth. Brack agreed with his recruitment and he joined T4 as an administrative lawyer. By January 1941, Brack appointed him as Bohne's replacement.

Allers was the liaison man between Aktion Reinhardt in Lublin, T4, and the KdF. He maintained an office in Lublin. Although he denied it, Allers frequently visited the three Aktion Reinhardt 'terminal stations' during their most active period. From the spring of 1944, Allers was the leader of Einsatz 'R' in Trieste. In this capacity, he was in charge of the Camp La Risiera San Saba, a former rice mill which served as a prison, a killing centre, and a transit camp for Auschwitz.

Dieter Allers lived in Hamburg after the war and appeared at Blankenburg's funeral as a mourner. He was arrested by the British and interned in the former Neuengamme concentration camp until 1947. Arrested again in 1948, he was released in 1949. In 1951, he stood for election to the Lower Saxony Landtag as a candidate of the subsequently prohibited Socialist Reich Party. He worked as a corporate lawyer in the Hamburg docks, despite his previous record with T4.

During the 1960s and 1970s, Allers appeared before a number of courts of law, both as a defendant and witness. His last appearance as a defendant was during

1967–69, together with Adolf Kaufmann, the T4 establishment's inspector, and two other former T4 officials. By the end of 1967, only Allers remained in the dock, the others having been released on 'health grounds'. In 1969, Allers was sentenced to eight years' imprisonment, of which he served only two years as the court deducted the time he had spent in Allied internment after the war. The sentence was imposed only in connection with his leading role in the euthanasia programme.

Despite several defendants and witnesses at various trials stating that they had seen Allers not only in Lublin, but also in the death camps, Allers would only admit to visiting Lublin to meet Globocnik and Wirth. He denied that these meetings had anything to do with Reinhardt. Dieter Allers's personal involvement in Reinhardt was never proved in court before his death. Allers married his secretary who worked for him in T4 and at Schloss Hartheim. Allers was director and the mainstay in the secret SS member's aid organisation 'Silent Help' supported by Gudrun Burwitz, the daughter of Heinrich Himmler. Allers died in Munich on 22 March 1975.

Dr Werner Catel was an expert paediatrician. He was born on 27 June 1894 in Mannheim and followed a grammar school education in Leipzig before studying medicine at Freiburg and Halle. He served in the First World War before returning to his studies and gained his doctorate in 1920. After working as an assistant at an anatomical and pharmacological institute, he found a position at the University Children's Hospital in Leipzig under Georg Bessau. He was an acquaintance of the eugenicist, Alfred Hoche, and was greatly influenced by him. In 1932, Catel moved to Berlin as a senior physician. By the following year, he transferred back to Leipzig as a professor of paediatrics.

A member of the NSDAP from 1937, Catel was the consultant paediatrician approached by the father of Gerhard Kretschmar to grant his son a mercy killing. After the involvement of Dr Karl Brandt, Catel was granted immunity and he administered a lethal injection for the child on 25 July 1939. This heralded the beginning of child euthanasia in the Reich.

Catel expanded the paediatric hospital at Oststrasse in Leipzig by opening an annexe at Leipzig-Dösen, under the direction of Arthur Mittag, and a further establishment at the Children's Clinic Leipzig. Catel administered the paediatric euthanasia programme at these sites, by the use of the drugs scopolamine and phenobarbital. Hermann Paul Nitsche tested and developed phenobarbital at Leipzig-Dösen during 1940, for use in the murder of patients considered 'unworthy of life'. All carried out under the supervision of senior physicians Georg Renno and Herbert Schulze. The Luminal Scheme allowed for an overdose of the drug for a period of three days, combined with a withdrawal of nourishment. Pneumonia soon developed, resulting in death. In the first series of experimental overdoses in Leipzig-Dösen, sixty children were murdered. Following the general adoption of the scheme throughout the Reich, around 5,000 disabled or ill children were murdered by the state. Its use was continued in the so-called 'Brandt Aktion' from 1943 in order to create bed spaces for war casualties.

Catel was one of three paediatric reviewers for T4 from late 1939. The others were Hans Heinze and Ernst Wentzler (see appendices).

The building in Oststrasse was destroyed in an air raid on 4 December 1943, and Catel transferred his office to Klinga. The murder of children proceeded unabated. By 1945, Catel was aware that he would be considered a criminal and he instructed his staff to weed out incriminating information from his files. It is estimated that approximately 500 children were murdered in Leipzig alone. Catel remained as hospital director until 1946.

In 1947, Catel moved to Hamburg where he was acquitted of Nazi crimes in 1949. He administered the Mammolshöhe paediatric TB sanatorium in Königstein until 1954 where he conducted experiments using unauthorised drugs, allegedly resulting in the deaths of at least four children. He was appointed as professor of paediatrics at Kiel University in 1954. He was forced to retire early in 1960, still declaring that malformed and severely disabled children should be administered a mercy death. He died in Kiel on 30 April 1981. The Catel-Manzke Syndrome condition bears his name.

Of all the physicians connected to T4, Professor Max de Crinis was one of the more remarkable. He was born Maximinus Friedrich Alexander de Crinis on 29 May 1889, in Ehrenhausen near Graz, the son of a physician. From 1895 until 1907, he attended elementary school in Graz, followed by the Imperial Royal Grammar School in the same city. As was common of the time, his upbringing was religious, but he converted to the Protestant faith from Catholicism in 1907. After school, he studied medicine in Graz and Innsbruck, qualifying as a doctor in Graz in 1912. His specialty was neurological psychiatry at the University Nursing Clinic in Graz. During the First World War, de Crinis became intensely interested in war neuroses. In 1916, he married actress Lili Anna Szikora. He was appointed a senior physician on 1 May 1918. He presented a thesis on the process of epileptic seizures and in 1924 was appointed as an associate professor, followed by a full professorship in 1927.

Having grown up in a city in south-east Austria, not far from the hometown of Odilo Globocnik, de Crinis was a strong German nationalist. He supported the formation of a single Greater German Reich. He joined the Freikorps and participated in the Styrian fight to remain part of German-speaking Austria. He joined the Austrian NSDAP in 1931 and was arrested on 22 May 1934 for political activities. He fled to Germany following the Dollfuss assassination and failed Nazi coup of July 1934.

In Cologne, de Crinis was hired as a professor of psychiatry and neurology at the University Clinic of Psychiatry, and he became a German citizen. In the National

Socialist state, he was free to practice his eugenic and racial hygiene theories without fear of opposition. He became an advisor to the Society of German Neurologists and Psychiatrists and was used as an expert for the Hereditary Health Court in Cologne. He studied and promoted the development of a special form of brain cell fixation. He undertook questionable procedures using brain punctures in his research on brain tumours. He also conducted research into schizophrenia. According to his thesis, he attributed mental illness to protein-decomposition toxicosis. From 1940, de Crinis also dealt with the human facial expression.

In 1938, the professorship and directorate of the Psychiatric University Hospital of the Charité in Berlin became vacant. De Crinis applied for the post but was not favoured by the hospital board. The dean wrote to the Reich Ministry, which had promoted the application of de Crinis:

> His exemplary personality and political commitment do not seem to match his achievements in the field of psychiatry. He has dealt mainly with physiological-chemical and purely brain anatomical investigations, but in the realm of psychiatry is hardly active. His work on the structure and degradation of cerebral performance and its anatomical foundations are strongly challenged....
>
> As much as I personally appreciate de Crinis, I cannot convince myself after detailed inquiries that he would be able to cope as a psychiatrist with the requirements of the local clinic.[3]

This was after the faculty had consulted various psychiatry experts throughout the Reich. Apparently, his only support came from Carl Schneider of Heidelberg. Despite reservations, de Crinis was appointed as professor of psychiatry and neurology and director of the mental hospital of the Charité on 1 November 1938.

Max de Crinis joined the SS in 1936, finally reaching the rank of SS-Standartenführer in 1942. He became a close personal friend of Reinhard Heydrich and would go horse-riding with him, accompanied by Walter Schellenberg. The Heydrich and de Crinis families socialised, a rare occurrence in the case of the ever suspicious Heydrich. Schellenberg spoke kindly of de Crinis, describing him as 'Elegant, stately, highly intelligent and cultured'.[4] Schellenberg actually recruited de Crinis for an undercover operation in Venlo where the British agents Best and Stevens were seized and transported across the frontier into Germany in October 1939. De Crinis masqueraded as a German general.

In addition to his SS connections, de Crinis acted as a consulting army psychiatrist in 1939. He held the army rank of Oberstarzt—equivalent to Oberst (colonel)—from December 1942. He was awarded both classes of Iron Cross. From October 1944, he was appointed as the Supreme Advisory Army Psychiatrist and the chief psychiatrist of the Military Medical Academy. He was also a health inspector for the Waffen-SS and the Army. As a convinced Nazi, de Crinis enjoyed the sponsorship of the party. In 1939, he was appointed to the board of trustees of the Kaiser Wilhelm Institute for Brain Research. He was also utilised as a representative for the Reich Ministry of Education and Science. De Crinis had a close professional relationship with the Reich Health Leader, Leonardo Conti, and the Reich SS-Physician Ernst-Robert Grawitz. In 1944, de Crinis worked for Karl Brandt as an advisor on psychiatric matters. For his services to the party, de Crinis received the NSDAP Golden Honour Badge.

After Hess's flight to England on 10 May 1941, de Crinis was commissioned to prepare a report on the deputy Führer's mental state in preparation for the political explanation of mental illness. He was also allegedly commissioned by Schellenberg towards the final days of the war, to provide reports on the mental health of both Hitler and von Ribbentrop, without their knowledge. He diagnosed Parkinson's disease for Hitler, but refused to produce a report that indicated a lack of control, in favour of Himmler.

On 21 April 1945, de Crinis attended his clinic for the last time. He withdrew to his home on the Wannsee to await the arrival of the Red Army. On 1 May, he and Lili failed in an attempt to break out of encircled Berlin in their car, reaching only as far as the Teltow Canal. The two killed themselves by inhaling potassium cyanide ampoules on 2 May 1945. Max de Crinis lies buried in the South-Western Cemetery at Stahnsdorf.

As the most influential Nazi in the structure of German psychiatry, the role of de Crinis in the T4 programme cannot be underestimated. Despite not holding any known official position in the organisation or implementation of the procedure, his status in German psychiatry alone indicates participation. The destruction of pertinent files by staff at the Charité does not help matters—not from the researcher's perspective. However, witness statements do incriminate de Crinis. He was identified as a member of the selection body, which identified the necessary reviewers for recruitment to T4. Dr Mennecke included the name of de Crinis as a probable member of the recruitment board:

> Then we were asked if we would be willing to participate.... It was not the individual who was asked, but in the circle, as we sat, more was treated in the open colloquium, this whole subject. The older gentlemen, Professor Nietzsche [*sic.* Nitsche] and Falthauser, took part in the main thing at this colloquium, then a gentleman whose name I no longer know, but who possibly was Professor Dekrinis [*sic.* de Crinis] from Berlin. I do not know him personally, and the résumé of this colloquium was that in those circumstances you could join in and support those measures. No one expressed any concerns about the measures...[5]

Purely by his connections alone, Max de Crinis must have been not only aware of the euthanasia being practiced, but must have agreed to it and physically participated in it, in one form or another.

The role of other physicians is not so ambiguous. Yet another Austrian, Dr Irmfried Eberl was born in Bregenz on 8 September 1910. He studied medicine at the University of Innsbruck and joined the NSDAP as a student on 8 December 1931. He qualified as a medical practitioner in 1934 and from February 1935, he worked as an assistant physician. His specialty was psychiatry. Eberl was a willing participant when he was recruited for the T4 programme. He was present at the first experimental gassing at Brandenburg and subsequently was appointed as the medical director of that facility on 1 February 1940 where he personally carried out numerous murders. He was transferred to Bernburg in the autumn of 1940 where he continued the murderous campaign.

When the euthanasia programme was scaled down after August 1941, Eberl was unemployed, but he was soon summoned to Tiergartenstrasse where he was allocated a new role in the General Government, under the command of the SSPF Lublin, SS-Brigadeführer Globocnik (his disastrous role in the subsequent Aktion Reinhardt will be highlighted later).

Eberl returned to Bernburg for a short period following his return from Poland, and in 1944, he joined the Wehrmacht for the remainder of the war. After the war ended, Eberl continued to practice medicine in Blaubeuren. Eberl was arrested in January 1948, and hanged himself on 16 February 1948 to avoid trial.

Dr Bodo Gorgass was born in Leipzig on 19 June 1909. Another confirmed Nazi, he was a member of the SA. He studied medicine at Leipzig and spent three years at the Eichberg Asylum as an assistant to Dr Hinsen. Gorgass did not have any consultation role in the selection procedure or administration procedure at Tiergartenstrasse, but he was one of many doctors whose role was important to the successful management of the programme. He was employed at the Hadamar killing centre where he operated the flow of gas into the death chamber. This was one stipulation of Viktor Brack, which was meticulously observed—only qualified doctors were authorised to administer the lethal gas. Gorgass considered that handicapped individuals were a financial and social burden upon their families and the state. At his post-war trial in 1947, he declared that the state should kill them in order to spare their families the task.[6] He was sentenced to death by the area court in Frankfurt, but the death penalty was abolished before the sentence could be carried out. It was commuted to fifteen years in prison. He was released in 1958 and died on 10 October 1993 in Bielefeld.

The medical director of the T4 programme was Professor Werner Heyde. In 1959, living under the name of Fritz Sawade, Heyde became embroiled by chance in a dispute involving a colleague, Professor Dr Helmuth Reinwein, in

Kiel-Düsternbrook. Reinwein was a former Nazi and held the posts of chair of internal medicine and rector of Kiel University. Dr Sawade was practising as a sports physician and neurologist in nearby Flensburg. Reinwein took civil action against his student neighbours for continuous bawdy parties during the night, but was dissatisfied with the court ruling. He felt mistreated by the courts and flew into a rage, refusing to teach. The dean of the faculty of medicine attempted to soothe the angry Reinwein, but the aggrieved professor blurted out that the authorities would be interested in the true identity of Dr Sawade. An investigation was launched and Sawade disappeared. A week later, he turned himself into the police at Frankfurt.

A major police investigation followed, which revealed many facts about the euthanasia programme. Other renowned medical doctors were implicated and it became obvious that eminent medical staff had been aware that Dr Sawade was, in truth, Werner Heyde, the former medical director of T4. Heyde was charged with 'the insidious, cruel and deliberate killing of at least 100,000 people'. His co-defendants before the Limburg District Court were Gerhard Bohne, Friedrich Tillmann, and Hans Hefelmann, and the hearing was set for 18 February 1964. Heyde killed himself in his cell at the Butzbach Prison on 13 February 1964. His farewell letter concluded: 'Before God, I stand firm and submit to his verdict. I intended no harm, as far as I can judge as a human being. He will decide'.[7]

Werner Heyde was born in Forst-Lausitz on 25 April 1902, the son of a cloth manufacturer. In the autumn of 1914, the family moved to Cottbus where Heyde graduated in 1920 with top marks. He had volunteered during the war and served as a telephonist in Reval. He then joined the Freikorps in Estonia. He returned to Cottbus and fought in the Kapp Putsch in March 1920. From 1920 until 1925, he studied medicine at Berlin, Freiburg, Marburg, Rostock, and Würzburg. He held temporary intern positions in Cottbus and Berlin-Wittenau before he was appointed as an assistant physician at the University Psychiatric Hospital in Würzburg. By 1926, he was fully qualified to practice medicine, having achieved excellent grades in all his classes. From November 1928, he was employed at the Chemical Institute of the Bavarian Academy of Science in Munich. His thesis 'Investigations on Brain Ferments', once again back in Würzburg, saw him appointed as a Privatdozent (outside lecturer) in psychiatry and neurology at the University of Würzburg on 10 August 1932. In February of the previous year, he had married Erika Precht. The union produced two children.

In March 1933, a patient under his care at the Würzburg Sanatorium was Theodor Eicke. Eicke had entered a dispute with Gauleiter Josef Bürckel and Himmler had ordered Eicke to admit himself for psychiatric evaluation. Heyde found nothing wrong with Eicke and declared so in a letter to Himmler: '[Eicke had] conducted himself here in an exemplary manner and was very pleasant by his calm, controlled nature; he did not give the impression of unusual personality'.[8]

Encouraged by Eicke, Heyde joined the NSDAP on 1 May 1933. He was a member of the Racial Political Office in Würzburg, eventually rising to manager of the office. He became an associate of the local Hereditary Health Tribunal, which received and assessed applications for enforced sterilisation. After Heyde authored a memorandum on the practice of the court, Arthur Gütt, the NSDAP and SS 'expert' on race, recommended Heyde to Grawitz, the chief SS physician. As a result, Heyde joined the SS on 1 June 1936. He was assigned to the Sanitary Department of the SS-Totenkopfverbände as head of psychiatry. This department was responsible for medical matters in the concentration camps. In this capacity, Heyde decided on possible sterilisation cases in the camp system. He was also responsible for the SS troops and was a consultant psychiatrist for the SS hospitals in Berlin.

In addition to his new responsibilities, he did not shirk from his duties at Würzburg. He became an associate professor on 5 April 1939 and from 1 December 1939, he succeeded his patron Martin Reichardt as chair of psychiatry and neurology at Würzburg. With this post, he became the Würzburg Hospital director.

Heyde was accused of homosexuality in October 1939, dating from 1927–1928, but the accusations proved unfounded following an investigation by the Gestapo.

He was almost certainly involved in the initial stages of the T4 programme, including child euthanasia, from the end of July 1939. He was a member of the governing panel of psychiatrists and physicians who assessed each case. Topics of the discussions may have included the organisation, the procedure and the secrecy of the scheduled mass killings, and the delimitation and selection of the sick. At the latest, from May 1940, Heyde was appointed as the medical director of T4. According to post-war testimonies, all fundamental questions were decided by him. He conducted all correspondence with the reviewers and nursing homes, and prepared statements on any protests received against the mercy killing.

From 9 October 1939, under the authority of the KdF, Heyde directed that all nursing homes and hospitals must register patients who fell in the categories of interest to T4. The registration of these unfortunate individuals was administered by Herbert Linden. The file of each patient was then reviewed by three doctors who signified death by a red '+', reprieved by a blue '–', and undecided by a question mark. The file was then submitted to a supervisory assessor who made the final decision, based on the pertinent marks inscribed. The supervisory assessors were Werner Heyde, Herbert Linden, and Hermann Paul Nitsche, Heyde's deputy. When institutions were suspected of falsifying their submissions, a special commission visited them and local 'independent' examinations were conducted. Heyde often participated as a member of this commission.

In December 1941, Heyde's alleged homosexual past once again rose to haunt him. Apparently, Heydrich insisted on his replacement for reasons of his homosexuality. However, it appears that Himmler did not wish the matter to become public and secrecy was maintained. Heyde was quietly replaced by Nitsche. Heyde was allowed to remain in the SS and eventually reached SS-Standartenführer. He returned to his medical duties at Würzburg and was involved in various atrocities connected to concentration camps. He was also head of the SS hospital in the town. After a heavy air raid on Würzburg, the SS hospital was relocated to Denmark in March 1945 and rebuilt under Heyde's leadership in Gråsten. It was in Denmark that Heyde fell into Allied hands. He subsequently 'disappeared' under the new identity, Fritz Sawade, supporting documents for which he obtained on the black market in Kiel.

Herbert Linden was born in Konstanz in 1899 and graduated from high school in 1917. He was drafted for military service, and served as a rifleman in several army units. From 16 October to 1 November 1918, Linden took part in the battle on the Western Front for which he received the Iron Cross 2nd Class. On 2 March 1919, Linden was discharged from the army and began studies at medical school. On 17 December 1923, he obtained his doctorate and qualified to practice medicine on 17 January 1925. He joined the NSDAP on 23 November 1925.

He worked as a medical assistant until 1928 at the Hygiene Institute and from 1929, as an assistant at the Institute for infectious diseases in Heidelberg. From 1 April 1931, he worked as a research assistant at the Reich Health Office in Berlin. On 1 November 1933, he was employed as an unskilled worker in the Reich Ministry of the Interior. He then received an established position on 1 December 1933. In the summer of 1934, he was promoted to senior councillor and advisor in department IV (People's Healthcare). His direct supervisors included Arthur Gütt and Leonardo Conti. Linden also worked in the Advisory Council on Population and Racial Policy of the Reich Ministry of the Interior. He was an advocate of the Reich Committee for the Protection of German Blood and established a research programme into the racial biology of Gypsies as part of the German Research Foundation.

From February 1939, Linden was instrumental in the planning of children's euthanasia. By the end of July 1939, he was also involved in the preparation planning of adult euthanasia. He suggested the use of the homologation institute at Schloss Grafeneck as a suitable location for the T4 programme, which resulted in an inspection visit by Brack. Shortly afterwards, the castle was sequestered for T4.

Linden was present at the trial gassing in January 1940 at Brandenburg and was subsequently responsible for the registration of patients dealt with by T4. He was one of the three final arbiters who had the final say over life or death. When approached by a nurse from Vienna in 1940 who complained of the mercy killing, Linden was somewhat taken aback: 'Herr Dr Linden, a small inconspicuous man, was visibly surprised when I met him. He recounted that he had spent a lovely time in Vienna.'[9] In response to a suggestion that lethal injections should at least be given on the spot, he replied: 'But … but, people do not understand injections; it's a big deal!'

Linden became the Reich Commissioner for Nursing and Nursing Homes, and was technically the nominal head of German institutional psychiatry. He was involved in the lethal injection murders carried out at Hadamar in August 1942. From 1942 until 1944, Linden is considered by many historians as the key figure in euthanasia. One witness, Kurt Gerstein, identified Ministerialrat Dr Herbert Lindner [*sic.*] as being present at Bełżec in August 1942.

Linden killed himself in Berlin on 27 April 1945. He was buried in the Waldfriedhof Berlin-Zehlendorf, but the grave was removed following protests.

The third supervisory assessor was Hermann Paul Nitsche. He was born on 25 November 1876 in Colditz, the son of a doctor employed at the local mental institution. He attended the Kreuzschule in Dresden, and then proceeded to study medicine at Leipzig and finally Göttingen, where he received his doctorate in 1902. He specialised in memory disorders in cases of brain disease. From 1904 until 1908, he worked as an assistant doctor at the mental asylum in Frankfurt, and the university hospitals in Heidelberg and Munich. By 1913, he was a senior physician in Dresden. From 1914 until 1918, he was employed at Schloss Sonnenstein in Pirna. He became director of the nursing home at Leipzig-Dösen in April 1918. He was appointed as a professor in 1925, and two years later was elevated as a consultant advisor to the state government of Saxony.

Nitsche was appointed as director of the health and nursing institute at Pirna-Sonnenstein on 1 August 1928. He had always been outspoken on the issue of restricting reproduction by the mentally ill and he called for legalised sterilisation in 1929. Even before 1933, he was a leading representative of racially hygienic psychiatry. He considered the termination of 'unworthy life' to be a necessary step towards preservation of humanity.

In 1933, Nitsche joined the NSDAP. He was appointed to the Hereditary Health Tribunal in Dresden, and in 1935, he was appointed as managing director of the Society of German Neurologists and Psychiatrists. In 1936, at Nitsche's instigation, the medical staff at Sonnenstein initiated a starvation diet for those patients considered by Nitsche's concepts as 'a burden on society'. Nitsche remained at Sonnenstein until the beginning of mercy killing under the T4 programme. He transferred to the hospital at Leipzig-Dösen and took over the directorship on 1 February 1940.

Viktor Brack approached Nitsche and discussed methods of mercy killing. Nitsche opted for the use of phenobarbital and carried out experiments during 1940. On 1 May 1940, Nitsche was seconded to T4 in Berlin. Initially he was an assessor, but he replaced Werner Heyde as medical director in December 1941.

Nitsche was arrested in Sebnitz in the spring of 1945. He was handed over to the German judicial authorities on 20 June 1946. In January 1947, he was brought before the district court in Dresden. Nitsche continued to declare that the killing of terminally ill patients and the mentally sick was scientifically and socially justified: 'It is wonderful when we in the institutions get rid of the ballast and are able to do proper therapy'.[10] Nitsche was sentenced to death on 7 July 1947 and was beheaded on 25 March 1948. His body was handed over to the medical faculty in Leipzig for research.

A name that has appeared several times already is that of Albert Widmann. He was born in Stuttgart on 8 June 1912. His father was a railroad engineer and young Albert showed an interest in science from an early age. He studied chemical engineering at the University of Stuttgart and gained a doctorate in September 1938. Just the sort of recruit favoured by Reinhard Heydrich for his security service, Widmann was hired by the Technical Institute of the Security Police, first as a consultant, but then as a permanent member of staff. Widmann specialised in chemical analysis and by 1940, he was head of that office.

Widmann had been a member of the NSDAP since May 1937, and a member of the NSKK since July 1933. His new status with the security police afforded him the rank of SS-Untersturmführer. As has been seen already, Widmann was approached to assess the effects of carbon monoxide gas on human beings; the consistency and the amount required to achieve the required result. He tested various doses—probably on animals—before the initial test gassing at Brandenburg. In conjunction with two other chemists, August Becker and Helmut Kallmeyer, Widmann advised T4 on suitable gas available, and obtained the necessary supplies. He remained employed by the RSHA and was not on the staff of the KdF or T4. Widmann also obtained supplies of lethal drugs needed for child euthanasia and intravenous killing methods.

Widmann experimented with different methods of killing adults, including explosives. He went to Minsk in September 1941 to assist the leader of Einsatzgruppe B, Arthur Nebe. The two men tried blowing up mental health patients in a bunker, but the result was unsatisfactory. They then tried using engine exhaust fumes, piped into a room from a car engine. The carbon monoxide began seeping into the room. After eight minutes, the people in the room were still alive. A second car was connected to the other pipe in the wall. The two cars were operated simultaneously, and a few minutes later, all those in the room were dead. This successful experiment led to the development of gas vans and the method used by the three terminal stations of Aktion Reinhardt in Poland. Widmann discovered that an adjustment of the ignition timing would result in an increase of exhaust fumes. The war ended with Widmann in the rank of SS-Sturmbannführer.

After the war, Widmann was interned by the US occupying forces for a short period before taking a job in a paint factory. His wartime duties remained undiscovered. He had worked his way up to chief chemist by the time of his arrest in January 1959. During his interrogation, he insisted that he was on anti-partisan duties during his time with Einsatzgruppe B. When faced with questions about the murder of mental patients in Russia, he shrugged and said that mental patients were being killed in Germany, so there was nothing for him to question. He was imprisoned for six years and six months. He died on Christmas Eve 1986.

Rudolf Höss commented on the use of gas vans in his post-war memoirs, written in pencil in his Krakow cell. He described a conversation with Adolf Eichmann:

> We further discussed how the mass annihilation was to be carried out. Only gas was suitable since killing by shooting the huge numbers expected would be absolutely impossible and would also be a tremendous strain on the SS soldiers who would have to carry out the order as far as the women and children were concerned.[11]

Walter Rauff, the head of technical services, including vehicles, in the RSHA, voluntarily described on 28 June 1972, one of the advantages of gas vans over the open air shootings carried out by the Einsatzkommandos: 'The main issue for me at the time was that the shootings were a considerable burden for the men who were in charge thereof, and this burden was taken off them through the use of the gas vans'.[12]

This is confirmed by August Becker:

> … the men in charge of the Einsatzgruppen in the East increasingly complained that the shooting commandos couldn't withstand the psychological and moral stress of the mass shootings in the long run. I know that the people of the commands were even in mental houses, and that therefore a new and better killing method needed to be found.… When I was transferred to Rauff in December 1941, he explained to me the situation that the psychological and moral stress on the shooting commandos was no longer sustainable and that therefore the gassing operation had been started.[13]

August Becker was born on 17 August 1900 in Staufenberg-Hesse, the son of a factory owner. He was called up to the German Army towards the end of the First World War. After the war, Becker studied chemistry and physics at the University of Giessen where, in 1933, he earnt a PhD in chemistry. From 1933 to 1935, he remained as an assistant at the university.

Becker joined the NSDAP in September 1930, and five months later, he also joined the SS. He was a member of the SS-Regiment 'Germania' in Arolsen from May 1935 until 28 February 1938, when he was recruited by the Reich Security Service. His main job was to detect the use of invisible inks in communications. He was promoted to SS-Untersturmführer. As described previously, he was placed at the disposal of Viktor Brack in the KdF in December 1939.

After the initial test gassing at Brandenburg, Becker arranged for the T4 facility at Grafeneck to become operational. Around the end of January 1940, Becker delivered bottles of CO gas to Grafeneck. Originally, Dr Schumann was designated to operate the gas valve, but he opened it too far to produce a loud hissing sound, which alarmed the victims in the chamber. Becker took control and slowed the flow of gas, with the result that the victims calmed and then died quietly.

In October 1941, Becker was assigned to department II D 3 A of the RSHA. This was responsible for the Kraftfahrwesen of the state police. The director of department D—technical affairs—was SS-Obersturmbannführer Walter Rauff. In December 1941, he assigned Becker to the inspection of the gas vans of the various Einsatzgruppen.

After his work as a gas van specialist, Becker was employed at the Central Commercial Company East (Zentralhandelsgesellschaft Ost), a monopoly company for agricultural products in the territories of the occupied east, and afterwards in the Foreign Defence Office (Auslandabwehr) of the RSHA. In 1943, he was promoted to SS-Obersturmbannführer.

Becker was sentenced post-war with a three-year prison sentence for membership of the SS, which had been declared an illegal organisation. Afterwards, he worked as a salesman and industrial worker. In 1959, he suffered a stroke and moved to a nursing home in the upper Hessian town of Laubach.

In 1959, the public prosecutor's office in Stuttgart began a preliminary investigation into offences committed by Becker and Widmann. Becker was condemned to ten years in prison, but on 15 July 1960, due to his state of health, he was released from detention and admitted to a home for the elderly in Butzbach. In 1967, the State Criminal Court in Stuttgart issued a summons for Becker, but he had been previously removed from the Butzbach home on 3 January 1966, by persons unknown, and his current whereabouts could not be determined. On 16 June 1967, the Baden-Württemburg State Criminal Police issued a 'wanted' bulletin for Becker. It was subsequently discovered that he returned to the nursing home in Laubach, where he remained in a state of almost complete mental and physical breakdown, ironically similar to the very same conditions experienced by the unfortunate souls for whom he had been instrumental in developing a method to end their lives prematurely. He died in Laubach on 31 December 1967.

The third chemist primarily involved in the development of mercy killing methods, and quite probably the establishment of extermination facilities for Aktion Reinhardt, was Helmut Kallmeyer. However, Kallmeyer denied any involvement in the T4 programme and maintained his innocence until his death on 27 September 2006, just short of his ninety-sixth birthday. There is no record of his membership of the NSDAP, the police or the SS, and it appears he acted as a consultant chemist for the KdF, as a member of the Criminal Technical Institute of the Security Police. However, he was a member of the SA. His name crops up in a number of letters which incriminate him. A letter from Alfred Wetzel of the Reich Ministry of the Occupied Eastern Territories to Hinirich Lohse attests that Viktor Brack wanted disabled Jews in Riga to be gassed by 'Brack's devices'. For this purpose, Brack offered his chemist, Dr Kallmeyer, and other assistants. Ultimately, this plan was not carried out in the Baltic States. Kallmeyer's name does appear on Criminal Technical Institute documentation concerning the delivery of gas and poisons to the T4 killing centres. On 2 May 1944, Kallmeyer ordered fifteen bottles of 'Kohlenoyd'. A German term for carbon monoxide is 'Kohlenmonoxid'.

Kallmeyer was born in Hamburg on 8 October 1910, the son of a government surveyor. He qualified as a chemist at the Berlin Technical University in 1939, and received his doctorate the following year, but was drafted into the navy. At the end of 1940, he married Gertrud Fröse, who had been working at the Grafeneck Institute. She had previously been a secretary for Viktor Brack, and he was a guest at the wedding. In September 1941, Kallmeyer was released from the Navy for 'special duties' at home. Kallmeyer immediately began his work for the KdF.

After the war, Kallmeyer insisted he knew nothing of the T4 programme, but he admitted being in Lublin in early 1942. He had no recollection of his duties while there. This was the crucial period in Aktion Reinhardt when the three extermination facilities were planned and built. Allegedly, Kallmeyer returned to Berlin after only one week.

During their post-war interrogations, Kallmeyer and his wife only admitted to events that could be proved by documentary evidence. There was little written evidence against them, and although the judicial authorities disbelieved their stories, they avoided prosecution. Kallmeyer worked as a civil servant until his retirement.

Worthy of mention in connection with T4 is Professor Dr Hans Heinze (1895–1983), an eminent paediatric psychiatrist and neurologist. One of the three child assessors of T4, he despatched numerous children to their early deaths. He served seven years' penal servitude in the Russian Sector, but continued to practice medicine after his release. Although proceedings against him for the euthanasia programme were considered in 1962, Heinze's poor health precluded any court action. He was never convicted for his part in the T4 murders and died in Wunstorf on 4 February 1983.

Another is Dr Carl-Heinz Rodenberg (1904–1995). Rodenberg is unusual among the group of T4 doctors because his young son suffered from encephalitis—inflammation of the brain.[14] Long-term problems with this condition include memory loss, frequent seizures, behavioural and personality changes, an inability to concentrate, and fatigue. One wonders if Rodenberg discussed his son with either Drs Catel, Heinze, or Wentzler.

The son of a physician, Rodenberg qualified as a doctor in 1930. He specialised in psychiatry and neurology. He was recognised as an expert on racial matters and was an outspoken advocate of compulsory sterilization. He worked as a criminal biologist in the Reich Office for Health. An early member of the NSDAP and the

SA, Rodenberg later applied to transfer to the SS. His application was backed by a confirmation from Himmler that he had been a useful informant for the SD.[15] In 1940, Rodenberg was attached to the RuSHA, but transferred to the RSHA in August 1942. He was an assessor for T4 from 28 February 1940 to 14 October 1940, as an expert in psychiatry.

On 27 October 1942, he took part in a conference chaired by Adolf Eichmann of RSHA Referat IV B4 (RSHA Sub-Department IV-B4), which was the follow-up to the Wannsee Conference. On the agenda was the sterilisation of half-Jews. On 1 July 1943, Rodenberg was transferred to Amt V of the RSHA as a speaker on issues of sexual psychology. He was also appointed as scientific director of the Reich Central Office for the Combating of Homosexuality and Abortion (Reichszentrale zur Bekämpfung der Homosexualität und der Abtreibung). In this capacity, he was given orders to research the castration of sexual offenders. This category included homosexuals, pyromaniacs, and habitual offenders. He ended the war as a SS-Obersturmbannführer.

Post-war, Rodenberg denied any wrongdoing in the various roles he held under the Nazi administration. He was nearly prosecuted for his participation in the meeting chaired by Eichmann, but he was never investigated for his role in T4. He died in 1995 aged ninety.

When questioned, Dr Georg Renno lied repeatedly about his time with T4. A member of the NSDAP since 1930, and the SS since 1931, he qualified as a doctor in 1933. He worked as a medical assistant at Leipzig-Dösen and took part in the trials of phenobarbital use on children. In June 1940, he was appointed as deputy medical director of Hartheim T4 facility, under Rudolf Lonauer. Together with Christian Wirth and Dr Lonauer, Renno organised the murder of countless individuals at Schloss Hartheim. Under interrogation, Renno denied actively participating in the gassing procedure, blaming Wirth and Lonauer who were already dead. He denied introducing gas into the system and denied any knowledge of the gassing procedure, insisting he was never present. Renno insisted that at Hartheim there was a single person known as the 'Brenner' who operated the gas valve. He stated that the 'Brenner' would also play a flute while administering the lethal gas.

Renno suffered from a heart condition that precluded court proceedings, and the case against him was eventually dropped. He spent his old age in Bockenheim in the district of Frankenthal (today Bad Dürkheim). He declared in a letter just before his death in 1997:

> I myself have a quiet conscience. I do not feel guilty, in the sense of—yes, like someone who shot someone.... Having seen how people have died, I have to say that it was not an ordeal, I would like to say ... it was a salvation.... With this feeling, I can leave here. I can go back to eternity, where I came from. Everything else does not matter.[16]

He died unrepentant on 4 October 1997, aged ninety, in Neustadt an der Weinstrasse.

Ernst Albert Max Wentzler, whose father was a leather manufacturer, was born in Hannoversch-Münden on 3 September 1891. He studied medicine after leaving school. His studies were interrupted by the First World War, and he served as a field doctor at a reserve hospital in Hanover. He completed his medical studies in 1918 at the University of Göttingen. He was an assistant physician under Erich Peiper at the University Children's Hospital, Greifswald. Wentzler eventually worked as a pediatrician in Berlin and converted his own home on the Veltheim Promenade (today, Zeltinger Straße 44 in Berlin-Frohnau) to a private children's hospital. It evolved into the Kinderklinik Frohnau. He bought the building in May 1934. In the 1920s, he developed the Wentzlersche Wärmewanne, a kind of incubator.

Wentzler joined the NSDAP on 1 April 1936, despite a ban on new admissions. He also belonged to the SA. From 1938, he was a member of the Association of German Children's Hospitals. During the Nazi period, Wentzler's hospital was known as the Deutsches Kinderkrankenhaus, and it achieved a status whereby the children of high-profile party members were treated there. These included the children of Hermann Göring, Walther Darré, Viktor Brack, Werner Blankenburg, and Hans Hefelmann. Not all cases ended happily—the son of Dr Kurt Blome died there after an immunisation went wrong.[17]

Karl Brandt recruited Wentzler in 1939 for the planning of child euthanasia, and he formed with Hans Heinze and Werner Catel the triumvirate that decided on the question of life or death of the children registered at T4. He was thus responsible for thousands of murders in the context of the child euthanasia specifically. It is suggested by available documents that the killing of handicapped children occurred on site at Wentzler's hospital. In addition, patients were transferred to the State Institute at Görden, and to the municipal mental hospital for children and adolescents, Wiesengrund, in Berlin-Wittenau, where they died.

After the war, Wentzler moved to Hannoversch-Münden, where he settled and practiced as a pediatrician. On 19 April 1949, in the course of a preliminary investigation before the District Court of Hamburg against almost twenty persons accused of the crimes committed in the context of child euthanasia, the First Criminal Division suspended the accused from prosecution, including Wentzler. The court declared insufficient evidence to prove a case. Wentzler died on 9 August 1973.

Carl Schneider is today regarded as a key member of the euthanasia programme, having worked at T4 from 20 April 1940. He was also an eminent expert in the fields of schizophrenia, dementia, and epilepsy, and he remains the author of the book considered the best on the subject of schizophrenia therapy. He was the director of the University Hospital for Psychiatry in Heidelberg. An outspoken supporter of compulsory sterilisation for mentally handicapped people, he stands accused of experiments on children at his hospital before transporting them to the Eichberg

Institute near Eltville where they were killed. After the war, he fled from Heidelberg, but was arrested. He killed himself in his cell at Frankfurt on 11 December 1946.

Horst Schumann is best remembered for his experiments on prisoners at Auschwitz. From October 1939, he worked for T4 and was appointed as director of the facility at Grafeneck in January 1940. He transferred to the killing centre at Sonnenstein in the summer of 1940. He was responsible for the deaths of many hundreds of patients, in addition to victims of Aktion 14f13 in which he was an active member. He served at Auschwitz from 28 July 1941. He conducted experiments for typhus and sterilisation by X-Rays. He left Auschwitz in September 1944 and returned to Sonnenstein, which had been converted to a military hospital.

He was interned for a short period after the war, and then fled from Germany and travelled to various countries, ending in Ghana where he obtained protection from President Nkrumah. Eventually extradited to Germany in 1966, his trial was opened in September 1970. By 1972, he had convinced the judicial authorities that his health was so bad, he did not have long to live, and he was released from custody. He died on 5 May 1983, eleven years after his release.

Haus Schoberstein, on the shores of the Attersee at Weissenbach in Austria, was a recreation facility for T4 personnel. For a time, it was run by the wife of Adolf Gustav Kaufmann. He was head of the Inspection Office of the T4 Central Administration and was an engineer by profession. His two brothers, Rudolf and Reinhold, both worked for T4. As a precautionary measure, the main T4 office was transferred to Haus Schoberstein in 1944 to avoid the bombing. Until then, it had been used only as a recreation centre for relaxation in the mountain lake area. Aktion Reinhardt staff had also used the villa for short breaks during their murder campaign in Poland. On 11 October 1944, the T4 headquarters moved to Schloss Hartheim. Haus Schoberstein still exists under the same name.

After the war, Kaufmann worked for BMW. He was finally arrested on 21 July 1965 and stood trial in 1967, accused with Dieter Allers. On 29 June 1967, Kaufmann was declared unfit to stand trial following a heart attack four days earlier. Charges against him were dropped in 1969. He died in Freising on 20 August 1974.

As can be seen, the entire operation of Aktion T4 was not only reliant upon the qualified and, in many cases, eminent physicians. Without the multitude of support staff, such as the nursing staff, orderlies, porters, maintenance men, cooks, crematoria operators, and pharmacists, the system would have faltered at a very early stage. A large section of these support staffers provided personnel for the subsequent Aktion Reinhardt in Poland when the T4 operation was largely scaled down. Many of these subsidiary workers received their initial training for the greater task to come, and a large number discovered a brutality within themselves that served them well in their later roles. They were well versed in the secrecy required by Reinhardt. Some took their secrets to the grave; others faced their crimes in open court. A number of post-war trials wreaked justice for the innocents, but in many cases, the guilty went unpunished.

Nurses, both male and female, were active participants. They were sworn to secrecy. Many reported that they were following the doctors' orders. Many obeyed through fear of retribution. Some even said that they considered death as a kind of release for the patients. Others struggled with their consciences, but still did what they were told. A few carried out their duty willingly. Some administered lethal injections of phenobarbital on the instructions of a doctor. There is even a suggestion that nurses left children outside on verandas to die of hypothermia.

On arrival at a killing centre, the patients were taken from the buses and led by a nurse to the reception room where they were recorded and photographed. They were then undressed and told they were to be bathed. Trusting the nurses, nearly all victims went to their deaths unsuspecting and willingly.

During this early 'killing period' in the Reich, the public were informed by propaganda means. Many parents of disabled children felt ashamed that their child was a burden on society. The voices of protest were few and far between, but a groundswell of opinion began to question and criticise the programme. When the church became involved, through the likes of Bishops Galen and Wurm, Hitler had doubts. As public opinion changed, Hitler could not afford this negative opinion in time of war. On 24 August 1941, he ordered a cessation to adult euthanasia. Paediatric murders continued, but in utmost secrecy. Aktion 14f13 also occurred and in fact gained pace after Hitler's directive. Some adults continued to be murdered, but usually by injections and tablets. Carbon monoxide had not, however, ceased to be used as a killing agent. A larger, even more sinister use had been found.

# 10

# THE ROAD TO HEAVEN

*The Jews are now being pushed out of the General Government, beginning near Lublin, to the East. A pretty barbaric procedure is being applied here and it is not to be described in any more detail, and not much is left of the Jews themselves. In general, one may conclude that 60% of them must be liquidated, while only 40% can be put to work. The former Gauleiter of Vienna, who is carrying out this action, is doing it pretty prudently and with a procedure that doesn't work too conspicuously ... the Führer is the guiding spirit of this radical solution both in word and deed...*

Reich Minister Joseph Goebbels, 27 March 1942.[1]

It is widely suggested that the operation to destroy the Jews of Poland was given the cover title Aktion Reinhardt—or Einsatz Reinhardt—as a mark of honour to the fallen SS General Reinhard Heydrich. His death on 4 June 1942 preceeded the period of the highest kill-rate of Polish Jews. However, Einsatz Reinhardt had been operational for a number of months by the time of Heydrich's death, albeit quite possibly under a different guise.

The first chronological document discovered referring to the operational name in Lublin is dated 6 June 1942 and is part of the Majdanek archive. It is a request for fifty empty suitcases from the operation, and it is addressed 'An den SS-u. Polizeiführer—Reinhardt—Lublin, Chopinstrasse 27'. It bears the printed heading 'Waffen-SS Standortverwaltung Lublin' and is ink signed by SS-Sturmbannführer Georg Wippern. Globocnik has underlined the word 'Reinhardt' and added a note and his signature in blue crayon. Was the apparently already established operation named in honour of the fallen Obergruppenführer as many people accept? Within two days of his death, the name appeared on Wippern's request. In which case, was

Reinhardt so named following the attack on Heydrich on 27 May, but before his death on 4 June? And how did the confusion over the two different spellings occur?

Unless documentary evidence surfaces, nobody knows who gave the operation this title, or when, but it can be safely assumed that whoever dreamed up the title was either a member of the operational staff, or someone highly placed who had knowledge of the secret policy. Awareness of the intention to exterminate the Jews wholesale was not common knowledge initially, nor is it certain that this outcome was the original operational intention, although resistance to that idea would have been minimal in the Nazi Party hierarchy.

Einsatz Reinhardt began as a manoeuvre to rob the Jews and the Poles of their assets upon resttlement, and it is likely that it evolved into a murder operation by force of circumstances and a change in policy ordered from above. Although those ethnic groups had to go, they would not be allowed to take their belongings with them. It is referred to in contemporary documents and post-war literature as both 'Reinhardt' and 'Reinhard'. Both spellings appear in documents originating from the participants themselves, creating uncertainty. In one particular document, both versions appear. Globocnik himself, the overseer of the operation, used both forms.[2]

The suggestion that the operation was named after Fritz Reinhardt, the State Secretary in the Ministry for Economics, has some substance, and gains credibility if one accepts that Aktion Reinhardt began as a fiscal robbery operation.[3] There is some evidence that Aktion Reinhardt was referred to as 'Katholisch Aktion' for a short time in early 1942. The building at ul. Chopina 27, subsequently used as a sorting and storage facility by Aktion Reinhardt, was built and owned by the organisation Catholic Action.[4] Today, it is occupied by the archives and library of the Catholic University. Was the name 'Katholisch Aktion' replaced as a result of the assassination of Heydrich?

Fritz Reinhardt was born in Ilmenau on 3 April 1895. His background was one of finance—economics and tax. He joined the NSDAP in 1923 and on 1 June 1928, Hitler appointed him as Gauleiter of Oberbayern-Schwaben. This post changed to Oberbayern in October 1928, and Reinhardt retained control. At his own request, he withdrew from the post on 1 November 1930. He was the economics representative for the Reich leadership of the NSDAP from 1932. A member of the Reichstag, Reinhardt was the deputy chairman of the Reichstag budget committee from March 1933.

On 1 April 1933, he was appointed as State Secretary in the Reich Ministry of Finance. In this capacity, he introduced the Reinhardt Programme, which promoted the use of manual labour, except where mechanical aids were absolutely necessary. He was a member of the general council for the Four-Year Plan, and he held the rank of SA-Obergruppenführer from 1937. Recognised as the foremost tax expert of the NSDAP, he often took decisions regarding taxation without further consultation. He died in Regensburg on 17 June 1969.

In summary, the debate over the name continues. If one considers the importance of Fritz Reinhardt in pecuniary affairs, and if one accepts that Aktion Reinhardt began as a financially driven concern, the cover name 'Reinhardt' attracts credence. However, if one is of the opinion that Fritz Reinhardt was too far removed and of relative insignificance to the SS-led operation, then the name 'Reinhard' gains ground. Reliance cannot be placed upon those operating the campaign, as both titles were used in correspondence. Globocnik, the primary authority in the action, used both titles on occasions, but in his winding up report to Himmler, he unremittingly referred to 'Reinhardt', and it is therefore that version that is used in this study. As Joseph Poprzeczny succinctly points out, it matters not which is correct, as the final outcome was still the same—the operation stripped the assets of hundreds of thousands of victims and resulted in the deaths of approximately 1.7 million people, the greatest single murder and plunder campaign in the history of mankind.

Unperturbed by his failures, Globocnik felt secure in his position in Lublin. It was glaringly obvious that the tank ditch project on the River Bug was a monumental waste of time, with only 13 km completed before the enterprise was cancelled, and its value proved militarily useless following Barbarossa. In response to a letter dated 13 May 1941 from the Lublin administration of civil governor Zörner, which indicated that Jewish policy had altered, Globocnik stressed that Jewish affairs remained the sole responsibility of the SSPF. In his reply of 15 May, Globocnik pointed out that SS-Obergruppenführer Krüger had not passed on any information that altered the held belief that the Jews were a matter for the SS. He also pointed out that he had the support of Heydrich.

Lublin's civilian governor, Ernst Zörner, had proclaimed the establishment of a ghetto in the historical Jewish district in the old town centre of Lublin in March 1941. This had been preceeded by the expulsion of about 14,000 Jews to outlying small towns of the region. Initially, for the first year, the ghetto area was not sealed off, but Jews were prohibited from the Aryan streets. The ghetto population rose to approximately 40,000. The conditions were not as bad as other ghettos, such as Lodz and Warsaw, but the site was the poorest area of the city. Despite severe restrictions on the sale and purchase of necessary supplies, food and some other essential commodities were smuggled readily into the ghetto, but at great risk. The better living conditions attracted Jews who had escaped from harsher similar communities. Overcrowding became a problem, and coupled with the unhygienic conditions, this led to outbreaks of disease epidemics, such as typhus.

On 16 July 1941, Himmler discussed Globocnik at a meeting with Krüger. After a working lunch with Rosenberg, Lammers, and Bräutigam on his special train 'Heinrich' on 17 July 1941, Himmler appointed Globocnik as the representative of the RFSS for the Establishment of the SS and Police Bases in the Occupied Eastern Territories.[5]

Himmler visited Lublin on Sunday 20 July 1941 after postponing his visit originally planned for 18 July. His inspection tour included a visit to the camp at Lipowa Street. He was accompanied by Globocnik, Krüger, Oswald Pohl, Karl Wolff, and Hans Kammler. Kammler was the building and construction expert for the SS-WVHA. In Lublin on 20 July 1941, Himmler ordered Globocnik to liaise with Oswald Pohl and erect a new large concentration camp in Lublin, and to completely Germanise the region of Zamość.[6] He also ordered the expansion of the Lipowa Street camp. Globocnik was very satisfied with the visit and wrote to Wolff on 22 July:

> The Reichsführer was here and gave us a lot of new work, that all our most secret wishes come true. I am so thankful for that because I am certain that his wishes will be fulfilled in a short time. I also give my thanks to you, Gruppenführer, because it is clear to me that you played a part in this visit.[7]

Around this time, Globocnik entertained Rudolf Höss in Lublin. Höss later remarked that he was surprised how casually Globocnik mentioned that he wished to seize the belongings of the people—Jews and Poles—that were evacuated in the resettlement. He intended to gather the property in large warehouses to exploit for the use of the SS.

Himmler followed his verbal instructions delivered during his Lublin visit with a written directive dated 21 July in confirmation of his orders. In addition to his order to build a new extensive camp in Lublin, Himmler outlined an economic strategy for Lublin. This included an immediate expansion of the German Supply Works (DAW—Deutsche Ausrüstungswerke), which had existed since 1940 at the Lipowa Street camp, as well as Globocnik's Clothing Works (Bekleidungswerke), which he had established earlier in 1941. Himmler also ordered the creation of a SS settlement on the site of the former Lublin airfield. He envisaged a new SS estate for approximately 60,000 SS men and considered the new intended camp as an integral part of his plans for the economic future of Lublin. The camp inmates would provide a ready workforce for the construction and development of a major military base for SS and police units participating in the campaign in the East.

Globocnik gained official recognition for his ideas of German colonisation of the Zamość region with Himmler's written approval on 21 July 1941 and his order:

> The action of searching for German blood will be extended to the whole General Government, and a vast settlement area will be set up near the German colonies in the environs of Zamość. In order to give a purely German character as quickly as possible, it is necessary to start early the establishment of farmsteads and the tilling of land.[8]

Himmler appointed Karl Otto Koch as the new commandant of the planned Lublin camp. Previously, he was the commandant of Buchenwald concentration camp near Weimar. The formal order to construct the camp was issued on 22 September 1941 by Kammler: 'On the order of the Reichsführer-SS it is necessary to set up in Lublin immediately a concentration camp for 5,000 prisoners. The camp will be the first building section in an area allocated for a future concentration camp for 50,000 prisoners'.[9]

Koch was the first in a line of infamous camp commandants. He was extremely experienced in the camp system and had learnt to utilise his various positions to benefit himself financially. He had previously served at Sachsenburg, Columbia Haus, Esterwegen, Sachsenhausen, Lichtenburg, Dachau, and Buchenwald. He was married to the infamous Ilse Koch, of Buchenwald fame. His rank of SS-Standartenführer did not save him from a death sentence when he was shot on 5 April 1945 in Buchenwald, following his conviction by a SS court for corruption.

Koch was succeeded at Majdanek by Max Koegel on 6 August 1942. Koegel had learnt his trade at Ravensbrück and was a brutal task master. The new gas chambers opened for business under his supervision, but he was quickly transferred in late October 1942. He committed suicide in his cell on 27 June 1946.

The third Majdanek commandant was Hermann Florstedt who had been Koch's adjutant at Buchenwald. His tenure at the camp is aptly described by survivors as a reign of terror. Commencing in November 1942, Florstedt oversaw the mass killings in the gas chambers of Majdanek. Prisoners were regularly hanged on Florstedt's orders, and it is alleged he personally took part in selections from Jewish transports, callously despatching women, children, and old folk to their deaths in the gas. Florstedt enriched himself by plundering valuables from his unfortunate victims. The subsequent investigation carried out by SS judge Dr Konrad Morgen discovered that Florstedt and several other members of the SS staff pilfered jewelry, currency, and precious metals from the transports and kept the ill-gotten gains for themselves. He was dismissed and indicted on charges of corruption, resulting in his conviction by a SS court and his execution on 15 April 1945.

Florstedt's replacement in November 1943 was Martin Weiss. Born on 3 June 1905, Weiss was the youngest Majdanek commandant. He had served in the camp system at Dachau, Arbeitsdorf, and Neuengamme. He had previously been active during the Aktion 14f13 when T4 doctors made thousands of selections for 'special handling'. He was also responsible during his tenure as camp commandant at Majdanek for the deaths of several thousand chronically ill prisoners transferred to his camp from various other camps throughout the Reich. At Majdanek, they were refused medical aid and deprived of sanitary installations, resulting in the deaths of the majority. Weiss was transferred to SS-WVHA Amt D on 18 May 1944. While still on Amt D staff, Weiss went to Muhldorf, a sub-camp of Dachau. At the end of the war, Weiss was at Dachau where he helped arrange the hand over of the camp to the Allies. He was hanged at Landsberg Prison on 29 May 1946.

The last commandant at Majdanek was Arthur Liebehenschel, but he rarely spent time in the camp as a result of poor health. The camp was liberated by the Red Army on 23 July 1944. Liebehenschel had been head of Amt DI at the SS-WVHA before his transfer to command Auschwitz on 1 December 1943. He was replaced at Auschwitz by Rudolf Höss the following summer as a more efficient commandant was required to carry out the genocide of the Hungarian Jews. Liebehenschel then transferred to the staff of Globocnik in Trieste. He was arrested by the Americans and handed over to the Poles who hanged him in Krakow on 24 January 1948.

Five days after his first order, Kammler issued a second directive:

> In Lublin and Auschwitz, camps for prisoners-of-war will be set up immediately, as of 1 October, with the possibility of accommodating 50,000 prisoners-of-war each, according to the instructions given in Berlin and the received documentation.... Work should start immediately and should proceed at the quickest pace possible.[10]

Koch established an office for the camp management at 12 Ogrodowa Street in Lublin and immediately set about erecting the first section of the camp, near the existing camp in Lipowa Street.

This second order from Kammler indicates a dual purpose for the intended camp—a concentration camp and a POW camp. The invasion of the Soviet Union, which began on 22 June 1941, netted a vast number of prisoners. Most were kept in open enclosures, with little or no shelter. Food and essential supplies were totally insufficient, and Soviet prisoners were forced to dig holes in the ground in which to live. Himmler was not planning a POW camp through compassion, but his idea was to utilise a number of the newly acquired masses as a workforce for the benefit of the German war effort; the excess could perish through natural wastage. It was also his plan for the SS to control all POWs.

An agreement was reached in September 1941 between Himmler and Generalfeldmarschall von Brauchitsch that the SS would take over responsibility for all 325,000 Soviet POWs. This resulted in Kammler's order of 27 September 1941, but there was no mention of funding. However, on 28 October, Globocnik allocated 2 million RM from the funds of the SS garrison in Lublin towards the new camp. On 1 November 1941, Kammler instructed the SS and Police Central Construction Board in Lublin to establish a POW camp in Lublin of sufficient size to house 125,000 prisoners. This time, he allocated 5 million RM from the account of Amt II of the SS-WVHA for the purpose. On 8 December 1941, he authorised an expansion of the camp to accommodate 150,000 POWs or detainees. He stipulated that workshops and economic facilities should be included in the camp, including a large laundry, a delousing station and a crematorium.

From this latter order, it became clear that the new camp would have a dual function—that of a POW camp administered by the SS and a concentration camp. This was confirmed by Himmler in April 1942 when he wrote: '… the POW camp in Lublin is to serve at the same time as a concentration camp'.[11]

Himmler's rather vague order of the 20 July 1941 gained some meat on the bone when the guidelines became more specific during October and November of the same year. The entire strategy was also given the name 'Programme Heinrich'. The military base would serve as a SS support and supply depot for the SS bases in the occupied Soviet territory. It consisted of the SS housing district, a supply works, a clothing works, a military storehouse, large workshops in the camp, and also a storage facility for the HSSPF Southern Russia.

With the expansion of the plans for the size of the camp, the initial site near Lipowa Street had to be abandoned. Koch faced the now daunting and urgent task of identifying a new suitable location for the camp. On 26 September, Koch obtained a large parcel of land from Governor Zörner to the south-east of the town, on the main route to Zamość. It was 5 km from the city centre. The police authorities designated the district of Kosminek and the village of Dziesiata, plus sections of Abramowice and Kalinowka, as the site of a new camp. Those inhabitants affected by the planned construction site were resettled. The eventual total area, including the surrounding protective zone, amounted to 1,275 acres.

The new camp was given the Polish name 'Majdanek', derived from the district of Majdan Tatarski, but the name was never used in official communications. It was referred to as 'Kriegsgefangenenlager der Waffen-SS in Lublin' until 1943, when it changed to 'Konzentrationslager der Waffen-SS Lublin—KL Lublin'.

To erect the camp, Globocnik entrusted the Zentralbauleitung der Waffen-SS und Polizei Lublin (Central Construction Board of the Waffen-SS and Police in Lublin), which had been established immediately following the visit of the RFSS in July 1941. Initially, it was administered by SS-Untersturmführer Hautz. He was succeeded by SS-Hauptsturmführer Naumann in 1942, and by SS-Untersturmführer Grothe in 1944.[12] This organisation was made responsible for all aspects of the design and construction of SS building projects in the Lublin district. It offered jobs for tender to outside builders, in addition to supply of materials. It was subordinate to the central office of the SS and Police Building Inspectorate for the General Government in Krakow, and from July 1942, to Amt C of the SS-WVHA.

The first plan for the new camp, dated 7 October 1941, shows the protective custody area only. Some 236 barracks were planned, 207 of which were to be accommodated by prisoners, conforming to Himmler's orders and those issued by Kammler. Work commenced in October 1941, carried out by Jewish Polish POW from the Lipowa Street camp. They were soon joined by Soviet POWs who were quartered on site, without shelter. The perimeter fencing and the barracks in Compound I were the first structures to be erected.

By 11 November 1941, Kammler was able to report to Oswald Pohl that 10,000 prisoners could already be accommodated, with an additional 10,000 within days. The final plan for 150,000 prisoners was approved by Koch on 23 March 1942. The complex included the SS Clothing Works, a tailors' barracks, furriers, hosiers, and shoe workshops, in addition to facilities for sorting and storage. All were complemented by living quarters for both prisoners and SS staff, plus buildings for administrative functions. By May 1942, the construction was limited to eight compounds, to be erected in two phases.

Each compound had a gallows for the public execution of prisoners, and the crematorium building had eight hooks attached to the ceiling for hanging larger groups of prisoners. From August to October 1942, purpose-built gas chambers were built beside compound I, opposite the bath barrack number 41. They were constructed of ceramic brick, covered with a ferro-concrete roof, standing on a concrete floor. The gassing installation, described in documentation as a 'delousing facility', comprised three chambers—one 10 metres by 5.5 metres by 2 metres, and two of 4.8 metres by 3.6 metres by 2 metres. There was a small annex room that accommodated the metal gas cylinders, operated by a SS man. He also had a small reinforced and grated viewing window through which he could watch proceedings. Carbon monoxide gas was used in the larger chamber and one of the smaller chambers. The other was adapted for the use of Zyklon B crystals—poured through an opening in the roof. Potassium cyanide crystals became the preferred method of gassing at Majdanek and another gas chamber was added in barrack 41. All chambers were supplemented with a hot air fan, which increased the lethal effect of potassium cyanide when released into the atmosphere.

In October 1941, a five-furnace crematorium was placed on order from the Berlin firm Kori. As an immediate stop-gap, a twin-furnace oven was transferred from Sachsenhausen and installed in a new barrack erected between two compounds. This also consisted of a morgue, accommodation for the cremation Sonderkommando, and an office for SS-Hauptscharführer Erich Muhsfeldt, the chief of the crematorium. The daily burning rate of each furnace was 100 corpses, with 'refills' every hour. The later purpose-built brick crematorium was completed by early September 1943 and the incineration rate was reduced to a new furnace load every ten to fifteen minutes.

Thus, Majdanek could be considered as the first major camp of Aktion Reinhardt, although the sole purpose of the camp was never regarded as a death camp, unlike the 'terminal stations' of Bełżec, Sobibor, and Treblinka. Despite the presence of purpose-built gas chambers after 1942, the function of Majdanek was first and foremost a POW camp, in conjunction with a concentration camp, providing labour and economic exploitation. Unlike other concentration camps, Globocnik, as SSPF Lublin, had unique power over the administration of Majdanek. He considered it as 'his' camp. Majdanek was subordinated to the SS-WVHA like other camps, but exclusively through the HSSPF in Krakow. This gave Globocnik, as Krüger's representative in Lublin, ultimate authority over the camp. It is no small coincidence that Karl Koch and several other of the camp staff were subsequently investigated by the SS on suspicion of corruption.

Majdanek can claim to be the site of the winding up of Aktion Reinhardt on Polish soil, with the massacres conducted in Aktion Erntefest—Harvest Festival—of November 1943. This was executed during the tenure of Jakob Sporrenberg, Globocnik's successor as SSPF Lublin, but there is little doubt that Globocnik's fingerprints were all over it.

The final area covered by the camp stretched over 667 acres of land and was surrounded by an electrified double wire fence incorporating nineteen timber watchtowers. Other than the construction groups, the first transport of prisoners arrived in October 1941. During the almost three years of its existence, approximately 150,000 people were incarcerated in Majdanek, from twenty-eight different countries. Estimates vary as to the death toll, and this is not helped by the failure to register large numbers of prisoners who went directly into the gas chambers. The most accurate estimation was provided by a Polish researcher, Tomasz, who calculated that 78,000 perished at Majdanek, the largest group as a result of Aktion Erntefest in November 1943.

The Lublin Ghetto was established in March 1941. By October 1941, the Nazi administrations of Governor Zörner and the SSPF prepared the eventual expulsion of the Jews of Lublin, apart from around 25,000 working for the German Army, the SS, and police. The Jews in the city lived initially in an unsealed area around Lublin Castle and to the east of Lubartowska. Early in 1942, the ghetto was divided into two parts, Ghetto A and Ghetto B, and in March 1942, the ghetto was sealed off.

Ghetto A was known as the 'Big Ghetto' and was where unemployed Jews lived. Ghetto B was located in several streets, Grodzka Street, Kowalska Street, and Rybna Street. The Judenrat and its institutions were located in Ghetto B. Jews who worked for the Germans and doctors who worked in the Jewish hospitals also lived in Ghetto B, which was fenced in with barbed wire. Jews living in Ghetto A and Ghetto B were allowed to visit each other at special times during daylight hours only, and this required special prior permission. At 10 p.m. on 16 March 1942, the first deportations to Bełżec commenced and signalled the beginning of the liquidation of the Lublin Ghetto. This was carried out by SS units and Ukrainians trained at the Trawniki facility. Many of the Jews, especially the elderly and sick, were shot immediately. Two hours later, SS-Obersturmführer Hermann Worthoff, who was responsible for Jewish affairs in the Lublin Gestapo, met representatives of the Judenrat and ordered that around 1,500 people had to be deported every day 'to the East for work'. This was a blatant lie—they were destined for the newly constructed gas chambers at Bełżec.

Without the benefit of any written evidence, the only guide to the decision to physically destroy all the European Jews is provided by Adolf Eichmann during his post-war interrogation in Israel. When questioned by Avner Less of the Israeli police, Eichmann stated:

> The war with the Soviet Union began in June 1941, I think. I believe it was two months later, or maybe three, that Heydrich sent for me.... He said to me, 'the Führer has ordered physical extermination'. These were his words ... and as though wanting to test their effect on me, he gave a long pause, which was not his way at all. I can still remember that. At first I didn't grasp the implications because he chose his words so carefully. Then I understood; I didn't say anything ... he then said to me, 'Eichmann, go and see Globocnik in Lublin'.[13]

This statement pinpoints the decision by Hitler to murder European Jewry as no later than August–September 1941, and coincides with the decision a little later to build the Reinhardt 'terminal station' at Bełżec.

On 15 November 1941, Rosenberg had lunch with Himmler, followed by a meeting that lasted four hours.[14] It is more than likely that Rosenberg was informed of the plans to kill the Jews by poison gas at this meeting. Three days later, Rosenberg stated at a press conference:

> In the East some six million Jews still live, and this problem can only be solved in a biological eradication of the entire Jewry of Europe. The Jewish question is only solved for Germany when the last Jew has left German territory, and for Europe when not a single Jew lives on the European continent up to the Urals ... for this reason it is necessary to expel them over the Urals *or eradicate them in some other way*.[15] [Italics added.]

In a note on 16 December 1941, following the US entry into the war, Rosenberg alluded to an agreement with Hitler over a planned speech:

> With regard to the Jewish question, I said that my remarks about New York Jews would perhaps have to be changed now.... My position was that the extermination of the Jews should not be mentioned. The Führer agreed. He said they had brought the war down on us; they had started all the destruction, so it should not come as a surprise if they became its first victims.[16]

For many historians of the Jewish Holocaust, the liquidation of the Lublin Ghetto marks the beginning of Aktion Reinhardt. It certainly coincided with the start of transports to the first of Globocnik's three terminal stations at Bełżec. For transportation 'to the East', the Jews were ordered to gather at the Great Marhaszala Synagogue at the foot of the Castle Hill, from where they were directed to the Umschlagplatz (congregation and forwarding point) at the site of the city slaughterhouse in ul. Zimna. The route took them along ul. Ruska, ul. Kalinowszczyzna, and ul. Turystyczna. The location of the Umschlagplatz—until 2016, it was known as Lublin Death Square—was chosen for its suitability as an onward despatch point for large numbers of people. In order to achieve this, a rail link was necessary. The railway infrastructure in the area of the slaughterhouse was created when the first industrial buildings were erected on the site between 1926 and 1928. The railway siding was in existence by the beginning of February 1929, but the construction of the railway siding and platforms was probably not completed until May–June 1930. Today, the site is derelict, and the rail lines have disappeared, but archeological investigations in 2006 have confirmed the presence of former rail tracks, which were connected to the rail link between Warsaw, Lublin, and Bialystok. This rail connection was accessed from the site, not only by the slaughterhouse, but also the marketplace, the local wire and nails factory, a mill, and the Lublin sugar refinery.

The Umschlagplatz was selected as a suitable congregation and forwarding point by the German Security Police in Lublin, under the supervision of the SSPF, Odilo Globocnik. The route to the site was sparsely populated, thereby affording a minimum number of eyewitnesses. Local inhabitants were ordered to screen their windows and close their doors and gates. To minimise possible witnesses, the transfers were carried out at night. The site itself had a tower that could serve as a watchtower, and it was surrounded by a wall that ensured further security.

As a young girl witness, Wiesława Majczak watched Jews being marched to the railway siding:

> Jews were being led to the railway platform, to the slaughterhouse, right outside our windows. It always started around 10 or 11 in the evening. We knew it to be the beginning of the march, because they would start to shout and shoot. And to this day I have a rustling ringing in my ears, because it's difficult to call it anything else. It was the rustle of feet dragged over cobblestone and this sound of talking, more like a buzzing noise. And then there was the obvious shouting and shooting.[17]

The unsuspecting Jews had no indication of their eventual destination or fate. The official information stated they were being resettled in a different location. Rumours persisted among the Jews, ranging from resettlement in a labour camp to being murdered by electrification at a place called Bezea (this was Bełżec). The tense ghetto atmosphere was interrupted by the sound of sporadic machine-gun fire, which only added to the anxiety.

Deportees were allowed to take a maximum of 15 kg of luggage, plus valuables and money. Some 200 children from the Jewish orphanage in the ghetto were shot, along with their teachers. Patients from the Jewish hospitals were taken to the nearby Niemce Forest and shot with their doctors and nurses. On 30 March 1942, Worthoff ordered the arrest and transportation of the members of the Judenrat, plus thirty-five members of the Jewish ghetto police, along with their families. They too died in the gas chambers of Bełżec.

The scenes at the Umschlagplatz were appalling. The Jews were forced into freight wagons, 100 at a time. No facilities were provided. The corpses of those murdered and the old and weak were thrown in also. The wagons were then sealed and sometimes the occupants had to wait for hours without food, water, or hygiene facilities provided before the train moved off towards Bełżec. By the time the ghetto liquidation ceased on 14 April 1942, it is estimated that approximately 28,000 men, women, and children were despatched from the Umschlagplatz in Lublin. Around 7,000 Jews remained in hiding within the ghetto. They were ordered to be moved to the small ghetto at Majdan Tatarski, near the airfield in the area of the present-day Bronowice district.

Before the establishment of the ghetto on 16 April 1942, the area had been inhabited by workmen employed in Tatary and Bronowice who, as a consequence of the Jewish resettlement plan, were forced to leave their homes and relocate into the city itself. The area of the so-called 'residual ghetto' was intended for only 4,000 Jews, but additionally it became a shelter for a similar number of 'clandestine' inhabitants, the total number of its inhabitants eventually rising to about 8,000. The historical Rolna Street was the main road of the ghetto. On 22 April 1942, about 2,500 Jews were shot in the Krepiecki Forest. Around 300 young men were also transported to Majdanek. Approximately 4,000 Jews officially lived in the Majdan Tatarski Ghetto, which was now sealed with a barbed wire fence. Only Jews in possession of the J-Ausweis cards were permitted to reside in the ghetto, with work permits simultaneously serving the function of a legal pass enabling chosen ghetto inhabitants to leave for work outside the enclosed area. Jews found taking unauthorised leave of the assigned housing zone were punished with death. Polish citizens were only allowed in for official reasons.

Small pockets of Jews were still to be found within the city limits as late as December 1942. An example was the small group of Jewish prisoners who were employed at the SS-Standortverwaltung. It consisted of a small number of Lublin jewellers who were involved in segregating and smelting the valuables taken from victims of Aktion Reinhardt. However, some within this group were also employed in tidying the SS men's living quarters in addition to maintaining the gardens in the surrounding grounds. The work undertaken by the jewellers was carried out in the strictest of secrecy. Even before the liquidation of the Majdan Tatarski Ghetto, those confined at Wippern's SS-Standortverwaltung were prohibited from returning to the Lublin closed district. They were also not permitted to be in contact with their families. One among this group was Zaurman, who, before the war, was a well-known Lublin watchmaker and jeweller who had been brought in from Majdan Tatarski. This group was tasked with receiving, sorting, recording, and storing currency, and the precious metals and stones in the basement of the building before onward transport to Berlin.

The president of the new Judenrat was Dr Marek Alten, but the most powerful Jew was restauranteur, former barber, and pimp Szama Grajer. He was known within the ghetto as the 'King of the Jews'. Grajer had owned a restaurant and brothel at 15 ul. Lubartowska in the old town, which was frequented by the SS and Gestapo. The German authorities turned a blind eye to his nefarious black market dealing, which enabled him to provide the very best food, drink, and female company. He was not averse to selling Jewish permits for work and he even participated in selections with the Gestapo. Heavily involved in the corruption of the ghetto, it is not surprising that there existed the suggestion of a direct telephone connection to Globocnik.

A further selection took place in September 1942 when approximately 1,000 Jews were deported to the ghetto at Piaski and this should have signalled to the inhabitants that the Germans were not finished. On 24 October 1942, the so-called privileged Jews who had considered themselves as exempt until then found themselves on their way to Majdanek. Finally, on 9 November 1942, the remaining 3,000 inhabitants of Majdan Tatarski Ghetto were deported to Majdanek. Approximately 180 inhabitants were shot in the ghetto, including Dr Marek Alten, Moniek Goldfarb, the erstwhile commander of the Jewish ghetto police, and the 'King of the Jews', Szama Grajer. These were personally shot by Hermann Worthoff on the strict orders of Globocnik in order to eliminate any prospective witnesses to SS corruption in the ghetto. Selections continued in Majdanek where the gas chamber engineers were kept busy.

Some survived the initial selections and were transferred to the Lipowa Street camp or the sorting and storage warehouses at the old airfield. Others were transferred to the Sportplatz camp or the Gestapo prison in the old castle. Nearly all fell victim to Aktion Erntefest in November 1943, or they were shot on 21–22 July 1944, just prior to liberation by the Red Army. Worthoff's hand in these executions was evident. Worthoff survived the war and lived under an assumed name, Hermann Josef Schmitz, until 1953, when he reverted to his real name. In 1975, he was sentenced to twelve years in prison for assisting in the deaths of

8,000 inhabitants of the Lublin Ghetto. Of approximately 42,000 Jews of Lublin, only 200–300 survived the Holocaust, either by hiding or surviving various camps.

Globocnik recognised that to physically destroy the Jews of the General Government, he required manpower. At the end of 1941, he established a camp at Trawniki in a former sugar factory, approximately 25 miles south-east of Lublin. Following the outbreak of hostilities between Germany and the Soviet Union, the camp was set up to provide POW facilities for the thousands of Soviet prisoners. The German authorities recognised that many of the Soviet prisoners were from Baltic States and were reluctantly fighting for Moscow. Teams entered the POW camps and offered improved conditions for those willing to fight for Germany. Thousands of Lithuanians, Estonians, Latvians, and Ukrainians took the offer and swapped allegiance. Many were transferred to Trawniki for retraining, and it was from this cadre of former prisoners that Globocnik found his manpower for Aktion Reinhardt.

The Trawniki men were known as 'Hiwis' (non-German personnel willing to help; the German abbreviation for Hilfswilliger). They trained for their role in Reinhardt on inmates of a small concentration camp set up within the Trawniki facility. Many Jews from the Reich and Czechoslovakia were deported to Trawniki, where large numbers perished through ill treatment, the lack of medical care, and starvation. Trawniki men were used as auxiliary guard units in death and labour camps, in the liquidation of ghettos and as escorts for the deported Jews. It is estimated that between 2,000 and 3,000 men went through training at Trawniki. Each death camp was allocated between ninety and 130 men and the vast majority of squad commanders were of Volksdeutsche extract. The largest contingent nationality of 'Hiwi' men was Ukrainian.

Not only did Globocnik require strength in numbers, but he also had a need for technical ability and experience in killing groups of people. The obvious source for these necessary skills was the euthanasia programme, which from August 1941 was being scaled down. T4 staff possessed the know-how and a large contingent was becoming available. Globocnik's Reinhardt operation consisted of around 450 personnel, including ninety-two KdF staff transferred from T4 by Viktor Brack for the purpose. Some of their names remain obscure to this day, but many were destined to become household names.

# 11

# AKTION REINHARDT

*Nobody liked doing this job … we sensed the threat over us that after the war was won, we would have paid for this 'special duty' with our lives—I more or less feared that we belonged to a doomed group.*

Hans-Heinz Schütt, SS-Oberscharführer, T4 and Aktion Reinhardt

THE LUBLIN *ALTER FLUGPLATZ* (Old Airfield) Camp took the name of its location on the airfield of the former aircraft manufacturer, E. Plage and T. Laskiewicz, on ul. Wronska, to the north of the Lublin concentration camp. This was the very first Polish aeronautical company, manufacturing aircraft from 1921 until 1935. The large plant was first located at ul. Fabryczna 26 and produced small fighter aircraft and bombers for the Polish airforce. The company soon added passenger aircraft to its stable. From 1924 to 1933, the company also produced car bodies and buses. With the success of the company, the plant was expanded to include the airfield at ul. Wronska. The renamed Lubelska Wytwornia Samolotow (LWS) aircraft factory dated from the end of 1935, after it had been nationalised following a period of economic hardship. The airfield was attacked by German bombers on 2 and 4 September 1939 when there were numerous casualties. Most of the airfield buildings remained intact, but the landing and take-off areas were severely damaged, as were a number of aircraft of the factory and the local flying club.

When the Germans arrived, they used the airfield for holding Polish POWs and the hangars were converted into warehouses for storing seized weapons and armoured equipment. At the end of hostilities on Polish soil in October 1939, there were approximately 200 Polish POWs under guard at the site. This prisoner facility was terminated in January or February 1940, when the airfield was converted again to house the 2. SS Cavalry Regiment. Stables were introduced into some of the buildings, but the hangars remained as storage buildings for SS clothing.

In the spring of 1940, Jewish prisoners from Lipowa Street were employed at the airfield as forced labour. Delegates from this group complained to the Arbeitsamt on 18 May 1940 of brutality and ill treatment by their guards at the airfield. The workers numbered eighty-four people, who stated that they were beaten and abused without exception by the guards. At the end of July 1940, a temporary camp was erected on the airfield site by Jewish labourers. This housed around 570 prisoners who were initially used to dismantle concrete structures connected to the former aircraft industry. Their numbers were swelled by a round-up carried out in the town on 9–10 August 1940.

As early as July 1941, Globocnik suggested the creation of a female camp in Lublin for approximately 500 women prisoners. Initially, the camp was to be situated in Field V of KL Lublin. However, the plans altered to be replaced by a new idea to locate the female camp in the newly constructed Alter Flugplatz. The first female prisoners arrived at the camp at the end of 1942.

This ever-expanding camp developed into a system of camp barracks and warehouses at the site, which included the main supply camp for the Higher SS and Police Leader Russland-Sud und Kaukasien (South Russia and the Caucasus). A Sonderkommando of approximately 1,200 prisoners was initially brought daily from KL Lublin and Lipowa Street for employment at the construction site of the Alter Flugplatz camp. From mid-September 1942, all prisoners were confined to the barracks of the Alter Flugplatz camp on a permanent basis.

All seized goods were transported to the SS garment factory to be recycled by Jewish tailors and furriers brought from the ghetto. *Globocnik was soon to recognise the value of having skilled tailors and furriers at his disposal at the SS garment factory. Himmler ordered all SS supply warehouses to use the SS garment factory which, from March 1942, was placed under Globocnik's supervision. The Alter* Flugplatz was incorporated into the so-called Pelzaktion, aimed at collecting furs, articles made of fur, and woollen garments. The action, which was carried out in the entire territory of the General Government, started in Lublin on Christmas Day 1941. At the beginning of 1942, the Jewish Lublin labour force was joined by a group of artisans brought from other towns and villages. The SS Garment Factory was closed down in 1942. A sorting facility for goods plundered from Jews during Aktion Reinhardt was established in its place.

In 1942, the rapidly developing *Deutsche Ausrustungswerke GmbH (*German Equipment Works—*DAW)* opened a tar paper factory at the Alter Flugplatz, and the following year, it set up shoe repair shops, launching the production of wooden shoe soles and munitions boxes.

During the summer of 1942, the camp was significantly expanded and became part of the close economic co-operation between the SS Business Administration

Main Office (*WVHA)*, headed by Oswald Pohl and Globocnik. Globocnik was interested in intensifying the exploitation of Jewish forced labour in the Lublin region and the profitable recycling of the property of deported and murdered Jews. Pohl was interested in increasing the efficiency of the SS economic enterprises. This created a conflict of interest between Globocnik and the KL Lublin administration. The authorities of Majdanek expected the Alter Flugplatz to become a sub-branch of the mother camp, which was contrary to that envisaged by Globocnik when he planned for the Alter Flugplatz camp to be part of the SS economic empire.

On 19 July 1942, the Reichsführer-SS ordered Friedrich-Wilhelm Krüger to 'resettle' the entire Jewish population of the General Government by 31 December 1942. By this, he meant liquidate all the Jews of the General Government with a few exceptions.

On 12 March 1943, Pohl founded the SS-Wirtschaftsunternehmen Ostindustrie GmbH (OSTI) for the forced labour of Jewish prisoners in the armaments industry. It began with a share capital of 100,000 RM. In October 1942, Himmler had ordered the creation of armaments factories in the east of the General Government, owned by the SS. They were termed 'KL-Großbetriebe'. He added a codicil to this order: 'But there too, one day the Jews will disappear according to the wish of the Führer'.[1] Pohl intended to profit from the availability of free labour. The company was registered in Berlin on 30 April 1943 with Globocnik and Dr Max Horn as managing directors. According to Dr Horn, the OSTI was to build and operate critical war and armament manufacturing facilities with Jewish forced labour, and to exploit the movable Jewish assets generated by Jewish resettlement.[2]

In January 1943, Himmler formulated contracts with the owners of the two largest Warsaw Ghetto factories, Walther Többens and Schultz GmbH, to relocate their companies to the camps at Poniatowa and Trawniki, in the district of Lublin. The ghetto inhabitants were to be deported, with the exception of 10,000 forced labourers, who were then to demolish all the buildings in the residential district and the vacated factories. These plans were not fully implemented as the Jewish inhabitants began resisting the deportations which culminated in the Warsaw Ghetto uprising of April–May 1943.

At the Alter Flugplatz site, a brush factory and a basket-weaving workshop were set up under the name Plant III. A metal works was created as Plant V for armaments production for the Luftwaffe, with metalworking and electrical engineering workshops. In August 1943, the OSTI transferred two further production sites to Lublin—a brickworks, including a cement plant and tile factory (Plant VII) and an orthopaedic workshop (Plant VIII) for prosthetic limbs. By the autumn of 1943, the Ostindustrie GmbH was compiled by a series of various concerns administered by the SS, using free enforced Jewish, and in some cases Polish, labour, which had not yet realised its full potential for productivity.

Aktion Erntefest in early November 1943 deprived the OSTI of its workforce. Himmler was alarmed by the various Jewish rebellions in 1943, which resulted in his review of the economic value of holding so many Jewish enforced labourers whose extermination had been temporarily postponed for exploitation. The workers in Plants II, III, V, VI, and VII were all murdered, and Pohl ordered the liquidation of the OSTI on 23 November 1943, after only eight months of operation. Some workshops survived as satellite camps of Majdanek, and others were transferred to the DAW. The collapse of the company was inevitable prior to its inception as a result of Hitler's decision to kill all Jews in late summer 1941 and Himmler's order to Krüger in July 1942. These took precedence over any plans to exploit the Jews for financial or political gain.

Before his departure from Lublin in September 1943, Globocnik had pulled a master stroke by tasking Christian Wirth with the reorganisation of the Alter Flugplatz camp. Wirth was the first commandant of Bełżec death camp, and from August 1942, he had been appointed as inspector of all Aktion Reinhardt camps. He was officially appointed as Alter Flugplatz camp commandant in March 1943, but prior to that appointment, his security position alone afforded him the power to influence the functions of the camp. Wirth replaced the camp staff with men he knew and returned the KL Lublin personnel to Majdanek. From then on, only the camp perimeter guards were Majdanek men.

The sorting and storage warehouses at the Alter Flugplatz camp served as the main reception point for all goods plundered from the murdered Jews of Aktion Reinhardt. The items were segregated, disinfected, and packaged before onward shipment to the Reich by the nearby rail link. This role, carried out by both Jewish men and women, was entrusted by Globocnik to SS-Hauptsturmführer Josef Obermeier. There was also a selection square where transports of Jews could be segregated into groups destined for the death camps, Majdanek or other labour camps and ghettos.

The August Frank memorandum of 26 September 1942, was a directive from SS-Brigadeführer Frank of the SS-WVHA. The document provides a measure of the detailed planning that the SS hierarchy put into the implementation of Aktion Reinhardt and the widespread murder of the European Jews. It sets out clear instructions as to the disposition of plundered assets of the Jewish victims. It illustrates that the Nazis were intent in removing everything of value from their victims. The memorandum contains an instruction that the yellow stars the Jews were ordered to wear on their clothing, were to be removed prior to the clothing being redistributed to ethnic Germans who were being resettled in occupied Poland. The memorandum, when it was discovered post-war, played a key role in refuting Frank's claims that he had no knowledge that Jews were being murdered *en masse* in the extermination camps of Aktion Reinhardt. The highly secret memorandum, produced in a number copies, was sent to interested parties, including Georg Wippern of the SS-Standortverwaltung in Lublin, and the chief of the camp administration at Auschwitz. It was translated into English for the trial of major war criminals in Nuremberg:

> Volksdeutsche Mittelstelle
>
> Without taking into account the overall regulations which are expected to be issued during October, pertaining to the utilization of mobile and immobile property of the evacuated Jews, the following procedure has to be followed with regard to the property carried by them—property, which will in all orders in the future be called goods originating from thefts, receiving of stolen goods, and hoarded goods:
>
> 1. a. Cash money in Reichsbank notes have to be paid into the account: Economic and Administrative Main Office 158/1488 with the Reich Bank in Berlin-Schöneberg.
>    b. Foreign exchange (coined or uncoined), rare metals, jewelry, precious and semi-precious stones, pearls, gold from teeth and scrap gold have to be delivered to the SS Economic and Administrative Main Office. The latter is responsible for the immediate delivery to the Reichsbank.
>    c. Watches and clocks of all kinds, alarm clocks, fountain pens, mechanical pencils, hand and electrical razors, pocketknives, scissors, flashlights, wallets, and purses are to be repaired by the Economic and Administrative Main Office in special repair shops, cleaned, and evaluated; and have to be delivered quickly to front line troops. Delivery to the troops is on a cash basis through the post exchanges. Three-fourth price grades are to be set and it has to be made sure that each officer and man cannot buy more than one watch. Exempt from sale are the gold watches, the utilization of which rests with me. The proceeds go to the Reich.
>    d. Men's underwear and men's clothing, including footwear, has to be sorted and valued. After covering the needs of the concentration camp inmates and in exceptions for the troops they are to be handed over to the Volksdeutsche Mittelstelle. The proceeds go to the Reich in all cases.
>    e. Women's clothing and women's underwear, including footwear; children's clothing and children's underwear, including footwear, have to be handed over to the Volksdeutsche Mittelstelle against payment. Underwear of pure silk is to be handed over to the Reich Ministry of Economics according to orders by the SS Economic and Administrative Main Office. This order refers also to underwear, under letter d.
>    f. Featherbeds, quilts, woolen blankets, cloth for suits, shawls, umbrellas, walking sticks, thermos flasks, ear flaps, baby carriages, combs, handbags, leather belts, shopping baskets, tobacco pipes, sun glasses, mirrors, table knives, forks and spoons,

knapsacks, and suitcases made from leather or artificial material are to be delivered to the Volksdeutsche Mittelstelle. The question of payment will be decided later.

The needs in quilts, woolen blankets, thermos flasks, ear flaps, combs, table knives, forks and spoons, and knapsacks can be furnished from Lublin and Auschwitz from these stocks against payment from budget funds.

g. Linen, such as bed sheets, bed linen, pillows, towels, wiping cloths, and tablecloths are to be handed over to the Volksdeutsche Mittelstelle against payment. Bed sheets, bed linen, towels, wiping cloths, and table cloths can be furnished for the needs of troops from these stocks against payment from budget funds.

h. Spectacles and eyeglasses of every kind are to be handed in to the medical office for utilization. (Spectacles with golden frames have to be handed in without glasses together with the rare metals). A settlement of accounts for the spectacles and eyeglasses need not take place with regard to their low value and their limited use.

i. Valuable furs of all kinds, raw and cured, are to be delivered to the SS-WVHA.

j. Ordinary furs (lamb, hare, and rabbit skins) are to be reported to the SS-WVHA, Amt B II, and are to be delivered to the clothing plant of the Waffen-SS, Ravensbrück near Fürstenberg (Mecklenburg).

k. All items mentioned under the letters d, e, and f, which have only one-fifth or two-fifths of the full value, or are useless altogether will be delivered via the SS-WVHA to the Reich Ministry for Economics for utilization.

For the decision on items which are not mentioned under the letters b–i, application for a decision as to their utilization should be made to the chief of the WVHA.

2. The SS-WVHA will establish all prices under observation of the legally controlled prices. This estimation, however, can be made later on. Petty evaluations which only waste time and personnel may be eliminated. Average prices for single items have to be established in general. For instance, one pair of used men's trousers 3.00 RM, one woolen blanket 6.00 RM, etc. For the delivery of useless items to the Reich Ministry for Economics, average Kilo prices will have to be established.

It has to be strictly observed, that the Jewish Star is removed from all garments and outer garments which are to be delivered. Furthermore, items which are to be delivered have to be searched for hidden and sewed-in values, this should be carried out with the greatest possible care.

[signed] Frank
SS-Brigadeführer und Generalmajor der Waffen-SS.[3]

Thefts from the warehouses were rife, especially by the SS personnel. Clandestine trade deals between prisoners and guards were another common practice in the camp. Money and valuables were often exchanged for food. However, if caught, the prisoners were punished for plundering with death and the SS were severely punished, sometimes with a sentence of imprisonment. A small warehouse was established where SS officers were able to purchase items. One particular SS man, Oberscharführer Heinrich Birmes, was a keen philatelist and he took great pleasure in seizing stamp albums.

Nearly all the Jewish inmates of the Alter Flugplatz camp fell victim to Aktion Erntefest on 3 November 1943. Today, only a small memorial marks the location of one of Globocnik's brutal enterprises. It bears the following inscription:

> During the German occupation a labour camp for Jews and, initially, small groups of Poles, was located in the area of the former factory airfield. Between 1942 and 1943, as part of the Third Reich plans to exterminate the Jews in 'Aktion Reinhardt', the site was the central sorting facility for property of the victims murdered in Nazi death camps in Bełżec, Sobibór and Treblinka. On 3 November 1943, the Jewish prisoners of Flugplatz were shot at the concentration camp at Majdanek.

As stated, the camp served as the central sorting facility of Aktion Reinhardt, a critical cog in the wheel of plunder and death operated under the supervision of Odilo Globocnik.

Another Globocnik led enterprise worthy of mention was situated at the site of the former Jewish cemetery, not far from Globocnik's residence. It was known as the Sportplatz and was located within the Wieniawa District of Lublin, bordering the designated German district. It was incorporated into Globocnik's SS district. This prohibited any non-German residents, and consequently the entire Jewish population of Wienawa was resettled in the Lublin Ghetto. The buildings formerly occupied by the Jews were demolished by Jewish work gangs brought into the district for the purpose. The whole area was designated a recreational area for Germans.

During 1940, the former Jewish cemetery was totally destroyed, with the tombstones being used as building material in the recreation area. In 1941, the construction of a sports arena and outdoor lido was commenced on the site by ghetto labour and some French POWs who were housed in a barrack on ul. Leszczynskiego. In the spring of 1942, a labour camp was erected on nearby ul. Ogrodkowa. The main camp building was located in a former cosmetics factory confiscated from its Jewish owner, Roman Keindel. He also owned the cosmetic company, Erika. Keindel was appointed as Kapo of the Sportplatz camp. Prisoner barracks were constructed near the factory building.

The camp was a sub-camp of Majdanek and was officially known as the Lublin SS-Polizeiführerkommando Sportplatz. The prisoners numbered about 600 in 1942. Conditions were not as bad as other camps as there were greater opportunities for contact with the Poles and food was more readily available. Each day, the Sportplatz inmates were supplemented by prisoners from Lipowa Street and consequently, there were exchanges of information and food.

The former cosmetics factory building was used for storage of cosmetics, medicine and surgical equipment plundered in Aktion Reinhardt. There was also a workshop for the repair of artificial limbs, which were sent to military hospitals and the Reich. The camp commandant was Standortarzt SS-Sturmbannführer Dr Kurt Sickel. He had an affair with a woman called Frau Radischat who some also suspected of having an affair with Globocnik and his adjutant, Max Cichotzski. This woman supervised the prisoners in the factory and was corrupt, pilfering Jewish property. She had a cruel reputation with the prisoners. This camp was also liquidated on 3 November 1943. The factory buildings were demolished in the late 1970s, but no memorial marks the spot, which is today occupied by apartment blocks. The sport stadium is still in use by the Lublinianka Sports Club, but is falling into disrepair through lack of maintenance funds.

On a street named after the Polish composer, Frederic Chopin, stood an enormous five-storey building at number 27. It was here that better quality goods were sorted and stored. Often referred to as the 'Chopin Lager', it has been described as a vast department store. Gangs of work Jews laboured daily, sorting the plundered goods into their various categories. In one big room, there were thousands of trunks and suitcases, deposited by the unsuspecting victims on arrival at the death camps, and fully expecting to regain their possessions once the bathing process was complete. Many had stuffed their most prized and valuable possessions into their luggage, which had carefully written labels identifying the owners. Others secreted their valuables in their clothing, expecting the possibility of losing them during searches.

There were various rooms at ul. Chopina 27. One marked 'Men's Shoes', another 'Women's Shoes'. In these rooms were deposited thousands of the better quality leather shoes and boots; far better than those sorted at the Old Airfield camp. In a corridor hung thousands of women's dresses; another with thousands of overcoats. One room contained large wooden shelves, which ran the length of the room, both against the walls and down the centre. On them were piled hundreds of safety razors, shaving brushes, penknives, and pencils. In another room, there were thousands of children's toys—teddy bears, dolls, tin cars, jigsaw puzzles, etc. Another room contained paper manuscripts and sheet music. The list is endless.

SS-Unterscharführer Eicholz and Dorl had twenty work Jews assigned to them. At first, these were guarded by members of the Lublin Schutzpolizei, but when they were withdrawn, they were not replaced. Apparently, conditions at the Chopin Lager were not as bad as at other locations. When valuables were discovered secreted in the clothing and furniture, they were immediately separated for transfer to Wippern's Standortverwaltung facility. Valuables were registered, but were not stored at the Chopin Lager. Any prisoner caught pilfering was executed.

The ground floor office was inundated with requests for supplies from various organisations and typed orders and circulars, some from Globocnik's office. One letter, dated 3 November 1942, was later discovered to be requesting blankets, table linen, crockery, bed linen, towels, and kitchen utensils for Company 934 of the Hitler Youth Camp. Apparently, the letter stated that the items were required for 4,000 evacuated children from the Reich. Another letter requested articles for 2,000 German children who required sportswear, gym shoes, warm underwear, gloves, and scarves. A German woman, living in Lublin, even asked for a pram and a complete layette for her new baby. The letters were addressed to the Altsachenverwertungsstelle, Lublin (Lublin Disposal Centre for Secondhand Goods). Any requests for goods had to be sent to Wippern or one of his deputies, SS-Obersturmführer Huber, who authorised any transfer of goods on the returned letter.

At Majdanek camp, an enormous warehouse contained about 850,000 pairs of boots and shoes, including baby shoes. After the liberation, within weeks, around half had disappeared, scavenged by the Lublin locals.

An important aspect of the development of Aktion Reinhardt were the intended SS and Police strongpoints in the East. The concept was basically the construction of a line of fortified defence farm villages, originally from Tallinn in the north, to Transylvania in the south, through the Zamość lands. Intended as a protective bulwark for the Germanic settlements in Eastern Europe, this defence wall would gradually move east, over the coming years, with the further strongpoints established as far as the Urals. According to Rudolf Höss's recollection of Globocnik, written in his cell in Krakow after the war, this Himmler assignment provided the Lublin SSPF man with an air of superiority and importance. Höss states:

> He [Globocnik] worked out fantastic plans for a series of strongpoints stretching to the Urals. He could see no difficulties in this, and he waved aside all objections. He wanted to destroy every Jew in this area on the spot, except those whom he needed for work on 'his' police positions. He proposed to put all their property into a collecting centre and utilise it for the SS. He talked about all this in his Viennese dialect in an easy-going way sitting in front of his fire in the evening, as though it were a most innocent adventure. I was extremely shocked by Globocnik, who according to Glucks' account was supposed to be extremely competent and to be held in high regard by the Reichsführer-SS.[4]

Höss went on to describe Globocnik as a pompous busybody who was prone to exaggeration in an effort to promote his own influence with Himmler. Höss had been advised by Glücks to see Globocnik in Lublin to obtain supplies for the camp at Auschwitz. Höss recalled that his visit to Lublin with his administrative officer, Wagner, had produced meagre supplies of surgical instruments and medicines which were 'indiscriminately heaped together in a factory building'.[5]

With the expansion of the war in the East, Globocnik was able to plan further strongpoints in the former Soviet Union. Three were created in Riga, Minsk, and Mogilev, with the fourth finally established in Kiev. These constituted the main strongpoints; subsidiary bases were set up by local the HSSPF and the Ordnungspolizei head office in Berlin. Erich von dem Bach established sites at Bialystok, Baranovichi, Bobruisk, and Vitebsk, in Weissruthenia. Globocnik's staff were ordered to liaise with local SS and police commanders in addition to the construction inspectorate created specifically by Oswald Pohl for the establishment of these sites. A fifth major site at Lvov, evolved into the Janowska labour and transit camp in Galicia.

All the strongpoint staff selected to run the sites were Globocnik men. Overall planning was the responsibility of Gustav Hanelt who was also tasked with 'Jew cleansing' operations. In Riga, Georg Michalsen; in Minsk, Kurt Claasen; in Mogilew, Hermann Dolp; and in Kiev, Richard Thomalla. Also involved was Hermann Höfle. Their involvement in the occupied eastern territories gave these men the opportunity to 'experiment' with gassing techniques for later use in Aktion Reinhardt. Höfle even used this posting to Mogilev in order avoid exposing his major role in Aktion Reinhardt when interrogated post-war.

On 1 October 1941, Globocnik wrote to Himmler:

> Reichsführer!
> In line with the implementation of your aims regarding the district, I passed on the detailed proposal to Obergruppenführer Krüger yesterday. SS-Obergruppenführer Krüger wished to present them immediately to you. He regarded this as urgent in the light of the emergency in which ethnic Germans now find themselves. This has taken such serious proportions that one can easily claim their situation in Polish times was better.... Since the preparations for concentrating them are now complete, implementation could commence immediately.... In this connection, I would also like to point out that by bringing them together in concentrated settlements and by a radical and thorough forced removal of alien ethnic elements here in the Lublin district, we can achieve a substantial political pacification. Because both of the political activism among the Poles and Ukrainians and the influence of the Jews, augmented by the influx of thousands of escaped POWs, have taken on a form here ... that simply in regard to implications for security policy, necessitates a rapid response.... SS-Obergruppenführer Krüger has ordered me to request you, Reichsführer, for the possibility of an audience with you in the near future.[6]

This meeting occurred on 13 October 1941, between 6 p.m. and 8 p.m.[7] No details of the meeting, or the detailed proposals referred to, exist today. This meeting is often referred to as the catalyst for the order to construct Bełżec extermination facility and possibly that at Sobibor.

Globocnik met Hans Frank in Lublin on 17 October 1941, with Ernst Böpple and Ernst Zörner. They discussed the Jewish question. It was agreed that all Jews would be evacuated from Lublin across the Bug River, with the exception of a few essential craftsmen. Responsibility was placed with the SSPF authority. Soon after, on 1 November 1941, construction work began on Bełżec death camp.

After the 17 October meeting, Globocnik travelled to Berlin to meet with the supremo of the SS Race & Resettlement Central Office, SS-Gruppenführer Otto Hofmann. On 4 November 1941, Globocnik convened a conference for his strongpoint leaders. He then visited Riga on 20 November. His grandiose plans never fulfilled their potential and his intended construction schemes brought him into conflict with Hans Kammler and therefore the powerful Oswald Pohl. The result was that Globocnik was relieved of his responsibilities for SS and police strongpoints, which Himmler placed under Pohl's SS-WVHA umbrella in March 1942. Globocnik was hindered by shortages of personnel and materials, in addition to disagreements over spheres of responsibility. He had to rely upon the SS Budget and Construction Central Office for fiscal and material support. His disagreements with Kammler prevented the strongpoint construction projects from getting past the preparatory stage.

By December 1941, only two T4 personnel had been transferred to Lublin—Christian Wirth and Josef Oberhauser. Himmler's service diary records a meeting with Viktor Brack at midday on 14 December 1941. Euthanasia was discussed.[8] Following this meeting, larger numbers of T4 staff began arriving in the Lublin District. Construction of the basic facilities at Bełżec was completed on 22 December 1941 and it was around this time that about ten T4 personnel arrived at the camp, including SS-Scharführer Erich Fuchs. Some SS officers and NCOs were already there, Wirth and Gottfried Schwarz among them.

Before deportations arrived at the camp in earnest the following March, the relatively small staff used the time to 'try out' the facilities with gassing experiments. In his testimony dated 10 November 1964, Oberhauser declared:

> [Initially] … only Jews unfit for work from various ghettos were to be liquidated. There was no talk yet of any extermination on a grand scale. I learned of the plan to systematically exterminate the Jews when Brack went to Globocnik in Lublin in April or May 1942 and informed him the members of Aktion T4 would be placed at his disposal for exterminating the Jews.[9]

This confirmed Adolf Eichmann's contention that Globocnik had initially been authorised to liquidate around 100,000 Jews, before obtaining further authorisation from Heydrich to increase this figure by another 150,000 to 200,000.[10]

The terminal facility at Bełżec was to become a prototype death processing plant and the Jews of Lublin were to be used as the guinea pigs. Elsewhere, the murder of Jews by shooting continued apace. In Mogilew, the Jewish population was decimated. Arthur Nebe conducted experimental gassing using the carbon monoxide exhaust of a car. Himmler visited Mogilew on 23 October 1941 when 279 Jews were shot in his presence, and soon after, the city was declared practically free of Jews. However, in November 1941, the SS Main Office for Budget and Construction ordered a massive crematorium consisting of thirty-two cremation chambers with a potential daily capacity in excess of 2,000 corpses from Topf of Erfut. The ovens were to be fired by wood instead of the normal coke. The first four chambers arrived on 30 December 1941. Was this crematorium intended for a huge death camp planned for Mogilew? What other explanation was there when the local Jewish population had been all but wiped out by then? As a result of events, these ovens were not eventually required, and the remaining undelivered components were redirected to Auschwitz.

Generalfeldmarschall Hermann Göring had lunch with Himmler on 2 July 1941. It is entirely feasible that the two men discussed the Jewish question. On 31 July 1941, Göring signed a letter to Heydrich, ordering him to find an end solution to the Jewish situation in Europe. This gave Himmler the authority for the SS to act as the sole responsible organisation for dealing with the Jews. Heydrich ordered Eichmann's IV B 4b office into action. Eichmann's deputy for Judicial Affairs, Claims and Damages, was Dr Friedrich Suhr.

Suhr was a legal expert on so-called 'atonement payments'. This euphemism first appeared after the Reichskrystalnacht of November 1938 when the decision was reached to get the Jews themselves to pay for the damage inflicted upon their property. He was born on 6 May 1907, in Lüneburg, and studied law at Göttingen and Freiburg Universities. He had been a member of the SS since 1 February 1933, but did not join the NSDAP until 1 May the same year. Suhr had often represented his former boss, Werner Best, after the latter's transfer to the military administration in France during 1940. From July 1941, Suhr was a department head in Eichmann's office, dealing with Jewish Affairs and Evacuation Matters. Suhr was almost certainly responsible for collating the Jewish population figures presented at Wannsee by Heydrich.

According to his wife, Suhr was transferred to the Eastern Front as a punishment duty for objecting to Eichmann's methods. There he commanded Sonderkommando 4b of Einsatzgruppe C, followed by command of Einsatzkommando 6. After his Einsatzgruppe service, he transferred to the west and finished the war on the staff of SSPF Upper Alsace. Former SS-Obersturmbannführer Dr Suhr took his own life in his cell at Bendahl Prison in Wuppertal-Elberfeld on 31 May 1946.

His role in the Jewish Holocaust cannot be underestimated. As a member of Eichmann's staff, he attended a meeting on 29 January 1942, at the Reich Ministry for the Occupied Eastern Territories (Rosenberg) at which the decision was reached to define a Jew. A Jew should be considered to belong to the Jewish religion, or to have at least one parent belonging to the Jewish religion. The slightest signs should be sufficient for Jewish religious affiliation. The category of 'half-breeds' was to be eliminated in the occupied eastern territories. Suhr also participated at meetings convened following decisions reached at the infamous Wannsee Conference of 20 January 1942.

Hitler 'went public' on 12 December 1941. At a meeting of Reichsleiter and Gauleiter, he announced the policy of physical Jewish extermination, again using ambiguous language.

On 16 December 1941, Dr Hans Frank held a high level conference in Krakow, attended by the district governors of the General Government. In his opening address, he informed them of the decision to kill all the Jews of the General Government. He did not use plain murder language, but his meaning was clearly understood by all present. He stated:

> We must put an end to the Jews, that I want to say quite openly. The Führer once spoke these words: if united Jewry should once more succeed in unleashing a world war, then the peoples who have been incited to this war will not be its only victims, because the Jew in Europe will also have found his end.... Before I continue to speak I would ask you to agree with me on the following principle: we want to have compassion only for the German people, otherwise for no one in the whole world. Others have had no compassion for us. As an old National Socialist, I must also say: if the Jewish tribe were to survive the war in Europe, while we had sacrificed our best blood for Europe's preservation, then this war would be only a partial success. Thus *vis-a-vis* the Jews I will in principle proceed only on the assumption that they will disappear. They must go. I have entered into negotiations for the purpose of deporting them to the east. In January, a large meeting will take place in Berlin on this topic, to which I will send State Secretary Dr Bühler. This meeting will be convened in the RSHA by SS-Obergruppenführer Heydrich. In any case a large migration of Jews will be set in motion.
>
> But what is to happen to the Jews? Do you believe that they will be lodged in settlements in the Ostland? In Berlin, we were told: why all this trouble, we cannot use them in the Ostland or the Reichskommissariat [Ukraine] either, liquidate them yourselves! Gentlemen, I must ask you, arm yourselves against any thoughts of compassion. We must destroy the Jews, wherever we encounter them and wherever it is possible, in order to preserve the entire structure of the Reich.... One cannot apply previous conceptions to such a gigantic, unique event. In any case we must find a way to achieve our goal.... The Jews represent for us also extraordinarily malignant gluttons. We have an estimated 2.5 million Jews in the GG, perhaps with the half-Jews

> and all that that entails some 3.5 million. We cannot shoot these 3.5 million, we cannot poison them, but nonetheless we will take some kind of action that will lead to a successful destruction, and indeed in conjunction with the important measures to be discussed in the Reich. The GG must become just as free of the Jews as the Reich.[11]

Himmler and Heydrich now had everything in place in order to carry out the systematic eradication of the Jews in the geographic sphere of influence exerted by the Third Reich. All they required now, before pressing the start button, was the tacit agreement of the pertinent Reich Ministries. To achieve this last goal, Heydrich issued invitations to a working lunch on 9 December 1941 at 56–58 Am Grossen Wannsee, in the Berlin suburb of Wannsee. The original date had to be postponed as a result of the USA entering the war, and the conference was rescheduled for 20 January 1942, at the same location.

Heydrich chaired the meeting, and presented an outline estimate of the total Jewish population in each European country. He included those unconquered by the German hordes. Eichmann was ordered to record the minutes and prepare copies in language that disguised the actual words used, but which gave a correct resumé of the facts whilst sanitising the true meaning. Heydrich's plan was to march columns of Jews eastward for road construction. He expected only the fit and healthy would survive, while the sick and disabled would fall by the wayside through natural wastage. Eichmann declared later that plain language of killing was used.

Dr Josef Bühler, the General Government State Secretary representing Frank, insisted that the final solution of the Jewish problem should start in the General Government. Heydrich obtained the ministerial agreement he sought, and immediately the meeting closed, he triumphantly informed Himmler. The way was now clear for Himmler's SS to take control of racial policy and to implement a solution as it saw fit.

By the summer of 1942, Himmler was secure in his position as the racial cleansing supremo. On 19 July 1942, he issued an order that sounded the death knell for the remaining Polish Jews:

> I herewith order that the resettlement of the entire Jewish population of the General Government be carried out and completed by 31 December 1942. From 31 December 1942, no persons of Jewish origin may remain within the General Government, unless they are in collection camps in Warsaw, Krakow, Czestochowa, Radom, and Lublin. All other work on which Jewish labour is employed must be finished by that date, or, in the event that this is not possible, it must be transferred to one of the collection camps.
>
> These measures are required with a view to the necessary ethnic division of races and peoples for the New Order in Europe, and also in the interests of the security and cleanliness of the German Reich and its sphere of interest. Every breach of

> this regulation spells a danger to quiet and order in the entire German sphere of interest, a point of application for the resistance movement and a source of moral and physical pestilence.
>
> For all these reasons, a total cleansing is necessary and therefore to be carried out. Cases in which the date set cannot be observed will be reported to me in time, so that I can see to corrective action at an early date. All requests by other offices for changes or permits for exceptions to be made must be presented to me personally.
>
> Heil Hilter!
> H. Himmler
> NO-5574.[12]

Hermann Höfle's office was upstairs in the former Stefan Batory College building in Lublin, now renamed the Julius Schreck SS Kaserne. His residential accommodation was located in the same premises, under the roof beams in the attic. Höfle supervised a small cadre of SS administration personnel, including the Einsatz Reinhardt personnel office, run by SS-Oberscharführer Willi Häusler.

According to Häusler's testimony on 23 May 1960, he had previously worked as a bookkeeper for T4 in Berlin and was not transferred to the staff of Einsatz Reinhardt until 1942:

> In Lublin I did my service in the office of Operation Reinhard. When referring to this office, people talked about it as Operation 'R'. It was in a barracks in Lublin. To speak more precisely, the office space was there. Housing was in a small villa near the barracks. Only Wirth and I worked in the office. I lived with Oberhauser in this villa. Oberhauser was Wirth's adjutant. Wirth was in command of a camp in the immediate area around Lublin. This was an internment or concentration camp. Wirth repeatedly visited different camps in the Lublin area. I remember the names Treblinka, Sobibor, Bełżec. I assume that these camps were under his command. I first discovered during my stay in Lublin that the last of these camps was one in which Jews were exterminated. Whenever Wirth drove to the extermination camps he was often accompanied by Oberhauser.[13]

As is the case with testimony provided by accused perpetrators in the post-war period, Häusler's evidence should be treated with caution. The vast majority of those interrogated made various attempts to distance themselves from the crimes committed. Häusler gives the impression that he suddenly discovered that Bełżec (and only Bełżec) was an extermination site. However, he drops his guard when describing the extermination camps in the plural being visited by Wirth and Oberhauser. The internment or concentration camp to which he refers is most likely the Alter Flugplatz camp.

The man chosen to command the first death camp in the General Government was Christian Wirth. He was experienced in gassing procedures during the T4 operation and was ideally suited for the job as a middle ranking police officer with exceptional organisational skills. A rabid Jew-hater and a diehard Nazi, he had few or no scruples that would interfere with the smooth running of Globocnik's plans.

Wirth was born on 24 November 1885 in Oberbalzheim, Württemberg, the son of a master cooper. His family followed the Evangelical faith. After an elementary school education from 1891 until 1899, Wirth learned the sawyer's craft on a course from 1899 until 1901. He was an apprentice carpenter with the Buhler Brothers timber firm in Oberbalzheim from 1901 until 1905. He enlisted in the Württemberg Grenadier Regiment 123 'König Karl' on 11 October 1905, and served until 23 September 1907. He was appointed as an instructor on 7 April 1908, until 6 April 1910. Wirth joined the police service in Heilbronn on 7 April 1910, but he soon transferred, first to Stuttgart-Cannstatt on 18 July 1910, and then to Büchsenstrasse, Stuttgart, where he became a criminal police detective on 17 July 1913.

On 5 November 1910, he married Marie Bantel, born 19 August 1888 in Ersingen. They had become engaged to marry on 18 May 1910. The union produced two healthy sons—Eugen was born on 22 May 1911 and Kurt on 22 September 1922—but the couple also lost two children. Frau Wirth died on 1 October 1979.

During the First World War, he volunteered as a non-commissioned officer with Reserve Infantry Regiment 246 in Ulm from 10 September 1914. He saw active service on the Western Front in Flanders; at Bellewaarde on 16 June 1915; the Somme; and Aisne-Champagne. He distinguished himself in battle, sustaining a wound to his upper right arm on 27 November 1914, and he was decorated. Wirth was awarded the Iron Cross 1st and 2nd Class, the Black Wound Badge, and the Württemberg Golden Military Service Medal. He was promoted to non-commissioned officer rank in 1915, and became a military police officer in December 1917 with the Replacement Battalion of Infantry Regiment 119 in Stuttgart. A fervent nationalist, Wirth was devastated by the defeat of Germany and attempted to shoot himself in his bedroom, but was prevented from doing so by his mother.

Discharged as a military policeman from the Army on 31 May 1919, Wirth returned to the Stuttgart police on 1 June 1919 as an acting Kriminalwachtmeister at Dienstelle 11, Büchsenstrasse 37, on the corner with Hospitalstrasse. It was nextdoor to the prison, known locally as 'the Grease Tin'. The original police office no longer exists. His rank as Kriminalwachtmeister was confirmed on 1 July 1919. A diligent detective, promotions quickly followed: Kriminalinspektor, 1 April 1920; Kriminalkommissar, 1 January 1923; and Kriminaloberkommissar, 1 October 1923. Wirth's unconventional methods of interrogation attracted attention, and on one occasion resulted in his arraignment before the Württemberg Landtag. This resulted in a reduction of two ranks to Kriminalinspektor on 1 November

1932. By 1 January 1938, Wirth was chief of Kriminal Kommissariat 5. In addition, he held senior posts in the Reichsverband der Kriminal Beamte Deutschland (1921–1933), the Kamaradschaftsbund Deutscher Polizei Beamte (1933–1939), the Landesbund Württemburg, the Amtes für Beamte der Fachschaft 9 Polizei, and the Amtes für Beamte Kreis Stuttgart. His last criminal investigation was a murder case in February 1939, which involved a serial sex murderer by the name of Johann Strössenreuther, who, having initially denied any wrongdoing, eventually admitted five murders. He was sentenced to beheading by the court in Kempton.

Wirth's police file describes him as 'tall and slim', but his height of 175 cm cannot be described as 'tall' by the standards of today. It also notes that he was in good health and of satisfactory stature. During the two years period from 1 April 1936 until 1 April 1938, he never reported sick for a single day. His reports show him to be mentally very agile and flexible, energetic, and very persistent, with a combination of good ability, general education, and expertise. His character was described as unblemished, impeccably professional, and morally reliable. There is a note that Wirth practised regularly with his service pistol. His leadership qualities were described as good and reasonable, suggesting that he possessed a reasonable attitude with his subordinates. The report, dated 30 May 1938, rounds off by stating that Wirth should be viewed as an example of a quality police officer.[14]

Wirth joined the NSDAP on 1 January 1931, but he had been an active member of the first Nazi Party cell outside of Bavaria from 1921 until 1924 when it was declared illegal. His NSDAP number was 420 383. He supported the German People's National Party in 1925. From 1 June 1933 until 1938, he was a member of the SA in Suttgart, attaining the rank of SA-Sturmführer on 9 November 1936, on the staff of SA-Sturm 119. From May 1934, he was active in the NSV—National Socialist Welfare Organisation. He was an Ortsgruppenleiter in the Kamaradschaftsbund of Ortsgruppe Stuttgart, and the equivalent of a shop steward for the Stuttgart NSDAP Kreisleitung. Wirth was recruited by the SD-Hauptstelle Stuttgart on 1 December 1937, and he was accorded the Allgemeine-SS rank of Untersturmführer on 10 August 1939. His SS number was 345 464. On 1 October 1939, he was promoted to SS-Obersturmführer.

He held the post of Head of Police Disciplinary Court from 28 February 1939 and was on attachment to the Gestapo in Vienna from 14 March 1939 on special inspection duties. This was followed by a special police duty attachment to the chief of SIPO and SD in Prague, from 15 July 1939, on the staff at Olomouc in Czechoslovakia. Wirth joined the SS on 10 August 1939 and was immediately promoted to SS-Untersturmführer. Three weeks later, he was elevated to SS-Obersturmführer. He was listed as a member of the Administrative and Legal Office of the RSHA in Berlin on 27 September 1939, following the reorganisation of that department. Although still posted to the police in Stuttgart, effectively he never worked for them again. Despite this, Wirth continued to gain police promotion within the criminal police department. Despite his nomination for promotion to SS-Sturmbannführer und Polizeimajor being rejected on grounds of insufficient service in his current rank on 30 January 1943, on 4 February 1943, well into his service in Poland, he was promoted to Kriminalrat by the State Criminal Police Office in Stuttgart. This police rank equates to the SS rank of Haupsturmführer. In a well-known photograph of Wirth, he is wearing rank insignia of a SS-Sturmbannführer. Although confusion reigns over Wirth's promotion to SS-Sturmbannführer, Himmler ordered his promotion on 12 February 1943 during a visit to Lublin. This was augmented on 17 March 1944, by the ward of the clasp to the Iron Cross 2nd Class on direct orders of Himmler.

At the end of 1939, Wirth, along with other Kripo police officers, was detached from the police for service with the T4 euthanasia programme. These police officers served as non-medical supervisors at the killing centres of the euthanasia programme, responsible for security measures. At the age of fifty-four, Wirth was one of the oldest personnel involved in T4. A memo from the office of the Police President of Stuttgart, dated 13 January 1941, states: 'Wirth was seconded to the Regional Institute Brandenburg by the Reich Criminal Police Office on 10 January 1940 for special duties. At present, he is Hauptmann of Police for carrying out a special mission in Linz'.[15] The memo finishes with the declaration that Wirth is an 'energetic, capable, reliable and well trained official who works with skill and untiring zeal for the service. His behaviour in and out of service is faultless. On the grounds of his abilities, his personality, his extraordinary ability … he is suitable'. High praise indeed.

Wirth initially set up administrative procedures at the euthanasia centre at Grafeneck Castle in Württemberg. Shortly afterwards, he was transferred as administrative director of the euthanasia facility at Brandenburg. The medical director there was Dr Irmfried Eberl.

First and foremost, Christian Wirth was a police officer. He committed man's greatest crime countless times, but believed it was lawful, acting on orders from the most senior authority. That he did not gain personally from his actions is extremely doubtful. He remained a committed Nazi and believed in Hitler and his cause, unswervingly to the end. Why was he chosen to administer such a dark and callous secret?

The answer almost certainly lies in geography. The planned programme of euthanasia was intended to commence at Grafeneck Castle in the German state of Württemberg. Research showed that the Swabian region in Württemberg had the highest instances of physical deformities and learning difficulties in Europe. The infant death rate, miscarriages, and stillbirths were also the highest in the German Reich. The Reich Chancellery had the location for its new policy, and where better than the selected region to find suitable personnel to execute it? Wirth himself was the tenth child in a family that suffered nine infant deaths before little Christian arrived and survived.

The next important aspect of his selection was his service record. Viktor Brack asked the Württemberg Ministry of the Interior to nominate a suitable police officer with excellent organisational and administrative skills for an important, but confidential post. He had to possess the ability to make decisions and display leadership qualities. Wirth was the obvious candidate. He had already gained a reputation as a leading detective, with twenty years' experience, and had attended an Interpol training course in Switzerland. Ironically, he was currently in charge of a serious crimes unit, specialising in murder and robbery.

In reply to Brack's enquiry, the Interior Ministry wrote:

> [Wirth is] an exceptionally capable, experienced and energetic criminal police officer who, is totally absorbed in his profession … a superior officer beyond reproach and is a generally good comrade who has attained well-deserved awards and promotions, thanks to his extraordinary professional ability, strength of personality, and his long years of service to the Party. His exemplary devotion to duty is stimulating.… He displays an outstanding will and personal toughness, has outstanding capabilities on duty, discipline and administration.… As a National Socialist police officer, Wirth has a clean, decent character, and an aggressive attitude.[16]

Some of this assessment is questionable. A 'good comrade'? His later colleagues would strongly disagree. Brack was suitably impressed, and no doubt summoned Wirth to Berlin in order to undergo the customary personal interview.

Wirth was present at the first gassing experiment in Brandenburg on 8 January 1940 when about eighteen to twenty patients were subjected to a gassing procedure using carbon monoxide bottled gas. The following day, Wirth personally gassed eight psychiatric patients himself, using the same apparatus. It was at Brandenburg that the idea to disguise the gas chamber as a shower room was first suggested and subsequently introduced. Wirth immediately displayed a total lack of compassion for the victims and he used any subterfuge to coax reluctant patients to their deaths.

Witnesses identified Wirth as being seen frequenting the offices of the Reich Chancellery over the following few weeks. On 4 February 1940, Wirth reported at Grafeneck wearing the police uniform of a Hauptmann, and for the remainder of his duty in the euthanasia programme, he wore only the green police uniform. Initially, his official position was registrar, in charge of security, but his enthusiasm soon gained him control of the entire administration of the castle. His responsibilities included all records, maintenance of secrecy, and the entire killing process. He soon displayed his violent temper when things did not run smoothly, and he quickly gained the reputation of an abusive bully; a figure of fear and hatred.

On 21 March 1941, with the personal recommendation of Reinhard Heydrich, Wirth was promoted to Kriminal Kommissar, ending his probationary period in that rank. Heydrich pointed out in his recommendation that Wirth 'was assured the personal protection of the Führer'. This effectively gave him *carte blanche* to do as he pleased.

He became a roving inspector of T4 centres and visited them all in order to sort out any problems. He temporarily transferred to Hadamar and then Hartheim, near Linz, as head of personnel and administration, with responsibility for security and discipline. He was unpopular and feared by all the staff for his course and brutal methods, regularly threatening his subordinates for breaches of security or any failure in procedures. His brutality extended also to the patients. On one occasion, four female inmates were suspected of contracting typhus and were incapable of walking to the gas chamber. Wirth shot them to simplify matters and to prevent any spread of the disease.[17] At Hartheim, one of his colleagues was Franz Stangl, the later commandant of Sobibor and Treblinka death camps. Interviewed by Gitta Sereny in 1971, Stangl described Wirth in the following terms:

> Wirth was a gross and florid man. My heart sank when I met him. He stayed at Hartheim for several days that time and often came back. Whenever he was there, he addressed us daily at lunch. And here it was again, this awful verbal crudity, when he spoke about the necessity of this euthanasia operation, he was not speaking in humane or scientific terms, the way Dr Werner at T4 had described it to me. He laughed; he spoke of 'doing away with useless mouths', and that 'sentimental slobber' about such people made him puke.[18]

Dr Georg Renno, at Hartheim, described Wirth:

> ... a conceited, self-opinionated ogre—an evil man, sadistic and violent, who at every opportunity harassed and tormented people. With his course voice and manners, he terrorised the staff to restore order. He did his best to set one against another. At the slightest misdemeanour or protest, his temper exploded. He was awful to his own men, a vulgar, horrible person, the evil spirit of Hartheim.[19]

In mid-1941, Wirth was involved in the euthanasia programme in western Poland. In late August 1941, he was transferred 'on loan' to Chełmno. He arrived in September to assist with the gassing of Jews and Gypsies there using gas vans. On 22 December 1941, Wirth arrived in Bełżec as the new camp commandant. After a final inspection of the camp facilities by SS-Hauptsturmführer Neumann of the Waffen-SS Construction Office in Lublin, Neumann and Thomalla transferred responsibility over to Wirth before leaving for the planned construction site at Sobibor. Wirth apparently went home for Christmas, before returning in early January 1942 with his new deputy commandant, Gottfried Schwarz, and Josef Oberhauser. The latter was given responsibility of supervising the approximately seventy Ukrainian guards from Trawniki who had arrived at Bełżec in late December. Wirth arrived in his car, at the head of a small convoy of three trucks which carried other T4 personnel, including Erich Fuchs, Siegfried Graetschus, Johann Niemann, and Werner Borowski. They were soon joined by Kurt Franz, Erwin Fichtner, and Heinrich Barbl.[20]

With regard to Wirth's transfer from T4 to Aktion Reinhardt, Dr Bodo Gorgass stated in 1947: 'Police Captain Wirth, whom I knew personally and who was administrative director in several euthanasia institutions, told me late in summer 1941, that he had been transferred by the "foundation" to a Euthanasia institute in the Lublin area'.[21] Wirth came to the conclusion that the exhaust emitted from a heavy duty combustion engine was preferable to the carbon monoxide gas produced by chemical firms and supplied in large heavy metal bottles. Transporting these bottles could arouse suspicion and the empty containers still had to be transported back to the suppliers for refilling. There was also the risk of a breakdown in supplies. Combustion engine exhaust could be produced on site, without the need for storage and transportation. Petrol and diesel were readily available.

Prior to Bełżec becoming operational on 17 March 1942, Wirth carried out experiments to determine the most efficient method of receiving and processing the transports of Jews, from the time of their arrival at the camp, until their murder and burial. He developed some basic concepts for the process of extermination and for camp organisation. These would be adopted in other death camps. The configuration of the camp, and the various procedures the victims were forced to do as soon as they left the train were intended to ensure that they would believe they had arrived in a labour or transit camp, not delivered for liquidation. The gas chambers were camouflaged as baths.

The second principle of the extermination procedure was it should be carried out with the utmost rapidity. The deportees should be rushed, made to run, so that they had no time to look round, to reflect, or to understand what was going on. This also supported the basic principle of deceipt. Any sign of reluctance or resitance must be brutally dealt with immediately in order to prevent a spread of rebellion or an explosion of defiance. The speed of the extermination process served yet a further purpose, in that it increased the killing capacity of the camp. More transports could be brought and processed in one day.

Wirth ordered his staff to use whips and vicious dogs to create panic and to drive the victims onward. According to Wirth's annihilation strategy, the Jews themselves should carry out all physical work involved in the extermination process of a transport. The death camp Sonderkommando was born, a child of Wirth's fertile mind.

Fellow T4 man Erich Fuchs, a civilian driver and mechanic prior to his service at Bełżec, described his impression of Wirth from his brief interaction with him during T4 and at Bełżec:

> Polizeihauptmann Christian Wirth conducted the actions in Bernburg. Subordinate to him were the burners, disinfectors and drivers. He also supervised the transportation of the mentally ill and of the corpses. One day in the winter of 1941, Wirth arranged a transport to Poland. I was picked together with about eight or ten other men and transferred to Bełżec.... I don't remember the names of the others. Upon our arrival in Bełżec, we met Friedel Schwarz [*sic.*] and the other SS men, whose names I cannot remember. They supervised the construction of barracks that would serve as a gas chamber. Wirth told us that in Bełżec 'all the Jews will be struck down'. For this purpose, barracks were built as gas chambers. I installed shower heads in the gas chambers. The nozzles were not connected to any water pipes; they would serve as camouflage for the gas chamber. For the Jews who were gassed it would seem as if they were being taken to baths and for disinfection.[22]

Wirth held no respect for his staff and never attempted to engender a feeling of comradeship between his men. Despite this, many of the Aktion Reinhardt staff remember a comradely attitude between Wirth's subordinates. This never included Wirth himself. When SS-Scharführer Hans Girtzig was appointed quartermaster to Reinhardt, Girtzig insists it was only after his posting that he became fully aware of Bełżec's purpose. When Wirth ordered him to the ramp to unload Jewish resettlement transports, Girtzig states he refused. Wirth detained him at gunpoint, restricted him to his quarters under guard, and threatened to send him to a concentration camp. Girtzig complained to Dieter Allers who was visiting the site. Allers advised Girtzig to hold on, as he said Wirth would be leaving the camp very shortly. In August 1942, Wirth was appointed inspector of all Aktion Reinhardt camps by Globocnik. Wirth's new official title in this capacity was Abteilung Reinhardt Inspekteur des SS-Sonderkommandos beim SSPF Lublin. He was replaced as commandant of Bełżec by Gottlieb Hering.

SS-Unterscharführer Franz Suchomel testified about Wirth:

> From my activity in the camps of Treblinka and Sobibor, I remember that Wirth in brutality, meanness, and ruthlessness could not be surpassed. We therefore called him 'Christian the Terrible' or 'The Wild Christian'. The Ukrainian guardsmen called him 'Stuka'. The brutality of Wirth was so great that I personally see it as a perversity. I remember particularly that on each occasion, Wirth lashed Ukrainian guardsmen with the whip he always kept...[23]

When in Lublin town, Wirth used a house opposite the offices of the SSPF Lublin. Today, the building still exists, but it is in urgent need of renovation.

Wirth was appointed as inspector of SS-Sonderkommando Aktion Reinhardt on 1 August 1942 and Gottlieb Hering, a Kriminalsekretär from the Stuttgart Police and a former colleague of Wirth, replaced him as commandant of Bełżec. Wirth took two rooms at the Julius Schreck Barracks as temporary offices. Josef Oberhauser, Wirth's immediate aide, also gained extra responsibilities. These two were joined by a third new member, sent from T4 in Berlin, Willi Häusler. Häusler was an accountant by profession and his new role incorporated the salaries of Aktion Reinhardt personnel, in addition to staffing matters such as leave, transfers in and out, and sick reports. He would accompany Wirth to the various Reinhardt sites in the General Government in order to pay the staff wages. During these visits, he also participated in discussions on management problems with the camp commandants. Häusler subsequently declared that the orders for Reinhardt came from T4 and not from Globocnik's office. They were delivered by courier in a sealed metal box and only Wirth or Oberhauser were authorised to open it. According to Häusler's account, the Reinhardt staff were segregated from other SS personnel, even to the extent that they were forbidden the use of the SS canteen.

At least one SS member of Aktion Reinhardt took his own life under the brutal administration of Wirth. Erwin Krainer had worked at Hadamar and was transferred to Poland. Wirth ordered Krainer to form a Jewish work brigade and clean up the mountain of rotting corpses left by Eberl's mismanagement. Krainer refused and was sent to Sachsenhausen concentration camp for six weeks. He ended up shooting himself out of desperation and fear of Wirth. The pile of bodies was eventually dealt with by Wirth himself, assisted by some staff from Bełżec.

Soon after his arrival at Treblinka, Wirth ordered new larger gas chambers to replace the original inadequate facilities. He placed Heinrich Matthes and August Miete in charge of the new building, and introduced whips to be carried by all SS NCOs. Wirth himself often toured the camp on horseback. He loved riding and kept three horses in the stable at Treblinka. His visits to all the camps produced panic among the SS and Ukrainian staff, who could be seen scurrying about on the days of his visits. Wirth was escorted on his outings by a troop of around ten men, usually from Police Regiment 25, acting as bodyguards. This was particularly necessary in the area around Sobibor where the partisans were especially active.

Upon his appointment as inspector of the German Equipment Works (Deutsche Ausrüstungswerke—DAW) in December 1942, Wirth and Oberhauser moved their office setup to a two-storey building on ul. Chelmska, at the south-west corner of the former Lublin airfield, adjacent to the railway link between Lemberg and Warsaw. The DAW had facilities at Trawniki, Poniatowa, Dorohucza, Budzyn, and the Lublin Airfield camp, where new timber barracks were erected east of the factory buildings. At the Lublin airfield location, the Jewish prisoners were employed sorting the textiles and items of less value. This location was previously used to greet new T4 staff on their arrival in Lublin. They congregated at the airfield where they were greeted by Wirth and one or more of the camp commandants. The last and greatest group of newcomers to assemble here was in early July 1942. Many of them had no formal military training, so they were posted initially to Trawniki.

Wirth's new office building at ul. Chelmska comprised of offices on the ground floor, occupied by Wirth, Oberhauser, Häusler, and two female secretaries from T4. On the first floor, living quarters for Wirth and his staff were located, in addition to a good-quality dining room, which had previously been frequented by SS officers from the Majdanek camp. Globocnik entertained Himmler to lunch here on 21 August 1942.[24] The elegant dining room was later described by one guest, Erich Bauer: 'I remember this dining room because I was once invited there to dine. The serving staff were several young pretty Jewesses, dressed as real waitresses with white aprons … one had the impression of dining in the best hotel'.[25]

Until Wirth's arrival at the airfield complex, the camp had been administered by SS-Stubaf. Josef Obermeier, not to be confused with Josef Oberhauser, and his deputy, SS-Oberscharf Birmes. The two men did not get on as Obermeier was appalled at Wirth's brutality towards the Jewish workers.

Disinfection of the clothing was carried out using Zyklon B crystals in a concrete bunker near the end of the railway ramp, and another concrete building inside a timber barrack. Jews who fell ill, or who were considered no longer capable of work, were gassed by Heinrich Birmes in these structures, using Zyklon B. Subsequently, Lorenz Hackenholt used these to gas Jews following his transfer to the airfield.

The process of sorting began with separating the men, women, and children's clothing into piles. Footwear was placed in a separate pile. The clothes were then searched methodically for valuables, which were placed in six or seven large wooden crates. Each evening at 6 p.m., the valuables crates were carried to Wirth's office. There was no system of recording each item, and pilfering was rife among the SS and Ukrainian personnel. From Wirth's office, the valuables were transported to Georg Wippern's office at the SS-Standortverwaltung, where it was recorded and stored for onward transportation to Berlin.

One innovation of Wirth was to rename the sorting depot as the Used Materials Administration Depot of the SS Garrison Administration of Lublin (Altsachverwaltungsstelle der SS-Standortverwaltung Lublin). This move was probably forced upon him by Globocnik as it meant surrendering the airfield complex to the command of Wippern.

By March 1943, Wirth had supervised the complete transition of the sorting depot at the airfield to a highly organised enterprise. By early June, around 50 per cent of the airfield prisoners were employed by the Ostindustrie. Wirth was officially appointed as commandant of the Lublin Airfield camp, including the Reinhardt sorting complex in the former hangars, on 3 June 1943.

Wirth worried that the mounds of clothing that accumulated in Bełżec harboured lice and fleas, which were the cause of outbreaks of disease in the camp, mainly typhus. He complained to Globocnik who arranged for Dr Kurt Gerstein, an expert on disinfection from the SS Hygiene Department to visit Lublin (see Appendix X). Gerstein's advice was to spray the mounds of clothing with Detanoline as a temporary measure, until sufficient quantities of Zyklon B could be obtained to enable proper disinfection. Wirth had the piles of clothing moved to the old locomotive shed on the main railway line where they were sprayed with the chemical. He also ordered the spraying of the barracks. Fastidious as ever, Wirth also ensured the camp was thoroughly cleaned each evening.

The first high-profile figure to visit Bełżec was SS-Brigadeführer Dr Hans Kammler on 16 June 1942. Wirth went to extraordinary lengths to impress his visitor, including issuing new uniforms to the SS and Ukrainian contingents, and arranging for Jewish work Kommandos to clean the route he would take to the camp. Kammler was escorted by a protection unit from Police Regiment 25 under the command of Oberstleutnant Hermann Kientrupp. Wirth was aware of Kammler's role in the expansion of Auschwitz-Birkenau and the construction of new crematoria. The purpose of Kammler's visit remains a mystery. Wirth made himself available to greet every important visitor to his camps, and he ensured that he personally accompanied them on their inspection tours. Globocnik apparently visited his camps at least once every three months.

There is a recorded visit to Sobibor by Himmler on 12 February 1943. Karl Frenzel was given the responsibility of securing the camp perimeter for the visit. Himmler witnessed the gassing of 300 Jewish women in Camp III, followed by the cremation process. The party was then treated to a banquet in the SS dining room. Himmler ordered the speeding up of the whole process, and as a result, Wirth arranged for SS-Hauptscharführer Johann Niemann's transfer from Bełżec to Sobibor. Obviously satisfied with the whole operation, Himmler promoted Wirth and the three camp commandants soon after, referring to them as 'the commanders at the forefront of the operation in Aktion Reinhardt'.[26]

Christian Wirth was both hated and feared by all under his command. He was not averse to the use of his fists or his whip on his own men. He maintained that he ill-treated his men to preserve discipline. It was suggested that, had any of his subordinates the courage to kill him, as many wished him dead, Aktion Reinhardt would not have been so successful in its aims; no other figure possessed the attributes to efficiently and heartlessly carry out the tasks demanded. Under Globocnik, Wirth really was the 'face of Aktion Reinhardt'.

It is worth highlighting here that Aktion Reinhardt was not restricted to Globocnik's area of Lublin District alone. Certainly, Treblinka was sited roughly midway between the major ghetto cities of Bialystock and Warsaw, on the main railway line. This was not an *ad hoc* choice for the location of a death camp. It was positioned for the sole purpose of liquidating both ghettos. Reinhardt also extended south-east, into the district of Galicia. An interesting document was presented at Nuremberg—a report to Friedrich-Wilhelm Krüger on the operation in Galicia. Major Walsh, of the prosecution team, quoted from the report:

> Since we received more and more alarming reports on the Jews becoming armed in an ever increasing manner, we started during the last fortnight in June 1943, an action throughout the whole of the District of Galicia, with the intention of using the strongest measures to destroy the Jewish gangsterdom ... [we] had to act brutally from the beginning in order to avoid losses on our side. We had to blow up or burn down several houses ... the surprising fact arose that we were able to catch about 20,000 Jews instead of the 12,000 who had registered. We had to pull at least 3,000 Jewish corpses out of every kind of hiding place; they had committed suicide by taking poison.
>
> Despite the extraordinary burden heaped upon every single SS police officer during these actions, the mood and spirit of the men were extraordinarily good and praiseworthy....
>
> Together with the evacuation action we executed the confiscation of Jewish property. Very high amounts were confiscated and paid over to the Sonderkommando Reinhard. Apart from furniture and many textile goods, the following amounts were turned over...

There followed a list of property, which included golden rings, complete stamp collections, pocket knives, fountain pens, propelling pencils, and furs. Major Walsh added that even 11.73 kg of gold teeth and inlays had been looted from the defenceless people.[27]

# 12

# BEŁŻEC

UNTIL THIS POINT, the sites used for gassing victims outside the Reich relied upon mobility. Gas vans and gas trailers could be transported from one location to another. However, Globocnik discounted the use of gas vans or the alternative method of shooting. He considered that, in order to submit large numbers of people to 'special handling', static sites were required that would cope with ever-increasing numbers. A necessity was an operational rail link, which could deliver the 'raw material', as Heydrich put it euphemistically, to the given point for processing. To maintain an element of secrecy, the sites had to be in rural, underpopulated locations. The village of Bełżec was such a place, but it was not the only site considered. Plans were also in evidence to erect static gas chambers at Chełmno, Sobibor, and Riga, in addition to the huge death camp intended for Mogilew. Globocnik ordered Richard Thomalla to inspect the sites at Bełżec and Sobibor for suitability.

Richard Thomalla was born on 23 October 1903 in Sabine-bei- Annahof (today, Sowin in Polish Silesia) in the Falkenberg District of Upper Silesia. A builder by profession, he was bilingual in German and Polish. He joined the *SS* on 1 July 1932, and the NSDAP a month later. On 5 October 1935, he married Margarete Bruckner. He served his military draft in Falkenberg and Oppeln, followed by service in the SS in Wohlau (Wolow) and Breslau (Wroclaw).

On 6 September 1940, Thomalla was transferred from Breslau to the General Government where he was a member of the *SS-Hilfspolizei (*auxiliary police) in the cities of Czestochowa and Radom. On 22 August 1940, he was transferred by Friedrich-Wilhelm Krüger, *HSSPF Ost,* for service under Globocnik in Lublin District. From August–October 1940, Thomalla was a Section Leader of the *SS* Border Defence Construction Service (*SS-Grenzschutz Baudienst*) in Bełżec. His first task was the establishment of a construction depot of the *Waffen-SS* and Police in Zamość. Thomalla maintained a construction office in Zamość where he spent most of his time.

After the German invasion of Russia, Thomalla was also in charge of constructing SS and Police Strongpoints in the Ukraine, with branch offices in Zwiahel and Kiev. He was recalled to Lublin in late 1941 to supervise the construction of the death camp in Bełżec, which commenced on 1 November 1941. He also oversaw the design and construction of the other two *Aktion Reinhardt* extermination camps at Sobibor and Treblinka, which were both based upon the prototype camp at Bełżec, but with improvements. Both gassing facilities were this time constructed of bricks and mortar—an improvement over the timber construction of the gassing building at Bełżec. The death chambers at Treblinka were designed to be a much larger scale, with an increased capacity. As such, he was the senior SS officer at each respective site until the camps became operational. At Sobibor, one of the Polish railway workers, Jan Piwonski, later recalled: 'The next day a German SS officer who spoke very good Polish came to the station cafeteria. He came from Poznan or Silesia. When the woman behind the counter asked him what was being built there, he replied that she would find out soon enough'.[1]

Erwin Lambert later recollected:

> Hengs [T4 man] and I went to Treblinka by car. SS-Hauptsturmführer Richard Thomalla was the camp commander. The Treblinka camp was still in the process of construction. Thomalla was in Treblinka for about four to eight weeks. I was attached to a building team there. Thomalla was there for a limited time only and conducted the construction work of the extermination camp. During that time, no extermination actions were carried out. Then Dr Eberl arrived as camp commander. Under his direction the extermination actions of the Jews began.[2]

In 1943, Thomalla headed *Waffen-SS* construction offices in Riga and Mogilew. Later, during 1943–1944, Thomalla also played a role in the 'pacification' operation of the SS and police in the Zamość district. Thomalla was last seen in Zamość in June 1944. He was arrested by the Russian forces near Jicin, on the Czechoslovakian side of the Czech–Polish border. He was held in a special prison nearby for members of the SS and Nazi Party officials at Karthaus–Walditz (Kartouzy–Vladice). On 12 May 1945, Thomalla was ordered out of his cell with his belongings. It is believed he was executed later that day.

Thomalla arrived in Bełżec in late October 1941, accompanied by SS-Hauptscharführer Gottfried Schwarz and SS-Oberscharführer Josef Oberhauser. They selected a site for the camp on the north side of the road between Zamość and Lvov, approximately 500 metres south-east from the Bełżec railway station. The rail line ran past the camp site. Bełżec was a small hamlet with a sparse population, situated approximately 70 miles south-east of Lublin as the crow flies. A labour camp for construction of Globocnik's defensive tank ditch had been in existence in the Bełżec vicinity since early 1940. The selected site was more than adequate for Globocnik's purpose and some existing buildings were incorporated into the camp design.

Local craftsmen and labourers were selected by the mayor, Ludwig Obalek, for the camp construction. All the workmen were local Polish men and Obalek was able to name them individually post-war. The first buildings erected were three barracks, with a walkway between two and the third. The third barrack housed the future gas chambers.

The gassing barrack consisted of three separate chambers, with an internal corridor running the length of all three, providing access to each chamber separately through three doors. The three chambers each had its own exit doorway onto a wooden platform running the length of the building, outside on the opposite side to the building entrance and access walkway. The platform was about 1 metre off the ground, and beside it was a small narrow-gauge rail track of the type found in coalmine pit faces. All six chamber doors were of sturdy construction and had rubber gaskets to seal them shut. The building was 12 metres long by 8 metres wide, and each internal chamber was 6 metres by 4 metres, with a height of 2 metres. The building walls were constructed of double boards, with sand poured in between each layer. The interior walls were covered with tarpaper and sheets of zinc. Zinc sheets were also covering the floor. There were no windows. Each door was 1.8 metres high and 1.10 metres wide. All doors opened outwards and were very strong, made from boards 7 cm thick. The doors were secured with heavy wooden locking crossbars, which fitted into large metal hooks on either side. As in the T4 euthanasia gas chambers, each chamber was served by a pipe at a height of 10 cm, hidden under benching against the wall. Another pipe was attached to the wall, at a height of 1 metre, with an elbow joint.[3]

The other buildings were almost certainly living accommodation for Jewish prisoners and the undressing barrack for the deportees, before being herded into the walkway. While the local Polish workmen were busy erecting the barracks, Ukrainians built the dense double barbed-wire fencing perimeter, surrounding the site. Once operational, a local railway engine driver, Michael Kusmierczak, enjoyed limited access to the camp. He befriended the Ukrainian guards who told him that the Jews were being killed with exhaust fumes from a 250-hp engine (some witnesses described it as a more feasible 350-hp engine), which was located a few metres from the gassing barrack.[4]

For the Kommandantur, Wirth commandeered a residential detached house on the road towards the railway station, about 250 metres west from the ramp. He used this building as his office and living quarters. The building still exists today.

Gottlieb Hering was no great improvement on Wirth. Hering was born and raised in Warmbronn, a district in the town of Leonberg. In 1915, he enlisted in the machine-gun company of Grenadier Regiment 123 and saw active service on the Western Front, attaining the rank of Feldwebel. He was awarded the Iron Cross 1st Class. After the First World War, Hering began his police career in 1919 as a detective sergeant in the criminal police investigation department in Göppingen, near Stuttgart. In 1920, Hering joined the Social Democratic Party. During the Weimar Republic he initiated vigorous actions against the NSDAP, SA, and SS and consequently was referred to as a 'Nazi-eater'. In 1933, local Nazis vehemently demanded Hering's dismissal from the police. However, Hering had known ardent Nazi Christian Wirth professionally since 1912. While working in the Kripo in Stuttgart, the two became acquaintances. Hering was able to continue working, despite the protests of local SA and SS men. In May 1933, Hering finally joined the NSDAP. In 1934, he was appointed head of the Göppingen Kripo and then transferred to Stuttgart-Schwenningen in 1939. After the outbreak of the Second World War, Hering, was posted to Gotenhafen (today, Gdynia). He was tasked with the resettling of Volksdeutsche to the General Government. From late 1940, Hering held various functions within the Action T4 programme. He was transferred to work at the Sonnenstein Euthanasia Centre. Hering served as an assistant supervisor. After Sonnenstein, Hering became the office manager at Hartheim Euthanasia Centre. He also worked in the special registry offices at Bernburg and Hadamar. Following his T4 service, Hering was posted briefly to the SD in Prague in June 1942, before being transferred to Aktion Reinhardt in Lublin. He replaced Christian Wirth as commandant of Bełżec extermination camp in August 1942, and served as the camp commandant until its closure in June 1943. Himmler was impressed by his visit to the Reinhardt camps in March 1943, and Hering was promoted to the rank of SS-Hauptsturmführer.

SS-Scharführer Heinrich Unverhau, who served at Bełżec, testified about him: 'Hering and Wirth were definitely wicked people, and the whole staff of the camp was afraid of them.... I heard that Hering shot two Ukrainian guards who expressed their dissatisfaction with what was going on in Bełżec'.[5] Camp survivor Rudolf Reder wrote of Hering's role in the killing of Jews:

> We knew that in the most beautiful house close to the station of Bełżec lived the commander of the camp.... He seldom was present in the camp and came only in connection with some event. He was a tall bully, broad shouldered, age around forty, with an expressionless face. He seemed to me as if he were a born bandit. Once, the gassing engine stopped working. When he was informed, he arrived astride a horse, ordered the engine to be repaired and did not allow the people in the gas chambers to be removed. He let them strangle and die slowly for a few hours more. He yelled

> and shook with rage. In spite of the fact that he came only on rare occasions, the SS men feared him greatly. He lived alone, with his Ukrainian orderly who served under him. This Ukrainian submitted to him the daily reports.[6]

Tadeusz Miziewicz, a Pole who lived in the village of Bełżec and worked at the railway station, testified about Hering on 15 October 1945:

> Once the major [*sic.*], the commander of Bełżec death camp, invented a new type of entertainment: he tied a Jew with a rope to his car; the Jew was forced to run behind the car and behind them ran the major's dog and bit the Jew. The major rode from the camp to the water pump, which was in Bełżec on Tomaszowska Street, and back. What happened to this Jew I do not know. This event was witnessed by the people of Bełżec.[7]

After the closure of Bełżec in June 1943, Hering was the commandant of the Poniatowa concentration camp, designated a sub-camp of Majdanek from September 1943. Globocnik conducted an inspection of the camp in August 1943, and he was dissatisfied with Hering's methods. A stricter regime was introduced, with an acceleration in executions. On 3–4 November 1943, German police massacred the remaining Jews at Poniatowa during Aktion Erntefest. Hering then transferred to Trieste. On 9 October 1945, Hering died of mysterious complications in the waiting room of St Catherine's Hospital in Stetten im Remstal.

Bełżec became operational on 17 March 1942 with the arrival of the first deportation transport from Lublin. This turn of events developed from a visit by Himmler to the General Government from 13 March 1942 until 15 March. Himmler discussed the security situation in preparation for the deportation of the Lublin Jews at meetings with Frank and Krüger in Krakow on 13 March, followed by further discussions on 14 March with Krüger, Schöngarth, and Scherner. Himmler had lunch with Frank before heading to Lublin where he visited the DAW factory. He had dinner with Globocnik at 8 p.m. prior to a meeting at 9.30 p.m. with Krüger, Wendler, Globocnik, Meyer-Hetling, Lechler, and Krug. He then stayed the night at Globocnik's villa and returned to Berlin on 15 March.[8]

Himmler reported to Hitler at the Wolfsschanze on 17 March 1942, the day upon which the first transport arrived at Bełżec. Unusually, he spent the whole afternoon and evening with Hitler.[9]

The ramp area at the camp was limited, so only one goods train at a time was allowed to use the rail spur. In addition, only a select few of locomotive drivers had permission to enter the camp. This resulted on occasions in trains having to 'queue' outside. Stefan Kirsz, a Polish railway worker, subsequently described the scene:

> As a co-driver of a locomotive, I led the Jewish transports from the station of Rava-Russkaya to Bełżec many times.... These transports were divided in Bełżec into three parts. Each part, which consisted of twenty freight trains, was taken to the railway spur inside the camp pushed by the locomotive, and stopped near the former border wall of 1939–1940. Immediately after the freight cars stopped inside the camp, they were emptied of Jews and their luggage. I saw that in addition to the living, corpses were taken out.... The Germans did not allow us to watch the camp, but I was able to see it when I approached the camp and deceptively pretended that I must put the coal closer to the entrance gate.[10]

Each freight car contained many dead. Those sick or injured were thrown into the wagons at the point of departure. The weakest often did not survive the journey. Those that had already died before being loaded were also thrown into the freight cars. There were no sanitary facilities and some died of suffocation during the journey through overcrowding.

On arrival, the deportees were herded into Camp I, which served as the reception area, and then segregated into sexes. The children stayed with the women. Wirth usually gave an address, reassuring the deportees that the camp in which they now found themselves was a transit camp, where they would be showered and re-clothed before being sent on to their final destination, a work camp further east. They were then ordered to undress. SS-Unterscharführer Karl Schluch testified on 11 November 1961, as follows:

> In the morning, or noon time, we were informed by Wirth, Schwartz [*sic.*], or by Oberhauser that a transport with Jews should arrive soon.... The disembarkation from the freight cars was carried out by a group of Jewish prisoners under the command of their capos. Two or three Germans from the camp staff supervised this action. It was my obligation to carry out such supervisions. After the disembarkation, the Jews were taken to the assembly square. During the disembarkation, the Jews were told that they had come here for transfer and they should go to baths and disinfection. This announcement was made by Wirth and translated by a Jewish capo.[11]

Kurt Franz, the last commandant of Treblinka, also confirms the deceipt practised by Wirth at Bełżec:

> I heard with my own ears how Wirth, in a quite convincing voice, explained to the Jews that they would be deported further and before that, for hygienic reasons, they must bathe themselves and their clothes would have to be disinfected. Inside the undressing barrack was a counter for the deposit of valuables. It was made clear to the Jews that after the bath their valuables would be returned to them. I can still hear,

> until today, how the Jews applauded Wirth after his speech. This behaviour of the Jews convinces me that the Jews believed Wirth...[12]

The men were first to enter the gas chambers as they were considered a greater potential threat of resistance. While the men were being killed, the women received haircuts. After the death chambers had been emptied and superficially cleaned, the naked women and children were pushed towards them along a pathway. This short route was euphemistically called 'the tube'. It was fenced and camouflaged with branches. Karl Schluch provided a description of the procedure:

> After the Jews entered the gas chambers, the doors were closed by Hackenholt himself or by the Ukrainian subordinate to him. Then Hackenholt switched on the engine which supplied the gas. After five or seven minutes—and this is only an estimate—someone looked through the small window into the gas chamber to verify whether all inside were dead. Only then were the outside doors opened and the gas chambers ventilated.... After the gas chambers were ventilated, the Jewish Work Kommando under the leadership of a Kapo and removed the corpses out of the chamber. Occasionally, I had to supervise at this place; therefore, I can describe the whole process, which I saw and witnessed personally.... The Jews inside the gas chambers were densely packed. This is the reason that the corpses were not lying on the floor but were mixed up in disorder in all directions, some of them kneeling, according to the amount of space they had. The corpses were besmirched with mud and urine or with spit. On the corpses, I could partially see that lips and also nose tips had a bluish discoloration. Some of them had their eyes closed, others' eyes rolled. The bodies were dragged out of the gas chambers and inspected by a dentist, who removed finger rings and gold teeth.... After this procedure, the corpses were thrown into a big pit.[13]

A further description of the murder process at Bełżec is provided by the Gerstein Report, and it is this version to which most historical studies of Bełżec refer. Kurt Gerstein was born on 11 August 1905, in Münster, the sixth of seven children. His father, Ludwig, was a former Prussian Army officer and a judge. The young Kurt rebelled against his authoritarian father and had a 'distant' relationship with his mother. His teachers described him as lazy. Despite this, he attended Marburg University in 1925 and then graduated from the University of Aachen as an engineer in 1931.

Although devoutly religious, he joined the NSDAP on 2 May 1933 and then the SA. His religious beliefs prevented his support of much of the Nazi policy. In 1935, he was physically attacked after protesting at a performance of an anti-Christian play by Edmund Kiss. This incident did little to dissuade him from voicing his feelings when the Nazis denigrated the Church. In 1936, he was arrested for possession of anti-Nazi literature and he lost his job. He strongly considered the church as a career, but chose to study medicine at the Protestant Missions Institute.

Kurt Gerstein married his long-term fiancée, Elfriede Bensch, on 31 August 1937. He continued his anti-Nazi work and in 1938, he was arrested and sent to a concentration camp. He was released after six months, owing to lack of evidence. With the help of the son of Hugo Stinnes, he got a job in a potassium mine in Thuringia.

In 1941, Gerstein's sister-in-law, Bertha Ebeling, became a victim of the euthanasia programme. Gerstein responded by joining the Waffen-SS in order to try to change the policies and to publicise the crimes being committed. In a letter to his wife, he told her that he had joined the SS as an 'agent of the Confessing Church'. Gerstein later claimed he was working for Martin Niemöller.

Gerstein was posted to the *SS-Führungshauptamt, Amtsgruppe D, Sanitätswesen der* Waffen-SS *Abteilung Hygiene*. While there, he designed a water filter for German troops. He constructed mobile and stationary disinfection facilities for the troops, for POW camps, and concentration camps. With this success, he was henceforth considered as a kind of technical expert. During 1941, he was able to control an epidemic of typhus in the camps. In January 1942, he was promoted and became head of the Technical Disinfection Service under the Reichsarzt-SS und Polizei, where he worked with highly toxic poisons. He was then promoted again to SS-Obersturmführer. He visited several concentration camps to examine the possibility of using the crystals of potassium cyanide, Zyklon B, on the inmates and supplied Höss at Auschwitz with canisters of Zyklon B from the Degesch company.

Kurt Gerstein visited the Lublin District with Professor Pfannensteil and was ordered to Bełżec to meet with Christian Wirth on 17 August 1942. While there, he witnessed the murder of an entire trainload of Jews from Lvov numbering some 3,000 souls (see Appendix X).

Gerstein later told a friend: 'One could tell families even in death. They were still holding hands, stiffened in death so that it was difficult to tear them apart to clear the chamber for the next load'. Gerstein was then shown how the bodies were processed:

> With gold to the left—without gold to the right.… Dentists hammered out gold teeth, bridges and crowns. In the midst of them stood Captain Wirth. He was in his element and, showing me a large can full of teeth. He said, '*See for yourself the weight of that gold! It's only from yesterday and the day before. You can't imagine what we find every day—dollars, diamonds, gold. You'll see for yourself!*'[14]

Kurt Gerstein voluntarily surrendered to French forces in Reutlingen on 22 April 1945. The following month, he was interviewed by Major D. C. Evans of the British

Army and Major John W. Haught of the US Army. He stated he had been present at meetings that dealt with the fate of prisoners in the concentration camps. When asked whether he was familiar with the use of gas chambers for killing prisoners, he replied that, as an engineer, he had often been called upon to advise on the workings of these installations. In June 1945, he was taken to Paris and held in the Cherche-Midi Military Prison as a war criminal. Gerstein was found dead in his cell on 25 July 1945. He appeared to have torn a strip from his thin blanket and committed suicide.

The first mass deportations to the Bełżec death factory were from Lublin and Lvov. The widely accepted date for the first large scale gassing is 17 March 1942, but it is possible that a transport of fifteen freight wagons reached Bełżec on 15 March.[15]

The arrival of the freight trains was prenotified to the Kommandantur, usually by telephone. The organisation of transports was collated by the RSHA in consultation with the AR office in Lublin. Therefore, it can be readily assumed that the notification call would come from a RSHA office. The Kommandantur at Bełżec then notified the camp gatehouse NCO. On arrival, the NCO signalled the locomotive to halt just outside the camp entrance, so that the required number of wagons was alongside a contingent of Ukrainian guards. The Jewish Sonderkommando then started the unloading process. Anyone unable to alight from the wagons was carried out by the Sonderkommando. Corpses were taken direct to a mass grave. The SS NCOs then checked each freight car to ensure it was empty. Anyone caught hiding inside was shot immediately or beaten to death by the Ukrainians. The empty wagons were then shunted back to the railway station and the camp gates were closed.

The sick, disabled, and elderly were often sent direct to the Lazaret, an area designed to resemble a makeshift field hospital where they were shot and unceremoniously dumped in a mass grave. In the first phase at Bełżec, these executions were probably carried out at the side of several small mass gravesites in the north-east corner of the camp. In the second phase, a mass grave in the southern section of compound II was used. Rudolf Reder testified that SS-Scharführer Fritz Irrmann was the Lazaret executioner:

> At the edge of the grave, the elderly, the children and the sick were waiting with insane expressions in their eyes, staring dully into the grave. They were waiting for death and were allowed to see their fill of the corpses, the blood, and the stench of putrefaction before SS-Scharführer Irrmann swept them into the grave with gunshots and the butt of his gun.[16]

Groups of between 700 and 750 people were forced into the largest barrack where Wirth delivered his reassurance speech, also conveyed by loudspeaker to the other groups outside the barracks:

> Jews! You have been brought here to be resettled, but before we organise this future Jewish State, you must of course learn how to work! You will learn a new trade which will be taught here. Our routine here is, first, everyone has to get undressed so that your clothing can be disinfected, and you can have a bath to ensure that no epidemics are brought into the camp.[17]

A totally plausible explanation for the unsuspecting deportees. Sometimes, Wirth's announcement was greeted by cheers. The Jews then willingly undressed and were directed in smaller groups of about eighty persons to the next barrack, where they deposited their valuables and personal papers, expecting to have them returned following their bath. From there, they were driven along the 'tube' to the 'bathing and inhalation' barrack.

Once inside, the doors to the three zinc-lined rooms were sealed and the large Soviet tank engine of the 'BT' series, a 350-hp, twelve-cylinder, was fired up. At first, it was Wirth himself who started the engine, but later SS-Scharführer Lorenz Hackenholt was placed in charge of the engine, assisted by the young Ukrainian driver and mechanic Edward Wlasiuk. The engine ran for twenty minutes with the exhaust fumes being pumped into the three chambers. From the sealed and darkened rooms, muffled screams could be distinguished.

After the engine was stopped, the Sonderkommando opened the gas chambers, via the back doors. The lifeless bodies inside were covered in excrement, vomit, and urine. The bodies were untangled and removed by the Sonderkommando. They were piled in two heaps beside the small gauge railway. Initially, the dead women had their hair cut off (this was later altered to before the gassing process) and a dental team extracted any gold fillings by ripping out the teeth. Jewellery was also removed, with fingers being amputated for difficult-to-remove rings. The Sonderkommando took about fifteen minutes to empty the chambers of sometimes around 1,000 cadavers in total.

On occasions, when clearing the death chambers, children were discovered still alive crouching below the bodies. This sometimes also happened with pregnant women. Apparently, the exit sliding doors were not sealed sufficiently, causing fresh air to seep into the chamber. Wirth solved this by ordering the Sonderkommando to pile sand against the doors to prevent fresh air encroaching into the chamber. Naturally, this sand had to be dug away each time prior to the doors being slid open, and it clogged the greased runners of the sliding doors. This problem was later solved long-term by the introduction of heavy doors, hinged at the top, as in garage style lift-up doors. Wirth also instructed the Sonderkommando to wait an additional twenty minutes, after the engine had stopped, before entering the chambers.

The property removed from the Jews was taken to the disused locomotive shed near the station, where it was sorted and stored before forwarding to Lublin. Former

T4 man Rudi Kamm was placed in charge of this facility. Under his supervision, another Jewish Sonderkommando worked at sorting and baling of the clothes.

With Bełżec fully operational and the teething problems resolved, Wirth was able to temporarily leave the camp to assist with the construction of the new camp at Sobibor. His deputy, Gottfried Schwarz, was left in charge. Schwarz continued to implement the strict procedures laid down by Wirth.

Following discussions between Viktor Brack and Globocnik, Wirth returned to Bełżec in mid-May 1942. Having assisted with the brick-built gas chambers at Sobibor, Wirth realised that the timber structure at Bełżec required updating. In fact, he decided to replace the barrack entirely. Bełżec ceased operations for one month between mid-June and mid-July 1942, when no transports were accepted.

The original gassing barrack was demolished and was replaced by a more efficient brick and concrete construction, consisting of six larger gas chambers. Each of the six gassing rooms was approximately 5 metres by 5 metres, thereby doubling the capacity, but descriptions of size of the phase 2 gas chambers vary.

In August 1942, Rudolf Reder was a new arrival at the camp and was one of the few survivors. He later described the new gas chambers:

> In the small yard you went up the steps to the entrance door, above which there was a sign saying Bade und Inhalationsraeume as well as a large flower basket, which made it look as though it was really the entrance to a health spa. From the entrance a corridor, which had three solid and tightly sealed single doors one either side, ran the length of the building. These doors led into the windowless chambers, which at the far end wall, adjoining the loading ramps I described earlier, had double sliding doors. On the other side of the building, i.e. behind the wall at the far end of the corridor, there was a small room where the engines were.[18]

The new building was euphemistically called the 'Hackenholt Foundation' and it bore a sign to that effect. Over the entrance doorway, a large metal Star of David was hung. Kurt Gerstein described the building at the time of his visit:

> After ascending a few small steps, we saw three rooms to our left and right, which looked like garages; 4 by 5 metres, 1.90 metres high. At the back, indiscernible, wooden exits. On the roof, a Star of David made of copper. In front of the building a plaque with Hackenholt-Stiftung. That is all I saw that particular afternoon.[19]

Gerstein was accompanied by SS-Obersturmbannführer Professor Wilhelm Pfannenstiel, the Nazi expert on 'racial hygiene'. Both men attended an 'action' the following day, and on 6 June 1950, Pfannenstiel described what he saw:

> Once the hair of the women had been shorn, the whole transport was led into a building containing 6 chambers. As far as I know, only 4 were needed that time. When the people had been locked into the chambers, the exhaust gases of an engine were fed into these chambers. Gerstein determined that it took 18 minutes for everything to become quiet in the chambers.... Once stillness reigned, the outer doors of the chambers were opened and the corpses brought out, checked for gold teeth, and then piled up in a pit. Again, this work was performed by Jews. No physician was present. I did not notice anything unusual about the corpses. Some were bluish in the face.[20]

Of note in Pfannenstiel's description is that the hair cutting process now occurred prior to gassing, and not *post-mortem*.

The actual combustion engine used to produce the lethal carbon monoxide-rich exhaust fumes has been the subject of much debate. Described by some as a petrol engine, and by others as a diesel engine, we must once again turn to prime evidence witnesses, as no trace of the engine used, in physical or documentary terms, was ever recovered.

On 22 September 1944, Rudolf Reder declared:

> There was an annex made to the 'bath' building from the side which was the farthest from the railway line, in which there was a compressor, working from a petrol engine. To this machine gas cylinders were brought. From the compressor, the pipes went into each chamber. In each chamber on the wall there was a small netting to which the gas-pipe went.[21]

Reder clearly states that the engine was petrol driven, although he appears to be under the impression that the gas may have been contained in bottles and pumped through the system by a compressor. Alternatively, the compressor could have been used to expel the deadly gas from the chambers, following the death of the deportees. Reder made a further statement on 29 December 1945:

> I myself saw that in that small room there was an engine with petrol fuel that looked very complicated. I remember that the engine had a flywheel, but I could not make out any other specific construction or technical features. This engine was always operated by two technicians, Russians from the armed camp staff. I know only that the engine used 4 cans of petrol each day, because that is how much petrol was brought to the camp every day. It was when the petrol was delivered to the engine room that I briefly had the opportunity to look inside the room.[22]

Again, Reder states the engine was petrol driven, and used four cans of petrol daily. The description of a compressor is no longer evident. Another witness testimony for the Bełżec engine is Kazimierz Czerniak, a Polish mechanic. Czerniak helped install the power supply to the camp, and he was able to get a glimpse inside the engine room:

> The motor of the small power station had 15 H.V., in contrast to the large power station which had the power of 200 H.V. From this motor, pipes led underground to take away the engine exhaust. Where these pipes went, I don't know.... The 200 H.V. motor was mounted on a base at the back of the barrack.... I have seen that on this barrack there were three doors from a wooden ramp and that from this ramp, a narrow gauged railway led to another part of the camp. The aforementioned doors were sliding doors which locked with hooks-pegs; they moved with the help of wheels on a track. The 'Blacks' laughingly told me that this barrack was a store. I understood that it was where the gas chamber was located.[23]

The skilled mechanic Czerniak helped to maintain vehicles used by the Germans at the camp and, as such, can be considered as an 'expert' witness on engines. From these testimonies, it is safe to say that the killing engine at Bezec was fuelled by petrol and not diesel. Alternative witness statements in favour of the diesel version did not have direct contact with the machinery actually used. In fact, Karl Schluch actually admits that his assumption was entirely based on the sound of the motor, as he never actually saw it: 'For the gassings, an engine was started up. I cannot give a more detailed description of the engine because I never saw it. I am certainly not a specialist, but I would say that based on the sound, it was a medium-sized diesel engine.'[24]

Former SS-Scharführer Heinrich Gley stated on 8 May 1961: 'After the doors of the gas chambers had been closed, a large engine-I don't know whether it was a diesel or an Otto (gasoline) engine-was started up by a mechanic from the Hiwi section. The exhaust fumes of this engine were fed into the chambers and caused the death of the Jews.'[25]

Aleksandr Semigodov, a former Ukrainian guard from Bełżec, declared on 24 May 1973: 'The people doomed to death were driven into these gas chambers or "dushegubki", as they were also known, where they were killed with exhaust gas from a diesel motor (found in the same building) or some other motor.'[26]

The resettlement transports to Bełżec ceased on 11 December 1942. By then, Himmler had ordered the exhumation and cremation of corpses in mass graves throughout the eastern territories. SS-Standartenführer Paul Blobel was handed responsibility for this gruesome assignment. At Bełżec, SS-Scharführer Fritz Tauscher and Heinrich Gley were ordered to carry out this task, with the assistance of SS-Scharführer Lorenz Hackenholt, who had access to a mechanical excavator. During the first week of November 1942, the exhumation and cremation operation began at the mass graves. By early December, a second cremation pyre was erected. Gley declared post-war: 'The grates were made by arranging standard gauge railway line sections on top of large stones. Narrow gauge line sections were then placed crossways on top to form a close meshed solid grate'.[27] The pyres were intermingled with wood and fuel, rising to a height of several metres and each one contained around 2,000 cadavers.

According to SS-Scharführer Heinrich Gley, a record was kept of the number of corpses dealt with in this way. Some 300,000 bodies were cremated on the first pyre, with another 240,000 on the second, making a total of 540,000.[28] The exact total number of victims of Bełżec terminal station in Aktion Reinhardt will never be known. Official estimates vary between 430,000 and 500,000 people murdered at Bełżec—the third largest killing facility in the Third Reich, after Auschwitz-Birkenau and Treblinka. The discovery of the Höfle Telegram in the UK National Archives at Kew puts the Bełżec total at 434,508 on 31 December 1942. By then, the camp had ceased to operate as a fully functioning death camp.

In December 1942, the transports to Bełżec suddenly ceased. The last deportees were the survivors of the ghettos that had been liquidated. On 4 December 1942, 600 Jews from Krosno were gassed. This was followed by 1,250 from Rohatyn, and several thousands from Rawa Ruska. Finally, three transports from Bursztyn, Bolszewce, and Bukaczowce ended the career of Bełżec as a terminal station for Aktion Reinhardt on 12 December 1942.

The Bełżec staff were informed that the camp was to be rebuilt. In June 1943, on the site of the camp itself, the planting of wild lupines and some fir trees occurred. A Jewish work commando began work on the demolition before being evacuated to Sobibor on 29–30 June. By this time, the corpses had been cremated and the sites of the mass graves were levelled. Bełżec was officially closed.

Local inhabitants descended on the now vacant site and began to dig in search of valuables. Some body parts were uncovered, which resulted in a report to AR headquarters in Lublin. An order was issued for the erection of a farm building on the site, with a caretaker to prevent further such incidents.

# 13

# SOBIBOR

AT THE SAME time Bełżec was becoming operational, a planned second installation at Sobibor was under construction. Polish railway worker Jan Piwonski testified:

> In the autumn of 1941 German officers arrived at the station of Sobibor on three occasions. During their visit to the station they took measurements of the platform, and the sidings leading away from the platform, and then went into the woods nearby. I have no idea what they were doing there. Sometime later some very thick doors, which had rubber strips around them, arrived by train. We speculated on what purpose the doors might be serving, and it dawned on us that the Germans were building something here, especially when trainloads of bricks were also being delivered, and they started to bring Jews over as well.[1]

After assisting with the erection of the Bełżec gas chambers, Erich Fuchs moved on to Sobibor:

> Sometime in the spring of 1942 I drove a truck to Lemberg on Wirth's orders and picked up a gassing engine, which I took to Sobibor. Upon my arrival at Sobibor, I found near the station an area with a concrete structure and several permanent houses. The special commando there was led by Thomalla. Other SS men present included Floss, Bauer, Stangl, Friedl, Schwarz and Barbl. We unloaded the engine. It was a heavy Russian petrol engine (presumably an armoured vehicle or traction engine), at least 200 HP (V-engine, 8-cylinder, water cooled). We installed the engine on a concrete base and connected the exhaust to the pipeline. Then I tried the engine. It hardly worked. I repaired the ignition and the valves, and finally got the engine to start.[2]

The site for Sobibor extermination facility was selected for much the same reasons as Bełżec. It was adjacent to the rail link between Włodawa and Chełm, situated in an unpopulated forest area next to the railway station at Sobibor, which was named after the small village approximately 4 km distant. The River Bug, which serves as the frontier with Ukraine, is about 3 km from the site of the camp. The rail station, the forester's cottage and the few other buildings in the immediate vicinity were all constructed of timber. The largest timber house, on the opposite side of the rail tracks from the quaint old station building, subsequently served as the camp commandant's quarters, and still remains to this day. The surrounding pine forest is aptly described as a thinly forested area.

Building work soon followed on from the initial architectural mapping and trains carrying building materials began to stop at the Sobibor station. One witness, Jan Piwonski, was employed as a pointsman at Sobibor railway station. He remembers one train delivering a heavy solid door with a rubber seal on all sides.[3]

In January or February 1942, the first 120 Jews arrived. This was a Jewish work Kommando. They were housed in a barrack next to the railway track, on the edge of the forest. As at Bełżec, Richard Thomalla was in charge of the construction. Much of the building material was organised by the Deutsch Horst Company and was brought from a camp at Krychow. Supplies were delivered under the authority of the Water Management Inspector in Chełm, Franz Holzheimer, an engineer from Hanover. Chełm architect Moser supervised the site. By the time of Thomalla's arrival at the site, much of the initial groundwork had been completed by Moser and his team.

During construction, the area was visited by SS-Hauptsturmführer Neumann, of the SS and Police Building Office in Lublin. The site of the intended camp was occupied by a building of the Sobibor Forestry Division, a small farm, a postal agency, a sawmill, and a timber chapel. All these buildings were requisitioned for the future camp. A dirt road ran parallel with the rail line.

The architects utilised some of the buildings and incorporated them into the structure of the camp. The existing farmhouse was a large timber building with a long porch running the length of the front façade. This was used as an administration office and later as a valuables store. A Jewish goldsmith subsequently worked there; also a pharmacist to sort and store cosmetics and medicines prior to shipment on to Lublin. The forestry buildings were demolished to make way for a yard used for undressing. At the north end of this yard, at the wall, a sorting barrack was built. There was a vegetable garden, a small stable, a henhouse, and a pigsty. A track led north-east from the site of the forester's farm, into the forest and the later site of the gas chambers. A rail spur led from the main line into the area of the camp.[4]

Pre-war aerial photographs of the region show a completely forested area at the site of the subsequent gas chambers and mass graves. These trees had to be felled and the area cleared to accommodate the required facilities. A drainage system was laid and a power source sufficient for a camp complex was installed. Local skilled workers were used at first by Moser, supplemented by the arrival of the aforementioned Jewish work Kommando.

By the close of March 1942, police from Wlodowa provided a military presence, ordered by Globocnik at a meeting in Lublin with Polizei Major Ferdinand Hahnzog, the local Gendarmerie commander, the previous November. Hahnzog was appalled when he discovered the true meaning of Sobibor and voiced his misgivings in his later discovered letters home to his wife. He made every effort to keep his men out of the annihilation process being being carried out against the Jews. Despite his plainly obvious objections, he was promoted to the rank of Polizei Oberstleutnant and was also accorded the rank of Obersturmbannführer in the SS. He was arrested by the Gestapo in Vienna in January 1945 and sentenced to death. He was liberated from his death cell by the Red Army, interviewed by the NKVD, and released. He died in 1969.

Sobibor was closed off from the outside world in March 1942, guarded by men from Trawniki and supervised by Thomalla. The wire perimeter fence had pine branches woven into it to prevent a clear view of the camp. This signalled the start of construction on the gassing installation and anything directly connected with the murder process. Not only were the death chambers erected, but also the 'Himmelstrasse' (road to heaven) and the pits for mass graves. Thomalla had gained experience by the construction of Bełżec, and this was added to with the experience of T4 men such as Gustav Wagner.

Wagner was born in Vienna on 18 July 1911. A committed Nazi, he was recruited by T4 and served at the Hartheim euthanasia centre. At Sobibor, Wagner served as one of the deputies to camp commandant Franz Stangl. He was primarily responsible for segregating out which prisoners would be used for work in the camp from the vast majority destined for the gas. His brutality was legendary among the prisoners. One survivor, Moshe Bahir, described Wagner in the following terms:

> He was a handsome man, tall and blond—a pure Aryan. In civilian life he was, no doubt, a well-mannered man; at Sobibor he was a wild beast. His lust to kill knew no bounds.... He would snatch babies from their mothers' arms and tear them to pieces in his hands. I saw him beat two men to death with a rifle, because they did not carry out his instructions properly, since they did not understand German. I remember that one night a group of youths aged fifteen or sixteen arrived in the camp. The head of this group was one Abraham. After a long and arduous work day, this young man collapsed on his pallet and fell asleep. Suddenly, Wagner came into our barrack, and Abraham did not hear him call to stand up at once before him. Furious, he pulled Abraham naked off his bed and began to beat him all over his

> body. When Wagner grew weary of the blows, he took out his revolver and killed him on the spot. This atrocious spectacle was carried out before all of us, including Abraham's younger brother.[5]

Wagner transferred to Trieste with other Aktion Reinhardt staff after the termination of the Lublin based enterprise in 1943. He escaped to South America with the help pf the Roman Catholic Church. He lived under a false name—Günther Mendel—in Brazil until he was exposed in 1978 by Simon Wiesenthal. Israel, Austria, and Poland requested his extradition. In a BBC TV interview in 1979, Wagner stated: 'I had no feelings.... It just became another job. In the evening, we never discussed our work, but just drank and played cards'.[6]

In October 1980, Wagner was discovered in Sao Paulo, Brazil, with a knife wound in his chest. He was declared to have committed suicide on 3 October, but the circumstances remain unclear.

The new camp commandant was identified, probably by Wirth, but authorised by Globocnik, as policeman and T4 recruit Franz Paul Stangl. He was born on 26 March 1908 in Altmünster, yet another Austrian. A weaver by profession, he decided to apply for a position in the police. To his surprise, he was accepted and reported for training. After uncovering a Nazi arms cache in 1934, he was rewarded with a posting to the criminal police investigation department. He transferred to the Kripo in Wels in 1935 and was married soon after. A diligent officer, Stangl had no qualms about targeting Nazis; it was a matter of duty and the NSDAP was illegal.

That all changed in March 1938 with the Anschluss. Stangl witnessed several of his colleagues being sent to concentration camps, or, worse still, shot without trial. Stangl and a friend pretended that they had been illegal Nazis.[7] In his revealing post-trial interviews with author Gitta Sereny, Stangl admits to being 'involved' with anti-Jewish policies within the police. In January 1939, Stangl's office was transferred to the provincial Gestapo HQ in Linz. His new boss was Georg Prohaska, a Bavarian with whom Stangl quickly fell out. Prohaska made life extremely unpleasant for Stangl.

In November 1940, Stangl received a personal transfer order, signed by Himmler, to report to Berlin—to the Foundation for Institutional Care. He was to present himself at the Kripo HQ in Werderscher Markt, and report personally to Kriminalrat Dr Paul Werner. Once there, he was informed that he had been especially selected for the post of police superintendent at an institute administered by the foundation, the main office of which was situated at Tiergartenstrasse 4 in Berlin-Charlottenburg. Werner also informed him of the true purpose of T4.

Stangl next reported to Tiergartenstrasse where he was interviewed by Viktor Brack. Stangl was promoted to Leutnant der Polizei and returned to uniform duty. He wore the green police uniform during his entire duty with T4 and then as commandant of Sobibor. In December 1942, when as commandant of Treblinka, he was entitled to wear the field grey uniform of the SS.

Stangl found himself posted to Hartheim euthanasia centre, near Linz, where he roomed with an old colleague from the police, Franz Reichleitner. Reichleitner introduced him to Hauptmann Christian Wirth, who informed Stangl that he would be responsible for the issue of death certificates. Stangl took an instant dislike to the uncouth Wirth, but had a reasonable relationship with the other members of staff: 'There were two chief medical officers—Dr Renno and Dr Lohnauer; and fourteen nurses, seven men and seven women. Dr Lohnauer was a rather aloof sort of man, but very correct. Dr Renno was very nice, friendly'.[8]

In October 1941, Stangl was sent to Bernburg to assist with the winding up process. Things were not going so well there, as at Hartheim. Dr Eberl was at Bernburg and Stangl would subsequently have further dealings with him in Poland. He returned briefly to Hartheim in February 1942 to gather his things together and say his 'goodbyes'. He was ordered to T4 in Berlin, where he was apparently offered the choice of returning to Linz (and Prohaska) or accepting a posting to Lublin in Poland. He understood this to be an anti-partisan posting. He chose the latter.

In March 1942, Stangl was ordered to report to SS-Brigadeführer Globocnik in Lublin. He travelled to Lublin with nineteen other T4 personnel, with Stangl as the ranking officer. The circumstances surrounding his arrival provide a point of contention. During his Sereny interview on the fourth day of their meeting in the Frankfurt Remand Prison in April 1971, Stangl described his first meeting with Globocnik:

> I reported to the SS HQ in Lublin as soon as I arrived.... The SS HQ was in the Julius Schreck Kaserne—a kind of palace surrounded by a large park. When I gave my name at the gate, I was taken through the building into the park. They said the General would meet me there....
>
> It was a beautiful Spring day, the grass was very green, the trees in bud and there were new flowers everywhere. I cam upon Globocnik sitting by himself on a bench about ten metres away from—and with his back to—the building. There was a lovely view across lawns and trees to buildings far away.

Stangl was told to sit beside Globocnik who asked about his service history and his family. Stangl quickly realised that Globocnik was quizzing him to ascertain if he was suitable for the job:

> ...The park seemed empty ... it was very quiet and very beautiful. When I finished, he said that no doubt I knew that the army had just had some major setbacks in the East. The SS was going to have to help. It had been decided, he told me, to open a number

> of supply camps from which the troops at the front could be re-equipped. He said that he intended confiding to me the construction of a camp called Sobibor. He called an aide, who must have lurked somewhere nearby, and told him to bring the plans.
>
> … the plans arrived and he spread them out on the bench between us and on the ground in front of us. They showed a design for a camp—barracks, railway tracks, fences, gates. Some of the buildings—bunkers they were—were crossed out with red ink. 'Don't worry about those,' he said, 'concentrate on getting the rest done first. It has been started, but they've got Poles working there. It's going so slowly, I think they must be asleep. What the place needs is someone to organise it properly and I think you are the man to do it.' And then he said he'd arrange for me to leave for Sobibor the next day—that was all.[9]

This impromptu meeting lasted for three hours. Stangl insisted in 1971 that not a single word about Jews was uttered. Globocnik offered that Stangl might like to visit Wirth, but Stangl declined, admitting that Wirth and him did not 'see eye to eye'.

Sereny doubts the validity of Stangl's version of his first meeting with Globocnik, citing the improbability of a general receiving a junior police officer with such informality. I believe she is mistaken in this assumption, accounting for the character of Globocnik and the secrecy surrounding Aktion Reinhardt. After all, Stangl was being posted to the command of the second major static killing facility in Aktion Reinhardt. Of course, it is entirely feasible that Globocnik wished to interview the man for such an important role personally. Secondly, and more importantly, is the dubious insistence of Globocnik in keeping the true nature of the camp from its future commander. Sereny agreed that Dieter Allers viewed the meeting as entirely possible.

The other inconsistency with Stangl's story is the location. The Julius Schreck Kaserne, although a fairly large building, could not be mistaken for a former palace. It was the former Stefan Batory School and it resembled then, as it does today, an educational establishment. The gate entrance is at one end of the building, and to access what was the rear garden, there was no need to enter the building at all. The garden ran alongside the building, easily accessed from the gate to which Stangl refers. It is now a car park. It is feasible that Stangl was mistaken over the location and that the correct building was that occupied by the SS-Standortverwaltung. That particular building was a former palace and was surrounded by parkland, with a view across lawns and trees. The nearest buildings at the rear were some distance away and Stangl's description fits in with that site. However, Sereny describes finding the building in 1972, then being used as a school for domestic science. She states the bench was still *in situ* as described by Stangl.

He spent his first night in a billet in Lublin. The next morning, a car and driver picked him up and they drove direct to Chełm where Stangl met the architect

Moser. He then visited a small farmstead camp called Krychow, midway between Chełm and Sobibor. After arriving at Sobibor village, Stangl noticed another small work camp in the village. Both these camps had Jewish female prisoners. From this point, Stangl's story varies concerning his very first sight of the new site of the death camp.[10]

A few days prior to Stangl's arrival at Sobibor, the camp construction site was visited by Dr Irmfried Eberl. The purpose of his visit is unconfirmed, but was likely for experience as he was the intended commandant of yet another planned camp at Treblinka.

It appears that Stangl did not stay at the camp site, but returned three days later with six men, one of whom was an old colleague from Hartheim, Hermann Michel. Allegedly, it was Michel who first drew Stangl's attention to a strange new brick construction in the forest. He came running soon after arrival and said to Stangl: 'I think there is something fishy going on here. Come and see what it reminds you of'.[11]

Stangl went on:

> It was about ten or even fifteen minutes' walk away from the railway stationwhere we were building the main camp. It was a new brick building with three rooms, three metres by four. The moment I saw it, I knew what Michel meant; it looked exactly like the gas chamber at Schloss Hartheim.[12]

According to Stangl, the structure was built by Poles without knowledge of its intended use. It had remained unseen by Stangl and Michel until then as neither had found time to explore the area before. Stangl realised that this was a building crossed out in red ink on the plans shown to him by Globocnik.

It contained three internal rooms, 3 metres by 4 metres. The building was constructed in late March or early April 1942. This structure was partly, or wholly, demolished in the autumn of 1942. It was replaced by an enlarged structure. All descriptions of the gas chamber building are based on memory of locals and/or staff, as there were no survivors of Camp III, which is where the gas chambers were located. The descriptions all vary to some extent.

A comprehensive description of the gas chamber building was prepared for the jury in a court case against Karl Frenzel. Sobibor historian Marek Bem considers this description as the most likely accurate version:

> About 500 metres west of that chapel, the preliminary works squad put up a building with a gas chamber inside it, a small massive construction on a concrete foundation. Inside the building were three separate gastight chambers of 4 metres by 4 metres, parallel with each other. Each chamber had an insulated door in the opposite empty walls, with one door serving as the entrance to the chamber, and the other as the

exit—for taking corpses out. The building team had had all fittings installed and a special annexe built by the back gable wall. In the annexe, there was an engine which fed exhaust fumes to kill the Jews. The gas chamber building was situated in the so-called Camp III, which was a fenced yard. It had its own separate fence made of barbed wire. The building with the gas chambers in it was located in the southernmost part of that area. The annexe with the engine was beside the building with the gas chambers. The exhaust pipe of the huge engine 'Otto' was connected to the system of cables which ended in the shower nozzles on the ceilings of the particular gas chambers. The engine received specifically calculated settings for the carburettor, and the number of revolutions. With the gas chamber doors locked, it was possible to create such a high degree of concentration of poisonous exhaust fumes from the engine inside the chambers (carbon monoxide and carbon dioxide) that the people trapped inside suffocated in agony for about 20–30 minutes. In time, the gas chambers turned out to be too small, and the 'efficiency' of the Sobibór camp proved to be too low. The old building with the gas chambers was partially torn down by the Lublin headquarters building crew under Lambert's technical guidance. It was replaced by a new massive building with twice as many chambers. Each of them had an area of 4 metres by 4 metres and a height of 2.20 metres. They were positioned on both sides of the corridor or formed just one row. Each of the chambers could hold about 80 people, if they were tightly squeezed. Since then, after the building works that lasted only for a few weeks, in the six chambers about 480 people could be killed at the same time. The old chambers proved to be impractical also due to too small an exit door, which was used for taking corpses out of the chamber. During the renovation, the door was replaced by a broader 'pendular' one. Since then, the working squad of Camp III could more easily get out of the chambers tightly huddled corpses, often extremely dirty, standing next to each other or twisted together, and then transport them to the pits along the narrow-gauge tracks. A special squad of prisoners in Camp III was to clear the chambers of blood and excrement as quickly as possible, before the next group of victims got inside...[13]

Marek Bem also notes:

On 8 September 2014, the archaeologists unearthed remains of red brick walls. All the indications are that these are the remains of the gas chamber. The excavated area lies between the (so-called) 'road to heaven,' the crematorium, the remains of the barrack which, at the time when the camp was operational, belonged to the special commando unit, and the well. A panel of experts from the Museum of the Auschwitz-Birkenau Nazi German Concentration and Extermination Camp have officially confirmed the find. Undoubtedly, this remarkable discovery will be of vital importance in further research into the Holocaust because it might enable researchers to, firstly, arrive at a more accurate estimate of the Sobibór camp's victims, and, secondly, to obtain more precise information as to the exact way in which the victims were murdered.[14]

Stangl described the Polish workers he discovered at Sobibor as unreliable and drunkards. Globocnik was still expressing dissatisfaction with the rate of progress. A sergeant who arrived from Lublin in a drunken state informed Stangl that Globocnik had told him: 'If these Jews don't work properly, just kill them off and we'll get others'.[15] Stangl drove to Lublin the following day to complain to Globocnik, and was informed that he had misunderstood the message. Stangl did not ask Globocnik about the gas chamber building.

He soon had the opportunity to discover his new role with a visit to Wirth at Bełżec:

> I can't describe to you what it was like. I went there by car. As one arrived, one first reached Bełżec railway station on the left side of the road. The camp was on the same side, but up a hill. The Kommandantur was 200 metres away, on the other side of the road.... The smell, oh God, the smell. It was everywhere. Wirth wasn't in his office. I remember, they took me to him ... he was standing on a hill, next to the pits ... the pits ... full ... they were full. I can't tell you; not hundreds, thousands, thousands of corpses ... oh God. That's where Wirth told me—he said that was what Sobibor was for...[16]

The date of this visit is open to question, but it was certainly before the arrival of the first transports in Sobibor in the first week of May 1942.

According to Stangl, the first trial gassings were carried out soon after his arrival at the camp. During the construction phase at Sobibor, Wirth certainly visited the incomplete site, and conducted an experimental gassing of twenty-five Jewish labourers. However, witness Jakob Engelhardt, commander of the first group of Ukrainian guards, places the very first trials using the gas chamber in early April 1942, when Thomalla was still in command, and not in the presence of Wirth. It is likely that there were several such trials.

The engine used to kill at Sobibor, as in Bełżec, was petrol driven. This was confirmed by Erich Fuchs, Erich Bauer, and Franz Hodl. Bauer and Fuchs were qualified car mechanics. Their only disagreement was whether it was a Soviet tank engine or a Renault. A diesel engine was used at Sobibor, but only to drive the power generator.

The gas chambers at Sobibor were situated in Camp III, which was located in the north-west section of the camp zone. There appears to have been two tracks into Camp III from Camp II. Access by camp staff was via a guarded southern gate upon delivery of a secret password which was subject to change on a daily basis. The entrance used by prisoners was via 'the road to Heaven'. This allowed access through a point in the wire a few metres from the entrance to the gas chamber building.

By the beginning of May 1942, the whole camp zone was surrounded by a single 2-metre-high barbed-wire fence. A rail spur provided direct access into the camp zone for locomotive traffic via a wooden gate in the south-east corner of the camp. This was closed each time a train rolled into the camp siding. Along the same southern perimeter fence was the main wooden camp gate, used by pedestrians and vehicular traffic. Internal camp buildings were separated by a complex of barbed-wire fences, which had passages for access.

Wirth inspected the camp during the first days of May 1942, prior to it becoming operational. He delivered a speech in his usual coarse manner and ordered that any Jew not performing up to standard would be eliminated immediately. He threatened any member of staff with similar treatment if they objected.

The very first recorded gassing action at Sobibor was that involving 250 Jews from Krychow labour camp. No record survives of the actual date or the sex of the victims. Wirth was apparently present during this test and it may have been that mentioned in the paragraph above, or even earlier in mid-April. Stangl was certainly the undisputed commandant of Sobibor by the time of the arrival of the first mass transports. The first verified transport of 2,000 Jews from Komarów was gassed on 3 May 1942. This was followed by another transport of 2,000 on 5 May from Opole Lubelski.

Large transports then began rolling in with regularity: 6 May, 2,500 from Demblin-Irena; 7 May, 2,500 from Ryki; 7 May, 1,270 from Józefów; 8 May, 1,500 from Baranów; 8 May, 1,580 from Końskowola; 9 May, 1,500 from Markuszów; 9 May, 200 from Łęczna; and 10 May, 2,500 from Michów. This totals 17,550 in the first week of operational service alone.[17]

Procedures for reception of transports ran along similar lines to those in operation at Bełżec. The deportees were unloaded from their train at the concrete constructed ramp inside the camp and parallel to the main railway track. This part of the camp was called the 'Vorlager'. The ramp was opposite the Sobibor railway station, but it was shielded from view by the newly erected wire fence, intertwined with pine branches. The deportees were then segregated into sexes and age groups in an open area. Hermann Michel, wearing a doctor's white coat, announced the same deception as at Bełżec; this was a transit camp and bathing was necessary to prevent infestation and disease. Next came the undressing and seizure of suitcases and property in Camp II. The women had their hair cut short before being forced naked with their children into the 'road to Heaven'. This was about 3–4 metres wide and 150 metres in length. Later, a barber station was introduced towards the end of the 'tube' and haircutting in the open ceased. At the far end of the 'tube' was the gas chamber building, surrounded by barbed wire, in Camp III.

Also in Camp III were the burial pits, approximately 50–60 metres in length, 10–15 metres wide, and 5–7 metres in depth. The sandy soil in this location allowed for ease of excavation. The pits were oblique to allow for ease of burial, and they varied in size. There was a narrow gauge railway track, which served Camp III from the ramp area in the Vorlager. To the east of Camp III, near the main railway line, stood a timber constructed forester's chapel. Behind this chapel, a further pit was excavated for use as the camp Lazarett.

Michel was replaced after a few months by Gustav Wagner as Stangl's deputy. He subsequently shared this responsibility with Johann Niemann who was appointed as permanent deputy commandant upon his promotion to SS-Untersturmführer in summer 1943. Camp I was commanded initially by SS-Scharführer Otto Weiss, who was also in charge of the station Kommando. A brutal anti-Semite, Weiss took great comfort in forcing the Jews to sing derogatory songs. He contracted TB and was transferred in early 1943 on grounds of ill health. His replacement was SS-Oberscharführer Karl Frenzel who previously supervised the Jewish prisoners in Camp II. Frenzel was a sadist who killed without compunction and was lucky to survive the prisoners' revolt as he was taking a shower at the time. He was transferred to Trieste in 1943 and was taken prisoner by US troops. Released, he lived as a free man until his arrest on 22 March 1962. He denied his involvement in any murders and protested that his treatment of the Jews was always humane:

> After the disembarking of the train, the children and the feeble Jews were forcibly thrown onto the trolley. Terrible scenes happened then. The people were separated from their families, pushed with rifle butts, lashed with whips. They cried dreadfully, so I could not cope with this task. Reichleitner complied with my request, and he appointed Bredow to escort the trolley....
>
> As I already pointed out, under the prevailing war conditions, which are now difficult to comprehend, I unfortunately believed that what was going on in Sobibor was lawful. To my regret, I was then convinced of its necessity. I was shocked that just during the war, when I wanted to serve my homeland, I had to be in such a terrible extermination camp. But then I thought very often about the enemy bomber pilots, who surely were not asked whether they wanted to carry out their murderous flights against German people in their homes in such a manner.[18]

Erich Bauer said of Frenzel:

> ... In the canteen at Sobibor I once overheard a conversation between Karl Frenzel, Franz Stangl and Gustav Wagner. They were discussing the number of victims in the extermination camps of Bełżec, Treblinka and Sobibor and expressed their regret that Sobibor 'came last' in the competition.[19]

A former T4 man, Frenzel was given a life sentence and served sixteen years in prison. He was released on account of ill health and died on 2 September 1996 in an old peoples' home in Garbsen-Hannover.

Camp III was commanded by SS-Oberscharführer Kurt Bolender. A former crematorium worker for T4, Bolender was in charge of the gas chambers from April 1942 until the autumn of 1942. Of his duties at Sobibor, Bolender stated: 'I assigned the Arbeitsjuden [work Jews] to different groups. Some had to empty out the gas chamber after the cremation was completed; others had to transport the dead bodies to the graves'.[20]

Erich Bauer had this to say about Bolender:

> Bolender was in charge of Camp III. In Sobibor there was a working Jew whom Bolender ordered to box with another working Jew, and for his pleasure they hit each other almost until death. Bolender had a big dog, and when he was in charge of the platform workers, he set the dog at the Jews who did not work quickly enough.... I was blamed for being responsible for the death of the Jewish girls, Ruth and Gisela, who lived in the so-called forester house. As it is known, these two girls lived in the forester house, and they were visited frequently by the SS men. Orgies were conducted there. They were attended by Bolender, Gomerski, Karl Ludwig, Franz Stangl, Gustav Wagner, and Steubel. I lived in the room above them and due to these celebrations could not fall asleep after coming back from a journey...[21]

Moshe Bahir, a Sobibor survivor, wrote about Bolender:

> It is hard to forget Oberschiarführer Kurt Bolender, with his athletic body and long hair, who used to go walking half naked, clad only in training breeches, carrying a long whip with which he brutally lashed the camp prisoners whom he came upon on his way. On his way to lunch he was in the habit of passing the main gate and swinging a whip with all his strength upon the heads of the Jews who went through. Once, when I was still working in the platform commando, the group was accused of carelessness when we had left a window open on one of the train cars. Each one of us was punished with 100 lashes. Bolender was very active in this task. More than once I saw him throwing babies, children, and the sick straight from the freight cars into the trolley with the load that went to the Lazarett. He was the one who chose the ten men to deliver the food to the workers in Camp III. When he had a yen to accompany the group, not one of them would return to us when the task was done.[22]

In the autumn of 1942, Bolender was put in command of the Ukrainian guards. Bolender's duties at Sobibor were interrupted in December 1942, when he was convicted by a German court of influencing a witness to lie during divorce proceedings with his wife. Bolender was sentenced to a short prison term in the Krakow SS prison camp, Danzig Matzkau. After serving the sentence, he returned to Operation Reinhardt duties. Bolender was posted to the labour camp at Dorohucza before transferring to Trieste. After the war, he lived under two assumed names, Heinz Brenner and Wilhelm Vahle, while working as a doorman. After his arrest, police discovered a whip with a silver-engraved handle bearing the initials 'KB'. This had been created for him at Sobibor by one of the prisoners, the goldsmith Szlomo Szmajzner. Bolender hanged himself in his cell on 10 October 1966.

As a result of his duties at Sobibor, SS-Oberscharführer Erich Bauer gained the nickname 'the Bathmaster'. He was also known as 'Gasmeister—the Gasmaster'. Bauer had charge of the gas chambers. He was an untidy man who overindulged regularly in alcohol. He worked as a labourer following the defeat of Germany. Recognised at a fairground in 1949, he faced trial accused of crimes against humanity. Bauer denied any involvement in the murders at Sobibor, but four witnesses proved he not only operated the engine for the gas chambers, but he also personally shot countless prisoners. He was sentenced to death in 1950, but this was commuted to life imprisonment. He died in Berlin Tegel Prison on 4 February 1980.

Quotes attributed to Erich Bauer:

> Usually the undressing went smoothly. Subsequently, the Jews were taken through the 'tube' to Camp III—the real extermination camp. The transfer through the 'tube' proceeded as follows: one SS man was in the lead and five or six Ukrainian auxiliaries were at the back hastening the [Jews] along. The women were taken through a barrack where their hair was cut off. In Camp III the Jews were received by SS men.... As I already mentioned, the motor was then switched on by Go[t]ringer and one of the [Ukrainian] auxiliaries whose name I don't remember. Then the gassed Jews were taken out.[23]

> I cannot exclude any member of the Sobibor camp staff of taking part in the extermination operation. We were a 'blood brotherhood gang' in a foreign land.[24]

> We were a band of 'fellow conspirators' ['verschworener Haufen'] in a foreign land, surrounded by Ukrainian volunteers whom we could not trust.... The bond between us was so strong that Frenzel, Stangl and Wagner had had a ring with SS runes made from five-mark pieces for every member of the permanent staff. These rings were distributed to the camp staff as a sign so that the 'conspirators' could be identified. In addition, the tasks in the camp were shared. Each of us had at some point carried out every camp duty in Sobibor (station squad, undressing, and gassing).[25]

According to Kurt Bolender, the name of the Ukrainian operating the engine with Bauer was Emil Kostenko. Bolender also stated the gas chambers were emptied of the dead by a Jewish work Kommando. At first, the elderly and infirm were taken direct to the burial pits in Camp III by carts, pushed by Jewish workers. The carts were later replaced by small gauge railway tippers pulled by horses. Once at the pits, instead of promised medical attention, they were shot.

A small number of deportees were saved from the gas to provide skilled work in the camp. These were segregated out immediately after arrival in the Vorlager. Carpenters, tailors, strong young labourers, cobblers, and even a goldsmith were reprieved. This did not guarantee survival, however, as their numbers were often reduced by the brutality of the staff. After all, there was a never-ending supply of skilled craftsmen and women arriving with each transport. The Sonderkommando in Camp III numbered between 200 and 300 Jews. They were separated from the prisoners in other sections of the camp and were liquidated from time to time. Theirs was the worst job of all.

The transports arriving at Sobibor for 'special handling' were not exclusively from the General Government. Many started their journey to the Polish pine forest in places as far afield as Holland, France, Czechoslovakia, the Reich, and even the Soviet Union. The final transports came from Lida, Minsk, and Vilno. Some of the Western European transports were carried in rail compartments, instead of the usual goods wagons.

A break in transports occurred at the end of July 1942 as a result of repair work to the main railway link between Lublin and Chełm, but the stoppage was only temporary. The original gas installation building was demolished and replaced by a new structure designed by Erwin Lambert and Lorenz Hackenholt. This is how it became known as the 'Stiftung Hackenholt' ('Hackenholt Foundation'). Their expertise gained in T4 and at Bełżec was applied to this new building and also the similar construction at Treblinka. The killing capacity was increased by the addition of more gassing rooms and a redesign of the layout.

The new gas chambers numbered six—three either side of a central corridor to feed all rooms, accessed from the 'tube'. The building was of brick and concrete construction and it is believed to be the building unearthed by the archeological dig in September 2014 (see above). At the far end of the building was a separate engine room containing the large horsepower petrol engine. This new structure allowed for the gassing of up to 1,300 people at a time.

Stangl was replaced as commandant by SS-Obersturmführer Franz Reichleitner on 1 September 1942, with his transfer to the command of Treblinka camp. Reichleitner was born on 2 December 1906 and had also served at T4 and he knew both Stangl and Wirth from Hartheim. A former Gestapo officer in Linz, Reichleitner had a reputation as a heavy drinker. He moved into the large timber house occupied by Stangl and selected members of his staff, and he was rarely seen at selections, preferring to delegate responsibilities. He was a well-dressed man, whose renowned efficiency preceeded his arrival at the camp. His tenure as camp commandant was marked by an increase in strictness, but was also marred by the prisoners' revolt, which eventually led to the closure of the camp. Survivor Moshe Bahir's memory of Reichleitner was as follows:

> Reichleitner, a man in his late forties, with an Austrian accent, was dressed always with great elegance and wore gloves. He did not have direct contact with the Jews and the transports. He knew that he could rely on his subordinates, who were very frightened of him. He ran the camp with German precision. During his time, the Aktionen went smoothly, and all the transports that arrived on a certain day were liquidated. He never left them for the following day...[26]

In the second half of September 1943, one of the transports from Minsk included a Red Army Jewish POW, Alexander Pechersky, who escaped selection for the gas chamber. He became the leader of a group of prisoners intent on revolt and escape. On 14 October 1943, this group killed ten of the SS staff and seized the armoury. A fire fight ensued and around 300 prisoners, mainly from Camp III, broke out of the camp and fled into the surrounding forest. Many were killed crossing the no-man's-land outside the wire, where the Germans had planted landmines to prevent such an escape. A large number were either shot or recaptured, only to be executed on their return.

Dutch historian and Sobibor survivor Jules Schelvis estimates that 158 prisoners perished in the Sobibor revolt, shot by the guards or in the minefield surrounding the camp. A further 107 were killed either by the SS, Wehrmacht, or Ordnungspolizei search squads pursuing the escapees. Some fifty-three insurgents died of other causes between the day of the revolt and 8 May 1945. There were fifty-eight known survivors, forty-eight males and ten females. Their time served in the camp ranged from several weeks to almost two years. Further escapes occurred during the felling of trees for the body disposal pyres. A number of the escapees joined partisan brigades to fight the Germans. Reichleitner was not present at Sobibor at the time of the revolt.

The SS fallen included Johann Niemann, the senior SS man present in the camp that day. Niemann was an experienced SS man who had seen service with SS-Totenkopf at Esterwegen and Sachsenhausen concentration camps. From the camp system he had transferred to T4 and served at Grafeneck, Brandenburg, and Bernburg before being appointed to Belzec and Sobibor. Known for his brutality, when he was informed of a planned prisoner revolt in Sobibor, he ordered all seventy-two suspected prisoners to be executed. On 14 October 1943, with

Reichleitner temporarily absent, he was in command at Sobibor. He was one of the first to die that day, when Alexander Shubayev killed him with an axe blow to the head in the tailor shop.

Globocnik had been replaced as SSPF Lublin prior to the revolt. His successor, Jakob Sporrenberg, circulated a message on 15 October that approximately 700 Jews had escaped from Sobibor. This erroneously assumed that all the Jewish inmates of the camp at the time had escaped.

In the wake of the revolts at Auschwitz II earlier in October 1943, at Treblinka in August 1943, and now at Sobibor, Himmler ordered that Sobibor should be closed forthwith. On 23 November 1943, Wagner ordered the execution of the last remaining thirty Jews at Sobibor. They were shot by Jührs, Sporleder, and Zierke, assisted by Trawniki men. The gas chambers were dismantled and the site of Camp III levelled. The other barracks were used by the German Baudienst until evacuation prior to liberation by the Red Army in July 1944.

The Höfle Telegram records the total victims of Aktion Reinhardt at Sobibor, until 31 December 1942, as 101,370. The final official total is estimated to be in the region of 170,165, although some post-war estimates put the figure much higher, in excess of 250,000. This total includes a minimum of 93,500 confirmed deportees from outside Poland. Citizens of the Greater German Reich, the Czech Republic, Slovakia, Holland, France, and the Soviet Union all succumbed to the gas at Sobibor. On 8 June 1942, 1,266 Dutch children were gassed.

The area around the former camp continued to be used for resettlements of Ukrainians in the few years immediately following the war. The ramp was used for this purpose in 1947, and remained in use until 1960. Reichleitner and Stangl's residence still exists today as a residential home. The railway station still stands, but it was closed in 1999 when the main railway line fell into disuse for passenger services.

# 14

# TREBLINKA, THE ASSEMBLY LINE OF DEATH

APPROXIMATELY 85 KM north-east of Warsaw, set back from the southern bank of the Bug River, lies the small village of Treblinka. Had it not been for the deeds carried out here by the Germans in the Second World War, the insignificant name of Treblinka would be lost to posterity. Today, it is associated with the German attempt to wipe out the European Jews, and it sits just behind Auschwitz as the names that spring to mind in the genocide perpetrated by Himmler's SS. What few people realise is that the site of the former camp facility associated with the infamous gassing operation is not at Treblinka, but is actually located about 3 km away, at a clearing just south of another small village called Poniatowo.

The new auto route 627 now bypasses the village of Poniatowo, and if one heads east out of the village on foot, it is possible to trace the old road. About 100 metres from Poniatowo, where the new road passes over the original track, there is an obvious slice through the trees that cuts diagonally across the old road, indicating the route of an old railway line, no longer existant. Approximately 500 metres south along this old rail clearing through the trees, one comes across an elongated open area with concrete rail sleepers marking the route of the rail spur. A further 200 metres takes one to more concrete rail sleepers uniformly laid beside a raised platform. This marks the original ramp of Treblinka death camp.

A witness to the construction phase, Lucjan Puchala, later recalled:

> Initially we did not know the reason for building the branch track, and it was only at the end of the job that I found out from conversation among the Germans that the track was to lead to a camp for Jews. The work took two weeks and it was completed on 15 June 1942. Parallel to the construction of the track, earthworks continued.... The

> SS-men and Ukrainians supervising the work killed a few dozen people every day, so that when I looked from the place where I worked to the place where the Jews worked, the field was covered with corpses. The imported workers were used to dig deep ditches and to build various barracks. In particular, I know that a building was built of bricks and concrete, which as I later learned, contained people to be exterminated.[1]

Since June 1941, a labour camp was located in the forest about 4.5 km south of Treblinka. It was under the control of the SSPF Warsaw. At its height, it held around 2,000 prisoners who were mainly Poles. Nearby, was the reason for the camps existence—a gravel pit. The prisoners were also employed on road construction and tree felling. This camp became known as Treblinka I, and should not be confused with the later death camp, Treblinka II.

A former guard from Trawniki, employed at Treblinka I, described the camp where he worked:

> At the end of July 1943, the exact date I cannot give, together with a group of about 20–25 guards whose names I don't remember now, I was sent to the camp in Treblinka. While I was in Treblinka I found out there were two camps located there, about two kilometres from each other. One of these camps, which was situated closer to the Malkinia railroad station, was a death camp where mass executions of Jews occurred.... This camp was surrounded by barbed wire and was camouflaged by spruce branches. The second camp I was sent to, to perform guard duty, was a labour camp—These two camps in Treblinka were called camp number one and camp number two by the guards...Near the entrance to the work camp where I served, there was a barrier and guard tower. The portion of the camp that contained the prisoners was isolated from the camp in general. This area that contained the prisoners was surrounded by a double barbed-wire fence, which in turn contained a patrolled region between the two fences. This controlled region consisted of a strip of ploughed earth where the footprints of anyone who crossed it would be left. The entire camp area was surrounded by a single barbed wire fence, there were buildings situated in the camp that held clothing; there were warehouses and stables also. There were barracks where the guards lived, and there were barracks where the Germans from the camp administration lived. None of the guards were permitted to enter the area where the prisoners were kept, and the guards were forbidden from entering the controlled region. One section contained a kitchen, stoves and sewing shops. The Jewish prisoners who were artisans, lived there along with Jewish tailors, barbers, stove workers and drivers. They were dressed in civilian clothes; each wore their own clothes. In the next section, the Jews who were used for forced labour lived. They were dressed in striped uniforms and they wore wooden shoes on their feet. I do not know if there were skilled labourers among these Jews.... They were sent to work in the sand pit where they hauled sand, they

> were also taken to work in the forest removing tree stumps. The sand from the sand pit was sent off in the direction of the Malkinia station.... In the third section of the camp were kept the Polish prisoners. As a rule, the Poles were used for auxiliary work in the camp—they were dressed in civilian clothes, like the Jewish skilled workers. I do not know if their food was on the same level as that of the other prisoners.... The guards were divided into four sections, platoons and companies. The camp administration was made up of Germans only—they occupied the supervisory positions.... Besides providing security for the camp, the guards took the prisoners to work by convoy and they guarded them during work.... I do not know who shot prisoners on the way to work. I personally had occasion to take prisoners by convoy to the sand pit and accompany them into the forest to remove tree stumps and to auxiliary jobs—in general wherever they went to work.... I also often led prisoners by convoy to the Malkinia railway station where they worked unloading and stacking. In the area of Treblinka labour camp, while leading prisoners to work by convoy and, in particular, to the Malkinia railroad station, I was constantly seeing a thick black smoke rising above the Treblinka death camp. At those times, I smelt the pungent odour of burning flesh. I understood they were burning human bodies in the death camp—other guards said so too, but who in particular said so, I do not recall now.[2]

From April to June 1942, a group of prisoners from the Treblinka labour camp were employed digging foundations at the intended site of the new Treblinka death camp. A concrete road that ran from Kosow Lacki village, through the forest to the labour camp, was built by the prisoners of Treblinka labour camp. This was known as the Czarna Droga—Black Road. It is still visible today.

The area around Poniatowo was considered suitable for a remote and secret gassing establishment as it fulfilled the required criteria for such a facility. It was close to Malkinia Gora, an important rail junction on the Warsaw to Bialystok rail link, and could therefore receive the Jewish population of the large ghettos in those nearby cities. There was a ready-made workforce in the vicinity at the Treblinka labour camp and in the local villages of Wegrow and Stoczec Wegrowski. A few SS men earmarked a plot of sandy, infertile land, around 32 acres in size, between the borders of Poniatowo and Wolka Okraglik. The selected site was in a pine forested area, well away from populated areas and it was hidden from view. A Leipzig firm, Schonbronn, and a Warsaw-based firm, Schmidt-Munstermann, were contracted to supervise the construction.

Soon afterwards, construction materials such as pipework, sanitary installation parts, bags of cement, and boards arrived on trucks. A telephone line was installed between the site and the local post office. Materials were supplied by SS-Untersturmführer Heinz Auerswald of the Warsaw Ghetto administration office. Trees from the local forest were felled to provide timber. After the construction of barracks, a barbed-wire perimeter fence was erected with pine branches interwoven, and watch towers were built at strategic locations. A concrete ramp was installed at the rail spur, to accommodate a locomotive and up to twenty wagons. The construction took about two months in total.

The camp design was very similar to Sobibor. At the area designated for the future killing operation in the south-east corner of the site, an excavator was used to dig large pits about 30 metres in length. An anti-tank wall was also constructed around the outside perimeter of this area to shield it from the outside world.

Both the Germans and the Ukrainians were brutal in their treatment of the Jewish workers. Murders were commonplace, and not a single Jewish worker employed on the construction of Treblinka II survived. The finished site had a dedicated power station, an armoury, living quarters for the camp personnel and a contingent of work Jews, undressing buildings and storage facilities, a roll-call square and a separate reception square, a barber's room, a valuables deposit, a Lazaret, and, remarkably, a zoo. These were all located near the arrival rail spur. A large sorting building was disguised as a station, even with a large station clock. From the undressing buildings, the usual fenced 'tube' served as a gated access to the gas chambers.

At Treblinka, the 'tube' was about 100–120 metres in length and 2 metres wide. On the ground was white gravel and it was lined with flowers. The Jewish prisoners referred to it as 'the pipe', while the German euphemism was 'Himmelstrasse'. The 'tube' was in the open, about 10 metres from the nearest trees. It was constructed of barbed wire, with interwoven pine branches. For the evacuees, this was the only living access route to the Totenlager (death camp), which housed the gas chambers and burial pits, in addition to a barrack for the Totenjuden (death Sonderkommando).

The first gas chamber building consisted of three chambers of about 5 metres by 5 metres, connected to a small engine room. The structure was built about 50 metres from the end of the 'tube', which afforded a view of burial pits prior to entering the gas chambers. This created panic for those about to meet their fate and was soon recognised as a design flaw. The capacity was around 200 persons per chamber and was similar to those operated initially at Bełżec and Sobibor. One of the bricklayers used in the construction, Jan Sulkowski, described the building:

> SS men said it was to be a bath. Only later on, when the building was almost completed, I realised that it was to be a gas chamber. What was indicative of it was a special door of thick steel insulated with rubber, twisted with a bolt and placed in an iron frame, and also the fact that in one of the building compartments there was put an engine, from which three iron pipes led through the roof to the three remaining parts of the building.... A specialist from Berlin came to put tiles inside and he told me that he had already built such a chamber elsewhere.[3]

There was no minefield surrounding the camp as at Sobibor. The perimeter fence stood at between 3 and 4 metres in height. Signposts along the approach road from the direction of Malkinia announced any road users that they were approaching a prohibited area of the forest. Within one kilometre of the camp, they were liable to be shot.

The first camp commandant was Dr Irmfried Eberl, the practised T4 specialist who had recently spent some time at Chełmno for further experience. On 7 July 1942, he advised Heinz Auerswald that Treblinka would be in a position to accept transports of Jews for resettlement from 11 July 1942. The camp was officially designated 'SS-Sonderkommando Treblinka' and was referred to in official documents as 'T II'.

The 'Grossaktion Warschau' (the Warsaw Great Action), as the clearance operation became known, was part of Aktion Reinhardt. At 10 a.m. on 22 July 1942, Hermann Höfle informed Adam Czerniakow, the president of the Judenrat, about the 'resettlement' operation destined for the East. The Jewish Ghetto Police were ordered to assist the action. Its role was to assist with round-ups, facilitate requisitions, and escort those to be deported to the Umschlagplatz (the collection and loading point). They were told that deportees were to be transported to a labour and forwarding camp, from whence they would be evacuated to the East. Their true final destination was Treblinka.

The Warsaw Umschlagplatz was located at ul. Stawki 4–6. At this place, in 1921, a large warehouse complex stood beside a railway ramp. By 1935, a large new school building was added. In December 1940, the Umschlagplatz was used by the Transfer Office, which eventually controlled the trade between the later ghetto and the Aryan side. This was the location of the subsequent official customs office of the ghetto. It was also through this point that new arrivals to the ghetto passed. From July 1942, this site was the scene of detention, selection, and loading of deportees.

Regular transports left the Umschlagplatz, destined for the gas chambers in the countryside at Treblinka. In the final phase of the action, between 6 September and 11 September 1942, under Höfle's command, approximately 90,000 people were rounded-up from the area of ul. Smocza, ul. Gęsia, ul. Zamenhofa, ul. Szczęśliwą, and Plac Parysowski. In the resultant selection, about 32,000 people were spared and remained in the ghetto. Approximately 2,600 were shot, and over 54,000 were deported to Treblinka.

The Yom Kippur festival on 21 September 1942 was the final day of the Great Action. That day, the Jewish Police numbers were reduced from 2,400 to 380. The majority of Jewish policemen and their families were deported to the gas chambers. In total, around 265,000 Jews were deported during the operation. About 10,000 were murdered on the spot, and approximately 70,000 people remained in the residual ghetto, some in hiding. Approximately 75 per cent of the inhabitants of the ghetto were transported to Treblinka. The remaining area of the ghetto was limited to the buildings occupied by the production facilities in the northern part of the closed district, and the Tobbens' factory in the area of ul. Panska.

The first transport of 6,500 Jews departed from the Warsaw Ghetto on the evening of 22 July 1942. The vast majority of evacuees were murdered on arrival at Treblinka II the following morning. The camp became fully operational that day with the arrival of a further 7,300 Jews from Warsaw. This was followed on 24 July by a transport of 7,400. By the end of the first week, 51,950 Jews from Warsaw had arrived at Treblinka, nearly all dying in the gas chambers. The pattern of daily arrivals of large transports continued into August. On 5 August 1942, the first transport of Jews from the liquidation action in the Radom Ghetto was one of two transports to arrive on the same day.

Eberl's ambition to surpass previous figures achieved at Bełżec and Sobibor, resulted in his exaggeration of the capabilities of his killing facility. SS-Unterscharführer August Hingst stated: 'Dr Eberl's ambition was to reach the highest possible numbers and exceed all the other camps. So many transports arrived that the disembarkation and gassing of the people could no longer be handled'.[4]

SS-Unterscharführer Willi Mentz subsequently described Eberl's mismanagement of the camp:

> He was very ambitious. It was said that he ordered more transports than could be processed in the camp. That meant that trains had to wait outside the camp because the occupants of the previous transport had not yet all been killed. At the time, it was very hot and as a result of the long wait inside the transport trains in the intense heat, many people died. At that time, whole mountains of bodies lay on the platform…[5]

The regular daily arrivals gathered pace in August 1942, putting the camp gassing facility and the staff under increasing pressure. Mechanical breakdowns of the Soviet tank engine were commonplace and chaos reigned with queues awaiting their turn to die. Without the combustion engine to provide carbon monoxide exhaust gas, the SS and Ukrainians resorted to shooting the deportees. The sound of gunfire from the camp was frequent. When the gas chambers were operating at full capacity, the Sonderkommando were unable to despose of the corpses fast enough and the gas chambers were not cleaned sufficiently after each action. The deception of a transit camp for new arrivals was soon abandoned as the sight of dead bodies and piles of clothes littering the arrivals area gave away the true nature of the camp. Oskar Berger, who arrived on 22 August in one of the four transports that day, stated:

> As we disembarked, we witnessed a horrible sight: hundreds of bodies lying all around. Piles of bundles, clothes, valises, everything mixed together. SS soldiers, Germans and

> Ukrainians were standing on the roofs of barracks and firing indiscriminately into the crowd. Men, women and children fell bleeding. The air was filled with screaming and weeping. Those not wounded by the shooting were forced through an open gate, jumping over the dead and wounded, to a square fenced with barbed wire.[6]

Abraham Goldfarb, who arrived at Treblinka on 25 August from the Miedzyrzec Podlaski Ghetto, described his experience:

> When we reached Treblinka and the Germans opened the freight car doors, the scene was ghastly. The cars were full of corpses. The bodies had been partially consumed by chlorine. The stench from the cars caused those still alive to choke. The Germans ordered everyone to disembark from the cars; those who could were half-dead. SS and Ukrainians waiting nearby beat us and shot at us…[7]

Christian Wirth, in his new role as inspector of Aktion Reinhardt, paid a visit to Treblinka with Josef Oberhauser on 19 August 1942. Appalled at what they found, they hurriedly drove to the Brühl Palace in Warsaw where they reported to Globocnik who was in the city.

Odilo Globocnik received reports of the chaotic scenes at Treblinka with dismay. The repairs to the railway between Warsaw and Sobibor which had caused a temporary halt to the actions at Sobibor camp, added to the already high numbers of transports from Warsaw to Treblinka. On 26 August 1942, Globocnik, Wirth, and Oberhauser, accompanied by two unidentified civilians, visited Treblinka to see for themselves. By the time of their inspection, a total of 307,622 evacuees had arrived at Treblinka, the vast majority of whom had been gassed or shot. This staggering figure had taken a few days in excess of one month to achieve.

The only post-war survivor of this visit, Josef Oberhauser, later declared:

> In Treblinka everything was in a state of collapse. The camp was overstocked. Outside the camp, a train with deportees was unable to be unloaded as there was simply no more room. Many corpses of Jews were lying insidE the camp. These corpses were already bloated. Particularly, I can remember seeing many corpses in the vicinity of the fence. These people had been shot from the guard towers…[8]

Globocnik was appalled at what confronted him. He immediately set plans in motion to relieve Eberl of his command. Rumours of Eberl pilfering valuables from the seized Jewish property, and passing the ill-gotten gains to his superiors at the Reich Chancellery as gifts, had not bypassed Globocnik's ears. Globocnik was also shocked by Eberl's apparent lack of regard towards the supposed clandestine nature of the work at Treblinka. With the camp at Sobibor experiencing a lull in activity as a result of the temporary suspension of the rail service there, Franz Stangl was available as an immediate replacement. Globocnik had been impressed by Stangl in his first few months at Sobibor. He also had a replacement in mind for the vacancy created at Sobibor—SS-Obersturmführer Franz Reichleitner, also a T 4 specialist.

Stangl described his arrival in Treblinka:

> Treblinka that day was the most awful thing I saw during all of the Third Reich … it was Danté's Inferno.… When I got out of the car on the square I stepped knee-deep into money … I waded in notes, currency, precious stones, jewellery, clothes. They were everywhere, strewn all over the square. The smell was indescribable; the hundreds, no the thousands of bodies everywhere, decomposing, putrefying.[9]
>
> When I arrived at Treblinka the first time, a large board was located in the reception square. As I remember, on this board were noted ten clauses … it alluded to the fact that all have to go to the baths and in the meantime the clothes would be disinfected.… Wirth ordered the signboard removed. In its place, the SS men would verbally announce the directions … these short announcements were translated by the working Jews.[10]

Stangl insisted that Eberl was still in post when he first arrived at Treblinka, and that it was Eberl who showed him around the camp:

> There was shooting everywhere.… I asked him what was happening to the valuables; why weren't they being sent to HQ? He said … 'The transports are being ransacked before they ever leave Warsaw'.
>
> I went straight back to warsaw and told Globocnik that it was impossible. No order such as he had given me could be carried out in that place. 'It's the end of the world,' I said to him, and told him about the thousands of rotting corpses. He said, 'It's supposed to be the end of the world for them.'[11]

Wirth was summoned to Warsaw for an immediate meeting with Globocnik the following day and he then accompanied Stangl back to Treblinka where Stangl took over command of the camp from Eberl who was ordered back to T4. Four of his staff members also joined him. Wirth stayed in Treblinka for the first two weeks of Stangl's command and totally tidied up the chaos left by Eberl.

According to Stangl's post-war account, all transports from Warsaw were halted on Wirth's orders until organisation was resumed. This directive must have had Globocnik's agreement. Existing records corroborate Stangl's memory. There were no transports from Warsaw to Treblinka for the period 28 August 1942 until 2 September 1942 inclusive. On 3 September 1942, transports resumed from Warsaw with the departure of a train carrying 4,609 victims. They were gassed on arrival the following morning.

SS-Unterscharführer Franz Suchomel, a former photographer for T4 at Hadamar, arrived on the staff of Treblinka in August 1942. His post-war evidence appears to be generally reliable. Suchomel insists that Eberl had already left the camp by the time of Stangl's arrival. He recalled:

> The first suggestion I heard Stangl make after he arrived, was to put buckets in the tube for the women. They all defacated you know, while they ran, or stood there waiting. Stangl said he had put buckets in the tube in Sobibor and it had proved helpful. Wirth answered, 'I don't care a damn what you did with the shit in Sobibor. Let them beshit themselves. It can be cleaned up afterwards.'[12]

This led to two men from the Sonderkommando being assigned the job of cleaning up excrement from the tube between transports.

Suchomel also declared on 14 September 1967 in Düsseldorf, during the investigation into Franz Stangl:

> I went to Treblinka at the end of August 1942. Before that I was at the Welfare Institute Hadamar and occasionally worked in Berlin at T4. As I remember, I came to Treblinka with Hirtreiter, Post, Loffler, Sydow, and two people from Frankfurt; also with Matthes. One of the two Frankfurters could have been called Schuh, whose name has just been mentioned. I cannot remember the name of the other one. It was not Post.
>
> When I arrived in Treblinka Dr Eberl was still Commandant. I stayed in Treblinka until October 1943 when I was posted to Sobibor. I went several times on home leave from Treblinka. Once, for the birth of my youngest daughter on the 18 September 1942. Altogether there were four occasions when I had home leave from Treblinka.
>
> From Sobibor I later went to Italy.
>
> At the end of the war I was captured by the Americans, but released as early as August 1945. Since 1949, I have lived in Alotting. I could of course not return to my home town of Krummau-Bohmerwald after the war.
>
> Under Dr Eberl there was chaos in the camp. So many transports were arriving that it was impossible to deal with them. In my opinion, when these transports arrived two thirds of those transported were already dead. At that time, I had to work on the ramp and I therefore know this accurately.
>
> After I had been in Treblinka quite a short time, one night Wirth appeared there. He had a fierce argument with Dr Eberl. At that time, my quarters and those of the other NCOs were in the Commandant's hut and so I heard what was going on.
>
> In the course of this dissension Wirth dismissed Dr Eberl.
>
> Wirth then went off for a day and returned accompanied by a detail consisting of Germans and Ukrainians. In Warsaw, he arranged for a three day break in the arrival of transports, and immediately commenced a total reorganisation of the camp.

> The method of operation was changed and the 'tube' relocated. The erection of a new gas chamber was started. At that time Wirth stayed in Treblinka throughout and supervised the new arrangements which included the creation of Jewish work details in both the upper and lower camps. Until then there had only been the so-called 'Court Jews.' i.e. craftsmen and others who had to carry out personal services for the Germans.
>
> As I remember it Stangl arrived in Treblinka at the beginning of September 1942. I know for certain that he signed my leave pass. That was on 18 September 1942. My daughter was born on 19 September. I recollect that when I reached Berlin my daughter had already been born.
>
> I also remember the date because on the advice of a railway employee from Malkinia I took a normal civilian train and not the train carrying personnel on leave. I learned later that this train had been in collision with a train from Lodz and there had been many casualties.
>
> On my written application Stangl also granted me some additional days of leave as I needed to take my son to hospital.
>
> When I returned to Treblinka on 1 October I ran into Hauptmann Schemmel. I assumed that Stangl was looking after Sobibor or was himself on leave. At any rate, he was not in Treblinka when I returned. I remember that the new gas chambers had been completed and were in use.[13]

Franz Suchomel was interviewed by Claude Lanzmann for his epic documentary film about the holocaust. *Shoah* was directed by Lanzmann and released in 1985. Suchomel's interview was secretly filmed without his knowledge and it was conducted only on agreement that his identity would not be revealed. Suchomel described the the process at the gas chambers of Treblinka:

| | |
|---|---|
| Suchomel: | In the meantime, the new gas chambers were built. |
| Lanzmann: | When, in which month? |
| Suchomel: | September. |
| Lanzmann: | And who built the gas chambers? |
| Suchomel: | Hackenholt. Under the leadership of Hackenholt and Lambert these gas chambers were built by Jews. |
| Lanzmann: | The Jews worked? Built them? |
| Suchomel: | The Jews worked. The Jews built the gas chambers, eh. That is, the brickwork. The doors, those were made by the Ukrainian carpenters. The Ukrainians made those. And the doors in the gas chambers, those were iron doors from bunkers. Those were brought, I think, maybe from Bialystok—there were Russian bunkers there. |
| Lanzmann: | Yes. And what was the capacity of the new gas chambers? There were two gas chambers, weren't there? |

Suchomel: Yes. The old one was shut down, but not demolished. When a lot of transports came, that is, a lot of people, then this gas chamber was used too.

Lanzmann: Yes, of course.

Suchomel: And here—the Jews say five on each side; I say four, but only the ones on this side were used—during operation, this side, see?

Lanzmann: And why not the other side?

Suchomel: Because then the transportation of the corpses would have been too complicated.

Lanzmann: Aha. Too far?

Suchomel: Yes. Because Wirth then had this camp built and for up here, had worker Jews assigned. That was a regular Jewish Detachment of around 200 people.

Lanzmann: Those in the death camp…

Suchomel: Who always worked in the death camp. And then there were…

Lanzmann: Only 200?

Suchomel: 200, yes.

Lanzmann: Women too?

Suchomel: They came later. So, the men could stand it better. The most beautiful young Jewesses, eh.

Lanzmann: The most beautiful?

Suchomel: Yes, yes—Steiner got that right. Very beautiful, eh. Imagine—with this inferno. There is nothing to laugh about.

Lanzmann: Oh no.

Suchomel: There's nothing to laugh about. Because love was the only comfort.

Lanzmann: Yes. Ah—love was the only comfort?

Suchomel: Yes. They were such poor people, eh? Such poor people.

Lanzmann: Yes.

Suchomel: Then stretchers were built. Say, can you translate that for him? Stretchers for carrying. Primitive stretchers were built…

Lanzmann: Primitive ones?

Suchomel: Yes. And then the corpses were put on them and carried to the trench.

Lanzmann: Yes. But what was the capacity of the new gas chamber?

Suchomel: The new gas chamber—well, you could be done with 3,000 people in two hours.

Lanzmann: Yes. Done. But how many people could [fit into] the gas chamber?

Suchomel: That—I can't tell you exactly as a German. The Jews say 200.

Lanzmann: 200?

Suchomel: Yes. 200. You have to imagine that in one room that's the size of the room over there.

Lanzmann: In Auschwitz, it was a lot more.
Suchomel: Yes, Auschwitz was a factory.
Lanzmann: And Treblinka, that was a …?
Suchomel: I'll give you my definition. Remember it. Though Treblinka was very primitive, it was a well-functioning assembly line of death.
Lanzmann: Assembly line?
Suchomel: … of death. Do you understand?
Lanzmann: Yes, yes, yes. I think you're right. But primitive.
Suchomel: Primitive. Granted, primitive. But a well-functioning assembly line of death.
Lanzmann: And Bełżec was primitive?
Suchomel: Bełżec was the studio. Wirth was the camp commandant there. And Wirth tried everything out there.
Lanzmann: Experienced it?
Suchomel: Yes. At the beginning, he had bad experiences. The trenches were overfilled, the sewer went to the front of the dining room, it stank…
Lanzmann: In front of the dining room?
Suchomel: In front of the dining room. In front of the barrack.
Lanzmann: Did you ever see Bełżec?
Suchomel: No. Wirth tried things there with his people—with Franz, with Oberhauser, with Hackenholt. Then they were supposed to put three corpses into the trench, so Wirth would know how much room he'd need. When they didn't want to do that—Franz didn't want to—he beat Franz with the whip, and Hackenholt too, eh?
Lanzmann: Kurt Franz?
Suchomel: Kurt Franz. That's how Wirth was. And Wirth came to Treblinka with these experiences.
Lanzmann: To Treblinka and to Sobibor too.
Suchomel: Sobibor was behind him. He'd already been there. Yes, he was also an Inspector at Sobibor, but for him, the main camp was Treblinka. The main camp, eh. Wirth reorganised everything, then new transports came, then he constantly selected. Understand? Choosing a thousand or five hundred men, having them stand at attention, here, from those thousand men, he selected again and sent so and so many off to be shot. People heard that, that there was shooting here.[14]

Oberhauser agreed with Suchomel's recollection of events surrounding Eberl's dismissal. He recalled that Globocnik dismissed Eberl during his visit of 26 August, and issued orders to totally reorganise the camp, putting Wirth in temporary command. Oberhauser stated that Globocnik decided there and then, leaning against a barrack door in the square, how the camp should be run and that Franz Stangl was the ideal replacement for Eberl. Globocnik would arrange matters through his office the following day. This appears the more likely sequence of events and would explain the way in which Stangl took over command of Treblinka on 1 September 1942. Stangl probably altered the events for the sake of minimising his guilt.

Soon after Stangl's arrival in Treblinka, he was joined by Kurt Franz, a former cook at T4. Franz was born on 17 January 1914 in Düsseldorf. A member of the NSDAP since 1932, Franz joined the SS-Totenkopfverbände in 1937 and served at Buchenwald concentration camp near Weimar. He was selected in late 1939 for service at T4 and was appointed as a cook at Hartheim, Brandenburg, Grafeneck, and Sonnenstein euthanasia institutes, before a posting at Tiergartenstrasse in Berlin.

On 20 April 1942, Franz was promoted to SS-Oberscharführer and he was then transferred to Lublin. He soon found himself at Bełżec where he remained until his transfer to Treblinka in early September 1942. At Treblinka, as a result of his boyish good looks, Franz was known as 'Lalke' by the Jewish prisoners. In Yiddish, lalke means 'doll'. His behaviour was nothing like that of a doll. He was feared by all the prisoners for his brutality and willingness to kill. He owned a large St Bernard dog named Barry, which accompanied his master on his rounds of the camp. Barry was trained to attack prisoners on command and was renowned for his ability to bite the buttocks or genital area of the unfortunate victim.

Franz was Stangl's successor as camp commandant after the latter's departure and he was given responsibility for the demolition of the camp site following its closure. He then transferred to Trieste and remained a free man until his eventual arrest in 1959. A search of his apartment uncovered a photo album with the words 'Schöne Zeiten' ('lovely times') written on one of the pages displaying photographs taken in Trieste and Treblinka. On 3 September 1965, Franz was given a life sentence for his complicity in the murder of at least 300,000 people. He was released in 1993 on health grounds, and he died on 4 July 1998 in Wuppertal. He never admitted his guilt. An interview following his release from prison revealed his continued denials:

> Interviewer: Mr. Franz, I assume it was clear that Treblinka was an extermination camp.
> Franz: Yes, people died there or had their lives taken.
> I: By gas?
> F: By gas.
> I: How was the gas produced?
> F: I haven't seen that, but I knew there was a French truck. If I am not wrong, a Saurer, or a Saurer engine. And there, exhaust gas was fed into the cells. The cells had been on the side.

I: How long did the people suffer?

F: I cannot say this, you know. It was said 4 to 10 minutes, but I cannot say it. I was not in charge up there. An Oberscharführer Matthes was in charge, but he was not a real Oberschaführer, more a police officer. In Treblinka all were police officers, whereas in Bełżec some SS officer named Nieman did the work which was done in Treblinka by this man.

I: You have seen gassings in two camps? Not only 'seen', you attended gassings?

F: I know that it had happened, I know it. I wasn't sent to Treblinka to be told those things. Everything was done secretly, under camouflage, but I knew it; I saw it; I was pissed, even in Treblinka.

I: You ddn't want to assist?

F: I didn't want to particpate and that meant death to Jirmann, and it ment death to the Ukrainian Alexejew Pior, who was shot.

I: I have here in front of me a Treblinka plan. Can you show me how the gassing procedure happened?

F: People were driven inside by wagons. I think 20 wagons were fitting inside, and then the doors were swept open. Those were always Jews, even when I arrived there. If from Stangl or Eberl, I don't know. I never experienced Eberl. The Jews were unloaded and led to this place [indicating the selection square on a plan of Treblinka II]. I don't remember it having been sided by two huts or one, but I think one. Those people had to enter the hut und undress. So far, I can say that.

I: Stripped naked?

F: Naked. And there was a corner where the women's hair was cut off. This was done by Suchomel, with whom I am really mad because he accused me. And then those Jews, and to be honest I never saw children, were lead through the so called 'tube', which was completely covered with tan, it was hidden like everything in the camp. They had an extra camouflage command, led by someone named Südow, or so. He was responsible that no one could see a thing. The Jews were then led up here and entered the so-called gas chamber. And there they were gassed. That is a fact. From this positon I do not move.

I: Did you see the mountains of dead bodies?

F: No. I hadn't seen it. I knew from where I probably could have seen it, but that would have meant to peek through a hole, or cut some wire. I didn't go there. I was disgusted. I cannot stand such things. I couldn't see people burn. They had been put here on a roast and burnt. Here they were burnt.

I: What happened to the ashes?

F: I cannot say. There was initially no roast. When I was there, there was none. Some other Unterführer made the roast. Before that, there were pits, in which the corpses were laid … by crane. They came from the gas chamber and had been carried to the pits. That's how I see it. And after the roast was available, they had been torn out by crane and put on the roast.... Jews did that.... I didn't take notice of it.... They had been placed on it ... even the ones out of the soil ... and they were burnt. And then there were sieves. Anglulated ones like for sieving sand ... and the ashes were sieved through it, and what was remained as solid was mangled and whipped until all ...

I: Disappeared?

F: Disappeared.

I: Have you seen 'Furuncle SS'?

F: Who?

I: 'Furuncle SS'; someone named 'Booz'; he was in the SS, not wanting to participate in gassing, so he scratched his own furuncles [boils] until they were infected. He then was discharged.

F: In Treblinka?

I: Yes.

F: Never heared of him.

I: You said the women's hair was cut off. Wasn't it the gold Jews who took the jewellery and the dentists, tearing out the teeth? You know from that?

F: I never heared from something alike. I haven't seen it. That was an internal affair; not my business. Up there, Matthes was responsible. Up there where the Jews were killed, Küttner was the one in charge. I was in charge for the guards. That was the assignment. This Küttner didn't take orders fom me. He was a police officer in a superior rank.

I: Did you see how the items were delivered, like the gold?

F: In this cottage, the clothing was sorted. That was the clothing cottage. Where the rail track was. Those garments were simply stockpiled by some work Jews ... garments and glasses ... you could see that without any problem; it was in the middle of the place.

I: From which army branches did the German forces derive?

F: All from police, with a very few exceptions from the general SS.

I: Waffen-SS?

F: I was Waffen-SS, and probably one more person named Willi Mätzig, aka 'Bubi'. He was the paymaster. He was in charge, he was Waffen-SS.

I: The rest Ukrainians?

F: Ukrainians and German speaking ones you cannot call Ukrainians.

I: Volksdeutsche?

F: They were Russian and came from behind the Urals. They spoke fluently with a Württemberg accent. They had lived there for a longtime, like their parents and grandparents. They spoke perfect German. Probably Volksdeutsche. In former times we nicknamed them 'booty Germans'.

I: Those mass murders happened half a century ago. What do you think of them today?

F: If I had known what would have come after I changed from the Wehrmacht to the SS, I never would I have changed. For the simple reason I cannot stand what happened there, at Treblinka and Bełżec.

I: Why were those people killed? Criminals?

F: What, why? I never ever have had any problems with Jews. And I have to insist that the co-accuser, a Dr Neumann, had testified that I had been in his appartment long ago having threatened him—I didn't know this man. I didn't have anything against Jews—I played handball with them in Ratingen and I played with them in Düsseldorf against Maccabi. I hadn't any dspute. I don't see differences between catholics, protestants or Jews. I had a Jewish friend named Ballach who owned a pub in Ratingen, that is a friend of mine. When I was young I went into some dancing club called Hirsch—at the age of 18 or 19. The owners name was also Hirsch, Kurt Hirsch. He was my friend. I had no reason to kill those people.

I: In Bełżec and Treblinka, tens of thousands were killed, women children and men. What did you think?

F: I was against it. In the beginning, nobody knew it anyway. Some pits were dug. In 1942, when I came, nothing happened. I didn't know what the pits were for. There was an old border line—the old Austrian-Russian frontier—between Bełżec and Rawaruska. That I knew. I didn't know what was to come.

I: What would you do, receiving the same orders today?

F: Never, ever.[15]

Treblinka II operated purely as a centre for murdering the Jews of the General Government by carbon monoxide gas. The vast majority of the victims of Treblinka came from the large ghettos in Warsaw and Bialystok, in addition to those of smaller towns. A few locations outside the General Government supplied victims for the gas chambers situated in the pine forest at Poniatowo. The Höfle Telegram provides a total of victims at Treblinka, until 31 December 1942, as 713,555.[16] The final estimate for deaths at Treblinka is in the region of 870,000.

These sorts of figures divorced reality from fiction for the perpetrators. Franz Stangl recalled:

> To tell the truth, one did become used to it … they were cargo. I think it started the day I first saw the Totenlager [extermination area] in Treblinka. I remember Wirth standing there, next to the pits full of black and blue corpses. It had nothing to do with humanity—it could not have. It was a mass—a mass of rotting flesh. Wirth said, 'What shall we do with this garbage?' I think unconsciously that started me thinking of them as cargo. I rarely saw them as individuals. It was always a huge mass. I sometimes stood on the wall and saw them in the 'tube'—they were naked, packed together, running, being driven with whips…[17]

The small area occupied by the two gas chamber buildings at Treblinka was the scene of one of the greatest crimes committed by man on his fellow man, second only to the death factory at Auschwitz-Birkenau. It was shielded from the rest of the camp by a row of trees. The tube was about 60 metres longer prior to the new gas chambers being erected. There was a well next to the original building, and the machine pump room stood approximately 15 metres from the old gas chamber building. The gas chamber building was constructed of brick, covered in grey concrete, and was of a rectangular shape, resembling a little bathhouse, set in trees. Four steps of narrowing width, flanked by wooden screens, led up to the entrance, about 2.1 metres high and 1.8 metres wide. The building had a flat roof, which was concealed from the air by a green net. Underneath the netting, but above the roof space, a tangle of piping was evident. Some descriptions give the roof a slight slant.

The entrance opened to an internal timber corridor, with steel doors that opened into the corridor and were hermetically sealed when shut by a rubber-mounted surround. They were secured shut by heavy metal bolts on the outside. Each of the three doors to the internal chambers had a small peep window of reinforced glass. The doors were 1.8 metres high and 90 cm wide. The door frames were also made of metal.

The external whitewashed doors were made of heavy timber and were also sealed with rubber. They were opened from the outside like up-and-over garage doors and were secured open by means of a heavy metal support. When closed tight, they were secured by a large timber bar bolt which rested in metal hooks either side of the door. The doors were 1.80 metres by 2.50 metres.

There were three internal rooms, accessible from the corridor, each approximately 4 metres by 4 metres and 2.6 metres in height. The walls were part-tiled with small white porcelain tiles, up to about half the height of the chamber. The floors were covered by terracotta tiles, which sloped slightly towards the external door side of the chamber. Nickel-plated shower heads were set into the ceiling. There was no internal piping. Each individual chamber had its own gas pipe inlet, which was fed from the engine room outside. There was a small grated window outlet, approximately 0.5 metres by 0.5 metres, in the roof of each chamber for the extraction of gas following each action. They were sealed by a hermetic cap during each action. This opening also allowed for chlorine to be poured into each chamber.

Outside the chambers, on the side of the external doors, was a raised concrete platform, about 80 cm above ground level. It was 2 metres in width and stretched the whole length of the building, with four steps at either end. The engine room contained a former Soviet tank engine that was used to produce the exhaust gas for the gas chambers. It was operated by Ivan Marchenko. In the same room was a generator for the electricity supply for the camp.

After the old gas chambers ceased to operate as a killing facility, wooden planks were set on the floors of each chamber and the building was used as a tailor's shop.

The new gas chamber building was erected soon after Stangl's arrival in Treblinka. It was 18 metres wide and about 36 metres long and was also constructed of brick, covered in a pale grey concrete shell on a concrete base. The finished single-story structure resembled a ritual Jewish bathhouse, along the lines of an old fashioned synagogue. It was much larger than previous similar gas chamber buildings built by the Germans.

It was reached via a shortened 'tube', which ended opposite the main entrance of the building. This entrance, on the north side, was reached by climbing five wide concrete steps with flowerpots either side. Along the north side of the building were flower boxes on the ground. Above the door was a copper Star of David, attached to the end roof gable, and a Hebrew inscription that read, 'This is the gateway to God. Righteous men will pass through'. The 2 metres wide entrance was covered by a dark coloured curtain.

Inside was a 2-metre-wide central corridor that ran the length of the building. Either side were five heavy steel doors uniformly spaced along the length of the corridor.[18] At the far end was another door, which led to the engine room. There was probably no ceiling to the corridor, revealing the timber frame beneath the roof. The corridor walls were covered in grey plaster. Each of the ten steel doors were 1.8 metres by 0.90 metres and they retained rubber seals around the inside edges. The material of the door frames is unknown, but may well have also been of metal construction as in the old gas chamber door frames. Each door had a reinforced glass observation window at the left side at chest height, which was also barred on the inside. The doors were secured by three hinged metal bars and were illuminated by a light above each one.

Upon entering a gas chamber, the victims would have seen shower heads and pipework at the ceiling level. Opposite the entrance door was a larger sealed doorway, about 2 metres by 1.8 metres. The door was of heavy timber covered in sheet metal and could only be opened from the outside. It was of up and over design, hinged at the top. The only light emanated from the peep window. The ceiling was clad in zinc metal and was almost certainly of timber construction. The walls and floor were constructed of brick and concrete. The floor was covered in terracotta tiles, and the walls had orange porcelain tiles up to a height of one metre. The floor sloped slightly towards the large exit doorway in the outside wall. Each chamber was 2 metres in height and 7 metres by 7 metres in area, giving a total of 490 square metres for the gassing process.

The outside doors were secured by a large wooden beam that rested in large metal hooks either side of the doorway. Wooden wedges were hammered into place to seal the door tight. Each door was hinged at the top and was clad in sheet metal on the inside. The wooden locking beam served as a support for the door when opened. When supported open, this doorway was where cadavers were extracted by the Sonderkommando for transfer to the burial pits and later the cremation grids, on a rolling narrow gauge platform.

The building itself had a sloping saddled roof with ventilation grilles to aid ventilation of the carbon monoxide gas after an action. The saddle was directly above the length of the internal corridor. The roof had a pitch of about 15 degrees and was covered with tar paper. It was almost certainly of a timber truss construction with spacing of 1.3 metres.

As in the two other death camps of Aktion Reinhardt, there is controversy over the type of fuel used in the combustion engines to produce the carbon monoxide exhaust gas. Witness evidence, although sometimes contradictory, indicates that the engines at Bełżec and Sobibor were petrol driven and not diesel driven. It is the same for Treblinka, where the key testimony is provided by Nikolay Shalayev, one of those identified as operating the engines. The operators were known as the Treblinka 'motorists', the other one being Ivan Marchenko. Shalayev testified in 1950:

> It was an ordinary, four-cylinder engine which used gasoline and, according to the story of the German machine operator, was of Russian make. The engine was installed on a wooden frame and started as soon as people were herded into the gas chamber rooms, whereupon the exhaust pipe was covered up and the valve of the pipe was opened, through which the exhaust entered the 'bath'.[19]

One of the Ukrainian guards, Ivan Shevchenko, also disputed the layout of the gassing building, under interrogation in September 1944:

> A stone building, the so-called 'dushegubka', had nine chambers inside, in which people were murdered by asphyxiation with gases. In the tenth chamber, there was an engine of high power which pumped the gas into the chambers.... In the last chamber on the right side in the north-eastern corner of the building, there was a high power engine which worked on petrol or ligroin.[20]

The confusion over gasoline or diesel may have arisen over the insertion of a diesel-driven power generator in each of the engine rooms. On balance, it appears that the more reliable witnesses—those that had direct contact with the engines—indicate the use of gasoline to produce carbon monoxide exhaust in all three death camps, and not diesel.

The introduction of the new gas chambers increased the capacity to kill from 200 per chamber in the old building, to between 1,000 and 1,200 per chamber in the new building. This achieved the primary objective of Wirth and Stangl. Lorenz Hackenholt was summoned from Bełżec to assist with the new construction.

On 18 January 1943, the Germans recommenced the clearance of the Warsaw Ghetto. The first clearance operation of six months earlier had met little, or no, resistance from the ghetto inhabitants, as the belief of evacuation to labour camps in the east was promulgated. This time, however, word had reached the remaining inhabitants of people 'disappearing' in gas chambers. They built bunkers and imported weapons in order to put up a fight. While Jewish families hid in their bunkers, fighters of the right-wing Jewish Military Union (ZZW) were joined by elements of the left-wing Jewish Combat Organisation (ZOB) and engaged the Germans in direct resistance. Both sides suffered casualties and the deportation measures were halted after a few days, with only 5,000 deported out of Globocnik's planned 8,000.

The Germans lost control of the ghetto, and the resistance fighters blatantly 'thumbed their noses' at the Nazi oppressors by kidnapping and executing Jewish policemen, Gestapo, and Abwehr agents, and collaborators. The former head of the Ghetto Police, Jozef Szerynski, killed himself, and Dr Alfred Nossig, a member of the Judenrat and a known collaborator, was executed on 22 February 1943.

Deputy SS and Police Leader of Warsaw SS-Oberführer Dr Ferdinand von Sammern-Frankenegg ordered SS and Police troops into the ghetto once more at 6 a.m. on 19 April 1943, the eve of Passover, in order to complete the deportation operation within three days. They were ambushed by Jewish resistance fighters and suffered fifty-nine casualties, with the loss of two combat vehicles.

Himmler was furious and replaced von Sammern-Frankenegg with SS-Brigadeführer Jürgen Stroop, transferring him to Croatia four days later. Stroop proceeded to wage a military campaign against the fighters. He recalled, post-war, an incident which occurred on the very first day of fighting, where two boys raised the Polish national flag and the banner of the ZZW. The flags remained flying for four days:

> The matter of the flags was of great political and moral importance. It reminded hundreds of thousands of the Polish cause; it excited them and unified the population of the General Government, but especially Jews and Poles. Flags and national colours are a means of combat exactly like a rapid-fire weapon, like thousands of such weapons. We all knew that—Himmler, Krüger and Hahn. The Reichsführer shouted into the telephone, 'Stroop, you must bring down those two flags at all costs!'[21]

The battle raged until 16 May 1943. Stroop produced his now famous 'Stroop Report' (see Appendices) and his daily telegraphed bulletins to Himmler's headquarters attest to the ferocity and bravery of the resistance. Stroop later recalled:

> 1 May was memorable for a number of reasons. I witnessed an extraordinary scene that day. A group of prisoners had been herded into the square. In spite of their exhaustion, many of them held their heads high. I stood nearby, surrounded by my escort. Suddenly I heard shots. A young Jew—in his midtwenties I'd guess—was firing a pistol at one of our police officers—one … two … three … fast as lighning. One of the bullets hit the officer's hand. My men sprayed the Jew with fire. I managed to whip out my own pistol and hit him as he fell. As he lay dying, I stood over him, watching his life ebb away. Such are the ways of war. I'll never forget the hate in his eyes. Do you know what he did? With all his remaining strength, he spat at me. When my men saw what he had done, they pumped him so full of lead that he looked like a flattened sack full of bloody meat.[22]

Jürgen Stroop was captured by Americans in 1945 and extradited to Poland where he was tried, convicted, and hanged in 1952. Von Sammern-Frankenegg was killed by partisans in Bosnia on 20 September 1944.

By early 1943, a resistance circle within the camp of work Jews at Treblinka was created. The members decided to rebel against the guards and the provisional date of 15 June 1943 was set for the uprising. This was postponed as a result of a grenade being smuggled into the camp on a transport from Warsaw in May. It was detonated inside the undressing area, causing panic among the SS personnel. Following the incident, most transports from Warsaw were redirected to Majdanek. The reduction in the number of actions made the Sonderkommando realise that their days were numbered and a new date for rebellion was fixed for 2 August 1943.

This date was a Monday, and Mondays were traditionally rest days from actions. A number of guards went for a swim in the River Bug in the hot August weather. At 3.45 p.m., approximately 700 prisoners set barracks ablaze and attacked the guards with stolen arms. The response of the camp guards was a slaughter, using automatic weapons and explosives. The camp Kommandantur appealed for help from the local police and Wehrmacht units. Around 200 prisoners escaped from the camp, pursued on horseback and by car. About half of them were subsequently killed, and seventy survived to the end of the war. One famous escapee, Richard Glazar, attended the post-war trials of guards and wrote his memoires of the camp, but he killed himself in Prague on 20 December 1997.

Himmler was beside himself following the revolt and Stangl attended a meeting with Globocnik and Wirth in Lublin. It was decided that Treblinka had achieved its goal and there was no point in rebuilding the facility. With Himmler's authority, Globocnik ordered the destruction of Treblinka II. Stangl would subsequently transfer to Trieste and Kurt Franz was appointed as the last commandant of Treblinka, to oversee its demolition and cover-up operation.

The uprising had left the gas chambers completely untouched and still fully operational. Although greatly reduced in size and regularity, transports continued to arrive and the gassing process continued. The final transports arrived on 18 and 19 August 1943. Thirty-seven wagons were processed on 18 August, and thirty-nine on 19 August. Both transports contained a combined total of 7,600 survivors from the Bialystok Ghetto uprising. All were gassed upon arrival.

Beginning on 22 August, single freight cars loaded with the clothes of murdered victims left Treblinka:

> Such wagons left the camp on 2, 9, 13 and 21 September.... On 30 September, the German railwayman, Rudolf Emmerich, who was employed to watch the transports entering the death camp, left the Treblinka station and went to Warsaw. At the beginning of October, it was noticed at the station in Treblinka that elements of disassembled barracks, wooden planks, chlorinated lime ... were being shipped out of the death camp. Later, the digger-dredger machine which was no longer needed was taken away.[23]

The barbed-wire perimeter fence was wound up and removed to Treblinka I. Both the old and new gas chamber buildings were demolished. The two combustion engines used to produce carbon monoxide gas were shipped out to Lublin on 21 October. The remaining majority of prisoners were evacuated to Sobibor on 20 October and 4 November, where they were gassed. The armoured vehicle used to transport valuables was shipped out on 5 November. Until 17 November, when the last Ukrainians left the camp, over 100 wagons of planks, rubble, bricks, and pipework were shipped out. Even Barry the dog was given away by Kurt Franz. A farmhouse was built for a Ukrainian family named Strebel, and the ground was ploughed and planted with lupins. The last twenty-five or thirty Jewish prisoners were shot by Willy Mentz, Paul Bredow, and a SS NCO from Treblinka I.[24] Franz, Mentz, and Bredow were the last to leave the site, *en route* to Sobibor by truck. The farm buildings were burned down by the former Ukrainian guard, Strebel, when the approach of the Red Army became imminent.

# 15

# JILTED

One could not describe the SS and Police Leader of Lublin as a handsome man. In his mid-thirties by the time of his appointment in the General Government, he was overweight and stood at a little under 5 feet 8 inches tall. His obvious love of champagne, brandy, and good food did not contribute to a healthy lifestyle. He was, however, generally liked, and possessed a sense of humour, attractive to the opposite sex. A little short of being described as charismatic, Globocnik's powerful position in the SS and police administration of Lublin certainly held him in high regard by the female fraternity, and he was not short of willing lovers. One young blonde secretary in particular caught his eye at one of his many parties held in the villa at Ostlandstrasse.

Irmgard Rickheim was born in Berlin on 8 December 1920. She was Globocnik's junior by sixteen years and was typical of the young German women of the time. Her blonde hair and slim shapely figure drew the attention of several male admirers, including that of her boss, Hans Maubach. Irmgard worked as a secretary in his office and had travelled to Lublin with him in January 1940. She was pretty, but not beautiful, and her immature inexperience led to her becoming more than a little attracted to her dashing and handsome boss. Not one to deter the interest of a young attractive woman, Maubach invited her along to Globocnik's villa parties.

The party host, Odilo Globocnik, had several lovers during his stay in Lublin, their numbers reputedly included his secretary Marianne Hillmann, a certain Frau Radischat, and a member of the local BDM, a Frau Hamacher. Many onlookers also believed that his other secretary, Mimi Trsek, was also too close for her not to be enjoying intimate relations with her boss. All Globocnik's affairs in Lublin were conducted in an air of secrecy, but this was all about to change.

The young Irmgard Rickheim had worked for Maubach's foreign affairs department in the headquarters offices of the Hitler Youth since 1938. On his transfer to Lublin, Maubach resolved to take her with him. Whether or not this was because the pair were involved in an extramarital affair at the time was not confirmed, but Maubach convinced Irmgard's family that the move would not compromise her integrity and could only result in a positive development in her secretarial career. She was the only girl from the pool of secretaries to receive such attention. Maubach obviously went to great pains to ensnare the young woman and he even included her in his travelling party. It is difficult to avoid the assumption that the couple were already heavily 'involved', despite Maubach being a married man.

Irmgard was very popular with the men surrounding her boss, Maubach, and she was soon referred to by her pet names of 'Irmschen' or 'Ricky'. She worked at the offices of the SSPF in the typing pool, but she attended certain meetings to take minutes and prepare typed reports. She certainly came to the attention of Globocnik during work sessions, and along with other girls from the secretarial pool, she was included on the guest lists of Globocnik parties. At one particular party thrown by Globocnik at his Ostlandstrasse villa, she attended accompanied by a young Leutnant, and she caught the eye of the host. She loved to dance, and the vision of a slim, attractive, young blonde woman swirling around on the dancefloor was one temptation too much for the thirty-something bachelor. Globocnik decided he wished to know the girl, and in a somewhat immature move, he enquired after her with his staffer, Maubach. Liking what he saw and heard, Globocnik asked Ernst Lerch to approach the girl on his behalf and advise her of his interest. Maubach's own feelings about the approach are unknown, but he realised that to offend Globocnik would be a disaster. At the first opportunity, Lerch informed Irmgard of Globocnik's interest.

Lerch called at Irmgard's quarters and, invited in, sat on her bed. Although the young woman was aware of the general's interest in her, she was flabbergasted that he had not made the approach himself. She had seen the looks Globocnik had cast in her direction, and she was expecting some sort of a move from him, but this indirect strategy was unexpected. Lerch was an amiable chap and she admired his obvious high regard for his superior officer. A little embarrassed by his task, Lerch suggested that she sit next to Globocnik at the next staff meeting and engage him in friendly conversation.

Irmgard later admitted that she did not love Globocnik, but she was flattered to be the one singled out by the police general.[1] At their next staff meeting a couple of days later, Globocnik was under the influence of too much liquor and her efforts to strike up a reasonable conversation resulted in his blurted request for them to get together. She politely pointed out that he was inebriated, and she asked him to repeat the question when he was sober. The following day, Globocnik called on her with a picnic basket and invited her to go riding with him. She loved horseriding, and mentioned this to Maubach who obviously passed on the information to his boss. Impressed by his efforts to please her, she readily accepted.

The pair found that they relaxed in each other's company and they rode out of Lublin into the surrounding countryside. They stopped for their picnic and were intimate. Although she did not love Globocnik, everything was quickly decided and she moved into his villa a couple of days later. Globocnik was soon to announce the couple were engaged. It was mid-summer 1940.

Irmgard moved into the small room, which she called the 'sewing chamber', next door to Globocnik's bedroom. She ceased to work as a secretary in the office of the SSPF at the end of August 1940, but continued to take dictation and type reports and letters for her suitor. Irmgard flatly denied any knowledge of what Aktion Reinhardt entailed, and she may innocently have been fooled by the camouflaged language and terms used in reports and communications. It is not unreasonable to accept that Globocnik may have decided to omit Irmgard from the circle of knowledge of what was happening to the Jews in the General Government. However, her period of intimacy with the architect of genocide coincided with the maximum operational status of Bełżec, Sobibor, and Treblinka. It would have been difficult for her to ignore the questions of from where the luxurious lifestyle, the mountains of expensive gifts, foodstuffs, and drink, were sourced.

Irmgard declared that she was only ever confronted by the ill-treatment of Jews on one single occasion. In one version, she described visiting the Lipowa Street camp on horseback with her fiancé when they encountered a male Jew, in Middle Eastern dress, who angrily demanded that the Brigadeführer shoot him then and there. In a separate version of the same incident, she stated: 'One day Globocnik and I rode through the Lublin ghetto. I clearly recall one Jewess running up to us saying, "Dear Sir, please shoot me. Come on, shoot me". Globocnik, however, didn't react at all'.[2]

The impressionable young woman began to live a fairytale life of luxury. Globocnik had extravagant taste and this was reflected in his lifestyle, described by one of the fifteen identified secretaries employed in the office of the SSPF: 'I dared criticise Globocnik publicly because of his lifestyle. As a woman, I was disgusted by the way he lived'.[3]

In later life, Irmgard still maintained that Globocnik was a sort of 'cheeky chappie' with an appealing sense of humour. She did not consider him a fanatic or an ideologue. She could not reconcile the man she knew as the same man responsible for over one million murders. Globocnik's persona allowed her to view his light-hearted side. She described how he joked on one occasion when talking to Friedrich-Wilhelm Krüger on the telephone. Lying on his back on the floor, with the phone to one ear, his contribution to the conversation was limited to the odd subservient 'Jawohl' in agreement with his superior's wishes. Every time Globocnik uttered the word, his right leg shot up in the air at an angle of 90 degrees to the floor. Irmgard witnessed her fiancé's joke and was highly amused by his antics.

She admitted that she was more attracted to the younger and more handsome Reinhold von Mohrenschildt than her overweight fiancé. Globocnik's lack of military bearing and style, with his slightly bloated features and his obvious paunch, disappointed and irked her. However, Irmgard described him as 'a nice person who had a heart'.[4] At the office, she referred to Globocnik as 'SS-Brigadeführer', but in private she addressed him as 'Globus'. In public, she used the term 'Sie', but alone, she used the familiar 'Du'. In his company, she experienced a highly elevated status, and she enjoyed all the trappings which accompanied his position.

Globocnik was obviously enchanted with the young attractive woman who had responded to his advances, and it is hard to believe her insistence that he did not shower her with gifts. He took her to the theatre and she accompanied him to Krakow and to Zakopane on several occasions. On one outing, he took her to Salzburg and to Klagenfurt in a chauffeur-driven limousine. In Salzburg, he introduced her to Friedrich Rainer. In Klagenfurt, she met Anna Globocnik. The meeting did not go well.

Contrary to all other evidence, Irmgard insisted that Globocnik was a reluctant police chief whose true wish was to work as an engineer in the mountainous region of Austria. She described his secret desire to hang up his SS uniform and concentrate on building bridges and power stations.

In the meantime, she was happy to live as part of the feudal lord's entourage. In her new home, she had three servants at her beck and call—two Polish girls and a Polish handyman. The German-speaking girl, Charlotte or 'Lotta', and the other girl took care of the cooking and cleaning of the villa, so Irmgard had time on her hands. She often went riding, sometimes alone and sometimes accompanied by Globocnik. They kept two horses in a nearby stables. Security was so relaxed that they were never worried about an attack. Irmgard declared that in the almost two years of their relationship, they never had a crossed word. Irmgard and Globocnik had a very active sex life and his recessed bed at the villa was often put to good use.

Despite enjoying the good life, Irmgard showed concern over the amount of alcohol consumed by her lover. He would also take pills to pep himself up before late night meetings, at which Globocnik often appeared inebriated. However, she was at pains to point out that he was always in command of all his faculties and was never too far gone to be unaware of proceedings. The Globocnik villa was used as an office by the SSPF who preferred to work from home than to go to the office. His home was also the location for two or three parties every week, and Globocnik played host to important visitors travelling to or from the Eastern Front. Many such visitors were left with a positive impression of their host, having been supplied with the best meat, bacon, ham, and butter, all difficult to obtain in time of war. They were also recipients of expensive leather goods, furs, textiles, and boots, in addition to rugs and carpets. All gifts were gratefully received with no questions asked. Willy Natke stated that Globocnik's villa basement was full of bags stuffed with paper currency. This was all part of Irmgard's new life.

Globocnik was served by a personal Jewish tailor who attended every day at 8 a.m. Irmgard was also served by a Jewish seamstress for her dresses. Suddenly, they stopped coming. One of the kitchen assistants, a Jewess from the ghetto, also disappeared suddenly. All this allegedly passed Irmgard by.

When he considered the time right, Globocnik informed Himmler of his engagement and his intended marriage. On 5 July 1941, Globocnik sent Himmler a simple and direct letter:

> Reichsführer!
>
> I am engaged to Miss Irmgard Rickheim and ask you, Reichsführer, to give your permission for a marriage.
>
> Heil Hitler!

Odilo Globocnik.[5]

Himmler's reply, dated 14 July 1941, followed enquiries by Rudolf Brandt, in Himmler's office, on 8 July to the RSHA, requesting any knowledge of the intended marriage. The answer came back from SS-Untersturmführer Kaiser, within a day, that the RuSHA had no record of Globocnik's intended marriage. This was not entirely correct. On the very same day that Globocnik informed Himmler of his engagement to be married, SS-Oberführer Richard Kaaserer, the head of the Sippenamtes (Geneology and Marriage Office) in the SS Race and Settlement Main Office, wrote to Globocnik in reply to a letter he had sent SS-Gruppenführer Otto Hofmann on 1 July 1941.[6] Hofmann was chief of the RuSHA, and Globocnik had obviously mentioned his forthcoming marriage. Kaaserer had even allocated a Sippenamt reference number, 67 613. Unfortunately, Globocnik's letter to Hofmann is not included in his RuSHA file.

Himmler wrote to his protégé from the Führer's field headquarters:

> Dear Globus!
> I am pleased in principle that you have finally decided to get married. Please do not be cross, but I have no idea who Miss Rickheim is. I will learn the particulars once you forward the formal marriage application, which should not be too difficult in wartime, since all regulations are simplified. I am looking forward to receiving this application and am certain that then I will be able to grant your wish for a marriage.
>
> Heil Hitler!
> H.H.[7]

Himmler also supplied a copy of the communication to Friedrich Rainer. Later the same week, Himmler travelled to Lublin and was no doubt introduced to Irmgard on this occasion as he stayed at Globocnik's villa overnight and she was already living there. It was during this visit that Himmler ordered the creation of Majdanek. Rieger pinpoints Irmgard's first meeting with Himmler as September 1941, but Himmler had only intended to meet with Globocnik during the Reichsführer's trip to the Ukraine at the beginning of September, as Globocnik was staying nearby in Starokostyantyniv at the time.[8] However, Irmgard refers to Himmler's September visit in a subsequent letter to him dated 25 November 1942 (see below).

Irmgard remarked that security police thoroughly searched the villa prior to the visit of the Reichsführer-SS. Following Globocnik's description of his mentor, she expected a charismatic character, but was sorely disappointed by the man who appeared. Polite introductions were followed by dinner, where Himmler remained quiet and aloof, taking time to admonish a maid for grating his carrots instead of cutting them into small strips the way he liked them. He hardly spoke to Irmgard.

She found him to be unimpressive, arrogant, irritable, and pompous. Himmler was concerned about the age difference between Irmgard and Globocnik. Author Berndt Rieger suggests he may also have had reservations about her as he had discovered her grandmother to have been Jewish, but this is not borne out by the evidence in Irmgard's background checks contained in Globocnik's RuSHA file. Over dinner, Himmler declared that he wished to have sight of Irmgard's Ahnentafel (her heritage chart). Unknown to both Irmgard and Globocnik, according to Rieger, Himmler had another candidate in mind for the wife of his protégé—Gisela Mauermayer, the German discus gold medallist at the Berlin Olympics in 1936.

Irmgard found Himmler's extraordinary influence over her fiancé most concerning. She was unaware of the complete tale of Himmler's rescue of her lover from the party wolves after his abject failure as Gauleiter of Vienna. Globocnik, however, was totally indebted to Himmler, and was consequently entirely submissive. Irmgard pinpoints the beginning of the decline of her relationship with Globocnik as Himmler's initial visit. It declined further in December 1941 when Anna Globocnik moved into the house across the street.

On 18 November 1941, Globocnik was Rainer's guest of honour at the inauguration ceremony in Klagenfurt for his appointment as Gauleiter of Carinthia. The two men held each other in high regard and their close bond was obvious. At the end of the month, Globocnik loaded his car with females for his return trip to Lublin. The party included his mother, Anna Globocnik, his sister, Erika von Gayl, her baby daughter, and his sixteen-year-old niece, Henny Pomerantz, the daughter of his other sister, Lydia. They all moved into the small house opposite Globocnik's villa.

Although Anna Globocnik did not dislike Irmgard following their first meeting, it was obvious straightaway that she considered the young woman to be unsuitable for her son. Anna Globocnik soon allied herself with Mimi Trsek, who had obvious designs on her boss herself. Not only was Trsek Austrian, but she possessed a more relaxed personality than the Berlin-born Rickheim. Trsek was by now regarded as the private secretary of the SSPF. Irmgard suspected Trsek to be scheming with Anna Globocnik to influence her fiancé away from the arrangement. Globocnik supported his fiancée, but the situation affected Irmgard, and resulted in mood swings and the reappearance of a childhood skin complaint.

Globocnik suggested a short vacation in Zakopane with his niece, Henny. He was too busy to accompany them, so he sent along a friend, Emilie Thomas, a nurse known to both Globocnik and Irmgard. Irmgard and Henny got on well as they were of a similar age. Zakopane was, and still is, a popular resort in the foothills of the Tatra Mountains in southern extreme of Poland. The young women visited the resort for two weeks in February and March 1942, and spent their vacation skiing during the day and attending parties in the evening. At one particular tavern, Irmgard accompanied Henny and Emilie in a sing-along. Irmgard recalled years later that she was in a particularly bad mood that evening, but she denied any inappropriate behaviour. She was still suffering from a form of eczema, which made her irritable. According to Irmgard, nothing of note occurred and she returned to Lublin at the end of her holiday.

Meanwhile, arrangements had proceeded for the upcoming nuptuals. On 24 November 1941, SS-Oberführer Kaaserer had written again to Globocnik, requesting completion and return of the necessary marriage forms, including details of geneology for both parties. The pertinent questionnaires and health forms were duly completed and submitted. It appears that it was Globocnik who was the cause of delay, as Irmgard's RuSHA forms are all dated October and early November 1941.

Her health questionnaire shows her to have been 5 feet 3 inches tall, 128 lb in weight, with a round face, blue-grey eyes, and a bust measuring 33 inches.

The following typed anonymous letter was subsequently received by Himmler's office:

Berlin, 10 April 1942.
[*Find out who the sender is*—handwritten note]
To
Reichsführer-SS and Chief of the German Police
Berlin

Reichsführer!

A few weeks ago during my stay in Zakopane I had the opportunity to meet the fiancée of the SS and Police Leader of Lublin in a local restaurant.

The eye-catching, absolutely impossible behaviour of the guests at a nearby side table drew the attention of some Luftwaffe officers, as well as my own, to a girl in the company of a lady and a young girl, as well as a few NCOs of the Luftwaffe. As I later found out, it was the fiancée of SS-Brigadeführer Globotschnik [*sic.*], who in the most generous way romped around in the public tavern and otherwise caused all to be upset and disgusted by her attentions and behaviour.

Reichsfuhrer, I have come to know the SS and Police Leader of Lublin as a great, idealist and worthy human being, and I would like to obediently consider, out of sheer camaraderie, whether such informal women, as a result of their behavior, have the reputation of being public high SS leaders and thus undermine the entire SS are worth connecting to such high leaders.

[indecipherable signature]
SS-Sturmbannführer.[9]

Enquiries to discover the identity of the author were carried out at the highest level, but proved unsuccessful. Bruno Streckenbach wrote to SS-Obergruppenführer Walter Schmitt, the chief of the SS Personnel Main Office, on 29 July 1942: 'A comparison with existing and known signatures unfortunately did not lead to the establishment of the name of the letter writer. By the volatility of the signature it is also safe to assume that this is not a representation of a real name, but rather a fictitious signature'.[10]

While this was going on in Berlin, it appears that Globocnik was unphased by the accusation aimed at his fiancée. That situation was altered by Rudolf Brandt's memo to him dated 30 July 1942 when he had his first sight of the allegation:

In the enclosed I send a copy of a letter that was received here some time ago. I have the original. I have just confirmed whether the SS-Sturmbannführer can be found out due to his illegible signature. But maybe you can comment briefly on these remarks. I have not informed the Reichsführer-SS about the letter.[11]

On 10 August 1942, Dr Brandt informed Globocnik that all investigations into the originator of the anonymous letter had proved fruitless and that the identity of the author remained unknown. Globocnik replied to Brandt on 30 August 1942 in a handwritten double-sided letter:

Dear comrade Brandt,

I would have liked to speak to you personally about the letter concerning my fiancée. Even more so as I also want to clear the matter with the Reichsführer. I enquired about the letter and discovered the following:

1) A flier captain Vogt, who is said to be a SS leader, has already stated in Zakopane that he wants to turn to the Reichsführer because of the behavior of my fiancée. Is the signature similar to this name? Either way, I would like to have it clear.
2) Should, as other acquaintances have told me, but not as blatant as the letter says, in the general behavior of my fiancée there is some truth. I have also been made aware of this by others. My fiancée denies the contents of the letter.

I do not want to do anything wrong and break something over my knee. But when I consider how much the Reichsfuhrer was against this connection, I do not want to disappoint him now, but above all make it dependent on his will. I take that view because I do not want to somehow damage me as a SS leader.

So I ask you comrade Brandt to question the Reichsführer what he wishes me to do. If one also has to consider the youth of my bride, the reputation should not be damaged. I thank you for your help and I send my best regards and

Heil Hitler!
Yours
Odilo Globocnik[12]

All this manoeuvring in his private life coincided with the most active period of the murder of the Jews in the General Government. The irritating spectre of Schwarz's antipathy towards him had also not entirely disappeared and he continued to exchange letters with Karl Wolff on the subject. At some point, Globocnik thought it prudent to relocate his fiancée and she was moved out of his Lublin villa to the small rural village of Sobieszyn, some 50 km north-west of Lublin. Sobieszyn was surrounded by forests and was secluded sufficiently for the purpose. Irmgard took her horse and her dog.

To the south of the village lies the River Wieprz, with man-made carp lakes between its banks and the southern perimeter of the village. The Kickich Palace stands on the north side of the lakes and in 1942 it was occupied by the Hilse family. Hilse was a farmer and a SS man who cared for the requisitioned building and farm. Globocnik arranged for SS-Sturmbannführer Hermann Dunkel, who was responsible for SS-administered estates in the Lublin District, to find a suitable secluded location where Irmgard would be out of the gaze of scheming factions. Globocnik's mother and her ally, Mimi Trsek, must have been elated.

Australian biographer Joseph Poprzeczny suggests that the move occurred in May, or even June, 1942, as a result of Himmler's involvement and Globocnik's own immersion in Aktion Reinhardt. It is more likely to have happened in August as Brandt's memo of 30 July states clearly that Himmler was unaware of the Zakopane scandal. I consider Aktion Reinhardt to have played no part in Globocnik's decision. His ambition, the desire for advancement without more blemishes on his character, and the wish to avoid any form of confrontation with his mother are much more likely to have been at the root. Anna Globocnik, Mimi Trsek, or even Himmler himself may have been behind the anonymous tip off. All had reason to want the break-up of the engagement. Irmgard suspected the jealous Trsek. However, would the anonymous writer have misspelled 'Globotschnik' had he been well known to them? A simple mistake such as this indicates the strong possibility that the anonymous author was not well acquainted with the SSPF Lublin. The most likely scenario was that the writer interpreted Irmgard's youthful and friendly behaviour as 'unbecoming that of a future wife of a senior SS officer'.

Irmgard insisted then, and also in later life, that she had done nothing wrong, and this is supported by the statement provided by Emilie Thomas to the Lublin Gestapo on 21 September 1942:

> In February/March of this year I was in the company of Miss Rickheim, the fiancée of the SS and Police Leader of Lublin and his niece, Henny Pommerhanz, on a holiday of about fourteen days. Over time we got to know a captain of the Luftwaffe (a Sturmbannführer of the Allgemeine-SS), who was there in the N.S. War Victims Home for recreation. On the occasion of a comrades evening of the NSKOV Home for wounded soldiers, this captain invited us to the 'German Home'.
>
> Together with Miss Rickheim and Henny Pommerhanz, I spent this evening at a table of badly wounded soldiers, at which various Red Cross Sisters and female telecommunications staff also sat. The endeavour of the organizers of this evening was to prepare these heavily and severely wounded soldiers for return to the front in a rehabilitation camp for war disabled, by preparing a happy and cheerful evening. Since I am a nurse in the SS Central District of the SS and Police Leader in Lublin, it was not difficult for me to create a happy atmosphere around me and I also asked Miss Rickheim repeatedly to go out and join in a little. Miss Rickheim, however, was currently being treated for a skin eczema by Dr. Beck, Zakopane, and was therefore not in the mood for the evening.
>
> The captain joined our table temporarily. After a short greeting, however, he soon left, and when I saw him again, he was already drunk. However, there was still the possibility that Henny Pommerhanz obtained the address of the captain for the purpose of a stamp exchange. During the evening, Miss Rickheim was approached by a SS-Unterscharführer, who had learned from the captain that Miss Rickheim was the bride of SS-Brigadefuhrer Globocnik, whom he, the captain, also knew. The SS-Unterscharführer enthusiastically told Miss Rickheim that he himself knew Brigadeführer Globocnik from SS-Standarte 'Germania' and that they had both joined the Polish campaign together and he was happy to tell Miss Rickheim about the experiences of this campaign, and then asked to send greetings to the Brigadeführer.

Later, when I wanted to go home with Miss Rickheim and Henny Pommerhanz, our attention was once again drawn to the already very heavily drunk captain, who had a violent confrontation with severely wounded soldiers who were carriers of the EK1 and 2. We heard the captain's words, he did not intend getting shot at and letting his bones break at the front, and he came up to say goodbye. Miss Rickheim, always ready to go home, went first after she had said goodbye to the captain, and waited for us at the door, which the captain did not tell us about. Later, we followed Miss Rickheim to go home together.

As witnesses to this evening, the paratrooper NCOs Schoffler and Stein could still be mentioned, whom I have recently heard from at the disabled military school of the Luftwaffe at Standal.

Signed: Emilie Thomas
Sister in the SS Central District
of the SS and Police Leader Lublin.[13]

From this statement, it is clear that Irmgard was totally innocent of any misbehaviour. It also appears that witnesses to corroborate her blameless conduct were readily available. But Himmler had already made up his mind—Irmgard Rickheim was an unsuitable wife for 'Globus'. The relationship was doomed.

Himmler wrote to Globocnik on 11 September 1942 from his field headquarters in East Prussia, by now fully informed of the allegation. The Reichsführer was suffering from stomach cramps at the time and received Felix Kersten that morning at 8.30 a.m. for a massage session.[14] He dictated the typed letter:

Dear Globocnik!

I have read your letter of 30.8.1942 to Dr Brandt.

Find out if your fiancée went out to coffee with other men. If so, break the engagement.

Be assured that nothing is to be excused by the youth of your bride, for if the girl is immature as a result of her youth, she would constantly disappoint you in all her work, during which you could care little about your wife—do not only take my word for the deception. Your marriage would be a burden for you instead of a strengthening. And worst of all, the moment may come when you doubt whether your children really are yours.

You write in your letter, you have been made aware of this fact by another side. From this I can see that the letter warning is to be taken seriously.

All in all, I can only advise you to break the engagement.

Friendly greetings and
Heil Hitler!
Yours,
H. Himmler.[15]

In this letter, Himmler displays his aversion to Irmgard and his arrogant attitude towards the relationships of others. As a young man, he disapproved of a particular choice of his elder brother, Gebhard, for a girlfriend, and made clear his dissatisfaction. It mattered not that Irmgard would be found innocent and the letter was from an anonymous source who was drunk on the evening in question. It suited Himmler's opinion, and despite Globocnik's initial reluctance to break with Irmgard, he was one who would not wish to contradict his mentor.

Irmgard was surrounded by the trappings of a priveledged life during her stay in Sobieszyn, but for a town girl, the rural setting, although beautiful, was somewhat tedious. She spent the majority of her time isolated, reading, walking, and riding in the surrounding forests. Her fiancé visited her at least twice, once during a visit by her mother, a beautician from Berlin. After about two months in the Kickich Palace, Irmgard left the General Government and returned to Berlin. It was early October 1942 and the relationship was finally at an end, although neither wanted to admit it.

When asked about the relationship in 1998, Irmgard stated:

> I just would like you to know that I was 19 years old when the war started and I was in Lublin with my employer from January 1940 until spring [*sic.*] of 1942. During that time I had met the staff of Odilo Globocnik and him also. As a young girl, I was not interested in O.G. since he was 16 years older than I was at that time. Mr E. Lerch, who was his adjutant, arranged that O.G. approach me one day to ask for an engagement. I was flattered because some older girls from Austria were eager to get close to him. There was a lady from Austria who hated me; her name was Mimi Trsek. It could have been she who wrote some hate mail. I just don't know. Mimi Trsek also had O.G. mother on her side and both did not approve of my engagement with O.G.[16]

Globocnik not only arranged for an apartment in Berlin for Irmgard, but he ordered his adjutant, Max Cichotzski, to drive her there. Globocnik also arranged for her to work at the Ministry of Propaganda and Enlightenment in the office at Mauerstrasse 45. From there, she transferred in 1943 to the Office of the General Council for Armaments and Buildings in the Propaganda Ministry at Luisenstrasse 31a. Allegedly, Irmgard's move to Berlin also involved the bulk transfer of furniture and trunks of her possessions. She later insisted that she preferred to live at her parents' apartment as it was closer to work. Apparently, the furniture was stored in the basement of her office. She states that a large amount of her personal belongings, including all the engagement presents that had been received by Globocnik and her, were stored in a large Mercedes Benz trunk on a farm in Pomerania, worked by a relative of her step-father. Apparently, the trunk went missing at some point and she lost everything.

By way of acknowledgement for his endeavours as SSPF Lublin and the head of Aktion Reinhardt, and for being an obedient servant of the Reichsführer-SS, Hitler promoted Globocnik on 9 November 1942 to SS-Gruppenführer und Generalleutnant der Polizei. Unknown to his mentor, and while she was working at Mauerstrasse, Globocnik visited Irmgard and invited her, and her mother and stepfather, out to dinner in Berlin. Despite Himmler's objection to her, Globocnik found it difficult to expel her from his life. It appears that he held a true affection for her. She also made one last effort to repair the damage to the relationship caused by the clandestine writer of what became known as the 'Zakopane note'. Irmgard decided to approach the one man she knew could influence the outcome. At the time, it appears the engagement was still officially on. On 25 November 1942, she penned a handwritten letter of three sides to the Reichsführer-SS:

> Reichsführer!
>
> I had the great honour and good fortune to be presented to you personally by my fiancé SS-Gruppenführer Globocnik in Lublin, during your September 1941 visit. I write today therefore to give you my full trust and ask you to assist me. Through my fiancé I have heard of a letter, which was addressed to you, Reichsführer, in which my honour was attacked in the lowest possible manner. This letter, the writer of which remains unknown to me to this day, was sent in July of this year [*sic.*] and relates to a farewell evening for wounded SS personnel in the German Home in Zakopane during February/March of this year. I attended that evening on the invitation of a Captain of Luftwaffe together with a nursing sister, Emilie Thomas, who nurses in the Central SS Hospital in Lublin, as well as Henny Pommerantz, who is the niece of my fiancé. A statement of what occurred this evening has been given by Sister Emilie Thomas to the commander of the SD in Lublin. I enclose a copy for your information. I attempted, through the commander of the Sipo and SD in Lublin, SS-Obersturmbannführer Müller, to obtain the address of the person who had sent that letter. I only know that he was a Sturmbannführer, but it has been impossible for me to learn more. All my attempts until now have been in vain so the only thing I am able to do now is to approach you, Reichsführer. I ask you now Reichsführer to give me the name of the writer. I have waited a long time and ask you Reichsführer to believe me that I would not have dared to take your time if I could envisage another possible way. Reichsführer, as a German girl and the fiancée of a SS leader, I have to

try with all my power to get myself rehabilitated and ask you Reichsführer to give me the name of the man so I can speak with him if that is at all possible.

Heil Hitler!
Irmgard Rickheim.[17]

An internal memo, dated 19 January 1943, states that the office was having trouble locating a letter dated 19 December 1942. It also mentioned that Irmgard's letter had been received and was probably being dealt with by SS-Oberscharführer Bartdorff—not something Irmgard would have wished. The date 19 December 1942 is significant in that Dr Rudolf Brandt, Himmler's Personal Referent, not only replied to Irmgard's letter, but also wrote to Globocnik:

Dear Gruppenführer!

Today, I briefed the Reichsführer-SS on the letter that Miss Irmgard Rickheim sent to the Reichsführer-SS on 25.11.42.

The Reichsführer-SS now desires that the captain of the Luftwaffe, who is also a Sturmbannführer of the Allgemeine-SS, should be heard on the matter. I would therefore be grateful if you could tell me the address of this SS-Sturmbannführer (if I remember correctly, you told me you had found out which SS leader was involved).

Friendly greetings and
Heil Hitler!
On behalf of
Yours
RB [penciled initials]
SS-Obersturmbannführer.[18]

Brandt's letter to Irmgard the same day stated:

Dear Miss Rickheim!

Today I just want to confirm the receipt of your letter of 25.11.42. I was only able to brief the Reichsführer-SS on the content of your letter and also on the statement of Sister Emilie Thomas.

Still, I hope that the necessary findings will have arrived by mid-January—the time of the return of the Reichsführer-SS from various sightseeing trips at the front—so that you can then receive news from the Reichsführer-SS.

> Heil Hitler!
> On behalf of
> RB [penciled initials]
> SS-Obersturmbannführer.[19]

The final letter on the matter was addressed to Dr Rudolf Brandt on 29 December 1942, handwritten and signed by Globocnik:

> Just as your letter from 19 December arrived I wanted to send a letter to Miss Rickheim to inform her that our engagement was at an end. I kept the letter as I don't know when the whole matter will be finalized and what I shall do. Among other things, I was forced to write this letter as I had read the letter of the Reichsführer-SS of 11 September, about 20 times and I also asked my 16-years-old niece, who was in Zakopane, and had seen everything. She gave me the address of the Luftwaffe Hauptmann. The address is Ottokar Pieschel, Hauptmann of Luftwaffe, Nieder-Prausnitz 115, über Arnau a.[n] d.[er] Elbe, Riesengebirge, Sudetengau.[20] She also thinks he is a leader of the SS and told my niece that he wanted to write a letter to the Reichsführer-SS about the way Miss Rickheim behaved. Dear Brandt, it is not very easy for me that the Reichsführer-SS has to deal with this matter. It would be better if this could be avoided and I had already taken his advice. Would you be so kind and tell me if I should write to this captain, if I should show Miss Rickheim my letter or not? I do not want to do anything which would upset the Reichsführer. Please send me a reply as soon as possible…[21]

This letter illustrates Globocnik's submissive and sycophantic behaviour towards Himmler. It is unknown what, if any, reply Irmgard received upon Himmler's return from the front. At some point, Globocnik submitted his letter to her, informing her that their arrangement was terminated. After almost a year, Irmgard wrote to the SS-Race and Settlement Main Office and requested the return of her personal documents. She asked for them to be sent to her place of employment at the Propaganda Ministry. She never saw Globocnik again. As the Red Army approached Berlin, she fled to southern Germany where she met a US Army sergeant, William Lakin. The couple were wed and she emigrated to the USA. They lived in Texas before moving to Sacramento where Irmgard died in a rest home for the aged, on 21 October 2015, at the age of ninety-four. She had outlived her former lover by seventy years.

# 16

# HARVEST FESTIVAL IN UTOPIA

GLOBOCNIK SEEMED TO attract controversy. His constant disputes with the local civilian governor of Lublin, Ernst Zörner, over which of the two had authority, was highlighted by the Winterfeld Affair. Zörner had been Dr Frank's representative in Lublin since 1 February 1940. He openly criticised the SS occupation policy which brought him into conflict with not only the local SS leader, but also with the Reichsführer-SS. Eventually, Himmler was able to pressurise Dr Frank into replacing Zörner on 10 April 1943. Before then, however, Zörner's intention was to usurp Globocnik and 'see him off'.

Henning von Winterfeld was the ardent Nazi administrator of the Janów Lubelski and Krasnystaw districts in the Lublin region. A rabid anti-Semite, he hated Jews and Poles equally, taking brutal revenge on any form of Polish resistance. On one occasion, he publicly hanged a Jew. On 20 January 1941, he kept an appointment with Globocnik to discuss his application for the post of party chief in Krasnystaw. According to von Winterfeld's version of the meeting, Globocnik informed him that he would discuss the matter in Krakow, but he could not foresee any problem. Before he left, von Winterfeld thought it prudent to mention that his wife had non-Aryan blood in the family, but the Führer had been informed and had issued von Winterfeld with a certificate of pardon on 19 April 1939. As far as he was concerned, this dealt with the problem. He offered to produce documents in support of his claim. Apparently, Globocnik nonchalantly waved this matter aside and gave the impression that the matter was resolved.

On 19 June 1941, von Winterfeld was summoned to the office of Ernst Zörner, where the governor told him that Globocnik had informed him von Winterfeld's spouse was a half-Jew. Appalled at von Winterfeld's impudence, Zörner fired him on the spot.

On 24 June, von Winterfeld wrote to the Brown House in Munich from Breslau. He complained that Globocnik had lied. He stated that his wife, Lotta Freiin Laur von Münchhofen's great-grandmother, although of non-Aryan birth, was not Jewish and had converted to Christianity at the age of thirteen. He pointed out that this flaw in his wife's ancestry had been purged by the Führer's intervention. He appealed against the decision to fire him and stated Globocnik had been untruthful as he was aware that the Führer had issued the pardon. An investigation ensued in which Globocnik declared in a statement on 30 September 1941 that he did not have a personal problem with von Winterfeld, but had refused his appointment in Krasnystaw because he considered von Winterfeld as unsuitable for the post. His version was supported by other witnesses. The dispute continued until 20 April 1943, when both parties agreed it had gone on long enough. Globocnik did not apologise.

It appears that the entire affair was manipulated by Zörner in an unsuccessful effort to unseat his SS rival. Zörner had underestimated Globocnik's abilities and the affair only resulted in Zörner's vulnerability in the battle for power. Zörner finally capitulated on 10 April 1943, when Himmler convinced Dr Frank that he had to go, and the unfortunate governor was ordered to return to the Reich. Globocnik was triumphant.

His final victory over Zörner occurred at a time when he was under immense pressure. Not only was he in constant conflict with the civilian administration in Lublin, but Aktion Reinhardt had been operating as a murder machine for hundreds of thousands of victims for over a year, in addition to the geographical realignment of whole populations. The tide of war was turning against the Reich, with all the worries of the possible consequences of the crimes perpetrated by the SS. Globocnik himself was beginning to doubt the superiority of the Nazi doctrine. Not only was there a chink in his protective armour—Himmler had begun to have reservations that Globocnik was still the best man for the job and was considering a replacement, but his protégé was no longer the convinced Nazi he once had been. Added to these was the burden of dealing with the enforced breakdown of his recent engagement to Irmgard Rickheim, a young woman for whom he had a strong affection and probably loved deeply. His extremely close relationship to his mother provoked an inner struggle in coming to terms with her animosity to his former lover.

A report in the Polish underground press trumpeted an attempt on the life of the SSPF Lublin which resulted in the deaths of his driver and one of the SS escorts.[1] The incident was not recorded anywhere else.

In addition to all these problems, Globocnik's reputation in the party came under intense pressure. His old powerful adversary, Franz Xaver Schwarz, was the NSDAP official who headed the office that dealt with the award of the coveted Blood Order. To be the bearer of this prestigious medal was an honour which had few equals. The Blood Order was introduced in 1934 to commemorate the failed

Munich Putsch of November 1923. The first issue of the decoration was struck in 99 per cent pure silver. It was awarded to 1,500 participants in the Putsch who had also been continuous members of the NSDAP or one of its formations before January 1932. Cadets from the Munich Infantry School, who marched in support of General Eric Ludendorff, were also entitled to wear it. Unlike other medals, the ribbon was worn on the right breast of the uniform tunic in the form of a half-rosette, and the actual medal was suspended below.

In May 1938, to the consternation of the putsch participants, the award was extended to persons who had served time in prison for Nazi activities before 1933, or who had received a death sentence, which was later commuted to life imprisonment for Nazi activities before 1933, or who had been severely wounded in the service of the party before 1933. Subsequently, it was further extended to members of the Austrian Nazi Party who had participated in the 1934 February Uprising or July Putsch, or those who had received significant prison time or injuries for National Socialist activities. The subsequent medals were struck in 80 per cent silver, with serial numbers above 1,500.

Odilo Globocnik applied for the medal under the clause, which specified a qualified term of imprisonment for Nazi activities. On his application, he referred to his sentences to prison and indicated that he had documentary proof. He failed to mention that he had been granted an amnesty that resulted in his early release from detention and that reduced his total time in prison to below that required to qualify for the medal. His application landed on the desk of Schwarz.

The NSDAP Treasurer wasted no time in conducting an enquiry with the authorities in Vienna and Klagenfurt. It subsequently became evident that Globocnik's amnesty disqualified him from the award. Despite the support of Martin Bormann and Philipp Bouhler, Schwarz denied the application and informed Himmler of the circumstances on 19 July 1941. Humiliated, Himmler undertook to rebuke his protégé. Why Globocnik risked his status in the party with a devious move that was easy to establish remains a mystery, but his reputation was undoubtedly damaged.

In July 1942, the 'demotion affair' began. It appears that Globocnik discovered on 9 July that he had lost the title and rank of 'Gauleiter' in the party. As a former Gauleiter, he expected to retain the rank and status afforded that exalted position. He was dismayed to discover that he had been demoted to NSDAP Hauptbereichsleiter on 9 November 1941. During a visit by Himmler to Lublin, he protested to the Reichsführer and followed this up with a letter to Karl Wolff on 22 July on the advice of Himmler. Globocnik asked Wolff to take steps to cancel his demotion. Wolff replied on 13 August 1942 to the effect that the demotion would stand. Apparently, a former Gauleiter who had served for less than four years was not entitled to retain that rank. Wolff had spoken to Martin Bormann on the matter, and Bormann, although sympathetic to Globocnik's wishes, reminded him that this was a Führer directive. His lower rank of Bereichsleiter der NSDAP was confirmed. Karl Wolff stated in his letter: '…Do not hang your head, but continue to be active in your beautiful work and I am certain you will find satisfaction…'[2]

Faced with such formidable obstacles, Globocnik capitulated, and in his reply dated 24 August, he assured Wolff that he would not dwell on the matter, despite feeling that his previous time as Deputy Gauleiter and Staff Leader of the Austrian Nazi Party for five years before the Anschluss would have contributed to his argument. He informed Wolff that Himmler had recently allocated new tasks, which would keep him busy.

Globocnik's health understandably suffered during his period in Lublin. The results of a medical examination, carried out in 1939 by a Luftwaffe doctor, survive in his SSO file, and are referred to, towards the end of chapter four, above. His health questionnaires for the SS Race and Settlement Central Office, completed for his marriage applications, are no longer in his RuS file. Therefore, no accessible written record of his later physical condition exists. His post-war surviving close associates provide verbal evidence of his health.

Irmgard Rickheim states he took many pills and drank far too much alcohol. His diet was not the healthiest option, and his love of partying late into the night on a regular basis would not have lent itself to maintaining a healthy lifestyle. The result was a complete breakdown.

There is no record in Globocnik's files of the nervous breakdown which overtook him in the spring of 1943. It is more than likely that Himmler did not want any trace of a mental breakdown in his man in the East. Professor Dr Wilhelm Pfannenstiel apparently examined Globocnik, but his findings are unknown. Our best indication of this mental abrogation in Globocnik's mental health was provided post-war by Max Cichotzski before the court in Wiesbaden:

> It must have been in the spring of 1943. One day Globocnik left his office in the evening without his cap and coat. Sometime later he appeared in Wippern's flat from where I was called. I met him and he was completely oblivious to events around him. Only some hours later was he able to leave the house. Wippern had already mentioned to me that Globocnik had suffered a nervous breakdown. When I went back with Globocnik to his office, I tried to find out what had really happened. He always said everything was terrible and I should not ask him further. Then he begged me that if he should not survive that I should look after his mother and sisters.… Pfannenstiel was announced by Himmler's adjutant that he would come from Berlin. In this connection, I received the order that I should accommodate Pfannenstiel in Globocnik's house. I told Globocnik about my order and he said Pfannenstiel should be accommodated in a guest house. When he arrived, Pfannenstiel, after dinner, had a long talk with Globocnik near the fireplace where they remained undisturbed…[3]

The distance from Globocnik's villa to Wippern's apartment is roughly a ten-minute direct walk, through a secuded part of Lublin, in those days segregated from the local population and only entered by authorised Germans, mainly SS or police. The overnight extreme temperatures at that time of year can fall to -20 degrees centigrade in Lublin. Without a top coat and hat for protection in those circumstances can result in very fast deterioration of human functions. For Globocnik to experience such an event, his mind was obviously disturbed.

The catalyst for the future of not only the Jews of Poland, but a large section of the Polish population of the General Government, was the visit of Himmler to Globocnik in Lublin on 20 July 1941. To recap on the importance of this meeting, Himmler ordered:

1. The creation of a new large concentration camp in Lublin (Majdanek).
2. The preservation of the SS Equipment Company (Deutsche Ausrüstungswerke) as a motor repair shop and a carpentry shop.
3. A new labour camp, with workshops for clothing, leather goods, cobblers, ironworks, and wheelrights, to be reinstalled east of Lublin.
4. The Waffen-SS clothing factory in Lublin must obtain its supplies from the Lublin workshops, and a new branch office of the Berlin textile factory will open in Lublin.
5. A new SS and Police district will be created at the site of the former Lublin airfield, with the construction of new buildings.
6. The SS-Führungshauptamt will create a new spare parts plant in Lublin for motor spares and will make available all parts required.
7. The training of skilled workers for the East will be the responsibility of the original equipment manufacturers.
8. New sewing workshops are to be opened using Jewish female labour.
9. The market place in Zamość must be retained, but updated with new services, such as central heating.
10. Apartments currently confiscated by the Treuhandstelle Ost will be made available for the SS.
11. A new guesthouse for the Reichsführer-SS will be created.
12. The action to search for German blood in the area will be extended to the entire General Government.
13. A German colonial settlement area is to be created in the region of Zamość.
14. SS-Brigadeführer Globocnik, as the delegated deputy of the Reichsführer-SS, will report on the progress of the measures taken for the erection and supply of SS and Police strongpoints, by autumn at the latest, etc.[4]

> The victory of German weapons in the East must, therefore, followed by the victory of the German race over the Polish race, if the regained Eastern sphere—according to the Führer's will—should henceforth remain for all time an essential constituent part of the Greater German Reich. It is therefore of great importance to infiltrate German laboratories, civil servants, merchants, and artisans into the regained German region so that it can be considered a protective wall against foreign penetration and possibly as a starting point for the racial infusion of the territories farther east'.
>
> SS-Gruppenführer Wilhelm Koppe, 1941.[5]

Prior to his Lublin visit, on 15 July 1941, Himmler received the second version of the General Plan East from Konrad Meyer-Hetling of the RKF in Berlin. Professor Meyer-Hetling was born on 15 May 1901, in the Saxon town of Einbeck-Salzderhelden. An agronomist by profession, Meyer-Hetling was a highly respected authority on spatial planning and agricultural science. A member of the NSDAP since 1932, he joined the SS on 20 June 1933. He worked as a consultant for the Reich Ministry of Education and Science under Bernhard Rust. In 1939, he was appointed as head of planning in Himmler's RKF, on the Staff of the RFSS. He attained the rank of SS-Oberführer. In the later stages of the war, he saw active service with the Waffen-SS. He was imprisoned after the RuSHA trial in Nuremberg and was released in 1948. He was subsequently a professor of agriculture and regional planning at the University of Hanover. He died on 25 April 1973.

The 1996 MA thesis by Karsten Schulz, 'Nationalsozialistische Nachkriegskonzeptionen für die eroberten Gebiete Osteuropas vom Januar 1940 bis zum Januar 1943', presented at the Berlin Technical University Institute for Political Science, contains a description of the various versions of the General Plan East (Generalplan Ost) in addition to other, competing plans for German domination of the conquered Soviet territories, submitted by Alfred Rosenberg's Reich Ministry for the Occupied Eastern Territories, the German Labour Front, and various other individuals.

Schulz suggests there were six versions of the General Plan East, which need to be carefully distinguished from each other in terms of what they actually propose. Four of them were prepared by the planning staff of the Reichskommissariat für die Festigung deutschen Volkstums (RKF) headed by Professor Meyer-Hetling, and two by the RSHA, specifically by SS-Standartenführer Erich Ehlich, director of Group III B (Racial Conciousness) of Section III of the Inland SD:

1. The General Plan of the RKF, dating from about January 1940. This is preserved in a document bearing the title 'Planungsgrundlagen für den Aufbau der Ostgebiete', and deals only with the planned germanization of the annexed

western Polish territories (Danzig-Westpreußen, Wartheland, Zichenau, Suwalki, and Ost-Oberschlesien).

2. General Plan East of the RKF, dated 15 July 1941. The plan itself has not been found, and is known only from a covering minute from Meyer-Hetling to Himmler with the above date. Judging from material contained in the unpublished autobiography of Professor Meyer-Hetling, in addition to the annexed territories included in the General Plan, it proposed German settlement in the east of the General Government, thereby encircling the ethnic Polish population. The estimated settler requirement is 4.55 million persons over 30 years.
3. General Plan East of the RSHA, dated around the end of 1941, or the beginning of 1942. The plan itself has never been found, but its main points can be reconstructed from the detailed (and highly critical) commentary on it by Dr Erhard Wetzel of Rosenberg's Ministry of the Occupied East, dated 27 April 1942.

   This is the plan that is usually indicated when the General Plan East is referred to in secondary literature. It is the plan that, judging from Wetzel's comments, proposed the resettlement in West Siberia of 31 million (including 5–6 million Jews) of the estimated 45 million non-German inhabitants of the specified areas designated for German settlement, over a period of 30 years. The plan calls for the settlement of 10 million Germans on the territory, consisting of Danzig-Westpreußen, Wartheland, Oberschlesien, General Government, south Ostpreußen, Bialystok, the Baltic States, Ingermanland, Weißruthenien, and some areas in Ukraine.

   Wetzel is highly critical of the RSHA plan and clearly considers it infeasible, although he supports the concept of germanization of territory and the deportation of population groups considered hostile to Germany. He proposes alternative actions, which are most probably to be regarded as representing the views of Rosenberg. There is no indication that this plan was ever given official approval in full by either Himmler or Hitler.
4. The Total Plan East—Gesamtplan Ost—of the RSHA. The existence of this extended plan can only be inferred indirectly. It is referred to in a letter of 12 June 1942 from Himmler to Ulrich Greifelt, representative head of the RKF. It also seems that comments made by Wetzel in April 1942, refer to this extended plan, rather than the original RSHA plan.

   The Total Plan East of the RSHA extended the area of proposed German settlement to the line Lake Ladoga–Valdai Heights–Briansk, and added as settlement areas Zhitomir, Kamianets-Podilsk and parts of Vinnytsia.
5. The later General Plan East of the RKF. This is known from a document of 71 pages dated 28 May 1942. In addition to the germanization of the Polish territories annexed to the Reich, it proposes the establishment of three 'border lands' (Marken), Ingermanland, Narew-West Lithuania, and Gotengau (Crimea and

Kherson province), and of 36 settlement bases, 14 in the GG, 14 in Ostland, and 8 in Ukraine. The period for the proposed resettlement is 25 years. The plan also gives a detailed estimate of the costs of the proposed ethnic German settlement, totals of 45.7 billion RM for the annexed Polish territories and 20.9 billion for the borderlands and bases, the greater part of which is to be raised by borrowing in the private capital market.

Nowhere does this plan talk of deporting any part of the existing non-German population to Siberia. Rather, it proposes the resettling of the population of land required for German settlement on alternative kolkhozes and sovkhozes within the area under German rule; the rationale for that mild treatment is stated to be the need to retain the cooperation of the native population. The previous method of 'evacuation' is explicitly rejected. The desired level of germanization will be reached when 50% of the population of the border lands is ethnically German, and 25–30% of the population of the bases. The process of germanization is estimated to take 25 to 30 years.

6. The Global Settlement Plan—Generalsiedlungsplan—of the RKF. This is known from a preliminary draft dated 23 December 1942, written by Ulrich Greifelt. There appears never to have been a final draft.[6]

The strategy defined seven settlement areas, comprising a 'Volksraum'—Luxemburg, Lorraine, Alsace, Upper Carinthia, Lower Styria, Bohemia-Moravia, and the Incorporated Eastern Territories annexed from Poland. To them was added six future regions—Lodz, Krakow, Lviv, Lublin, Warsaw, and Bialystok. These would eventually become known as Gau within the Eastern Settlement Area ('Ostsiedlungsraum'). The Baltic area was to be expanded with the addition of Pskov and Ingermanland, the latter atributed to Estonia, but it would not be considered as part of the 'Ostsiedlungsraum', for reasons unknown.

The plan proposed a future population of around 23.1 million persons in the settlement areas of the 'Volksraum' and in the 'Ostsiedlungsraum', consisting of an existing ethnic German population of 5.3 million, a residual germanized native population of 5.4 million, and 12.4 million German immigrants. It indicated the existing combined population of the two regions to be 36.3 million, of which 5.6 million were already German citizens, ethnic Germans, and German settlers. There was a further 5.4 million who were considered as 'germanisable' natives. The plan thus implied the deportation of around 25 million people, although such a deportation was not explicitly mentioned.

The same applied to the Baltic area. Of a population of 7.2 million, which included a neglible number of those considered as ethnic Germans, 2.1 million were deemed capable of being germanised. The remaining 5.1 million would simply 'disappear'. Around 3.1 million German settlers were thus required to increase the total population to 5.2 million inhabitants. The plan, therefore, implied the deportation of a total of around 30 million non-Germans to be expelled from the settlement areas. On 12 January 1943, Himmler ordered the inclusion of the Baltic area, the Crimea and Tauria in the 'Ostsiedlungsraum'. However, the fall of Stalingrad caused a halt in all further planning activity.

The plan assumed a victorious campaign in the East. Events dictated that the General Plan East could not be implemented. Had the fortunes of war taken a different turn, Himmler's intentions should not be underestimated. It is likely that various modifications would have occurred, but experienced has shown that Himmler would have pushed through his strategy for major geographical upheavals in population realignment. As it transpired, it appears that Himmler and Meyer-Hetling's ideas never progressed past the planning stage.

As described earlier, Zamość is a beautiful city, built in the Italian Rennaisance style. It was the birthplace of Rosa Luxemburg and a later president of Germany, Horst Köhler, was born in Skierbieszów in 1943, a small village about 15 km north of the city. Köhler was of Bessarabian German descent and his immigrant parents were moved into the region as part of the Himmler-Globocnik settlement strategy of General Plan East. Zamość is located on an extension of the 'Hellweg', the medieval east–west trade route of the Hanseatic League. At the opposite end stood the castle of Wewelsburg in Westphalia. In Nazi legend, Wewelsburg was the starting point of a final battle between east and west.

Himmler decided he needed a summer retreat in the east, and his gaze fell upon Zamość. At one point, Zamość was to be renamed 'Himmlerstadt,' but this never came to fruition, with Himmler settling upon the name 'Pfugstadt'—Town of the Plough. A rather fitting name for the centre of his agricultural plans for the area. Himmler's initial idea was to totally demolish the city buildings and rebuild from scratch, but the city administrator, Helmut Weihenmaier, shrewdly planted a question of design in Himmler's mind. The Reichsführer had not formulated a plan for the new city, and he agreed to stall the demolition to enable architects to move into Zamość and draw up designs. The city gained a reprieve, but plans for the region would be put in motion.

> The settlement is based on the direct order of the Reichsführer-SS. This order is for us a commitment that goes beyond the normal execution of the order, because the Reichsführer-SS expects us not only to carry out his will formally, but to let all of us from different parts of the European Volksdeutsche they built a new homeland here, they gave a healthy base of existence and created conditions for the development of future generations.
>
> Odilo Globocnik, 22 November 1942.[7]

This directive launched the ethnic cleansing operation of the Zamość region. Sourced to an order of the Reichsführer-SS, dated 1 July 1941, Globocnik declared the Zamość region to be the first settlement area in the General Government. A launch pad for further Germanisation of the East. The first trial deportation of Poles occurred in the Hrubieszów district in November 1941. Taken by surprise, the frightened Polish inhabitants offered no resistance. Buoyed by their success, the Germans formulated more specific plans for large-scale deportations.

The Germans commenced the action during the night of 27–28 November 1942. In secret orders, the officers who took part in the operations were ordered to treat Poles with the 'necessary severity' required to achieve success. The deported Poles were beaten and tortured in order to pacify them. They were also subjected to murder and their villages were set ablaze. Terrified residents were driven to transit camps in Zamość, Biłgoraj and Zwierzyniec. Some of the people were sent as enforced labour to the Reich; some were deported to Mazovia; some were transported to the concentration camps at Auschwitz and Majdanek. Small children with Aryan racial features were kidnapped and sent to the Reich. The mortality rate among the displaced persons was extremely high.

The German authorities displayed no regard for the lives and the feelings of Poles. The least chance of survival of those deported from the Zamość region was in Auschwitz. Of the 1,301 Poles who were deported to this camp, only 18 per cent survived. The main causes of death were exhaustion, disease, and blatant murder.

The initial stage of the pacification operation was met with little or no resistance, but the Poles soon reacted to the brutality of the Nazis. On 24 December 1942, General Stefan Grot-Rowecki, the commander of the Polish Home Army, issued an order recommending counter-action. He directed that abandoned farms were to be burnt in order to destroy property. He suggested the use of axes, forks, and shovels as makeshift weapons. He encouraged the rape and assault of the new occupants, and he promised subversive action by combat units against the police and administrative authorities involved in the deportations. The numbers of Polish partisans grew with new groups springing up in the forests of the Zamość region.

Himmler became alarmed at the news reaching Berlin in numerous reports of attacks on German outposts, the destruction of rail links, the emergence of road blocks, and the blowing up of warehouses. German troops on patrol outside the security of their barracks were regularly the subject of partisan attacks. The Police and security forces were unable to protect the new settlers, from as far afield as Bessarabia, Bosnia, Ukraine, Serbia, and Slovenia. In February 1943, an attempt was made to protect the areas populated by ethnic Germans with a belt of villages inhabited by Ukrainians. Some 14,739 of the local Polish farmers were expelled. The hope was that this 'Ukrainian action' would exploit national differences. A total of 13,000 people were relocated in settlements seized from Poles. Rifles were issued for their protection, but proved of little use against the Polish partisans. Many resettled villages, including Nawoz, Siedliska, Udrycze, Janiowka, and Cieszyn, witnessed the killing of settlers, including women and children.

The displacement action in the Zamość region ceased on 15 August 1943, by order of Globocnik. It had resulted in the suffering and death of large numbers of the Polish civilian population, but also the death of large numbers of the resettled peasants from abroad and the devastation of the region. Out of 293 villages, approximately 110,000 inhabitants were deported. Today, only ruins mark the locations of many previous Polish villages. The local infrastructure was completely devastated, with much of the livestock decimated. The Germans were unable to permanently defeat the numerous partisan units and to completely pacify the area. Groups of bandits continued to cause problems until the end of the war. In the spring of 1944, a mass evacuation campaign for the new settlers was organized by the German authorities. In July 1944, the last Volksdeutsche finally abandoned the region. The displacement action in the Zamość region, the brainchild of Heinrich Himmler and Odilo Globocnik, can only be described as a total catastrophe and an abject failure.

Himmler began to lose interest in the fortunes of his protégé, Globocnik. The Zamość debacle only contributed towards the doubts that the SS chief was nurturing. He now also had a spy in Lublin. Richard Wendler was Gebhard Himmler's brother-in-law and from 21 June 1943, was a SS-Gruppenführer. He was Ernst Zörner's replacement as governor of Lublin, and he lost no time in updating Himmler with the finer details of Globocnik's performance. Changes were afoot, but before leaving Lublin, Globocnik would stamp his mark on the surviving sparse Jewish population one more time, and in a way that only he could achieve.

Globocnik recommended SS-Brigadeführer Richard Wendler as Ernst Zörner's replacement as governor of Lublin. He implored the Reichsführer-SS to exert influence on his brother's brother-in-law, but also pointed out that the governor of Warsaw, Ludwig Fischer, might prove an obstacle in negotiations. Wendler was eventually appointed to the post on 26 May 1943.[8]

However, Wendler failed to support his fellow SS comrade. Instead, he complained to Himmler that civil unrest in the region was at an all-time high, and he considered this to be the result of inadequacies in Globocnik's police and security work. He was of the opinion that the SSPF was far too impulsive and acted without thinking. At a time when Himmler's own opinion of Globocnik was at an unprecedented low, the Reichsführer was quick to react. On 4 July 1943, on Himmler's direction, Globocnik was stripped of his State Secretary rank, one that he had held since 12 March 1938. Furthermore, Himmler decided to replace Globocnik as SS and Police Leader in Lublin. He no longer considered Globocnik as the man to direct the SS economic and Germanisation policies in the East. With the scaling down of the extermination process in the General Government, and the increased status of Auschwitz-Birkenau in the solution of the Jewish problem, 'Globus' could no longer be considered as the 'manager of death'.

Himmler's first inclination, on 5 July 1943, was to transfer him to the post of Higher SS and Police Leader of Russland-Mitte as replacement for Gerret Korsemann.[9] The idea was to direct Globocnik with the important task of counter-partisan operations. A surprising choice, given Globocnik's record with the aftermath of the ethnic cleansing operation in the Zamość region, and Wendler's subsequent report of ineffective policing of the Lublin District. Himmler delayed Globocnik's transfer out of Lublin until September to complete Aktion Reinhardt, but in the meantime, the situation in central Russia demanded a more urgent resolution and Curt von Gottberg filled the vacancy. Globocnik was replaced as SS and Police Leader Lublin on 12 July 1943, but he remained in the city. His successor, SS-Gruppenführer Jakob Sporrenberg, was on compassionate leave as his wife had been diagnosed with progressive cancer of the face, before taking up his post on 16 August.[10]

By the time of his arrival in Lublin, Sporrenberg was a forty-year-old experienced SS officer. He had seen service in Königsberg, Minsk, and the Ukraine, and had been involved in anti-partisan warfare. He had been the RKF representative for East Prussia and these credentials made him the ideal candidate to replace the troublesome Globocnik in Lublin. Himmler briefed Sporrenberg in a long and detailed talk on policy. He told Sporrenberg that his main task would be to administer to the German settlers in the Lublin region, and he advised him to avoid Jewish matters. He expected the entire region to be germanised by the end of 1944. In answer to Sporrenberg's enquiry about the destination of the incumbent Poles, Himmler said they would go to the Ukraine. On no account were they to be moved westward. When Sporrenberg pointed out that the Red Army was moving towards the Ukraine at an alarming rate, Himmler ordered him to build fortifications along the River Bug and the former Russo-German border of pre-June 1941. Himmler also desired that Sporrenberg nurture a friendly relationship with the new governor, Dr Wendler.[11]

Following his spell in Poland, Sporrenberg was transferred to southern Norway where he fell into British captivity. Interrogated by the British in Oslo, he was transferred to Island Farm POW Camp in South Wales, and thence to the London Cage in Kensington. He was handed over to the Polish authorities in October 1946 and was sentenced to death on 16 September 1950. He was hanged on 6 December 1952 in Warsaw.

Sporrenberg encountered problems immediately upon his arrival in Lublin. Himmler's reluctance to relocate Globocnik at once caused the new SSPF untold difficulties. Despite Himmler's advice not to get involved in Jewish affairs in Lublin,

Sporrenberg felt obliged to make himself familiar with the workings of the economic production of Aktion Reinhardt. He was soon to discover that, as a non-member of the 'Reinhardt club', the so-called 'Globocnik unit', doors were closed to even the new SS and Police Leader. His attempt to gain access to the Reinhardt hangars at the airfield camp was unsuccessful. He was met by Christian Wirth who refused admission and told him that Globocnik had been commissioned by Himmler himself to solve the Jewish problem. He would need Globocnik's authority to gain admission. Sporrenberg soon discovered the same was true for Majdanek, Sobibor and the DAW factory in Lipowa Street. At Sobibor, Reichleitner informed him that only Himmler and Globocnik were authorised to enter.

Sporrenberg had previously met Globocnik on one occasion, in the Berlin headquarters of the Ordnungspolizei, when the latter politely informed him that no matter what tasks he had been given, they were nothing in comparison to those he, Globocnik, had completed during his tenure as SSPF. The new man was met with distrust and aloofness. He complained to Wendler, who informed Himmler that in the two weeks since Sporrenberg's arrival, he had received no briefing of any description from the outgoing SSPF. Whatever Sporrenberg had discovered about his new role, was purely by chance, and he felt that he could not execute his duty as SSPF with the current staff in Lublin as they were all loyal to his predecessor.

Globocnik left Lublin temporarily on 16 August 1943, in order to administer the clearance of the ghetto in Bialystok. By this time, Himmler had heard rumours of Globocnik's silent partnership with Walter Többens, the industrialist who used Jewish slave labour from the Warsaw Ghetto, and who subsequently became a millionaire as a result. Himmler now began to experience doubts about his former protégé's financial dealings in Vienna. He instructed the SS judge, Dr Konrad Morgen, to visit Lublin and investigate.

Bialystok is the largest city in north-east Poland, situated in the Podlaskie Plain. According to the 1931 census, the population was 1,263,300. Polish records from April 1939, indicate the population of Bialystok voivodship was divided as follows—71.1 per cent Poles; 13.5 per cent Belorussians; 11.9 per cent Jews; 2.2 per cent Russians; 0.9 per cent Lithuanians; and 0.5 per cent Germans. It bordered East Prussia to the north-west, and Lithuania to the north-east. Some 56,000 Jews lived in the city.

The Jewish ghetto in Bialystok was created on 26 July 1941, between ul. Lipowa to the south, ul. Sienkiewicza to the east, ul. Przejazd to the west, and ul. Poleska to the north. The River Biala dissected the ghetto in two halves. On 1 August 1941, the ghetto was closed to the outside world, trapping 43,000 people inside. A Judenrat of twenty-four members was set up on 2 August, with Efraim Barasz, a forty-nine-year-old mechanical engineer, as the first president. Within a short time, the ghetto grew to over 50,000 Jewish inhabitants. It was surrounded by a wooden wall topped by barbed wire, with three entrances manned by the Jewish Police, supervised by the Germans. Textile and armament factories were established by the Judenrat.

The first deportations commenced in September 1941, in order to reduce the numbers living within the ghetto. Bribery and corruption was rife, and the first Jewish resistance group was founded in December 1941. Initially, this group distributed leaflets and carried out minor acts of sabotage in the factories. The first deportation to Treblinka amounted to forty freight cars on 21 November 1942, followed by a similar number the following day. A further transport of 10,000 souls were evacuated to Treblinka on 9 February 1943, and about 2,000 were shot in the city. Approximately 7,600 inhabitants were relocated to a new central transit camp within the city for further selection. Those deemed fit to work were sent to Majdanek where another selection procedure was carried out. Many were forwarded on to Poniatowa labour camp and Auschwitz. A number considered too emaciated to work were murdered in Majdanek. Among the deportees, more than 1,000 Jewish children were sent first to Theresienstadt, and then to on to Auschwitz-Birkenau, where they were murdered in the gas chambers.

As part of the death throes of Aktion Reinhardt, Globocnik commanded an action against the Bialystok Ghetto, commencing on 16 August 1943. He used SS and Trawniki men in an effort to finally clear and destroy the ghetto. Realising the end was nigh, the resistance group staged a fightback. During the night of 16 August, several hundred Polish Jews began an armed insurrection against the troops carrying out the liquidation of the ghetto. The battle lasted several days, but the fight was destined to fail as the insurgents were armed with small arms and Molotov cocktails, pitted against heavily armed troops and armour deployed by Globocnik. A small number of resistance fighters managed to break out and they joined partisan groups in the surrounding countryside. Out of almost 60,000 Bialystok Jews, only a few hundred survived the war. By 21 August, Globocnik was back in Lublin.

Sporrenberg was fully occupied initially, by his own admission, following the orders and advice of the Reichsführer-SS. Anti-partisan warfare occupied a major part of his time. He also had to supervise fifteen SS strongpoints holding stocks of supplies previously confiscated from the civilian population. These were intended for the Wehrmacht. The estates and buildings requisitioned by his predecessor had to be guarded.

After informing the commandant, Hermann Florstedt, that Himmler himself had authorised his admission to Majdanek, he was finally able to gain access. On inspection, Sporrenberg states he was surprised at the high standard of cleanliness and hygiene in the camp barracks, although they were overcrowded. When asked to inspect the gas chambers, Florstedt informed him that they did not exist, but showed him the delousing barrack instead.[12]

In order to gain access to the DAW factory in Lipowa Street, Sporrenberg obtained authority from Globocnik's office. He was escorted around by a specially appointed guide from the 'Globocnik unit'. The Gruppenführer also inspected the prison in the fortress. He noted that many of the prisoners were Polish adolescents who, it was explained were Polish 'footpads'. Here also, he saw much overcrowding. At this juncture, Sporrenberg did not attempt to inspect Poniatowa camp or Trawniki camp.

Some time towards the end of August 1943, Sporrenberg was summoned to Krüger's office in Krakow, along with Walter Bierkamp, the head of the SD and Sipo in the General Government. Krüger produced a communication from Himmler:

> To the HSSPF Obergruppenführer und General der Polizei Krüger
> Krakow
>
> The Jews in the district of Lublin have developed into a serious danger.
>
> This situation must be cleared up once and for all. I have charged the Globocnik unit with the execution of this matter.
>
> The HSSPF East, and the SSPF Lublin, are requested to assist Globocnik with all resources at their disposal.
>
> Heinrich Himmler.[13]

Sporrenberg stated subsequently that none of the three participants at the meeting agreed with the order. They were mystified as to the source of Himmler's information. Krüger advised his two subordinates that he would contact Himmler and correct the misinformation, as all agreed that the Jews posed no threat to security. Sporrenberg returned to Lublin, where he was contacted a few days later by Krüger. He said that Himmler was not willing to change his mind. The remaining Jews of the Lublin region were on course for destruction.

Some 2,000 additional SS and Police troops were placed at the disposal of the SSPF, the majority being Waffen-SS. These were to be used as cordon manpower. The commander of the security police in Lublin, SS-Sturmbannführer Dr Karl Pütz, informed Sporrenberg that a Sonderkommando unit of 150 men had already arrived at Majdanek from Auschwitz. Wirth arrived at Sporrenberg's office and showed the SSPF an order from Himmler to Globocnik, which stated that the 'Globocnik unit' was to exterminate all Jews in the district of Lublin. This order contained the codename for the operation—Erntefest (Harvest Festival). The action was to include the camp at Poniatowa, the DAW factory in Lipowa Street, and the OSTI and DAW concerns at the Airfield Camp. Wirth also produced a strategy for the cordons, to which Sporrenberg objected.

Sporrenberg then dictated a revised directive at Pütz's office, based mainly upon the original order, which roughly stated:

1. On orders of the RFSS, an action called 'Erntefest' will be carried out in the district of Lublin, for which the cordoning-off troops under the command of the SSPF are to be used.
2. For this purpose, the units in question will be disposed as follows: [Here Sporrenberg gave detailed instructions on the sketches, of which every commander was to have a copy given to him by Wirth].
3. The troops will be used for cordoning-off purposes only and are under the direct command of the SSPF Lublin. [Sporrenberg also gave detailed instructions that no-one was to be allowed in or out of the cordoned-off area].
4. In the case of the two camps at Lipowa Street and the airfield, the prisoners will be led out of the camps and taken to Majdanek under guard of the cordoning-off units. At Majdanek, the troops are to form a cordon round the camp while the action was being carried out and they are to remain there until recalled.
5. The commanders of the troop are to go into Majdanek Camp on arrival and report to Wirth, in order to establish contact and obtain information when the troops are no longer needed.
6. On returning from Majdanek, the officers are to report to the SSPF Lublin.
7. On the second day, the troops will surround the camp at Poniatowa at 0600hrs. Commanders will report there to Sturmbannführer Wirth.[14]

Sporrenberg was then informed by Pütz that around 150 prisoners at the Lipowa Street camp were Polish POWs. Sporrenberg telephoned Krüger with this information, but Krüger only advised him to contact Himmler himself. Sporrenberg immediately sent a telegraph message to Berlin requesting the action be postponed. An hour later, he received the following reply:

> Teleprint of the SSPF Lublin confirmed.
> All without exception to participate in operation.
> RFSS requests Sporrenberg to refrain from further queries.
> [Signed] Grothmann.[15]

Aktion Erntefest commenced at 5 a.m. on 3 November 1943. It was still dark when the prisoners in Majdanek stood for roll-call. Whether any of them had noticed three ditches being excavated beyond compound numbers 5 and 6, south of the crematorium, is unknown. In case anyone enquired, they were described as anti-aircraft ditches. They were dug in a zig-zag fashion, and were each about 100 metres long, 2 metres deep, and about 3 metres wide. The Jewish prisoners were separated from the others, including women and children. They were directed to compound number 5 and ordered to strip in one of the barracks. During the morning, Jewish prisoners from Lipowa Street, the castle prison and the airfield were escorted to Majdanek.

The men and women were separated in compound 5 and ordered through an opening in the fence to the ditches, past a contingent of Reserve Police Battalion 101. They were ordered to lay down in the ditches, where they were sprayed with automatic gunfire. Loud music was played over loudspeakers in a forlorn effort to drown out the machine-gun fire. Victims who entered the ditches down a slope, were ordered to lay upon those already shot. The action continued until 5 p.m.

Most studies of Erntefest rely heavily on the testimony of Erich Muhsfeldt, delivered on 14 August 1947 in Polish captivity:

> One day in late October 1943, the excavation of pits was begun behind compounds V and VI, approximately 50 metres behind the structure of the new crematorium. 300 inmates were put to this work; they dug without interruption for three days and nights, in two shifts of 150 each. In the course of these three days, three pits were excavated; they were more than two metres deep, zigzag-shaped, and each about 100 metres long.
>
> During these three days, special commandos from the concentration camp Auschwitz as well as SS and Police commandos from Krakow, Warsaw, Radom, Lvov and Lublin gathered in Majdanek. Otto Moll and Franz Hössler came from Auschwitz with 10 SS men. Altogether, some 100 SS men arrived from the cities I mentioned, and these SS men made up the Sonderkommando. On the fourth day—it may have been November 3—reveille was sounded at 5am. Therefore, I went to that part of the camp where I usually stayed. The entire camp was surrounded by the police; I would estimate that there were about 500 policemen. They stood guard with their weapons at the ready. They were armed with heavy and light sub-machine guns, as well as with other automatic weapons.
>
> A truck mounted with a radio transmitter was parked near the new crematorium; a second such truck stood near the camp entrance, not far from the administration building. When I arrived at the camp grounds, both transmitters were already on. They broadcast German marches and songs as well as dance music from records. The two trucks had been provided by the Propaganda Office [of the NSDAP] in Lublin.
>
> I want to stress that up to that day, I had no idea of the storm that was gathering. While the pits were being dug, I had thought that they were air-raid trenches, since an anti-aircraft battery was stationed nearby. I asked a SS man what they were for, but I received no answer, and I got the impression that he himself didn't know what it was all about. The Jews who had been put to digging the pits replied to my questions that these pits were surely intended for them. I wouldn't believe that; I laughed at

them and said that no doubt they were air-raid trenches. It was an honest remark, for at that time I really thought that.

Around 6am—or maybe it was already near 7am—the operation began. Some of the Jews who were gathered on compound V were herded into a barrack, where they had to strip naked. Then Commander [Anton] Thumann cut the wires of the fence separating compound V from those pits, making a passageway. Armed policemen formed a human chain from this passageway to the pit. The naked Jews were led past this line-up to the pits, where a SS man from the Sonderkommando chased them into one of the pits, in groups of ten. When they were in one, they were chased to the other end of the pit, where they had to lie down, and then a SS man from the Sonderkommando shot them from the edge of the pit. The next group was likewise driven to the same end of the pit, where they had to lie down on the bodies already there, so that the pit gradually filled with layers of corpses lying crosswise almost up to the edge. Men and women were shot separately, in separate groups.

This operation went on without a pause until 5pm. The SS men in charge of overseeing the execution took turns; after their replacements arrived they went to the local SS barrack to eat, and the execution continued without respite. Music was blaring from the two radio transmitters the entire time. I observed these events from the new crematorium, where I had my own room for myself and the inmates assigned to my unit.

That day all the Jews in the Majdanek camp were shot, also those who were quartered with various enterprises such as the DAW and the clothing works, as well as all those in the units working outside the camp. Jews who had been brought in from the castle were also shot. The entire operation was organised along military lines—a radio transmitter was used to keep in contact with the Chief of the SS and Police in Lublin and with other higher officers. The SD officer supervising the operation on-site (I don't recall his name) used this transmitter to give updates on the progress of the operation by periodically announcing the number killed. I heard that a total of more than 17,000 Jews of both sexes were shot that day. This also included all the Jews from my own kommando. In the morning, after I had arrived in the camp, I had made enquiries as to what was going on, and I had asked Commander Thumann to please leave me my kommando. He told me that was impossible; the operation, he said, was being conducted by Globocnik and the SD, and all the Jews of Lublin were to be killed, on the order of Governor General Frank. He added that instead of the Jews I would be assigned a unit of Russians.

However, 300 Jewesses were left alive that day; they were needed to sort the things that had been piled up in the barrack where the unfortunate victims had undressed before being led to the slaughter. Another 300 Jews were kept in the camp, at the disposal of the so-called Sonderkommando 1005. They were all quartered on compound V. The women from this group had arrived in Majdanek in March and April

1943. A couple of dozen days later, the men were gradually incorporated into the Sonderkommando.

After all the Jews had been shot on 3 November, the pits were covered over with a thin layer of soil.

On the day this operation was carried out, the camp received a new commandant. SS-Sturmbannführer Florstedt was recalled, and SS-Sturmbannführer Weiss of Amtsgruppe D, took over his post. Florstedt was relieved of duty because he had appropriated Jewish possessions. The matter was investigated by a Special Unit of the Reich Criminal Police led by SS-Sturmbannführer Morgen. To try and save his neck, Florstedt pretended to be insane. Even before he was relieved of office he had ordered me to remove the bodies of those murdered on 3 November. Commandant Weiss later repeated this order. I was assigned 20 Russians for this purpose. The fourth day I gathered wood and boards, and on 5 November 1943, I began to burn the corpses.

Since a section of the pits (that end at which the victims had climbed down into them) was not filled with bodies, I piled a bit of soil there so that a small incline was formed, making it easier to climb down. The following day I set up a sort of wooden grate in the pit; that's where the inmates placed those bodies that were in the farthest part of the pit. When the pyre was ready I poured methanol over it and set it on fire. I set up the next pyres closer towards the far end of the pits, on those spots where the bodies had lain that were already cremated. Once the ashes cooled off after the pyre burned down, the inmates from my unit brought it up, and then the bones were pulverized in a special, gasoline-powered mill. This powder was then put into paper bags and taken on cars to a SS factory near the camp, where this bone meal was later used to fertilize the soil. My work was supervised by an SD functionary from Lublin who saw to it that all the bodies were cremated, that no unburned bodies remained in the pits, that any gold teeth were pulled from the bodies prior to cremation, and that all jewels they wore were removed....

By Christmas 1943, I had finished cremating the bodies of the more than 17,000 Jews murdered on 3 November. After cremation was concluded, the pits were filled with earth and leveled off....

Construction of the [new] crematorium was completed after New Year 1944. I cremated the bodies of those who had died in the camp up to that time, together with those of the victims of 3 November 1943.[16]

Erich Muhsfeldt was born in Brandenburg in 1913. Professionally, he was a qualified baker in civilian life. He joined the SA in 1933, and in 1939 he became a member of the NSDAP. In 1940, he switched to the SS, where he underwent a short training course in Sachsenhausen Concentration Camp before his transfer to Auschwitz in August of the same year. Initially, he supervised various prisoner work squads and soon he was appointed a Blockführer.

According to his own statement, Unterscharführer Muhsfeldt was transferred to Majdanek on 15 November 1941, again as a Blockführer. According to his story, a few months after his arrival, in the summer of 1942, the then camp commander, Karl Koch, transferred to him the so-called 'funeral squad'. He stated that he accepted this job reluctantly: '… but I did not like the work. This is why, after I returned to Lublin and had to show Kommandant Koch how I operated the furnaces, I started a fire, where the roof of the barrack where the two furnaces were housed burned down'.[17]

To provide him with assistance, Muhsfeldt was given SS-Unterscharführer Robert Seitz as his deputy. Seitz was born in 1911 in Liedolsheim and transferred to Majdanek in late 1941, or early 1942.

According to this post-war testimony of Erich Muhsfeldt, around 17,000 Jews were murdered in Majdanek on 3 November 1943. A Polish-Soviet Commission estimated the total to have been 18,000, with 8,100 of them being Majdanek inmates; 1,660 were women. Similar actions took place simultaneously at Trawniki, Annopol-Rachow, Puławy, Dorohucza, and other minor locations. Through lack of manpower resources, the Jews in Pionatowa were spared for twenty-four hours. In Trawniki, the Jews were shot in ditches excavated in the garden of a former sugar mill along the road leading to the River Wieprz. Loud music was again broadcast through loudspeakers. Between 7 a.m. and 5 p.m., groups of men, women, and children fell victim to the bloodlust.

On 4 November, a similar action was carried out at Poniatowa as at Majdanek. The camp had been cut off from the outside to prevent news of the atrocities the previous day. Roll-call at 4.30 a.m. was the beginning of the nightmare. Jewish prisoners who had the privilege of living outside the camp perimeter in a settlement, were brought inside. Once inside, all Jewish prisoners were forced to strip naked and then were driven along the road to the sugar mill in groups of fifty. The same fate awaited them as at Majdanek. Once the action was over, the trenches were covered with pine branches. Subsequently, all the Harvest Festival cadavers were exhumed and cremated.

Erntefest was the final act of Aktion Reinhardt in Poland. It is estimated that between 42,000 and 43,000 Jews lost their lives in a period of forty-eight hours on 3–4 November 1943. Although Odilo Globocnik had left Lublin for Trieste by then, there is little doubt that he was aware, if not participated, in the planning stage, possibly just in the role of a consultant. His men certainly played a major role in the operation. It proved to be the single largest German massacre of Jews in the entire war. It surpassed the notorious massacre of more than 33,000 Jews at Babi Yar outside Kiev by the staggering figure of approximately 10,000 victims. It was exceeded only by the October 1941 Odessa massacre committed by Romanian troops of more than 50,000 Jews.

# 17

# GOLDEN BOY TARNISHED

Georg Konrad Morgen had the reputation of being a bloodhound when investigating corruption in the SS. A former judge in civilian life, Morgen enlisted in the Waffen-SS at the outbreak of war, and was later appointed as a SS judge. Himmler tasked Morgen with investigating wrongdoing and corruption in the concentration camp system. Most famously, he investigated corruption and murder perpetrated by the senior staff at Buchenwald concentration camp. The former commandant, Karl Koch, was tried and executed in Buchenwald on 5 April 1945. Among other investigations, Morgen also looked into the rumoured corruption and abuse of power at Auschwitz. Rudolf Höss and Max Grabner were both subjects of his enquiries.

Morgen was instructed by Himmler, in the late summer of 1943, to investigate the staff of Aktion Reinhardt, following justified rumours of corruption. Morgen was used as a witness at several post-war trials, and it will be useful to reproduce part of his testimony before the International Military Tribunal at Nuremberg:

[*Source: Yale Law School. Lillian Goldman Law Library. The Avalon Project. Nuremberg Trial Proceedings, volume 20.*]

One Hundred and Ninety-Seventh Day
**Wednesday; 7 August 1946**

MORGEN: One day I received a report from the commander of the Security Police in Lublin. He reported that in a Jewish labour camp in his district a Jewish wedding had taken place. There had been 1,100 invited guests at this wedding
HERR PELCKMANN: Go on witness, a little faster.

MORGEN: As I said before, 1,100 guests participated in this Jewish wedding. What followed was described as quite extraordinary owing to the gluttonous consumption of food and alcoholic drinks. Among these Jews were members of the camp guard, that is to say some SS men, who joined in this revelry. This report only came into my hands in a roundabout way, some months later, due to the fact that the Commander of the Security Police suspected that the circumstances indicated that some criminal acts had occurred. This was my impression as well, and I thought that this report would give me a clue to another big case of criminal corruption. With this in mind, I went to Lublin and called at the Security/ Police there, but all they would tell me was that the events happened at a camp of the Deutsche Ausrüstungswerke. But nothing was known there. I was told it might possibly be a rather odd and shrouded (this was the actual term used) camp in the vicinity of Lublin. I found out the camp and the commander, who was Kriminalkommissar Wirth.

I asked Wirth whether this report was true or what it meant. To my great astonishment, Wirth admitted it. I asked him why he permitted members of his command to do such things and Wirth then revealed to me that on the Führer's orders he had to carry out the destruction of Jews.

HERR PELCKMANN: Please go on, Witness, to describe your investigations.

MORGEN: I asked Wirth what this had to do with the Jewish wedding. Then, Wirth described the method by which he carried out the extermination of Jews, and he said something like this: 'One has to fight the Jews with their own weapons, that is to say "pardon me for using this expression" one has to cheat them.'

Wirth staged an enormous deceptive manoeuvre. He first selected Jews who would, he thought, serve as column leaders, then these Jews brought along other Jews, who worked under them. With that smaller or medium-sized detachment of Jews, he began to build up the extermination camps. He extended this staff of Jews, and with these Jews Wirth himself carried out the extermination of the Jews.

Wirth said that he had four extermination camps and that about 5,000 Jews were working at the extermination of Jews and the seizure of Jewish property. In order to win Jews for this business of extermination and plundering of their brethren of race and creed, Wirth gave them every freedom and, so to speak, gave them a financial interest in the spoliation of the dead victims. As a result of this attitude, this sumptuous Jewish wedding had come about.

Then I asked Wirth how he killed Jews with these Jewish agents of his. Wirth described the whole procedure that went off like a film every time. The extermination camps were in the east of the Government General, in big forests or uninhabited wastelands. They were built up like a Potemkin village. The people arriving there had the impression of entering a city or a township. The train drove into a dummy railroad station. After the escorts and the train personnel had left the area, the cars were opened and the Jews got out. They were surrounded by these Jewish labour detachments, and Kriminalkommissar Wirth or one of his representatives made a speech. He said, 'Jews, you were brought here to be resettled, but before we organize this future Jewish State, you must of course learn how to work. You must learn a new trade. You will be taught that here. Our routine here is, first, everyone must take off his clothes so that your clothing can be disinfected, and you can have a bath so that no epidemics will be brought into the camp.'

After he had found such calming words for his victims, they started on the road to death. Men and women were separated. At the first place, one had to deliver the hat; at the next one, the coat, collar, shirt, down to the shoes and socks. These places were faked cloakrooms, and the person was given a check at each one so that the people believed that they would get their things back. The other Jews had to receive the things and hurry up the new arrivals so that they should not have time to think. The whole thing was like an assembly line. After the last stop they reached a big room, and were told that this was the bath. When the last one was in, the doors were shut and the gas was let into the room.

As soon as death had set in, the ventilators were started. When the air could be breathed again, the doors were opened, and the Jewish workers removed the bodies. By means of a special procedure which Wirth had invented, they were burned in the open air without the use of fuel.

HERR PELCKMANN: Was Wirth a member of the SS?

MORGEN: No, he was a Kriminalkommissar in Stuttgart.

HERR PELCKMANN: Did you ask Wirth how he arrived at this devilish system?

MORGEN: When Wirth took over the extermination of the Jews, he was already a specialist in mass-destruction of human beings. He had previously carried out the task of getting rid of the incurably insane. By order of the Führer himself, whose order was transmitted through the Chancellery of the Führer, he had, at the beginning of the war, set up a detachment for this purpose, probably composed of a few officials of his, as I believe, the remainder being agents and spies of the Criminal Police.

Wirth very vividly described how he went about carrying out this assignment. He received no aid, no instructions, but had to do it all by himself. He was only given an old empty building in Brandenburg. There he made his first experiments. After much consideration and many individual experiments, he evolved his later system, and then this system was used on a large scale to exterminate the insane.

A commission of doctors previously investigated the files, and those insane who were listed by the asylums as incurable were put on a separate list. Then the asylum concerned was told one day to send these patients to another institution. From this asylum, the patient was transferred again, often more than once. Finally, he came to Wirth's institution, where he was killed by gas and cremated.

This system, which deceived the asylums and made them unknowing accomplices, enabled him with very few assistants to exterminate large numbers of people, and this system Wirth now employed with a few alterations and improvements for the extermination of Jews. He was also given the assignment by the Führer's Chancellery to exterminate the Jews.

HERR PELCKMANN: The statements which Wirth made to you must have surpassed human imagination. Did you immediately believe Wirth?

MORGEN: At first Wirth's description seemed completely fantastic to me, but in Lublin I saw one of his camps. It was a camp which collected the property or part of the property of his victims. From the piles of things-there were an enormous number of watches piled up-I had to realize that something frightful was going on here. I was shown the valuables. I can say that I never saw so much money at one time, especially foreign money-all kinds of coins, from all over the world. In addition, there was a gold smelting furnace and really prodigious bars of gold.

I also saw that the headquarters from which Wirth directed his operations was very small and inconspicuous. He had only three or four people working there for him. I spoke to them too.

I saw and watched his couriers arrive. They actually came from Berlin, Tiergartenstrasse, the Führer's Chancellery, and went back there. I investigated Wirth's mail and I found in it confirmation of all this.

Of course, I could not do or see all this on this first visit. I was there frequently. I pursued Wirth up to his death.

HERR PELCKMANN: Did Wirth give you names of people who were connected with this operation?

MORGEN: Not many names were mentioned, for the simple reason that the number of those who participated could be counted, so to speak, on one's fingers. I remember one name: I think the name was Blankenburg, in Berlin.

HERR PELCKMANN: Blankenburg?

MORGEN: Blankenburg, of the Führer's Chancellery.

THE PRESIDENT: Well, we had better adjourn now. We have already been 50 minutes.

[The Tribunal adjourned until 8 August 1946 at 1000 hours.]

Thursday; 8 August 1946

HERR PELCKMANN: We will go back to the mass exterminations, one case of which you described. You spoke of Kriminalkommissar Wirth, who was not a member of the SS and whose staff did not consist of SS men. Why was Wirth given the assignment?

MORGEN: I have already mentioned that Wirth was Kriminalkommissar with the Criminal Police in Stuttgart. He was Kommissar for the investigation of capital crimes, particularly murder. He had quite a reputation in discovering clues, and before the seizure of power lie became known to the general public for unscrupulous methods of investigation which even led to a discussion in the Wurttemberg Landtag [Diet]. This man was now used in order to cover up the traces of these mass killings. It was thought that on the basis of his previous professional experience this man was unscrupulous enough to do this job, and that was true.

HERR PELCKMANN: You mentioned the Jewish prisoners who aided in the killings. What became of these people?

MORGEN: Wirth told me that at the end of the actions he would have these prisoners shot and in doing so, would despoil them of the profits which he had allowed them to make. He did not do this all at once, but by means of, the deceptive methods already described he lured and segregated the prisoners and then killed them individually.

HERR PELCKMANN: Did you hear from Wirth the name Höss?

MORGEN: Yes. Wirth called him his untalented disciple.

HERR PELCKMANN: Why?

MORGEN: In contrast to Wirth, Höss used in principle entirely different methods. I would best describe them when we come to the subject of Auschwitz.

HERR PELCKMANN: Was the name Eichmann mentioned at that time?

MORGEN: I cannot remember that the name Eichmann was mentioned at that time, but later I heard of it, too.

HERR PELCKMANN: How did you come on the trail which led to Auschwitz?

MORGEN: I got a clue by a remark of Wirth himself. Now I had only to find a reason to institute investigations in Auschwitz itself. I beg to bear in mind that my assignment was limited; I had to investigate crimes of corruption and crimes committed in connection with them.

THE PRESIDENT: Dr Pelckmann, didn't he explain how he came to investigate Auschwitz yesterday?

HERR PELCKMANN: No, it was something entirely different, Your Lordship.

MORGEN: Yesterday I spoke only of Lublin and Wirth. I said I received information about Höss and wanted to try to get into the camp and needed a reason. I found this reason very soon.

The Protectorate Police had heard about the smuggling of gold in the Protectorate. The traces led to Berlin. The customs officials for Berlin-Brandenburg had found out persons who were on the staff of the Concentration Camp Auschwitz, and had turned over the proceedings to the SS and Police Court in Berlin. I learned of it there and I took charge of these proceedings-they dealt with enormous gold smuggling-and shortly thereafter went to Auschwitz.

HERR PELCKMANN: Then you were in Auschwitz proper?

MORGEN: Yes, I went to Auschwitz, and before I started with the investigation itself…

THE PRESIDENT: When did you go there?

MORGEN: I cannot give the date exactly, but it must have been the end of 1943 or the beginning of 1944.

HERR PELCKMANN: The method of extermination there was probably similar to the one you described yesterday?
MORGEN: I thoroughly investigated the entire stretch of territory and studied the layout and installations. The prisoners arrived on a side track in closed transport cars and were unloaded there by Jewish prisoners. Then they were segregated into able-bodied and disabled, and here already the methods of Höss and Wirth differ. The separation of the disabled was done in a fairly simple way. Next to the place of the unloading there were several trucks and the doctor gave the arrivals the choice to use these trucks. He said that only sick, old persons and women with children, were allowed to use them. Thereupon these persons swarmed toward the transportation prepared for their use, and then he needed only to hold back the prisoners that he did not want to send to destruction. These trucks drove off, but they did not drive to the Concentration Camp Auschwitz, but in another direction to the Extermination Camp Monowitz, which was a few kilometres away. This extermination camp consisted of a number of crematories which were not recognizable as such from the outside. They could have been taken for large bathing establishments, and that is what they told the prisoners. These crematories were surrounded by a barbed wire fence and were guarded from the inside by the Jewish labour details which I have already mentioned. The new arrivals were led into a large dressing room and told to take their clothing off. When this was done…
HERR PELCKMANN: Is that not what you described yesterday?
MORGEN: Of course.
HERR PELCKMANN: What precautions were taken to keep these things absolutely secret?
MORGEN: The prisoners who marched off to the concentration camp had no inkling of where the other prisoners were taken. The extermination camp Monowitz lay far away from the concentration camp. It was situated on an extensive industrial site and was not recognizable as such and everywhere on the horizon there were smoking chimneys. The camp itself was guarded on the outside by special troops of men from the Baltic, Estonians, Lithuanians, Latvians, and also Ukrainians. The entire technical arrangement was almost exclusively in the hands of the prisoners who were assigned for this job and they were only supervised each time by an Unterführer. The actual killing was done by another Unterführer who let the gas into this room. Thus, the number of those who knew about these things was extremely limited. This circle had to take a special oath…
THE PRESIDENT: Were these Unterführer in the SS?
MORGEN: They wore SS uniforms.
THE PRESIDENT: Didn't you take the trouble to ascertain whether they were proper members of the SS?
MORGEN: I said that they were people from the Eastern territories.

THE PRESIDENT: I do not care what you have already said. What I asked you was, didn't you take the trouble to ascertain whether they were members of the SS?
MORGEN: I beg your pardon, Your Lordship. I do not understand your question. They could not be members of the General SS. As far as I could learn, they were volunteers and draftees who had been recruited in the Baltic countries where they had carried out security tasks, and who were then somehow especially selected and sent to Auschwitz and Monowitz. These were special troops, who had only this particular task and no other. They were completely outside of the Waffen-SS...
THE PRESIDENT: I didn't ask you if they were in the Waffen-SS. Did you ask questions as to why they were put into SS uniforms?
MORGEN: No, I did not ask that question. It seemed incomprehensible to me. It is probably due to the fact that the commander of the Concentration Camp Auschwitz...
THE PRESIDENT: Wait a minute. You said, as I understand it, that you considered it incomprehensible why they wore the SS uniforms. Didn't you say that?
MORGEN: Yes.
THE PRESIDENT: Were there no officers of the SS there at all?
MORGEN: One officer, the commander of this company, I believe a Hauptsturmführer Hartenstein [*sic.*], or something like that.
THE PRESIDENT: Why didn't you ask him why these men were put into SS uniforms?
MORGEN: The extermination camp was under the direction of SS-Standartenführer [*sic.*] Höss. Höss was commander of the concentration camp Auschwitz, and also of the extermination camp Monowitz. Around Auschwitz were a number of labour camps and I have already said...
THE PRESIDENT: I didn't ask you where. What I am asking you is why you didn't ask these two SS men why they put these men into SS uniforms?
MORGEN: I assumed that this was done for camouflage reasons so that this extermination camp would not be distinguished outwardly from the other labour camps and the concentration camp itself. As a soldier, it was incomprehensible to me that this damage to the reputation of the SS was tolerated as it had nothing to do with this extermination.
THE PRESIDENT: You, yourself, were a high SS officer, were you not?
MORGEN: I was Sturmbannführer of the Waffen-SS.
THE PRESIDENT: Well, what I am asking you is this: why, in those circumstances, you made no inquiry about it, and why you didn't ask these high SS officers there, 'What is the meaning of these men being put into SS uniforms?'
MORGEN: I did not understand the question.
THE PRESIDENT: Go on.
HERR PELCKMANN: Witness, I should like to ask you the question myself. Why did you not ask the higher SS leaders whom you met there why these people were working in SS uniforms?

MORGEN: I said that I had the impression that this was clone for reasons of camouflage so that the camp would not be distinguished from the other camps through the use of different uniforms.

HERR PELCKMANN: This explanation which you gave yourself is the reason why you did not question the officers, is that true?

MORGEN: At any rate, I cannot remember having asked the officers about it. I did not speak to any officers except to the commander, Höss, and the commander of the guards of the extermination camp.

HERR PELCKMANN: Have you described everything which…

THE PRESIDENT: Go on.

HERR PELCKMANN: Have you said everything in answer to the question as to how secrecy was secured?

MORGEN: Another important point may perhaps be mentioned. Certain Jewish prisoners with connections abroad were selected and were made to write letters abroad telling how well-off they were in Auschwitz, so that the public got the impression that these well-known people were alive and could write that they were doing well.

HERR PELCKMANN: Thank you. Now, Witness, under normal circumstances what would you have had to do after you had learned of all these terrible things?

MORGEN: Under normal circumstances I would have had to have Kriminalkommissar Wirth and commandant Höss arrested and charged with murder.

HERR PELCKMANN: Did you do that?

MORGEN: No.

HERR PELCKMANN: Why not?

MORGEN: The answer is already entailed in the question. The circumstances prevailing in Germany during the war were no longer normal in the sense of State legal guarantees. Besides, the following must be considered—I was not simply a judge, but I was a judge of military penal justice. No court-martial in the world could bring the Supreme Commander, let alone the head of the State, to court.

HERR PELCKMANN: Please do not discuss problems of law, but tell us why you did not do what you realized you should have done?

MORGEN: I beg your pardon; I was saying that it was not possible for me as Obersturmbannführer to arrest Hitler, who, as I saw it, was the instigator of these orders.

HERR PELCKMANN: Then what did you do?

MORGEN: On the basis of this insight, I realized that something had to be done immediately to put an end to this action. Hitler had to be induced to withdraw his orders. Under the circumstances, this could be done only by Himmler as Minister of the Interior and Minister of the Police. I thought at that time that I must endeavour to approach Himmler through the heads of the departments and make it clear to him, by explaining the effects of this system, that through these methods the State was being led straight into an abyss. Therefore, I approached my immediate superior, the chief of the Criminal Police, SS-Obergruppenführer [*sic.*] Nebe; then I turned to the chief of the Main Office SS Courts, SS-Obergruppenführer Breithaupt. I also approached Kaltenbrunner and the chief of the Gestapo, Gruppenführer Müller, and Obergruppenführer Pohl of the Economic and Administrative Main Office, and the Reichsarzt, Gruppenführer Dr Grawitz. But, aside from taking these necessary steps, I saw a practical way open to me by way of justice; that is, by removing from this system of destruction the leaders and important elements through the means offered by the system itself. I could not do this with regard to the killings ordered by the head of the State, but I could do it for killings outside of this order, or against this order, or for other serious crimes. For that reason, I deliberately started proceedings against these men, and this would have led to a shake-up of this system and its final collapse. But these activities had another far-reaching effect in the near future, for through the big concentration camp trials against commandant Koch, of whom I spoke earlier, and against the head of the political section at Auschwitz—Kriminalsekretär Untersturmführer Grabner, whom I charged with murder in 2,000 cases outside of this extermination action—the whole affair of these killings had to be brought to trial. It was to be expected that the perpetrators would refer to higher orders also for these individual crimes. This occurred; thereupon the SS jurisdiction, on the basis of the material which I supplied, approached the highest government chiefs and officially asked, 'Did you order these killings? Is the legal fact of murder no longer valid for you? What general orders are there concerning these killings?' Then the supreme State leadership would either have to admit its mistakes and thereby bring the culprits definitely under our jurisdiction, also with regard to the mass exterminations, or else an open break would have to result through the abrogation of the entire judicial system. If I may anticipate, on account of the trial in Weimar against Koch and Grabner, this problem became acute as I had foreseen; the proceedings were suspended and the SS jurisdiction put these questions, which I mentioned before, publicly and officially to the Reich Security Main Office. For this very purpose, a judge was sent there, who had the task of investigating all sections of the Reich Security Main Office, to see whether such orders were in existence. As I heard, the result was negative. Thereupon an attempt was made to take direct steps against Höss, but in the meantime the front had advanced, Auschwitz was occupied and the judge who had, been sent there had to stop at the beginning of his fruitless investigations, and in January 1945, complete disorganization set in which made further legal prosecution impossible. If I may go back, the immediate effects of the judicial investigation were that in all concentration camps the killing of prisoners by so-called 'euthanasia' stopped immediately, because no doctor could feel sure that he would not be arrested from one moment to the next. Everybody bore in mind the example that was set by the case of the doctor of Buchenwald. I am convinced that through this intervention and action, the lives of thousands of prisoners were saved. The killing system was severely shaken; for it is noteworthy that on my second visit to Lublin, shortly after I first approached Kriminalkommissar Wirth, I did not find him there. I learned that in the meantime Wirth had suddenly received orders to completely destroy all his extermination camps. He had gone to Istria with his entire command, and was guarding streets there, and while doing so, he was killed in May 1944. When I heard that Wirth and his command had left Lublin, I immediately flew there in order to find out whether he was merely transferring his field of activity and would continue elsewhere, but that was not so.

HERR PELCKMANN: Witness, were you in danger of your life in all these investigations?

MORGEN: It was clear that the discovery of these horrible crimes was extremely unpleasant to those responsible for them. I knew that a human life meant nothing to these people and that they were ready for anything. As proof, I may cite the following: after I had arrested Grabner, the chief of the political section in Auschwitz, and the investigating commission…

THE PRESIDENT: You aren't forgetting that you said you were going to take 45 minutes with this witness, are you, Herr Pelckmann?

HERR PELCKMANN: No, Your Lordship, I have not forgotten, and I regret exceedingly that it is taking longer than I expected, but I believe that I owe the tribunal this explanation of the facts.

THE PRESIDENT: It seems of very little importance whether this man was in danger of his life or not.

HERR PELCKMANN: From the point of view of the defence, Your Lordship, I am of a different opinion, since for the conditions and possibilities of opposing this system, and for Number 1 of the ruling of the Court of 13 March, or rather Number 2, compulsion and orders are of decisive importance.

THE PRESIDENT: Go on, Herr Pelckmann. The tribunal does not think it is important.

MORGEN: May I say one more sentence on that subject? The investigating commission of the Reich Criminal Police Department at Auschwitz was quartered in wooden huts, and after it had worked with success for some time, unknown persons at night destroyed the huts by fire, with all the documents. The investigations in Auschwitz were interrupted and made difficult for a long time. You may see from that, how ruthless was the opposition to us. I, myself, received enough warnings and threats, but whether I was actually in danger of my life, I cannot say.

HERR PELCKMANN: Did the directing personnel of the concentration camp Auschwitz in any way justify the assumption that they knew of these exterminations? I emphasize again—if I understood you correctly the concentration camp Auschwitz, with its many labour camps, had nothing to do with the extermination camp and was separate from it?

MORGEN: As I have already said, Höss was simultaneously commander of Auschwitz and Monowitz; he is to be considered the chief of the personnel, aside from the one leader of the Monowitz troops. I dealt only with these two, and these two knew about it.
HERR PELCKMANN: Did you speak to the doctor of the concentration camp Auschwitz?
MORGEN: Yes. When I arrived, the doctor showed me the mortality figures at the time he took over. He pointed out with a gleam in his eye how, since his transfer to Auschwitz, these huge figures had dropped precipitately through extensive hygienic measures and changes. In this connection, he came to talk about Grabner. Grabner had expected him to kill pregnant Polish women. The doctor had refused since it was irreconcilable with his professional duties. Thereupon Grabner had reproached him for not realizing the importance of his, Grabner's, tasks. The doctor did not give in and a quarrel arose which was carried on before the commander, and neither Höss nor Grawitz said anything. Thus, the doctor, at the time when I met him by accident, was in a distressed frame of mind and said 'What shall I do?' I said to him, 'What you have done so far; absolute refusal is quite in order, and tomorrow I will arrest Grabner.'
THE PRESIDENT: What does this have to do with the SS unless the doctor was in the SS; perhaps he was?
HERR PELCKMANN: It is well known that the doctors were SS doctors, and the witness is describing how an SS doctor in this concentration camp Auschwitz opposed the suggestion of Grabner. He is describing that as a typical case.
THE PRESIDENT: Herr Pelckmann, the Tribunal thinks you have been quite long enough over this witness. You are going into matters in too much detail.
HERR PELCKMANN: You said previously that you had reported to the various agencies and named three of them, I believe. Please describe how Nebe reacted. What was Breithaupt's attitude? What did Kaltenbrunner and Müller say? What was Pohl's attitude, and how did the Reich Physician, Grawitz, react?
MORGEN: First I reported to my immediate superior, SS-Gruppenführer Nebe, as chief of the RKPA. Nebe was an extremely taciturn man, but I could see that his hair stood on end when I made my report. He was absolutely silent. Then he said that I must immediately report this matter to Kaltenbrunner. The chief of the Hauptamt SS Courts, Obergruppenführer Breithaupt, also became very much excited. He said that he would immediately go to see Himmler and report this to him and try to have a personal interview with Himmler arranged for me. The Reich Physician also did not know what to say. Obergruppenführer Pohl, however, took another attitude. Previously, or about the same time, I had had the commander of the concentration camp Hertogenbosch arrested, who had caused the death of 10 women through punitive measures. When I reported this to Pohl, he said these were trifles. He said, 'What do the lives of 10 women matter in view of the thousands of German women dying every night in the air raids?'

HERR PELCKMANN: Please be more brief on the others.

MORGEN: After I had already reported to Obergruppenführer Kaltenbrunner about the actual corruption crimes, the deadly crimes which I discovered about 6 months later, a conversation took place in the presence of Nebe, Kaltenbrunner, and Müller. This discussion was extraordinarily one-sided. Kaltenbrunner and Nebe were absolutely silent while Müller, white with rage, was infuriated with me and did not give me a chance to get in a word. When I looked at him calmly, he suddenly jumped up and rushed out of the room and left me alone, while the other two gentlemen turned away from me. In the afternoon, I went to see Müller again and personally told him my point of view once again, but Müller was still absolutely against it.

HERR PELCKMANN: Very well, did you …?

THE PRESIDENT: What was the date of this conversation with Kaltenbrunner?

MORGEN: That was immediately after the charge was raised against Grabner. I assume in July or August 1944.

HERR PELCKMANN: Did you report these things to other circles of the SS?

MORGEN: No. I wanted to inform and win over those people, who really had something to say, to my point of view. Nothing else counted. Besides that, I was bound by Basic Order Number 1, concerning secrecy on State affairs, and could only approach the chiefs of the main offices personally. Any mistake I would have made in contacting other offices would have had serious results for we and would have given my enemies a pretext for protracting the investigation.

THE PRESIDENT: Dr Pelckmann, he said he did not report it. Surely that is sufficient. We don't want to know more about it. He did not report. We are not trying the witness …

[contd.]

DR RUDOLF MERKEL (Counsel for the Gestapo): Mr. President, I should like to be permitted to put three brief questions to this witness, concerning non-participation and ignorance on the part of the Gestapo as far as the mass extermination is concerned.

THE PRESIDENT: You may.

DR MERKEL: Witness, if I understood you correctly, the crimes of Kriminalkommissar Wirth in Lublin were discovered because of a report of the Security Police in Lublin.

MORGEN: Yes.

DR MERKEL: Did the Security Police in Lublin participate in these crimes in any way?

MORGEN: No. As I saw it that was not the case.

DR MERKEL: The witness, Best, stated that the camps at Treblinka and Majdanek were under the supervision of the Security Police. Is that correct?

MORGEN: I know nothing about that. Wirth explained that he had four extermination camps. I believe the name Treblinka was mentioned in that connection.

DR MERKEL: According to your conviction, this camp as well was under Wirth?
MORGEN: I assumed that.
DR MERKEL: Did you wish to execute an order of the SS court to arrest Eichmann?
MORGEN: I asked the SS court at Berlin to investigate Eichmann on the basis of my report. The SS court in Berlin thereupon submitted to the chief of the Reich Security Main Office, SS-Obergruppenführer Kaltenbrunner, in his capacity as highest judge, a warrant to arrest Eichmann.

Dr Bachmann reported to me that on the submission of this matter rather dramatic incidents took place.

Kaltenbrunner immediately called in Müller, and now the judge was told that an arrest was in no event to be considered, for Eichmann was carrying out a special secret task of utmost importance entrusted to him by the Führer.

DR MERKEL: When was that?
MORGEN: That was in the middle of 1944.
DR MERKEL: Thank you, I have no further questions to put to this witness.
DR GAWLIK: Your Lordship, may I be permitted to put a few questions, please?
THE PRESIDENT: Yes.
DR GAWLIK: Witness, you spoke about orders of the Reich Security Main Office. From which offices of the Reich Security Main Office did these orders come?
MORGEN: Do you mean the orders for the mass extermination?
DR GAWLIK: Yes.
MORGEN: I stated that the SS jurisdiction…
DR GAWLIK: Answer the question briefly, please. Which offices issued these orders?
MORGEN: I said that the investigating judge could not establish the origin of such orders to my knowledge.
DR GAWLIK: You spoke of the orders of the Reich Security Main Office, did you not?
MORGEN: I said that the accused Koch and Grabner, in answering for their killings, referred to, orders of the Reich Security Main Office and maintained that these orders had to be destroyed as soon as they were received. That was purely an assertion and therefore this statement had to be investigated.
DR GAWLIK: Did you ascertain that the Offices III, VI, and VII were in any way participating in these measures?
MORGEN: I have already testified that Wirth's undertaking directly…
DR GAWLIK: Can you answer this question with a 'yes' or 'no'?
MORGEN: I could not determine that.
DR GAWLIK: Thank you. I have no further questions to the witness.
THE PRESIDENT: Does the Prosecution wish to cross-examine?
SIR DAVID MAXWELL-FYFE: The Prosecution very carefully considers the question of cross-examining this witness. We do not accept his evidence as to Buchenwald,

Dachau, and as to conditions in concentration camps generally. We feel, however, the tribunal has been shown such an overwhelming amount of evidence, including films and exhibits of the consistent pattern of cruelties in the concentration camps, of the smelling chimneys of the crematoria, and of the persons who carried out these actions, that we consider that any further discussion of these matters should be by way of comment and that it would not be right to take up the time of the tribunal by confronting this witness with the details of that evidence which is so fully in the tribunal's mind.
THE PRESIDENT: The witness may retire. Is that your case?
HERR PELCKMANN: Yes.

[The witness left the stand.]

Morgen was not the only investigator looking into the misappropriation of property in Globocnik's kingdom. Heinrich Wied was a career policeman. He was born in Oschersleben on 9 June 1909, but grew up in Düsseldorf. He joined the criminal police service in August 1937 and attended various courses. He was automatically accorded the rank of SS-Untersturmführer on completion of training. Wied had been a member of the NSDAP since 1933, but on his own admission was not politically active. In August 1939, he was called-up and joined a flak unit, but was soon recalled to the Kripo. Ordered to attend a special course at the Sipo School in Berlin, Wied became bored with Sipo studies and arranged another call-up with the Brandenburg Lehrregiment. This lasted only until September 1941, when he was again recalled to the Kripo where he headed an office dealing with fraud cases. In April 1942, he was posted to the RSHA in Berlin.

At the RSHA, Wied specialised in a Luftwaffe corruption case, and various cases of swindling, including one by railway construction contractors, and another of swindling over the supply of razor blades for the Wehrmacht. He was also tasked with the investigation into alleged corruption at the Bekleidungswerk in Lublin from December 1943 until April 1944. This unit had been set up to collect and utilise property seized from prisoners entering Majdanek, the labour camp at Puławy and several other camps in the Lublin area.

The Bekleidungswerk used three disused hangars at the former Lublin airfield as warehouses. Wied discovered that, apparently, some seventy SS staff were employed there. He also uncovered the responsible authority to be the Reich Chancellery in Berlin, which had created a specialist department, the 'Gemeinnutzige Stiftung für Anstaltspfleg' ('Charitable Foundation for Institutional Care') for the purpose. Unwittingly, Wied had uncovered the storage facility for the extermination of Jews and inmates of mental asylums—Aktion Reinhardt. He identified those responsible were Oberregierungsrat Allers, Sturmbannführer Wirth, Haupsturmführer Hering, and Gruppenführer Globocnik.

Wied's investigations proved fruitful. They uncovered that eighteen SS men, the majority employed on the staff of the Bekleidungswerk, were guilty of corruption on a large scale. Wied experienced many obstacles to his investiogations, including minor acts of sabotage to his car. He was even obstructed by senior Gestapo officers and when Allers was interviewed on behalf of a SS man discovered in possession of a large quantity of obviously stolen goods, Allers stated blatantly that the man had appropriated the property with the authority of the Stiftung.

The cases against the eighteen accused were submitted for hearing by the SS and Police Court sitting in Kassel. Some received terms of imprisonment of up to three years, but in several cases no verdict could be reached as the defendants were 'at the front'.[1] Although, by then, Globocnik had been in Trieste for several months, he was heavily implicated. No recorded action was taken against him, and not for the first time he escaped retribution for his dishonest transactions.

Historian Robin O'Neil, in his masterful study of Bełżec, *Stepping Stone to Genocide*, suggests that there were two types of criminality—authorised and unauthorised. If one committed a crime against the Jews or the Polish populace, if it was against the party, then it was 'not authorised', and the perpetrator would feel the full weight of Nazi justice. If, however, the offence was not against the party, it could be construed as 'authorised'. There is substance to this argument. On 4 October 1943, before his senior SS cadre in Posen, Himmler declared the SS had a 'right' to seize the Jews wealth (see Appendix I). Amon Göth, an early member of Reinhardt and the commandant of Plaszow labour camp, did not suffer the same fate as Karl Koch, at the hands of the SS, despite his corruption being plain to see to all concerned. He was considered as 'loyal to the Party'. Koch, on the other hand, transgressed against the party, according to his indictment.

Globocnik considered himself as the SS business executive with access to untold assets. He recognised the SS claim of right to plundered property, but skimming off his share of the spoils was also his own right. To achieve this benefit, he realised that others too had to be included in the embezzlement fellowship, and he turned a blind eye towards the pilfering by his SS staff. Even certain characters at the Reich Chancellery ensured they had their cut. The real mastermind behind the numerous SS business enterprises was SS-Obergruppenführer Oswald Pohl, the chief of the SS-WVHA at Unter den Eichen in Berlin. Pohl quickly supplanted Globocnik in Himmler's plans for the East. Where Globocnik's methods and ideas were impetuous and without substance, Pohl was the opposite; an astute businessman. Where Globocnik's financial acumen was lacking, Pohl possessed it in bundles. And where Globocnik's dishonesty was lurking just below the surface for all to see, Pohl was shrewd.

Oswald Pohl has been described as Himmler's 'Graue Eminenz' ('grey eminence'). He was the mastermind behind the vast SS financial empire, the tentacles of which extended into numerous commercial concerns, some of which still exist to this day. He born on 30 June 1892 in Duisberg-Ruhrort, the fifth child of eight offspring, to parents Emil Otto Hermann Pohl, a locksmith, and his wife, Emilie Auguste. Young Oswald was sent to the local school in Duisburg-Laar from 1898 until 1904, and from 1904, he attended the upper high school in Hamborn, until joining the navy on 1 April 1912. Pohl was posted to the Shipyard Division in Wilhelmshaven as a trainee paymaster.

At the outbreak of hostilities in August 1914, Pohl was attached to the pay office of the Shipyard Division. From December 1915 until July 1916, he enjoyed a stint as ship's paymaster on board the ships *Santa Elena* and *Answald*, at which point he was reallocated to command the pay section in the engineer and deck officer school. He was posted as paymaster to the mines clearing division in Flanders during December 1917. He passed his examination in naval pay and pensions at the naval school in Kiel in 1918. This afforded him the rank of Leutnant zur See from 1 April 1918. The same month he was reassigned to Flanders, where he stayed until returning to Kiel on 16 October 1918.

Pohl remained in the German Navy, with various postings as paymaster. He studied law and political science at the Christian-Albrecht University in Kiel during 1919 and 1920, and joined the Freikorps 3 Marine Brigade von Loewenfeld in 1920. Typical of many young German men, he belonged to the political group of the so-called '1918ers' who were defined by their war enthusiasm in 1914, and their subsequent disillusionment, frustration, and anger with the German defeat of 1918. Pohl first joined the NSDAP in Kiel on 1 July 1922, but was subsequently allocated number 30 842 on 22 February 1926, after the NSDAP was resurrected following the period of prohibition. He joined the SA in Swinemünde in 1925, and transferred to the Marine Sturm of SA-Sturmbann III in SA-Standarte 163, Kiel after he was posted to the city by the Navy. From January 1932, Pohl began to climb the promotion ladder in the SA, eventually attaining SA-Sturmbannführer on 2 August 1933.

On 15 May 1933, Heinrich Himmler wrote to Wilhelm Canaris, the commander of the battleship *Schlesien*, requesting if he knew of anyone whom he could use in the SS. Canaris ordered the ship paymaster, Rudolf Grossmann, to reply to Himmler on 21 May 1933, bringing Himmler's attention to Oswald Pohl. The two men later met in a Kiel hotel, resulting in Pohl's official application to join the SS on 24 May 1933. Pohl then attended a course at the SA Leadership School in Munich. On 31 December 1933, he was promoted to Marinestabszahlmeister, a naval rank equivalent to Kapitänleutnant, and the same day, he left the navy.

On 15 January 1934, still not an official SS member, Pohl took charge of Department IV (Commercial Administration) on the Staff of RFSS. Meanwhile, he was appointed by the SA leadership as commander of SA-Marinestandarte 2 in Kiel on 1 February 1934. Himmler wrote an official request on 16 February 1934 to the Supreme SA Leaderhip, asking that authority be given for Pohl to transfer to the SS. On 12 March 1934, Pohl joined the SS with the rank of SS-Standartenführer. His SS membership and rank were both backdated to 1 February 1934. He was placed in charge of Section IV of the Staff RFSS, dealing with all economic administrative matters in the SS. On 29 August 1934, Pohl was promoted to SS-Oberführer, effective from 9 September 1934.

On 1 June 1935, the SS departments were reorganised, and Pohl was transferred to the SS-Hauptamt as chief of the economic administration office (Department IV in the SS Central Office). He also attained the rank of SS-Brigadeführer the same day. In effect, he became the chief cashier of the SS.

Pohl was a founder member and the commercial director of the company for the building and maintenance of cultural monuments from 1 February 1936. This included the SS School at Wewelsburg Castle in Westphalia, and was one of many commercial enterprises that Pohl controlled in the name of the SS.

On 30 January 1937, Pohl was promoted to SS-Gruppenführer. He was a member of the 'Circle of Friends of the Reichsführer-SS' in 1937. He was later appointed as the treasurer of the German Red Cross. In April 1937, Himmler gave him responsibility for buildings construction and maintenance. On 8 May 1937, Pohl was made responsible for the financial administration of Lebensborn. Himmler also entrusted him with his beloved King Heinrich Memorial Foundation in Quedlinburg on 1 January 1938. Pohl continued to collect business titles and companies, all under the umbrella of economic administrative head of the SS. He became head of the SS Main Office for Administration and Economics in the major SS reorganisation of departments on 20 April 1939, simultaneously acquiring the government rank of Ministerialdirektor. Pohl acquired Waffen-SS rank on 21 June 1940 when he was made a Generalleutnant der SS-Verfügungstruppe. Himmler included Pohl among his trusted circle when he called twelve of his loyal lieutenants for a meeting at Wewelsburg in June 1941. Globocnik was not among them. Discussion focused on imparting the secret information regarding their roles attached to the upcoming Operation Barbarossa.

Following the period December 1941 to January 1942, Pohl's involvement in the financial aspects of POWs, the seized assets of the Jews and the prisoner labour force was formalised. Himmler nominated him as chief of the reorganised SS Economic Main Office (WVHA—SS-Wirtschafts-Verwaltungshauptamtes). Its departments included Amt D, the Inspectorate of the Concentration Camps, under Richard Glücks. On 1 February 1942, Pohl became responsible for all concentration camps, their construction and buildings, their inmates and the economic benefits derived from their labour force. He governed this economic empire from a large complex of offices at Unter den Eichen in Berlin-Steglitz. On 20 April 1942, the ex-naval pay clerk was promoted to SS-Obergruppenführer und General der Waffen-SS.

In his role as overall commander of the concentration camp system, Oswald Pohl was heavily implicated in scientific research work on camp inmates, the construction and functioning of the gas chambers and crematoria, and slave labour within the camps. Pohl attended numerous conferences regarding the physical extermination process and was present at Himmler's infamous speech to the Gruppenführer and Obergruppenführer at Posen on 4 October 1943. Pohl went on the run at war's end, but was arrested on 27 May 1946, living and working under the false name of Ludwig Gniss, on a farm at Verden. He was transferred to Nuremberg on 31 May 1946. The Pohl trial, also known as the WVHA trial, began on 8 April 1947. Pohl was found guilty and was sentenced to death by hanging on 3 November 1947. He was transferred to Landsberg Prison to await execution. There began a lengthy process of appeals for clemency and various officials from several countries spoke out, both in favour and against, the death penalty for Pohl. There were public demonstrations and the court reconvened on 14 July 1948 to hear additional evidence presented by the defence. On 11 August 1948, Pohl's death sentence was confirmed. All efforts to save him failed, and Oswald Pohl was hanged at Landsberg Prison on 7 June 1951. He was certified dead at 1.43 a.m. and was buried in the adjacent Spöttinger Prison Cemetery later that day.

Pohl had as good as admitted his personal involvement in Globocnik's murder and plundering operations in the General Government in his affidavit before the military tribunal in Nuremberg.[2] In this, Pohl declared that Himmler directed the secret deliveries of loot to the Reichsbank. He stated that Globocnik made frequent trips to Berlin from Lublin in order to deposit valuables at the Reichsbank. To his knowledge, the first shipment of which he was personally aware was in the autumn of 1943 (by this time, Reinhardt had been operating for at least eighteen months and this statement should be viewed with scepticism). He admitted little doubt as to the source of the valuables, and stated that he had despatched Sturmbannführer Opperbock from his Hauptamt, to Lublin to take over the business enterprises founded by Globocnik. On completion of Aktion Reinhardt, Pohl also admitted incorporating all the economic elements of the operation into his WVHA. He even admitted receiving a letter of thanks from Himmler for his participation in Aktion Reinhardt.

The final judgement of the military tribunal in case no. 4, the USA *v.* Oswald Pohl, August Frank, Georg Loerner, Heinz Karl Fanslau, Hans Loerner, Josef Vogt, Erwin Tschentscher, Rudolf Scheide, Max Kiefer, Franz Eirenschmalz, Karl Sommer, Hermann Pook, Hans Baier, Hans Hohberg, Leo Volk, Karl Mummenthey, Hans Bober min, and Horst Klein, on 3 November 1947 at Nuremberg, was rather revealing, so it is worth reproducing a few extracts:

[Concerning] ACTION REINHARDT
The extermination and deportation of the Jews in the East produced a vast amount of valuable property, both real and personal, which the Reich was quick to recognise and seize. To marshal these resources, the Action Reinhardt was instituted, named approximately enough, for Reinhard Heydrich, formerly 'chief of the Security Police and SD, who met his death—and this, too, appropriately enough—in Czechoslovakia in 1942. The purpose of the action was to gather into the Reich all the Jewish manpower and wealth which could be reached. It was an ambitious and profitable undertaking for Germany. The Jews themselves were herded into concentration camps as slaves and their entire worldly possessions confiscated. The real property, where possible, was put to German use (largely through the WVHA agency of OSTI) and the movable property was shipped to WVHA, where it was inventoried, appraised, and distributed through prescribed channels. The thoroughness of this program of looting is evidenced by the articles listed: featherbeds, quilts, blankets, woolen yardage, shawls, umbrellas, canes, thermos bottles, flasks, baby carriages, combs, handbags, belts, pipes, sun glasses, mirrors, table silver, luggage, linens, pillows, eye glasses, furs, watches, clocks, and jewelry. Everything that could be lifted was moved. The defendant Frank listed as received up to 30 April 1943, 94,000 men's watches, 33,000 women's watches, and 25,000 fountain pens. Currency and precious metals seized reached a total value of 60,000,000 Reichsmarks. About 2,000 carloads of textiles reached Germany as a result of this plunder, and in all a grand total of over 100 million Reichsmarks in personal property was thus acquired. When Jews died in concentration camps, additional loot became available. The clothing was stripped from their bodies and, after being carefully searched for hidden valuables and the distinguishing Jewish star removed, was distributed to still living inmates or to German civilians. Camp commandants were cautioned not to ship clothing which was stained with blood or showed bullet holes. To complete the desecration, the hair was shorn from the heads of the dead (one report showed a carload of 3,000 kilograms) and all the dental gold was extracted and deposited through WVHA in the vaults of the Reich Bank. It was ordered by the defendant Frank that all property originating from Action Reinhardt be called 'goods originating from thefts, receiving of stolen goods, and hoarded goods'. In the true sense, this description is more accurate than Frank intended.

In the *Southern German Legal Gazette* of March 1947, crimes against humanity are defined as acts involving 'cruelty against human life, degradation of the dignity of man or destruction of human civilization'. The Tribunal is quite content to use this German concept as a standard in deciding whether or not the facts heretofore found constitute crimes against humanity. Only one conclusion is possible. These facts establish beyond a reasonable doubt the wholesale commission of both war crimes and crimes against humanity. It next becomes necessary to determine to what extent, if any, the several defendants are criminally responsible therefore, by reason of actual perpetration, participation, or taking a consenting part therein.

A defence which has been almost universally advanced is that all the criminal acts of the Reich were conducted under a cloak of secrecy which prevented the defendants from knowing about them. Hitler's famous secrecy order has been offered by nearly every defendant. It has been urged that there was strict censorship of the press, that listening to foreign broadcasts was prohibited, that concentration camp prisoners were required upon their release to be sworn to secrecy as to events which they had observed or experienced, and that the German people generally were kept in complete ignorance of what was going on. All these facts are true. But in the very nature of things, it was impossible to maintain complete secrecy or anything like it. It was impossible to keep hidden from public view the huge transports which carried the slave labourers from the East to the concentration camps. It was impossible to keep secret the public demonstrations against the Jews. Streicher's infamous *Der Stürmer* had a circulation of 600,000 copies. Himmler spoke openly about 'the final solution of the Jewish problem' at Poznan, Krakow, and Metz. When prisoners were liberated from concentration camps, it is impossible to think that they maintained the complete secrecy to which they were bound. Soldiers returning on leave from Poland, Russia, and the Ukraine must have talked to some extent. The pall of smoke from the crematory at Auschwitz could not be kept hidden. In spite of decrees, foreign broadcasts were heard. The systematic murder of millions of human beings, extending over 5 years, could not by reason of its very magnitude be kept secret. It is undoubtedly true that millions of obscure and unimportant German citizens had no way of knowing and did not know of the horrible wrongs which were being perpetrated. But if high-ranking officers of the SS, whose daily tasks for years brought them into immediate contact with the operation of the camps, claim that they had no suspicion of the events occurring within the barbed wire, that defence cannot be believed. Undoubtedly some knew more than others, and some limited few knew nothing. With this conclusion Pohl himself agrees. In his interrogation of 13 June 1946 (NO-4728, Pros. Ex. 693), Pohl was confronted by Kaltenbrunner's testimony before the International Military Tribunal that, '...there were only a handful of people in the WVHA who had any control or knew anything about concentration camps', to which Pohl commented: 'Well, that is complete nonsense. I described to you how these were handled in the WVHA. As for instance, in the case of the use of textiles and turning in of valuables, and also from Glücks and Loerner right on down to the last little clerk, must have known what went on in the concentration camps, and it is complete nonsense for him to speak of just a handful of men'.

In Liebehenschel's letter of 25 February 1943, written as chief of Amtsgruppe D [Amt D I] of the WVHA and addressed to all the concentration camp commanders, he states that the population in the East is beginning to be startled by the frequent casualties in the concentration camps. Apparently, in some areas at least, the secret was beginning to leak out.

The Tribunal is convinced that the ignorance professed by many of the defendants is the ignorance of convenience.

At the outset of the testimony, the Tribunal realised the necessity of guarding against assuming criminality, or even culpable responsibility, solely from the official titles which the several defendants held. It became apparent that, in conformity with the ancient German passion for high-sounding titles, many purely ministerial officers, performing perfunctory or even menial tasks, were designated by sonorous names which did not necessarily connote substantial power or authority. In some instances minor officers, engaged in purely routine tasks, were designated on the elaborate tables of organisation by lengthy and awe-inspiring titles, which upon closer inspection were found to cover nothing more than a few desks in a remote corner. The Tribunal has been especially careful to discover and analyse the actual power and authority of the several defendants, and the manner and extent to which they were exercised, without permitting itself to be unduly impressed by the official designations on letterheads or office doors.

... [Concerning Oswald Pohl and] The Destruction of the Warsaw Ghetto.

In the fall of 1942, Himmler's plans for the complete subjugation of Poland reached a pinnacle. The Jewish ghetto at Warsaw covered a total area of approximately 320 hectares, or 800 acres. It comprised a large residential area and, in addition, housed a great number of industrial enterprises, principally textile and fur manufacturing plants. The ghetto had a population of nearly 60,000 persons. In October, Himmler ordered that the entire Jewish population of the ghetto was to be gathered together in concentration camps in Warsaw and Lublin to be used as an immense labour pool for armament purposes. After the round-up was completed, the Jews were to be deported to large concentration camps in the East and Polish labour substituted in the Warsaw industries. Himmler added: 'Of course, there too, the Jews shall someday disappear in accordance with the Führer's wishes'. All private Jewish firms were to be eliminated and no Jew was to be employed in private industry. This order raised a strong protest from the armament firms in Warsaw, in which a large number of Jews were employed, but Himmler was obdurate and insisted on the letter of his order being carried out. The Jewish residents of the ghetto, however, resisted deportation vigorously, and a pitched battle, lasting over a week, was necessary to uproot them. In February 1943, Himmler directed that after the removal of the concentration camp the ghetto be completely demolished. In his order, he stated: 'A master plan for the pulling down of the ghetto has to be submitted to me. It has to be accomplished in any case that the living space, which accommodated 500,000 sub-humans and was never suitable for Germans, will completely disappear, and that the city of Warsaw, with its one million inhabitants, will be reduced in size, having always been a dangerous centre of rebellion'.

This gigantic task of destruction and deportation was committed to Pohl as chief of the WVHA. Himmler directed that the 'city centre of the former ghetto is to be flattened completely and every cellar and every canal is to be filled in. After the work is finished, the area is to be covered up with earth, and a large park is to be planted'.

By an order dated 23 June 1943, addressed to the Higher SS and Police Leader in the East and to Pohl, Himmler ordered the erection of a concentration camp in the vicinity of Riga, to which the largest possible number of the male Jews were to be transferred. Surplus Jews from the ghetto were to be evacuated to the East, which meant ultimate starvation or extermination. In the summer of 1943, Pohl set to work to carry out Himmler's order. The concentration camp in the Warsaw ghetto was established and Pohl appointed Goecke, a veteran of Mauthausen, as commandant. Pohl reported to Himmler that at first there were only 300 prisoners in the camp, but that this number would be increased as speedily as possible. In October, Pohl reported that Amtsgruppe C of the WVHA had been charged with the technical execution of the demolition order and Amtsgruppe D with the placing of the prisoners. Pohl engaged four private contracting firms, who guaranteed to pull down and remove 4,500 cubic metres daily. He advised that 1,500 prisoners were being used as labourers at the end of October, but that upon securing additional mechanical equipment, 2,000 more prisoners would be needed at once. In February 1944, Pohl reported that 3,750,000 cubic metres of buildings had been demolished, and that 2,040 prisoners were being used. By April, 6,750,000 cubic metres had been 'pulled down and blasted', and 2,180 prisoners were being used. By June, 10,000,000 cubic metres had been destroyed and the concentration camp had been completed. Thus was accomplished the most complete task of destruction of a modern city since Carthage met its fate many centuries ago, and in this nefarious undertaking Pohl stood hand in glove with Himmler and Stroop in accomplishing the task of total destruction. This was not a city taken in battle; it had long before been captured and occupied by the German armed forces. It was the deliberate and intentional destruction of a large modern city and its entire civilian population. It was wholesale murder, pillage, thievery, and looting, and Pohl's part in accomplishing this abominable project is recorded in his own handwriting. He cannot free himself from his share in Brigadeführer Stroop's shameful boast—'The total number of Jews dealt with is 56,065, including Jews caught, and Jews whose extermination can be proved'.

... [Concerning Oswald Pohl and] ACTION REINHARDT.

This action, as has been indicated, involved a plan for draining the Eastern occupied countries of their last vestige of wealth. It had the two-fold purpose of reducing the East to abject poverty so that starvation would be the inevitable result to the population and, at the same time, filling the Reich Treasury. It was a programme of deliberate wholesale brigandage which was, at the same time, an added aspect of the extermination programme.

In the execution of this programme, Pohl's WVHA played a major role. His organisation was the clearing house for all the booty. All of the stolen property was routed through WVHA, where it was inventoried, appraised, and distributed. That Pohl knew of the criminal source of this property is evidenced by his letter of 9 February 1944, to [Gerhard] Maurer, directing that valuables found in clothing were to be delivered in sealed boxes to Amtsgruppe D, and directing further, that nothing in the shipment should reveal its origin. The money which was stolen was secreted in the Reich Bank under the assumed name of 'Max Heiliger'. On 4 July 1944, Pohl, in a communication to the Main Office chiefs, announced the names of officers responsible for the property seized in several areas, and stated: 'As a matter of principle, it has to be kept in mind that the entire Jewish property is to be incorporated into the Reich property'. Property from the Action Reinhardt which had been delivered to the Reich Main Treasury was kept in a separate account, appropriately called, 'Department Booty'.

Moved by the Christian spirit of Christmas, Pohl, on 6 November 1943, wrote to Himmler, stating that he intended to make gifts of watches and fountain pens to SS units, and asked whether the gifts should be made in Himmler's name. Himmler approved Pohl's generous plan and added that 15,000 ladies' watches should be distributed to Germans coming from Russia for resettlement. Pohl thought it would be a generous gesture to distribute 3,000 clocks which had been repaired to guards at the concentration camps and to Berlin inhabitants who had been bombed. As an afterthought, he suggested to Himmler that 16 extra-fine gold precision wrist watches, valued at 300 Reichsmarks each, which had been repaired, be distributed among commanders of technical units.

Pohl's own statement as to his knowledge of the operation of Action Reinhardt and of his participation in the distribution of the loot is again quite sufficient. In his affidavit of 2 April 1947 (NO-2714, Pros. Ex. 535), he states that the action was instituted in 1941 or 1942, and was in direct charge of SS-Gruppenführer Globocnik; that by Himmler's direction he contacted the president of the Reich Bank to arrange for delivery of the valuables; these transactions were to be carried out in extreme secrecy. Together with Georg Loerner, Frank, and others, he visited the Reich Bank and was shown the accumulated valuables in the bank vaults. 'It was never doubted,' he said, 'that this loot was taken from Jews exterminated in the concentration camps. As I learned in 1943, gold teeth and crowns of inmates of concentration camps were broken out of their mouths after liquidation. This gold was melted down and delivered to the Reich Bank. When I received all the vouchers, setting out the economic assets received, I realised the extent of the operation. I realised that the greatest part of the textile goods listed in these reports had been taken from people who had been violently put to death and that the purpose of the operation had been the extermination of the Jews.'

In another affidavit, 15 July 1946 (4045-PS, Pros. Ex. 536), Pohl further indicates his knowledge of, and participation in the ghoulish scramble. The facts stated therein are cumulative and need not be specifically referred to.

The fact that Pohl himself did not actually transport the stolen goods to the Reich or did not himself remove the gold from the teeth of dead inmates, does not exculpate him. This was a broad criminal programme, requiring the co-operation of many persons, and Pohl's part was to conserve and account for the loot. Having knowledge of the illegal purposes of the action and of the crimes which accompanied it, his active participation, even in the afterphases of the action, make him particeps criminis [an accomplice] in the whole affair.

... [Concerning Oswald Pohl and] OSTI (Eastern Industry).

Eastern Industries, known as 'OSTI', was a running-mate of Action Reinhardt in the so-called final solution of the Jewish problem in the East. OSTI was organised on 1 March 1943, and was dissolved one year later. The whole history of this project is clearly described in the report of Johann Sebastian Fischer in a final audit, 21 June 1944 (NO-1271, Pros. Ex. 491). It was impossible to completely strip the Eastern territories of all Jewish property. Some, because of its nature, could not be removed and some could be operated best by the Reich on the spot. To utilise this unremovable property, OSTI was organised, with a capital of 100,000 Reichsmarks. Of this, Pohl held 75,000 and defendant Georg Loerner 25,000. Pohl was chairman of the Aufsichtsrat, or supervisory board, of which Georg Loerner was also a member. Globocnik and Dr Max Horn were the active managers. Fischer describes the corporate purposes as follows: 'OSTI had to administer all Jewish property within the territory of the Government General except cash, jewelry, and clothing; and in particular to utilise the manpower of the Jews living in the Government General for tasks benefiting the Reich'.

This involved:

(1) Utilisation of the working capacity of the Jews by erecting industrial plants in the Government General in connection with the Jewish labour camps.
(2) Taking over commercial enterprises which had previously been maintained by the SS in the Government General.
(3) Taking possession of movable property which was formerly Jewish, especially machines and raw materials. The machines were to be installed in plants and the raw materials to be used.
(4) Utilisation of machines, tools, and merchandise formerly Jewish property which had been transferred to non-Jewish ownership.

A partial list of the industries thus administered included a glass works in Wolomin, a peat-cutting plant near Lublin, an iron foundry, a large textile factory, a plant for the manufacture of brushes, and a stone quarry. Globocnik states that the entire manpower was brought together and kept in closed camps into which the manufacture of essential items for war had been transferred. 'Altogether 18 establishments had been built up and still more were to be added. About 52,000 labourers were available'.

The project continued as long as the supply of Jewish concentration camp labour was available, but when, due to the exigencies of the war, in the fall of 1943 this labour supply was withdrawn, it was determined to liquidate OSTI, and Dr Horn was designated as liquidating officer.

As will be observed, OSTI was simply another manifestation of the policy of slave labour and appropriation of private property. Linked with Action Reinhardt, it was the consummation of the Reich plan to leave the occupied Eastern countries as vast stretches of scorched earth. In the OSTI phase of this plan, Pohl had even a more direct connection than he had with Action Reinhardt. Here he was the directing head and the chief executive of the project. As an original incorporator, he was in it from its inception and he actively participated in every phase of it until its liquidation. This being true, he was guilty of war crimes and crimes against humanity.

Under a plan which was perhaps devised to give some semblance of legality to this inherently lawless plan, PohI was designated as a trustee of the properties seized in the East and operated by OSTI. This was a strange species of trusteeship. All of the interests of the trustee were violently opposed to those of the cestius qui trustent. The recognised concept of a trustee is that he stands in the shoes of his beneficiaries and acts for their benefit and in opposition to any encroachment on their rights. Here, however, the trustee was in the service of adverse interests and acted at all times under an impelling motive to serve those interests at the expense of his beneficiaries. Actually, the trusteeship was pure fiction. It cannot be believed that it was ever the plan of the Reich to return any of the confiscated property to its former Jewish owners, most of whom had fled and disappeared, or had been exterminated. The only probative value of this fictitious trusteeship is to furnish another cord to bind Pohl closer to OSTI's criminal purposes.

In an attempt at partial exculpation, Pohl has submitted in evidence (Pohl 3, Pohl Ex. 2) a decree, dated 28 February 1933, signed by Reich President von Hindenburg and Chancellor Hitler, suspending the provisions of the Weimar Constitution, which guaranteed personal freedom, freedom of speech and of the press, the right of assembly, privacy of communication, and immunity from search. The Secret State Police were given almost unlimited power over persons and property, independent of any obligations and free from restraint or review. They became the supreme authority of the land. This tyrannical agency was the partner of WVHA in the administration of the concentration camps. Upon the promulgation of this decree, Germany became a police state and the liberty and lives of all German citizens were dependent upon the whims of men like Heydrich and Kaltenbrunner. It is to be assumed that if this is the kind of national government the people of Germany preferred, they were entitled to it. If they consented to surrender their human liberties to a police force, that was their privilege, and any outsider who intruded could well be told to mind his own affairs. But when the attempt is made to make the provisions of such a decree extra-territorial in their effect and to apply their totalitarian and autocratic police measures

> to non-Germans and in non-German territory, they thereby invaded the domain of international law, where reason still rules. The Nazi leaders, drunk with power, could abuse and deceive the German people just as long as the German people submitted, but when they extended their tyranny into foreign lands and attempted to justify it by the provisions of local German Law, their arrogance became over-extended and a power superior to Hitler's came into play to stop them.[3]

No longer was Globocnik protected by his mentor and former saviour. Despite all efforts to remain as a favourite of the Reichsführer, his decline was evident for everyone. SS-Gruppenführer Max von Herff was one of an ever-diminishing number of senior SS comrades that had a good word to say about Globocnik. His report on the Carinthian was not glowing, but was very positive:

> A strong character in everything he does—be it good or bad. Careless as to his personal appearance. A fanatic, going to extremes in carrying out his tasks, neglectful of his own health and independent of appreciation by others. A daredevil knowing no limits, even if it means overstepping the lines of the SS code of honour. All infractions so far, however, have been the result of personal ambition, but done out of necessity in the relentless pursuit of his task. His success in achieving his goals speaks absolutely for him.... It is important that [he] get married, so that he, his wife and a home put an end to this restless and self-destructive pioneer existence. He would learn to pace himself and thereby be able to grow into more important assignments.[4]

On the contrary, Richard Wendler could not wait to see the back of him:

> Dear Heinrich!
> I cannot help telling you how grateful I am for your clear words regarding the SS and Police Chief of Lublin and how relieved I am that you have decided to deploy him elsewhere.... I am writing today to ask you to remove him from here as quickly as possible and to assign him to a new task since he is using the time left him to pull stunts in his infamous way. He disregards all agreements, even thos reached in the presence of the Obergruppenführer, either notifying no one or lying.[5]

Globocnik's feeble attempts to ingratiate himself again with Himmler included sending the Reichsführer a gift of some rasberry tea, because he knew his boss was rather partial to fruit tea. It changed nothing. Himmler showed the odd flash of sympathy and admiration for his former protégé, but the only post he could find for him was as the rather ineffective position of Higher SS and Police Leader of the Operational Zone of the Adriatic Coastland (OZAK). This posting was headquartered in Trieste, Globocnik's birthplace, a fact that would not have been lost on the Reichsführer-SS or Globocnik. Globocnik was nominated for the post on 13 September 1943 and the appointment was made official on 17 September 1943.

He departed from his former fiefdom in a convoy of vehicles carrying a number of his inner circle, but not all, and former members of Aktion Reinhardt. He would soon be joined by former Lublin personnel totalling around 120, but his personal entourage on that occasion included the likes of Wirth, Oberhauser, Stangl, Otto Stadie, Konrad Geng (previously the driver for Wirth), and Rudolf Baer.[6] His close collaborators, Lerch, Michalsen, Hanelt, and Bareuther, made up the total of sixteen men. In addition, around thirty Trawniki men joined the convoy. Höfle and Offermann were among those who remained in Lublin for the time being.

His one-time secretary and confidante, Mimi Trsek, was not among the select few. She had fallen out of favour with the object of her affections. In her own words, she described the circumstances of Globocnik's departure:

> During the course of 1943, I fell out of favour due to personal, strictly private reasons. I do not wish to talk about them, but from that moment on I had very little contact with office staff. I remained in charge of entertainment for the troops until summer of 1943. For a while, I was asked to take care of the needs of Globocnik's mother during the time she lived in Lublin. In late summer of 1943, I went to Klagenfurt with Globocnik's sister, Frau von Gayl, to pick up winter clothes for Globocnik's mother and the Gayl family. Herr von Gayl then lived in Klagenfurt, but his wife and children stayed with Globocnik's mother in Lublin. We were notified in Klagenfurt that Globocnik had departed for Trieste with part of his staff. This news came as a complete surprise. When I returned to Lublin, I was informed that I could remain or look for a position elsewhere, wouldn't be transferred to Globocnik's unit. I have no idea why Globocnik no longer wanted me on his staff. I returned to Vienna and then applied for a position at the civil administration of Trieste, since I had some acquaintances from Lublin there.[7]

For someone who had been so close to the former SSPF, her fall from favour for 'personal and strictly private reasons' was both spectacular and sudden. Did Globocnik suspect Trsek to have had a hand in the anonymous note from the infamous evening in Zakopane involving his former fiancée? She refused all attempts to encourage her to expand on the reason and she remained unresponsive on the subject.

The Globocnik convoy travelled via Rudolf Schleissner's restaurant at the Wörthersee. He established his temporary headquarters at Cividale del Friuli, before moving on to Trieste. The column arrived safely at it's destination on 21 September. Wirth and his men were billeted at the Hotel Grande Albergo della Citta, near the quay. Globocnik was provisionally lodged at via Nizza 21 (today via Coroneo 21) in the city centre, until more permanent lodgings could be arranged.

Trsek was not alone in being surprised at the sudden departure of Globocnik from Lublin. On 5 October 1943, Sporrenberg directed his personal servant to call on Anna Globocnik and inform her that the Reichsführer-SS had ordered her and her family to vacate the Globocnik villa forthwith. Anna telegraphed her son in Trieste and complained of the rude and abrupt orders. Globocnik contacted Sporrenberg at once and requested a short delay, but his request fell on stoney ground. Instead, Sporrenberg instructed construction workers to carry out renovations at the villa immediately. Added to this problem, Globocnik received information from the Gestapo that an assassination attempt against the Globocnik family was being planned in retaliation for the resettlement of Poles. By chance, a Polish underground member had weakened under interrogation, and the plan was uncovered. Globocnik complained to Himmler in a letter dated 25 October 1943, that his family were moved to Klagenfurt to live in an unguarded apartment. Max Cichotzski was despatched to Lublin to drive the Globocnik women to Klagenfurt. This incident alone graphically illustrates that Globocnik was no longer considered as Himmler's favourite.

Controversy followed him, even after his departure from the General Government. Krüger's replacement in Krakow, SS-Obergruppenführer Wilhelm Koppe, wrote to von Herff on 24 November 1943:

> Dear Comrade von Herff,
> SS-Gruppenführer Globocnik has carried off all imaginable equipment from here which was not bolted down, personnel as well as trucks.... I do not have the slightest regard for Globocnik's behaviour towards his former department. His claim that fewer staff would be needed in Lublin after his departure is objectively untrue. I have to tell you a lot more about this matter and will report extensively on your next visit.[8]

# 18

# OZAK

ITALY AGREED AN armistice with the Allies on 8 September 1943, resulting in the German occupation of northern and central Italy. Hitler created two operational zones—Alpenvorland (OZAV) and the Adriatic Littoral (OZAK). The latter comprised the existing border region of North-East Italy, plus parts of Slovenia and Croatia. Friedrich Rainer was nominated as the Oberster Kommissar, with the military command placed under General Ludwig Kübler. As HSSPF OZAK, Globocnik had command of the SS, SD, Sipo, and Ordnungspolizei. He was subordinate to Rainer and Karl Wolff, appointed as Höchster SS- und Polizeiführer (Highest SS and Police Leader) in Italy. Globocnik's main problem was combatting the various operational partisan groups that had sprung up in the region. In this respect, he had to rely upon co-operation from the Wehrmacht and his close neighbour, SS-Gruppenführer Erwin Rösener, the HSSPF Alpenland.

Globocnik and his old friend, Rainer, were therefore reunited, possibly by design, as Himmler had always viewed Rainer as a steadying influence on Globocnik. Apparently, Rainer had suggested Globocnik for the post to Hitler and Himmler. The only missing character from the triumvirate of the old Carinthian 'days of struggle' was von Mohrenschildt, although he was based nearby in Klagenfurt, in an office located in the ironically named Gasometergasse.

For the first few weeks in Trieste, Globocnik's men had no real defined purpose. Wirth and Oberhauser were posted temporarily to Pola, with a few other Reinhardt personnel. There they acted as criminal police investigators, until returning to Trieste some three or four weeks later. Back in Trieste, they were lodged at the Villa Segre on via Murat. Their main task was recruitment for the Wehrmacht. Wirth returned to Lublin in early November to participate in Aktion Erntefest.

On 27 October 1943, Globocnik formally requested more personnel from Lublin.

He pointed out that in Lublin he had been allocated ninety-two people from the Reich Chancellery staff and that he had only seconded six of those to Trieste. By the time of Globocnik's written request for an increase in manpower, the Reinhardt staff in Lublin had completed the dismantling of the terminal stations and were close to concluding the concealment operation that followed. This was achieved by the end of November, and the residue personnel was transferred to Trieste. By January 1944, most arrived in Trieste.

Wirth's expanded unit was given the title 'Sonderabteilung R', often shortened to 'Abteilung R'. It remained linked to T4 in Berlin. The senior faces of T4 were regular visitors to Trieste. The men of Abteilung R were authorised to wear SS and Police uniforms in the ranks they had been allocated. The unit was soon divided into three—RI, based in Trieste, RII in Fiume, and RIII in Udine—with the nominated commanders all former extermination camp commandants. Gottlieb Hering was given RI, Franz Reichleitner RII, and Franz Stangl got RIII.

Sub-section RI in Trieste was the largest, and it setup its new barracks at an old rice mill in the suburb of San Sabba. The Risiera di San Sabba consisted of a number of large buildings and warehouses, which served as a prison and transit camp for Jews, partisans and generally anyone considered to be opponents of the Nazi regime. It also served as the main support base for Abteilung R. It became the scene of torturing and murders, the victims' corpses being disposed of in the camp's own crematorium. Hering was the first commandant, but he was replaced by Globocnik in July 1944 for unconfirmed reasons, most probably a difference of opinion between Hering and Allers, who had come to Trieste following the death of Wirth. Hering's replacement at the rice mill was Josef Oberhauser. Both commandants lived in the small gatehouse building, which also served as the commandant's office.

Other key figures from Aktion Reinhardt joined the team in Trieste. Kurt Franz had stayed behind in Poland at first. He was the last commandant of Treblinka II and he oversaw the final gassings, the dismantling of the camp structures and the subsequent cover-up operation, before transferring to the Adriatic coast. Lorenz Hackenholt was another who would be a prominent figure at the Risiera di San Sabba.

Once ensconced in Trieste, Globocnik recommenced his deportation measures against Italians and Slovenes, Jews and non-Jews. Assisting him were Lerch, Wilhelm Gunter, Ludolf von Alvensleben, Hanelt, Michalsen, Hermann Altman, and Werner Mundhenke. Officially, he was authorised to take just twenty-two staffers with him, but ended up with a much larger proportion of his 450-strong staff from Lublin.

In Trieste, Globocnik was to use the facilities at Auschwitz-Birkenau for the final destination of his deportations. Joseph Poprzeczny quotes thirteen deportation transports by rail to Auschwitz between October 1943 and November 1944.[1] In total, during the period of Globocnik's stay in Trieste as HSSPF, twenty-two trains headed north towards Silesia.[2] This confirms Siegfried Pucher's claim that

San Sabba was used, not only as an extermination centre and prison, but also as a transit 'feeder' camp for Auschwitz. The facilities at San Sabba were limited and larger numbers of partisans, political prisoners, and Jews were assembled for their onward journey to the crematoria at Birkenau. The deportation trains rolled on until February 1945, when the last train from Trieste left for Ravensbrück. It was subsequently redirected to Bergen-Belsen. Old habits die hard, as the saying goes, and Globocnik's men also used the former rice mill buildings as warehousing for property seized from the victims of Abteilung R.

Jewish bank accounts were frozen and all those in credit were seized. Furthermore, any transfers after 15 July 1943 from Jewish accounts to non-Jewish accounts, had to be notified to the authorities. Despite protests from the Italian police, the contents in the warehouses at the free harbour were also seized. Freight cars were loaded with spoils such as carpets, paintings, porcelain, and jewellery, headed in the direction of Klagenfurt, Vienna, and Berlin. The mayor of Vienna, SS-Brigadeführer Hugo Blaschke, requested art objects be deposited in the museums of Vienna. Globocnik's own sister, Lydia Pommeranz, submitted a request on 13 December 1944 for books from Trieste to be sent to the SS-Junkerschule at Lensdorf.

Around 4 per cent of the population of Trieste was Jewish at this time, and the city had always had a strong anti-Semite element. The first arrests for Abteilung R occurred on 9 October 1943 when thirty prominent members of the Jewish community were detained. The unit was employed full-time on anti-Jewish measures. Many targets ended up in the crematorium constructed by Erwin Lambert at San Sabba. Two methods of murder were employed at San Sabba—asphyxiation by carbon monoxide exhaust fumes from truck engines, or being struck on the nape of the neck with a mallet. Siegfried Pucher states that the crematorium was, in fact, a garage into which poison exhaust fumes were fed and this method accounted for 3,000 victims.[3] However, witness testimony suggests that only gas vans were used at this location, with no static gas chamber. The crematorium building was demolished prior to evacuation by Abteilung R, but the outline remains visible on the structure of the former rice mill today.

On 28 July 1967, Heinrich Gley declared in Münster:

> I knew that there was a human incinerator in the rice factory in Trieste. This plant, like most others of its kind, has been built in the annihilation and euthanasia sites. As a flue, the existing large factory chimney was used. Of the other technical facilities of this plant, I have only a vague picture. At the foot of the chimney, an open oven measuring about 2×2 meters was built with bricks and had a large iron grate. In my estimation, 8 to 12 bodies could each have had space in the oven. The stove or fireplace was open. An iron door was not available. It was a very primitive facility, but it served its purpose through the high chimney. It was therefore a strong pull.[4]

Globocnik and his close collaborator, Rainer, were soon to experience the war at first hand. Trieste oil refinery was attacked by the RAF in February 1944, and the airfields at Klagenfurt, Udine, and Aviano were targeted by aerial bombardment. Partisan activity was on the increase, and when seven German soldiers were killed during an attack on a cinema in Poggioreale in April 1944, reprisal measures were carried out with the execution of seventy-one political prisoners from Coroneo Prison in Trieste. One report stated they were hanged from trees and telegraph posts along the main thoroughfare, but execution by gunshot is the more likely method adopted. Globocnik attempted to take control of all anti-partisan operations, much to the annoyance of Generalfeldmarschall Albert Kesselring. Himmler intervened on Globocnik's behalf and a compromise was reached which gave Globocnik authority in a zone of 30 km from the coastline. In May 1944, Globocnik declared Trieste a citadel or fortress, giving him control over all supplies. On 26 July, Hitler ordered the futile construction of a defence line between Trieste and the Swiss frontier. Rainer placed Globocnik in charge. This hairbrain scheme, dictated the allocation of hundreds of thousands of manual labourers for the work, and prompted the mass round-up of likely candidates. Stangl was appointed as liaison officer for the project and Globocnik informed him that 'money was no problem' if he needed it, and that the defence wall must be built at all costs. The section at Trieste was named 'Wirth West' after Christian Wirth. The size of the project far outweighed the defence excavations of the River Bug in 1940. Needless to say, completion was never realised.

For his efforts in the construction of the proposed defence wall, Rainer successfully recommended his friend for the German Cross in Silver on 18 December 1944:

> I hereby apply for the award of the German Cross in Silver for SS-Gruppenführer und Generalleutnant der Polizei Odilo Globocnik, Higher SS and Police Leader in the Operations Zone of the Adriatic Coast.
>
> Upon receipt of the Führer Directive concerning the construction of defensive positions, Party Comrade Globocnik was appointed as my Executive Representative for the overall organisation of all construction activities. Globocnik has performed his duties with exceptional perseverance, greatest political skill and a unique diligence in following my numerous increased demands for greater efforts concerning the conduct of construction, which the present high level of activity reflects.
>
> He has conquered all difficulties with the zeal of a revolutionary National Socialist and leads all of my colleagues in deserving the highest merit for his efforts. Deployment has taken place under combat conditions. During his many visits to construction areas in close proximity to the front, Globocnik has closely escaped repeated strafing and bombing attacks. He has fulfilled his operational duties with a special courage and disregard for his personal safety, even in view of the (Partisan) band situation.
>
> I have observed on repeated occasions that the performance and personal

contribution of Party Comrade Globocnik throughout the construction of defensive positions in Upper Italy has earned enthusiastic recognition by the Supreme Commander South-West. In addition to his role as Executive Representative, Globocnik also performs assignments for senior SS and Police authorities in such an enthusiastic manner that observers are filled with wonder. His construction responsibilities are carried out within a party cadre that includes 4,300 political officers who mobilise a daily workforce of approximately 120,000 local inhabitants.

I hereby apply for the award of the German Cross in Silver for Party Comrade Globocnik and request if possible that all award proceedings be completed by year end.

[Signed] R a i n e r[5]

The decoration was awarded on 20 January 1945, and was followed by the award of the German Cross in Gold on 7 February 1945. Globocnik became one of the few Germans awarded both classes of the German Cross, which was authorised to be worn on the right breast of the tunic.

One outcome of the increased partisan activity in the region was the assassination of Christian Wirth. Globocnik's order number 16/44 nominated SS-Sturmbannführer Wirth as security co-ordinator for the main road between Trieste and Fiume (today, Rijeka). This road was an important link to the coastline further south of Trieste, bypassing the Istrian peninsula, and was known to the Germans as Karststrasse. It passed through several areas of high partisan activity. On 3 January 1944, Franz Reichleitner was killed by a bandit ambush on the Karststrasse while driving to Trieste about 3.5 km north-west of Castelnuovo d'Istria. Globocnik demanded a security strategy for the entire road to be submitted by him before 14 May 1944. This plan had to be agreed with the local SS and police commanders, and Globocnik advised him to co-operate with the Wehrmacht and local administrations of Trieste, Fiume, and Istria. The order was undated, but is believed to be in late April or early May 1944. A translation of the actual order is as follows:

10. Order number 16/44 of the Higher SS and Police Leader

In accordance with my order 15/44, I nominate SS-Sturmbannführer Christian Wirth security commander for the Trieste–Fiume road. To it also belong the areas left and right of the road itself. He will himself suggest the borders [of the security zone] after identifying the area from which the enemy intervenes on the road. A plan in this regard is to be submitted to me by 14 May.

His actions must be agreed with the provincial SS and Police commanders.

In particular, I emphasise the necessity of collaborating with the Wehrmacht and the German administration of the provinces of Trieste, Fiume and Istria.

Signed: SS-Gruppenführer und Generalleutnant der Polizei.[6]

In his role as security overlord for the main road, Wirth frequently travelled in his black personal service car, described as a 'Vetura', to outposts in Kozina, Materija, Podgrad, and Divaca. He was usually accompanied by his driver, Konrad Geng, and normally one or two Ukrainians as escort. This did not go unnoticed by the locals and information was fed back to the 1. Battalion of the Istrian Partisan Detachment—Istrski Odred.

A group of the 1. Battalion, commanded by Rudi Mahnic–Zito, had been staying in the Socerb and Beka area and was informed about it. Group's member Rudolf Pozru, a local from Beka, recalled in 1972 that they learnt of the SS major's visits and informed the first battalion headquarters of it. They intended to attack the major, but then the group was visited by the battalion commander's deputy, Karel Vene, who forbade the attack and informed the group members that the attack on the major would be carried out by a company lead by the first battalion commander.

A group of eighteen partisans were ordered to attack the car of the SS major at a location on his inspection route. They appear to have been unaware of the identity of the SS officer, but knew he was important to the local security service. A spot on the road between Kozina and Krvavi Potok was chosen for the ambush, approximately 1 km north-west of Kozina. The terrain here was hilly and trees, bushes, and rocks provided sufficient cover. The group was armed with four light machine guns, a machine pistol, and Italian rifles. Under cover of darkness, in the early hours of 26 May 1944, the partisans took up their positions either side of the road at about 50 metres from the carriageway. At 7 a.m., a car approached from the direction of Trieste. They immediately attacked the moving car, riddling it with bullets, killing Wirth and wounding Geng and one of the Ukrainians named Nikolai. The vehicle came to a halt about 100 metres further on. A German Wehrmacht unit was in the area and responded to the incident, surrounding the ambush point so quickly that the partisans lost some of their equipment during their escape. The partisans suffered no casualties. As a reprisal, the Germans destroyed thirty-six houses and seized sixty-seven cattle. The village of Beka was razed to the ground.[7]

Wirth's body was removed from the scene and taken to the Risiera di San Sabba where it was prepared for subsequent burial at the German military cemetery in Opicina. There appears to have been a memorial ceremony at the rice mill prior to internment, confirmed by witness Franz Rum in 1967: 'The second time I was in the factory [Risiera di San Sabba] was on the occasion of the funeral of Wirth in May 1944'.[8]

Wirth's favourite son, Kurt, last saw his father at the family home, Kauzenhecke 22 in Stuttgart, in April 1942. This was also Wirth's last visit to the family home. Marie Wirth stayed on at this address after her husband's death, and died there in 1979 aged ninety-one. Kurt Wirth spent five months on the Eastern Front, before returning to Stuttgart in March 1942 with frost bitten feet. He was informed of his father's demise by a General of the Wehrmacht on 30 May 1944, while working at the U-boat pens in Le Havre. He was granted four days' compassionate leave and travelled out of Le Havre in a truck carrying torpedoes. The young man admired his father and remembered that he refrained from drinking alcohol at home, but he had a liking for strong cigars. The two sons had a disagreement after the war, which resulted in them not speaking and losing touch. By the time of their mother's death in 1979, Kurt had no knowledge of his brother's whereabouts and did not know if he was still alive.

There has been much speculation over the death of 'Christian the Terrible', fuelled by Stangl's suggestion that it was Wirth's own men who murdered him. Another version is that Lorenz Hackenholt was selling arms to the partisans and it was his paid information that alerted the bandit group. This is refuted by the obvious lack of knowledge of the identity of the target on that May morning. The death of Wirth and the partisan attack were not connected until the early 1970s when investigations revealed the true identity of the 'SS major'. Even the Germans were reluctant to reveal his identity at the time. No obituary or official notice appeared until months after his death. Christian Wirth was remembered as a professional soldier.

The Italian Prefect of Police in Trieste notified the Italian Ministry of the Interior and Political Police Division on 29 May 1944:

> Reference: Partisan Activity
>
> At 07.30 on 26th of this month, a German car from Trieste, driving in the direction of Castelnuovo d Istria, reached the valley of Nazire di San Doligo [Nasirec] and encountered machine-gun fire from bandits.
>
> A German major, whose name is unknown, who was aboard the car was killed, while the driver was injured.
>
> Investigations are in progress.
>
> The Prefect,
> B. Coceani.[9]

This was followed by a further message on 31 May 1944:

> From Police Headquarters Trieste.
> Attention of Ministry of the Interior,
> Valdogno.
> Subject: Weekly report on the political and economic situation.
> … information from the local command of the German Police …

> On 26th of this month, moreover, on the Trieste-Castelnuovo d Istria road, near the town of Naziri di S. Dorligo della Vale [Nazirec] a nucleus of rebels attacked a German military car with machine-gun bursts, killing an officer of the Wehrmacht.[10]

Wirth could easily have been the author of his own downfall. He clearly underestimated the abilities of the local partisans, and his regular trips along the same route were so fixed that one onlooker described his movements like a bus timetable. In connection with the 'unknown SS major', Wirth's name first appeared in print in April 1972 in the newspaper *Il meridiano di Trieste*. Konrad Geng, who was in hiding after the war, first brought up the connection in 1970, and then he repeated it under interrogation in 1972, when he stated that Wirth had been killed outright and that himself and a Ukrainian, named Nikolai, had been wounded in the attack.[11] Further evidence that Wirth's identity was unknown to the partisans is contained in the Report of Istrski Odred, No. 628/3, dated 27 May 1944 which reported that a car 'was attacked and a Major of Police Units was killed'.

Ernst Lerch was placed in command of the anti-partisan operations for the region in January 1944. Until the summer of 1944, he operated out of Trieste, but then relocated to Gradisca d'Isonzo. He was ordered on two separate occasions to visit the site of Wirth's ambush, in order to try and uncover new evidence. On one of his visits, he came under gunfire, but was able to escape uninjured.

Wirth's body was buried within days in the cemetery at Opicina in the presence of Globocnik, Blankenburg, Allers, and several of the high-profile members of Abteilung R. He was accorded full military honours before a large contingent of SS, foreign auxiliaries, and Police troops. His remains were exhumed in 1959 and transferred to the German Military Cemetery in Costermano, overlooking Lake Garda, where they lay to this day, alongside those of Reichleitner and Schwarz, who had both been killed in separate partisan actions.

In January 1944, Globocnik moved into the Villa Ara on Scorcola Hill, at the rear of Via Romagna. This luxurious villa was part of an estate built in 1935 for a wealthy Jewish insurance broker, Angelo Ara. The owner managed to escape to Switzerland before the Germans arrived. The house was in an elevated position overlooking the town and had a distinctive tower rising above the roof level.

Following a heavy air attack by the Allies on Trieste on 10 June 1944, bomb shelters were constructed in a tunnel system below the estate. This tunnel complex also gave underground access to Globocnik's administrative office in the Palazzo di Giustizia—Trieste Tribunal Building—on the square, Foro Ulpiano. The construction work was undertaken by the Schwarz Construction Company, but it remained incomplete by the end of the war. The air raid shelters were for the use of German personnel only, on orders of Globocnik. No Italians, other than a small number of electricians, were permitted access. This complex became known as 'Kleines Berlin'—Little Berlin. Today, the villa no longer exists, having been replaced by modern apartment blocks, but traces of the bunker entrance still exist and the tunnel complex below is now open to the public.

Friedrich Rainer moved into the Villa Modiano, a large family residence set in a huge park, along with twelve members of staff. Here, too, the Germans constructed bomb shelters. After the Germans evacuated in 1945, this villa was occupied by British officers until 1954. Rainer also occupied an office in the Palace of Justice at Foro Ulpiano.

Just as he had practiced in Lublin, Globocnik preferred to work from home and the Villa Ara became the scene of comings and goings of SS and police staff members, including secretaries. The Villa Ara soon took on the mantle of Globocnik's headquarters. The SS headquarters was nearby on the Piazza Oberdan.

On 7 December 1943, Dr Max Horn requested the presence of Globocnik and Wippern at a meeting in Berlin to finalise the liquidation of OSTI. Also under discussion was the final account of Aktion Reinhardt. Globocnik had submitted a final report, consisting of two portfolios, to the Reichsführer-SS on 4 November 1943. There remained some unanswered questions, which required Globocnik and his Reinhardt accountant, SS-Oberscharführer Alois Rzepa, to return to Berlin for a further meeting at the end of the following March. Globocnik submitted his closing account on 5 January 1944, and in his covering letter, he emphasised the importance of destroying all evidence of Aktion Reinhardt. He declares that any evidence on his side has already been destroyed and that, as a result of his previous experiences with financial dealings, these accounts had been prepared with the utmost care. Oswald Pohl accepted the accounts.

The year 1944 began with the supposed anti-partisan Aktion Edelweiss, in which the village of Lokve was destroyed on 20 January. Further destructive operations soon followed: on 15 February 1944, the villages of Komen and Rihemberk; to mark the Easter period, in March and April 1944, Aktion Osterglocke was enacted; and in April, Aktion Braunschweig began, lasting from 26 April until 13 May 1944. This targeted partisan bases in Istria. On 30 April, the village of Lipa near Bistrica was razed to the ground and 257 inhabitants of both sexes and all ages were killed. Additionally, the villages of Fabce, Kutezevo, and Podgraje were totally wiped out. The men of villages in the Brkini Mountains were disbled with shots to their legs, before being doused with petrol and set ablaze. The brutality of these anti-partisan units knew no bounds.

On 29 May 1944, thirteen young partisans from the prison in Udine, were executed before a crowd in Premariacco, with a further thirteen facing the same fate in San Giovanni al Natisone the same day. On 25 August, a massacre of thirty-six people was carried out in Torlano. This was followed on 29 September 1944 by the destruction of 452 houses in Nimis, where six people were executed and twenty-eight deported. The towns of Attimis, Faedis, and Sedilis were destroyed the same day.

These crimes, although under SS control, were not carried out solely by SS troops. Globocnik's forces were heavily supplemented by foreign volunteers, such as Cetniks, Croatians, Serbs, Slovenians, and Italians. Russian Cossacks from the Don region arrived in Carnia on 20 July 1944, and they were soon joined by other units from Georgia and the Caucasus. Globocnik put this new manpower to good use.

Meanwhile, the HSSPF had personal matters on his mind. His disasterous engagement to Irmgard Rickheim had damaged his relationship with the Reichsführer-SS. Himmler had made it plainly obvious that he considered marriage for Globocnik to be a positive move, but his choice of wife was totally unsuitable to satisfy the former Bavarian chicken farmer's pompous idea of a wife for a SS General. Possibly, Himmler still nurtured the idea of Gisela Mauermeyer as a suitable match for Globocnik, but the Carinthian totally misjudged the importance that the Reichsführer now placed on his marital status. He was desperate to regain the favour of his former mentor, and he decided that an acceptable marriage was one way of achieving it. He miscalculated Himmler's intentions towards him; although the Reichsführer had not totally abandoned him, Himmler's plans had moved on and the tide of war now heavily influenced his decisions.

Globocnik surveyed the available candidates until his choice fell upon a local Carinthian leader of the Bund Deutscher Mädel (BDM—the League of German Girls), a sort of female version of the Hitler Youth. Laurentia Antonie Peterschinegg, known as 'Lore', was born in Spittal an der Drau on 28 March 1917. By profession, she was a teacher, and she was a leading member of the local BDM, and unattached. Her character was without blemish, and she was attractive, although she was not pretty. Her position in Carinthia had brought her into contact with Globocnik previously, although it is safe to assume that the initial attraction he felt for Irmgard was not repeated. Thirteen years his junior, she was dependable, and no doubt flattered by his attention. She was intelligent and loved sport, having graduated at the top of her school class and the teaching academy that followed. She had been the leader of the Gaumädchen in Linz and was now the deputy leader of the Carinthian BDM. She came from a family of staunch Nazi supporters, the middle daughter of three sisters, all with a pre-Anschluss police record for political activities. Globocnik considered she would be more acceptable to the Reichsführer-SS. Suffice to say, she was a 'safe' choice.

Max von Herff had noted that 'it is important that [Globocnik] get married, so that his wife and a homelife put an end to this restless and destructive pioneer existence'.[12] The details of his courtship are unknown, but the enforced separation caused by their duties, dictated a long distance relationship. It appears that Globocnik had proposed by March 1944, as Stangl informed Gitta Sereny in a post-war interview that Globocnik ordered him to take home leave that month and requested he call in on his fiancée at Klagenfurt Hospital where she was helping out. Stangl described Lore as a 'buxom blonde', but her photograph clearly depicts a dark haired young woman, with rather plain features, brown eyes, and thick eyebrows. The exact opposite of Irmgard Rickheim. Stangl may have confused Lore with Irmgard, which would indicate that the death camp commandant may have met the latter socially in Poland. Unfortunately, we do not have a confirmed image of Grete Michner and it is therefore impossible to make any further comparison of Globocnik's taste in women.

Lore did fulfil his idea of what would be acceptable to Heinrich Himmler, but it was not until 1 August 1944 that he plucked up enough courage to inform his boss:

> Reichsführer!
>
> Please do not be irritated that I make a request at this time. I believe, however, that all this severity makes it all the more important to try to make up for past neglect. I think that I have found the girl whom you, Reichsführer, would allow me to marry. Friedl [Rainer], with whom I have already discussed the matter, is very much impressed. I have asked him to convey his opinion to you, Reichsführer. Perhaps there will be an opportunity for you to meet the girl, and then you can tell me your opinion. I would like to get married this year.
>
> With most obedient greetings,
> Heil Hitler!
> Your grateful
> Globocnik.[13]

This handwritten letter clearly illustrates that Lore Peterschinegg had been chosen, not for love, but to satisfy his master. It is apparent that Globocnik was well aware at this stage just how far his star had dimmed in the eyes of the Reichsführer-SS. Author Bernd Rieger suggests that Irmgard still figured highly in Globocnik's affections, and there is substance to this view.

Globocnik was to be disappointed by Himmler's reaction to the news. On 6 August, he replied benignly:

> Dear Globus!
>
> I received your letter of 1 August with great pleasure. Please submit your marriage application as soon as possible.[14]

The requested Race and Settlement forms were duly submitted and Reinhold von Mohrenschildt, as liaison officer for the HSSPF, handled the application process on behalf of his fellow Carinthian. Covering letters and memos give the address for replies as Gasometergasse 6/II (12b) in Klagenfurt. Correspondence was on the headed stationery of Der Höhere SS-und Polizeiführer in der Operationszone Adriatisches Küstenland.

In September 1944, Lore hand-delivered a letter from Globocnik to Dr Rudolf Brandt in Himmler's Berlin office which implored Brandt to persuade Himmler to attend the wedding ceremony in person to act as best man. Globocnik suggested 10 October, but was willing to delay proceedings to fit in with Himmler's busy schedule. The 10th happened to be Carithian Liberation Day and Rainer's hand in the selection of the date of the wedding is evident, as he had invited Himmler to Klagenfurt to attend the celebrations. Both Rainer and Globocnik were disappointed by Brandt's reply on 28 September, declining both invitations and suggesting that Rainer act as Globocnik's best man.

The marriage ceremony took place on 22 October 1944 in the registry office in Klagenfurt, in the presence of Friedrich Rainer as witness. Both men wore SS uniform. The marriage entry in the Family Book was completed under 310/1944. Globocnik gave his place of residence as Bahnhofstrasse 67 in Klagenfurt. Lore's address was recorded as Beethovenstrasse 11, Klagenfurt. However, when in residence in Klagenfurt, Globocnik by this time regularly lodged at Schloss Emmersdorf on the northern outskirts of the town. A marriage announcement appeared in the SS newspaper *Das Schwarze Korps* on 16 November 1944. Himmler presented the newly wed couple with a tea set.

Lore Globocnik maintained that their relationship remained distant and that she only saw her new husband on a few occasions after their wedding. She insisted that she stayed living in her rented room at Beethovenstrasse, but this is difficult to believe. She insisted that she visited Globocnik only twice in Trieste, and that he came to her room in Klagenfurt twice a month. Apparently, he not only wore his own wedding ring, but also that of his late father. He visited his wife on his forty-first birthday, on 21 April 1945, and she produced a son, Peter Globocnik, nine months later, on 21 January 1946. The disasterous war situation, and the obstacles of his increasingly pressing duties and distance clearly did not interfere with him performing his husbandly duties and satisfying his sexual appetite.

Globocnik's heavy drinking continued unabated. Gauleiter Hartmann Lauterbacher relates the details of one Globocnik drunken visit to Pörtschach. Allegedly, Globocnik proposed they call at the Pragser Wildsee Hotel in the Puster Valley and liquidate the distinguished prisoners being held there, including former Austrian Chancellor Kurt Schuschnigg and Hjalmar Schacht, the ex-German finance minister. According to his own account, Lauterbacher was able to delay Globocnik's plan by plying him with even more liquor.

Lore noticed that her husband carried a small poison phial in a watch pocket in October 1944. She described it in detail: 'It was 3 cm long, rounded, and 1 cm thick, a metallic capsule of a silver colour. I asked my husband what it was. He answered, "A poison known to work very quickly. I must not fall into the enemy's hands alive"'.[15]

It was not the British or the Americans that Globocnik feared, but the chance that he might be captured by the partisans. He knew that he stood no chance of avoiding humiliation, possible torture and certain death were this to occur. Globocnik's men had shown no compassion or mercy dealing with the local inhabitants and partisans during their numerous sweeping operations, and the boss expected nothing less had the fortunes been reversed. The brutal methods employed had been condoned by the ultimate SS and police authority in the region. In fact, he had encouraged the inhuman behaviour practised during the murderous and destructive exploits of his SS and police units while exercising their ethnic cleansing and anti-partisan warfare.

Unlike the clandestine gassing and plunder operations conducted in the General Government, the criminal evidence in northern Italy and Slovenia was there for all to see. Abteilung R, although not militarily trained, was employed on security for the Karststrasse from the first quarter of 1944. SS and Police outposts were established throughout the length of the security zone, with the main ones being at Castelnuovo and Mattuglie. Aktion Braunschweig was the first major operation conducted in the region. Abteilung R suffered casualties during this military operation, most notably the deaths of Max Gringers and Alfred Löffler, on 30 April 1944, by mortar bombardment. This day also saw the destruction of the village at Lipa—at minimum 280 villagers murdered, including seventy-two children.

The outposts were tasked with patrolling the road, escorting vehicle convoys, responding to attacks and providing manpower for sweeps in anti-partisan actions, such as the aforementioned Aktion Braunschweig. This anti-partisan operation was designed to eradicate the partisan presence from the area of the Maggiore Mountains and to destroy their supply bases in the eastern Ciceria region. It came under the direction of Globocnik, and personnel was supplied by the Wehrmarkt, SS, Police, Sipo-SD, Abteilung R, and a contingent of Italian troops. A number of villages were burned and the inhabitants relocated, ostensibly to prevent the partisan units from receiving succour.

Abteilung R maintained its security role until the death throes of the occupation. Its participation in anti-partisan operations became all the more important with the rapidly advancing front. Two parallel major operations were mounted on 19 March 1945; Aktion Winterende (Winter End) and Aktion Frühlingsanfang (Spring

Start) were joint operations between Globocnik's OZAK and Erwin Rösener's Alpenland. Kampfgruppe Lerch was involved in Winterende, with its leader proving himself popular with his troops and an efficient military leader. Kurt Bolender and Josef Oberhauser both sustained wounds during this final campaign which was terminated on 5 April 1945. In addition, both Kurt Franz and Karl Frenzel received wounds in the fighting.

Members of Abteilung R who were confirmed killed in OZAK were: Max Gringers, 30 April 1944; Alfred Löffler, 30 April 1944; Karl Pötzinger, 22 December 1944; Franz Reichleitner, 3 January 1944; Karl Richter, 13 August 1944; Gottfried Schwarz, 19 June 1944; Kurt Vey, April 1945; Willi Wendlandt, 28 December 1944; Christian Wirth, 26 May 1944; Emil Kostenko, 15 May 1944; and C. Schmidt, 09 April 1944.[16]

The days of the 'thousand-year Reich' were close to extinction. Despite the deteriorating situation, Friedrich Rainer remained outwardly optimistic. Globocnik, on the other hand, was more realistic. In reply to Rainer's declaration that the Reich could still be salvaged by a miracle weapon, Globocnik declared, 'It is not a quarter to midnight, but only a few seconds away'.[17] As the Yugoslavs neared their objective, Trieste, Globocnik fled north towards his beloved Carinthia before the city was surrounded on 30 April 1945. As the Yugoslav forces crossed into OZAK from the south-east, British and New Zealand troops from the Po Valley arrived from the west.

On 29 April 1945, the staff of Friedrich Rainer, the command staff (BdS) of the Security Police and SD, and the command staff (BdO) of the Ordnungspolizei, departed Trieste and the OZAK for Klagenfurt. Before leaving, they destroyed all documentary evidence. Globocnik and members of his OZAK staff, fled by road towards the same destination on 29 April, hours before the city was cut off.[18] His motorised column included characters such as Oberhauser, Geng, and Allers from Abteilung R. Oberhauser took the trouble to release the last inmates of the rice mill before blowing up the crematorium and abandoning the facility.

Having bypassed Udine, some vehicles were strafed by Allied aircraft on the road on 30 April, near Tarcento, and they suffered some casualties. It may have been during this incident that Vey was killed and Hödl seriously wounded, both members of Abteilung R. The column scattered, but regrouped and continued its journey north. Globocnik's convoy overtook the BdS column at Ospedaletto, north of Tolmezzo, and arrived at Arta the same day, where Globocnik established a temporary HQ. Here, they discussed the futile plans for the defence of the Austro-Italian frontier. Throughout the entire journey north in Italy, the convoy had been suscepitible to partisan attacks. Globocnik's column decamped to Austria via the Plöcken Pass, during the night of 3–4 May 1945.

Globocnik was accompanied by his trusted aide, Ernst Lerch, when he appeared on the town square in Kötschach soon after crossing the frontier into Austria. He made a speech in which he declared that the people had nothing to fear; German troops would retreat into the hills and defend Carinthia against the British from their elevated positions. Globocnik then headed east towards Klagenfurt, via Hermagor where the group were billeted in a RAD camp. He ordered his closest colleagues to return to Moggio, back in Italy. The reason he gave was to support SS-Brigadeführer Heinz Harmel's troops in their defence of the frontier. Globocnik ordered Ernst Lerch to proceed to Pörtschach to contact Friedl Rainer, but he was unable to do so. Globocnik himself struck out for Klagenfurt via Arnoldstein.

Lore Globocnik heard from her husband when he arrived at von Mohrenschildt's office on Gasometergasse in Klagenfurt. In 1964, she stated:

> It was on 5 or 6 May when my husband came to see me for the last time in Klagenfurt. I was then a BDM leader, working mostly at their offices in Bahnhofstrasse. My husband was busy at the RKFDV office and called me over. He was hurried and we saw each other for about an hour. When we said goodbye, neither of us felt that it was forever. He still believed that we would win the war and never uttered suicidal ideas.[19]

This statement is contrary to all other indications that Globocnik thought 'the game was up'. In the hour that the couple had to themselves, it is likely that Globocnik aired his plans to go into hiding and the subject of where he intended to hide must have come up in the conversation. Lore and her husband were both aware of the various remote locations in the Weißensee area that would be suitable to disappear until the dust settled, from their days of illegal political activity prior to the Anschluss. As a local girl, Lore had the right connections.

On 5 or 6 May 1945, Globocnik attended a meeting in Pörtschach with Rainer where the peaceful handover of power to the British was discussed. At the conclusion of the meeting, Globocnik went into hiding with friends in the Wörthersee area. The Rainer family had a lakeside villa at the Wörthersee, and their old friend paid them a visit. Ada Rainer stated that this was the last occasion on which she saw Globocnik. Saying his farewells, he admitted that this was a final goodbye, and he showed her his poison phial, dejectidely admitting he would have to use it as a result of what he had done in Poland. Concerned, she asked if her husband also had a similar poison capsule, but Globocnik reassured her that Rainer had done nothing wrong. This was a twofold lie, of course, as Rainer was found in possession of a glass poison ampule upon his being searched after arrest. It was normal practice for all senior Nazis to have access to such methods of suicide. Globocnik then left for a friend's house in Pörtschach. Rainer stayed with his family until 8 May when his driver took him to Mallnitz where he stayed in a mountain hut for a couple of weeks.

Following the meeting in Pörtschach, Lerch was ordered to proceed to Adelsberg in order to obtain a situation report from elements of 7. SS Mountain Division 'Prinz

Eugen'. According to Lerch's interrogation in June 1945, Globocnik intended to return to Hermagor and then Neusach at the Weißensee, where he would establish a HQ for the whole of Carinthia. A wireless transmission station was already at that location. Globocnik foresaw this HQ being operational by 20 May. Failing that, a retreat into the alpine redoubt to conduct resistance, or dispersal and hide among peasants, were the alternative plans.

Lerch claims that he was captured on his departure from Pörtschach by car *en route* to Adelsberg on 6 May, but escaped after ten hours. Allegedly, he then hitchhiked to Arnoldstein. Michalsen insisted that Globocnik moved from Hermagor to Moggio, but he may have made an assumption based upon his boss's order to return to Italy. The remnants of Globocnik's close staff, in the form of Höfle, Lerch, Michalsen, and Hellesberger, made their way to Neusach on the Weißensee. Apparently, they lodged at the Hotel Enzian at the lakeside. There, they discarded their weapons in the lake and began the trek to the Mößlacher Alm. They were accompanied by two female secretaries from OZAK, Fräulein Ziranka and Fräulein Espernheim, who joined them on 10 May. Reaching the shepherd's house overlooking the valley, they rested and organised their rations for a long stay.

On 13 May, twenty-five-year-old SS-Oberscharführer Siegfried Kummerer sought shelter at the Mößlacher Alm, but the group feared for their remote hiding place and their meagre rations. Kummerer was turned away and advised to seek shelter down in the valley at the Mößlacher farmstead. It subsequently transpired that the decision to exclude Kummerer would be their downfall, as he was captured by the British and bore no loyalty to the group who had shunned him.

Lerch wrote a letter to the British in Hermagor on 14 May, offering to negotiate the group's surrender, and he made his way down the mountain and handed it to a local peasant in Boden with instructions to pass it on to the authorities. Whether it was delivered is unknown, but nothing appears to have come of it. Lerch also claimed to have met Rainer accidentally on his trip, and the two men supposedly arranged a further clandestine meeting ten days later.

Globocnik discarded his SS uniform and wore civilian clothes. He must have made his way on foot, hitching lifts where he could, from Pörtschach to the Weißensee, taking quite a few days for the journey. He carried a rucksack and would not have been out of place among the many returning soldiers and displaced civilians. Careful to avoid army patrols, he eventually arrived at the Weißensee and negotiated the climb up to the Mößlacher Alm on 20 May. On arrival, he was fatigued and ill, and took to his bed for several days.

# 19

# RUMBLED

The Weissensee is a mountain lake in the Austrian Gailtal Alpine range. It is one of the most picturesque glacial lakes in Europe, surrounded by lush meadows set on part-forested mountains. In the summer months, the lake water appears as a turquoise blue. The water stretches along the valley for a distance of about 11.6 km and is 0.9 km at its widest point, 930 metres above sea level. Its maximum depth is 97 metres, and it is home to numerous species of fish, including trout, pike, perch, and carp. Near the western shore is located the Kreuzberg Saddle Pass on the Greifenburg–Hermagor road. The steep inclines of the eastern shore dictate a lack of habitation and provide ideal hideaways in the mountain retreats dotted around this end of the valley. Mountain huts and small shepherd houses settle in meadows on the steep hillsides. In Austria, a mountain pasture is known as an 'Alm', and it is to one of these shepherd houses that Globocnik absconded in May 1945.

The Mößlacher Alm is perched at 1,454 metres elevation, at the head of a mountain pasture, located at the eastern end of the Weißensee Valley. It can only be reached on foot after a steep climb negotiating a mountain path from the Mößlacher Farm below. Today, it is popular with hikers and mountain bikers.

Globocnik probably selected this particular hiding place after discussing various locations with his wife, Lore. She was well versed with the local Weißensee area and the two of them may have identified Mößlacher Alm as a suitable bolthole from their days of illegal political activity prior to the Anschluss. It has been described as a hideout for the BDM. It was well off the beaten track and offered a perfect 360-degree view of anyone approaching.

Today, the main building is a single construction, having undergone extensive alterations, but in 1945 it appeared to be two adjoining small structures. Witnesses confusingly described the Alpine huts as being 'back to back'. One half, on the left viewed from downhill, consisted of two floors and the other, on the right, was a single storey. The development was erected on a steep incline and therefore set into the hillside at the rear. The larger section on the left, was built of stone on the ground floor and had a timber constructed first floor with windows to the front and side aspects, under wooden roof shingles. From the rear, it appeared to have only one floor. There was an external wooden staircase at the left side, towards the rear, and a separate door. The right side single storey was also of stone, under wooden shingle roof tiles. Access today is gained by a central ground floor door at the front, which existed in 1945 in the centre of the flush adjoined front aspect, but then probably only served the right single-storey structure. There were windows on both ground and first floors, which provided a good view down the sloping meadow to the front. Today, the small complex has been converted into a single structure of two floors with the addition of an upstairs to the right side. At the rear, there are now two windows. It was used as a shelter for cowhands, shepherds, and forest workers, and was sparsely furnished with typical rural furniture of the time. Nearby was a further timber-constructed barn. Being the most important resident, Globocnik occupied the largest available room in the right single-storey building, initially having sole use.

The last days of May 1945 were occupied by discussions on surrender to the occupying forces, or the alternative of escape and going under cover. Globocnik must have been under no illusion as to his fate if he chose the former. His methods in Poland and later in Italy were starting to gain attention with the military authorities as past witnesses and collaborators came under scrutiny in interviews and interrogation sessions. His name had already cropped up several times in the Allied press. The idea of escaping to live another day must have been the more appealing alternative. Globocnik was certainly not the kind of man who would face up to his deeds and accept his fate for his numerous crimes. His past nefarious financial dealings were testament to that. Those of the party that were fit and strong enough, ventured out during the day to go fishing and replenish their meagre food supplies. Water was in plentiful supply from the mountain streams, but negotiating the path down to the farm below, and the return climb of one and a half hours, in order to obtain other supplies such as milk, was not above the realms of possibility. That being the case, the group's presence at the Mößlacher Alm was probably known locally.

Friedrich Rainer arrived at Mößlacher Alm on 30 May. His importance and personal friendship with Globocnik dictated that he shared the largest room in the single-storey section with Globocnik. The small hillside refuge was now the hiding place for Odilo Globocnik, Friedrich Rainer, Hermann Höfle, Ernst Lerch, Georg Michalsen, Karl Hellesberger, and the two secretaries Ziranka and Espernheim.

The two old friends from 1930s Klagenfurt must have talked about their dismal circumstances and the prospect of a National Socialist role in post-war Austria. Were they under the illusion, like Himmler, that they had a role to play in the administration of the region now that Hitler was dead? Probably not. Globocnik certainly realised that his record was a passport to a legal trial and a certain death sentence. He had said as much to his friends in the preceding months. It is therefore difficult to accept Lerch's assertion of 5 June that the two men decided to surrender to the British on 31 May 1945. That being the case, why on earth did Globocnik keep up the pretence that he was an innocent bystander member of the party following their arrest?

Rainer provides a possible account of their conversation during their last night together in a secretly recorded conversation between himself and Gauleiter Siegfried Uiberreither, at a detention centre in Austria, between 28 July and 5 August 1945. In this, he states a post-war Germany should preserve the German heritage and customs, shun the Jews, and live a simple life. Rainer planned to go to ground in Austria and Globocnik had the idea to return to Trieste via the Plöcken Pass and stay with obliging friends.[1]

Meanwhile, in the valleys below the Alpine hut, the search for Nazi criminals intensified. Reports of Nazi bigwigs hiding in the mountains were not unusual. The region had been occupied by the British Army and the 4th (Queen's Own) Hussars, under Lt-Col. A. M. Barne, had established a field headquarters at nearby Paternion on the River Drau on 11 May 1945, alongside elements of 'B' Squadron motorised units. A POW camp was established on 12 May at Molzbichl and a regimental camp was set up at the Weißensee on 14 May. The 4th (Queen's Own) Hussars was an armoured regiment that formed part of the famed 8th Army. Sir Winston Churchill had joined the 4th Hussars straight from Sandhurst in 1895.

On 29 May 1945, information was received from an informer named Rudolf Dürr, of Stockenboi, that Gauleiter Rainer was hiding in the mountains, south-west of Spittal. Major Kuhweide, of the Brandenburg Regiment, had taken up residence in Stockenboi with twenty of his men, and he was now trying to buy his freedom from the British. The Brandenburgers had laid down their arms and withdrawn to Stockenboi to avoid Yugoslavian partisans. Kuhweide accompanied Dürr and offered to assist the British. The British feared that German Werewolf units were operating in the local mountains. It was thought that Rainer's group consisted of between three and twelve men and was supported by the locals, as small caches of food had been discovered.

Kuhweide and Dürr reported at the castle in Paternion that Kreisleiter Hugo Herzog and Kreis Propagandaleiter Friedrich Plöb were hiding in a mountain hut on the Wiederschwing Peak at map reference C 640885.[2] They were being observed by Kuhweide's men who would prevent them from absconding. Lt Kenneth

Hedley, who spoke fluent German, and Sgt Sowler, armed with Thompson sub-machineguns, accompanied Kuhweide and an associate to the location of the hut, where the two Nazis were arrested without a struggle and then transported back to Paternion.[3]

At 6 p.m. on the same day, information came in that two SS men were in hiding in house number 34 at Stockenboi. These two were disguised as agricultural workers. At 11 p.m., the two suspects were arrested. They gave their names as Kummerer and Schutz. The first proved to be the same Kummerer who had been turned away from the Mößlacher Alm on 13 May.

Both men were interrogated at Paternion at 3 p.m. the following day. Schutz was extremely non-commital and was not considered of interest. He was, therefore, immediately released from custody. Kummerer admitted to previous service at Dachau, but insisted he played no role in any atrocities there. Probably seeking to gain favour, and having no feelings of loyalty towards the party up at the Mößlacher Alm, he volunteered information later that evening, when a party was underway in the officer's mess, that a SS-Gruppenführer, three SS-Sturmbannführer, another SS man and two women were hiding at this location. He added that the group only occupied their hiding place at night in order to sleep, and vacated the hut during daylight hours. They watched the British troops below bathing in the lake. Kummerer and Schutz were only allowed water as minimum prisoner rations in an effort to loosen their tongues, and Hedley believes that hunger prompted Kummerer to talk, but this is doubtful after such a short incarceration.

Kummerer's information was almost correct. He made no mention of Rainer, who only arrived at the alpine retreat that very day. However, on the day that Kummerer had been refused help at Mößlacher Alm, Globocnik's arrival was still a week away in the future. Yet the entry for 30 May 1945 in the diary log of the 4th Hussars clearly indicates the presence of a SS-Gruppenführer at the hut. This would indicate either the entry being made after the events of the following night and morning, or that Kummerer had been back to the hut after Globocnik's arrival on 20 May. The latter is the more feasible, and it subsequently transpired that Kummerer was used to supply the concealed group with food from the valley below.[4]

(Author's note: From this point, reliance is upon witness accounts and the recorded diary log of the 4th Hussars. Each account has slight variations—totally normal when dealing with several witnesses—and understandable when considering the time lapse involved with memory. In some cases, statements were revised and updated many years after the events. In studying the various accounts, the following narrative appears to be the most likely version.)

The decision to arrest the occupants of the Mößlacher Alm at dawn the following morning was reached. A small arrest contingent, consisting of five officers—Maj. Ramsey and Lt Birkett of Special Forces, Maj. Quarmby, Capt. Wheeler, and Lt

Hedley of the 4th Hussars—plus twelve soldiers, including a handful of Paras Special Forces, and Kummerer as guide, climbed aboard their truck and jeeps at 10 p.m. and headed out of Paternion, along the Stockenboi road, towards Weißensee.[5] On arrival at the Mößlacher Farm, they abandoned their vehicles and began the arduous trek up the steep gradient to the hillside meadow. No road existed then, and the decision to proceed on foot was therefore forced upon the group. In those days, the climb was a path through the trees and took several hours in the darkness, by the light of a single lamp. The British officer in command of this arrest party was Maj. Alexander Ramsay. The group reached the edge of the clearing at about 4.30 a.m. on 31 May 1945. It was still dark.

The small force took up positions covering any escape route, surrounding their objective. Once *in situ*, they observed a male occupant, dressed in civilian clothes, exit the small right-hand hut to urinate. When finished, he looked about himself before returning inside the building, and closed the door behind him. Having surveyed the scene, Maj. Ramsay then decided to force entry and secure the building and occupants.

At 5.10 a.m., Ramsay and two men forced the door of the small hut and entered (the regimental diary states Maj. Ramsay entered through a loft window and opened the door from within, but this does not sound feasible). Simultaneously, Lt Hedley and Sgt Sowler kicked in the door of the larger building, taking the half-dressed occupants by surprise. Rainer and Globocnik were the last to be discovered. Everyone was ordered outside, with hands held high. It was a chilly morning and the detainees felt the cold in their sparse attire. Rainer was helped along by LCpl Lee's boot to the backside, at which he complained bitterly, but soon fell silent when threatened with a firearm. The building and prisoners were then searched thoroughly. A poison phial was found on Lerch and an empty poison case was discovered in the small hut, but this did not ring any alarm bells. Rainer surrendered his poison phial quite freely.

Lerch and Rainer both admitted their true identities at once, but the others denied any connection to the SS. Rainer's identity was easily confirmed by the presence of a large duelling scar on his left cheek. They were ordered to empty the huts of all their belongings and to carry them to the transport. They were allowed to put on clothes and then started off on the long descent to the vehicles below in single file. Apparently, the two female secretaries were allowed to remain at the hut, probably under guard, until their arrest at 2.30 p.m. that afternoon. Hedley escorted Rainer down the mountain first and later declared that they had a lively conversation and that he found his prisoner to be a likeable fellow. Hedley stated that they had not expected so many prisoners and that this forced him to order up extra transport, but this is questionable.

The remainder of the party followed them down. Globocnik was accompanied by Birkett who found his charge to be pleasant and easy going. Globocnik was dressed in a dark blue civilian jacket and trousers. The prisoners were sat in the rear of the truck with two armed military policemen. Nothing is recorded about any comments from the prisoners addressed to the traitor Kummerer. Rainer and Hedley travelled separately and were the first to arrive at the castle. The released prisoner, Schutz, was subsequently rearrested on further information from Kummerer. In addition to Globocnik, the British had netted Rainer, Lerch, Höfle, Michalsen, and Hellesberger in this operation.

On arrival at Schloss Paternion that morning at about 11 a.m., the prisoners were ordered to sit on their belongings in the courtyard, and then they were offered hot coffee. All but Globocnik accepted. He acted indignant that he had been arrested, and said he felt unwell and was unable to eat or drink. He insisted that he was a civilian engineer from Klagenfurt, named 'König'—his undercover codename from the 1930s—and was there solely as a defence construction advisor to the Gauleiter who had pressed him into joining the group. He gave references in Klagenfurt, but Maj. Ramsay remained unconvinced and suspected they had bagged the infamous Gruppenführer Globocnik. Why would an engineer be sharing a room with a Gauleiter? However, his story was extremely plausible, and at one point, even Ramsay began to doubt it was Globocnik. They discussed the possibility of releasing him, despite Kummerer's insistence that the man was SS-Gruppenführer Odilo Globocnik from Trieste.

Wheeler had gone to the Regimental HQ in the village school when Ramsay ordered all the prisoners to be taken to the lock-up and secured. The 'prison' was a separate building about 150 metres east of the castle, up a slight incline. It no longer exists. Ramsay did not include Herr König, who was allowed to pace up and down in the castle courtyard as his identity was still in question. He was closely supervised by Provost Sgt Sowerby while Ramsay and Hedley discussed their next move.

It was decided to play a trick on Herr König. Ramsay went inside to the first floor, while Hedley watched the prisoner closely. Once in position at the open window of a small balcony overlooking the courtyard, Ramsay shouted 'Globocnik!' The detainee did not falter his step, but in response to the shout, he inadvertently slightly moved his head to the sound. With that involuntary movement, he sealed his fate. Hedley spotted the movement and shouted, 'You have given yourself away! You moved your head very slightly!' and then ordered Sgt Sowler to add him to the gang in the lock-up. Globocnik was escorted through a small gate and up to the lock-up, 150 metres distant, by Sgt Sowler and Lt Birkett. Hedley went for a bath, satisfied that they had their man.

As Globocnik, Sowler, and Birkett approached the lock-up, Birkett saw Globocnik suddenly raise his right arm and he appeared to smack himself in the mouth. He immediately collapsed to the ground making a blowing noise. He lay there, obviously stricken. In a panic, one of the two soldiers shouted, 'He's dead! He's dying!' Hedley heard the commotion from within and ran outside to discover Globocnik lying motionless on the pathway next to the lock-up. The time was approximately 11.25 a.m. on 31 May 1945.

Dr Morris Leigh, the regimental medical officer, arrived almost immediately. He discovered a comatose, heavily built man on the ground, with glass splinters in his mouth. He administered two injections in the patient's arm and one in his heart—almost certainly of adrenalin—but Globocnik died within one or two minutes. The doctor pronounced death at the scene.[6] The death was also witnessed by several soldiers of the 4th Hussars and two local youths from the village who happened to be at the castle.

Herbert Dunkl described himself as a local historian when interviewed by this author in 2008. He appears to be the same unnamed man interviewed by author Siegfried Pucher in 1995. Dunkl declared to me during a visit to the castle at Paternion, where he acted as my guide, that in May 1945, he was a young teenager whose cousin acted as an amateur translator for the British. The two young men saw a group of soldiers and civilians standing outside the lock-up, about 150 metres west of the castle. They were at a distance of approximately 25 metres, with an unrestricted view. He testified that he saw a civilian suddenly fall to the ground. There was no contact with him and no sound of a shot. He then saw the efforts to resuscitate the unconscious man who had collapsed on the path outside the former building used by the British as the lock-up. When the soldiers saw the two youths, they were ordered away in no uncertain terms. He said that the scene was chaotic, with the British soldiers appearing to be in a panic. The time was about 11.30 a.m. He described the prostrate man as wearing dark clothing and boots. He said that two other younger boys from the village were standing closer to the lock-up and they witnessed the incident from about 5 metres distance, but they have never wanted to be involved. Some time afterwards, at about 1.30 p.m., he was at an upper window of his parents' house in the village, when he saw the same boots on a lifeless man, dressed in dark clothes, being transported through the village in the rear of a small army truck, driven by British soldiers. He subsequently came across the scene of what he described as a burial, in a field outside the village, near the River Drau, where he stood and watched. He stated the grave was no more than a metre deep at most. He was later informed by his cousin that the dead civilian was Globocnik. Herr Dunkl took this author to the same field and indicated the unmarked spot.

The unofficial identification of Globocnik by Ramsay and Hedley, only moments earlier, had led to the chief executive of murders in the German General Government in Poland taking his own life. Now the identification required confirmation before the disposal of the remains. Rainer, Lerch, Michalsen, Höfle, and Hellesberger were all brought out of their cells and viewed the corpse. Rainer was searched by Dr Leigh one more time. On seeing the dead body, the prisoners identified it as that of the former SS chief in Trieste, Globocnik. Until this point, Höfle, Michalsen, and Hellesberger had denied being SS, but now they admitted their own identities. They were photographed next to the body by Ramsay, who allegedly also took a close-up of Globocnik's bloated face, *post-mortem*, with legs astride the body. The body was part-covered with an army blanket from inside the lock-up. All the original photographs have now disappeared.

Capt. Wheeler was informed and he telephoned the news to Divisional HQ. He ordered Sgt Sowler to bury the corpse outside hallowed ground. Wheeler did not witness the suicide or the burial, but was later shown the burial spot. Men from the 4th Hussars Regimental Police buried Globocnik in his dirty clothes. His pockets were apparently empty. A villager who states he saw the burial testified that the spot was driven over by 'tanks' to obliterate the location. He may have been confused by the use of an armoured personnel carrier, which had half tracks. No tanks were based in Paternion in May 1945. Sgt Sowler asked Wheeler if he should mark the grave, but the officer said that, in the circumstances, he did not think it was appropriate.

At 12.45 p.m., the remaining eight prisoners, not including Schutz or the two female secretaries, were handed into the custody of Capt. Willett of the 78th Division Provost Company for onward transportation to a holding centre.[7] Schutz remained at Paternion under interrogation. Further arrests were carried out over the following weeks, but none commanded the priority or importance of those captured at the Mößlacher Alm. Three SS men were arrested on 1 June, and SS-Obersturmführer Karl Peer of the KRIPO was apprehended on 9 June. Of interest, the diary entry extracts of June 1945 include:

> **10 June 1945**: Acting on information, a party of 2 Officers and 6 ORs arrested 5 members of the SS, including the Deputy Gauleiter of Carinthia, Freiderich Thimel, in a hut at 5686. The SS men carried arms but offered no resistance. A search produced a Solbuch in the name of Hauptsturmführerer Friedrich Ahrens. Becker, Dahl and Burdorf admitted their identity, but Steuer said he was only a Cpl in the Army. His Soldbuch was found later and he admitted his identity. Equally divided among the packs was the sum of approx 1.5 million Lire which was alleged by Steuer to be his Regtl funds. 1,400,216 Lire paid into the appropriate bank in VILLACH on order of the Property Control Office. Names of captured personnel: SS-Standartenführer Friederich Thimel, Obersturmführer der Waffen-SS Friedrich Steuer, Oberscharführer Ernst Dahl, Oberscharführer Albert Burdorf, Unterscharführer Albert Becker.
> **12 June 1945**: Ruth Doering, a secretary of the SS Staff in TRIESTE arrested and sent to KLAGENFURT.
> **13 June 1945**: Obersturmführer Fritz Jochim and Emmi Mokry both of the SS staff TRIESTE arrested and handed over to the appropriate authority for investigation.
> **23 June 1945**: 11 SS men arrested and sent to PoW cage SPITTAL.[8]

Friedrich Rainer was interned by the British at Jerolitsch Inn, near Klagenfurt, together with Gauleiter Dr Siegfried Uiberreither. Some of their conversations were secretly recorded. They indicate that they both believed they were innocent of any crimes and would eventually be approached to participate in the reconstruction of a post-war Austria. Rainer was moved on 1 October 1945 to a sanatorium at Lassnitzhöhe, near Graz, and then to the provincial prison at Salzburg on 12 October, in US custody. He was transferred to the Nuremberg city jail on 24 October 1945. At Nuremberg, Rainer was interrogated and then held until he appeared as a defence witness for Arthur Seyss-Inquart on 12 and 13 June 1946. After giving evidence, Rainer was transferred to the internment camp at the former Dachau concentration camp. He was handed over to Yugoslav authorities on 13 March 1947.

From 10 July 1947 until 19 July 1947, Rainer was tried by the Military Court of the 4th Yugoslav Army in Laibach (Ljubljana), under the presidency of Capt. August Bračič. Maj. Viktor Damjan and his adjutant, Jože Pavličič, conducted the prosecution, and Dr Jože Ilc acted for the defence. Rainer was found guilty of 'punishable actions against the people and state' and was sentenced to death by hanging on 19 July 1947. The date of execution has never been confirmed and there are several variations. One is that he was hanged immediately on 19 July 1947; another that he was hanged on the morning of 18 August 1947. A death certificate was issued giving this latter date, which was the accepted date of demise until 2010, when documents came to light in the Slovenian National Archives in Ljubljana. An entry in the diary of Boris Krajger, the former interior minister in Slovenia, indicates that Rainer was executed in Lubljana with a number of other prisoners in mid-November 1950, most likely on 18 November. In the diary, crosses are drawn next to the names of those executed, including that of Rainer.

Other than for agricultural purposes and one official survey conducted on behalf of the post-war Austrian government, Globocnik's unmarked gravesite has remained undisturbed since 1945. It is located in a field, subject to waterlogging, owned at the time of research by a farmer named Johann Santer, on the east side of Bahnhofstraße, between the River Drau and the Drautalstraße. It is listed as plot 4/2 of the Paternion land register. Lore Globocnik and her son, Peter Globocnik, had no desire to reclaim the remains. The grave has attracted interest from genuine historical researchers, but also that group of people who can only be described as 'treasure hunters' or 'sensation seekers'. In 1990, Guy Wheeler was at great pains to mention that he had been contacted post-war by several enquirers purporting to be book researchers, but nothing had transpired. He was adamant that Globocnik's body was interred with nothing other than 'the dirty shirt and trousers he was wearing when we took him, with nothing in his pockets'.[9] Wheeler died in 1994.

Globocnik's suicide has been the subject of much debate since 1945. Did he die that day in May 1945, or was he mysteriously whisked away by the US government or British Secret Service on the promise of revealing the location of his purported treasure trove of plundered Jewish assets? One story suggests he had buried riches at a secret location on the shores of the Weißensee prior to his arrival at the Mößlacher Alm. The lack of good-quality photographs of his dead body, or a *post-mortem* examination, does not help. Did his henchmen conspire to fool the British into believing they had captured the infamous and demonic overlord of life and death in wartime Poland? The varied accounts by witnesses to his capture and death contribute to the uncertainty. The conspiracy generators had a field day.

Much has been made of the low-resolution images of the corpse, apparently unceremoniously dumped and half-covered, at the side of the track outside the now non-existent lock-up at Paternion. When shown the images, some past associates could not identify the body as that of Globocnik. Let us examine the method used as a means to end his life.

Hydrogen cyanide, anhydrous, stabilised is a very volatile colourless or pale blue liquid or gas (above 78 degree Fahrenheit) with a bitter, almond-like odour. Often used as a 96 per cent solution in water, it is a deadly and effective human poison when administered by all routes. A hydrogen cyanide concentration in the range of 100–200 ppm in air will kill a human within ten to sixty minutes. A hydrogen cyanide concentration of 2,000 ppm (about 2,380 $mg/m^3$) will kill a human in about one minute. It was first used as a chemical weapon by the French in 1916, but it proved to be ineffective in the open as it rapidly dispersed in the atmosphere. The USA and Italians also used it in 1918. Hydrogen cyanide has been absorbed into a carrier for use as a pesticide. Perhaps the most infamous of these is Zyklon B (the 'B' standing for Blausäure—prussic acid; also, to distinguish it from an earlier product later known as Zyklon A). Used most effectively at Auschwitz-Birkenau as a killing agent, it is ironic that the method of death selected by Globocnik was the method rejected by him during Aktion Reinhardt. The toxicity is caused by the cyanide ion, which halts cellular respiration by acting as a non-competitive inhibitor for an enzyme in mitochondria called cytochrome c oxidase. Prussic acid is a potent, rapidly acting poison, which enters the bloodstream of affected carriers and is transported through the body. It then inhibits oxygen utilisation by the cells so that, in effect, the carrier dies from asphyxia. As such hydrogen cyanide is commonly listed among chemical warfare as a blood agent.

The prussic acid solution contained in the glass ampoule was released by crushing the glass in Globocnik's mouth. A quick ingestion of breath through the mouth would have been sufficient to provide a lethal dose to the respiratory system, resulting in almost instant asphyxia and death. Evidence of the particles of broken glass was discovered by Dr Leigh on initial examination of Globocnik's mouth, but he failed to mention any almond-like odour usually present in such cases. The dose would have been adequate and sufficiently rapid to outweigh any effect provided by the subcutaneous administration of adrenalin. Inhalation produces coma, apnea, and cardiac arrest. The more concentrated the dose, the more rapid the body's response. Globocnik's features appear bloated in the available images, and this is an expected and common symptom of prussic acid inhalation. This method of death was common in cases of murder and suicide from the middle of the eighteenth century and was also employed in the USA as a method of legal execution.

The actual device used by Globocnik was almost certainly from a batch manufactured at Sachsenhausen concentration camp, and probably supplied to senior members of the Nazi administration. Evidence of this was provided by Albert Widmann who was chief of the Chemical Department of the KTI (who himself had served rather light sentences for developing the technical means of the euthanasia program—see above). Dated 15 February, 1973, his testimony in a letter reads:

> On orders of our Department Chief, SS-Gruppenführer Nebe, Reich Director of Criminal Investigation, self-destruction devices were developed and manufactured. They were intended for distribution to German agents. It might have been 1943 or 1944, when approximately 950 of these devices were ordered by the Reich Chancellery for distribution to the senior leadership. For that reason the filling operation was supervised personally by Senior Criminology Secretary Karl Sacks. The self-destruction devices were given over to the courier from the Reich Chancellery by me. They were obviously in fact distributed, as they were used.
>
> Our Department Chief Nebe gave the order to manufacture self-destruction devices that were infallibly effective. Potassium cyanide tablets, according to his statement, were disapproved from the medical end, for the reason that in cases of subacid stomach and with diabetics due to synthesis of cyanohydrin, they may fail to function. This gave a clear directive for production of the self-destructor. As an effective agent anhydrous hydrocyanic acid was used as a filler. For stabilization, 2 percent oxalic acid was added. For this reason the liquid is still in perfect condition today. It was neither polymerized, coloured brown nor turned resinous, as was the case with the Polish ampoules. The dosage per ampoule was an even cubic centimeter. The lethal dose on inhalation, as I recall, is around 8 mg. The hydrocyanic acid was made from pure sodium cyanide. This work was done by a prisoner, Dr Kramer, who was a chemist. Manufacture of the hydrocyanic acid and loading the ampoules was done in a small building in the RKPA plant in the Sachsenhausen concentration camp. Supervision was by Senior Criminology Secretary Sacks and SS-Hauptscharführer Gerhard Maier. There were no accidents. Some 3,000 to 4,000 were made. We made the glass ampoules to fit the containers. The diameter was 9 mm and the total length after annealing about 35 mm. The bottoms of the ampoules were flat. The annealed

> top was tinted blue for reinforcement. Ampoules that had been tested for hermetic seal in a vacuum were marked with a small read spot on the blue.
>
> As containers for the self-destructors, spent infantry rifle cartridges were fashioned into small cases. The cartridge cases were cut away on a lathe below the narrowing point. Their length came to about 41 cm. The 9 mm long caps were also made from cartridge cases. The caps were simply pushed down over the cases. The total length of the self-destructor therefore came to 46 mm, the diameter about 11 mm.
>
> It should be added that we probably received 1000 empty ampoules from the Army Medical Centre, each at three different times. I do not know which lot went to the Reich Chancellery.[10]

On the subject of the ampoules used by high-profile members of the Nazi government, the famed Nazi aviatrix Hanna Reitsch subsequently declared:

> The description of the cartridge case agrees completely with the account given by Dr Widmann on page 2 of his letter of 15 February in the indentation beginning with 'Zur Aufbewahrung' … and ending at '11 mm.' I know this so precisely because I sewed the capsule inside the cartridge case myself into the lining of a uniform skirt. That was how I came to measure the size in comparision with my little finger, then immediately measured it…[11]

Hermann Göring, plus Globocnik's former mentor, Himmler, and other senior members of the SS employed the same method of suicide, and it is believed that Hitler simultaneously crushed an ampoule of prussic acid in his mouth as he pulled the trigger of his pistol. His wife, Eva Braun, also chose the prussic acid route. It is a most effective way to end one's life rapidly, and there is little doubt that the prisoner of Paternion, who gave his name as 'König', died late on the morning of 31 May 1945.

Siegfried Kummerer insisted it was Globocnik; Rainer, Lerch, Michalsen, Hellesberger, and Höfle insisted it was Globocnik; Ramsay and Hedley were convinced it was Globocnik. In fact, on 5 August 1945, in a secretly taped conversation, Rainer said: 'Globocnik's suicide is a classical example; he accepted the responsibility for his actions'.[12] In an undated letter to Michael Tregenza, Ernst Lerch declared: 'We were not in a prison camp, but were in a police arrest which no longer exists today, namely in Paternion. Globocnik came from an interrogation and committed suicide before entering the arrest room. Time about 11am'. Investigative journalist Gitta Sereny saw the original images of the body at Paternion, and in an article she wrote for the *Independent on Sunday* newspaper in 1992, she declared unequivocally that the body was indeed that of Globocnik.[13] Conspiracy theorists give credence to the suggestions that it was a substitute who died that day in his place, or that the prisoner was telling the truth—his name actually was König.

All subsequent enquiries have failed to discover an engineer or businessman by the name of König from Klagenfurt, whose description fits that of Globocnik, or the prisoner König. If he was an innocent engineer as he stated, why was he sharing a room with a Gauleiter? Why was he in possession of a poison ampoule which he had secreted about his person, probably slipping it into his mouth at the time of the raid on the Mößlacher Alm? His refusal of food and drink on arrival at the castle suggests he did just that. Rainer revealed to Uiberreither, several weeks later, that he spent his last night of freedom with his old friend Globocnik. Rainer and 'König' were discovered together in one room at the Mößlacher Alm at 5.10 a.m.

Post-war claims of Globocnik working for the US authorities or the British Secret Service have since been discredited. Documentary evidence has allegedly been planted in archives to lend credence to these claims. The existing hard evidence that it was Odilo Globocnik who killed himself at 11.25 a.m. on 31 May 1945 in Paternion is overwhelming, and unless contradictory proof comes to light, this researcher and author is satisfied that the remains lying in a field at Patendorf are those of Himmler's manager of death.

The three-month pregnant Lore Globocnik was arrested on 28 July 1945 by the British 88th Field Security Section, 78 Division, near Spittal. She was interred at Wolfsberg, where she gave birth to a baby boy on 21 January 1946. She died in 1974, hardly ever mentioning his father to their son, Peter. Ernst Lerch apparently refused all efforts by Peter Globocnik to contact him.

# 20

# A LIFE EVALUATED

Odilo Globocnik was dead. His existence on Earth devastated the lives of millions of people. His legacy is one of corruption and murder, intertwined with a callous disregard for the feelings of his victims or traditions which, in many cases, stretched back hundreds of years. He genuinely believed in his mission, but paid little or no regard to the methods employed to achieve his goals. It is an indisputable fact that, among the arch-criminals of the Third Reich era, his name ranks as a front runner, and his close association with the plunder and murder agenda known as 'Aktion Reinhardt', will forever cast a shadow over the history of mankind. As the chief executive and administrator of Aktion Reinhardt, Globocnik bears total responsibility.

Aktion Reinhardt developed into the greatest single murder programme of the entire Holocaust. Most victims perished in the hastily constructed gas chambers of Bełżec, Sobibor, and Treblinka, in the area known as the General Government, in occupied Poland. Despite the poorly documented record of this extreme event, it is safe to assume that this operation accounted for a figure close approaching 1.5 million victims. Approximately 25 per cent of all Jews murdered during the six years of warfare were slain in an intense surge lasting no more than 100 days. The Holocaust kill rate far outweighs estimates suggested by authorities on comparative genocide by ten times. The main source figures are gleaned from transportation records, population shifts, post-war disappearance reports, in many cases of entire communities, and, to a lesser extent, copies of documents that have been uncovered in archives.

The Reinhardt operation began in March 1942 and lasted no more than twenty-one months, concluding in November 1943. In this operation, the three key termination stations of Bełżec, Sobibor, and Treblinka were established with the intention of eliminating every Jew in German-occupied Poland, having first stripped them of their assets. The three death camps were infamous for their industrial scale and express mass killings, and their ability to rapidly liquidate entire Jewish communities with the aid of gas chamber technology. Detailed records of the killings are almost non-existent as a result of the tight security around Aktion Reinhardt and its killing sites. Any recorded information was deliberately destroyed by the Nazis during the war, for fear of future incrimination once the realisation of the vulnerability of Hitler's 'thousand-year Reich' was manifested. In addition, a large percentage of the massacres have to be ascribed to widespread shooting, which occurred in parallel both inside and outside the area of the General Government. Very few survived the terminal centres of Aktion Reinhardt, indicating a level of efficiency maintained by the staff.

Professor Lewi Stone discovered that it is possible to evaluate and quantify the kill rate, and explore the spatial and spatio-temporal dynamics of Reinhardt, with the aid of basic data analysis.[1] Himmler's directive of 19 July 1942 ordered that all the Jews within the General Government, with few exceptions, should be liquidated by the end of December 1942. This basically set a time limit for Aktion Reinhardt and influenced its efficiency and timeline, although it was not met in practice. In Gerstein's report of 15 August 1942, he stated that Globocnik had declared 'the Führer ordered all action speeded up!'[2] Historian Martin Gilbert highlights a memo from Viktor Brack on 23 July 1942, which states: 'Globocnik believes that we must carry out the entire operation against the Jews at a faster pace, for the difficulties that might arise can freeze the entire operation, and then we will be stuck midway through.'[3] Worried that time was running out, Brack further suggested castration of all male Jews, and physical extermination of the remainder. This was at a time which witnessed the first transports from the Warsaw Ghetto to Treblinka.

The rate of murders increased dramatically from 22 July 1942, until it fell away from 4 November 1942—a period of 105 days. By the end of December that year, the Jewish population of the General Government had been decimated. Professor Stone refers to this short period of activity as the 'pulse of death', a highly appropriate analogy. The subsequent rapid plunge in the death rate in November and December 1942 simply reflects that there were very few Jewish victims left alive to murder by this stage in the General Government, Reinhardt having already consumed the vast majority. Himmler's overall strategy was then revised to transport and murder the remaining Jewish populations of Europe using the purpose-built Auschwitz-Birkenau extermination facility. The kill rate here was maintained at a steady tempo until a high peak in the summer of 1944 with the despatch of the Hungarian Jews. This peak also marked the introduction of a new internal ramp at Birkenau to accommodate arrivals and provide a quicker turnaround. Crematoriums II, III, IV, and V often operated independently at full capacity utilising hydrogen cyanide in the form of Zyklon B crystals as a killing agent.

The figures generated by Aktion Reinhardt corroborate Eichmann's description of Globocnik as the central figure of the Jewish genocide. Apparently, Eichmann reached this conclusion when Heydrich informed him that the expert on the physical extermination of the Jews was Berlin's man in Lublin.[4] The Israeli interrogator to whom Eichmann was speaking had never before heard the name 'Globocnik'. This is all the more surprising when one considers the report submitted by POW SS-Obersturmführer Kurt Gerstein at the end of the war in American captivity.

Gerstein was the chief disinfection officer in the Hygiene Office of the SS-Sanitätsamt. As has been mentioned before, in the company of SS-Obersturmbannführer Professor Wilhelm Pfannenstiel, the chief hygiene advisor to the Waffen-SS, Gerstein visited Lublin in August 1942. He reported that SS-Sturmbannführer Rolf Günther of the RSHA had ordered him on 8 June 1942 to obtain 100 kg of prussic acid and to transport it to a secret destination. Puzzled, Gerstein apparently followed orders and arranged to obtain the material from the potash plant at Kolin, near Prague. According to Gerstein, Pfannenstiel and Gerstein arrived in Lublin on 17 August 1942, with the prussic acid. They were greeted by Globocnik who told them: 'This is one of our most secret matters; indeed the most secret. Anyone who talks about it will be shot. Only yesterday two babblers were shot'.[5]

Globocnik then revealed the existence of the three installations at Bełżec, Sobibor, and Treblinka, plus the camp at Majdanek. He said:

> You will have to disinfect large quantities of clothing ten or twenty times, the whole textile accumulation. It is only being done to conceal that the source of the clothing is Jews, Poles, Czechs, etc. Your other duty will be to improve the service in our gas chambers, which function on diesel engine exhaust [*sic.*]. We need gas which is more toxic and works faster, such as prussic acid. The Führer and Himmler—they were here on 15 August, the day before yesterday—instructed me to accompany personally all those who have to see these installations. When asked by Professor Pfannenstiel what Hitler had said, Globocnik replied, 'The Führer ordered all action speeded up…'[6]

The major problem with Gerstein's story is that on 15 August 1942, Hitler was at his field headquarters at Winniza in the Ukraine, where he was visited by Himmler. There is no record of Hitler ever having visited Lublin in his life. On 17 August 1942, Globocnik attended a meeting at Himmler's home, Lindenfycht, in Bavaria, around 875 km away. Did Gerstein get the dates mixed up, or was his story a fabrication in an attempt to exonerate himself, or at least distance himself from his true guilty participation? Historian Yitzhak Arad suggests that Hitler's visit was a fabrication, not of Gerstein's invention, but that of Globocnik's, in his attempt to stress the importance of his mission. However, Arad fails to acknowledge that Globocnik was not even in Lublin on the day in question. Whatever the reason for the falsehood, either through Globocnik's lie, a mistake, or Gerstein's guilt, or his desire to avoid prosecution, Gerstein killed himself on 25 July 1945, and therefore withdrew any possibility of resolving the matter through interrogation.

Gerstein admitted to a thorough inspection of Bełżec and Treblinka, accompanied by Wirth. Pfannenstiel and Gerstein left Lublin for Bełżec soon after (for details of Gerstein's reports, see Appendices X and XI). Gerstein pointed out in his report that no trouble was taken at either Bełżec or Treblinka to count the actual contents of each freight wagon; they were only estimated. Wirth requested that Gerstein refrain from recommending changes to his methods in Berlin as they were well established and well tried, indicating his protective attitude to his 'empire'.

Pfannenstiel himself had the opportunity to provide his version of events on 6 June 1950, before the Regional Court in Darmstadt. He stated that he was ordered to visit Lublin on disease prevention measures. In his evidence, he testified:

> As a disinfector, I received an order to go to Lublin in the summer of 1942. There I had to advise about the reconstruction of the city water supply and sewer system.… I could not get a car. I was told that Dr Gerstein was also going to Lublin.… Dr Gerstein explained to me that he had to travel via Prague … our car was followed by an empty truck.… Dr Gerstein told me that he had to pick up prussic acid from a factory in Kolin … it was obvious that it was for disinfection.…
>
> In the small factory, I discovered the prussic acid was in the form of gas … [in Lublin] I devoted my time to the task assigned to me.… I found out there was a camp in Bełżec where Jews were being murdered. I wanted to see this camp … [and] I made a request to visit the camp. Globocnik, who was very proud of his creation, gave permission. Globocnik took Gerstein and me to the camp.[7]

Pfannenstiel then proceeded to describe the arrivals procedure, confirming the version provided by Gerstein. He described the gas chamber building as consisting of six compartments, but only four were needed on that occasion. His version continued:

> When the people were closed in the chambers, the gas from an engine was piped in. When the Jews were led into the chambers, an electric light was on inside and everything went quietly. But when the light was extinguished, screams were heard from the chambers. Gradually they became silent. When silence prevailed in the chambers, the outside doors were opened. Then the corpses were taken out, checked for gold teeth, and afterward they were put, layer upon layer, in a pit. This work was again carried out by Jews. No physician was present. The corpses were not exceptional. Some of the faces were blue. This was not surprising, because death was caused by suffocation. As I remember, I travelled back to Lublin with Globocnik that same day.[8]

He gave his reason for wanting to visit Bełżec as 'curiosity'. Allegedly, he wanted to see for himself if atrocities were being carried out during the extermination process. His opinion that eighteen minutes for the carbon monoxide to take effect was an atrocity, he apparently passed on to Globocnik. In answer, Globocnik thought that prussic acid would accelerate the timing of death, but, according to Pfannenstiel, he changed his mind when Gerstein pointed out the dangers involved with the use of hydrogen cyanide. Gerstein gave the reason as the premature decomposition of the prussic acid, of which he then supervised the burial in Lublin. Pfannenstiel apparently did not consider the murder of thousands of innocent men, women, and children as an atrocity in itself.

Further incriminating evidence to cement Globocnik's legacy as one of history's major criminals lies in the two operations, codenamed 'Aktion Hühnerfarm' (Operation Chicken Farm) and 'Aktion Hasenschiessen' (Operation Hare Shoot). These two murderous operations against Soviet POWs are worthy of mention among the numerous crimes committed by the occupying German war machine. Soviet POWs are often referred to as 'the forgotten Nazi victims of World War II'. Approximately 3.3 million Soviets apprehended by the Axis forces lost their lives after capture. On 8 September 1941, three months into 'Barbarossa', the officer responsible for POW policy, General Hermann Reinecke, informed his subordinates, 'the Bolshevik soldier has forfeited every claim to be treated as an honourable soldier in keeping with the Geneva Convention'.[9] Some German senior officers, such as Admiral Wilhelm Canaris, chief of the Abwehr (German Military Intelligence), objected to Reinecke's assertions, but with little effect. Canaris was silenced by Generalfeldmarschall Wilhelm Keitel, who reminded the admiral: 'This struggle has nothing to do with soldierly chivalry or the regulations of the Geneva Convention'. However, it is interesting to note that while Hitler's Wehrmacht felt itself relieved from the convention of international law during the war in the east, the soldiers of their Axis allies regularly acknowledged the rights of Soviet POWs under their protection.

The Germans established a POW camp near Biała Podlaska, inside the General Government, west of the city of Brest-Litovsk, in Belarus. Stalag 359B subsequently accommodated between 40,000 and 50,000 Soviet prisoners, far in excess of its original intended capacity. Insufficient shelter was provided and Soviet soldiers often had to dig holes in the ground in which to sleep. The lack of supplies resulted in deaths from starvation and thirst. An epidemic of dysentery demanded action from the German authorities to reduce the population of prisoners.

It was decided that at least 5,000 should be segregated as a result of their ethnic appearance, or the mere suspicion of their acting as Communist functionaries. Globocnik decided in Lublin that the directive issued by the Wehrmarkt High Command on 6 June 1941—the infamous Commissar Order—and Heydrich's

Directive No. 8 on 17 July 1941, should apply to those segregated. These provided grounds to execute Bolshevik Commissars and Jews on the spot.

Police Battalion 306 was based in Lublin, under the command of Major Ernst Dreier. This unit had already excelled itself by its brutal and murderous methods employed in the resettlement of Polish farmers in the Lublin District. The 2nd Company was billeted in Biała Podlaska under Oberstleutnant Schwarz. An execution site was selected by Schwarz in the forest on the road between Terespol and Biała Podlaska. A large pit was excavated by forty Soviet POWs who were immediately shot on its completion. On 21 September 1941, members of the 2nd Battalion were plied with alcohol before they began a shooting spree. Trucks transported the victims to the site where they were shot from 3–5 metres by groups of ten executioners. After each man shot five victims, they were replaced in a rota. Some 3,261 men were executed on the first day. The executions continued until 28 September, with a final tally of between 5,000 and 6,000 victims. Daily reports of the numbers were transmitted to the office of the SSPF Lublin, in which the victims were euphemistically referred to as 'laid eggs' of Aktion Hühnerfarm.

A few weeks later, Police Battalion 306 were in action once again. This time, they were joined by mounted members of Police Regiment 25 and the SD, near Zamość. Soviet POWs in Stalag 325 who followed the ancient Jewish religion of Moses were denounced by their fellow prisoners in exchange for food. Their number, totalling 780 men, included some senior officers. Another forest execution site was selected on the road to Lemburg, about 6 km south-east of Zamość. Once again, the prisoners were transported to the site in trucks, where they were forced, mostly naked, into a pit. Ordered to lie down, they were shot from the edge of the pit. The next batch were ordered to lie down on top of their dead comrades, and then shot. In command of the Aktion Hasenschiessen massacre was Major Ernst Dreier, a career policeman.

Of significance is the personal relationship between the Reichsführer-SS and Odilo Globocnik. Just why did Himmler leap to Globocnik's rescue when other powerful elements in the Nazi Party appear to have forsaken him after his disasterous stint as Gauleiter of Vienna? To the outside world, and to a certain extent to himself also, politically speaking, he was a dead man walking. His accounting skills were naïve at best. Yet Himmler selected him to administer one of the most confidential operations, if not the most confidential task of the war. Was he just a front man for Oswald Pohl and Christian Wirth, the real wealders of power in Aktion Reinhardt? Did Globocnik have direct classified access to Hitler, by-passing the usual channels? His unique appointment in the General Government may well have allowed him this coveted benefit. Author Joseph Poprzeczny states that Max Cichotzski gives a clue to this scenario in his statement to the court in Wiesbaden in 1961. When questioned about the valuables of the Jews, Cichotzski replied:

> I would like to mention what happened one evening when Odilo Globocnik was absent as he was at the Führer Headquarters in Lotzow [*sic.*—correct, Lötzen] (East Prussia). On this night, a man called Blankenburg came from Berlin from the Chancellery—he came with a truck, which was full of suitcases and Blankenburg told me he had Odilo Globocnik's permission to store all the suitcases for safekeeping in the cellars. I did not want to give permission and rang the Führer Headquarters and Greitman [*sic.*—correct, Grothmann] said it is okay. I had to clear out a room in the cellar and a man, Natke, helped. Also, two police ordnances worked for us and lots of cases were left in the cellars.[10]

Cichotzski almost certainly confused Himmler's field headquarters with Hitler's field headquarters in this statement. Werner Grothmann was Himmler's adjutant, and Lötzen (today, Gizycko, Poland) was the location of the airfield that served Himmler's Feldkommandostelle 'Hochwald', not Hitler's HQ 'Wolfsschanze' at Rastenburg in east Prussia (today, Ketrzyn, Poland). Globocnik attended a meeting at Feldkommandostelle 'Hochwald' on 9 July 1942, and it may well be this conference to which Cichotzski refers. There is no direct evidence that Globocnik had access to Hitler during his period as SSPF Lublin, despite the unique assignment with which he had been tasked.

Oswald Pohl was always the front-runner in the business of SS enterprises, but in this respect, Globocnik was only useful to Himmler for the duration of the period of pillaging the Polish Jewish assets. As the available victims reduced drastically in numbers, due in the main to the success of Globocnik's mission, Himmler's interest in protecting his General Government 'cashier' also waned. Pohl regained poll position and Globocnik fell victim to his own success.

The other enigmatic senior figure of Aktion Reinhardt, Christian Wirth, appears to have been a law unto himself. He was considered by many of his contemporaries as highly motivated, but mentally ill. Dieter Allers certainly considered him as insane. Wirth possessed an autonomous and mystifying authority, far in excess of his official appointment as inspector of the Aktion Reinhardt facilities. From what source was this authority derived? Was he Globocnik's man, Himmler's man, or even Hitler's man? The latter seems too far-fetched, despite Heydrich's promotion recommendation in 1941, which alluded to Hitler's 'personal protection' for Wirth. This hitherto unsolved mystery certainly requires further investigation. A detailed biography of Wirth has yet to be published, but Michael Tregenza of Lublin is on the cusp of producing such a project. It will make interesting reading.

There is no doubt that the financial 'rewards' of Aktion Reinhardt were enormous, both for the state and the corrupt individual. Nobody was above temptation with such high stakes on offer. Even the SD was not above corruption and stored stolen silver and wine at the Saciletto Castle, north of Trieste, towards the final days of the war. Given his past record in Vienna, Odilo Globocnik would have gained substantial benefits from the valuables stolen from its victims. What better way of avoiding any subsequent claims to recover the proceeds of the crime than to make the lawful owners disappear? This begs the question, 'was murder a biproduct of Aktion Reinhardt, or was it the original reason for it?' Some argue that theft of Jewish assets was the original reason Reinhardt came into being, and murder was the natural development of the original crime. Did Reinhardt start as a plunder operation as a result of resettlement policies, which then produced the unavoidable, but simple solution of where to put the Jews after they had been stripped of their belongings? Or was it simply a way to eject the Jews from all forms of society once and for all?

The US Nazi Conspiracy and Aggression series suggests quite clearly that Reinhardt was a long-term 'act of plunder'. Whether this 'act of plunder' is as a result of the murder campaign or the cause of the killings is unclear, but the two elements go hand in hand. The various spelling of the operational title fuels the speculation. In the Majdanek archive, where a number of original documents pertaining to Reinhardt exist, there are a few variants—even Globocnik himself spells the title differently in a single letter. Yet the timing of the death of Reinhard Heydrich, and the strong possibility of naming the operation in his honour, is difficult to ignore. It is a question that will remain unanswered unless documentary evidence to resolve the matter is uncovered. All the prime witnesses are now long dead.

That the assets of those murdered were looted is an undeniable fact. Globocnik supplied a closing account of the robberies at the conclusion of the operation. Georg Wippern was a crucial figure in the financial aspect of Aktion Reinhardt. He administered the sorting, storage, pilfering, and eventual transfer of stolen currency, precious metals, and gemstones, on behalf of his masters. In colloquial terms, Wippern could justifiably be described as Globocnik's 'fence'.

One of Wippern's post-war statements illustrates his role in Lublin during the Second World War:

> In my capacity as leader of the SS Garrison Administration—Standortverwaltung—Lublin, I received an order in the Spring of 1942 from the leader of the Main Economic Administration in Berlin, Oswald Pohl, to take charge of and sort all the jewellery, valuables and foreign currency and other money confiscated from the Jews, and to maintain their correct delivery. Accumulated jewellery and valuables, as well as foreign currency, were delivered to the Central Economic Administration (WVHA) in Berlin, and then to the Reichsbank in Berlin on receipt. Jewellery was melted down, if the design was not of special value, and then delivered to the Reichsbank as gold bars. The same applied with the silver. Local currency, Polish Zloty was transferred by my office at the Emissionbank in Lublin to an account at the Reichsbank.[11]

Until the order of Pohl referred to here by Wippern, seized valuables were despatched to Berlin by Christian Wirth, in an unorthodox manner. This method was clearly unacceptable to Pohl who issued the new order as a result. Wirth reluctantly acceded to his superior's command.

Bełżec survivor Rudolf Reder described the process at Bełżec for transferring the valuables:

> Valuables, money and dollars were taken out of the storehouse each day. The SS men collected it themselves and put it into suitcases which workers carried to Bełżec to the Kommandantur. A Gestapo officer went first, with Jewish workers carrying the suitcases. It was not far; only a twenty minutes walk to the Bełżec station. The camp in Bełżec ... was under this headquarters. Jews working in administration said that the whole shipment of gold, valuables and money, was sent to Lublin, where the main headquarters was situated with authority over the Bełżec administration.[12]

The officials employed at the killing sites, and the sorting and storage facilities in Lublin, had access to untold riches. Despite the strict regulations imposed by Himmler to ensure the stolen belongings found their way to named bank accounts in Berlin, or recycled for use by the German war machine, an ever-increasing amount was skimmed off the surface for personal gain. Almost everything taken from the victims before they entered the gas chambers, was of value. Very little was destroyed along with the former legal owners. Had he survived, Globocnik would have had access to a vast personal fortune.

Globocnik also ensured that a selected few would also profit from the assets seized from the Jews and Poles. Corruption in his fiefdom stretched to dealing with the Jews themselves. He oversaw swindling them out of their assets in addition to downright robbery. On one occasion, Globocnik authorised the purchase of furs, valued at 30,000 RM, for the benefit of Reichsleiter Philipp Bouhler, the nominal head of T4. Whether or not the unfortunate Jewish fur dealer was ever paid remains to be seen.

It is clear that both Globocnik and Wirth prevented formal accounts from being drawn up for the Reinhardt camps. Aside from the fact that no concise record was made of the goods seized at the camps, there can be no other reason than to cover up what was going on. When Bełżec ceased to operate, George Wippern sent an accountant from his office, Wilhelm Schwarzkopf, to the camp in order to audit the camp accounts. Schwarzkopf was refused entry by Gottlieb Hering, on orders from Wirth, with the statement that 'no snoopers were allowed'.

Georg Wippern escaped prosecution, as did Ernst Lerch. An article appeared in the *Jewish Chronicle* on 1 October 1971: 'It was announced in Vienna on 27 September 1971 that SS officer Ernst Lerch (60), had been arrested. He is suspected of complicity in the murder of 1,800,000 Jews, as chief of staff of Aktion Reinhard. At the time of his arrest, Lerch was a café owner in Klagenfurt'.

Lerch stood accused with fellow SS member in Lublin, Helmut Pohl. The allegation was their participation in the murder of 1.8 million Jews in Eastern Poland during Aktion Reinhardt in 1942–43, and other violent crimes, as members of the staff of the SS and Police Leader, Odilo Globocnik, in Lublin. Specifically, desk crimes leading to death, mass murder crimes in camps, and other mass murder crimes in various locations in Poland. The main trial before a jury at the Landesgericht Klagenfurt was terminated on 17 May 1972 after two days and not resumed. On 11 May 1976, the Vienna Prosecutor's Office announced the termination of the proceedings by the Landesgericht Klagenfurt due to the resignation of the public prosecutor from the indictment, before reopening the main hearing. No further action was taken, prompting questions of influence exerted by the defence.

Georg Michalsen was not quite so lucky. As a member of the Aktion Reinhardt staff, he had been responsible for the size of the daily transports from Warsaw to Treblinka once the deportations commenced in July 1942. He had been transferred to the Adriatic coast with the Reinhardt cadre, and was appointed as the SS and Police commanding officer in Pola in February 1944. As has been previously mentioned, Michalsen actively participated in anti-partisan operations in that region. With Globocnik's backing, Michalsen was appointed as the SS and Police commandant in Trieste from September 1944. He carried out this role simultaneously with his duties in Abteilung II of the HSSPF OZAK. At times, he served as the deputy of SS-Brigadeführer Erasmus von Malsen-Ponickau in Fiume.

Michalsen was arrested at the Mößlacher Alm with Globocnik and Rainer on 31 May 1945. He was released in 1948, having convinced his captors of his innocence, and then lived under a false name in West Germany. He was discovered living a quiet life at Sachtestieg 10 in Blankenese, a sedate suburb of Hamburg, in 1973. On 2 August 1974, the *Jewish Chronicle* reported:

> Last week in Hamburg, Otto Hantke (67) was sentenced to life imprisonment for murdering four Jews in Poland. Former SS-Major Georg Michalsen (68), Hantke's superior officer, was sentenced to 20 years imprisonment for complicity in the murder of two Jews. However, Michalsen was released by the jury because of his health and his age.
>
> The Court was told that some 300,000 Jews from Warsaw, Bialystok and other Polish ghettos, were deported to Treblinka and murdered. Hantke and Michalsen were members of the staff of Globocnik's 'Aktion Reinhard'.
>
> Hantke shot the four Jews with his pistol. Michalsen 'only carried out the orders of a higher authority'.

Having evaded justice for many years after the end of the Second World War, the vast majority of Aktion Reinhardt personnel disappeared into obscurity. The security cordon thrown around their work at the time, and the destruction of physical and documentary evidence, on the face of it, appears to have been successful. That would explain the lack of recognition afforded to the Globocnik name. Deprived of a trial, such as that provided for Adolf Eichmann, Globocnik appears to have largely slipped under the radar of popular exposure. Only in recent years has attention focused on the crimes of Aktion Reinhardt in Poland to such an extent that the personalities involved are achieving recognition. One such well-publicised case was that of former Ukrainian John Demjanjuk.

Demjanjuk was born Ivan Mykolaiovych Demianiuk in Dubovi Makharyntsi, a small farming village in Western Ukraine, on 3 April 1920. In 1941, he was conscripted into the Red Army. Captured in the Crimea, as a Soviet POW, he was sent to a camp where he suffered degradation and starvation at the hands of his captors. To survive, he volunteered for the Germans and was sent to Trawniki. He subsequently served at Majdanek, Sobibor, and Flossenbürg. He survived the war and emigrated with his wife and child to the USA in 1952. Demjanjuk became a US citizen in 1958 and changed his given name to John. He worked at the Ford auto plant in Cleveland, Ohio, and fathered two more children.

In 1975, Demjanjuk was identified as a possible war criminal and a request was submitted in 1977 to revoke his US citizenship. He had been identified as a former guard at Treblinka death camp. In 1983, Israel submitted a request for the extradition of Demjanjuk and this prompted a lengthy legal dispute, mainly centred on the identification and Demjanjuk's Trawniki identification papers, which had been provided by the USSR. His appeal against deportation was dismissed and he arrived in Israel on 28 February 1986.

In his trial, which began on 26 November 1986, the prosecution alleged that Demjanjuk was 'Ivan the Terrible', a Trawniki guard who assisted with the gas engine at Treblinka. The defence case was that Demjanjuk had been misidentified and that his ID card from Trawniki was a forgery. Despite glaring inaccuracies and even contradictory evidence, Demjanjuk was found guilty on 18 April 1988 and sentenced to hang. His appeal was successful on 29 July 1993 when the Israeli Supreme Court overturned the original verdict. The defence produced evidence from former Treblinka guards that Ivan the Terrible's real name was Ivan Marchenko, and not Demjanjuk. His US citizenship was restored.

Questions over his service at Sobibor, Majdanek, and Flossenbürg remained, and Demjanjuk faced another trial in the USA in 2001. Once again, his US citizenship was revoked and a lengthy legal battle commenced. In 2008, Germany requested his extradition from the USA, and despite legal wranglings, he was deported to Germany, arriving in Munich on 12 May 2009. He was immediately arrested and transferred to Stadelheim Prison. He was charged with complicity in the murder of 27,900 people at Sobibor during his period there as a guard.

The trial began on 30 November 2009, resulting in the ninety-one-year-old Demjanjuk's conviction on 12 May 2011. He was sentenced to five years in prison and immediately lodged an appeal against conviction. The judge released him on the grounds that he had already served two terms of imprisonment. Before his appeal could be heard, Demjanjuk died at an old people's home in Bad Feilnbach, Germany, on 17 March 2012. He was buried in Parma, Ohio.

The fate of John Demjanjuk is indicative of that of the vast majority of the perpetrators of the Polish massacres. Many served minor prison terms, while a large number escaped altogether. One of the more vicious guards at Treblinka was SS-Unterscharführer Willi Mentz. Born on 30 April 1904, Mentz served at Treblinka, and also as a member of Abteilung R in Trieste. At Treblinka, he was known as 'Frankenstein', one of the many nicknames attributed by the prisoners to the worst of their guards. Kurt Franz was known as 'Lalka' (the Doll) as a result of his boyish good looks. Mentz was a T4 operative, having been responsible for the pigs and cows at Grafeneck before his transfer to Hadamar, where he worked in the food garden. Mentz was 'the gunman of Treblinka', having been ordered by Wirth to be the supervisor of the Lazaret, the fake infirmary. There, he wore a white coat and personally carried out thousands of executions by gunshot. From Treblinka, Mentz was sent to Sobibor for a very short period, before moving to the Adriatic coast. He survived the war and returned to Germany, where he worked as a milkman. He was arrested and in 1965, charged with being complicit in the murder of at least 700,000 people at Treblinka. Found guilty, he was sentenced to life in prison. Released on 31 March 1978 as a result of poor health, he died a free man on 25 June 1978 in Niedermeien.

The first trial specifically aimed at one of the three terminal stations was the Bełżec trial, which was held in Munich from 8 August 1963 until 30 January 1964. Eight defendants stood accused of being accessories to thousands of murders. The defendants and verdicts were as follows:

| | |
|---|---|
| Josef Oberhauser: | guilty; 4.5 years imprisonment and loss of citizen's rights for 3 years. |
| Erich Fuchs: | not guilty on grounds of acting under duress. |
| Heinrich Gley: | not guilty on grounds of acting under duress. |
| Werner Dubois: | not guilty on grounds of acting under duress. |
| Karl Schluch: | not guilty on grounds of acting under duress. |
| Heinrich Unverhau: | not guilty on grounds of acting under duress. |
| Robert Jührs: | not guilty on grounds of acting under duress. |
| Ernst Zierke: | not guilty on grounds of acting under duress. |

The prosecution case collapsed as a result of the post-war decision in West Germany not to introduce specific crimes relating to Nazi crimes. Investigations and trials were based upon existing German law, which created problems when attempting to differentiate between being an accessory to murder, or specifically committing the act of murder. Oberhauser was immediately rearrested in January 1964 and finally convicted on 21 January 1965. He was released after serving half his sentence and returned to his work in a beerhall in Munich where he was reluctantly filmed by Claude Lanzmann for his monumental documentary *Shoah*. He lived in Munich-Riem at Martin-Enpl-Ring 8 in a comfortable apartment. Oberhauser died a free man in Munich on 20 November 1979. He had avoided a life sentence imposed in his absence in Italy for crimes committed in OZAK, as the Italian request for extradition had failed.

The first Treblinka trial opened in Düsseldorf on 12 October 1964, with the verdicts passed on 3 September 1965. The defendants were as follows:

| | |
|---|---|
| Kurt Franz: | guilty; life imprisonment; served 28 years. Died 4 July 1998, five years after his release. |
| Otto Horn: | not guilty. Interviewed by author Gitta Sereny. |
| Erwin Lambert: | guilty; 4 years in prison, but immediately released having already served his time. Died on 15 October 1976. |
| Heinrich Matthes: | guilty; life imprisonment. Date of death unknown. |
| Willi Mentz: | guilty; life imprisonment. Died 1978, three months after his early release. |
| August Miete: | guilty; life imprisonment. He was allegedly released in the 1980s and died in 1987, having lived on the proceeds from Treblinka. |
| Gustav Münzberger: | guilty; 12 years imprisonment. Released in 1971 for good behaviour. He was interviewed by author Gitta Sereny in his home in Unterammergau in Bavaria, and died on 23 March 1977. |
| Albert Rum: | guilty; 3 years imprisonment. Date of death not known. |
| Otto Stadie: | guilty; 6 years imprisonment. Died 28 July 1977. |
| Franz Suchomel: | guilty; 7 years in prison. Released 20 December 1967 and died on 18 December 1979. Suchomel was secretly filmed during an interview for Claude Lanzmann's *Shoah*. |
| Kurt Küttner: | died in 1964, before the trial began. |

The second Treblinka trial had one defendant, Franz Paul Stangl, and was held in Düsseldorf from 13 May 1970 until 22 December 1970. Stangl was found guilty and sentenced to life imprisonment. He was interviewed extensively by Gitta Sereny, who published the result in her book *Into That Darkness* in 1974. Stangl died of a heart attack in Düsseldorf Prison on 28 June 1971.

The first Sobibor trial commenced in Hagen on 6 September 1965 and verdicts were passed on 20 December 1966. The defendants were as follows:

| | |
|---|---|
| Karl Frenzel: | guilty; life in prison. Released on a technicality in 1982, he was again tried and found guilty on 4 October 1985. Due to his advanced age, he was set free. He died on 2 September 1996 in a retirement home near Hannover. |
| Kurt Bolender: | hanged himself in his cell on 10 October 1966, before the end of the trial. |
| Franz Wolf: | guilty; 8 years in prison. Date of death unknown. His brother, Josef Wolf, was killed in the Sobibor uprising. |
| Alfred Ittner: | guilty; 4 years imprisonment. Died 3 November 1976. |
| Werner Dubois: | guilty; 3 years in prison. Died 22 October 1971. |
| Erich Fuchs: | guilty; 4 years imprisonment. Died 25 July 1980. |
| Erich Lachmann: | not guilty. Considered mentally incompetent. Died 23 January 1972. |
| Hans-Heinz Schütt: | not guilty. |
| Heinrich Unverhau: | not guilty. |
| Robert Jührs: | not guilty. |
| Ernst Zierke: | not guilty. |
| Erwin Lambert: | not guilty. |

The Soviets held two Sobibor trials in which the defendants were all former Ukrainian guards. All were found guilty, and all but one received death sentences. The most notorious guard at Sobibor was former T4 operative, Erich Bauer. Known as the 'Gasmeister' or the 'Badmeister', Bauer operated the gas chambers at Sobibor. He was arrested by the Americans in Austria in 1945. Released, he returned to Berlin where he worked as a labourer. He was identified by two former Sobibor prisoners at a fairground in Berlin in 1949. When confronted by them, he apparently said, 'How is it you are still alive?' He was convicted by a court in Berlin in 1950 and sentenced to death. This was commuted to life imprisonment, and he died in Berlin-Tegel Prison on 4 February 1980.

One important character who did not face judgement in the courts was Lorenz Hackenholt. When the scales of justice were balancing for many of his fellow comrades, Hackenholt was nowhere to be seen. The tall, well built man had totally disappeared. The West German authorities took steps to trace the man considered by many as the most culpable in the gassing process. In 2000, historical researcher Michael Tregenza pieced together the details of the West German

Police investigation in the period 1959–1963 into Hackenholt's background and his whereabouts, and he produced a detailed report entitled 'The Disappearance of SS-Hauptscharführer Lorenz Hackenholt'. It is this report that forms the basis of what follows.

Laurenzius 'Lorenz' Marie Hackenholt was born on 25 June 1914 in Gelsenkirchen, the son of Theodor and Elisabeth Hackenholt (*née* Wobriezek). After attending the local elementary school until the age of fourteen, he became an apprentice bricklayer. He passed the trade examination was employed on a number of building sites until 1933, when he volunteered for the SS. His Lebenslauf (CV) in his SS file states:

> After joining the SS, I was posted on 1 January 1934 to the Leadership School of SS-Abschnitt XVII, and remained there until the closure of the school. At that time, I reported to the army as a volunteer and was called up to the 12th Engineer Battalion. After two years military service, I was discharged. I then reported to the 2nd SS-Totenkopf Standarte. In November 1939, I was then posted to Berlin for 'special duty'.

He failed to mention that he belonged to the 2. SS-Totenkopf 'Brandenburg' Standarte, based at Oranienburg. In March 1938, a SS vehicle depot was established at the nearby Sachsenhausen concentration camp, and Werner Dubois and Hackenholt were then attached to the camp staff. Both SS men were skilled motor mechanics and drivers, with Class I–III driving licences. At Sachsenhausen, they also performed the more onerous task of camp guards, in addition to serving as drivers for the camp command staff.

In November 1939, with two other members of the camp staff employed in the vehicle depot, Josef Oberhauser and Siegfried Graetschus, Hackenholt and Dubois were ordered to report to the Reich Chancellery in Berlin. The four SS NCOs from Sachsenhausen met six other SS NCOs who had also been posted from the concentration camp service. All ten were interviewed personally by Viktor Brack and Werner Blankenburg. Dubois later recalled this interview:

> We were shown photographs of extreme cases of mental illness. We were told that … the institutions from which the mentally ill were to be taken were needed as military hospitals. We were further told that gas chambers were to be built in which the victims would be gassed, after which they would be cremated. We would not have anything to do with the killings; we would only have to cremate the corpses.[13]

As part of their duties, the SS drivers from Sachsenhausen would also collect the patients from the mental hospitals and deliver them to the euthanasia centres in buses. They were now employed by the 'Gemeinnutzige Stiftung fur Anstaltspflege' ('Charitable Foundation for Institutional Care') later referred to simply as 'die Stiftung' ('the Foundation'). In other words, they were now on the payroll of T4. The SS men were transported in a bus, driven by SS-Scharführer Lorenz Hackenholt, to Grafeneck Castle, south of Stuttgart. They were in civilian clothes. Hackenholt worked at Grafeneck and Sonnenstein T4 euthanasia centres.

After the termination of the T4 gassings, in the autumn of 1941, Hackenholt and a small group of SS NCOs from T4 were transferred to Lublin District in the south-east of Poland. They were placed under the authority of the SS-und Polizeiführer, SS-Brigadeführer Odilo Globocnik. Shortly after arriving in Lublin, Hackenholt was allowed home on leave to Berlin, in order to marry his neighbour, Ilse Zillmer, at the Registry Office in Berlin-Schmargendorf. She was twenty-nine years old. After the wedding and a brief honeymoon, Hackenholt returned to duty in Lublin. From there, he was sent to Bełżec. He had begun his career as the Aktion Reinhardt gassing expert.

Within the short space of time of only one month—mid-March to mid-April 1942—over 50,000 Jews were killed in the primitive gassing installation, by the exhaust fumes produced by an old Soviet tank engine, operated by Lorenz Hackenholt. Later that year, he designed and supervised the construction of new and extended gas chambers in Bełżec, and also at the Treblinka and Sobibor extermination camps. He transferred to Trieste with Globocnik in late 1943, where he continued to utilise his gassing expertise at the Risiera di San Sabba, and also participated in anti-partisan operations.

In 1945, Hackenholt disappeared. Before their marriage, the Hackenholts had been registered with the Berlin police as living in their own separate apartments in the same building at Kurfurstendamm 112. As this was Lorenz Hackenholt's last known address, it seemed the logical place for the investigators at the Ludwigsburg Central Office to begin their search for the wanted war criminal.

The Berlin police authorities had no post-war residential registration for Lorenz Hackenholt. However, there was a registration card for a masseuse named Ilse Barbara Hackenholt (*née* Zillmer), born on 19 November 1912 in Berlin-Charlottenberg. Until 22 December 1951, Frau Hackenholt had been registered as living at Munsterdamm 32, in Berlin-Steglitz, c/o Schimmelpfennig. On that date, she had moved to the village of Tiefenbach, near Oberstdorf in the Allgäu, in the vicinity of the border with Austria, close to Bodensee. She had registered there with the local Border Police on 3 January 1952. She lived with another woman in a small wooden chalet named 'Sonnenhuttle'. The two women shared the expenses and worked together in a sauna in Isny. The Berlin police report also stated that on 22 August 1953, Frau Hackenholt had requested that the court in Berlin-Schöneberg declare her husband as officially dead. She wished to claim a war widow's pension.[14]

Ilse Hackenholt stated that she had heard nothing from her husband since November or December 1944. According to her, he was at that time a SS-Oberscharführer on the Eastern Front. She was now unaware of the Feldpost number. Included in the file is also a deposition, dated 28 September 1953, by Hackenholt's widowed mother, Elisabeth Hackenholt, now living at Görrerstrasse 8, in Gelsenkirchen. This states that she too was unable to give the Feldpost number, and was no longer in possession of any letters from her son. She, too, had, apparently, received no news from her son after 1944. In the file, the date of Hackenholt's marriage is given as 4 November 1941, at the Berlin-Schmargendorf registry office. The last address for the Hackenholts was at Martin Luther Strasse 11, in Berlin-Schönenberg, c/o Gloth. The application for the declaration of death was granted by order of the Berlin magistrates' court on 1 April 1954, with effect from 31 December 1945.[15]

At the request of the Ludwigsburg Central Office for the Investigation of National Socialist Crimes, the local Border Police in Tiefenbach kept Ilse Hackenholt and the 'Sonnenhuttle' under surveillance. They were instructed to particularly note all male visitors to the premises. Frau Hackenholt apparently also had a second residence at Wilhelmstrasse 10 in Isny, in Allgäu, Württemberg. No visits by unidentified males were observed.

On 1 March 1961, two officers from Sonderkommission IIIa (SK IIIa), the war crimes investigation unit of the Munich Kriminalpolizei, travelled to Berlin to interrogate one of Hackenholt's former SS comrades. In Berlin-Tegel prison, they questioned Erich Bauer, who was serving the eleventh year of a life sentence, imposed by a Berlin court in 1950, for crimes committed at Sobibor. In 1942–1943, SS-Oberscharführer Bauer had been Hackenholt's opposite number in charge of the Sobibor gas chambers. On oath, Bauer swore that he knew that Hackenholt had definitely survived the war. He declared that they had met and talked at Zuchering, near Ingolstadt in Bavaria, in 1946. At that time, according to Bauer, Hackenholt was living under the name of Jansen, Jensen, Johannsen, or something similar. Bauer stated that Hackenholt had allegedly taken the identity from a dead soldier towards the end of the war. It was Bauer's impression that, under this alias, Hackenholt had obtained work as a delivery van driver. When pressed for further details, he said that he believed the vehicle Hackenholt was driving was a Faun van. He suggested that Hackenholt might be living with a woman called 'Monika' he had known in Trieste.

During the interrogation of another former SS guard from Sobibor, Fritz Rehwald, they learnt that the wanted war criminal had approached him for assistance sometime after the war. Rehwald could not recall exactly where, or when, the meeting had taken place. He recalled only that Hackenholt was apparently running a motor accessory shop at Neuburg-an-der-Donau. This was of particular significance to the investigators—Neuburg is only 15 km from Ingolstadt.

At 7 a.m. on 8 July 1961, the Hackenholt house at Görrerstrasse 8, in Gelsenkirchen, was searched by two officers from SK IIIa, accompanied by two officers from the Bundeskriminalamt in Wiesbaden, the headquarters of the West German Kriminalpolizei. The search warrant had been issued the previous day by a local magistrate in Gelsenkirchen, on the grounds that 'there was a strong suspicion that Hackenholt had, or still has, contact with his mother, and to find any correspondence or other evidence of his present whereabouts'.[16] In Tiefenbach, on the same day, another house search was carried out at the 'Sonnenhuttle' chalet, by two officers of the Border Police, on a warrant issued on the same grounds as the one in Gelsenkirchen. Both searches produced no result. A second search warrant was executed on business premises at Landhausstrasse 27, in Leutkirch, without success.

During the course of the investigation into the whereabouts of Lorenz Hackenholt and the crimes committed in the Bełżec extermination camp, nine former members of the camp SS garrison were traced and arrested. While being interrogated about their individual roles in the extermination process, they were also asked what they knew about Hackenholt's activities and responsibilities in Bełżec. They all agreed that, at first, he had been employed in the camp as a driver, and that the camp commandant, Christian Wirth, had made him responsible for procuring vehicles from the SS and Police depot in Lublin. Only later were suitable vehicles, mainly trucks, supplied to the camp by the Reich Chancellery in Berlin.[17] In the camp, Hackenholt soon acquired a reputation for being the type of person who, because of what his comrades called his 'outstanding ability to organise anything', could be relied upon for all kinds of jobs, especially of a technical or mechanical nature. Consequently, Wirth placed Hackenholt in charge of the camp motor pool, the procurement of spare parts and fuel, in addition to technical equipment for the camp generally. This included the installation and maintenance of an electricity generator near the garage.

While the first primitive gas chambers were being built in the wooden shed, Hackenholt and Siegfried Graetschus converted a big post office delivery van into a mobile gas chamber by connecting the engine exhaust pipe to the sealed rear compartment.[18] The van was then used to kill the mentally and physically disabled in nearby villages. It was an invention of which Hackenholt was very proud, and one which particularly endeared him to Wirth.[19]

After the completion of the Bełżec gassing facility, Wirth carried out various experiments in the three small gas chambers, using different kinds of poison gas. These included the exhaust fumes from the post office van, when the exhaust pipe was connected to the main gas pipe under the gassing shed. Among the first Jewish victims were around 150 labourers who had been brought to the camp from nearby towns to finish the construction work. They were killed with Zyklon B, a hydrocyanic acid based pesticide supplied to military units in the field. Further experiments, using carbon monoxide bottled gas from steel cylinders, the same method used in the T4 killing centres, were also carried out on Jews from the ghettos in Izbica and Piaski. These first ghetto victims of Bełżec, brought to the camp in several railway goods wagons, were almost certainly Jewish mental patients deported from the Reich. One former SS NCO, Hans Girtzig, commented about these experiments conducted by Wirth: 'Bełżec was the laboratory … he tried everything imaginable there. In Bełżec, Wirth tested the basics of the extermination machinery right through with his men'.[20]

Finally, influenced by the success of Hackenholt's gassing post office van, the exhaust fumes from a Soviet tank engine were decided upon as the most suitable and economic means for the mass murder of Jews. Former SS NCO Hans Girtzig, who served in Bełżec with Hackenholt, told officers from SK IIIa about this gassing installation in the camp: 'Hackenholt had installed the engine, this was explained to us at a duty conference.… I know for certain that, in the beginning, Wirth and Hackenholt, and later Hackenholt alone, that is, with the help of Ukrainians, operated the gassing engine'.[21]

It was unanimously agreed by all nine former members of the Bełżec SS staff in custody that Hackenholt's main area of responsibility from then on had been at the gassing installation, an area prohibited to all members of the camp staff, except for the select few who had business there, authorised by Wirth. Wirth's SS driver, Werner Dubois, stated about Hackenholt's gassing team:

> Hackenholt, with the work force assigned to him, operated the gassing engine … as assistants, Ukrainians and Jews were at his disposal. As I recall, there were one or two Ukrainians and one or two Jews. I take it that the actual work was carried out by the Ukrainians and Jews, and Hackenholt only carried out their supervision.[22]

Former SS NCO, Karl Schluch, assigned by Wirth to gas chamber duty, elaborated on Hackenholt's duties in the extermination process at Bełżec: 'After the Jews had entered the gas chambers the doors were shut tight by Hackenholt himself, or by one of the Ukrainians assigned to him. Then Hackenholt started the engine.… I cannot say for certain who looked through the peepholes … it could have been Hackenholt'.[23]

The deportees who were unable to proceed through the undressing and gassing procedure unaided through infirmity, advanced age, or sickness were left lying on the ground next to the railway ramp until everyone else had been processed. Karl Schluch described what happened next:

> A Jewish work brigade carried them on stretchers to a special grave close to the eastern boundary of the camp. There they were laid face down either at the edge of

> the grave, or in the grave itself with their faces on the corpses already lying there. In these early days at Bełżec they were shot in the back of the head by Hackenholt.[24]

In addition, Schluch testified that Hackenholt also shot Jews of the work brigades.[25]

After a break of one month in the extermination operation at Bełżec, in the spring of 1942, the original gassing shed was torn down and a bigger, solid installation of brick and concrete was constructed, which contained six chambers, three on either side of a central corridor. Two Soviet tank engines, each one serving three chambers, were installed in a machine room at the rear of the building. According to Werner Dubois: 'To my knowledge, the plans for the solid gassing building came from Hackenholt. The construction of the building itself was carried out by work Jews'.[26]

Hackenholt supervised the work personally and when the installation was completed a sign was placed on the wall next to the entrance which read 'Stiftung Hackenholt' (Hackenholt Foundation). Hackenholt again supervised the operating and maintenance of the gassing engines, assisted by Ukrainian guards and Jewish prisoners.

In September 1942, Hackenholt and a small Kommando of German and Ukrainian guards were transferred to Treblinka II by Wirth. In the first days after Hackenholt's arrival, Wirth also issued orders for the construction of new gas chambers. The plans were drawn up by Hackenholt, who was known as 'Hacko' at Treblinka; Erwin Lambert was summoned as the builder, after 'Hacko' had already done some preparatory work. Lambert, like Hackenholt, was a bricklayer by trade, now in the employ of T4 in SS uniform. Previously, he had carried out construction work at the T4 killing centres, mainly converting rooms into gas chambers and erecting chimneys for the crematoria. He had also worked previously in Treblinka for a short time when the camp was under construction. According to Lambert, confirming a statement by Franz Suchomel, he returned to Treblinka in August or September 1942, after the construction of the new gas chambers had already commenced.

The new gassing installation at Treblinka was modelled on the 'Stiftung Hackenholt' in Bełżec. On completion, Hackenholt and Lambert were both transferred by Wirth to Sobibor, where new gas chambers were also required. Lambert described their journey:

> First, I went with Hackenholt to a timber yard near Warsaw. There, Hackenholt placed a big order for wood for construction work at Sobibor. Finally, we travelled together to Sobibor.… I could have arrived there sometime in October, I cannot say exactly. I only remember that it was already cold when I arrived … we reported to the camp commander, Reichleitner. He then gave us suitable instructions for constructing the

> gassing installation. The camp was already in operation before our arrival and there was already a gassing installation there.[27]

Around six Ukrainian guards, employed in Treblinka as labourers, also went to Sobibor with Hackenholt and Lambert. Their leader, a Volksdeutscher bricklayer called Busche, acted as their interpreter.[28]

At the beginning of winter 1942, Hackenholt returned to Bełżec, where the exhumation and cremation operation had begun. For a few weeks, he operated a mechanical excavator, opening the mass graves and removing the decomposing contents. During this period, according to Bełżec villagers who met him in the local bars, 'Hackenholt stank of corpses'. On the instructions of SS NCO Herbert Floss, the Aktion Reinhardt cremation expert, the exhumed human remains were cremated on big grates, constructed of metal railway lines placed on top of squat concrete pillars, arranged around the rim of an emptied grave. At the beginning of December 1942, a second grate was constructed and between them, the two pyres consumed about 4,000 corpses every twenty-four hours. SS man Heinrich Gley, who supervised the cremations, estimated that over half a million corpses were burnt between the end of November 1942 and March 1943 at Bełżec.[29]

In December 1942, Hackenholt returned to Berlin on home leave to spend Christmas and the New Year with his wife. On his return to Poland at the beginning of 1943, Hackenholt was once more assigned to Treblinka by Wirth, in order to assist with the cremation operation, which had just commenced at the camp. Victims were now also cremated immediately after gassing, and not buried in the mass graves. The bodies already in the pits had to be exhumed in order to destroy the evidence. Hackenholt was used as the excavator operator, and Floss supervised the cremation. Later, a second excavator was brought to Treblinka and permanent operators were employed. Hackenholt returned to Bełżec, where he remained until the completion of the exhumation and cremation operation in March 1943. The camp was then disbanded, and the buildings and fencing were demolished. Hackenholt was promoted to SS-Hauptscharführer and reassigned by Wirth to supervisory duties at the Lublin Airfield camp.

Here, valuable furs were disinfected with Zyklon B in four specially constructed chambers. After the arrival of SS-Hauptscharführer Hackenholt at the airfield camp, he used the chambers for killing prisoners no longer fit for work.[30]

Among the Aktion Reinhardt camp personnel transferred to the airfield by Wirth, was SS NCO, Kurt Bolender, formerly a member of the Sobibor camp staff, and recently released from custody in a SS penal facility. After the war, Bolender took two false names—'Heinz Brenner' and 'Wilhelm Kurt Vahle', which he used to obtain work as a nightclub doorman in Hamburg. He had even gone to the trouble of having Kurt Bolender declared legally dead. He was recognised in May

1961 and was arrested under the assumed name 'Heinz Brenner'. During a search of his apartment, police found a whip with the silver initials 'KB' worked into the handle. It had been created at Sobibor by camp survivor Stanislaw Szmajzner.

On 31 October 1961, Ilse Hackenholt informed officers from SK IIIa, that she had visited her husband at the Lublin airfield camp at the end of October 1943:

> At that time, my husband was in a factory, or some such similar place in Lublin, in which Jews were interned and had to work. My husband lived at that time in Lublin in the camp complex … we lived a part of the time inside the camp complex, and on this particular day the whole camp was surrounded and the interned Jews were driven out. Although I myself saw that the camp was surrounded, I cannot say for sure to which units the soldiers belonged. I believe I heard from my husband that the camp was surrounded by the SS. The Jews were taken some distance from the camp and later I heard shooting.[31]

This incident, witnessed and described by Ilse Hackenholt, occurred on 3 November 1943, and it marked the beginning of the massacre, codenamed 'Erntefest'.

The few members of Aktion Reinhardt who had remained in Poland after Globocnik's transfer to OZAK included Lorenz Hackenholt, who was allowed home on leave at the end of the year in time to spend Christmas with his wife. However, one day before Christmas the whole group received telegrams from Wirth ordering them to report to him immediately in Trieste.

At the Risiera di San Sabba, bodies were burnt in a crematorium constructed by Erwin Lambert. The executions and cremations were finally stopped on Globocnik's orders in early May 1944, and the Abteilung R units were switched to anti-partisan duties on the Istrian peninsula.

In 1944, Hackenholt was awarded the Iron Cross 2nd Class, for his dedicated and loyal service to Aktion Reinhardt, and sometime in the spring of 1945, according to his fellow SS comrades, Josef Oberhauser, Hans Girtig, and Heinrich Gley, Hackenholt was allegedly killed in the fighting near Trieste. There was no mention of his body. It was known that eleven members of the former Aktion Reinhard and Abteilung R SS-Sonderkommandos who served in Poland and Italy had been killed in action in northern Italy in 1944. Their numbers included their commander, SS-Sturmbannführer Christian Wirth, who had been attacked and killed by Yugoslav partisans. They had all been buried in the German Military Cemetery at Opcina, overlooking Triest. Between 1957 and 1961, their bodies were exhumed and reburied with over 21,000 other German war dead in Italy, in a new German Military Cemetery at Costermano, overlooking Lake Garda. There was no record of a Lorenz Hackenholt ever being buried at either Opcina or Costermano. If Oberhauser, Girtig, and Gley were to be believed, what happened to his body?

Karl Schluch described Hackenholt as an inconsiderate, hard, and brutal man, without any sense of honour. In his opinion, he was characterless and had an indifferent attitude. He was a heavy drinker, which often got him into trouble, but he carried out his orders without question.

Willy Grossmann, who had known Hackenholt in both Treblinka and Trieste, described him with some difficulty: 'It is difficult for me to give an appropriate expression which suitably characterises him. I can say that he was stupid and brazen. He was, moreover, greatly feared, especially in the latter days. Hackenholt was often very drunk. He was rebellious towards his superiors'.[32]

Robert Juhrs, who served with Hackenholt in Bełżec and Trieste, provided the most succinct description of Lorenz Hackenholt: 'About his character I can use the following figure of speech which, to my mind, most appropriately describes it: 'He wanted to go and piss with the big dogs, but he couldn't lift his leg'.[33]

Lorenz Hackenholt appears to have been a loner with no close friends. Not one of the men he served with, some since the early days at the Gafeneck killing centre in 1939, would admit to being in any way friendly with him. They all agreed, quite independently, that he spent most of his free time alone. Robert Juhrs stated that in Italy, Hackenholt continued to use his 'organisational abilities', and he dealt extensively on the black market. Inevitably, Hackenholt overstepped the mark and began black market dealings with the enemy, a capital offence in wartime. He was arrested for selling ammunition to the partisans. Hackenholt was imprisoned for a time in the Risiera di San Sabba, pending court martial and certain execution by firing squad. However, Dieter Allers, who had taken command of the Abteilung R units after Wirth's death, knew that the war was lost and shrewdly released all the Jews still held in the mill, together with Hackenholt, who no doubt considered it prudent to disappear from Trieste. In doing so, he committed another capital offence in wartime—desertion.

Hackenholt was next seen on the outskirts of the city, driving a civilian bus. Karl Schiffner, a former member of the Treblinka SS staff, recalls: 'On 29 April or 2 May 1945, Lorenz Hackenholt was taken on by a private bus company near Trieste. He accepted work there. I even saw him in this job. It was between Trieste and Udine.[34]

Josef Oberhauser and Kurt Bolender also confirmed to the post-war investigators that Hackenholt was certainly still alive at the end of April 1945. They had allegedly come across him 'in the company of other former members of the Bełżec camp staff'. They had also seen him alive 'the day before Easter 1945'.[35]

Witnesses are certain that Hackenholt joined the withdrawal because they saw him driving a lorry on which was mounted an anti-aircraft gun. Werner Dubois recalls the retreating troops reaching Austria and his last sighting of Lorenz Hackenholt, still driving the anti-tank truck:

> I saw Hackenholt during the early days of May 1945 at Kirchbach, Carinthia, in Austria. This was immediately before we were disarmed by British troops. If I remember correctly, he was driving a 'Flak' lorry. I cannot say who was with him. I was with Hackenholt at the time mentioned, at our disbandment, that is, our dismissal by Dieter Allers.[36]

SS-Hauptscharführer Hackenholt was last seen outside the town of Kirchbach by Willy Grossmann, and other SS-men who were heading for the rallying point in a lorry. On the road into the town they came across Hackenholt, as Grossmann recalls: 'I saw Hackenholt outside Kirchbach, Carinthia, driving a horsedrawn milk float. On that occasion, he shouted joyously as we went by. Whether Hackenholt was in uniform at the time, or in civilian clothes, I cannot say. After that, that is until today, I have never heard of him again'.[37]

Heinrich Gley kept in contact with Frau Hering after the war. Gley had been particularly friendly with Gottlieb Hering, both in Poland and in Italy, and he revealed an interesting fact about Lorenz Hackenholt and the Herings. In Trieste in 1944, Frau Hering, at that time Fräulein Riegraf, was employed as Hering's secretary. She lived in a villa with Hering and Hackenholt. This was confirmed by other witnesses who were also certain that she had known Hackenholt well. Apparently, she had almost been shot and killed, together with her future husband, during a drunken prank by Hackenholt and Gley. It was because of this and other incidents that Fräulein Riegraf and Gottlieb Hering had been transferred, first to Udine, and then back to Stuttgart. There, she became a secretary in the Stuttgart Police Presidium, while Hering became Kriminalpolizei chief in Heilbronn. They married in March 1945 and settled in Stuttgart-Fellbach.[38]

By 1961, Frau Hering was married to another Stuttgart police officer and was now called Helene Schubert. On 3 August of that year, she was summoned to the police station in Waiblingen, near Stuttgart, where she swore on oath:

> I do not remember a man called Hackenholt … it is not correct that I lived together with Hackenholt in a villa. I have never lived in a villa.… I do not know whether Hackenholt had any friends or acquaintances because I do not remember a Hackenholt. I did not know such a man, who probably lived under a false name in Trieste.[39]

This was the first of several occasions when Frau Hering was to commit perjury by denying all knowledge of Lorenz Hackenholt. Her apartment had been used after the war as a central point for information about former comrades from the days in Poland and Italy. It is therefore impossible that she was not aware of Hackenholt, and almost certainly knew of his whereabouts in 1945 and 1946.

Lorenz Hackenholt's brother, Theo Hackenholt, declared:

> It is correct that in August 1959, I went for a short holiday to visit my sister-in-law, Ilse Hackenholt, in Tiefenbach-Allgäu. During a conversation with my sister-in-law, which lasted one-and-a-half hours, I told her that I believe that I saw my brother, Lorenz Hackenholt, in 1947.... I was driving a lorry and trailer from Dortmund to Gelsenkirchen on Bundesbahn 1. On the way, we met a delivery van which I cannot describe in detail. It could have been a converted private car. The driver of the approaching vehicle could have been my brother, Lorenz. I had no opportunity to observe the driver properly as everything happened too quickly. At this encounter I only had the impression that the driver could have been my brother...[40]

On 9 October 1962, the examining magistrate at the Regional Court in Frankfurt-am-Main wrote to SK IIIa in Munich, enquiring about progress in the search for Lorenz Hackenholt as he too was interested in the whereabouts of the former SS-Hauptscharführer. The State Prosecutor in Frankfurt was preparing indictments against several participants in the T4 'euthanasia' killings, and Hackenholt featured high on the list of the prospective defendants.

The SK IIIa reply to the Frankfurt Prosecutor informed the examining magistrate that if current enquiries did not produce any new leads, 'the investigation into the whereabouts of Lorenz Hackenholt would be terminated'.

The American military authorities in Heidelberg and Washington, DC, were unable to provide any further useful information, and the investigation was finally abandoned at the end of 1963. Former SS-Hauptscharfuhrer Lorenz Hackenholt, wanted for participation in the mass murder of over 70,000 German mental patients in the T4 killing centres in Germany, and participation in the mass murder of around 1.5 million Jews in the Aktion Reinhardt extermination camps in Poland, has never been found.[41]

Post-war justice comes in different guises. Retribution meted out by courts in the Soviet-influenced territories tended to be more severe than that in the west. Some would maintain that the crimes perpetrated in the east were greater, while a more balanced argument registers the point that it is not the magnitude of the crime, but the crime itself that counts. There is no escaping the fact that far more murders were carried out by the Nazis in the eastern theatres than in the western and North African campaigns. Much suffering was endured on German home turf in the concentration camps that sprang up before the outbreak of open hostilities, but it was the advent of warfare that opened the route to the establishment of mobile Einsatzgruppen murder squads and specific death camps. Only four specific death camps existed that had no other purpose than to kill—Chełmno, Bełżec, Sobibor, and Treblinka. All four were sited in occupied Poland, and three came under the authority of Odilo Globocnik.

Chełmno (German: Kulmhof) can best be described as a 'despatch centre for death', as the vast majority of its victims began their journey to oblivion from the old manor house in the village of Chełmno. Here, the victims were loaded into the mobile gas vans, before being driven to their final destination in the local forest. They never saw their place of cremation, as they were all dead before arrival. There was a series of Chełmno trials, conducted both in Poland and Germany. At the first trial in Poland in October 1945, the defendant Bruno König—also known as Bruno Israel—testified:

> In July or August 1944 … I was assigned to the Sonderkommando Kulmhof.… I took part in the escorting of the transports. When Jews asked where they were being taken, I answered … they were going to work. The Jews generally believed it and behaved peacefully.… They were given soap, unless they had their own. They were told they would get towels at the bath house. Then all of them, both men and women were herded into a corral at the exit of which there was a Sonderwagen [gas van].… The bodies were thrown into one of the [Waldlager] crematoriums. The furnaces were about 10 metres wide and about 5–6 metres long. They did not stick out above the ground level. They had no chimneys.[42]

König was convicted under the name Israel, and was sentenced to death. Commuted to life imprisonment in 1946, he was released in 1958. Walter Piller and Hermann Gielow were both found guilty and sentenced to hang. They were executed in 1949 and 1951 respectively. From 1962 to 1965, eleven defendants were tried in four separate trials in Bonn, West Germany, resulting in six acquittals and sentences ranging from thirteen months and two weeks to fifteen years. Henryk Mania, a Polish Volksdeutscher, was tried in a 2001 court case in Poznan. He was found guilty of helping to load prisoners into gas vans and collecting their watches and jewellery, which he also stole for himself. He was sentenced to only eight years in prison as a result of his advanced age.

The Majdanek trials were a series of consecutive trials held in Poland and in Germany. Although Majdanek was a much larger establishment, the prosecution case was somewhat simpler as much evidence still existed. The camp structures survived, as did many witnesses and much documentary evidence. There were also many satellite camps. To begin with, the Germans had tried two former commandants themselves—Karl Otto Koch and Hermann Florstedt. Both were charged by SS courts with corruption and theft during their tenures at the camp. Koch was executed on 5 April 1945, and Florstedt suffered the same fate on 15 April 1945.

The Soviet investigation team began its work before the war ended, and the first trial opened on 27 November 1944. Trials continued until the last one concluded in Düsseldorf on 30 June 1981. In total, only 170 defendants of a known total of named camp personnel reaching 1,037 stood trial. A large number were acquitted, most in the West German courts. The camp had operated for two months short of three years, during which time almost 80,000 victims died at Majdanek alone; 59,000 were Polish Jews. With its sub-camps, the final estimate rises to between 95,000 and 130,000, an exact figure impossible to calculate. Aktion Erntefest contributed 43,000 victims to this estimate, with 18,000 dying on one single day (3 November 1943) in Majdanek alone.

The camp at Majdanek was liberated by the Red Army on 23 July 1944, and the advancing troops were shocked to discover the camp intact. Six former camp staff were detained and put on trial on 27 November. All six were quickly found guilty and sentenced to hang. They included SS-Obersturmführer Anton Thernes, SS-Hauptsturmführer Wilhelm Gerstenmeier, SS-Oberscharführer Hermann Vögel, SS-Rottenführer Theodor Schöllen, and two Kapos, Edmund Pohlmann and Heinrich Stalp. Pohlmann killed himself on 2 December 1944, and the others died on the scaffold the following day in the grounds of the camp. A further ten death sentences were handed out during the ensuing years, with seven of them being carried out, all in Poland. Other sentences ranged from three years' imprisonment to life, the German courts being more lenient.

The last conviction for crimes at Majdanek was that of Karl-Friedrich Höcker on 3 May 1989. Höcker was the adjutant of Richard Baer, the last commandant of Auschwitz. Höcker's photograph album recently surfaced and attracted attention worldwide. In the court at Bielefeld, Höcker received a prison term of four years. The prosecution showed that between May 1943 and May 1944, he had acquired a minimum of 3,610 kg of Zyklon B crystals (prussic acid) from the Hamburg firm of Tesch and Stabenow for use at Majdanek. Höcker died on 30 January 2000.

The US military authorities instigated the first specific euthanasia trial, which sat from 8–15 October 1945 in Wiesbaden, West Germany. The defendants were former staff of the Hadamar institute and the indictment stated:

> Charge: Violation of International Law.
> Specification: In that Alfons Klein, Adolf Wahlmann, Heinrich Ruoff, Karl Willig, Adolf Merkle, Irmgard Huber and Philipp Blum, acting jointly and in pursuance of a common intent and acting for and on behalf of the then German Reich, did, from on or about 1 July, 1944, to on or about 1 April, 1945, at Hadamar, Germany, wilfully, deliberately and wrongfully, aid, abet, and participate in the killing of human beings of Polish and Russian nationality, their exact names and number being unknown but aggregating in excess of 400, and who were then and there confined by the then German Reich as an exercise of belligerent control.[43]

All the accused were found guilty. Klein, Ruoff, and Willig were sentenced to be hanged; Wahlmann was sentenced to life imprisonment; and Merkle, Blum, and Huber were sentenced to imprisonment for thirty-five years, thirty years, and twenty-five years respectively.

There were four trials in Frankfurt, between 1946 und 1948, for people involved in the T4 euthanasia programme. Amongst the forty-four defendants were doctors, nursing sisters, and male nurses from the Hadamar, Eichberg, and Kalmenhof institutions. All were alleged to have been involved in the murder of patients. Six death sentences were passed and nineteen were given prison sentences. Consequently, the death sentences were not carried out, and apart from two of those convicted, all were eventually pardoned.

In the Soviet occupation zone, a trial began in Dresden on 16 June 1947 to prosecute those who had worked at the Sonnenstein euthanasia institute in Pirna. Dr Paul Nitsche, the director of the T4 Medical Office, was one of the fifteen defendants. The others included Dr Alfred Schulze, Dr Günther Langer, Dr Robert Herzer, Dr Emil Eichler, Dr Walther, and Dr Ernst Leonhardt; the nurses were Hermann Felfe, Erhardt Gäbler, Paul Räpke, Elsa Sachse, Martha Friedrich, Marie-Luise Puschmann, Wedel, and Ackermann. Several of the nurses appeared in court dressed in their nursing uniforms.

Nitsche, Leonhardt, Felfe, and Gäbler were sentenced to death on 20 December 1945. Räpke received a life sentence; Herzer twenty years' imprisonment; Dr Langer and Sachse fifteen years'; and Wedel and Ackermann eight years'. Puschmann and Friedrich were sentenced to three years' imprisonment. The defendants, Dr Walther, Dr Schulze, and Friedrich, were acquitted.

The Grafeneck trial began in summer 1949 at Hohentübingen Castle with just eight defendants. They were accused of participating in the murder of 10,000 patients at the T4 facility. The accused were Otto Mauthe, Max Eyrich, the former state youth doctor, Alfons Stegmann, a former doctor in the Zwiefalten Sanatorium, Meta Fauser the senior female doctor at Zwiefalten, Jakob Wöger, and Hermann Holzschuh an official at the registry office, Heinrich Unvertau, a former nurse, and nursing sister, Maria Appinger. Only three received terms of imprisonment, ranging from eighteen months' to five years'.

The main Hartheim trial named sixty-one defendants. These included three doctors, twenty-three former nurses, sixteen administrators, four drivers, six furnace operators, and nine others. The doctors included Dr Georg Renno and Dr Rudolf Lonauer. The case against thirteen defendants was dropped, and twenty-two of the defendants named could not be traced. Seven defendants had died. Two received prison terms, proceedings against thirteen were set aside for another trial and three cases remained outstanding. The sentences were passed on 7 July 1947. The state prosecution had sought the death sentence in eleven cases, but only four were passed. The sentences on the nursing sisters generally proved more lenient than had been requested. The death sentences were carried out in Dresden during March 1948. Those with long prison sentences were released in 1956 as part of an amnesty.

During his trial at Nuremberg, Viktor Brack testified that he received an order in 1941 to discontinue the euthanasia programme. However, the Reich Chancellery and T4 supremos had no intention that the programme should cease permanently. In fact, 'mercy killing' continued on a smaller scale, using other methods to kill. Once the war was over, the intention was to restart the programme. With this in mind, it was decided to keep a nucleus of the T4 personnel together. Bouhler ordered Brack to transfer a large contingent to Lublin, under the authority of SS-Brigadeführer Globocnik. Brack states, unbelievably, that he found out at the end of 1942 or the beginning of 1943 that his men were used in the mass extermination of the Jews, a fact, he suggested, which was already common knowledge in senior party circles.

Brack insisted under examination by his own counsel that neither he nor Bouhler had any idea what Globocnik needed the T4 personnel for. He suggested that Globocnik only took Bouhler into his confidence at his second request for increased staff. According to Brack, Bouhler then protested that his T4 men were being utilised for 'such an inconceivable assignment'. He considered that it would make them unsuitable for use in further mercy killing. Brack was hanged at Landsberg Prison on 2 June 1948. Bouhler had already killed himself with an ampoule of cyanide on 19 May 1945.

Dr Hans Frank was convicted by the International Military Tribunal at Nuremberg and was hanged on 16 October 1946. If Himmler had his way, his executioner would have been wearing SS uniform and the execution would have occurred years earlier. Himmler knew that Frank was entirely corrupt and used his position for personal gain. He was astute enough to know that Frank had Hitler's support and gratitude for his role as the Party lawyer during its early years. Himmler's dossier on Frank was bursting with incriminating evidence of corruption and black marketeering. His illegal dealings were not restricted to himself. Even Frank's sister had negotiated with Jews from the ghetto in Krakow for the purchase of black market goods. Frank's HQ, the Wawel Castle in Krakow, was stuffed with furniture, carpets, tapestries, and ornaments obtained in the ghetto at knock-down prices. One of Frank's closest allies, Governor Karl Lasch, was arrested in January 1942 for corruption. Despite attempts by Frank to save his friend, he was executed on 1 June 1942 in Auschwitz. The Governor General was a different matter, and Himmler knew it.

At Frank's trial, former State Secretary in the General Government Dr Josef Bühler was called as a defence witness for the former Governor General. He was later to hang on the scaffold in Montelupich Prison in Krakow on 22 August 1948. At Nuremberg on 23 April 1946, his evasive answers under cross-examination by Soviet Chief Counsellor of Justice L. N. Smirnov produced some interesting testimony. Frank was represented by Dr Alfred Seidl, who also represented defendant Rudolf Hess:

Dr Seidl: Is it correct that the Governor General, because of this arbitrary resettlement policy, repeatedly had serious arguments with Himmler, Krüger, and SS-Gruppenführer Globocnik?
Bühler: That is correct. The intention of preventing such resettlements always led to arguments and friction between the Higher SS and Police Leader and the Governor General.
Bühler: During the years 1940 and 1941, incredible numbers of people, mostly Jews, were brought into the Government General in spite of the objections and protests of the Governor General and his administration. This completely unexpected, unprepared for, and undesired bringing in of the Jewish population from other territories, put the administration of the Government General in an extremely difficult position.
Bühler: [On 20 January 1942, at the Wannsee Conference] … Because of the special problems of the Government General, I had asked Heydrich for a personal interview and he received me. On that occasion, among many other things, I described in particular the catastrophic conditions which had resulted from the arbitrary bringing of Jews into the Government General. He replied that for this very reason he had invited the Governor General to the conference. The Reichsführer-SS, so he said, had received an order from the Führer to round up all the Jews of Europe and to settle them in the north-east of Europe, in Russia.… Heydrich said furthermore that the Führer had given an order that Theresienstadt, a town in the Protectorate, would become a reservation in which old and sick Jews, and weak Jews who could not stand the strains of resettlement, were to be accommodated in the future.
Bühler: The publications in the press during the summer of 1944 called my attention to the Majdanek camp for the first time. I did not know that this camp, not far from Lublin, was a concentration camp. It had been installed as an economic establishment of the Reichsführer-SS, in 1941 I think. Governor Zörner came to visit me at that time and he told me that he had objected to the establishment of this camp when he talked to Globocnik, as it would endanger the power supply of the city of Lublin; and there were objections, too, on the part of the Police with regard to the danger of epidemics. I informed the Governor General of this and he in turn sent for Globocnik. Globocnik stated to the Governor General that certain workshops for the needs of the Waffen-SS at the front had been erected on that site by him. He mentioned workshops for dressing furs but he also mentioned a timber yard which was located there.
In these workshops for dressing furs, as I heard, fur articles from the collection of furs were altered for use at the front. At any rate, Globocnik stated that he had installed these workshops in compliance with Himmler's command.

The Governor General prohibited the erection of any further installations until all questions were settled with the police in charge of building, and blueprints had been submitted to the state offices; in other words, until all rules had been complied with, which apply to the construction of buildings. Globocnik never submitted these blueprints.

Smirnov: Mr President, have I your permission to submit a document handed to us by the American Prosecution, Document Number 2819-PS? It is a directive issued by the Administration of the Economic Department of the Government General and addressed to the Governors of Warsaw, Radom, Lublin, and Galicia. May I submit this document?…

I quote the following from the text of this document:

> Subject: Transfer of Jewish movable property from the SS to the Government. I inform you herewith that on 21 February 1944, in the presence of various departmental directors, an agreement was reached by State Secretary Dr Bühler and the Higher SS and Police Leader, Obergruppenführer Koppe, that movable Jewish property, insofar as it is, or will be in the future, in storehouses, will be placed at the disposal of the Government by the SS. In execution of the agreement arrived at, I have ordered that the taking over of the goods stored in the various SS depots shall take place in the shortest possible time. Goods deriving from confiscation and safeguarding have likewise been turned over to me by the commander of the Security Police and the Security Service. Please get in touch with the local SS and Police Leader in order to come to an understanding …

Smirnov: In any case, the property of Jews murdered in the concentration camps of Poland was, as a result of your negotiations, transferred to warehouses in the Government General?

Bühler: That is not correct.

Smirnov: I ask you this: In 1944 when the machines of destruction were working at top speed at Auschwitz and Majdanek, what depots or warehouses existed for the storage of Jewish movable property, besides those which stored the movable property of Jews executed in concentration camps? Do you know of any other warehouses and where they were located?

Bühler: The Jews were deprived of their property on the spot.

Smirnov: I would draw your attention to the date—21 February 1944. At that time were there any Jews still alive in Poland, or were the Jewish ghettos already quite empty?

Bühler: The Jewish ghettos were empty, but there were still some Jews; I know that because they were being used in one way or another in the armament industry. Jewish property could not have been removed from the territory, it must have been somewhere in the Government General, very probably near the ghettos or wherever else the evacuation of Jews took place.

Smirnov: Then the Jewish ghettos were already empty. In that case, what happened to the Jews from Poland?

> Bühler: When these Jewish ghettos were emptied, I assumed they were resettled in the north-east of Europe. The chief of the RSHA had definitely told me at the conference in February 1942 [sic.] that this was the intention.[44]

The enormity of the crimes committed during Aktion Reinhardt has only recently begun to attract similar recognition as those committed at the more familiar Auschwitz complex in Silesia. The exact figure will never be known, but the estimate of the US Holocaust Memorial Museum puts the death toll at Auschwitz between the years 1940 and 1945 at 1,082,000. That is 83 per cent of the total number of prisoners sent to Auschwitz. The accepted figure of Aktion Reinhardt camps exceeds this number by far. The numbers provided by SS-Sturmbannführer Hermann Höfle in his telegraph message intercepted by Bletchley Park, provides the running total of 1,274,166, up until 31 December 1942. While it must be accepted that the numbers in the Höfle Telegram are based on those people sent to the four camps of Reinhardt, the overwhelming majority were gassed immediately upon arrival, or within hours of arrival. The figure does not include those murdered in 1943. Unlike Bełżec, Sobibor, and Treblinka, not all arrivals at Majdanek (Lublin) were murdered on arrival. A great number were admitted to the camp. However, it is known that a minimum of 78,000 prisoners lost their lives at Majdanek. Taking these into account, it is easy to arrive at the now accepted estimate of 1,467,228 deaths in camps created by, and to a large extent administered by, Odilo Globocnik.

On 18 January 1943, Heinrich Himmler tasked Dr Richard Korherr, the head of the SS statistics office, to produce a report on the progress of the solution of the Jewish problem in Europe. The resultant sixteen-page report was submitted to the office of Dr Rudolf Brandt on 23 March 1943. The satisfied Reichsführer came to the decision that the report should remain under wraps, but requested that Korherr submit a summarised version for presentation to Hitler. On 19 April 1943, Korherr submitted this version of six and a half pages, which was extended to include the three months period to 31 March 1943. The original report confirmed the figure of 1,274,166 Jews, quoted in Höfle's telegram, in section V of the report, entitled 'The Evacuation of the Jews'. That section is reproduced here:

> The evacuation of the Jews replaced the emigration of the Jews, at least on the territory of the Reich. It was extensively prepared since the prohibition of Jewish emigration in the autumn of 1941 and to a large extent carried out throughout the Reich territory in the year 1942. In the balance of Jewry it is referred to as 'off-going'.
>
> Until 1.1.1943, according to the records of the Reichssicherheitshauptamt, the following numbers went off:

From the Old Reich with Sudetenland 100,516 Jews
From the Ostmark 47,555 Jews
From the Protectorate 69,677 Jews
Sum 217,748 Jews

In these numbers the Jews evacuated to the old-age ghetto Theresienstadt are also included.

All evacuations on the territory of the Reich and including the eastern territories and further in the German area of power and influence in Europe from October 1939 or later until 31.12.1942 resulted in the following numbers:

1. Evacuation of Jews from Baden and the Palatinate to France … 6,504 Jews
2. Evacuation of Jews from the Reich territory incl. the Protectorate and Bialystok district to the East … 170,642 Jews
3. Evacuation of Jews from the Reich area and the Protectorate to Theresienstadt … 87,193 Jews
4. Transportation of Jews from the eastern provinces to the Russian East: … 1,449,692 Jews.

   The following numbers were sifted through the camps in the Generalgouvernement … 1,274,166 Jews through the camps in the Warthegau … 145,301 Jews
5. Evacuation from other countries, namely:
   France (insofar as occupied before 10.11.1942) … 41,911 Jews
   Netherlands … 38,571 Jews
   Belgium … 16,886 Jews
   Norway … 532 Jews
   Slovakia … 56,691 Jews
   Croatia … 4,927 Jews

------------------------------

Evacuations total (incl. Theresienstadt and incl. special treatment) … 1,873,549 Jews
w/o Theresienstadt … 1,786,356 Jews

6. In addition, according to data from the Reichssicherheitshauptamt there is the evacuation of … 633,300 Jews in the Russian territories incl. the former Baltic countries since the beginning of the Eastern Campaign.

The above numbers do not include the inmates of ghettoes and concentration camps.

The evacuations from Slovakia and Croatia were carried out by these states themselves.[45]

In recent years, archeological investigations have been carried out at all three extermination centre sites in the former General Government, Poland. Chełmno has also had similar examinations. Evidence of not only former wartime structures have been uncovered, in addition to interesting discoveries at the locations of former burial pits, but the results of those surveys are not within the scope of a biography of Odilo Globocnik, and they must be reserved for another day and another project.

What of Odilo Globocnik himself? How are we to judge the man who altered the lives of hundreds of thousands of innocent people. Not only will he be remembered as one of the most prolific of mass killers, but his name should also be associated with the Nazi attempt at demographic realignment to satisfy Hitler's dream of Lebensraum for the Germanic people. The author Joseph Poprzeczny puts it rather succinctly and correctly as 'the final solution of the Slavic question'. The enforced upheaval of whole Polish villages, the resettlement, and in many cases, the murder of their inhabitants is often overshadowed by Globocnik's executive role in the physical destruction of Polish Jews and the subsequent plunder of their assets.

He was an amiable character to many. Those he liked, he kept close and made sure they were comfortable. He turned a blind eye to those in his inner circle who benefited from shady dealings and the black market. He obtained the best quality clothing, textiles, and furniture from Lodz, the site of the massive ghetto; all at ridiculously low prices and obviously via the black market. Such illegal dealings were considered permissible in these circumstances. Others caught supporting such trading unknown to him paid the ultimate penalty. He made gifts of carpets, curtains, boots, leather coats, and furs to high-profile NSDAP guests and senior officials. Good wine, spirits, hams, butter, real coffee, and other fine foodstuffs found their way into the homes and offices of anyone who could be of benefit to his career and schemes. Various Reich ministers received gifts of exquisite quality from the SS man in Lublin. All obtained on the black market or from the proceeds of Aktion Reinhardt.

When Irmgard Rickheim left Lublin for Berlin, Globocnik's batman, Willy Natke, stated that around fifteen large boxes containing food, clothing and various valuables were loaded onto a truck bound for Berlin. According to Natke, a new apartment was fully furnished for her with fine quality furniture and fittings.

Max Cichotzski, Globocnik's adjutant from the Hitler Youth, revealed that sacks of money were stored in Globocnik's basement. From this private vault, Cichotzski and Globocnik both financed their personal expenses. It was this cash that Globocnik used to purchase goods on the Lodz black market. Cichotzski furnished a three-room apartment for Frau Radischat, with the knowledge of his boss. Fine-quality crystal and silver was evident in the flat. After Cichotzski's alleged relationship with Frau Radischat was ended following an intervention by the local BDM leader, Fräulein Hamacher, Globocnik ordered that the fixtures and fittings in the apartment should remain with Frau Radischat. When Cichotzski finally got married, he received the use of a furnished small villa near Globocnik's home as a wedding gift.

The inner circle members were treated like princes by the king of Lublin. However, no matter how far back their friendship went, if one fell out of favour with Globocnik, it was the end of the line. Paul Gasser, Sepp Nemec, and Hans Maubach all fell foul of Globocnik's easily changed opinion. In particular, Nemec and Maubach had benefited financially from their positions, so when the time came to depart, it must have been a major wrench. Even a number of the women in Globocnik's life suffered similar fates. Globocnik was renowned for bedding girls from the secretarial pool. Each one probably thought that they were 'the chosen one'. Irmgard Rickheim was the love of his life, but she was shown the door when it became obvious that Himmler did not approve. Marianne Hillmann, reputed to have Jewish ancestry, was ejected unceremoniously when her time was up. Mimi Trsek was dropped for upsetting her boss in mysterious circumstances.

Globocnik was plainly fickle. Friedl Rau, a member of Globocnik's staff in Lublin, commented that his boss was a bad character with poor vocabulary. He was easy to influence and was a bad judge of character. Always willing to listen to informants, Globocnik had difficulty filtering the information in his own mind. In his financial dealings, Rau described him as a 'fly-by-night'—not a businessman, despite the various enterprises in which he became embroiled.[46]

The spectre of advancing years dulls the enthusiasm to seek justice—some might say revenge—for the lives lost in order to serve the policies of a few megalomaniacs. Most recently, a statement was issued by the Szczecin branch head of the Commission for Investigation of Crimes Committed Against the Polish Nation, entitled 'Discontinuance of the investigation regarding the Nazi crimes in the euthanasia center in the Hartheim Castle'. It was dated 2 December 2009:

> Branch Commission for the Prosecution of Crimes against the Polish Nation in Szczecin announces that due to the decision of 2 December 2009, the investigation S 55/05/Zn has been discontinued. The investigation concerns the crimes carried out by officers of the Nazi Third Reich in the euthanasia centre located in Castle Hartheim, in Alkoven near Linz, Austria. There, from 2 April 1940 until mid-December 1944, no less than 1,143 Polish citizens were killed in a gas chamber.
>
> This is an offence under Article 1, subsection 1, of the Decree of 31 August 1944, on the punishment of Fascist and Nazi war criminals guilty of murdering and abusing civilians and prisoners-of-war. In accordance with the Article 3 of the Act of 18 December 1998, on the Institute of National Remembrance, the proceedings were discontinued against Adolf Hitler, Heinrich Himmler, Philip Bouhler, Leonardo Conti,

Rudolf Lonauer, Georg Renno, Christian Wirth, Franz Stangl, Franz Reichleitner, Gustav Wagner, Kurt Bolender, Hubert Gomerski, Josef Vallaster, Josef Grömer, Anton Streitwieser—on the basis of Article 17 § 1 point 5, due to the death of offenders. Against Karl Brandt, Victor Brack, Anna Griessenberger (Aichinger), Maria Hammelsböck (Auer), Hermina Gruber, Maria Raab (Draxler), Maria Witmann, Margaret Haider, Maria Brandstätter, Helena Hintersteiner, Franc Hödl and Herman Merta, Vincenzo Nohel, Karl Schulz, Erich Wasicky, Gerhard Bohne, Hans Bodo Gorgass, and Albert Widmann, the investigation has been discontinued on the basis of Article 17 § 1 point 7, due to the fact that the criminal proceedings against the perpetrators have been validly terminated. With regards to Stefan Schachermayer, Heinrich Barbel, Karl Schiffner, Franz Peterseil, Johann Anziger, Hans Lenz, Marianne Lenz, Rosa Haas, and Annelies Gindl, the investigation has been discontinued on the basis of the Article 17 § 1 point 1, due to the absence of sufficient data on committing the offence by the aforementioned defendants.

As a result of an extensive investigation proceedings, domestic as well as international, supported by the historical divisions of the Institute, it has been established that 1,143 Polish citizens had been killed at the Third Reich euthanasia centre in the Hartheim Castle. The fate of several victims has been documented during the process. The conducted proceedings also enabled the process of verifying false information provided by the authorities of the Third Reich on the victims' place and cause of death.

During the investigation, the centre's personnel, individual responsibilities, as well as the identities of other people responsible for the murders, especially from the administration of concentration camps at Mauthausen and Dachau-Gusen have been established.

In the course of the investigation rich process and historical material has been collected. It concerns the organization, implementation and the conduct of criminal plans regarding the murders—Aktion T4 and Aktion 14f13, Aktion H-13. The material reveals details of the centre's activities, its scope, and the course of execution. The collected information also contains data on the pending criminal prosecutions against Nazi criminals responsible for the crime in question and their fate after the war, as well as the activities of the Austrian resistance movement in Hartheim.[47]

Post-war conspiracy theories abound. The majority are centred on precious metals and gemstones stolen from the unfortunate victims of the gas. It is true that valuables were regularly discovered secreted into the clothing and even body orifices of those who died at the terminal stations of Aktion Reinhardt. It is also widely accepted that gold fillings and dental work were removed from cadavers. Often overlooked are the vast returns gained from recycled textiles and leather. The more prosperous of Jewish and gentile victims also had other posessions, such as farm machinery, sewing machines, artwork, etc. Everything had value, but it was the treasure hunters who followed the Globocnik trail in the hope of discovering the hidden location of the Globocnik horde.

To many, the Globocnik convoy that decamped from Trieste in a northerly direction must have carried riches accumulated by the arch-thief for a comfortable post-war existence. Despite this assumption, Peter Globocnik declared quite sincerely that he never witnessed any extravagance exhibited by his mother in the years immediately following her release from internment at Wolfsburg. Lore Globocnik died in 1974, having lived a frugal life and steadfastly refusing to agree or co-operate with any notion of exhuming her late husband's body at Patendorf. Amateur divers have even surveyed the lake bottom in the area of the Hotel Enzian at Neusach.

Inconsistencies in witness statements concerning Aktion Reinhardt, Globocnik's final movements, and his death all add fuel to the fire. Journalist Gita Sereny in her article for the *Independent on Sunday* in 1992 even declared that Lore Globocnik was half Jewish. This would mean that one of her parents was a full Jew. Having researched her lineage, I can confirm that this rumour has no substance. Sereny did not go into details because there was none. Despite clear and readily available evidence to the contrary, the rumour persists and is repeated by respected journalists, even in Slovenia. One even erroneously suggests that Globocnik invented the gas chamber. The slightest lapse can be misconstrued and used to inflame doubt. Such is the case where a witness stated that tanks were used to drive repeatedly over Globocnik's grave in order to disguise its precise location. It was correctly pointed out that the 4th Hussars had no tanks stationed at Paternion. However, they did have tracked armoured personnel carriers, which could easily have been described as armoured vehicles. There was even a suggestion that a double was used in order to facilitate the British using Globocnik for anti-Soviet purposes and even that he had bought his escape with his ill-gotten loot. Kenneth Hedley stated post-war that he had stood astride Globocnik's body and photographed his features close-up for identification purposes. This image has mysteriously disappeared, contributing to more speculation.

Ernst Lerch gave evidence post-war that he had seen Globocnik bite down on the cyanide capsule from his cell window in the lock-up at Paternion. He even added that he watched as Globocnik turned blue before expiring in front of his very eyes. Some feat indeed, as no cell window overlooked the track upon which Globocnik breathed his last.

Small wonder there are so many conspiracies when one considers the amount involved in the plunder of victims' assets. Globocnik's submitted final audit of the Aktion Reinhardt accounts is testament to the vast sums involved, as exhibited by the records (see Appendix III). There are no records of the 'under the counter' transactions and the effects that simply went missing. Globocnik's private lifestyle certainly benefitted from his positions. What is also not recorded is the abject misery inflicted upon thousands of innocent lives as a result of Odilo Globocnik's policies and actions, regardless of the motives. Posterity is left with the conclusion that the man, born to Austro-Hungarian parents on the Adriatic coast, conducted his life generated by ambition and the need to please a few men he revered. In order to do so, he was prepared to bend and break rules of humanity. For him, a satisfactory outcome far outweighed any notion of benevolence or emotion. Heinrich Himmler recognised in Globocnik a man upon whom he could rely to complete his task, regardless of cost or consequence.

*Those who cannot remember the past are condemned to repeat it.*

George Santayana, 1905

## APPENDIX I

# HIMMLER'S POSEN SPEECH

EXTRACT FROM THE speech of Reichsführer-SS Heinrich Himmler before a meeting of SS-Gruppenführer and SS-Obergruppenführer in the Golden Hall of the City Hall in Posen on 4 October 1943 (translation from sound recording).

I want to mention another very difficult matter here before you in all frankness. Among ourselves, it ought to be spoken of quite openly for once; yet we shall never speak of it in public. Just as little as we hesitated to do our duty as ordered on 30 June 1934, and place comrades who had failed against the wall and shoot them, just as little did we ever speak of it, and we shall never speak of it. It was a matter of course, of tact, for us, thank God, never to speak of it, never to talk of it. It made everybody shudder; yet everyone was clear in his mind that he would do it again if ordered to do so, and if it was necessary.

I am thinking now of the evacuation of the Jews, the extirpation of the Jewish people. It is one of those things that's easy to say: 'The Jewish people will be extirpated,' says every Party comrade, 'that's quite clear, it's in our program: elimination of the Jews, extirpation; that's what we're doing.' And then they all come along, these 80 million good Germans, and every one of them has his decent Jew. Of course, it's quite clear that the others are pigs, but this one is one first-class Jew. Of all those who speak this way, not one has looked on; not one has lived through it. Most of you know what it means when 100 bodies lie together, when 500 lie there, or if 1,000 lie there. To have gone through this, and at the same time, apart from exceptions caused by human weaknesses, to have remained decent, that has made us hard. This is a chapter of glory in our history which has never been written, and which never shall be written; since we know how hard it would be for us if we still had the Jews, as secret saboteurs, agitators, and slander-mongers, among us now, in every city—during the bombing raids, with the suffering and deprivations of the war. We would probably already be in the same situation as in 1916/17 if we still had the Jews in the body of the German people.

The riches they had, we've taken away from them. I have given a strict order, which SS-Obergruppenführer Pohl has carried out, that these riches shall, of course, be diverted to the Reich without exception. We have taken none of it. Individuals who failed were punished according to an order given by me at the beginning, which threatened: he who takes even one mark of it, that's his death. A number of SS men—not very many—have violated that order, and that will be their death, without mercy. We had the moral right, we had the duty to our own people, to kill this people which wanted to kill us. But we don't have the right to enrich ourselves even with one fur, one watch, one mark, one cigarette, or anything else. Just because we eradicated a bacillus, after all, doesn't mean we want to be infected by the bacillus and die. I will never permit even one little spot of corruption to arise or become established here. Wherever it may form, we shall burn it out together. In general, however, we can say that we have carried out this most difficult task out of love for our own people. And we have suffered no harm to our inner self, our soul, our character in so doing.

I will never see it happen, that even one bit of putrefaction comes in contact with us, or takes root in us. On the contrary, where it might try to take root, we will burn it out together. But altogether we can say: We have carried out this most difficult task for the love of our people. And we have taken on no defect within us, in our soul, or in our character…

# APPENDIX II

# THE STROOP REPORT

The destruction of the Jewish Ghetto in Warsaw in May 1943 was one of the major final acts of Aktion Reinhardt. It not only involved some of the staff from Reinhardt, but also a contingent of Trawniki men. The Stroop Report and daily situation reports provide the most comprehensive illustration of what was involved in the clearing of a ghetto. Although lengthy, they are reproduced here in almost their entirety to convey the Aktion as it occurred.

*The Stroop Report* (Pantheon Books 1979) and *Nazi Conspiracy and Aggression Volume 3 Translation of Nuremberg Document No. 1061-PS*

**THE JEWISH QUARTER OF WARSAW IS NO MORE!**

For the Führer and the Fatherland

The following fell in the battle for the destruction of Jews and bandits in the former Jewish Quarter of Warsaw: [There follows fifteen names.]

Furthermore, the Polish Police Sergeant Julian Zielinski, born 13 November 1891, 8th Commissariat * * * fell on 19 April I 1943 while fulfilling his duty. * * * They gave their utmost, their life. We shall never forget them. The following were wounded: [there follows the names of sixty Waffen-SS personnel, eleven guards from Training Camps, probably Lithuanians (to judge by their names), twelve Security Police Officers in SS Units, five men of the Polish Police, and two regular Army personnel engineers.]

| Units used in the action | Average number of personnel used per day |
|---|---|
| **SS Staff & Police Leader** | 6/5 |
| **Waffen-SS:** | |
| SS Panzer Grenadier Training and Reserve Battalion 3, Warsaw | 4/440 |
| SS Cav. Training and Res Bat. Warsaw | 5/381 |
| **Police:** | |
| SS Police Regiment 22/I. Bat. | 3/94 |
| III. Bat. | 3/134 |
| Engineering Emergency Service | 1/6 |
| Polish Police | 4/363 |
| Polish Fire Brigade | 166 |
| **Security Police:** | |
| Wehrmacht | |
| Light AA Alarm Battery III/8 Warsaw | 2/22 |
| Engineers Det. of Railway Armoured Trains Res. flat. Rembertow | 2/42 |
| Res. Eng. 14 Gora-Kalwaria | 1/34 |
| **Foreign Racial Watchmen:** | |
| 1 Bat. "Trawniki" men | 2/335 |
| **Total:** | 36/2054 |

[Translator's note: this obviously means thirty-six officers, 2,054 men.]

## I

The creation of special areas to be inhabited by Jews, and the restriction of the Jews with regard to residence and trading is nothing new in the history of the East. Such measures were first taken far back in the Middle Ages; they could be observed as recently as during the last few centuries. These restrictions were imposed with the intention of protecting the Aryan population against the Jews.

Identical considerations led us as early as February, 1940 to conceive the project of creating a Jewish residential district in Warsaw. The initial intention was to establish as the Ghetto that part of the City of Warsaw which has the Vistula as its Eastern frontier. The particular situation on prevailing in Warsaw seemed at first to frustrate this plan. It was moreover opposed by several authorities particularly by the City Administration. They pointed in particular that disturbances in industry and trade would ensue if a Ghetto were founded in Warsaw, and that it would be impossible to provide the Jews with food if they were assembled in a closed area.

At a conference held in March 1940, it was decided to postpone the plan of creating a Ghetto for the time being, owing to the above objections. At the same time a plan was considered to declare the District of Dublin the collecting area for all Jews within the Government General, especially for the evacuated or fugitive Jews arriving from the Reich. But as early as April 1940, the Higher SS and Police Leader, East, Krakow, issued a declaration that there was no intention of assembling the Jews within the Lublin District. In the meantime, the Jews had increasingly taken to crossing the frontiers without permission and illegally. This noted especially at the limits of the Districts of Lowicz and Skierniewice. Conditions in the town of Lowicz became dangerous from the point of view of hygiene as well as from that of the Security Police, owing to these illegal migrations of Jews. The District President of Lowicz therefore, began to install Ghettos in his district in order to avoid these dangers.

The experiences in the district of Lowicz, after Ghettos had been installed, showed that this method is the only one suitable for dispelling the dangers which emanate repeatedly from the Jews.

The necessity of erecting a Ghetto in the City of Warsaw as well became more and more urgent in the summer of 1940, since more and more troops were being assembled in the district of Warsaw after termination of the French campaign. At that time, the Department for Hygiene urged the speedy erection of a Ghetto in the interest of preserving the health of the German Forces and of the native population as well. The original plan of establishing the Ghetto in the suburb of Praga as intended in February 1940, would have taken at least 4 to 5 months, since almost 600,000 persons had to be moved. But since experience showed that greater outbreaks of epidemics might be expected in the winter months and since for this reason the District Medical Officer urged that the resettling action ought to be completed by 15 November 1940 at the latest, the plan of establishing a suburban ghetto in Praga was dropped; and instead, the area which hitherto had been used as a quarantine area for epidemics was selected for use as a Jewish residential area. In October 1940, the Governor ordered the Commissioner of the District, President for the City of Warsaw, to complete the resettlement necessary for establishing the Ghetto within the City of Warsaw by 15 November 1940.

The Ghetto thus established in Warsaw was inhabited by about 400,000 Jews. It contained 27,000 apartments with an average of 2 1/2 rooms each. It was separated from the rest of the city by partition and other walls and by walling-up of thoroughfares, windows, doors, open spaces, etc.

It was administered by the Jewish Board of Elders, who received their instructions from the Commissioner for the Ghetto, who was immediately subordinated to the Governor. The Jews were granted self-administration in which the German supervising authorities intervened only where German interest were touched. In order to enable the Jewish Board of Elder to execute its orders, a Jewish Police force was set up, identifier by special armbands and a special beret and armed with rubber truncheons. This Jewish Police force was charged with maintaining order and security within the Ghetto and was subordinated to the German and Polish Police.

II

It soon became clear, however, that not all dangers had been removed by this confining the Jews to one place. Security considerations required removing the Jews from the city of Warsaw altogether. The first large resettlement action took place in the period from 22 July to 3 October 1942. In this action 310,322 Jews were removed. In January 1943, a second resettlement action was carried out by which altogether 6,500 Jews were affected.

When the Reichsführer-SS visited Warsaw in January 1943 he ordered the SS and Police Leader for the District of Warsaw to transfer to Lublin the armament factories and other enterprises of military importance which were installed within the Ghetto including their personnel and machines. The execution of this transfer order proved to be very difficult, since the managers as well as the Jews resisted in every possible way. The SS and Police Leader thereupon decided to enforce the transfer of the enterprises in a large-scale action which he intended to carry out in three days. The necessary preparations had been taken by my predecessor, who also had given the order to start the large-scale action. I myself arrived in Warsaw on 17 April 1943 and took over the command of the action on 19 April 1943, 0800 hours, the action itself having started the same day at 0600 hours.

Before the large-scale action began, the limits of the former Ghetto had been blocked by an external barricade in order to prevent the Jews from breaking out. This barricade was maintained from the start to the end of the action and was especially reinforced at night.

When we invaded the Ghetto for the first time, the Jews and the Polish bandits succeeded in repelling the participating units, including tanks and armoured cars, by a well-prepared concentration of fire. When I ordered a second attack, about 0800 hours, I distributed the units, separated from each other by indicated lines, and charged them with combing out the whole of the Ghetto, each unit for a certain part. Although firing commenced again, we now succeeded in combing out the blocks according to plan. The enemy was forced to retire from the roofs and elevated bases to the basements, dug-outs, and sewers. In order to prevent their escaping into the sewers, the sewerage system was dammed up below the Ghetto and filled with water, but the Jews frustrated this plan to a great extent by blowing up the turning off valves. Late the first day we encountered rather heavy resistance, but it was quickly broken by a special raiding party. In the course of further operations, we succeeded in expelling the Jews from their prepared resistance bases, sniper holes, and the like, and in occupying during the 20 and 21 April the greater part of the so-called remainder of the Ghetto to such a degree that the resistance continued within these blocks could no longer be called considerable.

The main Jewish battle group, mixed with Polish bandits, had already retired during the first and second day to the so-called Muranowski Square. There, it was reinforced by a considerable number of Polish bandits. Its plan was to hold the Ghetto by every means in order to prevent us from invading it. The Jewish and Polish standards were hoisted at the top of a concrete building as a challenge to us. These two standards, however, were captured on the second day of the action by a special raiding party. SS-Untersturmführer Dehmke fell in this skirmish with the bandits; he was holding in his hand a hand-grenade which was hit by the enemy and exploded, injuring him fatally. After only a few days I realized that the original plan had no prospect of success, unless the armament factories and other enterprises of military importance distributed throughout the Ghetto were dissolved. It was therefore necessary to approach these firms and to give them appropriate time for being evacuated and immediately transferred. Thus, one of these firms after the other was dealt with, and we very soon deprived the Jews and bandits of their chance to take refuge time and again in these enterprises, which were under the supervision of the Armed Forces. In order to decide how much time was necessary to evacuate these enterprises thorough inspections were necessary. The conditions discovered there are indescribable. I cannot imagine a greater chaos than in the Ghetto of Warsaw. The Jews had control of everything, from the chemical substances used in manufacturing explosives to clothing and equipment for the Armed Forces. The managers knew so little of their own shops that the Jews were in a position to produce inside these shops arms of every kind, especially hand grenades, Molotov cocktails, and the like.

Moreover, the Jews had succeeded in fortifying some of these factories as centres of resistance. Such a centre of resistance in an Army accommodation office had to be attacked as early as the second day of the action by an Engineer's Unit equipped with flame throwers and by artillery. The Jews were so firmly established in this shop that it proved to be impossible to induce them to leave it voluntarily; I therefore resolved to destroy this shop the next day by fire.

The managers of these enterprises, which were generally also supervised by an officer of the Armed Forces, could in most cases make no specified statements on their stocks and the whereabouts of these stocks. The statements which they made on the number of Jews employed by them were in every case incorrect. Over and over again we discovered that these labyrinths of edifices belonging to the armament concerns as residential blocks, contained rich Jews who had succeeded in finding accommodations for themselves and their families under the name of 'armament workers' and were leading marvellous lives there. Despite all our orders to the managers to make the Jews leave those enterprises, we found out in several cases that managers simply concealed the Jews by shutting them in, because they expected that the action would be finished within a few days and that they then would be able to continue working with the remaining Jews. According to the statements of arrested Jews, women also seem to have played a prominent part. The Jews are said to have endeavoured to keep up good relations with officers and men of the armed forces. Carousing is said to have been frequent, during the course of which business deals are said to have been concluded between Jews and Germans.

The number of Jews forcibly taken out of the buildings and arrested was relatively small during the first few days. It transpired that the Jews had taken to hiding in the sewers and in specially erected dug-outs. Whereas we had assumed during the first days that there were only scattered dug-outs, we learned in the course of the large-scale action that the whole Ghetto was systematically equipped with cellars, dug-outs, and passages. In every case these passages and dug-outs were connected with the sewer system. Thus, the Jews were able to maintain undisturbed subterranean traffic. They also used this sewer network for escaping subterraneously into the Aryan part of the city of Warsaw. Continuously, we received reports of attempts of Jews to escape through the sewer holes. While pretending to build air raid shelters they had been erecting dug-outs within the former Ghetto ever since the autumn of 1942. These were intended to conceal every Jew during the new evacuation action, which they had expected for quite a time, and to enable them to resist the invaders in a concerted action. Through posters, handbills, and whisper propaganda, the communistic resistance movement actually brought it about that the Jews entered the dug-outs as soon as the new large-scale operation started. How far their precautions went can be seen from the fact that many of the dug-outs had been skilfully equipped with furnishings sufficient for entire families, washing and bathing facilities, toilets, arms and munition supplies, and food supplies sufficient for several months. There were differently equipped dug-outs for rich and for poor Jews. To discover the individual dug-outs was difficult for the units, as they had been efficiently camouflaged. In many cases, it was possible only through betrayal on the part of the Jews.

When only a few days had passed, it became apparent that the Jews no longer had any intention to resettle voluntarily, but were determined to resist evacuation with all their force and by using all the weapons at their disposal. So-called battle groups had been formed, led by Polish-Bolshevists; they were armed and paid any price asked for available arms.

During the large-scale action, we succeeded in catching some Jews who had already been evacuated and resettled in Lublin or Treblinka, but had broken out from there and returned to the Ghetto, equipped with arms and ammunition. Time and again Polish bandits found refuge in the Ghetto and remained there undisturbed, since we had no forces at our disposal to comb out this maze. Whereas it had been possible during the first days to catch considerable numbers of Jews, who are cowards by nature, it became more and more difficult during the second half of the action to capture the bandits and Jews. Over and over again new battle groups consisting of 20 to 30 or more Jewish fellows, 18 to 25 years of age, accompanied by a corresponding number of women kindled new resistance. These battle groups were under orders to put up armed resistance to the last and if necessary to escape arrest by committing suicide. One such battle group succeeded in mounting a truck by ascending from a sewer in the so-called Prosta, and in escaping with it (about 30 to 35 bandits). One bandit who had arrived with this truck exploded 2 hand grenades, which was the agreed signal for the bandits waiting in the sewer to climb out of it. The bandits and Jews-there were Polish bandits among these gangs armed with carbines, small arms, and in one case a light machine gun, mounted the truck and drove away in an unknown direction. The last member of this gang, who was on guard in the sewer and was detailed to close the lid of the sewer hole, was captured. It was he who gave the above information. The search for the truck was unfortunately without result.

During this armed resistance, the women belonging to the battle groups were equipped the same as the men; some were members of the Chaluzim movement. Not infrequently, these women fired pistols with both hands. It happened time and again that these women had pistols or hand grenades (Polish 'pineapple' hand grenades) concealed in their bloomers up to the last moment to use against the men of the Waffen-SS, Police, or Wehrmacht.

The resistance put up by the Jews and bandits could be broken only by relentlessly using all our force and energy by day and night. On 23 April 1918, the Reichsführer-SS issued through the higher SS and Police Führer East at Krakow his order to complete the combing out of the Warsaw Ghetto with the greatest severity and relentless tenacity. I therefore decided to destroy the entire Jewish residential area by setting every block on fire, including the blocks of residential buildings near the armament works. One concern after the other was systematically evacuated and subsequently destroyed by fire. The Jews then emerged from their hiding places and dug-outs in almost every case. Not infrequently, the Jews stayed in the burning buildings until, because of the heat and the fear of being burned alive they preferred to jump down from the upper stories after having thrown mattresses and other upholstered articles into the street from the burning buildings. With their bones broken, they still tried to crawl across the street into blocks of buildings which had not yet been set on fire or were only partly in flames. Often Jews changed their hiding places during the night, by moving into the ruins of burnt-out buildings, taking refuge there until they were found by our patrols. Their stay in the sewers also ceased to be pleasant after the first week. Frequently from the street, we could hear loud voices coming through the sewer shafts. Then the men of the Waffen-SS, the Police or the Wehrmacht Engineers courageously climbed down the shafts to bring out the Jews and not infrequently they then stumbled over Jews already dead, or were shot at. It was always necessary to use smoke candles to drive out the Jews. Thus, one day we opened 183 sewer entrance holes and at a fixed time lowered smoke candles into them, with the result that the bandits fled from what they believed to be gas to the centre of the former Ghetto, where they could then be pulled out of the sewer holes there. A great number of Jews, who could not be counted, were exterminated by blowing up sewers and dug-outs

The longer the resistance lasted, the tougher the men of the Waffen-SS, Police, and Wehrmacht became; they fulfilled their duty indefatigably in faithful comradeship and stood together as models and examples of soldiers. Their duty hours often lasted from early morning until late at night. At night, search patrols with rags wound round their feet remained at the heels of the Jews and gave them no respite. Not infrequently they caught and killed Jews who used the night hours for supplementing their stores from abandoned dug-outs and for contacting neighbouring groups or exchanging news with them.

Considering that the greater part of the men of the Waffen-SS had only been trained for three to four weeks before being assigned to this action, high credit should be given for the pluck, courage, and devotion to duty which they showed. It must be stated that the Wehrmacht Engineers, too, executed the blowing up of dug-outs, sewers, and concrete buildings with indefatigability and great devotion to duty. Officers and men of the Police, a large part of whom had already been at the front, again excelled by their dashing spirit.

Only through the continuous and untiring work of all involved did we succeed in catching a total of 56,065 Jews whose extermination can be proved. To this should be added the number of Jews who lost their lives in explosions or fires but whose numbers could not be ascertained.

During the large-scale operation, the Aryan population was informed by posters that it was strictly forbidden to enter the former Jewish Ghetto and that anybody caught within the former Ghetto without valid pass would be shot. At the same time these posters informed the Aryan population again that the death penalty would be imposed on anybody who intentionally gave refuge to a Jew, especially lodged, supported, or concealed a Jew outside the Jewish residential area.

Permission was granted to the Polish police to pay to any Polish policeman who arrested a Jew within the Aryan part of Warsaw one third of the cash in the Jew's possession. This measure has already produced results.

The Polish population for the most part approved the measures taken against the Jews. Shortly before the end of the largescale operation, the Governor issued a special proclamation which he submitted to the undersigned for approval before publication, to the Polish population; in it he informed them of the reasons for destroying the former Jewish Ghetto by mentioning the assassinations carried out lately in the Warsaw area and the mass graves found in Katyn; at the same time, they were asked to assist us in our fight against Communist agents and Jews (see enclosed poster).

The large-scale action was terminated on 16 May 1943 with the blowing up of the Warsaw synagogue at 2015 hours.

Now, there are no more factories in the former Ghetto. All the goods, raw materials, and machines there have been moved and stored somewhere else. All buildings etc., have been destroyed. The only exception is the so-called Dzielna Prison of the Security Police, which was exempted from destruction.

### III

Although the large-scale operation has been completed, we have to reckon with the possibility that a few Jews are still living in the ruins of the former Ghetto; therefore, this area must be firmly shut off from the Aryan residential area and be guarded. Police Battalion III/23 has been charged with this duty. This Police Battalion has instructions to watch the former Ghetto, particularly to prevent anybody from entering the former Ghetto, and to shoot immediately anybody found inside the Ghetto without authority. The Commander of the Police Battalion will continue to receive further direct orders from the SS and Police Führer. In this way, it should be possible to keep the small remainder of Jews there, if any, under constant pressure and to exterminate them eventually. The remaining Jews and bandits must be deprived of any chance of survival by destroying all remaining buildings and refuges and cutting off the water supply.

It is proposed to change the Dzielna Prison into a concentration camp and to use the inmates to remove, collect and hand over for reuse the millions of bricks, the scrap-iron, and other materials.

### IV

Of the total of 56,065 Jews caught, about 7,000 were exterminated within the former Ghetto in the course of the large-scale action, and 6,929 by transporting them to T.II, which means 14,000 Jews were exterminated altogether. Beyond the number of 56,065 Jews an estimated number of 5,000 to 6,000 were killed by explosions or in fires.

The number of destroyed dug-outs amounts to 631.

*Booty:*

Polish rifles, 1 Russian rifle, 1 German rifle, 59 pistols of various calibres
Several hundred hand grenades, including Polish and home-made ones.
Several hundred incendiary bottles
Home-made explosives
Infernal machines with fuses
A large amount of explosives, ammunition for weapons of all calibres, including some machine-gun ammunition.

Regarding the booty of arms, it must be taken into consideration that the arms themselves could in most cases not be captured, as the bandits and Jews would, before being arrested, throw them into hiding places or holes which could not be ascertained or discovered. The smoking out of the dug-out by our men, also often made the search for arms impossible. As the dug-outs had to be blown up at once, a search later on was out of the question.

The captured hand grenades, ammunition, and incendiary bottles were at once re-used by us against the bandits.

*Further booty:*
1,240 used military tunics (part of them with medal ribbons-Iron Cross and East Medal)
600 pairs of used trousers
Other equipment and German steel helmets
108 horses, 4 of them still in the former Ghetto (hearse).

Up to 23 May 1943 we had counted: 4.4 million Zloty; furthermore about 5 to 6 million Zloty not yet counted, a great amount of foreign currency, e.g. $14,300 in paper and $9,200 in gold, moreover valuables (rings, chains, watches, etc.) in great quantities.

State of the Ghetto at the termination of the large-scale operation: Apart from 8 buildings (Police Barracks, hospital, and accommodations for housing working-parties) the former Ghetto is completely destroyed. Only the dividing walls are left standing where no explosions were carried out. But the ruins still contain a vast amount of stones and scrap material which could be used.

Warsaw, 16 May, 1943.
The SS and Police Führer in the District of Warsaw.
[Signed] **Stroop**[1]
SS-Brigadeführer and Major General of Police.

**Daily Reports**

Copy
Warsaw, 20 April 1943.
Journal No. 516/43 secret.
SS Service Teletype message
From: The SS and Police Führer in the District of Warsaw
Ref. No.: I ab/St/Gr-16 07
Re: Ghetto Operation.
To: The Higher SS and Police Führer East, Krakow

Progress of Ghetto Operation on 19 April 1943:

Closing of Ghetto commenced 0300 hours. At 0600 order to Waffen-SS (strength: 16/850) to comb out the remainder of the Ghetto. Hardly had the units fallen in, strong concerted fire-concentration by the Jews and bandits. The tank used in this action and the two heavy armoured cars pelted with Molotov cocktails (incendiary bottles). Tank twice set on fire. Owing to this enemy counterattack, we had at first to take the units back. Losses in first attack: 12 men (6 SS men, 6 Trawniki men). About 800 hours second attack by the units, under the command of the undersigned. Although the counterattack was reported, this time we succeeded in combing out the blocks of buildings according to plan. We caused the enemy to retire from the roofs and elevated prepared positions into the cellars or dug-outs and sewers. During this combing-out we caught only about 200 Jews. Immediately afterwards raiding parties were directed to dug-outs known to us with the order to pull out the Jews and to destroy the dug-outs. About 380 Jews captured. We found out that the Jews had taken to the sewers. Sewers were completely inundated, to make staying there impossible. About 1730 hours we encountered very strong resistance from one block of buildings including machine gun fire. A special raiding party invaded that block and defeated the enemy, but could not catch the resisters. The Jews and criminals resisted from base to base, and escaped at the last moment across lofts or through subterranean passages. About 2030 hours the external barricade was reinforced. All units were withdrawn from the Ghetto and dismissed to their barracks. Reinforcement of the barricade by 250 Waffen-SS men. Continuation of operation on 20 April 1943.

| **Units at my disposal:** | |
|---|---|
| SS-Panzer-Gren. Res. Batl. | 6/400 |
| SS-Cav. Res. Batl. | 10/450 |
| Police | 6/165 |
| Security Service | 2/48 |
| Trawniki men | 1/150 |
| Wehrmacht: | |
| 1 10-cm-Howitzer | 1/7 |
| Flame thrower | 1 |
| Engineers | 2/16 |
| Medical detachments | 1/1 |
| 3 2.28-cm A.A. Guns | 2/24 |
| 1 French tank of the Waffen-SS | |
| 2 heavy armoured cars of the Waffen-SS | |
| Total: | 31/1262 |

I put Major of Police Sternagel in command of today's operations, subject to my further instructions if necessary.

At 0700 hours 9 raiding parties were formed, each 1/36 strong, consisting of mixed units, to comb out and to search the remainder of the Ghetto intensively. This search is still in progress; its first objective will be completed by 1100 hours. In the meantime, it has been ascertained that part of the Ghetto which is no longer inhabited but not yet released and which contains several armament factories and the like, there are several centres of resistance, which were so strong that the tank could not go through. 2 raiding parties defeated these centres of resistance and made a passage for the tank men. In this operation, we already had two wounded (Waffen-SS).

Enemy is much more cautious than yesterday, since he has of course learned of the heavy arms at our disposal.

My intention is first to comb out completely the remainder of the Ghetto and then to clean out in the same manner the so-called uninhabited Ghetto, which so far has not been released. It had been ascertained in the meantime that the latter part of the Ghetto contains at least 10 to 12 dugouts, some of which are even in armament factories. The whole operation is made more difficult because there are still factories in the Ghetto which must be protected against bombardment and fire, because they contain machines and tools.

A further report will follow tonight.

The SS and Police Führer in the District of Warsaw.
Signed: Stroop
SS-Brigadeführer and Major General of Police.
Certified copy:

[Signed] **Jesuiter** SS-Sturmbannführer[2]

Copy
Teletype message
Prom the SS and Police Führer in the District of Warsaw
Warsaw, 20 April 1943.
Ref. No. I ab St/Gr 16 07-Journal No. 517/43 secret.
Re: Ghetto Operation.
To the Higher SS and Police Führer East, SS-Obergruppenführer and General of Police Krüger—or deputy.
Krakow
Supplementing my teletype message of 20 April 1943-Ref. St/Gr 16 07, re Ghetto Operation-I beg to report as follows:

The resistance centres ascertained with the uninhabited but not yet released part of the Ghetto were crushed by a battle group of the Wehrmacht-Engineers and flame throwers. The Wehrmacht had one wounded in this operation, shot through the lungs. Nine raiding parties broke through as far as the northern limit of the Ghetto. 9 dug-outs were found, their inmates crushed when they resisted, and the dug-outs blown up. What losses the enemy suffered cannot be ascertained accurately. Altogether the 9 raiding parties caught 505 Jews today; those among them who are able-bodied were kept ready for transport to Poniatowo. At about 1500 hrs I managed to arrange that the block of buildings occupied by the Army Accommodation Office said to be occupied by 4,000 Jews is to be evacuated at once. The German manager was asked to call upon the Jewish workers to leave the block voluntarily. Only 28 Jews obeyed this order. Thereupon I resolved either to evacuate the block by force or to blow it up. The A.A. Artillery-3 2-cm. guns used for this operation had two men killed. The 10-cm howitzer, which also was used, expelled the gangs from their strong fortifications and also inflicted losses on them, as far as we were able to ascertain. This action had to be broken off owing to the fall of darkness. On 21 April 1943, we shall attack this resistance centre again, as far as possible it will remain blocked off during the night.

In today's action we caught, apart from the Jews reported above, considerable stores of incendiary bottles, hand grenades, ammunition, military tunics, and equipment.

*Losses:*
2 dead (Wehrmacht) 7 wounded (6 Waffen-SS, 1 Trawniki man)

In one case the bandits had laid pressure mines. I have succeeded in causing the firms W.C. Toebens, Schultz and Co., and Hoffman to be ready for evacuation with their entire personnel on 21 April 1943 at 0600 hrs. In this way, I hope to get the way free at last for cleaning out the Ghetto. The Trustees Toebens has pledged himself to induce the Jews, numbering about 4,000 to 5,000, to follow him voluntarily to the assembling point for being resettled. In case this has as little success as was attained in the case of the Army Accommodation Office, I am going to clean out this part of the Ghetto as well by force. I beg to acknowledge receipt of the order which the Obergruppenführer communicated to me by telephone today, and of the powers granted to me.

Next report on 21 April 1943 at noon.
The SS and Police Führer in the
District of Warsaw
Signed: Stroop
SS-Brigadeführer and Major General of Police.
Certified copy:
[Signed] **Jesuiter** SS-Sturmbannführer

Copy
Teletype message
From: The SS and Police Führer in the District of Warsaw
Warsaw, 21 April 1943.
Ref. Nr. I ab/St/Gr-16 07-Journal Nr. 527/43.
Re: Ghetto Operation.
To the Higher SS and Police Führer East,
SS-Obergruppenführer and General of Police, Krüger—or deputy.
Krakow
Progress of Ghetto Operation on 21 April 1943.
Supplementing the report which I made today about 1400 hours by telephone, I beg to report: Forces at my disposal as of 20 April 1943.

Start of operation: 0700 hours. The whole of the Ghetto has continued to be cordoned off since the start of the operations on 19 April 1943.

Inasmuch as the special operation concerning the block of buildings occupied by the Army Accommodation Office had to be interrupted yesterday because of darkness, one battle group reinforced by Engineers and heavy artillery was again sent into the block of buildings, which was found to contain an enormous quantity of dug-outs and subterranean passages firing from time to time. I resolved therefore to blow up these passages which we had discovered and subsequently to set the entire block on fire. Not until the building was well aflame did screaming Jews make their appearance, and they were evacuated at once. We had no losses in this operation. Precautionary measures were taken in order to ensure that the conflagration remained localized.

The main body of our forces was detailed to cleanse the so-called uninhabited, but not yet released, part of the Ghetto by proceeding from South to North. Before we started this action, we caught 5,200 Jews who had been employed in enterprises under the supervision of the Commissioner for Armament [Ru KoBetrieben] and transported them under armed guard to the Railway Station which had been chosen for use in the resettlement. I formed 3 search-parties to which were attached special raiding parties who had the duty to attack or blow up the dug-outs which I severe known to us. This operation had to be interrupted when darkness set in, after one half of the area mentioned had been combed out.

Continued on 22 April 1943, 0700 hours.

Apart from the Jews who were to be evacuated, 150 Jews or bandits were killed in battle and about 80 bandits were killed when their dug-outs were blown up. The enemy today used the same arms as on the previous day, particularly home-made explosives. Samples have been kept by the SS and Police Führer. For the first time, we observed the participation of members of the Jewish Women's Battle Association (Chaluzim Movement). We captured rifles, pistols, hand grenades, explosives, horses, and parts of SS uniforms.

Own losses: 2 policemen, 2 SS men, 1 Trawniki man.
(light wounds)

The SS and Police Führer in the District of Warsaw.
Signed: Stroop
SS-Brigadeführer and Major General of Police.
Certified copy:
**Jesuiter** SS-Sturmbannführer

Copy
Teletype message
From the SS and Police Führer in the District of Warsaw
Warsaw, 22 April 1943.
Ref. No. I ab St/Gr 16 07-Journal Nr. 530/43 secret.
Re: Ghetto Operation. (supplement to par. 1 of letter of 21 April 1943).
To: The Higher SS and Police Führer of Police Krüger—or deputy
Krakow

Our setting the block on fire achieved the result in the course of the night that those Jews whom we had not been able to find despite all our search operations left their hideouts under the roofs, in the cellars, and elsewhere, and appeared at the outside of the buildings, trying to escape the flames. Masses of them—entire families—were already aflame and jumped from the windows or endeavoured to let themselves down by means of sheets tied together or the like. Steps had been taken so that these Jews as well as the remaining ones were liquidated at once. During the whole night, there were shots from buildings which were supposed to be evacuated. We had no losses in our cordoning forces. 5,300 Jews were caught for the evacuation and removed.
The SS and Police Führer in the District of Warsaw.

Signed: Stroop
Certified copy:
**Jesuiter** SS-Sturmbannführer

Copy
Teletype message
From The SS and Police Führer in the District of Warsaw
Warsaw, 22 April 1943.
Ref. Nr. I ab/St/Gr-16 07-Journal Nr. 531/43 secret.
Re: Ghetto Operation.
To: The Higher SS and Police Führer East, SS-Obergruppenführer and General of Police Krüger or deputy.

Krakow

Progress of the Ghetto Operation on 22 April 1943 up to 1200 hours. One raiding party was despatched to invade once more the block of buildings which for the greater part had burned out or was still aflame, in order to catch those Jews who were still inside.

When shooting again started from one block against the men of the Waffen-SS, this block also was set on fire, with the result that a considerable number of bandits were scared from their hideouts and shot while trying to escape. Apart for those, we caught about 180 Jews in the yards of the buildings. The main body of our units continued the cleansing action from the line where we terminated this action yesterday. This operation is still in progress. As on the preceding days local resistance was broken and the dug-outs we discovered were blown up. Unfortunately, there is no way of preventing part of the Jews and bandits from taking refuge in the sewers below the Ghetto, where we can hardly catch them since they have stopped the flooding. The city administration is not in a position to frustrate this nuisance. Neither did the use of smoke candles or the introduction of creosote into the water have the desired result. Co-operation with the Wehrmacht splendid.

The SS and Police Führer in the District of Warsaw.
Signed: Stroop
SS-Brigadeführer and Major General of Police.
Certified copy:
**Jesuiter** SS-Sturmbannführer

Copy
Teletype message
From the SS and Police Führer in the District of Warsaw
Warsaw, 22 April 1943.
Ref. Nr.: ab/St/Gr-16 07-Journal Nr. 532/43 secret.
Re: Ghetto Operation.
The Higher SS and Police Führer East, SS-Obergruppenführer and General of Police Krüger—or deputy.
Krakow

Progress of operation of 22 April 1943. Report on action up to 1200 hours has already been submitted by my message of today. Continuing, I beg to report:

When the special raiding party searched the remainder of the blocks as already reported, they met with resistance at some places; they had the following success: 1,100 Jews caught for evacuation, 203 bandits and Jews killed, 15 dug-outs blown up. They captured 80 incendiary bottles and other booty. Units at my disposal: as reported by teletype message on 20 April 1943. Journal No. 516/43 secret.

*Our losses*: SS-Untersturmführer Dehmke (dead); enemy hit a hand grenade which he carried. (SS-Cav.Res. Batl.)

1 Sergeant of Police (shot through the lungs)

When the Engineers blew up the dug-outs, a considerable number of Jews and bandits were buried under the ruins. In a number of cases it was found necessary to start fires in order to smoke the gangs out.

I must add that since yesterday some of the units have been shot at time and again from outside the Ghetto, that is, from the Aryan part of Warsaw. Raiding parties at once entered the area in question and in one case succeeded in capturing 35 Polish bandits, Communists, who were liquidated at once. Today it happened repeatedly when we found it necessary to execute some bandits, that they collapsed shouting 'Long live Poland,' 'Long live Moscow.'

The operation will be continued on 23 April 1943, 0700 hours.

The SS and Police Führer in the District of Warsaw.
Signed: Stroop
SS-Brigadeführer and Maj. Gen. of Police.
Certified copy:
**Jesuiter** SS-Sturmbannführer

Copy
Teletype message
From the SS and Police Führer in the District of Warsaw
Warsaw, 23 April 1943.
Ref. No.: I ab/St/Gr-16 07-Journal No. 538/43 secret.
Re: Ghetto Operation.
To: The Higher SS and Police Führer East, SS-Obergruppenführer and General of Police Krüger—or deputy.
Krakow

Progress of Ghetto Operation on 23 April 1943. Start: 0700 hours.

The whole of the former Ghetto had been divided for the purposes of today's combing-out operations into 24 districts. One reinforced searching party was detailed to each district with special orders. These assignments had to be carried out by 1600 hours.

Result of this action: 600 Jews and bandits ferreted out and captured, about 200 Jews and bandits killed, 48 dug-outs, some of them of a quite elaborate character, blown up. We captured apart from valuables and money-some gas masks.

The units had been informed that we intended to terminate the operation today. In the morning, the Jews had already become aware of this-instruction. This is why a renewed search by the searching parties was undertaken after an interval of 1 to 1 1/2 hours. The result was, as always, that again Jews and bandits were discovered to be in various blocks. From one block shots were even fired against the cordoning units. An attack by a special battle group was ordered and in order to smoke the bandits out, every building was now set on fire. The Jews and bandits held out, every building was now set on fire. The Jews and bandits held their fire up to the last moment and then concerted their fire against the units. They even used carbines. A number of bandits who were shooting from balconies were hit by our men and crashed down.

Furthermore, today we discovered a place said to have been the headquarters of the 'PPR'; we found it unoccupied and destroyed it. It was on this 5th day of operations that obviously we

I found the worst of the terrorists and activists, who so far had always found ways and means to dodge every searching or evacuation action.

A racial German reported that again some Jews had escaped through the sewers into the Aryan part of the city. We learned from a traitor that there were some Jews in a certain house. A special motorized raiding party invaded the building and caught 3 Jews, 2 of them females. During this operation, their motor-car was pelted with one incendiary bottle and one explosive; 2 policemen were wounded.

The whole operation is rendered more difficult by the cunning way in which the Jews and bandits act; for instance, we discover that the hearses which were used to collect the corpses lying around at the same time bring living Jews to the Jewish cemetery, and thus they are enabled to escape, from the Ghetto. Now this way of escape also is barred by continuous control of the hearses.

At the termination of today's operation about 2200 hours, we discovered that again about 30 bandits had passed into a so-called armaments factory, where they had found refuge. Since the forces are storing goods of great value in this enterprise, this factory was requested to evacuate the building by noon on 24 April; this will enable us to cleanse that labyrinth of a building tomorrow.

Today 3,500 Jews were caught who are to be evacuated from the factories. A total of 19,450 Jews have been caught for resettlement or already evacuated up to today. Of these about 2,500 Jews are still to be loaded. The next train will start on 24 April 1943.

Strength as of 22 April 1943, without 150 Trawniki men; these have already been put at the disposal of the Eastern Command as reinforcement for another assignment.

*Our losses:*

2 Police corporals ('SB') wounded 1 Trawniki man wounded.

The operation will be continued on 24 April 1943, 1000 hours. This hour was chosen so that Jews who may still be in the Ghetto will believe that the operation was actually terminated today.

The SS and Police Führer in the District of Warsaw.
Signed: Stroop
SS-Brigadeführer and Major General of Police.

Certified copy:
**Jesuiter** SS-Sturmbannführer

Copy
Teletype message
From The SS and Police Führer in the District of Warsaw
Warsaw, 24 April 1943.
Ref. Nr.: I ab/St/Wdt-16 07-Journal No. 545/43 secret.
Re: Ghetto operation.
The Higher SS and Police Führer East, SS-Obergruppenführer and General of the Police-Krüger—or deputy.
Krakow

Progress of operation on 24 April 1943, start 1000 hours.

Contrary to the preceding days, the 24 searching parties which had again been formed did not start at one end of the Ghetto, but proceeded from all sides at the same time. Apparently, the Jews still in the Ghetto were deceived by the fact that the operation did not start until 1000 hours into believing that the action really had been terminated yesterday. The search action, therefore, had especially satisfactory results today. This success is furthermore due to the fact that the non-commissioned officers and men have meanwhile become accustomed to the cunning fighting, methods and tricks used by the Jews and bandits and that they have acquired great skill in tracking down the dug-outs which are found in such great number. The raiding parties having returned, we set about to clean a certain block of buildings, sit.

Dated the north-eastern part of the former Ghetto. In this labyrinth of buildings there was a so-called armaments firm which reportedly had goods worth millions for manufacture and storage. I had notified the Wehrmacht of my intentions on 23 April 1943 about 2100 hours, and had requested them to remove their goods by 1200 hours. Since the Wehrmacht did not start this evacuation until 1000 hours I felt obliged to extend the term until 1800 hours. At 1815 hours a search party entered the premises, the building having been cordoned off, and found that a great number of Jews were within the building. Since some of these Jews resisted, I ordered the building to be set on fire. Not until all the buildings along the street and the back premises on either side were well aflame did the Jews, some of them on fire, emerge from these blocks, some of them endeavoured to save their life by jumping into the street from windows and balconies, after having thrown down beds, blankets, and the like. Over and over again we observed that Jews and bandits, despite the danger of being burned alive, preferred to return into the flames rather than risk being caught by us. Over and over again the Jews kept up their firing almost to the end of the action; thus the engineers had to be protected by a machine gun when toward nightfall they had to enter forcibly a concrete building which had been very strongly fortified. Termination of today's operation; on 25 April 1943 at 0145 hours. 1,660 Jews were caught for evacuation, pulled out of dug-outs, about 330 shot. Innumerable Jews Swede destroyed by the flames or perished when the dug-outs were blown up. 26 dug-outs were blown up and an amount of paper money, especially dollars was captured; this money has not yet been counted.

Our forces; as on the preceding day, minus 50 men of the Waffen-SS.

Our losses: 2 SS men and 1 Trawniki man wounded.

Altogether there have now been caught in this action 25,500 Jews who lived in the former Ghetto. Since there are only vague estimates available of the actual number of inhabitants I assume that now only very small numbers of Jews and bandits still remain within the Ghetto.

Operation will be continued on 25 April 1943, 1300 hours.

I beg to acknowledge receipt of teletype messages Nos. 1222 and 1223 of 24 April 1943. As far as can be predicted, the present large-scale operation will last until Easter Monday inclusive.

Today large posters were affixed to the walls surrounding the Ghetto, announcing that everybody who enters the former Ghetto without being able to prove his identity will be shot.

The SS and Police Führer in the District of Warsaw.
Signed: Stroop
SS-Brigadeführer and Major General of Police.
Certified copy:
**Jesuiter** SS-Sturmbannführer

Copy
Teletype message
From: The SS and Police Führer in the District of Warsaw
Warsaw, 25 April 1943
Ref. No. I ab/St/Wdt-16 07-Journal No. 549/43 secret.
Re: Ghetto operation.
To: The Higher SS and Police Führer East, SS-Obergruppenführer and General of Police Krüger—or deputy.
Krakow

Progress of operation on 25 April 1943, start 1300 hours.

For today 7 search parties were formed, strength 1/70 each, each allotted to a certain block of buildings.

Their order was: 'Every building is to be combed out once more; dug-outs have to be discovered and blown up, and the Jews have to be caught. If any resistance is encountered or if dug-outs cannot be reached, the buildings are to be burnt down.'

Apart from the operations undertaken by these 7 search parties, a special operation was undertaken against a centre of bandits, situated outside the wall surrounding the former Ghetto and inhabited exclusively by Poles.

Today's operations of the search parties ended almost every- ~i; where in the starting of enormous conflagrations. In this manner, the Jews were forced to leave their hideouts and refuges. A total of 1,960 Jews were caught alive. The Jews informed us that among them were certain parachutists who were dropped here and bandits who had been equipped with arms from some unknown source. 274 Jews were killed. As in the preceding days, uncounted Jews were buried in blown up dug-outs and, as can be observed time and again, burned with this bag of Jews today. We have, in my opinion, caught a very considerable part of the bandits and lowest elements of the Ghetto. Intervening darkness prevented immediate liquidation. I am going to try to obtain a train for T II tomorrow. Otherwise liquidation will be carried out tomorrow. Today also, some armed resistance was encountered; in a dug-out three pistols and some explosives were captured. Furthermore, considerable amounts of paper money, foreign currency, gold coins, and jewellery were seized today.

The Jews still have considerable property. While last night a glare of fire could be seen above the former Ghetto, today one can observe a giant sea of flames. Since we continue to discover great numbers of Jews whenever we search and comb out, the operation will be continued on 26 April 1943. Start: 1000 hours.

Including today, a total of 27,464 Jews of the former Warsaw Ghetto, have been captured.

Our forces; as on the previous day.

Our losses; 3 members of the Waffen-SS and one member of the Security Police wounded.

**Total losses up to date:**

| | |
|---|---|
| Waffen-SS | 27 Wounded |
| Police | 9 Wounded |
| Security Police | 4 Wounded |
| Wehrmacht | 1 Wounded |
| Trawniki men | 9 Wounded |
| 50 Wounded and 5 dead: | |
| Waffen-SS | 2 Dead |
| Wehrmacht | 2 Dead |
| Trawniki men | 1 Dead |
| | 5 Dead |

The SS and Police Führer in the District of Warsaw.
Signed: Stroop

SS-Brigadeführer and Major General of Police.
Certified copy:
**Jesuiter** SS-Sturmbannführer

Copy
Teletype message
From: The SS and Police Führer in the District of Warsaw
Warsaw, 26 April 1943.
Ref. No.: I ab/St/Wdt-16 07-Journal Nr. 550/43 secret.
Re: Ghetto operation-supplementary report.
To: The Higher SS and Police Führer East, SS-Obergruppenführer and General of Police Krüger—or deputy.
Krakow

1. The operation on 25 April 1943, was terminated at 2200 hours. 2. General effects of the execution of this operation.

The Poles resident in Warsaw are much impressed by the toughness of our operations in the former Ghetto. As can be seen from the daily reports, the General situation has greatly calmed down since the beginning of that operation within the city area of Warsaw. From this fact, one may conclude that the bandits and saboteurs resided in the former Ghetto, and that now all of them, have been destroyed.

In this connection, the fact may be of some interest, that an illegal ammunition store was seen to explode when we burned down a certain building in the dwelling area on which we were working at the time.

The SS and Police Führer in the District of Warsaw.
Signed: Stroop
SS-Brigadeführer and Major General of Police.
Certified copy:
**Jesuiter** SS-Sturmbannführer

Copy
Teletype message
From: The SS and Police Führer in the District of Warsaw
Warsaw, 26 April 1943.
Ref. Nr.: I ab/St/Wdt-16 07 Journal Nr. 551/43 secret.
To: The Higher SS and Police Führer East, SS-Obergruppenführer and General of Police Krüger—or deputy.
Krakow

Start of operation: 1000 hrs.

The whole of the former Ghetto was once more combed through today by the same search parties, each of them allotted to the same district as before. In this way, I tried to bring about that the leaders of these parties work in thoroughfares, blocks of buildings, and courtyards which they know already and that thus they are able to penetrate deeper and deeper into the maze of dug-outs and subterranean passages. Almost every search party reported resistance, which however they broke either by returning fire or by blowing up the dug-outs. It becomes clearer and clearer that it is now the turn of the toughest and strongest among the Jews and bandits. Several times dug-outs have been forcibly broken open, the inmates of which had not come to the surface during the whole of this operation. In a number of cases the inmates of the dug-outs were hardly in a condition, when the dug-out had been blown up, to crawl to the surface. The captured Jews report that many of the inmates of the dug-outs became insane from the heat, the smoke, and the explosions. Several Jews were arrested who had kept close liaison with the group of Polish terrorists and collaborated with it. Outside the former Ghetto we arrested 29 Jews. During today's operation, several blocks of buildings were burned down. This is the only and final method which forces this trash and sub-humanity to the surface. We again captured arms, incendiary bottles, explosive charges and considerable amounts of cash and foreign currency. Today I also arranged that several so-called armaments and defence enterprises will evacuate their stores from the buildings at once, so that these buildings in which the Jews now have taken refuge, under the protection of the army of the German Wehrmacht and police, can be combed out. In one case we again discovered, as previously, that in a building which had been said to contain a giant enterprise there existed in fact almost no stores or goods. One factory was closed without further ado, and the Jews were evacuated.

Result of today's operation:

30 Jews evacuated, 1,330 Jews pulled out of dug-outs and immediately destroyed, 362 Jews killed in battle. Caught today altogether: 1,722 Jews. This brings the total of Jews caught to 29,186. Moreover, it is very probable that numerous Jews have perished in the 13 dug-outs blown up today and in the conflagrations.

At the time of writing not one of the Jews caught still remains within Warsaw. The scheduled transport to T. II had no success. [Note of translator: This probably means that no Jews were available for regular transport to the extermination camp.] Strength: as on preceding day.

Our losses: none.

End of today's operation at 2145 hours. Will be continued on 27 April 1943 at 0900 hours.

The SS and Police Führer in the District of Warsaw.
Signed: Stroop
SS-Brigadeführer and Major General of Police.

Certified copy:
**Jesuiter** SS-Sturmbannführer

Copy
Teletype message
From: The SS and Police Führer in the District of Warsaw
Warsaw, 27 April 1943.
Ref. No.: I ab/St/Gr-16 07-Journal No. 555/43 secret.
Re: Ghetto Operation
To: the Higher SS and Police Führer East, SS-Obergruppenführer and General of Police Krüger—or deputy.
Krakow

Progress of operation on 27 April 1943. Start: 0900 hrs.

For today's operation, I formed 24 raiding parties with the same task as on several days of last week; they had to search the former Ghetto in smaller groups. These search parties pulled 780 Jews out of dug-outs and shot 115 Jews who resisted. This operation was terminated about 1500 hrs.; some of the parties had to continue to operate because they had found more dug-outs.

At 1600 hours a special battle group, 320 officers and men strong, started cleansing a large block of buildings situated on both sides of the so-called Niska Street in the north-eastern part of the former Ghetto. After the search, the entire block was set on fire, after having been completely cordoned off. In this action, a considerable number of Jews were caught. As before, they remained in-the dug-outs, which were either below the ground or in the lofts of the buildings until the end. They fired their arms to the last moment, and then jumped down into the street, sometimes from as far up as the fourth floor, having previously thrown down beds, mattresses, etc., but not until the flames made any other escape impossible. A total of 2,560 Jews were caught today within the former Ghetto, of whom 547 were shot. Moreover, Jews in a not ascertainable number perished when dug-outs were blown up, or in the flames. The sum total of Jews, formerly residing in the Ghetto caught in this action, now amounts to 31,746.

We learned from an anonymous letter that there were a considerable number of Jews in a block of buildings adjoining the north-eastern part of the Ghetto, but outside of it. A special raiding party under the command of 1st. Lt. of Police Diehl was despatched to attack these buildings. The raiding party discovered a gang of about 120 men, strongly armed with pistols, rifles, hand grenades, and light machine guns, who resisted. They succeeded in destroying 24 bandits in battle and arresting 52 bandits. The remainder could not be caught or destroyed, since darkness intervened. The buildings, however, were surrounded at once, so that an escape will hardly be possible. This cleansing action will be continued tomorrow. Moreover, we arrested 17 Poles, among whom 2 Polish Policemen, who should have been aware, among other things, of the existence of this gang. In this operation we captured 3 rifles, 12 pistols, partly of heavier calibre, 100 Polish 'pineapple' hand grenades, 27 German steel helmets, quite a number of German uniforms, tunics and coats which were even furnished with ribbon of the East medal, some reserve magazines for machine guns, 300 rounds of ammunition, etc. The leader of the raiding party had a difficult task because the bandits were disguised in German uniform, but despite this fact, he did his duty with great efficiency. Among the bandits who were caught or killed, there were some Polish terrorists who were identified with certainty. Today we succeeded furthermore in discovering and liquidating one of the founders and leaders of the Jewish-Polish resistance movement. The external appearance of the Jews whom we are catching now shows that it is now the turn of those Jews who were the leaders of the entire resistance movement. They jumped from the burning windows and balconies, abusing Germany and the Führer and cursing the German soldiers.

SS-men who descended into the sewers discovered that a great number of corpses of perished Jews are being washed away by the water.

Our strength:

288 German Police

200 Trawniki men Cordon-

From 0700 to 1900 hours 140 Polish Policing

From 1900 to 0700 hours 288 German Police forces

250 Waffen-SS

140 Polish Police

Strength in the operation:

3/115 German Police

4/400 Waffen-SS

1/6 Engineering Serv.

2/30 Security Police

2/21 Engineers.

Our losses:

3 wounded:

2 Waffen-SS

1 Trawniki man

Termination of operation: 2300 hours. Will be continued on 28 April 1943 at 1000 hours.

The SS and Police Führer in the District of Warsaw.
Signed: Stroop
SS-Brigadeführer and Major General of Police.
Certified copy:
**Jesuiter** SS-Sturmbannführer

Copy
Teletype message
From: The SS and Police Führer in the District of Warsaw
Warsaw, 28 April 1943.
Ref. Nr. I ab/St/Gr-16 07 Journal Nr. 562/43 secret.
Re: Ghetto operation
To: The Higher SS and Police Führer East, SS-Obergruppenführer and General of Police Krüger—or deputy.
Krakow

Progress of operation on 28 April 1943. Start 1000 hrs.

Today, 10 raiding parties were formed for combing out the whole of the Ghetto. These raiding parties again discovered proceeding step by step, a number of dug-outs, which were found to have been prepared as far ago as the middle of last year for use in the resistance of the Jews. A total of 335 Jews were forcibly pulled out of these dug-outs. Apart from these operations, we continued to cleanse the resistance centre used by the Jewish military organization, situated at the borders of the Ghetto. We succeeded in shooting 10 more bandits, and in arresting 9, beyond those caught yesterday, and in capturing more arms, ammunition, and military equipment. In the afternoon, a battle group again was directed against a block of buildings which had already been combed out; the block was set on fire during this operation.

As on previous days, masses of Jews emerged, forced out by the flames and the enormous clouds of smoke. At another point, an Engineer officer, attached by the Wehrmacht to the units, with great trouble, opened a dug-out situated about 3 metres below ground. From this dug-out, which had been ready since October of last year, and was equipped with running water, toilet, and electric light, we pulled out 274 of the richest and most influential Jews. Today again we encountered very strong resistance in many places and broke it. It becomes clearer every day that we are now encountering the real terrorists and activists, because of the duration of the operation.

Result of today: 1,655 Jews caught for evacuation, of whom 110 were killed in battle.

Many more Jews were killed by the flames; moreover, Jews in an unascertainable number were destroyed, the dug-outs being blown up. By the results of today, the number of Jews caught or destroyed rises to 33,401 altogether. This number does not include the Jews who were killed by fire or destroyed in the dug-outs.

Our strength: as on the previous day. Our losses: 3 wounded (1 Police, 2 Waffen-SS)

Termination of operation: 2200 hours. Will be continued on 29 April 1943. 1000 hours.

The SS and Police Führer in the District of Warsaw.
Signed: Stroop
SS-Brigadeführer and Major General of Police.

Certified copy:
**Jesuiter** SS-Sturmbannführer

Copy
Teletype message
From: The SS and Police Führer in the District of Warsaw
Warsaw, 29 April 1943.
fief. Nr. I ab/St/Gr-16 07-Journal Nr. 566/43 secret.
Re: Ghetto Operation.
To: The Higher SS and Police Führer East, SS-Obergruppenführer and General of Police Krüger—or deputy.
Krakow

Progress of large-scale operation of 29 April 1943. Start 1000 hrs. As on the previous day I formed search parties, who red the special task of searching those blocks of buildings which had been recently separated. A larger raiding party was detailed to clean a certain block of buildings (formerly the Hall- j mann concern) and to burn this block down. 36 more dug-outs used for habitation were discovered altogether, and from them and other hideouts and from the burning buildings, 2,359 Jews, were caught, of whom 106 were killed in battle.

Captured are 2 rifles, 10 pistols, 10 kilograms of explosives, and ammunition of various types.

When a large dug-out was blown up, the entire building collapsed and everyone of the bandits perished. In the ensuing conflagration, loud detonations and darting flames showed that the building must have contained large stores of ammunition and explosives. Some sewer entrances were blown up. Two exits discovered outside the Ghetto were also made unusable by blowing them up or walling them up.

The depositions of some of the inmates of the dug-outs are to the effect that these Jews have been unable to leave the dug-outs for the last 10 days and that their food, etc., is now beginning to grow short because the large-scale operation has lasted so long. Furthermore, the Jews testify that bandits appeared at night who were Jews or sometimes Poles, wearing black masks, who walled the dug-outs up from the outside and admonished them not to give any signs of life, so that they could continue to live in the Ghetto when the action was finished. Some of the armaments factories are being evacuated very slowly. In several cases one gains the impression that this is done intentionally. Thus, I discovered with regard to one firm, Schulz and Co., which I had visited on Easter Monday and then instructed to start evacuation at once and to have it completed within 3 days, that up till today, Thursday, nothing had been done. Our strength: as on the previous day. Our losses: none.

Termination of operation at 2100 hrs. Will be continued on 30 April 1943, 0900 hrs.

Total caught or destroyed: 35,760.

The SS and Police Führer in the District of Warsaw.
Signed: Stroop
SS-Brigadeführer and Major General of Police.
Certified copy:
**Jesuiter** SS-Sturmbannführer

Copy
Teletype message
From: The SS and Police Führer in the District of Warsaw
Warsaw, 30 April 1943.
Ref No.: I ab/St/Gr-16 07-Journal No. 579/43 secret.
Re: Ghetto operation.
To: The Higher SS and Police Führer East, SS-Obergruppenführer and General of Police Krüger—or deputy.
Krakow

Progress of large-scale operation on 30 April 1943. Start 0900 hrs.

Combing out by search parties was continued. Although some giant blocks of buildings now are completely burned out, the Jews continue to stay in the dug-outs 2 to 3 meters below ground. In many cases we are not able to discover those dug-outs unless some Jew, whom we have already caught, gives us a hint as to their whereabouts. Repeatedly, during the last few days, Jews have testified that some armed Jews emerge at night from some hideouts or dug-outs and threaten the other Jews with shooting if they give any signs of life. We were able to ascertain beyond all doubt that several dug-outs had been closed from the outside by these bandits, who tried in this manner to prove that they meant business. Altogether, 30 dug-outs were discovered, evacuated, and blown up today. Again we caught a great number of bandits and sub-humans. Apart from the bombing-out operations effected by small parties, two larger battle groups were occupied with bombing out and destroying by fire several interconnected blocks of buildings.

A total of 1599 Jews were caught today, of whom 179 were killed in battle. The sum total of Jews caught up to date thereby rises to 37,359. 3,855 Jews were loaded today. The number of Jews in possession of arms was much higher than before among the Jews caught during the last few days. Today, we again captured arms and particularly parts of German uniforms from them. The operation against Fort Traugutta did not have any positive results. So far as we were able to discover subterranean exits, we either occupied them or blew them up. In attacking one of the blocks we had to use a gun today.

Our strength:

| **Used in the operation:** | |
|---|---|
| Police | 5/133 |
| Security Police | 3/36 |
| Waffen-SS | 6/432 |
| Engineer | 2/40 |
| Staff | 3/7 |
| **Cordoning forces:** | |
| Waffen-SS | 3/318 |
| German Police | 2/89 |
| Trawniki men | 200 |

moreover some Polish Police

Our losses: 1 wounded (Police)

Termination of today's large-scale action: 2100 hours. Will be continued on 1 May 1943, 0900 hours.

The SS and Police Führer in the District of Warsaw.
Signed: Stroop
SS-Brigadeführer and Major General of Police.
Certified copy:
**Jesuiter** SS-Sturmbannführer

Copy
Teletype message
From: The SS and Police Führer in the District of Warsaw
Warsaw, 1 May, 1943.
ref: Nr.: I ab/St/Gr-16 07-Journal No. 583/43 secret.
Re: Large-scale Ghetto operation.
To: The Higher SS and Police Führer East, SS Obergruppenführer and General of Police Krüger-or deputy.
Krakow

Progress of large scale operation on 1 May 1943. Start 0900 hours. 10 searching parties were detailed, moreover a larger battle group was detailed to comb out a certain block of buildings, with the added instruction to burn that block down. Within this block of buildings there existed a so-called armament factory which had not yet been entirely evacuated, although it had had enough time to do so. It was not exempted from the operation. Todays operation a total of 1,026 Jews were caught, of whom 245 were killed, either in battle or while resisting. Moreover, a considerable number of bandits and ringleaders were also caught. In one case a Jew who had already been made ready for transport fired three shots against a 1st Lieutenant of

Police, but missed his mark. All the Jews caught today were forcibly pulled out of dug-outs. Not a single one gave himself up voluntarily, after his dug-out had been opened. A considerable part of the Jews caught were pulled out of the sewers. We continued systematically blowing up or blocking up the sewer entrances. In one case the Engineers laid a strong concentrated charge and had to proceed to an adjoining entrance where they had something to do. In the meantime, a Jew emerged from the sewer, removed the fuse from the concentrated charge, and appropriated the charge. In the further course of this operation we succeeded in catching the Jew, still in possession of the concentrated charge.

In order to ascertain the movements of the Jews during the night, today I used for the first time 5 scouting parties, each 1/9 strong, at irregular intervals during the night. In General, it has to be stated that our men need extraordinary diligence and energy to discover the Jews who are still in so-called dug-outs, caves, and in the sewerage system. It can be expected that the remainder of the Jews who formerly inhabited the Ghetto will now be caught. The sum total of Jews caught so far has risen to 38,385. Not included in this figure are those who died in the flames or in the dug-outs. One patrol discovered an unascertainable number of corpses floating in a main sewer under the Ghetto. Outside of the Ghetto, in the immediate vicinity of Warsaw, the gendarmerie has shot a total of 150 Jews who could be proved to have escaped from Warsaw.

Again we captured pistols and explosives.

Our strength:

| **Used in operation:** | |
|---|---|
| Police (German) | 4/102 |
| Waffen-SS | 7/350 |
| Engineers (Wehrmacht) | 2/38 |
| Engineering Emergency Service | 1/6 |
| Security Police | 2/1 |
| **Cordoning units:** | |
| Waffen-SS | 300 |
| German Police | 1/71 |
| Trawniki | 250 |

Our losses: 1 policeman-wounded yesterday, died from wounds.

Termination of today's large-scale action: 2200 hours. Will be continued on 2 May 1943, 1000 hours.

The SS and Police Führer in the District of Warsaw.
Signed: Stroop

SS-Brigadeführer and Major General of Police.
Certified copy:
**Jesuiter** SS-Sturmbannführer

Copy
Teletype message
From The SS and Police Führer in the District of Warsaw
Warsaw, 2 May 1943.
Ref. No.: I ab St/Gr-16 07-Journal No. 584/43 secret.
Re: Large-scale Ghetto operation.
To: The Higher SS and Police Führer East, SS-Obergruppenführer and General of Police Krüger—or deputy.
Krakow

Progress of large-scale operation on 2 May 1943, start 1000 hrs. 9 raiding parties combed out the whole area of the former Ghetto; moreover, a larger detachment was detailed to clean out or destroy one block of buildings grouped around the two armament enterprises Transavia and Wischniewski. To find more dug-outs, the raiding parties took along with them some Jews caught on the previous day to act as guides. In these operations, the raiding parties pulled out 944 Jews from dug-outs; 235 more Jews were shot on this occasion. When the block of buildings mentioned above was destroyed, 120 Jews were caught and numerous Jews were destroyed when they jumped from the attics to the inner courtyards, trying to escape the flames. Many more Jews perished in the flames or were destroyed when the dug-outs and sewer entrances were blown up. The Jews were removed from two armaments concerns and the managers were requested to evacuate within a short time.

Altogether we caught today: 1,852 Jews. The sum total of Jews caught thereby rises to 40,237 Jews. 27 dug-outs were discovered, forcibly opened and destroyed, arms and ammunition captured. When the external barricade was shot at and when some Jews who broke out from a sewer entrance outside the Ghetto made an attack, we suffered 7 losses, 4 Policemen and 3 Polish Policemen. The scouting parties used during the night encountered armed resistance from some Jews who under the protection of darkness ventured to emerge from their holes and dugouts. We did not suffer losses thereby. On the other hands a considerable number of Jews were killed or wounded in this operation.

Our strength:

**Used in operation:**

| | |
|---|---|
| German Police | 3/98 |
| Engineering Em Service | 1/6 |
| Security Police | 3/12 |

| | |
|---|---|
| Engineers (Wehrmacht) | 2/37 |
| SS-Gren | 11/409 |
| SS-Cav. | 3/7 |
| **Cordoning forces:** | |
| German Police | 2/9 |
| SS-Gren | 1/300 |
| Trawniki | 200 |

Our losses:
4 Policemen wounded
3 Polish policemen wounded

Present at todays large-scale operation was the Higher SS and Police Führer East, SS-Obergruppenführer and General of Police Krüger.

Termination of operation: 2030 hours. Will be continued on 3 May 1943, 0900 hours.

The SS and Police Führer in the District of Warsaw.
Signed: Stroop
SS-Brigadeführer and Major General of Police.
Certified copy:
**Jesuiter** SS-Sturmbannführer

Copy
Teletype message
From: The SS and Police Führer in the District of Warsaw
Warsaw, 3 May 1943.
Ref. Nr.: I ab-St/Gr-16 07-Journal Nr. 597/43 secret.
Re: Large-scale Ghetto operation.
To: The Higher SS and Police Führer East, SS-Obergruppenführer and General of Police Krüger—or deputy.
Krakow

Progress of large-scale operation on 3 May 1943, start 0900 hours. l In the combing-out operation of the former Jewish Ghetto today 19 more dug-outs were discovered and the result was as follows:

Pulled out of dug-outs - 1,392 Jews

Shot – 95

Evacuated from former armament factories - 177

The sum total of Jews caught thereby rises to 41,806 Jews. In most cases the Jews offered armed resistance before they left the dug-outs. We had two casualties (wounded). Some of the Jews and bandits fired pistols from both hands. Since we discovered several times today, that Jewesses had pistols concealed in their bloomers, every Jew and bandit will be ordered from today on, to strip completely for the search. We captured among other things, one German rifle, model 98, two 08 pistols and other calibres, also home-made hand grenades. The Jews cannot be induced to leave their dug-outs until several smoke candles have been burned. According to depositions made yesterday and today, the Jews were asked during the second half of 1942 to erect air-raid shelters. At that time under the camouflage of erecting air-raid shelters, they began to build the dug-outs which they are now inhabiting, in order to use them for an anti-Jewish operation. Some of the scouting parties used in the Ghetto were shot at last night. One casualty (wounded). These scouting parties reported that groups of armed bandits marched through the Ghetto.

Strength: as on the previous day.

Losses: 3 SS-men wounded.

Termination of today's operation: 2100 hours. Will be continued on 4 May 1943. 0900 hours.

3,019 Jews were loaded.

The SS and Police Führer in the District of Warsaw.
Signed: Stroop
SS-Brigadeführer and Major General of Police.
Certified copy:
**Jesuiter** SS-Sturmbannführer

Copy
Teletype message
From: The SS and Police Führer in the District of Warsaw
Warsaw, 4 May 1943.
Ref. No.: I ab-St/Gr-16 07-Journal No. 603/43 secret.
Re: Large-scale Ghetto operation.
To: The Higher SS and Police Führer East, SS-Obergruppenführer and General of Police Krüger—or deputy.
Krakow

Progress of large-scale operation on 4 May 1943, start 0900 hours. For mopping up the dug-outs a raiding party was used, 1/60 strong and reinforced by an Engineers' detachment provided by the Wehrmacht. This raiding party pulled 550 Jews out of dugouts and killed in battle 188 Jews. Discovering the dug-outs becomes more and more difficult. Often they can only be discovered by betrayal through other Jews. If the Jews are requested to leave their dug-out voluntarily, they hardly ever obey; they can only be forced to do so by the use of smoke-candles.

The main forces were detailed about 1100 hours to comb out, mop up, and destroy two large blocks of buildings, containing the former firms Toebbens, Schulz and Co., and others. After these blocks had been completely cordoned off, we requested the Jews who were still within the buildings to come forward voluntarily. By this measure, we caught 456 Jews for evacuation. Not until the blocks of buildings were well aflame and were about to collapse did a further considerable number of Jews emerge, forced to do so by the flames and the smoke. Time and again the Jews try to escape even through burning buildings. Innumerable Jews whom we saw on the roofs during the conflagration perished in the flames. Others emerged from the upper stories in the last possible moment and were only able to escape death in the flames by jumping down. Today we caught a total of 2,283 Jews, of whom 204 were shot and innumerable Jews were destroyed in dug-outs and in the flames. The sum total of Jews caught rises to 44,089.

As is learned from depositions made by the Jews, today we caught part of the governing body of the so-called 'Party'. One member of the committee which leads the gang will be used tomorrow for mopping up some more fortified dug-outs with armed Jews inside. When the armament enterprises were evacuated, we again observed that the goods carted away were by no means valuable military equipment, as had been pretended, but trifles, like used furniture and other requisitioned items. We took appropriate measures against this at once.

The scouting parties who patrolled during the night in the former Ghetto again reported movements of the Jews in the burned out and destroyed streets and courtyards. In order to be better able to take the Jews by surprise, the scouting parties at night tie rags and other stuff round their shoes. In skirmishes between the scouting parties and Jews, 30 Jews were shot.

We captured 1 carbine, 3 pistols, and some ammunition. During the conflagration a considerable amount of stored ammunition exploded.

Our strength:

| **Used in operation:** | | |
|---|---|---|
| German Police | 4/101 | |
| Engineering Em. Service | 1/6 | |
| Security Police | 2/14 | |
| Engineers | 2/41 | |
| Waffen-SS | 11/407 | |
| **Cordoning forces:** | **Day** | **Night** |
| German Police | 2/87 | 1/11 |
| Waffen-SS | 25 | 1/300 |
| Trawniki | 200 | |
| Polish Police | 1/180 | 1/180 |

Our losses: None.

Termination of operation: 2330 hours. Will be continued on 5 May 1943, 1000 hours.

The SS and Police Führer in the District of Warsaw.
Signed: Stroop
SS-Brigadeführer and Major General of Police.
Certified copy:
**Jesuiter** SS-Sturmbannführer

Copy
Teletype message
From: The SS and Police Führer in the District of Warsaw
Warsaw, 5 May 1943.
Ref. Nr.: I ab/St/Gr-16 07-Journal No. 607/43 secret.
Re: Large-scale Ghetto Operation.
To: The Higher SS and Police Führer East, SS-Obergruppenführer and General of Police Krüger—or deputy.
Krakow

Progress of large-scale operation on 5 May 1943. Start 1000 hours. In the beginning of today's operations, the raiding parties seemed to have less results than on the preceding days. When the operation terminated, however, quite a number of dug-outs had again been discovered, owing to the tracking ability of the men and to betrayal; 40 of these dug-outs were destroyed. As far as possible, the Jews in these dug-outs were caught (1,070 altogether). The combing out patrols shot about 126 Jews. Today again the Jews resisted in several places until they were captured. In several cases the entrances (hatches) of the dugouts were forcibly held or bolted from the inside, so that only by using a strong explosive charge could we force them open and destroy the inmates. Today, we again captured arms and ammunition, including one pistol. From one enterprise still in existence (so-called Prosta) 2,850 Jews were caught for evacuation. This figure was included in the sum total reported earlier, so that only 1,070 have to be added; the present sum total therefore is 45,159.

Our strength: as on the preceding day.

Our losses: 1 SS man wounded, 1 Policeman wounded.

Sum total of losses to date: 8 dead, 55 wounded.

Termination of operation: 2200 hours. - Will be continued on 6 May 1943, 0900 hours.

The SS and Police Führer in the District of Warsaw.
Signed: Stroop
SS-Brigadeführer and Major General of Police.

Certified copy:
**Jesuiter** SS-Sturmbannführer

Copy
Teletype message
From: The SS and Police Führer in the District of Warsaw
Warsaw, 6 May 1943.
Ref. No.: ab/St/Gr-16 07-Journal No. 614/43 secret.
Re: Ghetto large-scale operation.
To: The Higher SS and Police Führer East, SS-Obergruppenführer and General of Police Krüger—or deputy.
Krakow

Progress of large-scale operation on 6 May 1943, start 0930 hours.

Today we combed especially those blocks of buildings which were destroyed by fire on 4 May 1943. Although it was hardly to be expected that any living person could still exist in those blocks, we discovered quite a number of dug-outs in which a burning heat had developed. From these dug-outs and from other dugouts which we discovered in other parts of the Ghetto, we pulled out 1,553 Jews. While resisting, and in a skirmish, 356 Jews were shot. In this skirmish, the Jews fired from 08 pistols and other calibers and threw Polish 'pineapple' hand grenades. One SS-Unterscharführer was wounded and a total of 47 dug-outs were destroyed.

2 men of the external cordoning forces were wounded. The Jews who had broken out from the Ghetto seem to be returning now with the intention of assisting the Ghetto Jews by force or liberating them. One Jew who had escaped from Lublin was caught just outside of the Ghetto wall. He was armed as follows: 1 08 pistol, ample reserve ammunition, 2 Polish 'pineapple' hand grenades. It could not be reliably ascertained so far whether the so-called 'Party Directorate' of the Jews ('PPR') have been caught or destroyed. We are on their traces. It is to be hoped that tomorrow we shall succeed in tracing down this so-called Party Directorate. In order to enable us to intercept more effectively the Jews and bandits who approach the Ghetto, covering detachments of the external barricade were shifted farther inside the Aryan part. The former miniature Ghetto 'Prosta' was searched by raiding parties today. We caught some Jews who had stayed behind. The firm Toebbens was requested to evacuate, this miniature Ghetto by noon on 10 May 1943. The so-called library, situated outside the Ghetto, was put at their disposal for temporary storage of their raw materials, etc.

The sum total of Jews caught so far rises to 47,068. The Polish Police take pains to deliver to my office every Jew who turns up within the city, because they are eager to win such premiums as have been paid in earlier cases. The undersigned received some anonymous letters in which he was notified of the fact that some Jews are staying in the Aryan part of the city. One anonymous letter draws a parallel between Katyn and the large-scale action within the Ghetto.

Our strength:

| **Used in operation:** | | |
|---|---|---|
| German Police | 4/101 | |
| Engineering Em. Service | 1/6 | |
| Security Police | 2/14 | |
| Engineers | 3/72 | |
| Waffen-SS | 10/500 | |
| **Cordoning forces:** | **Day** | **Night** |
| German Police | 2/87 | 1/11 |
| Waffen-SS | 25 | 1/300 |
| Trawniki | 200 | |
| Polish Police | 1/180 | 1/180 |

Our losses:
1 Policeman dead
1 Policeman seriously wounded
1 SS-Unterscharführer less seriously wounded. Termination of operation: 2100 hours. Will be continued on 7 May 1943, 0930 hours.

The SS and Police Führer in the District of Warsaw.
Signed: Stroop
SS-Brigadeführer and Major General of Police.
Certified copy:
**Jesuiter** SS-Sturmbannführer

Copy
Teletype message
Prom: The SS and Police Führer in the District of Warsaw
Warsaw, 7 May 1943.
Ref. Nr.: I ab/St/Gr-16 07-Journal Nr. 616/43 secret
Re: Large-scale Ghetto Operation.
To: The Higher SS and Police Führer East, SS-Obergruppenführer and General of Police Krüger—or deputy.
Krakow

Progress of large-scale operation on 7 May 1943, start 1000 hours. The combing-out parties today obtained the following results: 49 dug-outs discovered. Part of the Jews were caught. A considerable, not ascertainable, number of Jews who refused to leave the dug-outs and offered armed resistance were destroyed when the dug-outs were blown up. Altogether 1,019 Jews were caught alive today, 255 shot. The sum total of Jews caught so far rises to 48,342. Today we again encountered armed resistance in several cases, whereby we lost 1 SS man (wounded). We captured 4 pistols of various calibres and some stores of ammunition.

The location of the dug-out used by the so-called select 'Party Directorate' is now known. It is to be forced open tomorrow. The Jews testify that they emerge at night to get fresh air, since it is unbearable to stay permanently within the dug-outs owing to the long duration of the operation. On average, the raiding parties shoot 30 to 50 Jews each night. From these statements, it was to be inferred that a considerable number of Jews are still underground in the Ghetto. Today we blew up a concrete building which we had not been able to destroy by fire. In this operation, we learned that the blowing up of a building is a very lengthy process and takes an enormous amount of explosives. The best and only method for destroying the Jews therefore stir] remains the setting of fires.

Our strength: as on the preceding day. Our losses: 1 Waffen-SS man wounded.

Termination of operation: 2100 hours, will be continued on 8 May 1943 1000 hours.

The SS and Police Führer in the District of Warsaw.
Signed: Stroop
SS-Brigadeführer and Major General of Police.
Certified copy:
**Jesuiter** SS-Sturmbannführer

Copy
Teletype message
From The SS and Police Führer in the District of Warsaw
Warsaw, 8 May 1943.
Ref. No.: I ab/St/Gr-16 07-Journal No. 624/43 secret.
Re: Large-scale Ghetto Operation.
To: The Higher SS and Police Führer East, SS-Obergruppenführer and General of Police Krüger—or deputy.
Krakow

Progress of operation on 8 May 1943, start 1000 hours.

The whole former Ghetto was searched today by raiding parties for the remaining dug-outs and Jews. As reported some days a number of sub-humans, bandits, and terrorists still remain in the dug-outs, where heat has become intolerable by reason of the fires. These creatures know only too well that their only choice is between remaining in hiding as long as possible or coming to the surface and trying to wound or kill off the men of the Waffen-SS, Police, and Wehrmacht who keep up the pressure against them.

We continued today the operation against the dug-out of the so-called select 'Party Directorate' which we had discovered yesterday, as reported in my teletype message yesterday. We succeeded in forcing open the dug-out of the Party Directorate and in catching about 60 heavily armed bandits. We succeeded in catching and liquidating Deputy Leader of the Jewish Military Organization 'ZWZ' and his so-called Chief of Staff. There were about 200 Jews in this dug-out, of whom 60 were caught and 140 were destroyed, partly owing to the strong effect of smoke-candles, and partly owing to heavy explosive charges which were laid in several places. The Jews whom we caught had already reported that innumerable Jews had been killed by the effect of the smoke-candles. The fight of the first six days was hard, but now we are able to state that we are catching those Jews and Jewesses who were the ringleaders in those days. Every time a dug-out is forced open, the Jews in it offer resistance with the arms at their disposal, light machine guns, pistols, and hand grenades. Today we again caught quite a number of Jewesses who carried loaded pistols in their bloomers, with the safety catch released. Some depositions speak of 3 to 4,000 Jews who still remain in underground holes, sewers, and dug-outs. The undersigned is resolved not to terminate the large-scale operation until the last Jew has been destroyed.

A total of 1,091 Jews were caught today in dug-outs; about 280 Jews were shot in battle, innumerable Jews were destroyed in the 43 dug-outs which were blown up. The sum total of Jews caught has risen to 49,712. Those buildings which had not yet been destroyed by fire, were set on fire today and we discovered that a few Jews were still hiding somewhere within the walls or in the staircases.

Our strength:

| **Used in operation:** | | |
|---|---|---|
| German Police | 4/101 | |
| Engineering Em Service | 1/6 | |
| Security Police | 2/14 | |
| Engineers | 3/69 | |
| Waffen-SS | 13/527 | |
| **Cordoning forces:** | **Day** | **Night** |
| German Police | 1/87 | 1/36 |
| Waffen-SS | 25 | 1/300 |
| Trawniki | 160 | |
| Polish Police | 1/160 | 1/160 |

Our losses:

2 Waffen-SS dead

2 Waffen-SS wounded

1 Engineer wounded

A policeman wounded on 7 May 1943 died today from wounds. We captured about 15 to 20 pistols of various calibres, considerable stores of ammunition for pistols and rifles, moreover a number of hand grenades, made in the former armament factories.

Termination of action; 2130 hours, will be continued on 9 May 1943 1000 hours.

The SS and Police Führer in the District of Warsaw.
Signed: Stroop
SS-Brigadeführer and Major General of Police.
Certified copy:
**Jesuiter** SS-Sturmbannführer

Copy
Teletype message
From: The SS and Police Führer in the District of Warsaw
Warsaw, 9 May 1943.
Ref. No.: I ab/St/Gr 1607 Journal No. 625/43.
Re: Large-scale Ghetto Operation.
To: The Higher SS and Police Führer East, SS-Obergruppenführer and General of Police Krüger—or deputy.
Krakow

Progress of large-scale operation on 9 May 1943, start 1000 hours.

The operation carried out today had the following result: The raiding parties at work today discovered 42 dug-outs. From these dug-outs we pulled out alive 1,037 Jews and bandits. In battle 319 bandits and Jews were shot, moreover an uncertain number were destroyed when the dug-outs were blown up. The block of buildings which formerly contained the 'Transavia' concern was destroyed by fire; in this operation, we again caught a number of Jews, although this block had been combed through several times.

Again we captured some pistols and hand grenades.

Our strength:

| **Used in operation:** | | |
|---|---|---|
| German Police | 4/103 | |
| Security Police | 2/12 | |
| Engineers | 3/67 | |
| Waffen-SS | 13/547 | |
| **Cordoning Forces:** | **Day** | **Night** |
| German Police | 1/87 | 1/36 |
| Waffen-SS | ------ | 1/300 |
| Trawniki | 160 | ------- |
| Polish Police | 1/160 | 1/160 |

battle groups, had either been killed in battle or had committed suicide because they had realized the futility of continuing the fight. The search for the truck, which was ordered at once, had no results. The bandits testified further that the Prosta is now the refuge for the still existing Jews because the Ghetto has become too hot for them. For this reason, I resolved to deal with the Prosta in the same manner as with the Ghetto, and to destroy this miniature Ghetto.

Today, we again captured small arms and some ammunition.

The Security Police yesterday succeeded in capturing a workshop outside the Ghetto which manufactured 10,000 to 11,000 explosive charges and other ammunition.

Our strength: as on the preceding day. Our losses: 3 SS men wounded.

Owing to the excellent understanding between us and the Wehrmacht, the detachment of Engineers was reinforced. Moreover, a considerable amount of explosives was put at our disposal.

Termination of operation: 2200 hours. Will be continued on 11 May 1943, 0930 hours.

The SS and Police Führer in the District of Warsaw.
Signed: Stroop
SS-Brigadeführer and Major General of Police.
Certified copy:
**Jesuiter** SS-Sturmbannführer

Copy
Teletype message
From: The SS and Police Führer in the District of Warsaw
Warsaw, 11 May 1943.
Ref. No.: I ab-St/Gr-16 07 Journal No. 629/43 secret.
Re: Ghetto large-scale Operation.
To: The Higher SS and Police Führer East, SS-Obergruppenführer and General of Police Krüger—or deputy.
Krakow

Progress of large-scale operation on 11 May 1943, start 0930 hours.

The scouting parties sent out last night again reported that there must still be some Jews within the dug-outs, since some Jews were seen in the ruined streets. The scouting parties shot 12 Jews. On the basis of these reports, today I again formed raiding parties who in combing-out operations discovered, captured, and destroyed a total of 47 dug-outs. Today again we caught some Jews who had taken refuge in ruins which were still protected by a roof. The Jews and bandits are still seeking this new refuge, because staying in the dug-outs has become unbearable. One dug-out was discovered which contained about 12 rooms equipped with plumbing, running water, and separate bathrooms for men and women. Considerable amounts of food were captured or secured, in order to make it more and more difficult for them to get necessary food.

A total of 931 Jews and bandits were caught. 53 bandits were shot. More of them perished when dug-outs were blown up and when a small block of buildings was destroyed by fire. The total of Jews caught up to date has risen to 53,667. We captured several pistols, hand grenades, and ammunition.

We have not been able to smoke out the sewers systematically once more, since we are short of smoke-candles. 'OFK' is ready to provide new smoke-candles.

Our strength:

| **Used in operation:** | | |
|---|---|---|
| German Police | 6/126 | |
| Engineering Em. Service | 1/6 | |
| Security Police | 2/14 | |
| Engineers | 4/76 | |
| Waffen-SS | 12/308 | |
| **Cordoning forces:** | **Day** | **Night** |
| German Police | 1/112 | 1/86 |
| Waffen-SS | ------- | 1/130 |
| Trawniki | 160 | -------- |
| Polish Police | 1/160 | 1/160 |

Our losses: 1 SS man wounded.

Total of losses up to date: 71 wounded, 12 dead. Termination of today's operation: 2145 hours, will be continued on 12 May 1943, 0930 hours.

The SS and Police Führer in the District of Warsaw.
Signed: Stroop
SS-Brigadeführer and Major General of Police.
Certified copy:
**Jesuiter** SS-Sturmbannführer

Copy
Teletype message
From: The SS and Police Führer in the District of Warsaw
Warsaw, 12 May 1943
Ref. No.: I ab-St/Gr-16 07-Journal No. 637/43 secret.
Re: Large-scale Ghetto Operation.
To: The Higher SS and Police Führer East, SS-Obergruppenführer and General of Police Krüger—or deputy.

Krakow

Progress of large-scale operation on 12 May 1943, start 0930 hours.

When the raiding parties combed out the area for remaining dug-outs in which Jews were hiding, they succeeded in discovering 30 dug-outs. 663 Jews were pulled out of them and 133 Jews were shot. The sum total of Jews caught has arisen to 54,463.

Furthermore, today the units cordoning off the miniature Ghetto were reinforced and destroyed by fire. Probably a considerable number of Jews perished in the flames, no accurate information in this regard could be obtained since the fire was still burning when darkness set in. One concrete building in the Prosta, from which Jews had been removed, was heavily damaged by blowing-up operations in order to make it impossible for the bandits to use it as a base later.

It is noteworthy that the Poles, without having been warned, took appropriate measures for protecting their window-panes, etc., before the blowing-up started.

The transports of Jews leaving here will be directed to T.II beginning today.

Our strength:

| **Used in operation:** | | |
|---|---|---|
| German police | 5/126 | |
| Engineering Em. Service | 1/6 | |
| Security Police | 2/14 | |
| Engineers | 4/74 | |
| Waffen-SS | 12/508 | |
| **Cordoning forces:** | **Day** | **Night** |
| German Police | 1/112 | 1/86 |
| Waffen-SS | ------- | 1/300 |
| Trawniki | 160 | --------- |
| Polish Police | 1/160 | 1/160 |

Our losses: 1 Waffen-SS man wounded.Termination of today's operation: 2160 hours, will be continued on 13 May 1943, 1000 hours.

The SS and Police Führer in the District of Warsaw.
Signed: Stroop
SS-Brigadeführer and Major General of Police.
Certified copy:
**Jesuiter** SS-Sturmbannführer

Copy
Teletype message
From: The SS and Police Führer in the District of Warsaw

Warsaw, 13 May, 1943.
Ref. No.: I ate/ St/Gr 16 07 Journal No. 641/43 secret. Re: Large-scale Ghetto Operation.
To: The Higher SS and Police Führer East, SS-Obergruppenführer and General of Police Krüger—or deputy.
Krakow

Progress of large-scale operation on 13 May 1943, start 1000 hours. In combing out the Ghetto and the miniature Ghetto (Prosta) today we found 234 Jews. 155 Jews were shot in battle. Today it became clear that the Jews and bandits whom we are catching now belong to the so-called battle groups. All of them are young fellows and females between 18 and 25 years of age. When we captured one, a real skirmish took place, in which the Jews not only fired from 08 pistols and Polish Vis pistols, but also threw Polish 'pineapple' hand grenades at the Waffen-SS men. After part of the inmates of the dug-out had been caught and were about to be searched, one of the females as quick as lightning put her hand under her shirt, as many others had done, and fetched from her bloomers a 'pineapple' hand grenade, drew the safety-catch, threw the grenade among the men who were searching her, and jumped quickly to cover. It is only thanks to the presence of mind of the men that no casualties ensued.

The few Jews and criminals still staying in the Ghetto have for the last few days been using the hideouts they can still find among the ruins, retiring at night into the dug-outs whose location is known to them, to eat and get provisions for the next day. Lately we have been unable to extract information on the whereabouts of further dug-outs from the captured Jews. The remainder of the inmates of that dug-out where the skirmish took place were destroyed by using heavier explosive charges. From a Wehrmacht concern we evacuated 327 Jews today. The Jews we catch now are sent to T II.

The total of Jews caught has risen to 55,179.

Our strength:

| **Used in operation:** | | |
|---|---|---|
| German police | 4/182 | |
| Engineering Em. Service | 1/6 | |
| Security Police | 2/14 | |
| Engineers | 4/74 | |
| Waffen-SS | 12/517 | |
| **Cordoning forces:** | **Day** | **Night** |
| German Police | 2/137 | 1/87 |
| Waffen-SS | ------ | 1/300 |
| Trawniki | 270 | ------- |
| Polish Police | 1/160 | 1/160 |

Our losses:
2 Waffen-SS dead
3 Waffen-SS wounded
1 Policeman wounded. The 2 Waffen-SS men lost their lives in the air attack against the Ghetto.
33 dug-outs were discovered and destroyed. Booty: 6 pistols, 2 hand grenades, and some explosive charges.

Termination of today's operation: 2100 hours, will be continued on 14 May 1943, 1000 hours.
My intention is to terminate the large-scale operation on 16 May 1943 and to turn all further measures over to Police battalion III/23. Unless ordered otherwise, I am going to submit to the conference of SS and Police Leaders a detailed report of the operation, including an appendix containing photos.

The SS and Police Führer in the District of Warsaw.
Signed: Stroop
SS-Brigadeführer and Major General of Police.
Certified copy:
**Jesuiter** SS-Sturmbannführer

Copy
Teletype message
From: The SS and Police Führer in the District of Warsaw
Warsaw, 14 May 1943.
Ref. No. I ab/St/G 16 07 Journal No. 646/43 secret.
Re: Large-scale Ghetto Operation.
To: The Higher SS and Police Führer Fast, SS-Obergruppenführer and General of Police Krüger—or deputy.
Krakow

Progress of large-scale operation on 14 May 1943, start 1000 hours.

The raiding parties formed today went to work within the areas allotted to each of them under orders to force open further dwelling dug-outs and to catch the Jews. In this way a considerable number of bandits and Jews were caught, especially as some traces had been discovered during the night which were now followed up with good results. The night patrols clashed with armed bandits several times. These bandits fired a machine gun and small arms. In this operation we had four casualties—3 Waffen-SS men and 1 Policeman. Repeatedly, shots were fired from the Aryan part against the external barricade. In the skirmishes about 30 bandits were shot and 9 Jews and bandits, members of an armed gang, were captured. One dug-out was taken during the night, the Jews captured, and some pistols, among them one of 12-mm caliber, were captured. In one dug-out inhabited by 100 persons, we were able to capture 2 rifles, 16 pistols, some hand grenades and incendiary appliances. Of the bandits who resisted, some again wore German military uniform, German-steel helmets and 'knobeloecher'. Apart from the carbines, we captured 60 rounds of German rifle ammunition. One raiding party had a skirmish with a gang, 10 to 14 strong, on the roofs of a block of buildings at the border of the Ghetto (Aryan part). The bandits were destroyed; we suffered no losses.

The captured bandits repeatedly testify that still not all persons in the Ghetto have been caught. They confidently expect that the action will soon be over, and that they will then be able to continue to live in the Ghetto. Several bandits stated that they had long been in a position to kill off the leader of the action, the 'General', as they call him, but that they would not do so, since they had orders to that effect to avoid the risk of a further intensification of the anti-Jewish measures.

Today again some concrete buildings in which the bandits find refuge time and again were blown up by the engineers.

In order to force the bandits in the sewers to come to the surface, 183 sewer entrances were opened at 1500 hours, and smoke candles were lowered into them at an ordered x-time, thereupon the bandits, seeking escape from what they supposed to be poison gas, crowded together in the centre of the former Ghetto, and we were able to pull them out of the sewer entrances there.

I shall come to a decision after tomorrow's operations regarding termination of the action.

Today SS-Gruppenführer and Lieutenant General of Waffen-SS von Herff was present during the operations.

Our strength:

| **Used in operation:** | | |
|---|---|---|
| German Police | 4/184 | |
| Engineering Em. Serv | 1/6 | |
| Security Police | 2/16 | |
| Engineers | 4/73 | |
| Waffen-SS | 12/51270 | |
| Cordoning forces. | Day | Night |
| German Police | 2/138 | 1/87 |
| Waffen-SS | ------- | 1/300 |
| Trawniki | ------- | |
| Polish Police | 1/160 | 1/160 |

Our losses:

5 wounded, 4 Waffen-SS, 1 Police

A total of 398 Jews were caught today, furthermore 154 Jews and bandits were shot in battle. The total of the Jews caught has risen to 55,731.

Booty: rifles, pistols, and ammunition. Further, a number of incendiary bottles (Molotov cocktails).

Termination of action; 2155 hours, will be continued on 15 May 1943 0900 hours.

The SS and Police Führer in the District of Warsaw.
Signed: Stroop
SS-Brigadeführer and Major General of Police.
Certified copy:
**Jesuiter** SS-Sturmbannführer

Copy
Teletype message
From: The SS and Police Führer in the District of Warsaw
Warsaw, 15 May 1943.
Ref. No.: I ab/St/Gr 16 07 Journal No. 648/43 secret.
Re: Large-scale Ghetto Operation.
To: The Higher SS and Police Führer East, SS-Obergruppenführer and General of Police Krüger—or deputy.
Krakow

Progress of large-scale operation on 15 May 1943. Start 0900 hours.

The 5 scouting parties who patrolled the Ghetto last night reported that they encountered Jews only sporadically. In contrast to the preceding nights, they were able to shoot 6 or 7 Jews. The combing-out actions today also had little result. 29 more dug-outs were discovered, but part of them were no longer inhabited. A total of 87 Jews were caught today and 67 bandits and Jews were shot in battle. In a skirmish which developed around noon, and in which the bandits again resisted by using Molotov cocktails, pistols, and home-made hand grenades, the gang was destroyed; but subsequently a policeman was wounded by a shot through the right thigh. A special unit once more searched the last block of buildings which was still intact in the Ghetto, and subsequently destroyed it. In the evening the chapel, mortuary, and all other buildings on the Jewish cemetery were blown up or destroyed by fire.

The sum total of Jews caught has risen to 55,885.

Our strength:

**Used in operation:**

| | |
|---|---|
| German Police | 4/184 |
| Engineering Em. S | 1/6 |

| | | |
|---|---|---|
| Security Police | 2/16 | |
| Waffen-SS | 12/510 | |
| **Cordoning forces:** | **Day** | **Night** |
| German Police | 2/138 | 1/87 |
| Waffen-SS | ------- | 1/300 |
| Trawniki | 270 | ------- |
| Polish Police | 1/160 | 1/160 |

Our losses:
1 Policeman wounded.

We captured 4 pistols of larger calibres, 1 infernal machine with fuse, 10 kilograms of explosives, and a considerable amount of ammunition. Termination of operation: 2130 hours. Will be continued on 16 May 1943, 1000 hours.

I will terminate the large-scale operation on 16 May 1943 at dusk, by blowing up the Synagogue, which we did not succeed in accomplishing today, and will subsequently charge Police Battalion III/23 with continuing and completing the measures which are still necessary.

The SS and Police Führer in the District of Warsaw.
Signed: Stroop
SS-Brigadeführer and Major General of Police.
Certified copy:
**Jesuiter** SS-Sturmbannführer

Copy
Teletype message
From: The SS and Police Führer in the District of Warsaw
Warsaw, 16 May, 1943.
Ref. No.: I ab-St/Gr 16 07 Journal Nr. 652/43 secret.
Re: Large-scale Ghetto Operation.
To: The Higher SS and Police Führer East, SS-Obergruppenführer and General of Police Krüger—or deputy.
Krakow

Progress of large-scale operation on 16 May 1943, start 1000 hours.

180 Jews, bandits, and sub-humans were destroyed. The former Jewish quarter of Warsaw is no longer in existence. The large-scale action was terminated at 2015 hours by blowing up the Warsaw Synagogue.

The measures to be taken with regard to the established banned areas were handed over to the commander of police battalion III/23, whom I instructed carefully.

Our losses: None.

The total of Jews caught up to date has risen to 51,313. Outside the former Ghetto 254 Jews and bandits were shot.

Termination of operation: 2100 hours, will be continued on 10 May 1943, 1000 hours.

The SS and Police Führer in the District of Warsaw.
Signed: Stroop
SS-Brigadeführer and Major General of Police.
Certified copy:
**Jesuiter** SS-Sturmbannführer

Copy
Teletype message
From: The SS and Police Führer in the District of Warsaw,
Warsaw, 10 May, 1943.
Ref. Nr. I ab St/Gr 16 07 Journal No. 627/43 secret.
Re: Large-scale Ghetto Operation.
To: The Higher SS and Police Führer East, SS-Obergruppenführer and General of Police Krüger—or deputy.
Krakow

Progress of large-scale action on 10 May 1943 start 1000 hours.

Today raiding parties again combed out the area of the former Ghetto. As on preceding days we again pulled out of the dug-outs, against all expectations, a considerable number of Jews. The resistance offered by the Jews had not weakened today. In contrast to the previous days, it seems that those members of the main body of the Jewish battle group who are still in existence and have not been destroyed have retired into the ruins still within their reach, with the intention of firing from there against our men and inflicting casualties.

Today we caught a total of 1,183 Jews alive, 187 bandits and Jews were shot. Again, a not ascertainable number of Jews and bandits were destroyed in the blown-up dug-outs. The total of Jews caught up to date has risen to 52,693.

Today at 0900 hours a truck drove up to a certain sewer in the so-called Prosta. Someone in the truck exploded two hand grenades, which was the signal for the bandits who were standing ready in the sewer to climb out of it. The bandits and Jews—there are always some Polish bandits among them armed with carbines, small arms, and one machine gun, climbed into the truck and drove away in an unknown direction. The last man of the gang, who stood sentry in the sewer and had the duty of closing the sewer lid, was captured. It is he who gave the above information. He testified that most of the members of the gang, which had been divided into several

Total number of Jews dealt with 56,065, including both Jews caught and Jews whose extermination can be proved.

No losses today.

I will submit a final report to the Conference of SS Police Führer on 18 May 1943.

The SS and Police Führer in the District of Warsaw.
Signed: Stroop
SS-Brigadeführer and Major General of Police.
Certified copy:
**Jesuiter** SS-Sturmbannführer

Copy
Teletype message
From: The SS and Police Führer in the District of Warsaw
Warsaw, 24 May 1943.
Ref. No.: I ab-St/Gr 16 07 Journal Nr. 663/43 secret.
Re: Large-scale Ghetto Operation.
Ref: Your teletype message Nr. 946 or 21 May 1943.
To: The Higher SS and Police Führer East, SS-Obergruppenführer and General of Police Krüger—or deputy.
Krakow

I beg to reply to the above teletype message:

**Re No. 1:**
Of the total of 56,065 caught, about 7,000 were destroyed in the former Ghetto during large-scale operation. 6,929 Jews were destroyed by transporting them to T.II; the sum total of Jews destroyed is therefore 13,929. Beyond the number of 56,065 an estimated number of 5 to 6,000 Jews were destroyed by being blown up or by perishing in the flames.

**Re No. 2:**
A total of 631 dug-outs were destroyed.

**Re No. 3 (booty):**

7 Polish rifles, 1 Russian rifle, 1 German rifle.

59 pistols of various calibres.

Several 100 hand grenades, including Polish and homemade ones.

A few 100 incendiary bottles.

Home-made explosive charges.

Infernal machines with fuses.

Large amounts of explosives, ammunition for all calibres, including machine-gun ammunition.

With regard to the bag of arms one must take into consideration that in most cases we were not able to capture the arms themselves, since the Jews and bandits before they were captured threw them away into hideouts and holes which we could not discover or find. The smoke which we had developed in the dug-outs also prevented our men from discovering and capturing the arms. Since we had to blow up the dug-outs at once we were not in a position to search for the arms later on.

The hand grenades, explosive charges, and incendiary bottles captured were used at once against the bandits.

Furthermore, we captured:

1,240 used uniform tunics (partly equipped with medal ribbons, Iron Cross, and East Medal).

600 pairs of used trousers.

Pieces of equipment, and German steel helmets.

103 horses, 4 of them in the former Ghetto (hearse)

We counted up to 23 May 1943:

4.4 million Zloty. We captured moreover about 5 to 6 million Zloty, not yet counted, a considerable amount of foreign currency, including-

$14,300 in paper.

$ 9,200 in gold.

Large amounts of valuables (rings, chains, watches etc.)

**Re No. 4.**

With the exception of 8 buildings (police barracks, hospital and accommodations for working parties) the former Ghetto has been completely destroyed. Where blowing-up was not carried out, only partition walls are still standing. But the ruins still contain enormous amounts of bricks and scrap material which could be used.

The SS and Police Führer in the District of Warsaw.
Signed: Stroop
SS-Brigadeführer and Major General of Police.
Certified copy:
**Jesuiter** SS-Sturmbannführer

A pictorial report, consisting of 54 photographic images with 39 listed captions was then attached. [Author's note: TII refers to the death camp at Treblinka.]

# APPENDIX III

# THE GLOBOCNIK REPORTS

ONCE HIMMLER ORDERED Globocnik to wind up Aktion Reinhardt, the death camps were obliterated and a final accounting was prepared for the financial aspect of the operation. The result is what follows. The reports are remarkable documents in that they provide an overall economic tally of goods and currency seized by the SS masters. Note: the spelling 'Reinhardt' used here may be a translator error.

Nuremberg evidence document 4024-PS [Translation of original]

TOP SECRET
The Higher SS and Police Chief in the Operational Zone of the Adriatic Coast
Trieste, 5/1/1944.
Gl./Go.-Diary No. 1/44 Top Secret PK.
To the Reichsführer-SS and Reich Minister of the Interior, Heinrich Himmler, Berlin.

Reichsführer,
I am taking the liberty of submitting to you in the enclosed a report on the economic development of the Action Reinhardt, as you, Reichsführer, ordered in your letter of 22 Sept 1943 that I should have this completed and submitted by 31 Dec 1943. However, the recognition given me for the Action also impels me to give you, Reichsführer, an account of the economic side, in order that you, Reichsführer, may thereby see that in this respect also, the work was in order. Though SS-Obergruppenführer Pohl has not yet had time to take over, I nevertheless hope that these data will be of assistance.

A proper winding up and my relief is necessary because I carried out this activity within the framework of the SS and it must therefore be wound up in a proper manner with regard to the competent Reich authorities. The Action Reinhardt was also too dangerous.

In addition, however, a certain odium still rests upon me to the effect that in all economic matters I do not maintain the necessary order, and in this respect, I must advance indisputable proof that this is not so.

The total accounting is composed of two parts:

1. The economic part of the Action Reinhardt with the subdivisions a. Accounting and delivery of the assets seized and b. Accounting of the assets attained by the work.
2. The Settlers' Economic Association, the conduct of whose economy also rested on my work, and which is now being transferred to civilian hands.

There is one additional factor to be added to the total accounting of 'Reinhardt' which is that the vouchers dealing with it must be destroyed as soon as possible after the data have already been destroyed by all other works concerned in this matter. With regard to the SWG (Settlers' Economic Association), the question is not only the financial order, but also a transfer so that this institution may be maintained for the settlers.

Only after I have been relieved of both matters will my functions in both be terminated.

I request, Reichsführer, that you lay down a deadline by which the final winding up has to be completed on the spot on the basis of my data.

I have taken the liberty of sending a copy to SS-Obergruppenführer Pohl.

Heil Hitler!
Yours obediently,
[signed] Odilo Globocnik

[Rubber Stamp:] Personal Staff, Reichsführer-SS, Rec'd: 10/1/1944. Diary No. 1851[?]44 Top Secret To: RF
4 copies, first copy
Economic Aspect of the Action Reinhardt, gathered together in the SS Economic and Administrative Head Office—Special Task "G", which I am in charge of and of which I have not been relieved:

The entire Action Reinhardt is divided into four spheres: A. The expulsion itself. B. The employment of labour. C. The exploitation of property. D. Seizure of hidden goods and landed property.

A. The Deportation

This is settled and completed. In this case the prerequisite was to get hold of the people with the small forces available and to cause as little economic damage as possible to war production by methodically appropriate measures. On the whole, this was achieved. Considerable damage occurred only in Warsaw, where, owing to ignorance of the position, the methods applied in the final action were entirely wrong.

I was no longer able to carry out the action in Litzmannstadt (Lodz) myself because of my transfer.

The equipment which was provided for this action from seized goods, which however are to be considered as Reich property, have been removed completely. For reasons of surveillance in each camp a small farm was created which is occupied by an expert.

An income must regularly be paid to him so that he can maintain the small farm.

B. Employment of manpower

The entire manpower was put into closed camps, to which essential war production was transferred.

For this purpose, the following conditions had to be created:

1. Erection of all camps.
2. Erection of workshops with all the working equipment, such as the installation of machinery, power supply, etc.
3. The organization of provisions, by making use of the TWL's as well as by the creation of farms in the vicinity of the camps.
4. Equipment for the establishment of adequate sanitation and hygiene.
5. Security measures.
   a. Achieved by adequate security precautions
   b. By organizing a security organization within the camp
   c. By adequate guarding

   For this purpose, the SS guards were developed, the overwhelming majority of whom carried out their duties satisfactorily led by Germans.

   Their reliability was to be increased by mixing these guards with Reich German guards from the concentration camps.

   d. The pre-conditions for a satisfactory security system were created by these camps being taken over by the concentration camp department of the SS Economic and Administrative Head Office.
6. The proper administration and methodical treatment were made possible thanks to extensive training of the German leading personnel. It became apparent that the working capacity of the Jews in the camps was constantly increasing.
7. By the creation of a works management and factory conditions, the technical and commercial aspects were ensured. For this purpose, the 'Osti' was created and as second

works management the German Equipment Works [Deutsche Ausrüstungswerke]. A total of 18 works was established; it was intended to add more. About 52,000 workers were available. These conditions of work made it possible to accept urgent orders both from the Armament Inspectorate and from Reich Minister Speer, and thus to replace bombed out works.

The demand from these offices was considerable. 'Osti' and the German Equipment Works were firms under my own supervision, whereas other concerns, such as the Heinkel aircraft works were only looked after by me.

Enclosure 1 contained factory reports and output figures. The number of orders was so large that the German Equipment Works (DAW) was fully occupied up to March and the other factories had enough work for 2–3 months.

C. Exploitation of Property.
The exploitation of property which was carried out by Reinhardt. It has been completed as shown in Enclosure 2.

D. Seizure of Hidden Goods.
The seizure of hidden goods and exploitation of landed property is divided into:
1. Property such as machinery, raw material, etc., handed over by the 'Osti' to Aryans. To date the result is 6.3 million Reichsmarks; a further 7–8 million Reichsmarks are yet to be brought in. This seizure had furthermore the advantage that all those were affected who had built up industries for themselves in this manner, with the help of Jews without cost to themselves and had become rich without effort.
2. Seizure of Jewish assets at home and abroad in that the camp inmates were ordered to cede these claims to the 'Osti', which then carried out the recovery. The first attempt resulted in a cession of an amount of 11 million Zloty, at least half of which appeared obtainable. However, since it was also possible to discover money that had been smuggled abroad, this action could have brought valuable foreign currency to the Reich.
3. Real estate was transferred to the Real Estate Administration of the Government General for exploitation. All the above-mentioned arrangements were functioning satisfactorily at the time of my departure. As I received an indication from the Reichsführer-SS that a potential transfer might be possible some time during the year, I immediately go down to finally settling and consolidating the organization I had created, and for this purpose handed over the entire organization to the SS Economic and Administrative Head Office.

The measures taken were as follows:

1. On the 13 August 1943, the SS Training Camp of Trawniki was handed over to SS-Obergruppenführer Pohl (see letter of 18 August 1943—Chief A/Fr./S—Enclosure 3).

2. On the 7 September 1943, in a conference with SS-Obergruppenführer Pohl, the taking over of 10 SS Work Camps in the Lublin District as subsidiaries of Lublin

Concentration Camp was decided on and in addition the further handing over of further working camps in the Government General. The head of the Lublin Concentration Camp was provided with suitable contracts. This conference was brought about by SS-Obergruppenführer Krüger and SS-Standartenführer Schell (see file note of the Chief of the SS-WVHA (SS Economic and Administrative Head Office)) of 7 September 1943—D II/L (Ref. No. 29 Ma./F.) (Enclosure 4).

3. In pursuance thereof, a letter of the Commandant of the Lublin Concentration Camp, dated 14 September 1943 to the SS Work Camps announced that they had become subsidiaries of the Lublin Concentration Camp. The mixing of guards of foreign race with the German concentration camp guards from the Reich has also been initiated.

4. On the 22 October 1943, SS-Obergruppenführer Pohl announced that he had ordered taking over of the following Work Camps by Amtsgruppe D: (1) Old Airport Lublin (2) SS Work Camp Trawniki (3) SS Work Camp Poniatowa (4) Forced Labour Camp and SS Workshops in Radom (5) Forced Labour Camp and SS Workshops in Budzyn (6) Main Camp Krakow Plaszow (7) German Equipment Works, Lublin (8) Armament stores in Lemberg.

5. During the conference on 22 October 1943, SS-Obergruppenführer Pohl stated that I would be replaced as first manager of the 'Osti' by the second manager and a new second manager would be appointed. My relief was also approved. I also explained everything fully to my successor and called his attention to his supervisory duty. I thereby created all the conditions for the continuation. The principles of security existed and were guaranteed by the Leadership by the Concentration Camps. The relief has not yet been effected.

On 3 November 1943, the workers were withdrawn from the labour camps and the works shut down. The camp leaders were not informed of this action although the responsibility rested with them. I was thus impeded in my supervisory duty. I have ordered the camp leaders to wind up and continue determining the contracts and/or transferring stocks.

On the day before the evacuation of the camps, General Schindler of the Armaments Inspectorate, Krakow, arranged with the camp leaders on the basis of a promise from SS-Obergruppenführer Krüger, that (a) In the future only armament contracts were to be given to the labour camps. (b) He had received the assurance on 2 November that a further 10,000 Jews were to be removed for armament work.

It was no longer possible to carry out with this arrangement.

[Signed] Globocnik.
SS-Gruppenführer and Lt. General of Police.

These enclosures are the papers mentioned in SS-Gruppenführer Globocnik's letter of the 5 January 1944. They have been taken out to facilitate depositing.

**Report on the Administrative Development of Aktion Reinhardt**

I. All the assets acquired as a result of this Aktion were centrally mustered by an administration set up by me, duly classified and booked. The muster extends to the entire Government General. The personnel came from the SS Economic and Administrative Head Office (SS-WVHA).

The utilisation and winding up of the assets was carried out on the basis of directives by the Reichsführer-SS. During the course of the Action this was summed up in a directive of 26 September 1942 and 9 December 1943, and the SS Economic and Administrative Head Office was given the task of winding up with regard to the Reich authorities.

The assets I collected were regularly delivered to the SS Economic and Administrative Head Office against receipts, and they in turn passed on the assets to the Reichsbank, the Reich Ministry of Finance, textile concerns, etc.

On the orders of the Reichsführer-SS, necessary articles could be removed for the maintenance of persons of the German race. The Reichsführer-SS forbade any appropriation for the purposes of the SS.

What is remarkable about the accounting is that no hard and fast basis for the amount collected existed, as the collection of the assets was carried out under orders and only the decency and honesty, as well as the surveillance, of the SS men used for this purpose could guarantee a complete delivery. Nevertheless, what was seized and collected and received by the Department Reinhardt was listed and delivered without error and with the greatest accuracy. A preliminary examination up to 1 April 1943 by SS-Obersturmbannführer Vogt of the SS Economic and Administrative Head Office, has already taken place and has revealed perfect order. For the balance, the preliminary examination has still to be carried out.

In accordance with an agreement with the Reich Ministry of Finance, this preliminary examination is final and the vouchers and data will be destroyed in accordance with Security regulations, cutting out the Reich Accounting Office.

II. The assets accounted for are divided into:

1. Sums of Reichsmarks and Zloty. The entire expenditure transport costs, dues, etc. incurred as a result of this Aktion were covered from these receipts. By far the greater portion was placed at the disposal of the SS Economist in the Government General and the amounts were credited to the Aktion Reinhardtt in Reichsmarks by the SS Economic and Administrative Head Office by an accounting transaction and handed over to the Reichsbank.

A small portion was used for foreign currency reasons as a credit for various economic enterprises and then also credited by the SS Economic and Administrative Head Office by an accounting transaction.

In addition, differences arising from increases in the price of urgently required raw material supplies were covered. All these transactions were carried out with the consent of the SS Economic and Administrative Head Office. A further amount was placed at the disposal of the Concentration Camp currently for additional building operations, to develop the economic concern and to obtain the necessary agricultural machinery, etc. Exact accounts were kept of this, the purchases were always confirmed by me, and the documents covering this will also be attached to the final account. The accounts were kept by the Administrative Chief of the Concentration Camps and were actually kept separate from my administration, as the Concentration Camp Administration was independent of the SS Garrison Administration, Lublin, by order of the SS Economic and Administrative Head Office. The authority which finally takes over the concern will have to reimburse Reinhardt for these expenditures.

2. Foreign Currency in bank notes or coined gold was collected, sorted, and also handed over to the Reichsbank via the SS Economic and Administrative Head Office.

3. Jewels, jewellery, watches and such like, were sorted according to their value and delivered to the SS Economic and Administrative Head Office. On orders from this office, watches of non-precious metals were handed over to the troops, spectacles were repaired and placed at the disposal of wounded persons, and utensils of no value were principally handed over to Wehrmacht authorities to cover urgent needs. The necessary transfer vouchers are available.

4. Textiles, garments, underclothing, bed feathers and rags were collected and sorted according to their quality. The sorted articles had to be searched for hidden valuables and finally disinfected. More than 1,900 wagons were then placed at the disposal of the authorities named by the Reich Ministry of Economy by order of the SS Economic and Administrative Head Office. Out of these stocks not only foreign workers were clothed but a large portion was used for re-manufacture. No case of sickness became known, although these garments frequently came from persons suffering from spotted typhus. The disinfection therefore was adequate.

The best garments were separated and by order of the Reichsführer-SS were used for supplying persons of the German race. Shoes were also sorted according to how far they could be used and then either given to persons of German race or to concentration camps for supplying inmates, or else taken to pieces and used for wooden shoes for supplying inmates.

5. Individual valuables of a special kind, such as stamps, coins, and such like were sorted and delivered to the SS Economic and Administrative Head Office; worthless articles were destroyed.

6. Other articles received, such as soap, washing materials, crockery and cutlery, and the like, were used in the Jewish camps; glass, old iron articles, etc., were sent to the salvage centres for re-manufacture.

7. The food brought on the transports was used to help provision the Jewish camps.

8. Valuable furniture and household utensils were reconditioned and mainly put at the disposal of settlers of German race. But furniture was also loaned to German and

Wehrmacht authorities against an accommodation bill. Inferior goods were either destroyed or given to the population as a reward for good work at the harvest, etc.

It was attempted to take from articles which could no longer be used parts such as locks, hinges, and the like, and to use these elsewhere.

The vouchers pertaining to the loaned articles were submitted monthly to the Higher SS and Police Chief East [Krüger].

In accordance with the order of the Reichsführer-SS of the 22 September, the total takings are now closed, evaluated and passed on, so that there is hardly any mass left now.

Equipment which was necessary for carrying out the Aktion, such as barracks, camp equipment, vehicles, and such like, which had been purchased out of the monies obtained, is still on hand.

This equipment has been registered. A decision must, however, still be taken as to what purpose it is to serve.

The total value of the articles received is, according to the attached list, approximately 18 million Reichsmarks. However, minimum values have been assured, so that the total value is most likely twice as much, quite apart from the value of the articles obtained which are in short supply, such as textiles, of which alone more than 1900 wagons have been made available to German industry.

[signed] Globocnik
SS-Gruppenführer and Lt. General of Police

Assets delivered from Aktion Reinhardt
The following assets from the Aktion 'Reinhard' were delivered to the SS Economic and Administrative Head Office, Berlin, for further transmission to the Reichsbank or to the Reich Ministry of Economics:

a. Reichsmark sums totalling RM 53,013,133.51
b. Currency in banknotes from all the principal countries in the world (half a million dollars being particularly to be noted) to a total value of RM 1,452,904.65
c. Foreign currency in gold coins to a total value of RM 843,802.75
d. Precious metals (about 1800 kg. of gold and about 10000 kg. of silver in bars) to a total value of RM 5,353,943.00
e. Other valuables such as jewellery, watches, spectacles, etc. (the number of watches being particularly worthy of note about 16,000 in working order and about 51,000 requiring repair: they have been placed at the disposal of the troops) RM 26,089,800.00
f. About 1,000 wagons of textiles to a total value of RM 13,294,400.00.
   Total RM 100,047,983.91.

1,000 wagons of textiles and about another 50% of the above mentioned assets—which still have to be counted and valued—are warehoused here. It should be noted here that the estimated values were based on the officially established rates of exchange or prices, which however would be much higher on the open market, for instance in the sale of precious stones or precious metals abroad, as the flight to investments in articles whose value is not subject to much fluctuation is much greater there than with us. Besides these sales abroad bring us foreign currency. If these prices were taken as a basis of evaluation here, this was done in order to be able to give a picture of the assets delivered; in general, this evaluation is not authoritative. The value of the acquisition lies principally in the fact that such large quantities of urgently needed raw materials can thereby be gained and that, on the basis of the assets obtained, foreign currency can be brought in, with which raw materials can in turn be bought by Reich authorities.

[Signed] Globocnik
SS-Gruppenführer and Lieut. General of Police.
1 detailed list enclosed herewith.

List of Jewish property received for delivery up to 3.2.1943, showing values
[Editor's Note: The following tables are reproduced as they appear in original German document although accuracy of calculations is questionable.]
[rubber stamp]
Personal Staff Reichsführer-SS, Ref. No. Secret/115

1. Cash in hand:
   - RM 16,931,722.01;
   - Delivery SS-Economist, Krakow: RM 31.5 million;
   - SS-Econ.-Admin. Head Office Berlin-(RB): RM 5.58 million;

[Total]: RM 53 million

2. Foreign currency in notes:
   - USA Dollars: 505,046.00 Rate of exchange: 2.50 RM 1.26 million
   - Pal. Pounds: 1069/00/00 9.30 RM 9,941.70
   - Pengoes: 16,436.00 .60. RM 9,861.00
   - Roubles: 294,070.00 .10 RM 29,407.00
   - English Pounds: 3,822. 9.30 RM 36,644.60
   - Canadian Dollars: 3,840.76 2.60 RM 9,601.87
   - Pesetas: 131.00 2.40 RM 314.40
   - Czech Crowns: 789,630.00 .10 RM 78963.00
   - French Francs: 22,767.60 .05 RM 1138.37
   - Brazilian Francs: 8.00 .09 RM .72
   - South African Pounds: 28/10/00 4.40 RM 125.40
   - Turkish Pounds: .5/50/00 1.90 RM 10.45
   - Dutch Gulden: 1,720.00 1.33 RM 2287.60

- Swiss Francs: 7,530.00 5.80 RM 4,367.40
- Lira: 883.00 .13 RM 114.79
- Levas: 100.00 .01 RM 1.00
- Australian Pounds: 15/10/00 2.60 RM 38.75
- Lei: 13,486.00 .02 RM 269.72
- Egyptian Pounds: 4/l0/00 4.40 RM 19.80
- Belgas: 4,203.00 .40 RM 1681.80 Lats: 10.00 .10 RM 1.00
- Argent. Pesos: 90.00 1.00 RM 90.00
- Paragu.: 10.00 .60 RM 6.00
- Swedish Crowns: 455.00 .60 RM 273.00
- Norwegian Crowns: 165.00 .60 RM 99.00
- Dinars: 30.00 .05 RM 1.50
- Slov. Croons: 59,608.75 .10 RM 5,960.88
- Litas 140.00 .10 RM 14.00

[Total]: RM 1,452,904.65

3. Currency in gold coins:
   - USA Dollars: 116,425.00 Rate of exchange: 4.20 RM 488985.00
   - Roubles: 91,362.00 2.15 RM 196,428.30
   - English Pounds: 3,822/00/00 20.40 RM 77,969.00
   - Austrian Crowns: 30,940.00 .85 RM 26,299.00
   - Austrian Shillings: 1,975.00 [none] RM 1185.00
   - Ducats: 2,366.00 10.00 RM 23660.00
   - Finnish marks: 20.00 1.00 RM 20.00
   - Reichsmarks: 12,730.00 1.00 RM 12730.00
   - Zloty: 1,080.00 .50 RM 540.00
   - Danish Crowns: 230.00 .52 RM 119.60
   - Czech ducats: 2.00 10.00 RM 20.00
   - Portuguese reis: 15,000.00 (150 Ese) 1.00 RM 150.00
   - Pesetas: 25.00 1.50 RM 37.50
   - French francs: 8,005.00 1.62 RM 12,968.10
   - So. African Pounds: 2/00/00 20.40 RM 40.80
   - Turkish pounds: 47/00/00 3.50 RM 164.50
   - Dutch gulden: 315.00 17.00 (f.10 Hf1) RM 535.50
   - Swiss francs: 490.00 16.50 (f.20 Frs) RM 404.25
   - Lira: 1,210.00 .50 RM 605.00
   - Australian pounds: 8/10/00 20.40 RM 172.60
   - Lei: 1,140.00 .50 RM 570.00
   - Belgas: 140.00 .50 RM 70.00
   - Swedish crowns: 2.00 11.20 RM 22.40
   - Norwegian Crowns: 35.00 11.20 RM 39.20

- Dinars: 30.00 50 RM 5.00
- Cuban pesos: 10.00 4.20 RM 42.00
- Alb. francs: 20.00 .50 RM 10.00

Total: RM 843,802.75 4

4. Precious metals:
   - 1,775.46 kg. of gold in bars at RM 2,784.00 RM 4,942,870.00;
   - 9639.34 kg. of silver in bars at RM 40.00 RM 385,573.00;
   - 5.10 kg. of (?) platinum at RM 5,000.00 RM 25,500.00;

Total: RM 5.35 million

5. Other valuables:
   - 5 Gold revolving pencils: at RM 30.00 RM 150.00
   - 17 Gold fountain pens: at RM 70.00 RM 1,190.00
   - 4 Ladies' platinum watches: at RM 300.00 RM 1,200.00
   - 2,894 Gentlemen's pocket watches, gold: at RM 500.00 RM 1.42 million
   - 578 Gentlemen's wrist watches, gold: at RM 300.00 RM 173,400.00
   - 7,313 Ladies' wrist watches, gold: at RM 350.00 RM 1.82 million
   - 19 Platinum watch cases with brilliants and diamonds: at RM 1,000.00 RM 19,000.00
   - 280 Bracelets with brilliants and diamonds: at RM 3,500.00 RM 980,000.00
   - 6,245 Gentlemen's wrist watches: at RM 10.00 RM 62,450.00
   - 3,455 Gentlemen's pocket watches: at RM 20.00 RM 269,100.00
   - 1 Gentleman's pocket watch-gold with brilliants: at RM 600.00 RM 600.00
   - 179 Ladies' gold watches with brilliants and diamonds: at RM 600.00 RM 107,400.00
   - 7 Ladies' ring watches, gold: at RM 150.00 RM 1050.00
   - 4 Ladies' fob watches with pearls: at RM 200.00 RM 800.00
   - 394 Ladies' fob watches with brilliants: at RM 600.00 RM 236,400.00
   - 228 Ladies' platinum and brilliant watches: at RM 1200.00 RM 273,600.00
   - 293 Ladies' fob watches, gold: at RM 250.00 RM 73,250.00
   - 2,324 Spectacles: at RM 3.00 RM 66,972.00
   - 3 prs cuff links with brilliants: at RM 150.00 RM 450.00
   - 1,675 Rings, gold with brilliants and diamonds: at RM 1,500.00 RM 11,675,000.00
   - 7,200 Ladies wrist watches: at RM 10.00 RM 75,000.00
   - 40 Gold brooches: at RM 350.00 RM 14,000.00
   - 1,399 prs gold earrings with brilliants: at RM 250.00 RM 349,750.00
   - 169 Tie pins with brilliants diamonds: at RM 100.00 RM 16,900.00
   - 1,974 Gold brooches with brilliants and diamonds: at RM 2000.00 RM 3,948,000.00 70.00
   - 27 Gold bracelets with brilliants and diamonds: at RM 250.00 RM 6,750.00
   - 49 kg. Pearls: RM 4 million

- 7,000 Fountain pens: at RM 10.00 RM 70,000.00
- 130 Single large brilliants: at RM 1,000.00 RM 130,000.00
- 2 Necklaces with brilliants and diamonds: at RM 1,500.00 RM 3,000.00
- 1 Gold cigarette case: at RM 400.00 RM 400.00
- 1 Mother of pearl casket: RM 20.00
- 3 Gold Compacts: at RM 50.00 RM 150.00
- 2 Mother of Pearl opera glasses: at RM 50.00 RM 100.00
- 1.44 kg. Corals: RM 150 00
- 1,370 Watches requiring repair: at RM 5.00 RM 256,850 00
- 1,000 Revolving pencils: at RM 3.00 RM 3,000.00
- 350 Shaving equipment: at RM 2.50 RM 875.00
- 800 Pocket knives: at RM 1.00 RM 800.00 .00
- 3,240 Money purses: at RM 1.50 RM 4,860.00
- 1,316 Brief cases: at RM 2.50 RM 3,287.50
- 1,600 prs Scissors: at RM 0.50 RM 750.00
- 230 Flashlights: at RM 0.50 RM 115.00
- 2,554 Alarm clocks requiring repair: at RM 3.00 RM 7,662.00
- 160 Alarm clocks in running condition: at RM 6.00 RM 960.00
- 477 Sun glasses: at RM 0.50 RM 238.50
- 41 Silver cigarette cases: at RM 30.00 RM 1,230.00
- 230 Clinical thermometers: at RM 3.00 RM 690.00

Total: RM 26,089,800.00

6. Textiles
   - 462 Wagons of rags: at RM 700.00 RM 323,400.00
   - 261 Wagons of bed feathers: at RM 10,000.00 RM 2,510,000.00
   - 317 Wagons of clothing and underclothing: at RM 33,000.00 RM 10,461,000.00

Total: RM 13,294,400.00

Totals:

1. Cash and cash balance delivered: RM 53 million.
2. Foreign currency in notes: RM 1.45 million.
3. Foreign currency in gold coin: RM 843,802.76
4. Precious metals: 5,353,943.00
5. Miscellaneous: RM 26 million.
6. Textiles: 13.29 million

Total: RM 100 million.

Lublin, 27 February 1943.

/S/ [?] SS-Sturmbannführer

Situation with Regard to Orders of the Concerns of the SS and Labour Camps in Lublin District on 11/3/1943

- The situation with regard to orders, according to Industrial concerns:
  - Ostindustrie G.n.b.H. (Eastern Industry Co., F Ltd.), Lublin: ZI 5.55 million. Encl.
  - German Equipment Works, Lublin ZI 7.98 million. Encl.
  - Textile Works, Poniatowa ZI 13 million. Encl.
  - Fur Works, Trawniki ZI 4.63 million. Encl. Total: ZI 31 million. [As it is almost entirely a question of wage. contracts, the situation with regard to orders represents essentially only wage and administration costs. The actual value of production if the concerns had to produce their own materials would therefore have been at least 50% higher.]
- This total situation with regard to orders is divided up into the following manufacturing groups:
  - Lumber: ZI 5.72 million.
  - Metal: ZI 4.17 million.
  - Textiles: ZI 10,338,200.00
  - Leather: ZI 1.967 million.
  - Furs: ZI 4.81 million.
  - Others: [Under other manufacturing groups the following are included amongst others: Production of peat or generator coke, the only roofing felt factory in Lublin district, 2 metal-making factories, 1 brush factory, the largest bristle preparing establishment of the Government General, basket and straw plaiting, and printing concerns, production of concrete parts for building huts.] ZI 4.054 million Total: ZI 31.077 million

[signed] Globocnik

Situation with regard to orders of the 'Ostindustrie' G. Ltd., Lublin, the 11/3/1943

Factory:

- II Peat Mine Dorohucza

Orders:

1. 420 tons peat coke
2. 4.5 tons tar

Customer:

1. Waffen-SS
2. DAW

Total value in Zloty:

1. 210000
2. 4500

3. Of which Wehrmacht orders in Zloty:
    1. 210000 Civilian orders Zloty:
    2. 4500
- III. Brush Factory for bristles, Wicker works factory:
    1. 724,000 painting brushes and brushes of various kinds
    2. Repairs of 135,000 ammunition baskets
    3 . 15,000 kg bristles for dressing
- (1) W BA Berlin RWL II of the Waffen-SS etc. (2) Munition store Lublin (3) Various deliveries to Navy and to private firms (1) 1.592 million (2) 216,000 (3) 210,000 (1) 1.39 million (2) 216,000 (3) 105,000 (1) 200,000 (2) (3) 105,000
- V. Mechanical and other factories in Lublin
    1. Production of 1.5 million threaded fuses
    2. Production of 4.5 million buckles
    3. Repairs to 37,500 tin packing receptacles
    4. Taking to pieces of 3,000 gun carriage installations
    5. Repairs to 15,000 motor car component parts
    6. Repairs to about 3,000 watches (or clocks) and other repairs of various kinds
    7. Preparing 18,000 articles of military equipment

    (1) Navy (Planning Syndicate) (2) Cossack division (Army) others (3) Munition store, Lublin (4) Airforce (Planning Syndicate) (5) HKP Lublin (6) Navy and civilian firms (7) Factory Kienle Stuggart for Navy

    (1) 1.35 million (2) 1.62 million (3) 150,000 (4) 40,000 (5) 75,000 (6) 60,000 (7) 25,200

    (1) 1,350,000 (2) 1.62 million (3) 150,000 (4) 40,000 (5) 75,000 (6) 15,000 (7) 25,200 (6) 45,000

    [Totals]: Total value in Zloty: 5.55 million Of which Wehrmacht orders in Zloty: 5.198 million Civilian orders in Zloty: 354,500

    The above figures for orders include, together with the current orders for permanent orders, figures for 3 months only.

**Enclosure 2**

Situation with Regard to Orders of the German Equipment Works-Works Dublin on 3 Nov 1943

Manufacturing Group Wood: Total value in Zloty: 5,728,000.00

Of this: Wehrmacht Orders in Zloty: 3.899 million

Available Orders in Zloty: 1.82 million

Metal: 151,000.00 130,000.00 21,000.00

Textiles: 28,000.00 14,000.00 14,000.00

Leather: 660,000.00 570,000.00 90,000.00

Others: 1.422 million 162,000.00 1.26 million
[Total]: 7.989 million 4.775 million 3.21 million

Note: The above figures of orders contain, besides the current orders, figures for three months only for permanent orders.

The German equipment works were the best developed works.

41 Aryan leading personnel ran 5,445 Jewish workers who worked 1.115 million working days in the first 10 months of the year 1943 with 31 million Zloty in the bank and till.

Woodworking was in the foreground, 7,600 square metres [*Editor's note: cubic metres are obviously meant*] of wood being dealt with.

Shoemaking also rose to 337,250 pairs and was to be raised to 450,000 pairs by the repair work shop which is being newly added.

331,700 square metres of roofing felt were produced during this period.

Woodworking was to have been extended considerably by the purchase of a sawmill of their own and the by-products utilised—as the production of wood for producer gas and the making of charcoal; the tar produced thus could again have been used in the production of roofing felt.

Another considerable production was the manufacturing of 2,500 Finnish tents and the monthly preparation of 25,000 packing containers.

71,000 knapsacks and haversacks were also repaired.

5,000 optical instruments were taken to pieces.

1,270 motor cars were repaired.

Production in 1944 is said to have been:

Wood cut: 20,000 cubic metres; Manufacture of shelter equipment: 15,000 units; Doors, windows, shelves: 20,000 units; Bell tents: 5,000 units; Preparation of packing containers: 250,000 units; Wooden soles: 6,000 units; Brush handles: 4.8 million units; Fuel for wood-burners: 20,000 Rm.; Charcoal: 4,500 kg.; Roofing felt: 2 million sq. m.

The capacity is best shown by the fact that 312 working unions of the partisans in the government, generally, did not even have twice the turnover of the DAW alone. The orders were covered by 83% work for the Wehrmacht and 17% for the civil field.

Situation with regard to orders of the textile works 3 Nov 1943

Manufacturing Group: Textile orders

Orders:

- Production and repair of 1.53 million articles of clothing of all kinds.
- Customer: Wehrmacht primarily HBA. Warsaw and Posen and HBA, Berlin and civilian firms.
- Total value in Zloty: 10.28 million

Of this:

- Wehrmacht orders in Zloty: 7.2 million
- Civilian Orders in Zloty: 3.085 million

Fur clothing:

- Production of 28,100 articles of fur clothing of various kinds
- Wehrmacht 280,000 280,000

Leather goods.

- Production of 132,000 articles or pairs of leather goods of various kinds.
- Wehrmacht 1.31 million 1.31 million

Iron orders.

- Production of nuts.
- Working Syndicate D-OKH 725,000 725,000

Reinforced concrete construction.

- Production of 20,200 reinforced concrete nuts.
- Ministry of Armaments Speer (Armament-construction) 400,000 400,000
- [Total]: 13 million 9.91 million 3.085 million
- Note: The above figures of orders contain, besides the current orders, figures for 3 months only for permanent orders.

**Appendix 2**

Provisional balance sheet of the Action 'Reinhardt', Lublin, for 16 Dec 1943

The following money and stocks were brought to the German Reich during the course of the Action 'Reinhardt', Lublin, during the period 1 Apr 1942–15 Dec 1943 inclusive:

Cash:

- Cash in hand Income: RM 17,470,796.66
- To the Reichsbank Berlin, Reichsmark notes and coins RM 3,979,623.60
- To the Reichsbank Berlin, Zloty notes and coins RM 5,000,461.00
- To the SS economist, Krakow RM 60,416,181.37
- Loans for SS industrial concerns RM 8,218,878.36
- Income from title 21/E RM 656,062.40
- Total RM 85,741,903.28

Cash:

- Personal taxes, title 21/7a Expenditure RM 96,207.28
- Expenditure in goods (of which about 40% for J-Transports [Author note: Jewish transports] title 21/7b) RM 11,765,552.62
- Counterfeit money (Zloty notes) RM 28,062.64
- Total RM 11,889,822.54

Totals

- Income RM 85,741,903.28
- Expenditure RM 11,889,822.64
- Net income RM 73,862,080.74
- [Totals] RM 86,741,903.28 RM 86,741,903.28

Precious Metals:

- 236 Gold bars 2,909.68 kg at RM 2,800.00 RM 8,147,104.00
- 2134 Silver bars 18,733.69 kg at RM 40.00 RM 749,347.60
- Platinum 15.44 kg at RM 6,000.00 RM 77,200.00
- [Total]: RM 8,973,651.60

Foreign Currency in Notes:

- USA Dollars 1,081,521.40 at RM 2.50 RM 2,703,803.50
- English Pounds 15,646.11 at RM 9.30 RM 145,512.80
- Palestine Pounds 4,922.60 at RM 9.30 RM 45,779.25
- Canadian Dollars 8,966.25 at RM 2.50 RM 22,415.62
- Roubles 2,454,278.36 at RM 0.10 RM 245,427.84
- French Francs 1,468,486.35 at RM 0.05 RM 73,424.31
- Swiss Francs 119,302.33 at RM 6.80 RM 691,953.51
- Lire 6,465.08 at RM 0.10 RM 646.50
- Protectorate Croons 1,746,601.60 at RM 0.10 RM 174,560.15
- Turkish Pounds 39.60 at RM 1.90 RM 75.05
- Belgas 12,449.25 at RM 0.40 RM 4,979.70
- Lei 55,975.54 at RM 0.02 RM 1,119.51
- South African Pounds 119.50 at RM 4.40 RM 525.80
- Dutch Gulden 133,986.95 at RM 1.33 RM 178,202.64
- Levas 9,995,421.00 at RM 0.01 RM 59,954.21
- Australian Pounds 55.00 at RM 2.50 RM 137.50
- Diners 435,641.00 at RM 0.05 RM 21,782.06
- Karbowanetz 164,169.00 RM 0.10 RM 16,416.90
- Pengoes 28,392.50 at RM 0.60 RM 17,035.50
- Slov. Croons 103,538.35 at RM 0.10 RM 10,353.84
- Drachmas 4,875,419.70 at RM 0.02 RM 97,508.29
- Swedish Croons 4,377.00 at RM 0.60 RM 2,626.20
- Norwegian Croons 775.00 at RM 0.60 RM 465.00
- Argentinian Pesos 977.55 at RM 1.00 RM 977.55
- Pesetas 1,471.00 at RM 2.40 RM 3,530.40
- Finnish Marks 1,140.00 at RM 0.05 RM 57.00
- Danish Croons 1,270.00 at RM 0.52 RM 660.40
- Brazilian Milreis 63.00 at RM 0.09 RM 5.67
- Egyptian Pounds 20/00/00 at RM 4.40 RM 88.00
- Litas 175.00 at RM 0.10 RM 17.50
- Yen (Japanese) 4.00 at RM 0.50 RM 2.00
- Lats 20.00 at RM 0.10 RM 2.00
- Paraguayan Pesos 12.00 at RM 0.60 7.20
- Cuban Pesos 57.00 at RM 0.60 RM 28.20

- Uruguayan Pesos 1.00 at RM 0.60 RM 0.60
- Bolivian Pesos 4.50 at RM 0.60 2.70
- Mexican Pesos 3.00 at RM 0.50 RM 1.50
- Albanian Francs 195.44 at RM 0.10 RM 19.54
- Rhodesian Pounds 8/00/00 at RM 4.00 RM 32.00
- New Zealand Pounds 0/10/00 at RM 4.00 2.00
- Algerian Francs 30.00 at RM 0.10 RM 3.00
- Lux. Francs 40.00 at RM 0.50 20.00
- Javan Gulden 10.00 at RM 1.30 RM 13.00
- Danzig Gulden 1,038.00 at RM 1.00 RM 1,038.00
- Columbian Pesos 1.00 at RM 0.60 RM 0.60
- Mozambique Escudos 1.00 at RM 0.60 RM 0.60
- Manchukuo Cents 15.00 at RM 0.50 RM 7.50
- Chinese Dollars 1.00 at RM 1.50 RM 1.50
- Total RM 4,521,224.13

Currency in gold coins:

- USA Dollars 249,771.50 at RM 4.20 RM 1,049,040.30
- English Pounds 610/00/00 at RM 20.40 RM 12,444.00
- Roubles 189,053.00 at RM 2.15 RM 425,813.95
- Austrian Crowns 73,230.00 at RM 0.85 RM 62,245.00
- French Francs 38,870.00 at RM 1.62 RM 62,969.40
- Reichsmarks 23,485.00 at RM 1.00 RM 23,485.00
- Portuguese Reis 20,000.00 at RM 200 Esc 1.00 RM 200.00
- Swiss Francs 6,970.00 at RM 16.50 (f.20 Frs) RM 23,001.00
- Ducats 6,614.00 at RM 10.00 RM 66,140.00
- Lire 3,740.00 at RM 0.50 RM 1,870.00
- Austrian Shillings 2,925.00 at RM 2.3 RM 1.950.00
- Turkish Pounds 417/75/00 at RM 3.50 RM 1,462.12
- Belgas 1,740.00 at RM 0 50 RM 870.00
- Levas 30.00 at RM 0.50 RM 15.00
- Lei 1,177.50 at RM 0.50 RM 588.75
- South African Pounds 4/00/00 at RM 20.40 RM 81.60
- Dutch Gulden 905.00 at RM 17.00 (f.10 Fl) RM 1,538.50
- Australian Pounds 7/00/00 at RM 20.40 RM 142.80
- Dinars 41.00 at RM 0.50 RM 20.50
- Swedish Crowns 30.00 at RM 11.20 (f.10 Kr) RM 33.60
- Norwegian Crowns 55.00 at RM 11.20 (f.10 Kr) RM 61.60
- Pesetas 50.00 at RM 1.50 RM 75.00
- Finnish Marks 80.00 at RM 1.00 RM 80.00
- Zloty 2,060.00 at RM 0.50 RM 1,030.00

- Danish Crowns 360.00 at RM 11.20 (f.10 Kr) RM 403.20
- Czechoslovakian Ducats 17.00 at RM 10.00 RM 170.00
- Yen 2.00 at RM 0.50 RM 1.00
- Cuban Pesos 10.00 at RM 4.20 RM 42.00
- Mexican Pesos 111.50 at RM 4.20 RM 468.00
- Albanian Francs 20.00 at RM 0.50 RM 10.00
- Jugoslavian Ducats 1.00 at RM 5.00 RM 5.00
- Tunisian Francs 180.00 at RM 1.62 RM 291.60
- Peruvian Libre 1.00 at RM 1.00 RM 1.00
- Chilean Dollars 1.00 at RM 4.20 RM 4.20
- Total RM 1,736,554.12

Jewellery and other valuables:

- 15,883 Rings, gold, with brilliants and diamonds Average in RM: 1,500.00 [Total] RM: 23,824,500.00;
- 9,019 Ladies' gold wrist watches 250.00 2,254,750.00;
- 3,681 Gentlemen's gold pocket watches 500.00 1,840,400.00;
- 353 Bracelets with brilliants and diamonds 3,500.00 1,232,000.00;
- 1,716 Gold earrings with brill. and diam. 250.00 429,000.00;
- 2,497 Gold brooches with brill. and diam. 2,000.00 4,994,000.00;
- 130 Single large brilliants 1,000.00 130,000.00;
- 2,511.37 Carat Individual brilliants 100.00 251,137.00;
- 13,458.62 Carat Individual diamonds 50.00 672,931.00;
- 291 Tie pins with brilliants 100.00 29,100.00;
- 660 Gentlemen's gold wrist-watches 100.00 66,000.00;
- 458 Ladies' fob watches with brilliants 500.00 229,000.00.
- 273 Ladies' watches of platinum & brill. 1,200.00 327,600.00;
- 349 Ladies' gold fob watches 250.00 87,250.00;
- 362 Ladies' gold watches with brill. & diam. 600.00 317,200.00;
- 27 Armbands with brill. & diam. 250.00 6,750.00;
- 40 Gold brooches 350.00 14,000.00;
- 18 Cufflinks with brilliants 160.00 2,700.00;
- 114.20 Kg. Pearls 6,000,000.00;
- 63 Plat. & Brill. watch cases 1,000.00 63,000.00;
- 4 Ladies' platinum watches 300.00 1,200.00;
- 3 Gentleman's pocket watches with brill. 600.00 3,000.00;
- 4 Necklaces of brilliants and diamonds 1,500.00 6,000.00;
- 8 Ladies' golden ring-watches 150.00 1,200.00;
- 4 Ladies' fob watches with pearls 200.00 800.00;
- 18 Gold fountain pens 20.00 360.00;
- 5 Gold revolving pencils 15.00 75.00;

- 1 Gold cigarette case 400.00 400.00;
- 60,125 Watches of various kinds 10.00 601,250.00;
- 7.80 Kg. Coral 600.00;
- 3 Golden compacts 50.00 150.00;
- 103,614 Watches to be repaired 2.00 207,228.00;
- 29,391 Spectacles 3.00 88,173.00;
- 350 Shaving equipment 2.00 700.00;
- 800 Pocket knives 1.00 200.00;
- 3,240 Money purses 1.50 4,860.00;
- 1,315 Briefcases 2.50 3,287.50;
- 1,300 Scissors 0.50 750.00;
- 230 Flashlights 0.50 115.00;
- 6,943 Alarm clocks, to be repaired 1.00 6,943.00;
- 2,343 Alarm clocks, in order 4.00 9,372.00;
- 627 Sunglasses 0.50 313.50;
- 41 Silver cigarette cases 15.00 615.00;
- 230 Clinical thermometers 3.00 690.00;
- Total: 43,662,150.00

Textiles:

- 1901 Wagons of clothing, underclothing, bed feathers and rags to an average value of RM: 26,000,000.00;
- Camp articles to an average value of 20,000,000.00
- Total: 46,000,000.00

Total Compilation:

- Currency delivered, Zlotys and RM-Notes: RM 73,852,080.74;
- Precious metals RM 8,973,651.60;
- Foreign currency in notes RM 4,521,224.13;
- Foreign currency in gold coins RM 1,736,554.12;
- Jewellery and other valuables RM 43,662,450.00;
- Textiles RM 46,000,000.00;
- Total RM 178,745,960.59

[signed] Rzepa SS-Oberscharführer and Chief of Cash Office
[signed] Wippern SS-Sturmbannführer and Chief of Administration
[sgd] Globocnik [=] [Rubber Stamp:] Personal Staff Reichsführer-SS, Ref. No. Secret/115
[initialled] H. H. [Himmler]

Measures for Pacifying Foreign Nationals During Transfer of Populations
Z-Villages

1. Poles who are fit for work have already been resettled during previous expulsions on so-called z-farms within the colonization area, with an increase of their former property. These z-farms form the nucleus of the z-village, where the German settlers and Polish workers are lodged. Not only do these Polish workers receive a guaranteed wage and an employment book, but their food supply is also cared for through the SWG.

Security Questions.

2. Only elements with a bad record will be expelled for security reasons. For this reason, the security police are at present carrying out the following:
   a. Villages which lie within that part of the district of z-areas which is to be colonized will be combed for elements who are a danger to security, so that only the reliable part of the population will remain.
   b. Villages which lie outside the colonization area and are considered to be bandit infested are subject to same action. The population mentioned under paragraph a will then be invited to emigrate voluntarily to the uninhabited farms mentioned under paragraph 1. By this action the colonization area will be free and can be colonized by Germans.

   Security measures are always looked upon with understanding by the peaceful part of the population; this will therefore be a way to pacify the population.

The Question of Expropriation.

3. All Poles, including those who are being brought into the labour cycle in the Reich, are to be given certificates confirming what property they have left behind. They will be informed that they will receive a suitable compensation sometime in the form of goods or cash. This applies also to those who have already been expelled to date. The certificates are to be issued by the DUT. I request the Reichsführer-SS to give his approval to this.

State Property.

4. Admission of the whole of the expelled population into State property is not possible because of the overcrowding of the space.

Time for Colonization.

5. Owing to the favourable weather, spring tilling can take place five weeks earlier than usual this season. Owing to this shift in time, colonization will be carried out after the completion of spring tilling. This has the advantage on the one hand that the Poles can till their fields normally and production will not be upset, while on the other hand the settlers will not run the risk of not being able, in view of

the shortness of the time, to carry out their spring tilling, owing to ignorance of local conditions. The settlers will, therefore, have the benefit of the harvest, and their reconstruction work can be carried out without any hurry.

6. The classification into four groups could take place without any further ado, owing to the fact that Groups I and II, as racially valuable, have no objection to being transferred to the Reich anyhow; Group III, for the greater part, will remain here in any case, whereas Group IV will be sent for employment as labourers. The communications from persons previously sent to the Reich, reporting that they are getting on well there, and the people's realization of the fact that up to now nobody has been treated like the Jews have already taken away the frightening atmosphere surrounding this system of grouping. It is precisely in such cases that one has to await the results of measures; only then does the realization prevail. The rumour mongers are then proved to be liars without any further ado.
7. Again, I request you to consider whether my former proposal to lodge the expelled Poles, and especially also the Ukrainians in the Eastern territories, especially the Ukraine, may not be feasible after all. I believe that there is not only sufficient space today because of the events of the war, but also that this form of transferring population with new allocations of land would have the best results and that it facilitates the expulsion. For the Ukrainians, this would mean a return to their own area. A tendency in this direction exists already, and for the Poles it is a fact with which they have reckoned for a long time.

I therefore request the Reichsführer-SS to leave the hitherto existing measures as they are.

The above-mentioned facts may not have been known to Governor Wächter when the report was made.

[signed] Globocnik
SS-Gruppenführer and Lieut. General of Police

[Rubber stamp] Personal Staff, Reichsführer-SS Correspondence administration
File No. Secret/115

Measures for the further transfer of populations

As many quarters express themselves against the transfer of populations on the grounds that it causes too much unrest among the foreigners, thus disturbing production, the following measures have been decided upon:

1. Verbal propaganda will spread news about the discontinuation of these transfers.
2. No authority will announce anything before the actual moment when the transfer of populations is to be carried out. Planning will be done secretly.
3. The time for immigration will be fixed for after the spring tilling of the fields,

so that the foreigners will carry out the cultivation of the land, and the new settlers will already be able to make use of the harvest. This has the advantage that, under the above-mentioned pre-suppositions, the foreigners will till their fields in all districts, while the German settlers will not run the danger, in view of the shortness of the time, of possibly being hindered in their spring work.

4. The transfer of Poles should be carried out in such a manner that the good elements are put, as much as possible voluntarily, in districts cleared by the Security Police, and the transfer is entitled 'The Establishment of Security in the Partisan districts'. The bad elements will be taken away gradually, where they are not employed as auxiliary workers.
5. The announcement of the time of immigration will be made only on the day of the transfer of population.
6. All villages will be occupied in advance by the 'Landwacht' [country guard] in all parts of the organization formed by settlers, who, having received previous training, are to save the use of our own SS forces.

O. U. the 1 Jul 1943 [initialled] H. H. [Himmler]

1. In the course of the security operation Werewolf I, the area roughly west of the points colonization area via Biłgoraj-Tarnogród, bordered on the West by the district frontier, extending southwards are far as Bełżec and from there along the road via Tomasgow to Zamość as far as the southern border of the colonization area has been cleared of the native population.
2. The part to the South of the Biłgoraj wood will be handed over to the Ukrainians and in such a manner that-
    a. The Ukrainians already living there will receive more land up to an average area of 6 hectares, so that a part of the evacuated land will already be colonized in that way, and
    b. Where there are too few native Ukrainians, Ukrainian families will be moved from the Hrubieszówer area and resettled there. The Ukrainian inhabited area will thus be loosened there and ground will be freed adjoining the colonization area.
3. The Biłgoraj wood itself will be completely evacuated and will not be re-colonized.
4. The part to the north of the Biłgoraj wood, limited roughly by the Tomasgow-Krasnobród road and further, will also be newly colonized with Ukrainians as under 2b.
5. The area to the South of the present colonization area of Zamość will thus remain vacant, and racial Germans and persons of German stock can be settled there. Persons of German stock from the district of Hrubieszów have already been collected for this purpose. This is all the more necessary as they are not being abandoned to Polishdom as stray Germans.

6. In the course of the operations, the towns of Tomasgow and Zamość will also be evacuated of Poles, and Germans are to be settled there. Accordingly, the Security operation would have the following effect:
   a. The population of this area, who have lived on robbery and banditry for decades, is removed.
   b. About 30,000 workers are brought to the Reich.
   c. The territory surrounding the German settlement area will then be settled with Ukrainians, who form a sort of buffer and are more peacefully inclined toward Germandom.
   d. In addition, as a result of this colonization, the state of tension of the Poles will be transferred to the Ukrainians, and they are turned into defence forces.
   e. A new agrarian structure arises as proletarian ownership disappears and an average farm area of 6 hectares is formed, which contributes to intensification and increased production.
   f. The German colonization territory will be free for a further influx of Germans, this presupposing a security measure. But the German colonization territory will thereby be enlarged which helps toward the essential security of the territory. Pressure by the Poles can then be exerted only from the North and it is then easier to guarantee the security of the colonization territory from one side.

[Signed] Globocnik
SS-Gruppenführer and Lt. General of Police.
Trieste, 4 Nov 1943

The Higher SS and Police Chief in the Operational Zone of the Adriatic Coastal Area.
Gl./Go. Diary No. 225/43 [initialled] H. H. [Himmler]
To the Reichsführer SS and Chief of the German Police, Heinrich Himmler, Berlin

I concluded Operation Reinhardt, which I have been directing on the government-general, on 19 October 1943, and have dissolved all camps.

I take the liberty of submitting the attached portfolio to you, Reichsführer, as my final statement.

My observations on Lublin showed that a special centre of radiation existed in the Government General and particularly in the Lublin district, and I have tried, therefore, to capture these dangerous tendencies graphically. It may prove to be a good thing for the future if we can point to the elimination of this danger. I have, however, also endeavoured to give a picture of the employment of labour, from which one can not only gather the extent of the work, but also with how few Germans this fatal effort was made possible. It has at any rate grown to such proportions today, that well-known industries are interesting themselves in it.

I have meanwhile handed these labour camps over to SS-Obergruppenführer Pohl.

Please, Reichsführer, look through this portfolio.

During a visit, you, Reichsführer, held out to me the prospect that a few Iron Crosses might be awarded for the special performances of this hard task after the work had been concluded. Please advise me, Reichsführer, whether I may submit suggestions in this connection.

I beg to point out that such an award to the forces of the local SS and Police Chief was authorized for the work in Warsaw, which formed only a comparatively small part of the total work.

I should be grateful to you, Reichsführer, for a positive decision regarding this matter, as I would like to see the hard work of my men rewarded.

Heil Hitler!

[Signed] Globocnik
SS-Gruppenführer and Lieut. General of Police
Note for the files Action 'Reinhardt' also comes under 'Top Secret' 1851/43 Secret.
[Initialed] H

Field-Command Post, 30 Nov 1943
The Reichsführer-SS RF/M
[Rubber Stamp] Personal Staff, Reichsführer-SS Correspondence Administration.
File No. Secret 155

To the Higher SS and Police Chief in the Adriatic Coast zone of operations, SS-Gruppenführer GLOBOCNIK

Dear Globus,

I confirm receipt of your letter dated 4 Nov 1943 and your notification regarding the termination of Aktion Reinhardt. Also, I thank you for the portfolio you sent me.

I express to you my thanks and my acknowledgment for the great and unique services which you have performed to the entire German people by carrying out the Aktion Reinhardt.

Heil Hitler!

Sincerely yours
[Signed] H. H. [Himmler]

# APPENDIX IV

# DEPARTMENT OF THE ARMY PAMPHLET (EXTRACT)

*The German Campaign in Poland* (1939) by Robert M. Kennedy, Major, Infantry, US Army

DEPARTMENT OF THE ARMY
WASHINGTON 25, D.C., 18 April 1956
Department of the Army Pamphlet 20-255 is published for the information and guidance of all concerned.
[AG 385 (14 Sep 55)]

- BY ORDER of Wilber M. Brucker, Secretary of the Army:

MAXWELL D. TAYLOR,
General, United States Army,
Chief of Staff.

JOHN A. KLEIN,
Major General, United States, Army,
The Adjutant General.

**Army Group South, 1–6 September 1939**

**The Advance to the Warta (Warthe)**

The morning of 1 September was clear on the front of Rundstedt's *Army Group South,* which had the advantage of air reconnaissance as it moved into Poland. *Eighth Army,* on the left, advanced toward Lodz and protected *Tenth Army's* north flank. *Tenth Army,* in the centre of the army group line, struck out in the direction of Warsaw with the strongest concentration of armour in either army group. *Fourteenth Army,* on the right, moved toward the industrial area about Cracow and into Galicia, protecting the south flank of the main attack force.

Forward elements of *Army Group South* penetrated three to four miles into Poland by 0600. Steady progress was reported until 1400, when the army group commander was informed that the retreating Poles had demolished numerous bridges and even blown up stretches of roadway to slow the German armoured and motorized columns. *Tenth Army* also reported resistance by rear guards, an engagement with elements of the Wolynska Cavalry Brigade, and several incidents of civilians firing on German troops.

No protracted resistance was encountered, and by late afternoon some *Army Group South* units had advanced as much as 15 miles. The tactics of the new war of movement were first demonstrated during this period of operations. When their armoured columns were fired upon or held up by obstacles, the Germans deployed their tank units off the roads and continued their forward move. When necessary, the Luftwaffe was called upon to support the advance by dive bombing centres of Polish resistance. Polish units bypassed by the German armour were engaged by infantry units following the tanks.

*Eighth Army* reported the 10th Infantry Division of the Lodz Army withdrawing toward Kalisz (Kalisch) and the 14th and 25th Infantry Divisions and Wielkopolska Cavalry Brigade of the Poznan Army retreating to the north and east. *Tenth Army* reported the Polish 7th Infantry Division and Krakowska Cavalry Brigade of the Cracow Army and the 28th and 30th Infantry Divisions and Wolynska Cavalry Brigade of the Lodz Army to be withdrawing to the east. Most of the first day's fighting on the *Eighth* and *Tenth Army* fronts was carried on between Polish rear guards and German reconnaissance elements or the advance guard of German armoured and motorized units.

*Fourteenth Army* reconnaissance troops and Slovak units on the right of the army front captured a number of villages in the area immediately to the north of the Slovak frontier by the close of the first day. Other *Fourteenth Army* units drove elements of the Rzeszow Armoured Cavalry Brigade from the Novy Targ (Neumarkt) region, and cleared the Jablunka Pass and the area for several miles to the north of the pass of the Cracow Army's 21st Mountain Division after hard fighting. The Polish 5th Infantry Division from the general reserve and the 6th Infantry Division of the Cracow Army were forced to withdraw in the direction of Cracow, and the Cracow Army's 23d Infantry Division fell back to the northeast of the city. Units on the left flank of *Fourteenth Army* then found themselves confronted by strong permanent fortifications guarding the approaches to the industrial complex in the southwest of Poland.

The attack of *Army Group South* was resumed at 0600 on 2 September. The Poles resisted stubbornly at Mikolow (Nibolai), in the fortifications before Katowice

(Kattowitz), and about Czestochowa (Tschenstochau). *Eighth Army* crossed the upper Prosna, *Tenth Army* reached the Warta above Czestochowa in its zone of advance, and *Fourteenth Army* divisions fought their way forward to converge north of Novy Targ.

Their movements made it apparent to Rundstedt that the Poles intended to establish a defensive line along the Warta River, and hold out in such fortified areas as Katowice and Czestochowa as long as possible. The Germans also found an increasing number of demolitions and other obstacles to the movement of armoured and motorized units. A number of reservists sufficient to form two provisional divisions were sent to reinforce the Polish units facing *Eighth Army.* Elements of several infantry divisions from the Polish general reserve also moved into the area beyond the Warta in the *Tenth Army's* zone of advance.

Czestochowa was taken on the morning of 3 September, and *Tenth Army* seized several bridgeheads across the Warta despite determined Polish resistance. *Fourteenth Army* fought its way through the fortifications about Katowice and Mikolow in its zone of advance, and moved east along the Vistula. The southern Polish armies, bypassed in numerous places by the fast-moving German columns, began a hurried withdrawal. The troops on the front noted a marked decrease in Polish resistance and made extensive gains.

### The Advance across the Polish Plain and into Galicia

By the morning of 4 September *Army Group South* estimated the withdrawing Poznan Army incapable of launching a heavy attack on the exposed left flank of the *Eighth Army* as it advanced north-eastward. *Tenth Army* had virtually destroyed the Cracow Army's 7th Infantry Division and taken 1,000 prisoners, including the division commander. Heavy losses had also been inflicted on the Krakowska Cavalry Brigade. *Tenth Army's* Panzer divisions continued the drive eastward, moving beyond Radomsko, while two light divisions protected the right flank of the Panzer units and advanced to the Pilica River. *Fourteenth Army* reported the destruction of the Cracow Army's 6th Infantry Division and a general Polish withdrawal toward Cracow and the east.

The *XXII Corps* was operational under *Fourteenth Army* control on 4 September and advancing northward in the Novy Targ sector, with a Panzer, a mountain, and a light division attached. The *XVIII Corps,* which had controlled these three divisions the morning of the attack, had been withdrawn to assume control of two mountain divisions on the right front of the army and make a crossing into Poland farther to the east.

Additional gains were reported by all three armies on 5 September. *Eighth Army* was advancing rapidly to the northeast, while its *X Corps* presented a front to the north. Several battalions of the *IV Frontier Command,* a regiment of the *62nd Infantry Division,* and elements of the *252nd Infantry Division* crossed the Reich frontier to fill the gap formed as *Eighth Army* moved farther eastward. The frontier command

and the infantry units were immediately organized into a task force known as *Group Gienanth* and given responsibility for the defence of *Army Group South's* exposed left flank. As *Eighth Army* continued to move eastward the front presented by the *X Corps* became more extended despite the relief afforded by the commitment of *Group Gienanth.* The Poznan Army to the north had not been engaged as heavily as the other Polish armies in the frontier area and still possessed a considerable combat potential.

*Tenth Army* units were across the Pilica by 5 September, and the way was open for an advance across the Polish Plain to the capital. The Polish reserves had been committed and there were a few units to be drawn upon to reinforce the sagging defence line before Warsaw.

*Fourteenth Army* drove eastward on Cracow against stiffening resistance on 5 September. The *XXII Corps* below the Vistula moved in the direction of the San River, and the *XVIII Corps* fought a way into Poland through the eastern Carpathian passes.

Rundstedt's headquarters revised its earlier estimate of the Poznan Army's capabilities on the *Eighth Army* flank on 6 September and prepared to meet a Polish attack from the north. The army group commander requested additional cavalry for reconnaissance purposes but OKH could make no cavalry available. To restrict the Poznan Army's movement and channel its withdrawal, two infantry divisions of the army group reserve were sent into line between *X Corps* and *Group Gienanth,* strengthening that part of the *Eighth Army* front facing north.

*Tenth Army* continued to move northeastward on a wide front on 6 September, making deep penetrations with its Panzer divisions. The Poles contested the advance of the Panzer divisions bitterly, since they were closest to Warsaw and threatened the eastward retreat of the Lodz and Poznan Armies. The Panzer divisions were followed by infantry divisions, which quickly cleared the captured areas of bypassed Polish units and stragglers. The Panzer division on the northern flank beat off heavy counterattacks, inflicted severe losses on the Poles, and captured the commander of the Polish general reserve's 29th Infantry Division. *Fourteenth Army* captured the key city of Cracow the same day.

Intelligence reports indicated that the Poles were attempting to rally remnants of their Cracow Army in the area of Radom. The destruction of the forces concentrating at Radom and known to still be at Lodz would prevent the escape of more organized Polish units beyond the Vistula River. *Eighth Army* was directed to make a frontal attack against the force assembling near Lodz. *Tenth Army* was ordered to envelope the force at Radom from north and south while continuing the drive toward the Vistula.

Meanwhile an order from OKH assigned *Fourteenth Army* the mission of destroying the Polish forces escaping to the east of the Vistula. Strong armoured and motorized forces were to move to the northeast in the direction of Lublin. Polish units that managed to escape destruction west of the Vistula would be caught within this second envelopment in eastern Poland.

The first phase of *Army Group South's* operations was completed by 6 September. The Poznan Army had been forced to withdraw eastward. The Lodz Army was under heavy attack. Cracow had been taken and remnants of the Cracow Army at Radom were about to be enveloped by *Tenth Army.* The Carpathian Army had been forced to withdraw toward Lublin and Lwow.

No great number of prisoners had been taken in a single engagement, as had happened in the Corridor to the north a few days earlier. However, *Army Group South* reported several thousand captives in the Cracow area, and *Tenth Army* had bypassed thousands of Polish troops in its advance across the Warta; these were still being captured by the infantry units that had followed the armour. The Poles had also committed a larger proportion of their general reserve to stem the rapid advance of the stronger southern army group and to meet the threat Rundstedt posed to the capital and control centre of the Polish defence effort. *Tenth Army* had had innumerable obstacles with which to contend, as the Poles destroyed bridges and other constructions before its tank columns, and part of *Fourteenth Army* had had to fight its way through mountain passes defended by picked Polish mountain troops.

To retain control of its widening and moving front *Army Group South* displaced its headquarters to Lubliniec (Lublinitz), just inside the Polish frontier. *Eighth Army* moved to Gross Wartenberg, *Tenth Army* to Radomsko, and *Fourteenth Army* to Bielsko (Bielitz).

**Army Group South, 7–17 September**

All three of its armies reported progress as *Army Group South* entered the second phase of operations, and OKH cancelled its planned airborne attack on the Vistula crossing at Puławy. The three army headquarters had to displace forward again to maintain proper control over their advancing units. On 7 September *Eighth Army* moved to the vicinity of Lodz, as it pressed the attack against that city and the Lodz Army. *Tenth Army* moved to Konskie on 9 September as it prepared to destroy forces of the Cracow Army concentrated at Radom. *Fourteenth Army* moved to a point southeast of Cracow the same day and continued its drive to the east and northeast. *Army Group South* moved its headquarters on 13 September to Kielce where it remained until the end of operations.

A series of separate battles developed on each of the army fronts. These were simultaneous actions, with each German army attempting to envelop and destroy the Polish units on its front and prevent their escape to the east.

**Eighth Army**

The combat potential of *Eighth Army* was increased considerably at the outset of the second phase of *Army Group South's* operations with the attachment of the *XI* and

*XVI Corps* from *Tenth Army*. The *XI Corps* held the right of the army line, while *XVI Corps* reached the suburbs of Warsaw with its *4th Panzer Division* on 8 September and its *1st Panzer Division* penetrated to the Vistula.

The *Eighth Army's* successes against the Lodz Army and its deep penetration north-eastward across the Polish Plain were to work to *Eighth Army's* temporary disadvantage in the area of the *X Corps* at the outset of the second phase of operations, however. The *Gienanth Group* and the *213th Infantry Division* from the army group reserve on the army's north flank were left far to the west. The *221st Infantry Division* from the army group reserve was disposed on a very wide front and was also too far to the west to come to the support of *X Corps* units in case of an attack from the north. The continued advance of *Eighth Army* to the northeast made necessary an increasing prolongation of the line held by *X Corps* against the Poznan Army, particularly on the front of the German *30th Infantry Division.*

The *30th Infantry Division* made some redispositions to meet a possible attack, but was still in an unfavourable position for defence. Division units were strung out along an open flank for a distance of more than 20 miles and advancing north-eastward in column, with only small detachments thrown out for security. The division artillery was scattered throughout the column and a coordinated defensive fire would have been impossible.

At noon on 10 September the German *30th Infantry Division* reported itself under heavy attack from the north by a Polish force estimated at two or three infantry divisions and two cavalry brigades. The army commander first considered counterattacking with the *XIII Corps,* but discarded this plan in favour of directing the *X Corps* to turn its front to the north. The *30th Infantry Division* lost some ground to the Poles, but the support of the other two infantry divisions of the corps made it possible to establish a new line the following day.

A number of anti-tank and other army group units were made available to *Eighth Army* and hurried into line to bolster the front, and the *XI Corps* was directed to attack the Polish penetration on its eastern shoulder.

Despite the heavy losses incurred by the *30th Infantry Division,* the Polish attack served the Germans in that it hastened the encirclement of the Poznan Army at Kutno. The diversion of units to make the attack weakened the eastern front of the Polish force and the *XI Corps* succeeded in driving the Poles to the west of the Bzura and farther away from Warsaw and Modlin and any possible escape to the two fortress cities.

On 11 September OKH placed *Eighth Army* in control of operations against the Polish forces about Kutno, and the army moved its headquarters to Lodz. The German plan for the operation provided for attacking the Poles from the west, south, and east, while Bock's army group blocked escape north across the Vistula. A day later OKH directed the attachment of the *III Corps* of *Fourth Army* south of the Vistula to the *Eighth Army* as *Army Group North* prepared to regroup and shift *Fourth Army* to the drive east of Warsaw. A provisional force was organized to hold the north bank of the Vistula against Polish crossings from the Kutno area.

Included in the Kutno encirclement at this time were 12 Polish divisions, including the Poznan Army's 14th, 17th, 25th, and 26th Infantry Divisions, and the Wielkopolska and Kresova Cavalry Brigades; remnants of the Lodz Army's 2nd, 10th, 13th, 28th and 30th Infantry Divisions and Wolynska Cavalry Brigade; and battered units of the Pomorze Army's 4th, 15th and 16th Infantry Divisions that managed to escape destruction following the junction of the German *Third* and *Fourth Armies* across the base of the Corridor. This represented more than one third of the entire Polish land force. Some concern was expressed at OKH and the headquarters of both army groups about the capability of this Polish force to break out to the east to join the garrison of Warsaw. For the next few days this encirclement, a development of the original OKH plan to destroy the bulk of the Polish armies west of the Vistula, was to become a focal point of attention in the campaign.

*Eighth Army* controlled a total of six corps for the operation against the Polish force at Kutno, including the *XI* and *XVI Corps* attached from *Tenth Army.* These corps were deployed in a rough circle about the Polish force centred between the Vistula and Bzura. One more attempt by the Poles to break out of the encirclement and escape to the southeast on 12 September was thwarted despite the loss of some ground by the Germans. The desperate attacks of the Poles only served to exhaust further their few units still intact.

The *XI* and *XVI Corps* reverted from *Eighth* to *Tenth Army* control on 15 September, as *Tenth Army* was made responsible for operations against Kutno from the east. The commander of the Polish force was finally identified as General Bortnowski, of the Poznan Army. Despite his hopeless position, Bortnowski made one more effort to break through the German line on 16 September, this time to the north and east in an attempt to cross the Vistula and reach Modlin. This final attempt was fruitless, and the *Eighth Army* took advantage of the weakening Polish situation to compress the Kutno force into a compact mass and a target small enough for a concentrated air assault.

The following day, 17 September, German air units attacking Warsaw were diverted long enough from their target to deliver a series of heavy air attacks on the encircled Poles and expedite the movement of ground units toward Kutno. The Polish defensive organization collapsed, and 40,000 prisoners were taken. A strong Polish force managed to fight its way through the German line and moved toward the forested area southwest of Modlin, below the Vistula. This force was immediately engaged by *Tenth Army* and destroyed.

At the conclusion of the second phase of *Army Group South* operations *Eighth Army* was still occupied in clearing the Kutno area of the last remnants of its Polish force. While *Tenth Army* completed the destruction of those Polish units that had escaped east of the Bzura, *Eighth Army* destroyed all those remaining west of the river.

Since it was not in the area of the demarcation line between the Russian and German halves of the country and had no orders to move in that direction *Eighth Army* was not immediately affected by the sudden Russian advance into eastern Poland.

### Tenth Army

The deep penetration of *Tenth Army* prevented the Polish forces near Radom from completing their defensive deployment as the second phase of *Army Group South's* operations began. The Lodz Army, already under attack by the *Eighth Army* on the German left, could not prevent *Tenth Army* tank units from moving up the north bank of the Pilica toward the Vistula and Warsaw. Bypassed on the south, the Lodz Army was forced to fall back on the Polish divisions at Kutno, and *Tenth Army* could make its major effort against the Polish force at Radom.

The Radom force on 8 September consisted of survivors of the Polish 3rd, 19th, and 29th Infantry Divisions from the general reserve, the Krakowska Cavalry Brigade and 7th Infantry Division of the Cracow Army, and the 12th Infantry Division from the general reserve. All but the 12th Infantry Division had been heavily engaged and had but a fraction of their original strength. Depleted as this force was, it succeeded in slowing the German advance toward the Vistula.

*Tenth Army* was directed by Rundstedt to destroy the Polish force at Radom by an envelopment from north and south. This would enable *Tenth Army* to seize crossings on the Vistula and press forward to a junction with *Army Group North* at Warsaw. The *Tenth Army* order of the same date assigned *XIV* and *XV Corps* the mission of enveloping the Polish force from the north and south, while *IV Corps* tied it down with attacks from the west and southwest.

Hard fighting developed as Panzer units reached the Vistula north and south of the Polish force at Radom late on 8 September. The stubborn resistance of the Poles required the full attention of *Tenth Army,* and the *XI* and *XVI Corps* on the left flank of *Tenth Army* were temporarily attached to *Eighth Army.*

*Tenth Army* destroyed the Polish force at Radom by 11 September and took 60,000 prisoners. A few Polish units of regimental strength withdrew into the more wooded areas and continued a sporadic resistance that tied down a number of German divisions for several more days. Bridges across the Vistula, including the important crossing at Puławy, were secured. *Tenth Army* was directed to move the *IV Corps* across the river and in the direction of Lublin, to support the advance of *Fourteenth Army* on that city and its junction with *Army Group North.* The *XIV Corps* would remain west of the Vistula temporarily, and clear the area of Polish remnants still trying to escape across the river.

On 13 September *Tenth Army* was given control over the *VII* and *VIII Corps* on the left flank of *Fourteenth Army.* The two corps were directed to continue their advance eastward, enveloping the Polish force at Biłgoraj and supporting the movement of *Fourteenth Army* on Lublin. This shift gave *Tenth Army* control over all German forces moving on Lublin from the west.

The *IV Corps* in the centre of the *Tenth Army* front was across the Vistula on 14 September and moving east on a small Polish force at Kraśnik. The city of Kraśnik was taken on 15 September, and the corps moved rapidly past Lublin toward the Wieprz River. The *XIV Corps* concentrated on the west bank of the Vistula but did not cross in force, since some of its units were still occupied in clearing the area east of Radom of Polish remnants. On the *Tenth Army* right, the *VII* and *VIII Corps* attached from *Fourteenth Army* fought hard to destroy the Polish forces at Biłgoraj.

On 15 September *Tenth Army* reassumed control over the *XI* and *XVI Corps* that had been attached temporarily to *Eighth Army*, and *Tenth Army* became responsible for two fronts, one facing north toward Warsaw and the other east toward Lublin. The two corps on the Warsaw front would lay siege to the Polish capital from the south and move Panzer units between Warsaw and the Polish forces at Kutno, in support of the *Eighth Army* effort against the encircled western Polish armies. This would also provide flank protection for *Tenth Army* on the left, originally the mission of *Eighth Army*, and would free *Eighth Army* to concentrate on reducing the Polish force within the encirclement.

*Tenth Army* units on the Warsaw front held an east-west line. One infantry division was assigned to hold the southern approaches to the city, while the army concentrated stronger forces to move between Warsaw and the mass of Polish units at Kutno. The army commander directed the *XI Corps* to establish a bridgehead west of the Bzura River, to enable the *XVI Corps* to cross with its armour and attack the Poles from the east. This operation was worked out in close co-ordination with *Eighth Army*, pressing in on the Poles from the northwest, west, and southwest.

The bridgehead across the Bzura was established by 16 September, and the two Panzer divisions of *XVI Corps* prepared to attack immediately, with strong infantry support. A sharp spoiling attack by the encircled Polish force, in an attempt to break out to the east, prevented the implementation of this plan. Two infantry divisions were diverted to stem the attack, and a Panzer division was shifted northward to interpose itself between the Polish force and the capital. The disruption of the German plan mattered little, however, as the Polish force at Kutno expended its strength in attempts to break through the German encirclement.

*Tenth Army* was still committed against the eastern side of the Kutno encirclement as the *Eighth Army* and Luftwaffe launched a concerted attack the following day. The Polish units that escaped in the course of this action, most of them from the Poznan Army, were caught between the Vistula and *Tenth Army* units west of Warsaw. Twelve thousand prisoners were taken and *Tenth Army* moved on the Vistula to close the gap between Kutno and Warsaw.

On *Tenth Army's* eastern front, meanwhile, Biłgoraj was taken though stiff fighting continued southeast of the city, and Lublin was entered on 17 September. Advance units, passing between Polish concentrations to the north and south, reached the Wieprz Kiver the same day. *Tenth Army* units were moving on Chełm and street fighting raged in Lublin as the second phase of *Army Group South's* operations came to a close. *Tenth Army* moved its headquarters to a point a short distance southwest of Warsaw and continued its drive in the direction of the Bug River, which would form the limiting line for its advance.

**Fourteenth Army**

On 10 September the *XVII* and *XVIII Corps* on the *Fourteenth Army* right crossed the San north and south of Przemysl, forced the 24th Infantry Division of the Polish general reserve to withdraw eastward and drove elements of the Cracow Army's 11th Infantry Division into the fortress city. The two German corps moved rapidly in the direction of Lwow, where the Polish High Command had established headquarters a few days before in an attempt to rally the withdrawing Polish Army for a stand in the south-eastern part of the country. A task force under Colonel (later Field Marshal) Schoerner of the *XVIII Corps' 1st Mountain Division* reached the fortifications of the city on 12 September, and met spirited resistance from the garrison of 12,000 men. The mountain division quickly invested Lwow from the north and west, and cut all contact with the Polish force at Przemysl.

The city of Lwow is dominated by the Zboiska Heights to the north and northeast. It was important that these heights be seized without delay and that the exits from the city to the south and southeast be closed. Security would have to be provided against attacks from the west by the Polish force in Przemysl, and from the south-west, where the entire right flank of the division was exposed to Polish forces being moved up from the south-eastern region of the country.

The attack to secure the ridges north and north-east of the city was launched by *Group Schoerner* at 1000 on 13 September. The task force made rapid progress from the start, reaching the commanding height known as Hill 374 in the afternoon, and Zboiska and the surrounding ridges by dark. The major road to the north was cut by the capture of Zboiska, and the mountain troops dug in to hold their gains against a series of heavy Polish attacks. Other task forces moved out to secure the approaches from the southwest and Przemysl, and to close off exits from the city to the south and southeast.

On the left flank of *Fourteenth Army,* meanwhile, progress was slow, and *VIII Corps,* had to be shifted to clear the north bank of the Vistula as far as the junction with the San. The units opposing the forces on the left of the *Fourteenth Army* front comprised remnants of the Polish 21st and 22nd Mountain Divisions and the Rzeszow

Armoured Cavalry Brigade. The Polish units fought a strong rearguard action and withdrew across the San in a north-easterly direction to the dense forest and swamp area about Biłgoraj.

On 13 September *Army Group South* directed *Fourteenth Army* to send the remainder of its *XVIII* Corps to take Lwow, after which the corps was to move northward. The *XVII* and *XXII Corps* in the centre of the *Fourteenth Army* line were to move to the north-east in the direction of Wlodzimierz and Hrubieszów, to effect a junction with *Army Group North* east of the Bug River. The *VII* and *VIII Corps* on the left were attached to *Tenth Army*, freeing *Fourteenth Army* for its extensive operations deeper into south-eastern Poland. Army Headquarters moved to Rzeszow.

Lwow was completely encircled by *XVIII Corps* units by 14 September. Further west the Poles in Przemysl continued a stubborn resistance. Elements of several divisions had to be relieved from other missions for the assault on Przemysls defences.

Przemysl fell on 15 September, marking the end of organized Polish resistance on the *Fourteenth Army* front except at Lwow, in the area northwest of Lwow, and near Biłgoraj. The protracted resistance at Lwow led the *Fourteenth Army* to direct the *XXII Corps*, after the capture of Wlodzimierz and Hrubieszów, to execute a move to the south with Panzer and motorized units with the mission of destroying the Polish forces still attempting to reach the fortress city. Detachments were also sent to the east to secure the oil fields below Lwow and prevent the escape of more Polish units and small parties to Romania. Meanwhile, a desperate attempt by Polish remnants to reach the garrison at Lwow was thwarted, at the expense of heavy casualties to the *1st Mountain Division*, which held the *XVIII Corps* line north of the city and bore the brunt of the Polish attacks.

*Fourteenth Army* reported some local engagements on 16 September as isolated Polish units were encountered on the army front and in the rear areas. Heavy fighting continued at Lwow and in the area of Biłgoraj.

The intervention of the Red Army on 17 September made necessary some changes in the plan of operations. *Fourteenth Army* was ordered to advance no further than the line Stryj-Lwow-Bug River. The siege of Lwow would continue, temporarily, and the oil-producing area south of Lwow was to be secured.

### The Army Group South Area

Rundstedt reported the destruction of the Polish concentrations south of Biłgoraj during the several days preceding the receipt of orders to evacuate eastern Poland. *Fourteenth Army* on 20 September also reported the capture of 11,000 prisoners north-west of Lwow, ending operations in that area. The siege of Lwow was still in progress when *Army Group South* received orders to withdraw west of the Vistula-San River line.

The evacuation order instructed Rundstedt to leave the reduction of Lwow to the Russians. The attack planned by *XVIII Corps* for 21 September was cancelled, and the corps prepared to move to the west. Contact had already been established with the Russians when Red Army tanks had suddenly appeared at Winniki, southeast of Lwow.

The Polish garrison of Lwow abruptly and unexpectedly surrendered to the *1st Mountain Division* as it made ready to withdraw from its siege lines on 21 September. The occupation of the city was left to the Russians and the *1st Mountain Division* moved westward toward the San with the rest of the *XVIII Corps.*

*Tenth Army* ceased operations at Chełm and began its withdrawal to the west of the demarcation line. Chełm had already been taken under artillery fire and preparations were under way for an infantry assault when the withdrawal order arrived.

A heavy engagement was reported in the *Tenth Army* area on 23 September, when a strong Polish force attacked the withdrawing Germans in the Zamość region. *Tenth Army* reacted quickly, surrounding part of the Polish force southwest of Zamość and driving the remainder to the south and into the area to be occupied by the Red Army.

By 30 September Eighth Army was engaged in evacuating the Polish garrison of Warsaw and with the numerous tasks involved in establishing control over the Polish capital. *Tenth Army* was still in contact with Polish remnants east of the Vistula, and *Fourteenth Army* had completed its evacuation to the San River.

Several incidents occurred during this period in the *Fourteenth Army* area when German and Russian troops exchanged fire. The incidents were settled by the local commanders concerned and no further action was taken by either side.

On 1 October *Tenth Army* was alerted for movement back to Germany. At the same time, OKH informed *Army Group South* that the demarcation line had been changed again and would follow the Pisia and Narew Rivers to Ostroleka, thence past Ostrow Mazowiecka to the Bug, south along the latter to a point east of Tomaszow, west to the San, and south to the Slovak frontier. This would extend the German zone to the east, in places over 100 miles. The change had been made at the request of the Soviet Government, which desired to add Lithuania to its own sphere of influence. In exchange for Lithuania the Russians were willing to give the Germans that area of Poland between Warsaw and the Bug River.

*Army Group South's* commander was redesignated OB EAST (*Oberbefehlshaber Ost*) as of 3 October, with responsibility for all of occupied Poland. Under this reorganization, Rundstedt became the Commander-in-Chief East.

The last organized stand by the Polish Army was made at Kock, where heavy fighting raged from 4 to 6 October. Panzer and motorized infantry units of *Tenth Army* ended this last Polish resistance, and the Kock force surrendered on 6 October, adding 17,000 more to the total of prisoners taken by the Germans. The Polish Campaign was over, though sporadic fighting was to continue in some of the more remote areas for a considerable period.

### Results of the Campaign

The German Army suffered a total of 8,082 officers and men killed, 27,278 wounded, and 5,029 missing in its 36 days of operations in Poland. Luftwaffe and Navy losses were much lighter. The figure on missing Army personnel can be considered as high, in view of the fact that the German Army destroyed the Polish Army and recovered most prisoners taken by organized military units.

Two hundred and seventeen tanks were destroyed during the period 1-30 September, including 89 Mark I vehicles, 83 Mark II's, 26 Mark III's, and 19 Mark IV's. Neutral sources also reported over 400 German aircraft of all types destroyed. Sustained operations over poor roads and rough terrain far ahead of maintenance facilities was extremely wearing on armoured vehicles as well as trucks, requiring extensive repair work at the end of the campaign. German aircraft that participated in the campaign were in little better condition by the end of operations, having had to fly repeated sorties as the weather permitted, often from bases with only the most primitive landing and few if any maintenance facilities. The situation in the *XIX Corps* perhaps best exemplified the mate´riel situation by the end of operations when the entire corps was temporarily immobilized in East Prussia while its tanks, armured cars, and trucks were overhauled and repaired.

The Polish losses were staggering. The Germans claimed 694,000 prisoners of war, out of some 800,000 who had served in Poland's defence; the remainder were killed, captured by the Russians, had fled into Romania or Hungary, or had hidden in isolated areas of their own country. The Germans, by their own count, captured a total of 3,214 field pieces, 16,500 machine guns, 1,700 mortars, and enormous quantities of small arms and ammunition. The captured ordnance and other material was not considered suitable for issue by Wehrmacht standards, but could be put to use by Germany's various satellites.

The civilian population which came under German control as a result of the campaign comprised approximately 22½ million persons. Some three-quarters of a million were ethnic Germans and available for military service. Some of the other minorities, as the Ukrainians, were not opposed to cooperation and service with the Germans. However, the bulk of the Polish population under German control were considered as the people of an occupied country. As a result, sizeable military forces had to be maintained in Poland until the time that the Wehrmacht began to concentrate its forces in the east for the campaign against the Soviet Union more than a year later. The units assigned to this occupation duty were usually of far lower combat potential than those assigned to front-line service, but the necessity of keeping a military force in Poland at all tied down personnel and equipment that might have been put to use elsewhere in the major war effort in which the Reich now found itself engaged.

# APPENDIX V

# GENERAL GOVERNMENT AS AT 1 SEPTEMBER 1941

Extract from *Das Generalgouvernement* by Dr Max Freiherr von du Prel, 1942.

Generalgouverneur:
Reichsminister Dr. Hans Frank: 26.10.1939 – 17.1.1945
Reichsleiter des Reichsrechtsamts der NSDAP, Präsident der Akademie für Deutsches Recht, MdR.
Dienstsitz: Krakau, Burg

Stellvertreter des Generalgouverneurs:
Staatssekretär Dr. Josef Bühler
Dienstsitz: Krakau, Regierungsgebäude, Außenring 46

Bevollmächtiger des Generalgouvernement in Berlin:
Reichsamtsleiter Dr. Heuber, M.d.R.
Dienstsitz: Berlin W 35, Standartenstraße 14

Die Regierung des Generalgouvernements
(Was Amt des Generalgouvernements until 1 December 1940)
Der Staatssekretär in der Regierung des Generalgouvernements:
Dr. Josef Bühler
Dienstsitz: Krakau, Regierungsgebäude, Außenring 46
1. Stellvertreter: Staatssekretär Dr. Boepple
2. Stellvertreter: Ministerialrat Wolsegger

**I. Staatssekretäriat**

a) Kanzlei des Generalgouverneurs:

Chef der Kanzlei des GG.: Kammergerichtsrat Dr. Keith

Dienstsitz: Krakau, Burg

b) Regierungskanzlei:

Der Chefreferent des Staatsekretärs: Oberlandesgerichtsrat Klein

Dienstsitz Krakau, Regierungsgebäude, Außenring 46

| | |
|---|---|
| Hauptref. I: | Allgemeine Regierungsangelegenheiten, Behördenorganisation u. a. |
| Hauptref. II: | Ausbildungs-, Schulungs- und Präfungswesen |
| Hauptref. III: | Statistik |
| Hauptref. IV: | Bodenforschung |
| Hauptref. V: | Pressechef der Regierung des Generalgouvernements |

c) Amt für Gesetzgebung:

Leiter: Oberlandesgerichtsrat Dr. Weh

Dienstsitz: Krakau, Außenring 46

d) Amt für Preisbildung:

Leiter: Oberregierungsrat Dr. Schulte-Wissermann

Dienstsitz: Krakau, Scharffenbergplatz 3

e) Amt für Raumordnung:

Leiter: Oberregierungsrat Dr. Schepers

Dienstsitz: Krakau, Außenring 31

f) Personalamt:

Geschäftsführender Leiter: Freiherr von Medem

Diesntsitz: Krakau, Regierungsbebäude, Außenring 46

g) Betriebsamt:

Leiter: Notar Gutbrod

Dienstsitz: Krakau, Regierungsgebäude, Außering 46

h) Direktion der Archive des Generalgouvernements:

Leiter: Staatsarchivdirektor Dr. Randt

Dienstsitz: Krakau, Außenring 31

i) Dienststelle für Außenhandel:

Leiter: Außerordentlicher Gesandter und Bevollmächter Minister des Deutschen Reiches Rümelin

Dienstsitz: Krakau, Regierungsgebäude, Außenring 46

**II. Hauptabteilungen**

a) Hauptabteilung Innere Verwaltung:

Hauptabteilungsleiter: Ministerialrat Dr. Siebert

Dienstsitz: Krakau, Regierungsgebäude, Außenring 46

Abt. I: Allgemeine Staatsverwaltung
Abt. II: Kommunalverwaltung
Abt. III: Polizeiangelegenheiten
Abt. IV: Sonderdienst
Abt. V: Straßenverkehr
Abt. VI: Gesundheitswesen
Abt. VII: Veterinärwesen
Abt. VIII: Baudienst

b) Hauptabteilung Finanzen:
Hauptabteliungsleiter: Finanzpräsident Senkowsky
Dienstsitz: Krakau, Regierungsgebäude, Außenring 46

A. Hoheitsverwaltung:
Abt. I: Haushalt etc.
Abt. II: Zölle, Verbrauchssteurn und Monopole
Abt. III: Verwaltung der direkrion Steuern und Verkehrssteuern
Abt. IV: Besoldungsangelegenheiten etc, Gemeindefinanzen und Finanzausgleich

B. Generaldirektion der Monopole:
Leiter: Finanzpräsident Senkowsky, Krakau, Zipser Gasse 1
Abt. I: Organisation etc.
Abt. II: Tabakmonopol
Abt. III: Branntweinmonopol
Abt. IV: Salzmonopol
Abt. V: Beschaffung und Ausfuhr
Abt. VI: Zündholz-, Süßstoff- und Glückspielmonopol
Abt. VII: Mineralölmonopol

c) Hauptabteilung Justiz:
Hauptabteilungsleiter: Ministrialrat Wille
Dienstsitz: Krakau, Außenring 45
Abt. I: Verwaltung und Strafvollzug
Abt. II: Bürgerliches Recht, Handels-, Verkehrs- und Wirtschaftsrecht
Abt. III: Öffentliches Recht, Strafrecht und Internationales Recht

Warschau
Deutsche Gerichte in Krakau, Reichshof (Rzeszow), Lublin, Cholm, Radom, Petrikau, Warschau und Zyrardow
Sondergerichte in Krakau Reichshof (Rzeszow), Lublin, Radom, Kielce, Petrikau, Tschenstochau, Warschau, Zamość, Lemberg
Patentamt in Warschau

d) Hauptabteilung Wirtschaft:
Hauptabteilungsleiter: Ministerialdirigent Dr. Emmerich

Dienstsitz: Krakau, Außenring 45
Abt. S: Treuhandverwaltung und Sonderaufgaben
Abt. I: Allgemeine Verwaltungsangelegenheiten
Abt. II: Industrie und Bergbau
Bewirtschaftungsstelle für Eisen und Stahl
Krakau, Schönberggasse 13
Bewirtschaftungsstelle für Metalle
Krakau, Schönberggasse 13
Bewirtschaftungsstelle für Kohle
Krakau, Gotengasse 3
Bewirtschaftungsstelle für Spinnstoffe und Spinnstoffwaren
Krakau, Scharffenbergplatz 1
Bewirtschaftungsstelle für Leder und Pelze
Krakau, Schönberggasse 13
Bewirtschaftungsstelle für chemische Erzeugnisse
Krakau, Schönberggasse 13
Bewirtschaftungsstelle für Alt- und Abfallstoffe
Krakau, Schönberggasse 13
Abt. III: Handel, Handwerk und wirtschaftlich-techn.
Abt. IV: Geld,- Bank- und Versicherungswesen (der derzeitige Leiter der Bankaufsichtsstelle für das Generalgouvernement ist dem Staatssekretär unmittelbar unterstellt)
Abt. V: Devisen und Außenwirtschaft
Abt. VI: Verkehrswirtschaft
Dienststelle für den Vierjahresplan im Generalgouvernement

e) Hauptabteilung Ernährung und Landwirtschaft:
Hauptabteilungsleiter: Landesbauernführer SS-Brigadeführer Körner
Geschäftsführender Hauptabteilungsleiter: Kreisbauernführer Naumann
Dienstsitz: Krakau, Danziger Straße 11
Abt. I: Allgemeine Angelegenheiten
Abt. II: Erzeugung
Abt. III: Marktordnung
Abt. IV: Bodenordnung und Landarbeit
Hauptlandamt Krakau
Abt. V: Liegenschaftshauptverwaltung
Abt. VI: Wasserwirtschaft
Abt. VII: Genossenschaft- und Kreditwesen

f) Hauptabteilung Forsten:
Hauptabteilungsleiter: Oberlandforstmeister Dr. Eißfeldt
Dienstsitz: Krakau, Außenring 31

Abt. I: Verwaltung
Abt. II: Forstwirtschaft
Abt. III: Holzwirtschaft
Abt. IV: Jagdwesen

g) Hauptabteilung Arbeit:
Hauptabteilungsleiter: Reichshauptleiter Dr. Frauendorfer, M.d.R.
Dienstsitz: Krakau, Zipser Gasse 2
Abt. I: Allgemeine Angelegenheiten
Abt. II: Arbeitsschutz, Arbeitsrecht LOhnpolitik
Abt. III: Arbeitseinsatz
Abt. IV: Sozialversicherung
Abt. V: Wohnungswirtschaft und Baupolizei
Abt. VI: Militärversorgung
Abt. VII: Betriebsversorgung und Berufsverbände

h) Hauptabteilung Propaganda:
Hauptabteilungsleiter: Oberregierungsrat Ohlenbusch
Dienstsitz: Krakau, Klöppermarkt 4
Abt. I: Verwaltung
Abt. II: Presse
Abt. III: Propaganda
Abt. IV: Kultur
Abt. V: Film
Abt. VI: Rundfunk

i) Hauptabteilung Wissenschaft und Unterricht:
Hauptabteilungsleiter: Hofrat Dr. Watzke
Dienstsitz: Krakau, Außenring 40
Abt. I: Wissenschaft und Volksbildung
Zentralstelle für Denkmalsamt Krakau
Abt. II: Erziehung und Unterricht

k) Hauptabteilung Bauwesen: (eingegliedert die Baudirektion des Generalgouverneurs)
Hauptabteilungsleiter: Präsident Bauder
Dienstsitz: Krakau, Außenring 40
Abt. I: Hochbau
Abt. II: Straßenbau
Abt. III: Strombau
Abt. IV: Verwaltung und Recht

l) Hauptabteilung Eisnebahnen:
Hauptabteilungsleiter: Präsident Gerteis
Dienstsitz: Krakau, Matejkiplatz 12
Abt. I: Finanzen und Rechtsbteilung

Abt. II: Personal- und Verkehrsabteilung
Abt. III: Maschinentechnische Abteilung
Abt. IV: Betriebsabteilung
Abt. V: Bauabteilung
Abt. VI: Werkstättenabteilung
Abt. VII: Sonderbauvorhaben

m) Hauptabteilung Post:
Hauptabteilungsleiter: Präsident Lauxmann
Dienstsitz: Krakau, Poststraße 19
Abt. I: Post- und Organisationsabteliung
Abt. II: Fernmeldeabteilung
Abt. III: Personalabteilung
Abt. IV: Finanzabteilung

**III. Der Höhere SS- und Polizeiführer**

Der Höhere SS- und Polizeiführer:
SS-Obergruppenführer General der Polizei Krüger
Dienstsitz: Krakau, Regierungsgebäude, Außenring 46

a) Der Befehlshaber der Ordnungspolizei im Generalgouvernement:
SS-Brigadeführer und Generalmajor der Polizei Winkler
Dienstsitz: Krakau, Außenring 29

b) Der Befehlshaber der Sicherheitspolizei und des SD. im Generalgouvernement:
SS-Oberführer und Oberst der Polizei Dr. Schöngarth
Dienstsitz: Krakau, Magdeburger Straße 1

**IV. Der Bankdirigent der Emissionsbank des Generalgouvernements**

Reichsbankdirektor a.D. Bankdirigent Dr. Paersch
Dienstsitz: Krakau, Straße der Wehrmacht 20

**V. Das Oberste Rechnungsprüfungsamt des Generalgouvernements**

Präsident: Senatsrat Dr. Blauert
Dienstsitz: Krakau, Karolingerstraße 12

**Beauftragte von Reichs- und Parteidienststellen beim Generalgouvernement**

(Nicht zur Regierung des Generalgouvernements gehörig)

1. Der Beauftragte der Parteikanzlei beim Generalgouverneur:
   Reichshauptamtsleiter Pg. Schalk (zur Zeit bei der Wehrmacht)
   (Vertreter im Amt: Hauptabschnittsleiter Pg. Adolf Stahl)
   Krakau, Regierungsgebäude, Außenring 46
2. Der Verbindungsoffizier des Oberkommandos der Wehrmacht:

Oberstleutnant Fischer
Krakau, Regierungsgebäude Außenring 46

3. Der Verbindungsoffizier des Heeres und des Militärbefehlshabers im Generalgouvernement:
   Oberstleutnant von Tschammer und Osten
   Krakau, Regierungsgebäude Außenring 46
4. Der Verbindungsoffizier des Oberbefehlshabers der Luftwaffe:
   Major von Dazur
   Krakau, Regierungsgebäude Außenring 46
5. Der Beauftragte des Auswärtigen Amtes:
   Gesandter von Wühlisch
   Krakau, Regierungsgebäude Außenring 46
6. Der Reichsminister für Bewaffnung und Munition, der Beauftragte für das Generalgouvernement:
   Oberingenier Kobold
   Krakau, Invalidenplatz 4
7. Der Generalbevollmächtigte für die Regelung der Bauwirtschaft, der Gebietsbeauftragte für das Generalgouvernement:
   Präsident Bauder
   Krakau, Regierungsgebäude Außenring 46
8. Der Beauftragte des Reichsjugendführers:
   Gebietsführer Blum
   Krakau, Regierungsgebäude Außenring 46
9. Der Verbindungsführer des Reichsarbeitsführers:
   Oberstarbeitsführer Hinkel
   Krakau, Stefansplatz 5
10. Der Beauftragte des Deutschen Roten Kreuzes beim Generalgouverneur:
    DRK. Oberstführer Dr. Heller
    Krakau, Karolingerstraße 16
11. Der Sonderbeauftragte für die Sicherung der Kunst- und Kulturschätze:
    Staatssekretär Dr. Kajetan Mühlmann
    Krakau, Regierungsgebäude, Außenring 46

# APPENDIX VI

# THE JEWISH POPULATION OF LUBLIN DISTRICT

Source: Yad Vashem and YIVO Institute via www.Chelmfreeyellow.com

The Lublin district of Poland was the centre of Jewish life and had a high concentration of religious (orthodox/Hasidic) Jews. According to the 1931 census of Poland, Lublin district had 314,340 Jews. In the nearby Wolyn district [modern Ukraine], there were 207,792 in the same census.

In the Lublin district, there were more than 115 Jewish communities that had a Jewish population of more than 100 Jews each, prior to 1939. The following communities in the Lublin district had a pre-Holocaust Jewish population. Please note that in many cases these are estimates, as most of Lublin's Jews were murdered in the Holocaust. This is not an all-inclusive listing because records for the smaller communities were destroyed during the Shoah.

The below listing does not include communities north of Adamów, Kodeń, Łomazy, Radzyń Podlaski, and Ryki. Therefore Siedlce and Terespol are not included in the listing.

| Community Name | Community Estimated Pre-war Jewish Population | Estimated Number of Shoah Survivors from Community |
|---|---|---|
| Abramowka (Abramowice) | ? | No survivors |
| Adamów | ~650 Jews | 2 survivors |
| Adampol | ? | 2 survivors |
| Annopol | 1,250-1,400 Jews | 30 survivors |
| Andrzejów (near Kamien) | ? | No survivors |
| Baranów | 1,100 Jews | No survivors |
| Bekiesza (near Cyców) | ? | No survivors |
| Bełżec | 100 Jews | 10 survivors |
| Bełżyce | 2,100 Jews | 35 survivors |
| Berajow | 35 Jews | No survivors |
| Biała Podlaska | 7,000 Jews | 50 survivors |
| Białopole | ? | No survivors |
| Biłgoraj | 4,596 Jews | 40 survivors |
| Biskupice | 250-600 Jews | No survivors |
| Biszcza (near Tarnogród) | ? | No survivors |
| Blinów | 25 Jews | 1 survivor |
| Bobrowniki | 200 Jews | No survivors |
| Borowica | 10 Jews | No survivors |
| Brzeźnica | 35 Jews | No survivors |
| Buków (near Sawin) | 30 Jews | No survivors |
| Bussowno (Busówno) | 15 Jews | No survivors |
| Bychawa | 2,459 Jews | 50 survivors |
| Bystrzyca | 5 Jews | No survivors |
| Bystrzejowice | ? | No survivors |
| Chełm | 15,500 Jews | 525 survivors |
| Ciecierzyn | ? | No survivors |
| Chodel | 750-950 Jews | 10 survivors |
| Chrzanów (near Janów Lubelski) | 123 Jews | 1 survivor |
| Chutcze (near Sawin) | 100 Jews | No survivors |
| Chylin (near Wierzbica) | ? | No survivors |
| Cokolowka | ? | No survivors |
| Cyców | 181 Jews | No survivors |
| Czarnystok | ? | No survivors |
| Czemierniki | 1,000 Jews | 1 survivor |
| Debinie | 45 Jews | No survivors |
| Dęblin | 3,100-3,500 Jews | 55 survivors |
| Dolhobrod (near Sławatycze) | ? | No survivors |

| Community Name | Community Estimated Pre-war Jewish Population | Estimated Number of Shoah Survivors from Community |
|---|---|---|
| Dorohusk | 430 Jews | No survivors |
| Dratow (near Łęczna) | ? | No survivors |
| Drewnik (near Lubartów) | ? | No survivors |
| Dzierzkowice | ? | No survivors |
| Dzwola | ? | No survivors |
| Dubeczno | 400-650 Jews | 1 survivor |
| Dubienka | 2,500 Jews | 15 survivors |
| Dyle | ? | No survivors |
| Dzierżoniów | ? | No survivors |
| Fajsławice | 150 Jews | No survivors |
| Firlej | 167-250 Jews | 5 survivors |
| Frampol | 1,500-2,500 Jews | 15 survivors |
| Garbów | 100-125 Jews | 1 survivor |
| Giełczew | ? | No survivors |
| Głusk | 400-500 Jews | 6 survivors |
| Gołąb (near Puławy) | 30 Jews | No survivors |
| Goraj | 700 Jews | 15 survivors |
| Gorajec | ? | No survivors |
| Górka Lubartowska | 15 Jews | No survivors |
| Gorzków | 500-800 Jews | 7 survivors |
| Grabowiec | 2,356-2,500 Jews | 15 survivors |
| Hanna (near Sławatycze) | ? | No survivors |
| Hola | 30 Jews | No survivors |
| Holeszów | 118 Jews | 1 survivor |
| Holowno | 23 Jews | 2-3 survivors |
| Horodło | 1,000 Jews | 23 survivors |
| Horyszów | ? | No survivors |
| Hrubieszów | 11,750 Jews | 176 survivors |
| Husynne | 50 Jews | No survivors |
| Izbica | 4,000-6,000 Jews | 35 survivors |
| Janowiec | ~360 Jews | No survivors |
| Janów Lubelski | 3,500-5,000 Jews | 20 survivors |
| Janów Podlaski | 1,883 Jews | ? |
| Jarczów | 250-400 Jews | 2 survivors |
| Jarosławiec (near Hrubieszów) | ? | No survivors |
| Jastków | ? | No survivors |
| Jeziorzany | ~250 Jews | No survivors |

| Community Name | Community Estimated Pre-war Jewish Population | Estimated Number of Shoah Survivors from Community |
|---|---|---|
| Józefów, Chełm County | 6 Jews | No survivors |
| Józefów Ordynacki | 2,800 Jews | 10-30 survivors |
| Józefow nad Wisłą | 800-1,000 Jews | ? |
| Kamionka | 556 Jews | 2 survivors |
| Kanie | 20 Jews | No survivors |
| Karczmiska (near Opole Lubelski) | ? | No survivors |
| Kaznów (near Ostrów Lubelski) | 10 Jews | No survivors |
| Kazimierz Dolny | 2,500 Jews | 5 survivors |
| Kijany (near Spiczyn) | 50 Jews | No survivors |
| Kłątwy | ? | No survivors |
| Kock | 2,300 Jews | 8 survivors |
| Koczergi | ? | No survivors |
| Kodeń | 525-800 Jews | No survivors |
| Kodeniec | 125 Jews | No survivors |
| Kołacze | 50 Jews | 1-2 survivors |
| Komarów | 2,000-3,000 Jews | 10 survivors |
| Komarówka Podlaska | 500-700 Jews | 2 survivors |
| Końskowola | 750-1,200 Jews | 5 survivors |
| Konstantynów | 1,150 Jews | 5 survivors |
| Kosyń (near Zbereże) | ? | No survivors |
| Krasnobród | 1,200-1,800 Jews | 35 survivors |
| Kraśnik | 5,000-5,500 Jews | 329 survivors |
| Krasnowka | ? | No survivors |
| Krasnystaw | 2,200 Jews | 40 survivors |
| Kraśniczyn | 500 Jews | No survivors |
| Krępiec (near Świdnik) | ? | No survivors |
| Kryłów | 750-1,000 Jews | 25 survivors |
| Krynice (near Tomaszów Lubelski) | ? | No survivors |
| Krzeszów | 250-500 Jews | 10 survivors |
| Kurów | 1,800-2,000 Jews | 25 survivors |
| Łabunie | 25 Jews | No survivors |
| Łaszczów | 1,500-2,500 Jews | 7 survivors |
| Łęczna | 2,300-2,600 Jews | 10 survivors |
| Liszno | 45 Jews | No survivors |
| Liwcze near Dołhobyczów) | 50 Jews | No survivors |
| Łomazy | 1,000 Jews | 1 survivor |
| Łopiennik Górny | ? | No survivors |

| Community Name | Community Estimated Pre-war Jewish Population | Estimated Number of Shoah Survivors from Community |
|---|---|---|
| Lubartów | 3,411 Jews | 32 survivors |
| Lubień | ? | 6 survivors |
| Lublin | 42,500 Jews | 2,000 survivors |
| Lubycza Królewska | ~600 Jews | No survivors |
| Ludmiłówka | ? | No survivors |
| Łuków | 6,000 Jews | 150 survivors |
| Łukowa t(near Tarnogród) | 50-100 Jews | No survivors |
| Łukówek (near Sawin) | ? | No survivors |
| Luta | 20 Jews | No survivors |
| Łysobyki (near Jeziorzany) | ? | No survivors |
| Majdan Górny | ? | No survivors |
| Majdan Tatarski | ? | No survivors |
| Marianka | 50 Jews | 3 survivors |
| Markuszów | 2,000 Jews | 25 survivors |
| Matczyn (near Bełżyce) | ? | No survivors |
| Miączyn | 50 Jews | No survivors |
| Michów | 1,700-2,000 Jews | 6 survivors |
| Modliborzyce | 1,200 Jews | 5 survivors |
| Mokre | 10 Jews | No survivors |
| Mosty Małe | ? | No survivors |
| Mszanna (near Uhrusk) | 30 Jews | No survivors |
| Nadrzecze | ? | No survivors |
| Nałęczów | 250-400 Jews | 3 survivors |
| Narol | ? | No survivors |
| Niedrzwica Duża | ? | No survivors |
| Niedrzwica Kościelna | ? | No survivors |
| Nielisz | 20 Jews | No survivors |
| Niemce | 125 Jews | No survivors |
| Niewirków | 20 Jews | No survivors |
| Nowy Dwór (near Wysokie) | 20 Jews | No survivors |
| Nowy Orzechów | 25 Jews | No survivors |
| Obrowiec | 9 Jews | 2 survivors |
| Opatów | 5,200 Jews | 100 survivors |
| Opole Lubelski | 7,000 Jews | 5 survivors |
| Orchówek | 27 Jews | No survivors |
| Osmolice | ? | No survivors |
| Ostrów Lubelski | 1,994 Jews | ? |

| Community Name | Community Estimated Pre-war Jewish Population | Estimated Number of Shoah Survivors from Community |
|---|---|---|
| Parczew | 5,000 Jews | ~200 survivors |
| Pawłów | 50 Jews | No survivors |
| Piaski (near Wola Uhruska) | 35 Jews | No survivors |
| Piaski Luterskie | 4,165 Jews | 20-35 survivors |
| Pilaszkowice | 10 Jews | No survivors |
| Plosko | 10 Jews | No survivors |
| Podedwórze | 378 Jews | No survivors |
| Poniatowa | ? | No survivors |
| Potok Stany | 25 Jews | No survivors |
| Potok Wielki | 25 Jews | 3 survivors |
| Przeorsk | ? | No survivors |
| Puchaczów | ? | No survivors |
| Puławy | 3,600-3,700 Jews | 30 survivors |
| Rachanie | 80 Jews | No survivors |
| Radecznica | ? | No survivors |
| Radzanów (near Sawin) | 20 Jews | No survivors |
| Radziecyn | ? | No survivors |
| Radzyń Podlaski | 4,000 Jews | 50 survivors |
| Rejowiec | 2,500-3,500 Jews | 75 survivors |
| Rossosz | ~250 Jews | No survivors |
| Różaniec | ? | No survivors |
| Rozkopaczew | 45 Jews | No survivors |
| Ruda Huta | ~250 Jews | No survivors |
| Ruda Opalin | 25 Jews | No survivors |
| Rudka | 75 Jews | No survivors |
| Rudnik | ? | No survivors |
| Rybczewice | 20 Jews | No survivors |
| Ryki | 3,000-4,000 Jews | 35 survivors |
| Sajczyce | ? | No survivors |
| Sawin | 882 Jews | 19 survivors |
| Sernicki (near Lubartów) | 45 Jews | No survivors |
| Serock (near Firlej) | 10 Jews | No survivors |
| Serokomla | 250 Jews | No survivors |
| Siedliska | 100 Jews | No survivors |
| Siedliszcze | 1,000-1,500 Jews | 7 survivors |
| Sielec | ~250 Jews | No survivors |
| Siennica Różana | 150 Jews | 1 survivor |

| Community Name | Community Estimated Pre-war Jewish Population | Estimated Number of Shoah Survivors from Community |
|---|---|---|
| Sitaniec | 60 Jews | No survivors |
| Skierbieszów | 100-150 Jews | No survivors |
| Skorodnica | 15 Jews | 4 survivors |
| Skryhiczyn | 150-300 Jews | No survivors |
| Sławatycze | 900-1,300 Jews | 5 survivors |
| Sobibor | 40 Jews | No survivors |
| Sobieska Wola (near Bychawa) | ? | No survivors |
| Sobolew | 15 Jews | No survivors |
| Sosnowica | 300 Jews | 3 survivors |
| Stanin (near Łuków) | ? | No survivors |
| Stara Wieś (near Krasnystaw) | ? | No survivors |
| Staroscin | 10 Jews | 1 survivor |
| Stary Brus (Wołoskowola) | 4 Jews | 1 survivor |
| Stary Orzechów | ? | 1 survivor |
| Stare Załucze (near Cyców) | ? | No survivors |
| Staw | 25 Jews | No survivors |
| Stężyca | 125 Jews | No survivors |
| Strzelce (near Białopole) | ? | No survivors |
| Strzyżów | 60 Jews | No survivors |
| Studzianki | 45 Jews | No survivors |
| Suchodoly | 75 Jews | No survivors |
| Sułów | 18 Jews | No survivors |
| Świdnik | 10 Jews | 1 survivor |
| Świerże | 800 Jews | 1 survivor |
| Świerszczów | 25 Jews | No survivors |
| Szastarka (near Janów Lubelski) | 10 Jews | No survivors |
| Szczebrzeszyn | 3,000-4,000 Jews | ? |
| Szumów (near Kurów) | ? | No survivors |
| Syczyn (near Wierzbica) | ? | No survivors |
| Tarło (near Niedźwiada) | 40 Jews | No survivors |
| Tarno (near Wierzbica) | 25 Jews | No survivors |
| Tarnogród | 2,515 Jews | 60 survivors |
| Tarnogóra | 100-200 Jews | No survivors |
| Tarzymiechy (near Izbica) | ? | No survivors |
| Teodorówka (near Frampol) | ? | No survivors |
| Tomaszów Lubelski | 5,669 Jews | 49 survivors |
| Trawniki | 100 Jews | 1 survivor |

| Community Name | Community Estimated Pre-war Jewish Population | Estimated Number of Shoah Survivors from Community |
|---|---|---|
| Trzebieszów | ? | No survivors |
| Trzeszczany | ? | No survivors |
| Trzydnik | ? | No survivors |
| Tuchowicz | ? | No survivors |
| Turobin | 1,400 Jews | 5 survivors |
| Turno | 3 Jews | No survivors |
| Tyszowce | 3,800 Jews | 32 survivors |
| Uchanie | 1,161 Jews | 20 survivors |
| Uhnin | 10 Jews | 17 survivors |
| Uhrusk | 100 Jews | No survivors |
| Ulan (near Łuków) | ? | No survivors |
| Urszulin | 40 Jews | No survivors |
| Urzędów | 509 Jews | 4 survivors |
| Ustilug | 3,000 Jews | 5 survivors |
| Wanda (near Wierzbica) | ? | No survivors |
| Wasylow | ? | No survivors |
| Wąwolnica | 1,000-1,200 Jews | No survivors |
| Węglinek | 10-15 Jews | No survivors |
| Wereszczyn | 100 Jews | 1 survivor |
| Werbkowice | 75 Jews | No survivors |
| Wierzbica | 150-200 Jews | 4 survivors |
| Wisznice (near Radzyń Podlaski) | 950 Jews | 5 survivors |
| Włodawa | 5,650 Jews | 173 survivors |
| Wohyń | 1,025 Jews | No survivors |
| Wojcieszków | ? | No survivors |
| Wojsławice | 1,000-1,200 Jews | 23 survivors |
| Wola Czołnowska | ? | No survivors |
| Wola Uhruska | 20 Jews | No survivors |
| Wola Wereszczyńska | ? | No survivors |
| Wołczyny | ? | No survivors |
| Wólka Cycówska | ? | No survivors |
| Wólka Kańska | 32 Jews | No survivors |
| Wólka Okopska | ? | No survivors |
| Wólka Rokicka | 35 Jews | No survivors |
| Wożuczyn | ? | No survivors |
| Wytyczno | 50 Jews | No survivors |
| Wyryki | 20 Jews | 4 survivors |

| Community Name | Community Estimated Pre-war Jewish Population | Estimated Number of Shoah Survivors from Community |
|---|---|---|
| Wysokie Lubelskie | 350-550 Jews | 7 survivors |
| Zagrody | 14 Jews | No survivors |
| Zaklików | 2,000 Jews | 25 survivors |
| Zakręcie | ? | No survivors |
| Zakrzew | ~50 Jews | 1 survivor |
| Zakrzówek | 818 Jews | 13 survivors |
| Zamość | 12,000-15,000 Jews | 204 survivors |
| Zarzecze | 100 Jews | No survivors |
| Zagóźdź (near Baranów) | ? | No survivors |
| Zahajki | 25 Jews | 4 survivors |
| Zaliszcze | 10 Jews | 5 survivors |
| Zalucze (near Bychawa) | ? | No survivors |
| Zamek Modliborzycki | 212 Jews | No survivors |
| Zamołodycze | 50 Jews | No survivors |
| Zastawie | 9 Jews | No survivors |
| Zbereże (near Wola Uhruska) | ? | No survivors |
| Zdziłowice | 100 Jews | 1 survivor |
| Zezulin | 30 Jews | No survivors |
| Ziółków (near Spiczyn) | 35 Jews | No survivors |
| Żółkiewka | 1,500-1,800 Jews | 15 survivors |
| Zmiarka | ? | No survivors |
| Zosinek (near Chodel) | ? | No survivors |
| Żyrzyn (near Puławy) | ? | No survivors |
| Zwierzyniec | 1,000-1,500 Jews | No survivors |

Total from the above (prewar Jewish population in Lublin district): Approx. **277,455 Jews**

Total population of Holocaust survivors: Approx. **7,664**

Missing population data for more than 50 of these destroyed Jewish communities.

# APPENDIX VII

# AKTION REINHARDT CAMPS PERSONNEL

(With thanks to Robin O'Neil & Jewishgen.org)

| Name | SS Rank | T4 Service & Camp Service |
|---|---|---|
| Arndt, Kurt | SS- Scharführer | Hadamar/Treblinka |
| Bär, Rudi | SS-Scharführer | Bernburg/Treblinka |
| Bärbl, Heinrich | SS-Rottenführer | Hartheim/Bełżec/Sobibor |
| Bauch, Ernst | SS-Rottenführer | Bernburg |
| Bauer, Hermann Erich | SS-Oberscharführer | T4 driver. Sobibor |
| Baumann, Max | SS-Scharführer | Bełżec |
| Becher, Werner | SS-Unterscharführer | Sonnenstein/Sobibor |
| Beckmann, Rudolf | SS-Oberscharführer | Hartheim/Sobibor |
| Beulich, Max | SS-Scharfüher | Sonnenstein |
| Bielas, Max | SS-Scharführer | Bernburg/Brandenburg/Treblinka |
| Blauroch, | SS-Scharführer | Sonnenstein/Sobibor |
| Boelitz, Kurt | SS- Scharführer | Treblinka |
| Bolender, Kurt | SS-Oberscharführer | Bran/Had/Hart/Sonn/Sobibor |
| Bootz, Helmut | SS- Scharführer | Bernburg/Grafeneck/Treblinka/Sobibor |
| Börner, Gerhardt | SS-Scharführer | Sonnenstein/Sobibor |
| Borowski, Werner | SS-Untersturmführer | Bernburg/Treblinka/Bełżec |
| Bredow, Paul | SS-Scharführer | Grafeneck/Hartheim/Sobibor/Treblinka |
| Bree, Max | SS-Scharführer | Grafeneck/Hadamar/Sobibor/Treblinka |
| Cook | SS-Scharführer | Hartheim/Treblinka |
| Daschel, Arthur | SS-Oberwachtmeister | Sonnenstein/Bełżec/Sobibor |
| Dietz, Erich | SS- Scharfuhrer | Sonnenstein/Sobibor |
| Dubois, Werner +* | SS-Oberscharführer | Bernburg/Hadamar/Bełżec/Sobibor |

| Name | SS Rank | T4 Service & Camp Service |
|---|---|---|
| Eberl, Irmfried (Dr). | Obersturmführer | Bernburg/Brandenburg |
| Eehwald, Wenzel | SS-Unterscharführer | Lublin |
| Eisold, Johannes | SS-Scharführer | Sonnenstein/Treblinka |
| Feix, Reinhold | SS-Untesturmführer | Trawniki/Bełżec |
| Felfe, Hermann | SS- Scharführer | Grafeneck/Sonnenstein/Treblinka |
| Fereleng, Gustav | SS-Unterscharführer | T4. Bełżec |
| Fettke, Erich | SS-Unterscharführer | T4. Sobibor |
| Fichtner, Erwin | SS-Scharführer | Bernburg/Bełżec |
| Floss, Herbert | SS-Scharführer | Bernburg/Bełżec/Sobibor/Treblinka |
| Forker, Albert | SS- Scharführer | Sonnenstein/Sobibor/Treblinka |
| Franz, Kurt Hubert ** | SS-Untersturmführer | Brand/Graf/Sonn/Bełżec/Treblinka |
| Frenzel, Karl + | SS-Oberscharführer | Bernburg/Graf/Hadamar/Sobibor |
| Friedel, | SS-Schaführer | T4. Bełżec/Sobibor |
| Fuchs, Erich +* | SS-Unterscharführer | Bernburg/Bran/Bełżec/Sobibor/Treblinka |
| Gaulstich, Friedrich | SS-Unterscharführer | T4. Sobibor |
| Gentz, Ernst | SS-Scharführer | T4 Treblinka/Sobibor |
| Getzinger, Anton | SS-Oberscharführer | Hartheim/Sobibor |
| Girtzig, Hans * | SS-Scharführer | Grafeneck/Hartheim/Bełżec/Sobibor |
| Gley, Heinrich * | SS-Oberscharführer | Grafeneck/Sonnenstein/Bełżec |
| Gomerski, Hubert | SS-Oberscharführer | Hadamar/Sobibor |
| Goetzinger, Anton | SS-Oberscharführer | Hartheim/Sobibor |
| Graetschus, Siegfried | SS-Oberscharführer | Bernburg/Treblinka/Sobibor |
| Gringers, Max (Karl) | SS-Scharführer | Hartheim/Bełżec |
| Grömer, Josef (Ferdl) | SS-Sturmmann | Hartheim/Sobibor |
| Grossmann, Willi | SS-Scharführer | Hadamar/Sonnenstein/Treblinka |
| Groth, Paul | SS-Unterscharführer | Hartheim/Bełżec/Sobibor |
| Hackel, Emil | SS- Scharfuhrer | Sonnenstein/Sobibor |
| Hackenholt, Lorenz | SS-Hauptscharführer. | Grafeneck/Sonnenstein/Bełżec/Sobibor/Treblinka. |
| Haunstein | SS- Scharführer | Sonnenstein/Sobibor |
| Häusler, Willi | SS-Hauptscharführer | Lublin |
| Hengst, August | SS- Scharführer | Bernburg/Brandenburg/Treblinka |
| Hering, Gottleib | SS-Hauptsturmführer | Bern/Brand/Hart/Sonn/Bełżec |
| Herman, Erwin | SS-Scharführer | T4. Sobibor |
| Hiller, Richard | SS-Unterscharführer | T4 |
| Hirsch, Fritz | SS-Scharführer | Hartheim/Bełżec |
| Hirtreiter, Josef | SS-Scharführer | Hadamar/Treblinka/Sobibor |
| Hödl, Franz | SS-Unterscharführer | Hartheim/Sobibor |
| Horn, Otto ** | SS-Scharführer | Sonnenstein/Sobibor |

| Name | SS Rank | T4 Service & Camp Service |
|---|---|---|
| Irrmann, Fritz | SS-Scharführer | T4/Bełżec |
| Ittner, Alfred + | SS-Oberscharführer | T4-HQ Berlin/Sobibor |
| Jührs, Robert +* | SS-Unterscharführer | Hadamar/Bełżec/Sobibor |
| Kainer, Erwin | SS- Scharführer | Hadamar/Treblinka |
| Kaiser, Aleksy | SS-Oberscharführer | T4. Sobibor |
| Kamm, Rudolf | SS-Scharführer | Sonnenstein/Bełżec/Sobibor |
| Kielminsky, Otto | SS-Scharführer | T4. Sobibor |
| Klier, Johann (Josef) | SS-Unterscharführer | Hadamar/Sobibor |
| Kloss, Walter | SS-Scharführer | Sonnenstein/Bełżec |
| Konrad, Josef (Fritz) | SS-Scharführer | Grafeneck/Sonnenstein/Sobibor |
| Kraschewski, Fritz | SS-Scharführer | Grafeneck/Hadamar/Bełżec |
| Kramer, Johann | SS-Rottenführer | T4. Sobibor |
| Küttner, Karl 'Kiwi' ** | SS-Oberschaführer | T4. Treblinka |
| Lachmann, Erich + | SS-Scharführer | T4. Sobibor |
| Lambert, Erwin ** | SS-Unterscharführer | Bern/Had/Hart/Sonn/Sobibor/Treblinka |
| Lindenmüller, Alfons | SS-Hauptscharführer | T4. Treblinka |
| Löffler, Albert | SS-Unterscharführer | T4. Treblinka/Majdanek |
| Ludwig, Karl Emilr | SS-Scharführer | T4-HQ Berlin/Sobibor/Treblinka |
| Matthes, Heinrich ** | SS-Scharführer | Sonnenstein/Treblinka/Sobibor |
| Mauritius Schnur | SS-Unterscharfuhrer | Lublin |
| Mätzig, Willi | SS-Scharführer | Bernburg/Brand/Treblinka/Sobibor |
| Mentz, Willi ** | SS-Scharführer | Grafenesck/Hadamar/Treblinka/Sobibor |
| Michalsen, Georg | SS-Scharführer | T4. Sobibor |
| Michel, Hermann | SS-Oberscharführer | Grafeneck/Hartheim/Sobibor |
| Miete, August ** | SS-Scharführer | Grafeneck/Hadamar/Treblinka |
| Möller, Max | SS- Unterscharführer | T4. Treblinka |
| Müller, Adolf (Karl) | SS-Scharführer | T4. Sobibor |
| Münzberger, Gustav ** | SS-Scharführer | Sonnenstein/Treblinka |
| Niemann, Johann (Josef) | SS-Untersturmführer | Bernburg/Bełżec/Killed Sobibor revolt |
| Nowak, Walter (Anton) | SS-Scharführer | Sonnenstein/Sobibor |
| Oberhauser, Josef * | SS-Oberscharführer | Bern/Brand/Graf/Sonn/Bełżec |
| Pflanzer Alexander | SS-Unterschaführer | T4. Sobibor |
| Poul | SS-Scharführer | T4. Sobibor |
| Pötzinger, Karl | SS-Scharführer | Bernburg/Brand/Treblinka/Sobibor |
| Rehwald, Fritz | SS-Unterscharführer | Bern/Had/Hart/Sonn/Sobibor |
| Richter, Kurt (Karl) | SS-Scharführer | Hartheim/Sonnenstein/Sobibor/Treblinka |
| Reichtleitner, Franz | SS-Hauptsturmführer | Hartheim/Sobibor |
| Rost, Paul | SS-Scharführer | Hartheim/Sonnenstein/Sobibor/Treblinka |

| Name | SS Rank | T4 Service & Camp Service |
|---|---|---|
| Rum, Franz Albert ** | SS-Scharführer | T4-HQ Berlin/Treblinka/Sobibor |
| Ryba, Walter | SS-Unterscharführer | T4. Killed Sobibor revolt |
| Seidel, Kurt | Oberwachmann | Lublin |
| Schafer, Herbert | SS-Scharführer | Sonnenstein/Sobibor |
| Schemmel, Franz | SS-Scharführer | Hartheim/Sonnenstein/Sob/Treblinka |
| Schiffner, Karl | SS-Scharführer | Sonnenstein/Bełżec/Sobibor/Treblinka |
| Schluch, Karl * | SS-Scharführer | Grafeneck/Hadamar/Bełżec |
| Schmidt, Fritz | SS- Scharführer | Bernburg/Sonnenstein/Treblinka |
| Schreiber, Klaus | SS-Unterscharführer | T4. Sobibor |
| Schuh, Richard | SS-Unterscharführer | Lublin |
| Schulze, Erich | SS- Scharfuhrer | Graf/Had/Sonn/Sobibor/Treblinka |
| Schumacher, Ernst | SS-Unterscharführer | T4. Sobibor |
| Schütt, Heinz-Hans +** | SS-Scharführer | Grafeneck/Hadamar/Sobibor |
| Schwarz, Gottfried | SS-Untersturmführer | Bernburg/Grafeneck/ Bełżec |
| Sidow | SS-Scharführer | T4. Treblinka |
| Stadie, Otto | SS-Scharführer | Bernburg/Treblinka |
| Stangl, Franz Paul | SS-Hauptsturmführer | Bernburg/Hartheim/Sobibor/Treblinka |
| Steffl, Thomas | SS-Scharführer | T4-HQ Berlin/Sobibor |
| Steubel, Karl | SS-Scharführer | T4. Killed Sobibor revolt |
| Sporleder | SS-Scharführer | T4. Sobibor |
| Suchomel, Franz ** | SS-Scharführer | Hadamar/Treblinka/Sobibor. |
| Szpilny, Heinrich | SS-Scharführer | T4. Sobibor |
| Tauscher, Fritz | SS-Oberscharführer | Brand/Hart/Sonn/Bełżec |
| Thomalla, Richard | SS-Hauptsturmführer | (Builder) Bełżec/Sobibor/Treblinka |
| Unverhau, Heinrich +* | SS-Oberscharführer | Grafeneck/Hadamar/Bełżec/Sobibor |
| Valaster, Erich Josef | SS-Scharführer | Hartheim/Bełżec/Sobibor |
| Vey, Kurt | SS- Scharfuhrer | Sonnenstein/Bełżec/Sobibor |
| Wagner, Gustav Franz | SS-Oberscharführer | Hartheim/Sobibor |
| Wallerang, Bernard | SS-Scharführer | T4. Sobibor |
| Weiss, Bruno | SS-Hauptscharführer | T4. Sobibor |
| Wendland, Willi | SS-Scharführer | T4. Sobibor |
| Werner, Kurt | SS-Scharführer | T4. Sobibor |
| Widemann, Albert | SS-Obersturmbannführer | T4. Bełżec |
| Wirth, Christian | SS-Sturmbannführer | Brand/Graf/Had/Hart/Sobibor/Bełżec/Treblinka |
| Wolf, Franz + | SS-Unterscharführer | Hadamar/Sobibor |
| Wolf, Josef | SS-Unterscharführer | T4. Sobibor |
| Zanker, Hans | SS-Scharführer | Sonnenstein/Bełżec/Treblinka |
| Zierk, Ernst +* | SS-Unterscharführer | Graf/Had/Sonn/Bełżec/Sobibor |

* Prosecuted for crimes in Bełżec
\+ Prosecuted for crimes at Sobibor
** Prosecuted for crimes in Treblinka

Staff at all three 'AR' camps was interchangeable. It was more prevalent between Sobibór and Bełżec due to geographic reasons. In view of this, SS staff known to have been in these two camps has been listed. Only two of the SS-Garrison at Bełżec, and only seven at Sobibór were *bona fide* SS, the rest were civilians (police, nurses and tradesmen) in SS uniform.

Note: T4—euthanasia practitioner; KZ, concentration camp guard; PO, Police Officer; WSS, Waffen-SS.

# APPENDIX VIII

# THE KATZMANN REPORT

(Translation of Document L-18, in Nazi Conspiracy and Aggression. Volume VII)

Secret report of Fritz Katzmann to SS-Obergruppenführer und General der Polizei Friedrich-Wilhelm Krüger (HSSPF Ost) concerning the solution of the Jewish question in the District of Galicia), 30 June 1943:

To:
The Höhere SS- und Polizeiführer Ost, SS-Obergruppenführer und General der Polizei or deputy, Krakow
Enclosed I am submitting the 1st copy of the Final Report on the Solution of the Jewish Question in the District of Galicia for your information.

[Signed] ***Katzmann***
SS-Gruppenführer und Generalleutnant der Polizei

SOLUTION OF THE JEWISH PROBLEM IN THE DISTRICT OF GALICIA
Owing to the term 'Galician Jew', Galicia probably was the spot on earth which was best known and most frequently mentioned in connection with Jewry. Here they lived in immense multitudes, forming a world of their own, out of which the rising generations of world-Jewry were supplied. In all parts of Galicia, one found Jews in their hundreds of thousands.

According to obsolete statistics of 1931, the number of Jews then was about 502,000. This number should not have decreased from 1931 up to the summer of 1941. Precise statements on the number of Jews present at the time when the German troops invaded Galicia are not available. By the Committees of Jews, the number was stated to have been 350,000 at the end of 1941. That this statement was incorrect will be seen from the statement at the end of this report with regard to the evacuation of Jews. The town of Lemberg alone had about 160,000 Jewish inhabitants in July-August 1941.

The influence of this Galician Jewry, being considerable already under Austrian and Polish rule, increased to an almost incredible extent when the Soviets occupied this district in 1939.

Every important appointment within the country was filled by them. This explains the fact that in July 1941, after the occupation by German troops, Jews were found everywhere. Hence it was considered to be also our most urgent task to find a solution for this problem as soon as possible.

Our first measure consisted of marking every Jew by a white armlet bearing the Star of David in blue. By virtue of a decree of the General Governor, the Department of the Interior was responsible for the marking and registering of Jews as well as for the formation of Committees of Jews. Our task, that of the Police, was initially to counter effectively the immense black market carried on by Jews throughout the entire district and especially to take measures against loafing idlers and vagabonds.

The best remedy consisted of the formation, by the SS- und Polizeiführer, of Forced Labour Camps. The best opportunities for labour were offered by the necessity to complete the 'Dg. IV' road which was extremely important and necessary for the whole of the southern part of the front, and which was in a catastrophically bad condition. On 15 October 1941, the establishment of camps along the road was commenced, and despite considerable difficulties there existed after a few weeks, only seven camps containing 4,000 Jews.

Soon more camps followed these first ones, so that after a very short time the completion of 15 camps of this kind could be reported to the Höherer SS- und Polizeiführer. In the course of time, about 20,000 Jewish labourers passed through these camps. Despite the hardly imaginable difficulties occurring at this work, I can report today that about 160 kms of the road are completed. [*Photographs*].

At the same time, all other Jews fit for work were registered and distributed for useful work by the labour agencies. When the Jews were marked by the Star of David as well as when they were registered by the labour agencies, the first symptoms appeared of their attempts to dodge the orders of the authorities. The measures which were introduced thereupon, led to thousands of arrests. It became more and more apparent that the civil administration was not in a position to solve the Jewish problem in an approximately satisfactory manner. When, for instance, the municipal administration in Lemberg had no success in their attempts to house the Jews within a close district which would be inhabited only by Jews, this question too was solved quickly by the SS- und Polizeiführer through his subordinate officials. This measure became the more urgent as in winter 1941, big centres of spotted fever were noted in many parts of the town, whereby not only the native population was endangered, but also, and to a greater extent, the troops themselves, those stationed there as well as those passing through. During this removal of the Jews into a certain quarter of the town, several sluices were erected at which all the work-shy and a-social Jewish rabble were caught, during the screening and treated in a special way.

Owing to the peculiar fact that almost 90 of artisans working in Galicia were Jews, the task to be solved could be fulfilled only step by step, since an immediate evacuation would not have served the interest of war economy. With regard to those Jews, however, who had a place in the labour process, no real effect could be found of their work. They used their job mostly only as a means to an end, namely in order first to dodge the intensified measures against Jewry, and secondly to be able to carry on their black market activities without interference. Only by continuous police interference was it possible to prevent of these activities. After it had been found in more and more cases that Jews had succeeded in making themselves indispensable to their employers by providing them with goods in scarce supply etc., it was considered necessary to introduce really draconic measures. Unfortunately, it had to be stated that the Germans employed in the district, especially so-called 'operational firms' or the 'ill-famed trustees' carried on the most extravagant black market activities with Jews. Cases were discovered where Jews, in order to acquire any certificate of labour, not only renounced all wages, but even paid money themselves. Moreover, the 'organising' of Jews for the benefit of their 'employers' grew to such catastrophic extents, that it was deemed necessary to interfere in the most energetic manner for the benefit of the German name.

Since the administration was not in a position and showed itself too weak to master this chaos, the SS- und Polizeiführer simply took over the entire disposition of labour for Jews. The Jewish labour agencies which were manned by hundreds of Jews, were dissolved. All certificates of labour given by firms or administrative offices were declared invalid, and the cards given to the Jews by the labour agencies were revalidated by the police offices by stamping them.

In the course of this action, again thousands of Jews were caught who were in possession of forged certificates or who had obtained surreptitiously certificates of labour by all kinds of pretexts. These Jews also were exposed to special treatment.

Army administration offices in particular had countenanced Jewish parasitism by giving special certificates to an uncontrollable extent.

Of the great number of certificates seized, only three will be enclosed; you will be able to conclude what methods were used with the intention to sabotage the measures of the SS. [*Listing of aforementioned certificates*]

There were cases when arrested Jews were in possession of 10-20 of such certificates.

Where Jews were arrested in the course of these check-ups, most of their employers thought it necessary to intervene in favour of the Jews. This often happened in a manner which had to be called deeply shameful.

An especially exaggerated example is the action of a certain Schmalz, a wholesale butcher working for the army in Lwow, who sent from Berlin the following telegram to the Office of the SS- und Polizeiführer:

[*Report on the case of the aforementioned Schmalz, and further commenting regarding same*]

Despite all these measures concerning the employment of Jews, their evacuation from the district of Galicia was commenced in April 1942 and executed step by step.

When the Höherer SS- und Polizeiführer once again intervened in the solution of the Jewish problem by his decree of 10 November 1942, concerning the formation of districts inhabited by Jews, already 254,989 Jews had been evacuated, resp. resettled .

Since the Höherer SS- und Polizeiführer gave the further order to accelerate the complete evacuation of the Jews, again considerable work was necessary to regulate the status of those Jews who, for the time being were permitted to be left in the armaments factories. The Jews in question were declared labour prisoners of the Höherer SS- und Polizeiführer and they were put into barracks, either within the factories or in camps established for this purpose. For the town of Lwow a giant camp was established at the borders of the town, in which at the time of writing 8,000 Jewish labour prisoners are confined. The agreement with the army concerning the disposition and treatment of these labour prisoners was executed in writing. The decree which contained the measures now in force is attached herewith.

[*Decree of 23.10.1942 re: "Disposition of Jewish Labour..."*]

In the meantime, further evacuation was executed with energy, so that with effect from 23 June 1943, all Jewish residential districts could be dissolved. Therewith I report that the District of Galicia, with the exception of those Jews living in the camps being under the control of the SS- und Polizeiführer, is Judenfrei [*Free of Jews*].

Jews still caught in small numbers are given special treatment by the competent detachments of police and gendarmerie.

Up to 27.6.1943 altogether 44,329 Jews have been evacuated.

Camps for Jews are still in existence in:

Lwow, Weinbergen, Ostrow, Kurowice, Jaktorow, Lackie, Pluhow, Kosaki, Zborow, Jezierna, Tarnapol, Hluboczek, Borki-Wielki, Kamienki, Drohobycz, Boryslaw, Stryj, Belechow, Broschniow, Njebelow containing altogether 2,116 Jews. This number is being reduced currently.

Together with the evacuated action, we executed the confiscation of Jewish property. Very high amounts were confiscated and paid over to the Sonderstab 'Reinhard'. Apart from furniture and many textile goods, the following amounts were confiscated and turned over to Sonderstab 'Reinhard':

As per 30. June 1943:
25580 kg Copper Coins
53190 kg Nickel Coins

97581 kg Gold Coins
82600 kg Necklaces-Silver
6640 kg Necklaces-Gold
432780 kg Broken Silver
167740 kg Silver Coins
18490 kg Iron Coins
20050 kg Brass Coins
20952 kg Wedding Rings-Gold
22740 kg Pearls
11730 kg Dental Gold-Dentures
28200 kg Powder Boxes-Silver or Metal
44655 kg Broken Gold
482900 kg Cutlery-Silver
343100 kg Cigarette Boxes-Silver or Metal
20880 kg Rings, Gold with stones
39917 kg Brooches, Ear Rings etc.
18020 kg Silver rings
6166 kg Watches, all kinds
3133 kg Watches, Silver
3425 kg Wrist Watches-Silver
1256 Wrist Watches-Gold kg
2892 kg Watches-Gold
68 kg Cameras
98 Binoculars
7 Stamp Collections-complete
5 Trunks filled with loose stamps
100550 kg 3 bags with rings, not genuine
3290; 1 box with corals kg
460 kg 1 chest with corals
280 kg 1 chest with corals
7495 kg 1 box with fountain pens and propelling pencils
1 basket with fountain pens and propelling pencils
1 suitcase with fire tongs
1 suitcase with pocket knives
1 suitcase with watch parts
Banknotes:
Paper-Metal 261589.75 USA-Dollars
Paper Gold Dollars: 3 a 5, 18 a 10, 28 a 20, 2,515.75
Canadian Dollars 124
Argentine Pesos 18,766,64

Hungarian Pengoe 231,789
Roubles-Paper Gold Roubles: 1 a 7 1/2, 11 a 10, 29 a 5 4316
Rouble Paper 513
French Francs 2460
Swedish Francs 52
Austrian Ducats-Gold Austrian Crowns 36 a 10, 25 a 20 8 a 100 2229,18,60
English Pounds 23
African Pounds 13490
Roumanian Lei 25,671
Russian Cerwon 4600,70
Czechoslovakian Crowns-Paper 185
Dutch Florins 5277
Palestinian Pounds 9,300
Palestinian Mille 160
Lithuanian Oere 360
English Schillings 1
Irish Pounds 1
Hungarian Pengos 2
Mexican Pesos 10
Norwegian Crowns 381770
Slovakian Crowns 435
Karbowanez 16.79 million Zloty

Following the 'Fur-action' in December 1941 35 Wagons of Furs were handed over.

Earned Moneys from forced labour camps and from W. and R. factories 25.5.1943

1. Forced Labour Camps
a. Takings
Wages: 11,511,606.98 Zl.
Hidden money found in clothes: 1,232,143.71 Zl.
Proceeds from useless tools: 807.93 Zl.
[total:] 12,744,558.62 Zl.
b. Outgoings (Board for Prisoners)
1. Food, Clothes, Medicine: 3,108,866.62 Zl.
2. Wages, Custody by Ukrainian Police: 47,358.51 Zl.
3. Camp-sustenance Repairs, Rents: 118,063.15 Zl.
4. Means of Conveyance:
Horses: 1,448,863.57 Zl.
Cars: 83,324.14 Zl.
Tools: 3,037.10 Zl.
5. Purchases of Furniture: 2,410.15 Zl.
Postage and Telephone: 5,678.44-Zl.

Office needs: 29,005.59 Zl.
6. Buildings: 220,000.00 Zl.
[total:] 5,066,607.27 Zl.

2. W. and R. Factories Takings: 7,711,428.92 Zl. [total:] 7,711,428.92 Zl.
3. Amount paid over to the SS cashier:
a. Camp: 6,876,251.00 Zl.
b. W. and R. Factories 6: 556,513.69 Zl.
[total:] 13,423,764.69 Zl.

Further payments to the SS cashier are effected every month.

Owing to the great number of Jews and the vast area to be combed out, these actions were performed with the assistance of detachments from the Sicherheitspolizei, the Ordnungspolizei, the Gendarmerie, the Sonderdienst, and the Ukrainian Police, all acting together in numerous single sweeps. Page 19 of this report contains a map intended to show how Jews lived scattered throughout the whole of the District, until the special Jewish residence districts were established. The detachments continually were exposed to serious physical and mental strains. Again and again they had to overcome the nausea threatening them when they were compelled to enter the dirty and pestilential Jewish holes. During the searches there has been found, moreover, a number of leaflets in the Hebrew language, inciting the Jews to breed lice carrying spotted fever, in order to destroy the Police Force. In fact, several phials filled with lice were confiscated. Nothing but catastrophical conditions were found in the ghettos of Rawa-Ruska and Rohatyn. The Jews of Rawa-Ruska, fearing the evacuation, had concealed those suffering from spotted fever in underground holes. When evacuation was to start, the police found that 3,000 Jews suffering from spotted ever lay about in this ghetto.

* * * * *

[*MAP*]

From this map one is able to see how the Jews lived scattered throughout the whole of the district, until the special Jewish residence districts were established. The large dots refer to localities of more than 1,000 Jews, the smaller ones where less than 100 Jews lived.

At once every police officer inoculated against spotted fever was called into action. Thus, we succeeded to destroy this plague boil, losing thereby only one officer. Almost the same conditions were found in Rohatyn. Moreover, our detachments again and again discovered smaller or larger centers of pestilence in many towns and villages. Despite all our precautionary measures, 120 officers fell ill of spotted fever, of whom only 18 died, owing to the protective measures introduced by us.

Some photos of these dirt caves may give an idea of the degree of effort which every officer had to apply to force himself to merely enter these centers of dirt. [*Photographs*]

On the occasion of these actions, many more difficulties occurred owing to the fact that the Jews tried every means in order to dodge evacuation [Aussiedelung]. Not only did they try to flee, but they concealed themselves in every imaginable corner, in pipes, chimneys, even in sewers, etc. They built barricades in passages of catacombs, in cellars enlarged to dugouts, in underground holes, in cunningly contrived hiding-places in attics and sheds, within furniture, etc.

The smaller the number of Jews remaining in the district, the harder their resistance. Arms of all kinds, among them those of Italian make, were used for defence. The Jews purchased these Italian arms from Italian soldiers stationed in the district for high sums in Zloty currency. The ensuing photos give a small selection from the arms confiscated. Especially dangerous were the sawed-off carbines of all kinds. [*Photographs*]

Underground bunkers were found with entrances concealed in a masterly manner opening sometimes into flats, sometimes into the open. In most cases the entrances had only so much width that just one person could crawl through it. The access was concealed in such a manner that it could not be found by persons not acquainted with the locality. Here nothing succeeded, but the assistance of some Jews to whom anything whatever was promised in exchange. What these dug-outs looked like will be shown by the ensuing photographs together with their comments:
[*Photographs*]

In the course of the evacuation action we furthermore discovered that the Jews attempted more than ever to escape to foreign countries. These attempts were made by Jews in possession of considerable amounts of money, jewels, and of forged papers. They tried every means to effect their purpose and often approached members of the German and allied forces with the request to transport them to or beyond the frontier by way of military cars. They offered in exchange disproportionately high amounts, in many cases up to 5,000 Zl. and more a person. Although in a few cases members of foreign forces, especially Hungarians, came to an agreement with them and fulfilled their part, in by far the most cases the Security Police was informed in time by V-men so that the necessary counter-measures were applied, the Jews caught, and the valuables confiscated. By way of illustration, some cases are described:

In 09.1942 the office of the SS- und Polizeiführer was informed by an Italian soldier (of German blood resident in Switzerland) that some Jews were concealed within the Italian barracks in Lwow, who were to be smuggled across the frontier by members of the Italian forces within the next days. Shortly before they intended to start, two leaders in mufti entered the barracks and succeeded in arresting a group of seven persons and confiscating 3,200 gold dollars and a large amount of diamonds and jewels. They made the interesting discovery that already 970 gold dollars had been paid for bribing 4 members of the Italian forces. This money was confiscated also. The Italian soldiers thereupon were sent home.

On 13.05.1943 two German drivers of the Luftwaffe headquarters in Krakow reported that a Jew had approached them with the request to transport about 20 to 30 Jews from the Jewish camp Lwow to Brody; some of them were in possession of arms; they would provide forged transport orders; directed to these military drivers. In exchange they offered 20,000 Zl. The drivers were ordered to accept the offers, to load the Jews on the Luftwaffe car on 15 May at 5 p.m., to start in the direction of Brody, but to turn the car as soon as it passed the office of NSKK Lwow which was situated at this street, and to drive into the court yard of this office. In fact the car, manned with 20 Jews and one Pole, arrived in this court yard at 5.30 p.m. The Jews, some of whom were armed with charged pistols and sawed-off carbines with the safety devices released, were overwhelmed by a waiting detachment and disarmed. The following arms were confiscated:
[*list of weapons*]

The pistols, mentioned sub. 1. and 2. had been purchased by the Jews from members of the Italian forces for 2,000 Zl. each. The names of the sellers could not be ascertained. After a diligent search, considerable valuables were found and confiscated. A diligent interrogation of the arrested Jews led to the discovery that a certain Jew by the name of Horowitz who was staying in the woods near Brody together with a larger group of Jews, used to organise such transports. As a result of this interrogation it was possible moreover to arrest those Jews who forged identity papers for fugitives. The Pole who was arrested at the same time, confessed to be a member of the Polish resistance movement 'PPR'. Furthermore, he named the Jew Horowitz as the Chief Executive of the 'PPR' in Lwow. The place of communication in the woods near Brody having been discovered by these interrogations, the whole of this wood area was surrounded and combed out by detachments of the Gendarmerie and of the Ukrainian Police, and two companies of the German army on the same day. These forces met smaller forces of armed bandits who had established themselves in several furnished dug-outs and trenches dating from the Russian occupation. The bandits in all cases used their arms, but they all were overwhelmed and rendered harmless.

33 Jewish bandits were shot. Some sawed-off carbines and some quick-firing rifles and pistols of Russian make were confiscated. A Polish gamekeeper taking part in the combing-out action was shot dead by the bandits. During the arrests in Lwow, one SS-Mann was wounded by a shot into the left shank. The 2 German drivers were paid as recompense for their exemplary conduct 2,000 Zl. each. The forged marching orders and transport orders found in possession of the Jews are reproduced below.
[*Transport order*]

In the same way we succeeded on 21.5.1943 in destroying a Jewish gang who again were armed with 0.8 cal. pistols of Italian origin. [In the meantime, all Italian soldiers left the district of Galicia.]

Only some days later, the 31 May, we succeeded again, during a new comb-out, in destroying 6 dug-outs of major size containing 139 Jewish bandits.

On 02.06.1943, again some Jews who attempted to escape to Hungary by means of a military car owned by the Hungarian army, were arrested and, since they resisted, shot. Here again considerable values were confiscated. The Hungarian soldiers participating in the action were adequately rewarded.

The evacuation having been completed, nevertheless, still minor actions are necessary in order to track Jews in hiding and concealment. This is proved by the fact that every day some persons are caught in possession of forged identity cards and passes. Some forged identity cards, passes, marching orders, and leave passes are enclosed herewith. [*Cards and photographs*]

Since we received more and more alarming reports on the Jews becoming armed in an ever-increasing manner, we started during the last fortnight in 6.1943 an action throughout the whole of the district of Galicia with the intent to use strongest measures to destroy the Jewish gangsterdom. Special measures were found necessary during the action to dissolve the ghetto in Lwow where the dug-outs mentioned above had been established. Here we had to act brutally from the beginning, in order to avoid losses on our side; we had to blow up or to burn down several houses. On this occasion, the surprising fact arose that we were able to catch about 20,000 Jews instead of 12,000 Jews who had registered. We had to pull at least 3,000 Jewish corpses out of every kind of hiding places; they had committed suicide by taking poison.

Our own losses suffered in these actions:
Spotted Fever: dead 1
Men fallen ill: 120 men
Shot by Jews: dead 7 men
Wounded: 12 men
Stabbed by Jews: dead 1 man
Lost by accident in evacuation action: dead: 2 men,
Wounded: 5 men.

Despite the extraordinary burden heaped upon every single SS-Police Officer during these actions, mood and spirit of the men were extraordinarily good and praiseworthy from the first to the last day.

Only thanks to the sense of duty of every single leader and man have we succeeded to get rid of this PLAGUE in so short a time.

# APPENDIX IX

# T4 REVIEWERS

T4 assessors were medical evaluators appointed by the T4 central office, responsible for the organisation and conduct of the National Socialist euthanasia murders—Aktion T4—and by means of registration forms containing the data of the sick and the disabled, as the potential victims of the action decided, who were gassed in the purpose-built killing centres. [From an original document of an internal list of doctors of the T4 organization] 40 physicians who acted as reviewers for the action T4 can be confirmed—

| Doctor | Birth & death dates | Period as a T4 reviewer |
|---|---|---|
| Hermann Pfannmüller | 8 June 1886 – 10 April 1961 | from 17 November 1939 |
| Ernst Wagenknecht | 23 October 1880 – ? | 17 November 1939 – 16 February 1940 |
| Ernst Hefter | 11 January 1906 – 11 April 1947 | from 17 November 1939 |
| Hans Heinze | 18 October 1895 – 2 February 1983 | from 17 November 1939 |
| Walter Kaldewey | 10 December 1896 – 13 January 1954 | 28 February 1940 – 29 January 1941 |
| Carl-Heinz Rodenberg | 19 November 1904 – 1995 | 28 February 1940 – 14 October 1940 |
| Arthur Schreck | 15 August 1878 – 3 October 1963 | 28 February 1940 – 30 November 1940 |
| Theodor Steinmeyer | 7 December 1897 – 26 May 1945 | from 28 February 1940 |
| Hermann Paul Nitsche | 25 November 1876 – 25 March 1948 | from 28 February 1940 |
| Friedrich Mennecke | 6 October 1904 – 28 December 1947 | from 28 February 1940 |
| Friedrich Panse | 30 March 1899 – 6 December 1973 | 14 May 1940 – 16 December 1940 |
| Carl Schneider | 19 December 1891 – 11 December 1946 | from 20 April 1940 |
| Kurt Pohlisch | 28 March 1893 – 6 February 1955 | 30 April 1940 – 6 January 1941 |
| Konrad Zucker | 7 December 1893 – 31 August 1978 | from 8 May 1940 |
| Georg Renno | 13 January 1907 – 4 October 1997 | from 31 May 1940 |

| Doctor | Birth & death dates | Period as a T4 reviewer |
|---|---|---|
| Otto Reisch | 23 October 1891 – 1977 | 30 April 1940 – 2 July 1940 |
| Otto Hebold | 27 July 1896 – 4 January 1975 | from 8 May 1940 |
| Rudolf Lonauer | 9 January 1907 – 5 May 1945 | from 9 May 1940 |
| Hans Aloys Schmitz | 1 July 1899 – 6 March 1973 | 30 July 1940 – 14 November 1940 |
| Berthold Kihn | 10 March 1895 – 19 January 1964 | from 5 June 1940 |
| Günter Munckwitz | 13 March 1912 – 1970 | 25 July 1940 – 31 January 1941 |
| Wilhelm Schumacher | 19 November 1908 – ? | from 5 August 1940 |
| Oskar Begush | 21 January 1897 – 11 January 1944 | 2 September 1940 – 4 July 1941 |
| Ernst Sorger | 19 November 1892 – 9 August 1945 | 2 September 1940 – 8 March 1941 |
| Walter Schmidt | 9 July 1910 – 31 January 1970 | 2 September 1940 – December 1940 |
| Friedrich Mauz | 1 May 1900 – 7 July 1979 | from 6 September 1940 |
| Valentin Faltlhauser | 28 November 1876 – 8 January 1961 | from 6 September 1940 |
| Hanns Heene | 11 August 1896 – 13 April 1948 | 6 September 1940 – December 1940 |
| Franz Fehringer | 14 June 1903 – ? | 6 September 1940 – 13 January 1941 |
| Hans Bertha | 14 April 1901 – 3 January 1964 | 30 September 1940 – March 1941 |
| Erwin Jekelius | 5 June 1905 – 8 May 1952 | 14 October 1940 – February 1941 |
| Robert Müller | 14 January 1886 – 2 June 1945 | from 4 March 1941 |
| Werner Villinger | 9 October 1887 – 8 August 1961 | from 28 March 1941 |
| Erich Straub | 26 August 1885 – 29 April 1945 | from 8 July 1941 |
| Gerhard Wischer | 1 February 1903 – 4 November 1950 | from 2 August 1941 |
| Curt Schmalenbach | 24 February 1910 – 15 June 1944 | from 28 August 1941 |
| Victor Ratka | 27 December 1895 – 5 April 1966 | from 10 September 1941 |
| Curd Runckel | 4 August 1913 – ? | from 3 October 1942 |
| Alfred Schulz | 13 September 1890 – 1 November 1947 | from 7 May 1943 |
| Gustav Schneider | 15 April 1908 – ? | from 31 May 1943 (?) |

## Paediatric Reviewers

| Person | Birth & death dates | Period as a T4 reviewer |
|---|---|---|
| Werner Catel | 27 June 1894 – 30 April 1981 | from the autumn of 1939 |
| Hans Heinze | 18 October 1895 – 2 February 1983 | from the autumn of 1939 |
| Ernst Wentzler | 3 September 1891 – 9 August 1973 | from the autumn of 1939 |

The individual registration forms were printed in copies of three and sent to the above appraisers. The result was summarized by the T4 Central Service, which submitted it to one of the following three reviewers, to whom the final decision was reserved—

## Senior Reviewers

| Person | Birth & death dates | Period as a T4 reviewer |
|---|---|---|
| Werner Heyde | 25 April 1902 – 13 February 1964 | October 1939 – December 1941 |
| Hermann Paul Nitsche | 25 November 1876 – 25 March 1948 | from 28 February 1940 |
| Herbert Linden | 14 September 1899 – 27 April 1945 | from October 1939 |

# APPENDIX X

# THE CONFESSIONS OF KURT GERSTEIN (EXTRACT)

Written in the Cherche-Midi Prison in Paris, June 1945.

In January 1942, I became 'head of section' in the Technical Section of Health and I was at the same time assigned to double duty in the same sector by the chief medical officer (Reichsarzt) of the SS and of the police. In this capacity, I was assigned all the technical service of disinfection, including disinfection relating to highly toxic gases.

It was while in this capacity that I received, on 8 June 1942, the visit of SS-Sturmbannführer Günther, of the Central Office of Security of the Reich, Berlin W, Kurfürstenstrasse, a person I did not know till then. Günther came in civilian clothes. He gave me the order to have brought immediately, for an ultra-secret mission relating to the Reich, 100 kg of prussic acid and to transport it in an auto to an unknown place of which only the driver knew the name.

Then, some weeks later, we left for Prague. I could almost imagine the kind of mission this was, but I accepted it because in this way by chance it presented me with an opportunity, long awaited, of sticking my nose into these matters. In addition, in my position as expert on prussic acid, I possessed so much authority and competence that it had to be easy for me, in any circumstances, to declare under whatever pretext that the prussic acid was unusable because decomposed or something of that sort, and to prevent its being used with the murderous purpose he had in mind. With us, rather by chance, was Professor Pfannenstiel, doctor of medicine, SS-Obersturmbannführer, holder of the chair of hygiene at the University of Marburg-Lahn.

Next, we left by car for Lublin where SS-Gruppenfuhrer Globocnik as waiting for us. At the factory at Cholm, I had purposely thrown out hints that the acid was intended to kill human beings. Also, it was not long before that, in the afternoon, a person appeared who showed a great deal of interest in the vehicle and who, as soon

as he saw himself observed, ran away with all speed. Globocnik said, 'All this affair is one of the most secret things in existence at this moment; one can say: the most secret. Anyone who speaks about it will be shot on the spot. No later than yesterday two talkers were shot.' Then he declared to us: 'Actually [this was 17 August 1942] we have three installations in service, which are:
1) Bełżec, on the Lublin-Lemberg road and railway at the intersection of the demarcation line with Russia. Maximum output per day: 15,000 persons.
2) Sobibor. Also in Poland, I do not know exactly where. Maximum output: 20,000 persons per day.
3) Treblinka, 120 km north-north-east of Warsaw. Maximum output, 25,000 persons per day.
4) Still in Preparation: Majdanek, near Lublin.'

In the company of the director of these establishments, Police Captain Wirth, I personally inspected Bełżec, Treblinka and Majdanek right down to the details.

Globocnik addressed himself exclusively to me in saying: It is your task to carry out successfully the disinfection of very important quantities of textiles. The collection of textiles has in fact been done only in order to explain the origin of the clothes for the workers in the East etc. and to present them as the result of the sacrifice accepted by the German people. In reality, the output of our establishments is from 10 to 20 times superior to the whole of the collection of textiles. I afterwards discussed with firms capable of this work the possibility of disinfecting such quantities of textiles at least, it was a matter of about 40,000 tons, 60 full trains of merchandise, in the existing laundries and disinfection establishments. But it was completely impossible to place such large orders. I turned to profit all these negotiations, to make known or cleverly to hint at the fact of the murder of the Jews. Globocnik then expressed himself as satisfied that all this heap should be sprayed with detenoline so that it would have the smell of disinfection—which was then done.

Your second task— till much more important—is to adapt our gas chambers, which function at the moment with the exhaust gases of a diesel, to something better and more rapid. I am thinking above all of prussic acid. The Führer and Himmler were here the day before yesterday. In accordance with their instructions, I must take you there personally. I must not deliver passes or entry permits to anyone.

Thereupon, Pfannenstiel asked: What then did the Fuhrer say? Globocnik: More quickly! to carry out the whole operation more quickly! The ministerial counsellor, Dr Herbert Lindner, who accompanied him, then asked: 'Do you believe, Herr Globocnik, that it is well-done and judicious to bury all these cadavers instead of burning them? After us could come a generation who will not understand all that!' Globocnik replied: 'Gentlemen, if ever after us must come a generation so feeble and soft that it does not understand our great mission, then all the National Socialism will have been in vain. On the contrary, I am of the opinion that we should put down plaques of bronze commemorating that it is us, we, who have had the courage to accomplish this great work so necessary.' Then the Führer: 'Good, Globocnik, that is my opinion too.'

Afterwards, it was the other opinion which was imposed. The cadavers were burned on large grills improvised with railway rails, with the help of petrol and diesel oil.

The next day, we left for Bełżec. For this purpose, a special little station had been constructed close to a hill directly to the north of the route Lublin-Lemberg in the left corner of the demarcation line. To the south of the route some houses carrying the inscription 'Special Detachment of the Waffen-SS at Bełżec'. The actual head of all the murderous installations, Captain of Police Wirth, not yet being there, Globocnik introduced me to SS-Hauptsturmführer Obermeyer (of Pirmasens). This latter let me see that afternoon only what he absolutely had to show me. I did not see any dead that day, only the smell which prevailed in the surroundings was pestilential in that scorching month of August and there were flies everywhere by the million. Just the little station of two lines, there was a large hut, the so-called 'Cloakroom,' with a large service window 'Valuables. Then came a room with a hundred chairs; the premises of the hairdresser. Then a little alley in the open air planted with birch trees, bordered to the right and left with a double row of barbed wire, with the signs: Access to the inhalation rooms and baths! Before us, a kind of bath establishment, with to right and left in the front large concrete pots with geraniums, then a small stairway and afterwards to right and to left respectively 3 halls of 5 × 5 metres, 1.90 m high, with doors of wood like garages. In the wall at the bottom, not very visible in the darkness, large sliding doors of wood. On the roof, by way of a "'ubtle joke,' the star of David! In front of the building a sign: 'Hackenholt Foundation'. I did not see more on that afternoon.

The following morning, a little before 7 o'clock, I am told: the first transport arrives in ten minutes! Actually, at the end of some minutes, the first train coming from Lemberg arrives: 45 cars, 6,700 persons of whom 1,450 were already dead on their arrival. Behind the barred openings, terribly pale and frightened, children were looking outside, their eyes full of the anguish of death, as well as the men and women. The train entered the station: 200 Ukrainians brutally open the doors and make the people go out of the cars by lashing them with their whips of leather thongs. A big loudspeaker gives further instructions: to undress completely: also remove artificial limbs, spectacles, etc.... Deliver objects of value to the service window, without vouchers or receipts. Carefully tie up the shoes in pairs (in view of the collection of textiles), otherwise, in the pile which rose easily to 25 meters in height, no one would have been able to retrieve the shoes which went together. Then the women and the young girls pass to the hairdresser who, in two or three cuts with the scissors, cuts all the hair, so to have it disappear into large potato sacks. 'This is intended for some special purpose or other, for the submarines, for the caulking or something like that,' the SS-Unterscharführer who is on duty at this place tells me.

Then the procession starts to move. At the head, a very pretty young girl, they follow the road, all naked, men, women, children, without artificial limbs. I am standing above, on the ramp, between the chambers, with Captain Wirth. Mothers with nursing babies at the breast: they go up, hesitate enter in to the death chambers. In a corner is standing a man of the SS unit, corpulent, who says in an unctuous voice to these unfortunates: Not the least thing will happen to you! It will be necessary only to breathe deeply in the chambers, this develops the lungs, this inhalation is necessary because of the sicknesses and the epidemics. To those who ask what might become of them he replies: Yes, naturally, the men will have to work, to build houses or make roads, but the women will not have need to work. Only if they wish, they can help with the housework or in the kitchen. For some of these unfortunates a little glimmer of hope which suffices to make them walk without resistance the few steps which lead them to the chambers. The majority know what to prepare themselves for, the smell tells them their fate! They climb up the little stairway and then they see everything. The mothers with their children at the breast, the small naked children, the adults, men and women, all naked, they hesitate but they enter into the chambers of death pushed forward by others who are behind them or by the whips of leather thongs of the SS men. The majority without saying a word. A Jewess of about 40 years, with eyes full of flame, calls for the blood shed here to fall again on the murderers. She receives 5 or 6 blows of the horsewhip in the face from Captain Wirth personally, then she too disappears into the chamber. Many pray. I pray with them. I squeeze myself into a corner and I cry in a loud voice to my God and theirs. How I would have loved to go into the chambers with them, how I would have loved to die their death. They would then have found an SS officer in uniform in their chambers. They would have interpreted and treated the affair as an accident and it would have been quietly shelved. But I still do not have the right to do it; I must first reveal what I see here! The chambers are filled. Pack tightly! Captain Wirth has ordered. The people are stepping on each other's feet, 700–800 on 25 square metres, in 45 cubic metres. The SS men press them physically one against the other as much as they can. The doors close.

During this time, the others are waiting outside in the open air, naked. Someone says to me: even in winter it is exactly like this! Yes, but they can catch their death, I say. But that's exactly what they are here for! a man of the SS troop retorts in his dialect. Now, I also understand at least why the installation is called 'Hackenholt Foundation'. Hackenholt is the operator of the diesel engine, a little technician, at the same time the constructor of the installation. The people must be put to death by the exhaust gases of the diesel. But the diesel does not work! Captain Wirth arrives. One sees that it is painful to him that it should have to happen today just when I am here. Yes, I see everything and I wait. My stopwatch has recorded everything very well. 50 minutes, 70 minutes, the diesel does not start. The people wait in their gas chambers. In vain. One hears them weep, sob. 'Like at the synagogue,' remarks Professor Pfannenstiel, his ear against the wooden door. Captain Wirth beats the Ukrainian who has to help Unterscharführer Hackenholt get the diesel going, 12 or 13 times on the face with his horsewhip. At the end of 2 hours 49 minutes—the stopwatch has recorded everything—the diesel starts. Up to that moment, the people remain alive in these 4 chambers, 4 times 750 persons in 4 times 45 cubic meters. Once more, 25 minutes pass. Correct, 12 many are now dead, one sees it through the small window in which the electric light illuminates the chamber for an instant. At the end of 28 minutes only some still live; at the end of 32 minutes everyone is dead. From the other side the men of the work detail open the wooden doors. They have been promised for their dreadful work—even the Jews—liberty and so much per thousand of all the valuables found.

The dead are standing straight like pillars of basalt, ranged tightly one against the other in the chambers. There would not be place to fall or lean forward. Even in death one recognizes the families. They still hold hands, clenched in death, so that there is difficulty separating them to free the chambers ready for the next load. The bodies are thrown outside, damp with sweat and urine, dirtied with excrement and with menstrual blood on the legs. The cadavers of children fly through the air. There is no time. The horsewhips of the Ukrainians whistle on the work detail. Two dozen dentists open the mouths with hooks and look to see if there are gold crowns. Gold to the left, without gold to the right. Other dentists break the gold teeth and crowns with the aid of pincers and hammers to pull them out of the jaws.

In the middle of all these people, Captain Wirth leaps everywhere. He is in his element. Some workers check the genital organs and anus in the search for gold, brilliants and precious objects. Wirth calls me beside him: 'Just feel the weight of this fruit tin with the gold teeth. This is only from yesterday and the day before.' He says to me in language incredibly common and incorrect: 'You would not believe the quantities of gold and of brilliants—he pronounced the word with two L's—and dollars. But see for yourself.' And he took me to a jeweller whose job it was to look after all these treasures, and he showed me everything. Then again, I was shown a former manager of the 'Kaufhaus des Westens' of Berlin and a violinist. 'This is a Captain of the old imperial and royal army of Austria, knight of the Iron Cross 1st Class, who is now the senior of the Jewish work detail in the camp.' The naked cadavers were hauled on wooden barrows to only a few metres from there to pits of 100 by 20 by 12 metres. At the end of some days, the cadavers started to swell, then sank down tight together shortly afterwards, in such a way that it was possible to throw a new layer on top of them. Then 10 cms of sand was spread on top so that there only emerged some isolated heads and arms. At one of these places I saw Jews scrambling around on the cadavers and working in the graves. I am told that, by mistake, the people of a convoy who arrived already dead had not been unclothed. Naturally it was necessary to salvage that because of the textiles and the precious objects which, without that being done, they would have carried to the grave.

Neither at Bełżec nor at Treblinka was the least trouble taken to record or count those who were killed. The numbers were only estimates made according to the content of the cars. Over and above the Jews coming from all the sovereign states, above all the Czechs and the Poles, no ill were killed in the gas chambers. Commissions of SS men—some of them without even a full primary school education—went from village to village in fine limousines and with medical equipment, in white coats, making the population march by in front of them, making a show of examining them, and designating those who were alleged to be without biological value and should for this reason be killed, principally the old, the consumptives, and the sick. Yes, a Sturmbannfuhrer of the SS told me, without these measures, Poland, overpopulated, would be for us devoid of all value. We are only carrying out after the event that which nature looks after for herself in the animal and vegetable kingdoms, and unfortunately omits to do with mankind. Captain Wirth begged me not to propose to Berlin to change the installations and to leave everything just as it was, a good setup that was perfectly run in and had proven itself. As for the prussic acid, I had it buried under my supervision while giving as a reason that it had begun to decompose.

The next day, 19 August 1942, we went in Captain Wirth's auto to Treblinka, 120 kms to the north-northeast of Warsaw. The installation was almost the same, but quite a bit larger than at Bełżec. Eight gas chambers and veritable mountains of suitcases, of textiles, and under-wear. A banquet was given in our honor in the style of 'old Germany' in the common hall, typically Himmlerian. The meal was simple, but one could have all that one wished. Himmler himself had ordered that the men of these commands should have as much meat, butter, and other things, notably alcohol, as they wished. Professor Pfannenstiel made a speech in which he explained to the men the usefulness of their task and the importance of their great mission. Talking to me, he spoke of the 'very humane methods' and of the beauty of the work. I guarantee that he really said this incredible thing to me. He said in particular to the teams: 'When one sees the bodies of Jews, one then understands truly how much your task is worthy of recognition'. When we took leave, we were offered again several kilos of butter and many liqueurs to take away. I had difficulty in making them believe that I had sufficient of all that from my so-called estate, whereupon Pfannenstiel, entirely happy, grabbed my share. We then left by car for Warsaw. It was there, while I was vainly trying to obtain a bunk in the train, I met the secretary of the legation of Sweden in Berlin, Baron von Otter. Still under the very fresh impression of the terrible things I had seen, I told him everything, while begging him to make this known immediately to his government and to the allies, considering that each day of delay must cost the lives of thousands and dozens of thousands of other people. He asked me to give him a reference and in this respect I named Herr Superintendent

Gewera, Doctor Otto Dibelius, Berlin, Brüderweg 2, Lichterfelde-West, close friend of Pastor Martin Niemöller and a member of the ecclesiastical resistance against Nazism. I met Herr von Otter twice more in the Swedish legation. He had meantime made a report to Stockholm and stated to me that this report had had a considerable influence on German-Swedish relations.

I tried to make a report of the same matter to the apostolic nuncio. It was there that I was asked whether I was a soldier. Following which, they refused to have all further conversation with me and I was invited to leave the embassy of His Holiness. On leaving the embassy of the Holy See, I was pursued by a policeman on a bicycle who passed quickly in front of me, put his foot on the ground and let me then pass, in a totally incomprehensible way. After that I recounted the foregoing to hundreds of important persons, among others to the secretary of the Catholic Bishop of Berlin, Herr Doctor Winter, begging him expressly to transmit my information to the Apostolic See.

I must still add that SS-Sturmbannführer Günther of the Principal Security Office of the Reich—I believe he is the son of the 'Rassen' Günther—demanded again from me at the beginning of 1944 very large quantities of prussic acid for a very obscure purpose. He showed me in the Kurfurstenstrasse, in Berlin, a shed in which he was thinking of stocking the prussic acid. I then declared to him that it was out of the question that I take the responsibility. It was a matter of several freight cars, enough to put to death millions of human beings. He said to me that he did not know yet himself whether the poison would be used, nor when, for whom, by what method, etc., but it was to be held available at all times. Afterwards, I was often unable to put Goebbels' words out of my mind. I suppose they wanted to kill a large part of the German people, including surely the clergy and the unpopular officers. This would have to have been done in places such as lecture halls or clubs, or at least that is what I could deduce from the questions relating to execution techniques that Günther asked me. It is possible also that he would have had to kill foreign workers or prisoners of war—I do not know—in any case I made arrangements so that the prussic acid would disappear, serving for no matter what disinfection purposes as soon as it had arrived in the camps of Oranienburg and Auschwitz. This was dangerous for me, but I would simply have been able to say that the poison was already in a dangerous state of decomposition. I am sure that Günther wanted to obtain the poison to put to death eventually millions of human beings. There was enough of it for 8 million persons, 8,500 kgs. I have submitted the invoices for 2,175 kgs. I always had the invoices written in my name, pretending that this was for reasons of secrecy, but actually in order to be more free to dispose of the poison as I intended to get rid of it. Above all I avoided bringing the matter constantly to mind by presenting the invoices, but left the invoices totally unpaid, while asking the firm to be patient.

The manager of DEGESCH, Doctor Peters, Frankfürt a.M. and Friedberg, who made this delivery, told me that he has delivered prussic acid in ampoules intended to kill human beings.

Another time, Günther asked me whether it was possible to kill in the open air, in the moats of the fortress of Theresienstadt, the Jews who had permission to walk there. To thwart this terrible plan, I stated that it was impossible. I then afterwards learned that the SD-Commando Theresienstadt had obtained prussic acid another way and killed the Jews. The most horrible concentration camps moreover were not Oranienburg or Belsen or Dachau, but Auschwitz, where millions of people have been killed, part in the gas chambers, part in what were called the 'death caves'; and Mauthausen-Gusen near Linz. At Auschwitz, it was customary to kill children by holding pads soaked in prussic acid under the nose. Furthermore, I have myself seen at the Ravensbrück camp, near Furstenburg in Mecklenburg, the concentration camp for women, experiments made on the living. These were made on the initiative of SS-Gruppenfuhrer Dr Gebhardt—Hohenlychen, by SS-Hauptsturmfuhrer Dr Gundlach. At Buchenwald, as well, such experiments on living human beings were made, for example, with up to 100 Pervitin tablets or, failing that, until death occurred. Himmler himself reserved the right of approval for these experiments. In particular, it was down there that the vaccine against typhus, lymph and other serums was tested. The experiments were made each time on 100 to 200 persons, namely people condemned to death by the camp management or by the SD. I was astonished at Oranienburg that in just a few days all the homosexuals disappeared by hundreds, and this in the ovens.

I furthermore avoided making too frequent appearances in the camps, because sometimes they had the habit of hanging people or proceeding with executions in honour of visitors. SS-Hauptsturmfuhrer Dr. Fritz Krantz, who has seen great numbers of such things, often spoke to me in profound indignation. For example, at Gusen-Mauthausen, every day numerous Jews who had to work in a large quarry were pushed, to make them fall to the bottom of the steep cliff; and, down below, their cases were recorded as fatal accidents. At Auschwitz, such shameful actions were similarly perpetrated in much greater numbers than at Belsen. I had the luck in my service to meet some total anti-Nazis, like the SS-Hauptsturmfuhrer and chief of staff, Heinrich Hollander, a good Catholic, and Dr Fritz Krantz, whom I just previously mentioned. Hollander kept me informed of all the interesting things. His wife one day, on the occasion of a meal, made violent reproaches on the subject of the homicide committed against the Jews to Dr. Grawitz, SS-Obergruppenführer, of the Reich SS and Police medical service and, moreover President of the German Red Cross. As a consequence of this, she was severely reprimanded and forbidden ever to mention that subject again.

All the information I am supplying is the literal truth, absolutely accurate. I am fully aware, before God and all humanity, of the extraordinary import of the information which I am noting here in writing and I affirm under oath that nothing at all of what I have recorded is imagined or invented, but on the contrary, everything happened exactly as I have said.

At Bełżec, I had the impression that all were really dead although Captain Wirth had told me that they had seen the most unexpected things, for example, that they had found a child fully alive, in the morning, in a chamber which had been left full all night without emptying it. Notably, Wirth said, they had seen the most curious things and the most diverse reactions among the mentally ill.

The experimentation with different kinds of homicide must not have been extended to a great number. But more than one thing was tried. For example—undoubtedly on a fairly large number of people—death by compressed air in the old boilers into which the air was introduced from compressors of the type ordinarily used to break up asphalt. At Treblinka, I had the impression that many were still living. Nearly all had their eyes open and for this reason had a frightful appearance. However, I saw no more movement even though I paid great attention. The medical doctor Villing, of Dortmund, told me with very profound emotion the account of a truly heroic death. It concerned thousands of Polish ecclesiastics who had to dig the ditches themselves in front of which they were subsequently shot, naked.

When they were asked with mocking contempt if they still believed in Christ and Mary, they replied by firmly confessing their faith in Christ and invoked the Virgin of Czestochowa. This death had been gripping and convincing, Doctor Villing tells me. Other intellectuals also—notably teachers, men and women, died in the hundreds of thousands with similar exemplary dignity. A kind of death which was told me under every assurance of truth consisted of making people climb the stairway which led to a blast furnace, to finish them off once at the top, and to make them disappear afterwards into the blast furnace. Plenty of people must have been killed likewise in the brick kilns. But the source from which I have this fact is not sufficiently worthy of belief.

A high-ranking officer of the Police of Bromberg, the SS-Obersturmführer Haller, recounted, to me and the doctors in the course for the SS, that before his arrival at Bromberg it was usual to kill Jewish children without further ado by simply bashing their heads against the walls of houses. He put a stop to these stupidities and saw to it that execution by firearms was implemented.

He has the particularly tragic memory of two little girls who had knelt down before them to say their prayers—they were 5 and 8 years of age—and who 'had' to be shot however all the same. Hall[er] says moreover: at the mass executions of the Poles, they were forced to dig long ditches and to lie in them face down. Then they were executed from above with a machine gun. The following ones then had to lie down on the cadavers which were still warm, to be executed similarly. Many were still not dead, and when they tried to get out of the ditch by crawling under 5 or 6 layers [of bodies], it was necessary to finish them off at the edge of the ditch.

An important member of the German government of Krakow told me, while carving a turkey, of an especially fortunate capture they made. According to him, they had taken a leading member of the Polish resistance movement, a Jew. This one, during his interrogation, cloaked himself in silence. Upon which his wrists were broken. Even then he continued to be silent. Then he was seated by force on the plate of a stove, red-hot from the fire. You should just have seen how the fellow became talkative!

During a visit to the local office of the construction department of the Waffen-SS of Lublin, on 18 August 1942, two heads of the special works told me of an inspection made in the morning at the morgue of the prisoners-of-war camp of the SS, near Lublin. The cadavers there had been crammed in by the thousands. While they were taking measurements for an alteration of the premises, two men had suddenly moved. The SS-Rottenführer who was accompanying them had then asked: 'Where then?' Then he had taken an iron bar which he found at hand and he had smashed the skulls of the two men. It was not the action, the heads of the works thought, which had surprised them, but the natural way in which it had happened.

The day of my inspection at Bełżec, it happened that a Jewess made some cuts in the neck to some Jews of the work detail with a razor that she had kept hidden on her person. Wirth deeply regretted that the woman was already dead, she should have had to suffer some exemplary punishment. As for the Jews of the work detail who were wounded, he had them looked after attentively and receive medical treatment, as he said, in order to keep them believing that they would be resettled, remunerated, and kept alive. He—Wirth—found an inexhaustible source of astonishment and amusement in the fact that they believed it. 'And the fellows believe that, the fellows believe it!' he exclaimed to himself!

At Bełżec, the men and young boys were invited by loudspeaker, after the opening of the cars and the undressing, to fetch the clothes scattered everywhere straight away into the cars and with which they disappeared into a big warehouse. 'Whoever does the most can stay in the work detail!' Then began a race to the death between these naked people at the time of tidying up, under the sarcastic laughter of the men of the troop. Naturally, they all disappeared afterwards into the gas chambers. Only a few very old and very weak persons were set apart, and then shot. I think of some impressions profoundly moving for me: of a little Jewish boy of 3 or 4 years, who had a packet of strings for tying up the shoes by pairs put into his hand; of the way that, lost in a dream, he distributed the strings to the people; or again, of a little coral chain which a little girl lost one metre from the entrance to the gas chamber. I recall that a little boy, of perhaps three, bent down to pick it up. What pleasure it gave him, and that he was afterwards pushed—no, in that instance he is gently urged—to make him go into the gas chamber.

SS-Hauptsturmführer Obermeyer told me: I met in a village of the region a Jew and his wife, natives of my home town of Pirmasens. The man was a Wachtmeister during the World War and he is a very good fellow. When I was a child he saved me from death by preventing me from being run over. I am going to take them with me now and I shall enroll them in the work detail. As I asked him what would happen to those two, Obermeyer says: Afterwards, it will be as for the others, we must have no illusions. There is only one possibility. But, at least, I shall have them shot. I have similarly met a fairly large number of people within the SS who condemned these methods most severely and who, because of this, came to a rejection of or even a passionate hatred of National Socialism.

# APPENDIX XI

# THE FRANKE-GRIKSCH REPORT (EXTRACT)

National Archives, Kew; WO 309/374

**LUBLIN—WEDNESDAY 12 MAY 1943**

Visit to the concentration camp and salvage dump in Lublin, and the office for the disposition of salvage. There are the usual institutions, such as cobblers, tailors, blacksmiths, etc.

A great part of this place has been switched over to war production. In the salvage depot, all things gained from the deportation of Jews are rendered useful by the Jews. The blankets and linen coming from Jewish households are being collected, cleaned and repaired or reformed into raw material for new production of cloth.

This camp alone has delivered 1,800 trucks of textiles for the last big drive for old material.

In the workshops they are producing blankets, bed-linen and towels for the colonies and partly for the German Army.

After inspecting this camp, we go onto Trawniki. Here there is a small concentration camp to which a very big training camp is attached.

This training camp at Trawniki has been established to train Russian prisoners of war, who after having been specially trained, will be used as guards for the concentration camps and forced labour camps throughout Poland. The enormous shortage of SS-men for guarding concentration camps gave Gruppenführer Globocnik the idea of sorting out Russian prisoners of war and training them to make guards for the various camps under German supervision.

SS-Gruppenführer Globocnik received permission from the German Army High Command to take 10,000 prisoners out of the POW camps for this purpose. Out of this number, 4,000 Russian prisoners have been so far called up.

These Russian prisoners who are earmarked as guards are being trained by German NCO's, they learn how to give commands and whilst they are being trained they choose their own NCO's from their own ranks.

A company which is usually 200 men strong, is led by a company leader, who is German. These people from Trawniki Camp, or as 'Uskaris', as they are usually called, have made a very good show of guarding concentration camps. They keep their distance from the prisoners, they are hard and lend themselves willingly to German discipline, to which they get accustomed very quickly. It is a very queer experience to hear and see what is going on, on the square. German commands are being given and the men have got used in a few weeks to these commands.

The weapons are being explained to them in Russian by their own NCO's. The commands for the training are being given in German. These men are full of goodwill and they are eager to be trained. It is very comical to a certain extant when you see these companies march past singing German songs in their enthusiasm, when you can hear by the way they pronounce German, but that does not interfere with their enthusiasm and singing. These people are chosen from the Russian point of view and they are mostly tall, blue eyed, fair haired and so far experience has fully justified this new experiment. It is very typical for the development of Europe, if you see on this barrack square, how the SS-Scharführer's parade their companies and take great pains to instruct the NCO's to pick up the German drill.

People who a short while ago were prisoners of war and, not so long ago, faced us the other side of the trench, are now representatives of the German will to order in the East and are willing to serve the new European idea.

From Trawniki we travelled back to Lublin to inspect the 'Special Enterprise REINHARD'. This branch has had the task of realising all mobile Jewish property in the General Government. It is astonishing what immense fortunes the Jews have collected in their ghetto and even ragged and vermin infested dirty little Jews who look like beggars, carry with them, when you strip their clothes off them, foreign currency, pieces of gold, diamonds and other valuables. We wandered through the cellars of this 'special enterprise' and we were reminded of the fairy tales of the 'Arabian Nights'.

Whole boxes full of genuine pearls, cases full of diamonds, a basket full of pieces of gold and many cwts of silver coins, beside jewellery of every kind. In order to carry out a better realisation of all these valuables, the gold and silver are melted into bars. We inspected the melting process in the garden of the house. There is a small foundry where gold and silver are melted and then formed into bars and then delivered to the German National Bank on certain days. 'Special Enterprise REINHARD' has so far delivered 2,500 kilos of gold, 20,000 kilos of silver and six and a half kilos of platinum, 60,000 Reichsmark in currency, 800,000 dollars in money and 144,000 dollars in gold. The huge quantity of diamonds and pearls can hardly be evaluated. The best proof of the repercussion this enterprise has on the international market is the quotations on the Swiss Stock Exchange and the effects on the international market in diamonds and brilliants. The prices have all gone down and Switzerland could not absorb any more diamonds, because our enterprise has swamped the market.

In this respect alone, the 'Special Enterprise REINHARD' gives us the means for our political struggle and would have a decisive effect on the world market. Apart from other valuables there are 60,000 watches, most of them double-cased watches of high value, very often decorated with diamonds, 800,000 wrist watches and a huge quantity of other small valuables from tobacco and cigarette cases and gold fountain pens and silver bracelets etc.

In special workshops all these treasures are sorted out and examined by specially trained Jews, jewellers, bank clerks and goldsmiths. If necessary the diamonds are broken out in order to separate them and use the metal in a different way. The wrist watches will be repaired, if necessary and will be handed out to front-line troops.

When one goes through the cellar of this special branch it appears like a secret treasure and you get a very different idea of all the things for which people have sacrificed their lives and forgotten, through them the real issues. You get the right distance from these false values and, even if our eye is delighted by the shine of thousands of brilliants, some of them the size of a pea, for which the old world has paid hundreds of thousands, one recognises a people which saw its whole existence in the heaping up of such treasures. It is a pleasure to see with what indifference the Oberscharführer registers these valuables as if they were bits of coal or other things of everyday life. The real values of our life which carry us as human beings and as a nation become very clear and more precious still.

The treasure of these people of parasites prove that the age of the power of gold is over and a new time, which has new values, has begun.

## SS BARRACKS—LUBLIN

In the late hours of the afternoon we go and inspect SS Barracks in Lublin, and we are being shown round by SS-Gruppenführer Globocnik. In these barracks, the ideological planning for the reconstruction and colonisation of the General Government takes place. It is gratifying to see the whole work in this sphere is planned to every detail and people will be resettled only after this planning has been completed. This detailed planning makes it possible to occupy thousands of settlements in a few weeks and to effect the whole resettlement which means deportation of the Polish population and the settling of German farmers without great difficulty. The work of the SS in the sphere of preparing this resettlement is considerable. We see that the planning of the German settlements is thought out to the smallest detail, all the sanitary arrangements, canalisation, electric light, water, economic problems are being worked out by young experts. The entire decoration of the cottages is considered, halls for festivals are planned etc.

The preparation extends even to the personal life of the settlers. A form of life is being tried out in these settlements in small proportion which is the final object of the SS organisation for the whole of the German nation in the future. We realise with joy that this huge work which is being planned and carried out under such difficult circumstances is not only theoretical but it has become a reality in the Eastern sphere. For the first time, we can understand the whole colonisation plan of the Reichsführer. One can see how he is building up a big belt of German settlements against the masses of the Slav nations. It is proved by statistics how much German blood can be saved out of the Polish people and these problems of the Eastern sphere are being scrutinised with German scientific thoroughness.

After this very interesting inspection of the SS barracks, which gives us for the first time a clear picture of the situation of the German in the Eastern sphere, we attended a social function arranged by the SS-Gruppenführer Globocnik, General Moser and his staff.

## LUBLIN AREA—THURSDAY 13 MAY 1943

Early in the morning we proceeded to the Ostlager Erlenhof which is situated in the vicinity of **Lublin**. On this beautiful Polish estate, a school for SS men and various SS and police strongholds and SS farms are housed.

In a fortnights or three weeks' course the SS men are being trained and are given lectures on the special questions of the Eastern countries and particularly problems of agriculture.

## WORK CAMP PONIATOWA

We reached this big working camp in the afternoon. It lies completely off the big arterial roads and has been installed for 50,000–80,000 Jews.

These Jews work in big sheds and the larger part of the Warsaw Ghetto has been transplanted to this place and work for the German armament industry. Uniforms and furs for the German army are being produced here on the Ford system, and the results are very satisfactory.

Just as we entered the camp a large consignment of Jews from the ghetto in Warsaw are being brought in. It is an amazing thing what a turnout these people present, the women in the very best clothes, in furs and silk stockings, and the men in nicely fitting suits. They walk up and down in the camp and await their fate.

As the evacuation of the Warsaw Ghetto took place so suddenly there are tens of thousands of newly-arrived Jews for whom there are neither barracks nor anywhere to sleep. In consequence of this an open air life developed which presents itself in a most peculiar way to the spectator.

The larger part of the Jews seems to be content to get out of the ghetto, as they know that they have to work here they are pleased about it because they know that as long as they work and as long as they are able to work, nothing will happen to them.

If you watch these masses of Jews, in small groups sitting round a fire, you can see how they become very fat with composure and civility. The only explanation for this is that they look upon themselves as the chosen people and with this servility and toughness they represent a danger for the world as long as they are not wither done away with completely or put in vast areas where they are completely isolated from human culture and perish slowly.

In these camps in Poland now the Jews live in a Babylonian exile as in the olden days. They were suppressed by the Egyptians and they were exploited by the Romans and under the various systems of modern times which exploited them, but again and again they have succeeded in surviving and have created new positions for themselves and within a few generations made these positions into key positions.

Walking through this camp and watching these people in their servile attitude, one is bound to notice that again and again they try to make the best of every situation without any dignity and self-respect and one realises the alternative with which we are faced: either this generation of ours succeeds in clearing up the Jewish problem completely and to its last consequences or, if their liquidation is not completely achieved, the Jewish people will rise again after this wave of oppression. Some individual cases may appear hard or even brutal but seeing these people in large masses and knowing how dangerous their passive attitude is to the life of the nations, one comes to the conclusion that this problem has to be cleared up completely to free the world once and for all of this pestilence.

After having inspected the camp with all its institutions and the excellently organised munitions factories, SS-Gruppenführer Globocnik and his staff took leave of us and we proceeded to Radom.

Once more we pass through the old sleepy, formerly German, town of **Kazimierz**, cross the Vistula and reach Radom after two hours. Here we are greeted by SS-Oberführer Dr Böttcher and his staff and pass the evening with him and his staff.

### WARSAW—14 MAY 1943

We reached the outskirts of Warsaw in the early hours of the afternoon. Even from far off we could see the large dark clouds of smoke in the sky. They rise from the fires in the ghetto.

SS-Brigadeführer Stroop awaits the Gruppenführer in the SS-leaders house and reports on the situation in Warsaw and the Warsaw Ghetto. After a quick meal, we drive with him to the command post where the commandant of the SIPO and the SD gives a detailed report on the battles in the ghetto.

It is proved that the Jews of the ghetto not only directed the black market of Warsaw from their secret dumps but have used the munition factories in the ghetto to obtain economic advantages for themselves. Furthermore, the more active parties of the Jewish Youth used the workshops to manufacture explosives, so-called 'Molotov Cocktails' and handgrenades. They procured infantry weapons on the black market and thought that they could thus face armed interference of the police and SS in the ghetto.

When the ghetto was to be evacuated on the orders of the RFSS, the spearhead of the Waffen-SS was received with small arms fire and handgrenades.

The ghetto comprises of several districts of the town and has cellars everywhere and extensive underground passages and gangways and these had to be combed out, in a drawn-out action which lasted several weeks to apprehend the various groups of the Jewish Resistance Movement.

The whole of the ghetto affair was anything but pleasant for the SS-leaders and men engaged. If one sees these revolting types come out of the deep cellars and bunkers, where our men, over and over again, come up against their treacherous resistance, one can understand that these SS-men carry out their task with the utmost brutality. Systematically, one part of the town after the other is being combed out, evacuated and then burned down. Driving through the burning and already partly demolished districts, one meets shock troops everywhere with captured Jews, who were dragged out of this notorious quarter after long searches. It is amazing that this dirty lot, when stripped, is always found in possession of considerable amounts of money and cheques. It certainly is no heroic task to clear out and destroy once and for all this ghetto of Warsaw, which was for the whole Jewish world, a symbol of their independent life. All the more respect is due to the SS-men who dealt with this scum of the earth.

Evidence from witnesses proves beyond doubt that from this ghetto attempts were made again and again (and partly successfully) to get certain privileges for the Jewish community through connections with the Wehrmacht authorities.

For all these reasons, it was high time that this centre was liquidated.

We had another look at the Wehrmacht engineers blowing up considerable blocks of houses and then left the burning, smouldering ghetto.

In the evening, a meeting of all SS-leaders of Warsaw takes place, and SS-Gruppenführer Herff takes this opportunity of talking to the various departmental leaders about their respective departments.

**WARSAW—15 MAY 1943**

We drive through the town to obtain a better picture of it. It is crowded with people and one does not gain the impression of being in the fourth year of the war. It appears to strange to a German that huge numbers of young people are loafing, idly in the streets.

Inspection of Panzer Grenadiers Btn 'Deaths Head'.

Meeting with SS-Obst. **Bellwidt** and his staff. Inspection of army stores and other establishments of the SS Economic Department.

After a private talk with Brigadeführer **Stroop** we drive to the central station and leave **Warsaw** at 19:00 hrs for **Berlin**.

# APPENDIX XII

# LIST OF GLOBOCNIK'S AWARDS AND DECORATIONS

With thanks to Michael D. Miller and Andreas Schulz

| | |
|---|---|
| 07.02.1945 | Deutsches Kreuz in Gold as SS-Gruppenführer und Generalleutnant der Polizei; Höherer SS- und Polizeiführer in der Operationszone Adriatisches Küstenland |
| 27.01.1945 | Deutsches Kreuz in Silber as SS-Gruppenführer und Generalleutnant der Polizei, Höherer SS- und Polizeiführer in der Operationszone Adriatisches Küstenland (based on a recommendation submitted by Dr Friedrich Rainer, 18.12.1944 and approved by Reichsführer-SS Himmler on 18.01.1945) |
| 06.06.1944 | 1939 Eisernes Kreuz I. Klasse |
| 00.09.1943 | 1939 Eisernes Kreuz II. Klasse |
| 21.04.1942 | Kriegsverdienstkreuz I. Klasse mit Schwertern |
| 00.00.194_ | Kriegsverdienstkreuz II. Klasse mit Schwertern |
| 17.09.1944 | Bandenkampfabzeichen in Silber |
| 00.09.1939 | Medaille zur Erinnerung an den 1. Oktober 1938 |
| 00.00.1939 | Medaille zur Erinnerung an den 13. März 1938 |
| 30.01.1939 | Goldenes Ehrenzeichen der NSDAP |
| 15.05.1944 | Goldenes Hitler-Jugend Ehrenzeichen mit Eichenlaub |
| 00.00.19__ | Ehrenzeichen für Deutsche Volkspflege 2. Stufe |
| 00.00.194_ | Dienstauszeichnung der NSDAP in Silber |
| 00.00.194_ | Dienstauszeichnung der NSDAP in Bronze |
| 00.00.19__ | Deutsches Reichssportabzeichen in Silber |
| 00.00.19__ | SA-Sportabzeichen in Bronze |
| 00.00.1938 | Ehrendegen des Reichsführers-SS |

| | |
|---|---|
| 23.08.1939 | Totenkopfring der SS |
| 00.00.19__ | Julleuchter der SS |
| 00.00.193_ | Ehrenwinkel für alte Kämpfer (SS) |
| *c.* 1920 | Kärntner Kreuz für Tapferkeit (Carinthian Cross of Bravery—according to Globocnik's own account, although his name does not appear on the official list of recipients) |
| 14.11.1944 | Crown of the Order of King Zvonimir First Class with Star and Swords (Independent State of Croatia) |
| 00.00.19__ | Order of Merit First & Second Class (Hungary) |

Author's note: Globocnik applied for the award of the Blutorden der NSDAP on 03.03.1938. Application rejected by the NSDAP Treasurer, Reichsleiter Franz Xaver Schwarz on 22.06.1940.

# APPENDIX XIII

# CHRISTIAN WIRTH—OBSERVATIONS BY FRANZ SUCHOMEL

Manuscript translated from post-war recollection, undated.

I will try to describe the person that Wirth was as I experienced him myself, or as he was described to me by reliable comrades.

Today, I can no longer say what sort of post Wirth held in T4. Occasional snippets of conversation were heard, referring mostly to some trouble in one clinic or another. Wirth was sent there to keep order.

I know that Wirth was sent to Hadamar for example, a clinic which had sunk quite low in human and moral terms, and which lacked discipline, as a type of 'purge commissioner'. He sorted things out. Through various occurrences, in particular through the co-operation of the 'Grafeneckers' (A) who viewed themselves as 'old soldiers', and acted accordingly. There was rowdy behaviour in bars and events which led to public complaints, resulting in energetic steps to solve it. Also, many serious mistakes with the belongings of those killed in Hadamar (E) came to light. In short, Wirth stepped in with great energy and despatched two men—Kainer and Arndt—to a KZ for a few months. As I worked in E for a few months during the Spring of 1942, I gained a lot of experience of Wirth and his methods.

Wirth worked the same way at Hartheim (C), as confirmed to me by a 'Hartheimer'. He had a very strict regime there; cancelled leave, loss of privileges, and his general behaviour led to him being considered as a hard man there also. In C also, there were problems which needed to be eradicated. People like Gomerski and Konsorti had a poor reputation as a result of their behaviour. In C there were thefts, and excesses outside the clinic. Wirth acted with an iron hand and achieved success.

Whether or not he also worked in the so-called 'nut house', to use jargon, in Bernburg (Be), I don't know. What is certain is that he could not stand Dr Eberl; it was mutual. He had an aversion and suspicion of everything academic. But everyone who came under the special protection of the T4 circle enjoyed a special popularity.

I myself first experienced Wirth in Berlin in T4. Under the umbrella of 'voluntary applications' for the special task in the East under camouflage he had command and sent word to Viktor Brack. At that time, even the ladies of T4 were afraid of Wirth. He would call, 'Kommando women, step forward!' Here, as everywhere, the iron man.

When I was sent to Treblinka for duty and did not want to stay there, I first learned through Dr Eberl that Wirth was working in Lublin as the inspector of three camps, and that Wirth would not release me under any circumstances. Dr Eberl himself swore and threatened me and said he had no authority to release me. Therefore, here too was the ghastly spectre of Wirth.

Wirth was also the temporary commandant of Bełżec. His predecessor there was a certain Kaufmann [brother of an accused in Frankfurt trial] who was too soft and just could not cope. Wirth acted there with methods that far exceeded his authority. That he struck his subordinates is a fact which cannot be denied.

One thing is certain—in Bełżec, Wirth thoroughly tested the basics of the extermination machinery with his people, and then set it up. In order to achieve this, a man was required who had no feelings or consideration; who treated people, whether Germans, Jews or Ukrainians, as numbers, and often even worse. Wirth incorporated all these traits and had an exceptional talent for organisation. He despised and abused people. He only saw himself and was foremost a Jew-hater on an unimaginable scale. With his constant threats, the support he obtained from General Globocnik, and other illegal means and machinations, he finally gained an unimaginable position of power, in addition to a kind of fear-neurosis among all the men subordinate to him.

Sadly, his inhumanity shown to Jews rubbed off on some of his subordinates, but I will not elaborate on that here.

I myself first experienced Wirth in Treblinka, when the problems were to be sorted out, he suddenly appeared around midnight. This was at the end of August or could have been the beginning of September [1942]. We woke up—he was separated from us only by a thin wooden partition—as he laid into a man called Wengler in the next room. On this occasion I learned the full force of his usual expressions of strength and his threats. His introduction consisted of accusations of cowardice and other demeaning expressions. His threats included probationary periods and courts martial. When Wengler, a close associate of Viktor Brack, tried to speak, he threatened him with a court martial. Today, I find it impossible to recount all the horrible words and threats uttered by Wirth on this occasion. Wengler was a sick man with constant headaches who died a year later, ostensibly from a brain tumour. After this, we were all shocked and we went in constant fear of Wirth.

A similar confrontation occurred the next morning with Dr Eberl, who Wirth declared to be unfit as camp commandant and dismissed him forthwith. Although

Wirth was well aware of the circumstances of the situation, they provided the perfect excuse to oust and get rid of the self-confidant Dr Eberl. All this added to Wirth's power which could not be ignored. Camp commandants, such as Hering in Bełżec, the drunkard Reichleitner in Sobibor, and finally Stangl, who was not interested in duty and had to 'get round' Wirth whenever he could with his real Austrian charm, and with his great intelligence with which he was amply endowed, and who outwitted Wirth whenever possible.

Following the confrontation with Dr Eberl, Wirth left Treblinka for one day and returned accompanied by a Kommando of trained Germans and reliable Ukrainians. It took control of the whole [Treblinka] Kommando. In these days and weeks, the camp was completely reorganised to meet Wirth's exact specifications, including the preparations for transports. Although for these, some preparations were still necessary.

In the meantime, Wirth managed to arrange in Lublin a three-day halt for transports; an extremely necessary matter which had been constantly denied to Eberl, in spite of repeated telephone requests. From the last trains still arriving, Wirth ordered work Jews to be selected. Stangl, who had also arrived in the meantime, began to take charge. Thus, Oberkapo Blau, whom Stangl had known a long time, was chosen by him to oversee the camp.

At the same time the selected Jews were divided into work Kommandos. Owing to recurring new selections, a select core was created. Wirth repeatedly lined up the Jews and those he did not like were set apart and removed. Through his people brought from Bełżec [Oberhauser, Hackenholt, Franz, and Schwarz], Wirth initiated a few executions during these days. This was probably intended to encourage the remaining Jews to be more compliant and for the majority of them to participate in the mass murders.

First, Wirth had excavators dig long deep graves on the west side of the camp. The excavated earth was used as a rampart to obstruct the view of the pits. At the bottom of the pits he put the thousands of corpses which were lying about the camp and on them he covered them with chloride of lime before closing the pit. Right next to it he erected the so-called hospital [Lazarett] which was sheltered on two sides by a rampart. The remaining part of the pit was used to throw in the large and growing amounts of rubbish accumulating in the camp, in order to burn it.

At the same time, on Wirth's orders, the tube was laid; the former undressing room for those 'resettled', destined as a barrack for the Ukrainians who had until then led a very wild life, and for whom a post in the military sense was out of the question, were brought to heel by Wirth and two cronies with an iron hand, that is, whip and punishments. Their commander, SS-Oberscharführer Kretschus, was ousted by Wirth at the same time as Eberl.

For the German personnel too, there now began dark and difficult days. Work started at 5am and never finished before midnight. Wirth had initiated daily meetings which never began before 11pm. At these meetings, Wirth described point by point how he envisaged the winding-up of future transports. He divided individual areas of duty among the relevant NCOs. At one of these work meetings, he also set up the new camp leadership with Stangl at the head and Franz as deputy. Stadie remained company leader, Küttner became leader of the reception camp. No real decision had been made yet for Camp II. Only after Kainer's death was Matthes installed as there as leader.

At the above-mentioned meetings, Wirth went through all daily occurrences which, to his mind, were bad. And that was almost everything. He criticised all deeds and actions, he interviewed each NCO individually and briefed them. His constant threats and his extolling of total power which, in his own words, was combined in his person.

At one of these meetings he also said, 'The Jews come here in order to perish. The Ukrainians will be despatched after the Aktion, and what happens to us we still don't know today. Perhaps we shall also die'. This statement, as the whole conversation, made many of us very thoughtful.

On the other hand, he joked about the manner in which we tried to envisage, plan and implement the whole resettlement programme 'around the green table', as he called it.

There was a directive from the Führer which stated that the Wehrmarkt should have nothing to do with this matter. That is why initially the whole matter was placed in the hands of the Ukrainians, who carried out the whole proceedings in their own way. How they did it, I do not want to describe here. The few Germans on the ramp and the reception area acted solely as 'apostles of peace'. This sad affair could not continue like this, and Wirth therefore stood out as the organiser of the Final Solution.

On the directive of the Führer, no Jew was to be beaten or tortured. Wirth, however, introduced the whips! He did say that when the 'gentlemen from Berlin' came, the whips had to disappear, but who bothered about that? It was Wirth who, at every possible opportunity, became brutal and mean, thus setting a bad example.

As I have already recounted, he delegated the supervisors to the various work Kommandos. He had a preference for people he had known for a long time. Thus, the three 'M's—Müller, Mentz and Miete. He knew them from Hadamar (E). Mentz and Müller he assigned to the hospital, and Miete, whom he had also noticed while cleaning out the clothing barracks, was detailed to Küttner. Post he assigned to the Ukrainians. Thus Kainer, whom I shall mention later, became leader of Camp II.

In these days, one saw in Treblinka only people who were constantly running! They could be Jews, Ukrainians or Germans. The constant pressure from Wirth and his threats made them all do it. For he constantly brought into the conversation the KZ or the unity of proven Waffen-SS duty. He kept repeating that we were all under the control of, and answerable to, the SS law machine and that in the mentioned set up, only a hero's death could give ultimate credit. It was true!

If I recount here the dealings with Germans, the strict, even inhuman intervention by the Ukrainians, then I must consider what happened to the Jews in those days as absolutely inhuman. Beatings, executions, which I will mention again, were always in evidence. One could see it. How grateful they were for every friendly word, for orders which were given without threats or beatings. Or for gestures which during these first days consisted of only sufficient drinking water. All this had to be done in great secrecy, as Wirth had eyes everywhere, and there were people among us who unfortunately told him every little thing.

It was Wirth who later used every opportunity to boast that it was he who had managed to see to it that Jews helped to kill Jews.

Wirth also issued orders in these first days after his arrival for the erection of a new gas chamber. The plans were drawn up by a man in Wirth's retinue called Hackenholt, whom we all called 'Hacko'. Lambert was called in as builder after 'Hacko' had already done some preparatory work.

Writing about executions, which Wirth authorised in the first days of his work in Treblinka, they were to be carried out by Germans. This caused us a great deal of concern. Under Eberl, these things were done only by Ukrainians who were there for that. I have already written about the Führer's directive. Now it seemed that we too were to be involved in such things. We naturally criticised this. Most of us wanted nothing to do with the executions. Wirth's reaction to our stance was very sour; there was denigration and swearing.

Another topic of conversation was the treatment of the Ukrainians, who were beaten. How could one beat soldiers—and they were soldiers in our eyes—with whips? The Ukrainians were very bitter and began to realise what sort of a trap they had fallen into. They mentioned this to us secretly in conversations. I went to Stangl and told him our worry that one day the Ukrainians and Jews would, if this treatment were to continue, turn against us and kill us all. Stangl told Wirth this, as he too was of the same opinion, at least in part. As a request, the Ukrainians were ill-treated and beaten less, but the poor Jews even more so. Especially those under my control. Even then Wirth hailed me with the name 'Jew lover'.

As Wirth continually threatened us with legal proceedings, which he said he was entitled to do as the local commander, this also became a topic of conversation and brought doubts. What did Wirth do? He began to demonstrate his power over us. Through the camp police one morning he arrested around ten people, mostly so-called 'speculators', but also local peasants straight from the fields. Among them was a 10 years old boy! He sent them to the hospital, said his bit and had them shot. I wanted to say this in court, but refrained due to desperate pleas from Miete who was afraid he would be held responsible for this. The shootings were witnessed by a Ukrainian guard.

Thus, Wirth did everything to frighten us and to prove his power. His constant success is not in doubt. It has to be taken into account though, that we were all novices then and took these threats seriously. When he slackened his tight grip about 12 months later, this had to be viewed and evaluated in a different context.

The aforementioned halt in transports lasted three days, much too short a time. There were still corpses lying around in Camp II. In front of the old gas chambers there was quite a heap. With the resumed gassings which began immediately after the halt, this situation deteriorated, as the reorganisation was not yet ready to take effect. So the pile of cadavers in front of the gas chambers grew bigger and bigger. This caused Wirth to take even more drastic measures as the bad situation had to be solved at any cost. Kainer, who as the so-called 'courier' who quietly went about his business and liked to ride around the neighbourhood, was appointed chief of this camp by Wirth.

Owing to the heat, the corpses had become so swollen that they were unrecognisable and had been rotting for some time. Blood, excrement and other excretions had bound them into a pile almost 15 cms [sic.] high and riddled with worms. [It must be assumed that Suchomel meant 15 metres high.] Kainer had to take this in hand at once and dispose of the bodies. Nobody wanted to do this job. The Jews specifically detailed to this work preferred to be shot, and beatings had no effect. Some jumped into the well and drowned themselves. Kainer could not manage it. Wirth thereupon threatened him that if he were not capable of forcing the Jews to do the job, then he was to do it himself. All this happened at great speed. To Kaner's excuses that he could not, or would not, do it, Wirth again threatened him with a KZ. These threats drove Kainer to desperation and he could see no way out. On that particular day, I met and spoke to Kainer in front of the barracks containing the sorting room of the 'gold Jews'. He told me all this, and he opened his pocket and showed me his cocked pistol. He gave me to understand that if Wirth continued treating him like this, he would shoot himself. I talked to him to talk him out of it. He answered that he did not want to go to a KZ again. He knew he would not return from there. [Kainer shot himself soon afterwards.]

Kainer did not die immediately as was reported, but he could no longer speak. He lay on a bier in front of the German quarters, ready for the transport to Ostrow. I leaned over him and asked why he had done it. Küttner came up then and said to me, 'Don't bother about this cowardly pig'. That was how much human life was valued in Treblinka!

This testimony, which I presented like this, or almost like this, was not taken up in court in critical examination of the 'Kainer affair'. Only Kainer's corpse transport Kommando was mentioned. More note should have been taken of Wirth's attitude, especially in a case which was important to him and his ambition. If Wirth, as I stated in court, had fallen then, Aktion Reinhardt would have broken up. Berlin would not have found a single person with such energy for evil and nastiness. The mood of the German guard detachment had reached an all-time low.

After Kainer's death, Wirth now personally took a hand in dealing with the state of affairs in front of the gas chambers. He really did work at it. Colleagues told me this who were up there [in Camp II]. Using long leather straps, pulled under the arms, the corpses were dragged to the pits and disposed of. [Wirth, Oberhauser, and Hackenholt all participated.]

In front of the gas chambers, he had placed a large amount of chloride of lime first, over which was thrown a thick layer of sand. So, the gassing carried on with regularity. After getting rid of this trouble, he installed Matthes as the chief of Camp II. As far as I know—I lived with Matthes—against his will. He also forced Matthes to toe the line with further threats. Matthes, as far as I know, ran the place fairly, and even saw to it that the work Jews had three times as much food dished out to them. All improvements, such as decent toilets, a clean laundry, kitchen with cookers and baking ovens, he had built on his own initiative without waiting for a directive, which he would certainly not have received anyway.

In the meantime—Lambert had come back again—the building of the new gas chambers progressed quickly. The addition of a Star of David was done on Wirth's orders, as well as the hanging up of a curtain plundered from a synagogue. He even wanted a celebratory speech at the opening! Thank God this did not happen, as I was later informed. [Suchomel was on leave at the time of the new gas chambers becoming operational.]

On my return, I found the camp completely different. The outer camouflage was complete, the tube was re-laid and then camouflaged as best as possible. The chambers were also in full use and the extermination machinery running smoothly. Stangl, who had worked at Sobibor and was going on leave, was represented by Schemmel. He ran the place with quite a soft approach. At the end of October, Stangl took command again, Schemmel went home as he was ill.

Wirth kept returning to Treblinka, almost every week, in order to see how things were running. On such days the camp resembled a disturbed ant heap. Everyone was running, trying to avoid Wirth. His presence affected us all like a nightmare. Through various measures and orders he saw to it that he continued to inspire fear. The things which Stangl had secretly and quietly diverted away from us. Wirth never wanted us to rest or even have time to think. The order to burn all corpses, which nobody believed at first, caused chaos. Also, it was too cold, and the bodies had frozen hard in a short time. An even bigger shock came when we were suddenly told that the pits had to be emptied as well, in order to burn those corpses too. Here, too, Wirth took a hand with his specialist, 'Hacko', as excavator operator, and Floss as cremation specialist. As usual, Bełżec was once again used as an experimental camp. Thus, in Treblinka there began the most gruesome activity of its entire existence, besides the gruesome killings. It was the repeated inventiveness of a Wirth-hound whose unscrupulous lack of consideration finally enforced the implementation of this work and the impossible-sounding orders.

With the halt of all transports in the Spring of 1943, Wirth appeared less, but the fear and terror of him remained. The intervention and persuasion of Oberbereichsleiter Blankenburg was always needed to calm the men.

On Stangl's request, Treblinka II was to be converted into a labour camp and the Jews were to be set to digging peat. The setting up of extermination machinery had already begun at Auschwitz in grand style, but we knew nothing of this at the time. In future, all transports had to go there, and that is what happened. Due to these changes, Wirth also arrived in the camp and the negotiations with the District Commissioner in Sokolow progressed well. In mid-August 1943, the plan was to be put into effect. Before that, the well known uprising in the camp happened, which I need not describe here.

Wirth arrived the next day in a rage and screamed tirades at all present. I don't need to describe how. Franz was his scapegoat. All of us over a period of time, had become immune to his abuse, but not to the fear he instilled—that remained.

Treblinka was, as Stangl said, to be built bigger and better. The necessary parts for the barracks had arrived some time ago, and the necessary craftsmen found for the workshops from the last transports from Bialystok, and the work had begun again. There, too, Wirth appeared again.

One Sunday in August, Stangl, who arrived in Lublin in a very jolly mood, called the personnel together and informed us that the German staff and some of the Ukrainians were to be transferred to Italy. He did not say where exactly at first. So the dissolution of the camp was a decided fact. Up to the time of the removal of the Duce, Stangl remained at the camp, in order to go with an advance Kommando under Wirth to Trieste. I learned this later from Stangl. Franz was given the task of disbanding the camp. This happened just as described and verified at the trial. Franz's descriptions thereof are untrue. One can say that by mid-November 1943, only the guardhouse remained standing at Treblinka II. But how long for, none of us Germans know. At most, only until the dissolution of the Treblinka I camp.

# ENDNOTES

## INTRODUCTION

1 Wikipedia.org.
2 Adolf Hitler in *Mein Kampf*, volume 2, chapter 14.
3 Recording of Hitler speech, Berlin Reichstag, 6 October 1939; *Deutsches Rundfunkarchiv*.
4 Nazi Conspiracy & Aggression, vol. 3, pp. 619-621.
5 Joseph Poprzeczny manuscript.
6 Haaretz, 18 November 2018.
7 *Ibid*.
8 Planning and construction of the Reinhardt death camps was already underway.
9 1939 *Reichsgesetzblatt*, Part 1, p. 2,077.
10 Friedrich Gottlob Schmidt (1902–1973) Deputy Gauleiter (retd); SS-Brigadeführer; Chief NSDAP political administrator for the region of the General Government. Saw active service with the Waffen-SS and was captured by the Americans in August 1944. Sentenced to thirty months at a labour camp and his assets forfeited in July 1948.
11 Galicia was added to the General Government in August 1941. Otto Wächter (8 July 1901–14 July 1949) was Austrian by birth. He served as governor of Krakow and then Galicia. During his tenure, many thousands of the Jewish population lost their lives. He finished the war attached to the Reich Security Central Office. He evaded capture, under the false name Alfredo Reinhardt, with the help of the church, but he succumbed to a disease contracted by swimming in the polluted River Tiber. His son maintains that Wächter never supported the SS racial extermination policy.
12 Richard Wendler's sister was married to Gebhard Himmler, the older brother of the Reichsführer-SS.
13 Lukas, R., *Out of the Inferno* p. 13.
14 On 10 July 1941, at Jedwabne, a group of forty ethnic Poles attacked the local Jewish population, beating them and then allegedly locking them in a barn before setting it ablaze. A German *Ordnungspolizei* was present and did nothing to prevent the atrocity. Records of the Polin Museum Warsaw.
15 Hitler replied to an enquiry about the Jewish question from a Herr Adolf Gemlich.
16 Münchner Neuesten Nachrichten.
17 USHMM.
18 1935 *Reichsgesetzblatt*, Part 1, pp. 1,146-1,147.

19 Yad Vashem, Shoah Resource Centre; stenographic record of minutes of the meeting held at 11 a.m. on 12 November 1938 at Göring's Air Ministry office building in Wilhelmstrasse, Berlin.
20 See illustrations.
21 Gerhard Kretschmar was born in Pomssen, a village south-east of Leipzig on 20 February 1939. His parents were ardent Nazi supporters, Richard Kretschmar, a farm labourer, and his wife, Lina Kretschmar. Gerhard was born blind, with either no legs (or one leg), and with one arm (the original medical records are lost, and second-hand accounts vary). He was also subject to convulsions. Brandt later testified that the child was also 'an idiot', although how this was determined is not stated. Richard Kretschmar took the newborn Gerhard to Dr Werner Catel, a paediatrician at the University Children's Clinic in Leipzig, and asked that his son be 'put to sleep'. Catel told him that this would be illegal. Kretschmar then wrote directly to Hitler, asking that he investigate the case and overrule the law that prevented 'this monster' (as he described his own child) from being killed. As was usual with such petitions, it was referred to Hitler's private secretariat, headed by Philipp Bouhler. There, it was seen by Hans Hefelman, head of Department IIb, which dealt with petitions. Hefelman and Bouhler showed the petition to Hitler, aware of his frequently expressed support for the 'mercy killing' of people with severe disabilities. Hitler summoned Dr Karl Brandt, one of his personal physicians, and sent him to Leipzig to investigate the Kretschmar case. Hitler told Brandt that if Gerhard Kretschmar's condition was indeed as described in Richard Kretschmar's petition, then he, Hitler, authorised Brandt to have Gerhard killed, in consultation with the local doctors. If any legal action were taken, it would be thrown out of court. In Leipzig, Brandt examined the child and consulted with Catel and another physician, Dr Helmut Kohl. He also went to Pomssen and saw the Kretschmars. When Brandt informed the Leipzig doctors of Hitler's instructions, they agreed that Gerhard Kretschmar should be killed, although they knew this was illegal. The Pomssen church register says that Gerhard Kretschmar died at Pomssen of 'heart weakness' on 25 July 1939. He was buried in the Lutheran churchyard three days later. Although no medical records exist, and although the testimony of Brandt and Catel after the war was contradictory and evasive, there is a suspicion that Gerhard was killed in the Leipzig clinic with an injection of a common drug such as luminal, and that the church register was falsified to conceal this fact.
22 Nazi Conspiracy and Aggression, vol. VIII, pp. 606-619. Affidavit of Dieter Wisliceny.
23 Bayerisches Staatsbibliothek.
24 This figure was reported by Heydrich in January 1940.
25 Holocaust documents of Yad Vashem, Jerusalem, NG-2586-B.
26 Bayerisches Staatsbibliothek.
27 Death Dealer—Rudolf Höss.
28 Documents on the Holocaust, p. 197.
29 Mayer, p. 302.
30 Davidson, p. 438.
31 See illustrations.
32 Haus der Wannsee Konferenz; BA Koblenz.
33 See illustrations.
34 'Globus', from the Latin meaning 'globe' or 'sphere'.
35 Johannes Sachslehner, p. 12.
36 Heinz Höhne.

## CHAPTER 1

1 Emperor Franz Joseph I visited Prague on 30 September 1891 at the cadet school for the infantry, which was then located in the former Josef Barracks, next to the Powder Tower. The local newspaper, *Prager Tagblatt*, referred to this visit in great detail:

> Meanwhile, all riflemen were formed into a battalion; the commander reported; the Emperor took the salute at a parade followed by the scrolls.… From the big courtyard, the emperor went to the small courtyar … and from there he entered the winter gym. There was a large fresco in the vestibule in front of the first staircase representing the Viennese memorial of Maria Theresa. When questioned who painted the beautiful painting, the cadet school commander replied that the cadet and freelance artist, Globocnik, created the work during three weeks of holidays, copying a small photo. It was signed in the lower right corner of the picture: Franz D. Globocnik, Frek. 1891. The Emperor expressed admiration for a beautiful and faithful reproduction, praised the young artist and asked if he had studied painting. Globocnik replied that he had the basics from his father, a drawing professor at a high school in Laibach. The emperor enquired whether his father still lived. Globocnik replied that he had already died. The Emperor then reiterated that the picture was very beautiful and that he liked it very much. There were two frescoes with equestrian themes in Globocnik's school, which adorned the interior of the shooting range. The Emperor expressed his appreciation of the purposeful and surprisingly artistic decoration.

After graduation, Franz Globocnik was assigned to the 3rd Cavalry Regiment, and in 1896, he left the army as an Oberleutnant. Communication from Pavel Landa and Milan Hodik to Joseph Poprzeczny.

2 Joseph Poprzeczny.
3 Unusually, Lydia Globocnik was not confirmed until 21 May 1923 in Klagenfurt.
4 Schulz & Wegmann; and Miller & Schulz.
5 State Archives Austria.
6 Berndt Rieger.
7 Siegfried Pucher.
8 Kärntner *Amts- und Adressbuch* 1939, Klagenfurt. When Globocnik married Lore Peterschinegg in 1944, he gave his address as Bahnhofstrasse 67, which indicates he maintained an apartment next door to his mother.
9 Rieger.
10 There is disagreement over Grete Michner's year of birth. Rieger states she was born on 19 October 1908; Sachslehner offers 1906; Pucher declares 1907; Poprzeczny avoids providing a birthdate. Globocnik himself declared her as his wife when registering for the April 1938 plebiscite, and stated her birthdate was 19 October 1906.
11 Rieger.
12 BDC, Globocnik SSO file.
13 Pucher.
14 BDC, Globocnik SSO file.
15 Elste, p. 117.
16 *Ibid*, p. 120.
17 Wolf held the Austrian professional title of Kommerzialrat. He was not the mayor of Klagenfurt as some researchers state, but between 1934 and 1938, he was Regierungskommissar with the powers of a mayor. He was relieved of his duties following the Anschluss and died in 1952.
18 Sachslehner, p. 34.
19 Hubert Klausner (1 November 1892–12 February 1939) was subsequently appointed as Gauleiter and Landeshauptmann of Carinthia in 1938. He died of a stroke while in office. He held the rank of SS-Brigadeführer. Rieger states Globocnik introduced Rainer to Klausner, and Poprzeczny writes Globocnik and Rainer first met in Klausner's office. Sachslehner states that Globocnik and Rainer met at Klausner's villa 'Alpenheim' at Latschach, Faaker See, indicating that Klausner and Rainer were already acquainted.
20 Herta Michner in 'Kärntens braune Elite' by Alfred Elster.
21 Elster.

22 Max Grillmayr, SS-Obersturmbannführer, was born on 1 August 1908, the son of a railway official in Vordernberg in Styria. From 1930–1931, he was a member of the SA and also joined the National Socialist German Workers Party (NSDAP). He was sentenced to two and a half months' imprisonment in December 1932 as a result of the Gerngroß teargas attack. He also participated in the June 1933 bomb attack murder of Viennese jeweler Futterweit. As a result, he fled to Germany from June 1933. On 21 June 1934, he was expatriated, but was still illegal in Austria. He was killed in action on the Eastern Front on 23 May 1942.
23 Franz Novak subsequently gained notoriety as Adolf Eichmann's transport expert.
24 Tiefenthal commanded squads of Jewish prisoners forced to cleanse the gas chambers after each '*aktion*' in the initial phase of 'Reinhard'.
25 Ingeborg Capra-Teuffenbach, 1 October 1914–16 September 1992. Married SS-H'Stuf. Heinz Capra (Personal Advisor to Globocnik) in Berchtesgaden, 1937.
26 BDC, Lerch SSO file.
27 *Ibid*.

## CHAPTER 2

1 Michner Villa, Krumpendorf. On 6 December 1900, Ottilie Messiner sold a plot of land for 8,200 crowns, to Gustav Edler von Jahl, k.k. Major General in Bratislava, and his wife, Leopoldine. On the land, they built the Villa Jahl (later Villa Michner, Lannerweg 25). Emil Michner subsequently opened his home as a guest house.
2 Robert Rapatz (14 August 1890–17 December 1964) was an active member of the NSDAP. Post-war, he joined the Austrian Peoples' Party and was a member of the National Council.
3 Rieger, p. 17.
4 *Ibid*, p. 23.
5 Reinhold von Mohrenschildt, SS-Hauptsturmführer. Served under Globocnik in Lublin and Trieste. Died in Klagenfurt 1990 following surgery for a brain tumour.
6 Rieger, p. 21.
7 SS-Untersturmführer Ernst Natter, born 21 December 1904 in Krumpendorf; KIA 14 September 1942 with IR 8. Ebba subsequently remarried and took the married name Skreiner.
8 Information from Maurice Williams.
9 Sachslehner, p. 50.
10 *Ibid*, p. 53.
11 Kajetan Mühlmann, art historian and SS officer. He became Seyss-Inquart's art expert and followed him to Poland and the Netherlands where he was involved in the appropriation of artworks. Born in 1898, he died of stomach cancer in 1958.
12 Wilhelm Miklas, 1872–1956. Placed under house arrest for his initial opposition to the appointment of Seyss-Inquart, he gained protection from SS-Standartenführer Otto Skorzeny and survived the war.
13 Due to a legal technicality, Schuschnigg could not dissolve the cabinet until 5.30 p.m. when his resignation would take effect.
14 Sachslehner, p. 63.
15 Rieger, p. 29.
16 Sachslehner, p. 68.
17 August Edler von Meyszner (1886–1947) was a former Austrian police officer who fled to Germany via Yugoslavia following the failed Putsch of July 1934. An exponent of the extreme right-wing, he joined the SA and SS in Germany and took German citizenship in May 1935 which allowed him to join the German Ordnungspolizei in September the same year. As police officers were not permitted at that time to be members of the SS, he resigned from the SS in October 1935. Two years later, he was reinstated in the SS with the rank of Oberführer. From 12 April 1938, he was the inspector of Ordnungspolizei in Austria and reported directly to

Kaltenbrunner. During the war, promoted to SS-Gruppenführer, he served in Norway and Serbia, and he was executed for war crimes on 24 January 1947 in Belgrade.

18 One People! One Realm! One Leader! The unification of Germany and Austria was expressly forbidden by the Treaty of Versailles 1919. It was Hitler's argument that all German-speaking people should be merged under one authority. Therefore, it was Nazi policy that Austria, the Memelland, the Saarland, and the Sudetenlands should be unified under German rule.

19 Comicism.tripod.com.

20 The Speeches of Adolf Hitler, vol. 2, p. 1,423.

21 Stevenlehrer.com.

22 Nommeraadio.ee.

## CHAPTER 3

1 BDC, Globocnik SSO file; Michael D. Miller & Andreas Schulz, Gauleiter, p. 245.

2 *Ibid*, p. 249.

3 Pucher, p. 45.

4 Sachslehner, p. 77.

5 Herman Neubacher (1893–1960), SA-Gruppenführer, was the first Nazi mayor of Vienna from 13 March 1938 until 14 December 1940. Nothing more than a figurehead, his last months in office were spent in south-east Europe where he operated as part of the Nazi administration. He transferred to the Nazi diplomatic service as 'Special Representative for Economic Issues'. In October 1942, he was appointed Plenipotentiary for Greece. Captured by the Americans in 1945, he gave evidence on behalf of his friend, Kaltenbrunner, at Nuremberg. He was sentenced to twenty years' hard labour in Yugoslavia in 1946, but was released in 1952 for health reasons. He held various positions in Ethiopia and Austria, and died in Vienna on 1 July 1960.

6 Sachslehner, p. 83.

7 The Great Armorial Hall is located on the first floor of the west wing of Landhaus Klagenfurt. It extends over both upper floors and is 9.8 metres high. The base measures 23 × 13 metres, the dimensions of the hall are unchanged since 1581. The hall was originally decorated with frescoes and a ceiling painting by Anton Blumenthal, but these were destroyed in the fire in 1723. The walls and ceiling of the hall were then redesigned by Josef Ferdinand Fromiller, since then, only coats of arms have been added. On the ceiling, there is a fresco by Fromiller. The ceiling mirror is framed by a 'Perspective excellently constructed pseudo-architecture', which represents a circular arcade with niches in the corners. In the niches are Grisaillestatuen the Habsburg ruler Matthias, Ferdinand II, III, and IV. In the balustrades in the middle of each page are the cardinal virtues. Above the illusory architecture no sky opens, but it is the inheritance of Emperor Charles VI. This had taken place on 22 August 1728 in the Palais Rosenberg (now the city hall), but was moved by Fromiller architecturally in the Great Hall of Weapons. The emperor sits under a red canopy, and is surrounded by the decreed, the spiritual dignitaries, the ducal peasant, and the bearers of the eleven lands. The coat of arms of the latter as well as the coats of arms of Austria, Carinthia, the spiritual territories of Salzburg and Bamberg at the edge of the picture combine the homage scene with the illusory architecture. On the north wall is a framed panel painting and dated 1740 fresco. It shows the installation of the Carinthian duke at Fürstenstein near Karnburg. On the south wall there is an equally large fresco, which shows the handing over of the Gabbriefs (the deed of donation) by Maximilian I to the Carinthian estates (24 April 1518), with which Klagenfurt became a state-owned town. These two frescos symbolise the state and state consciousness of the Carinthian estates. The remaining wall surfaces are completely covered with 650 coats of arms (with ceiling, 665). On the long sides, the coats of arms of the landed nobility and the knights are painted: in the top two rows in alphabetical order the families who were estates before 1591, among them in chronological order the newly admitted families, ending with Count Hugo Henckel-Donnersmarck 1847. Nineteen coats of arms fields are empty, since

the coats of arms of these families could not be determined during the baroque period. On the south side are the coats of arms of the ecclesiastical estates on the left, on the right those of the provincial governors, ending with Leopold of Aichelburg-Labia (1909–1918). On the north side are the coat of arms of the Landesvizedome (sovereign prince) and on the right, the Landesverweser (deputy of the governor), both offices existed until 1747. From the Venetian Francesco Robba comes the marble floor in white, red, and black, the five door frames, the gate to the arms hall, and the southern fireplace. The northern fireplace was reconstructed in 1908 by Pietro d'Aronco from Gemona. Since March 2006, the Fürstenstein is again in front of this fireplace. (*Wikipedia*)

8 The seven putschists, plus another six who were indirectly involved in the attempted coup, were executed on the Choke (Würgegalgen) by Johann Lang, the official executioner. Of the seven SS Putschists involved in the Dollfuss murder, Otto Planetta and Franz Holzweber died on 31 July 1934. Their bodies were then cremated at the fire hall Simmering. After the *Anschluss*, the ashes were recovered and returned to the families for burial. Ernst Feike died on 7 August 1934; Ludwig Maitzen, Franz Loeb, Erich Wohlrab, and Josef Hackel died on 13 August. Lang was arrested by the Nazis and incarcerated in Dachau concentration camp where he died.

9 Rieger, p. 41.

10 Hanns Albin Rauter, SS-Obergruppenführer and Higher SS and Police Leader in Holland. Executed for war crimes in 1949.

11 Die Tagerbücher von Joseph Goebbels, vol. 1, p. 201.

12 Rieger, p. 38.

13 BDC, Globocnik SSO file.

14 *Ibid.*

15 *Ibid.*

16 During the Polish campaign, SS 'Germania' was a motorised infantry unit under the command of Karl-Maria Demelhuber. It served as a component of Army Group South. For a description of this Army Group's actions in the Polish campaign, see Appendix IV.

17 BDC, Globocnik SSO file.

18 *Ibid.*

## CHAPTER 4

1 *Ibid.*

2 *Ibid.*

3 Teatr NN.PL.

4 The administrator of the assets of a local clan.

5 State Archives Lublin.

6 Teatr NN.PL.

7 Yad Vashem archive.

8 Noted in the official diary of Dr Hans Frank; Sachslehner, p. 106.

9 Buchheim, pp. 182-187.

10 Clay & Leapman, pp. 94-96.

11 Prof. Dr Konrad Meyer-Hetling (1901–1973), SS-Oberführer on the staff of RFSS. Agronomist and rural planner, found not guilty of war crimes and crimes against humanity. Instrumental in the planning phase of General Plan *Ost*.

12 The General Plan *Ost* was the master plan for the expulsion of Slavic peoples and the resettlement of ethnic Germans in central and eastern Europe.

13 Josef Umlauf (1906–1989). Architect and town planner in the RKFDV.

14 Buchheim, pp. 187-188.

15 Williams, Heinrich Himmler, p. 57.

16 There was a bar, a cafeteria and a bowling alley for the use of SS personnel, situated at todays 15 ul. Wieniawska. This building survived the war until it was demolished in recent years, despite a

public outcry. After the war, the bowling alley was converted to a sports shooting range and the building was subsequently used by the prosecution team of the Insitute of National Remembrance.

17 Sachslehner, p. 106.
18 Testimony of Wilhelmine Trsek, 11 June 1964, held in the Michalsen file, BA Ludwigsburg.
19 Description of the house provided by the current owner, Jerzy Łobarzewski, the grandson of Gustaw Haberlau, and recorded in Sachslehner, p. 127.
20 Domagala, Lublin Gazeta Wyborcza.
21 *Ibid.*
22 Rieger, p. 53; BA Berlin-Lichterfelde.
23 Adrian Weale.
24 BA Berlin-Lichterfelde;
25 Rieger, pp. 55-57; BA Berlin-Lichterfelde.
26 Rieger, p. 57.
27 See letter from Globocnik to Himmler dated 28 January 1941 and Himmler's handwritten note (illustrations).

## CHAPTER 5

1 Krüger was awarded both classes of Iron Cross, the Austrian Military Service Cross 3rd Class, the Knights Cross of the Royal House Order of Hohenzollern with Swords, and the Wound Badge in Silver.
2 BDC, F-W Krüger SSO file.
3 *Ibid.*
4 *Ibid.*
5 The biographical details of F-W Krüger are taken from SS Elite, volume 2, by Max Williams; BDC Krüger SSO and RS files.
6 BA Berlin-Lichterfelde.
7 Nuremberg evidential document USA 299.
8 Nuremberg evidential document USA 300.
9 Nuremberg evidential document USA 302; Frank diary for period 25 October 1939–15 December 1939.
10 Reichsgesetzblatt, 1940, Part I, 1270.
11 Instruction for internal use on the application of the law of 17 September 1940, concerning property of Poles; copy of monthly report 31 May 1942, with statistics on farms and estates seized and confiscated in the Incorporated Eastern Territories; copy of letter from SS officer to Himmler, 20 November 1940; Nuremberg evidential document USA 312.
12 Nuremberg evidential document USA 304.
13 Nuremberg evidential document USA 306.
14 Nuremberg evidential document USA 307.
15 Copy of monthly report 31 May 1942, with statistics on farms and estates seized and confiscated in the Incorporated Eastern Territories; Nuremberg evidential document USA 312.
16 Polish Information Centre, 1939–1945.
17 Himmler's appointment dated 15 October 1939.
18 Memorial to the victims of Krychow; www.Chelm.freeyellow.com
19 Described by a witness (Ben-Tzion Bruker) as an Oberleutnant, but most likely a SS officer of the rank of SS-Obersturmführer.
20 www.jewishgen.org
21 Testimony of Franz Bertl, 29 April 1965, held in the Michalsen file, BA Ludwigsburg.
22 Testimony of Franz Eigner, 3 May 1965, held in the Michalsen file, BA Ludwigsburg.
23 Testimony of Marianne Dombrowsky-Hillmann, 21 November 1964, held in the Michalsen file, BA Ludwigsburg.

24 Testimony of Wilhelmine Trsek, 22 February 1968, held in the Michalsen file, BA Ludwigsburg.
25 *Ibid.*
26 ZDF TV interview.
27 Goldhagen, p. 299.
28 Rieger, p. 60.
29 IfZ Doc 04-133.
30 Sachslehner, p. 106.

## CHAPTER 6

1 Louise Guyon-Witzschel was arrested by the Allies and interrogated by the French and Americans. She was held in the US interrogation camp at Freising before being transferred to Nuremberg. She was a divorced secretary who had married a French journalist named Zesbron before the war, and she had worked for the Wehrmacht in Vichy and Paris. At the approach of the Allies in 1944, she fled to Berlin where she worked at the SS-Hauptamt for SS-Hauptsturmführer Adalbert Schindlmayer, a liaison officer with the Cossack volunteers. Schindlmayer transferred to Udine Province in Italy and took Guyon-Witzschel with him. They were based at Tolmezzo and she met Globocnik on three or four occasions, but never worked directly for him. She insisted that she had no knowledge of atrocities. See interrogation of Louise Guyon-Witzschel in IWM FO645 Box 156.
2 Teatr NN.PL
3 BDC, Lerch SSO file.
4 Mike Tregenza states in correspondence that his room was behind the circular window in the roof space, above the main entrance. Georg Michalsen states that Hofle's room was on the second floor; Poprzeczny, p. 103.
5 BDC, Höfle SSO file.
6 Poprzeczny, p. 102.
7 BDC, von Mohrenschildt RS file.
8 *Ibid.*
9 BDC, Höfle SSO file, copy of letter dated 17 February 1942 regarding promotions.
10 Wippern's wounds are described in his BDC SSO file on a SS-Führungshauptamt memo, dated 4 July 1942, following a report from the Waffen-SS General Government Welfare Officer the previous 1 June. See also Poprzeczny, p. 116.
11 ZStL 251/59, Sobibor case, Statement by Josef Kölbl, 23 January 1962.
12 ZStL 252/59, Bełżec case, Statement by Erich Bauer, 7 December 1962.
13 NA Kew, WO 208/4673.
14 Wehrwolf was a German nationalist league of men with paramilitary roots. Its members consisted mainly of Freikorps fighters in the Weimar Republic.
15 Fricke, p. 838.
16 Possibly the brutal Rosalie Benesch who was accused post-war of the murder of a number of Jewish prisoners, but appears to have escaped prosecution. See recherche.staatsarchiv.hamburg.de/ScopeQuery5.2/detail.aspx?Id=1198995.
17 BDC, Maubach RS file.
18 BDC, Maubach RS file. Irmgard Rickheim states that Maubach arrived in Lublin on 7 January 1940, having left Berlin two days earlier by car. She further states they travelled with Friedrich Schmidt, the SS-Brigadeführer and temporary governor of Lublin district, visiting Krakow *en route*.
19 Maubach cites the reason for his departure from Lublin as a desire to escape the constant 'jockeying for favour' between Globocnik's Austrian insiders. See Rieger, p. 89.
20 recherche.staatsarchiv.hamburg.de/ScopeQuery5.2/detail.aspx?Id=1198995.
21 Perz, p. 410.

22 Sachslehner, p. 135.
23 Rieger, p. 63.
24 Christian Ingrao, p. 176.
25 Recent information from his grandson suggests that Claasen received a gunshot wound to his lung and was subsequently hospitalised in Berlin from where he was declared 'missing'.

## CHAPTER 7

1 Marszalek, p. 20.
2 *Ibid.*
3 Sachslehner, p. 139.
4 Sachslehner, p. 140.
5 BDC, Katzmann SSO file.

## CHAPTER 8

1 Walter Benjamin, A Berlin Street Boy, from the series 'Enlightenment for Children', which the author wrote in the years 1929 to 1932 for the youth hour of the Berlin Broadcasting Company 'Funk Hour AG'.
2 Landesarchiv Berlin.
3 Reichsausschuss für Volksgesundheitsdienst. Berlin, Reichsdruckerei, 1935. (Official translation of the law into English).
4 The date of composition and actual signing is open to conjecture. It is widely accepted that this occurred at the end of September or early October 1939, towards the conclusion of the Polish campaign, or immediately after it had ended on 6 October. The wording is attributed to a committee of senior members of the medical profession who agreed on the content, which was then passed on to Werner Blankenburg and Viktor Brack at the KdF. A leading member of this committee, Professor Max de Crinis, is believed to have discussed the wording with his close personal friend and boss at the Reich Security Office, Reinhard Heydrich, but this requires confirmation.
5 Hamburg State Archives, 631A/300.
6 Nuremberg evidence document NO-203. Harvard Trials Project HLS item no. 1245.
7 Klee, Dressen and Riess, p. 229.
8 Nuremberg evidence document NO-205.
9 HLS Nuremberg Trials Project, transcript for NMT 1: Medical case, testimony of Viktor Brack 14 May 1947.
10 SS-Sturmbannführer Karl Freiherr Michel von Tüßling (1907–1991) was a member of the Motorized Unit of SS-Standarte 1 where he became acquainted with Viktor Brack. Both men were avidly interested in motor sport. Philipp Bouhler was a well known amateur racing driver, and he appointed Michel von Tüßling as his pre-war Chief of Staff. Brack and Michel von Tüßling became close friends. The latter prepared an affidavit in Brack's defence, in which he stated that Brack had always acted honourably and had often supported victims of injustice. He declared that both Brack and himself had Jewish acquaintances whom they had helped. He also stated that Brack was an outspoken enemy of Martin Bormann. See HLS Nuremberg Project, item no. 312, Exhibit Brack 10.
11 Archives of the Prosecutor General, Frankfurt am Main. Werner Kirchert was the director of Grafeneck Clinic and a consultant to the Reich SS Physician, Ernst-Robert Grawitz.
12 Bohne was subsequently replaced in 1941 by the more efficient Dieter Allers.
13 Götz Aly, Peter Chroust & Christian Pross, pp. 36-37. Dr Karl Heinz Rodenberg of Heydrich's SD was added to the governing body as an expert advisor from February 1940 until October 1940.

14 Vernehmungsprotokoll der Sonderkommission des Hessischen Landeskriminalamtes Wiesbaden, V/1 of 4 April 1960.
15 Burleigh, p. 133.
16 www.holocaustresearchproject.org
17 Deposition by Wentripp on 2 February 1961, contained in Holocaust Controversies, p. 279.
18 Nazi Conspiracy & Aggression, volume 3, pp. 418-419.
19 Burleigh, p. 132.
20 Aly, Chroust & Pross, pp. 251-256.

## CHAPTER 9

1 *Ibid*, p. 245.
2 Williams, Max; SS Elite, vol. 1, p. 190.
3 Archive of Humbolt University, personal file Karl Bonnhoefer.
4 Schellenberg, p. 86.
Eichberg Process, 2 December 1946. Quoted in Ernst Klee, Euthanasie im NS-Staat, p. 119.
6 Kreitmair thesis.
7 Klee, Ernst. Was sie Taten, p. 50.
8 BDC, Eicke SSO file. Upon his discharge, Eicke was appointed as the commandant of Dachau concentration camp where he formulated the regulations adopted by all camps in the system. Eicke was subsequently appointed as the first Inspector of Concentration Camps. He finally commanded the SS-*Totenkopf* Division with the rank of SS-Obergruppenführer until he was killed in action on 26 February 1943.
9 Aly, Götz. Aktion T4, 1939–1945. *Die Euthanasie* -Zentrale in der Tiergartenstraße 4. Berlin 1989.
10 Attributed to Paul Nitsche by Georg Andreae, the Department for Welfare and Nursing Homes of the Provincial Administration of Hanover, on 8 August 1961.
11 Höss, Death Dealer, p. 28.
12 Rauff deposition to West German investigators in Chile. Online at www.nizkor.org
13 Klee, Dressen, Riess, p. 69.
14 BDC, Rodenberg RuS file.
15 BDC, Rodenberg SSO file.
16 Letter to journalist Walter Kohl.
17 Professor Dr Kurt Blome was a defendant in the Doctors' Trial at Nuremberg. He was accused of experiments on concentration camp inmates. He was an expert on biological warfare and research around the disease cancer. Evidence suggests that he practised euthanasia and carried out experiments on humans he infected with the plague. He was acquitted of all charges, but historians believe he was spared in exchange for information for the Americans about biological warfare. He died on 10 October 1969.

## CHAPTER 10

1 Joseph Goebbels Tagebücher, p. 1,776.
2 I have opted for the Reinhardt version for this study, as that is the option recorded in the first document to which the operation is referred, but as Joseph Poprzeczny succinctly puts it, it matters not what name the campaign was given; it remains one of the most murderous events in history during which literally hundreds of thousands of innocent people lost their belongings and their lives.
3 This version is sourced to Rudolf Höss during his post-war captivity.
4 Poprzeczny, p. 256.
5 Himmler Dienstkalender 1941–1942, p. 185.

6 *Ibid*, p. 186; the planned new camp was subsequently erected in the south-east suburb of Lublin at Majdanek, on the main route to Chełm.
7 Sachslehner, p. 175.
8 Marszalek, p. 20.
9 Marszalek, p. 21.
10 *Ibid.*
11 Marszalek, p. 22.
12 *Ibid*, p. 24.
13 Eichmann's interrogation record in 'Eichmann Interrogated: Transcript from the Archives of the Israeli Police', pp. 74-75.
14 Der Dienstkalender Heinrich Himmlers 1941–42, p. 262.
15 Rosenberg speech in Politische Archiv, Auswärtiges Amt, Berlin, XIII, VAA Berichte.
16 Remark by Rosenberg following a discussion with Hitler on 14 December 1941; Nuremberg IMT document 1517-PS.
17 Oral testimony provided on 8 April 1999 contained in archive of Grodzka Gate NN Theatre Centre.

## CHAPTER 11

1 Schulte, p. 48, note 34.
2 *Ibid*, p. 57.
3 Nuremberg Military Tribunal, Judgment of the Tribunal (regarding August Frank), 3 November 1947, *United States of America v. Oswald Pohl, et al. (Case No. 4)* pp. 992-997; Jump up to: Frank, August; Memorandum, 26 September 1942, in NO-724, Pros. Ex. 472, *United States of America v. Oswald Pohl, et al. (Case No. 4)*, V, pp. 965-967. (Under 1e, the original states 'The same applies to underwear [or laundry or linens] under letter d [men's clothing]'.
4 Höss, Commandant of Auschwitz, p. 258.
5 *Ibid*, p. 257.
6 BDC, Globocnik SSO file.
7 Der Dienstkalender Heinrich Himmlers 1941–42, p. 233.
8 *Ibid*, p. 290.
9 Pohl, pp. 125-126.
10 Longerich, p. 331.
11 Bełżec, Sobibor, Treblinka, p. 192.
12 Documents on the Holocaust, Selected Sources on the Destruction of the Jews of Germany and Austria, Poland and the Soviet Union, Yad Vashem, Jerusalem, 1981, Document no. 124.
13 Bryant, p. 55.
14 Hauptstaatsarchiv Stuttgart, police personnel file Christian Wirth.
15 *Ibid.* The special mission in Linz referred to here denotes his attachment to the euthanasia institute at Schloss Hartheim.
16 Tregenza manuscript, Christian Wirth—Architect of Aktion Reinhardt lecture, Brussels 3–4 November 2018.
17 Testimony of Hartheim stoker, Vinzenz Nohel, on 4 September 1945. Contained in Holocaust Controversies, p. 282.
18 Sereny, p. 54.
19 Tregenza manuscript, Christian Wirth—Architect of Aktion Reinhard lecture, Brussels 3–4 November 2018.
20 O'Neil, p. 118.
21 Affidavit of Dr Hans Bodo Gorgass, 23 February 1947, contained in Holocaust Controversies, p. 282.
22 Arad, p. 24.

23 *Ibid*, p. 183.
24 Der Dienskalender Heinrich Himmlers 1941–42, p523, note 77. Grothmann also confirms lunch was taken in the 'Airfield Restaurant' in BA Koblenz NS 19/1446, p. 22.
25 ZStL 208 AR-Z 252/59, Bełżec case, Statement by Erich Bauer, 7 December 1962.
26 BDC, Wirth SSO file, copy held in Yad Vashem archive (the original Wirth SSO file in Berlin is badly water damaged).
27 Nuremberg document USA 277.

## CHAPTER 12

1 holocausthistoricalsociety.org.uk/Richard Thomalla.
2 Arad, p. 40.
3 Description provided by local locksmith Stanislaw Kozak who was employed on the initial construction. Quoted on pp. 116-117 of O'Neil. Other witnesses state the gas feed pipes were below floor level.
4 O'Neil, p. 116.
5 *Ibid*, p. 187.
6 *Ibid*, pp. 187-188.
7 *Ibid*, p. 188.
8 Der Dienstkalender Heinrich Himmlers 1941–42, pp. 378-380.
9 *Ibid*, p. 381.
10 Arad, p. 69.
11 *Ibid*, p. 70.
12 *Ibid*, p. 70.
13 *Ibid*, pp. 70-71.
14 www.Spartacus-Educational.com/KurtGerstein.
15 Witness testimony from Alojzy Bereszowski and Viktor Skowronek; O'Neil, p. 120.
16 O'Neil, p. 173.
17 *Ibid*, p. 122.
18 Holocaust Controversies, p. 292.
19 *Ibid.*
20 *Ibid*, p. 293.
21 *Ibid*, p. 318.
22 *Ibid.*
23 *Ibid*, p. 319.
24 *Ibid*, p. 323.
25 *Ibid*, p. 324.
26 *Ibid.*
27 O'Neil, p. 179.
28 *Ibid*, p. 180; evidence of Heinrich Gley.

## CHAPTER 13

1 Holocaust Controversies, pp. 282-283.
2 *Ibid*, p. 283.
3 Bem, p. 49.
4 For an initial description of the camp, see Bem, p. 52.
5 Arad, pp. 191-192.
6 BBC TV Archives, Tom Bower, 19 August 1979, *'The Tracking and Freeing of a Nazi Killer'*.
7 This was the subject of much discussion at Stangl's trial. Stangl may, in fact, have secretly contributed to Nazi funds prior to the Anschluss. He wore the Old Fighter's chevron on his

tunic. See Sereny, pp. 32-34.
8 Sereny, p. 54.
9 *Ibid*, pp. 102-103.
10 See Sereny, pp. 108-109 for the differing versions of Stangl's first visit to Sobibor.
11 Sereny, p. 109.
12 *Ibid.*
13 Bem, pp. 59-60.
14 *Ibid*, p. 61.
15 Sereny, p. 110.
16 *Ibid*, p. 111.
17 Figures provided by the research of survivor Thomas Blatt.
18 Arad, p. 192.
19 Klee, Dressen, Riess, p. 232.
20 Sobiborinterviews.nl.
21 Arad, pp. 116-117, 193.
22 *Ibid*, p. 193.
23 *Ibid*, p. 77.
24 Burleigh, p. 188.
25 Klee, Dressen, Riess, p. 230.
26 Arad, pp. 188-189.

## CHAPTER 14

1 Chrostowski, pp. 25-26.
2 Alexsei Kolgushkin, a former Trawniki SS guard, made a statement on 24 September 1980, in the city of Rybinsk, regarding his service at the Treblinka Labour Camp.
3 Chrostowski, p. 31.
4 Arad, p. 87.
5 Klee, Dressen, Riess, p. 245.
6 Arad, p. 84.
7 *Ibid.*
8 *Ibid*, p. 91.
9 Sereny, p. 159.
10 Arad, p. 92.
11 Sereny, p. 160.
12 *Ibid*, p. 161.
13 www.HolocaustResearchProject.org.
14 Excerpt from the translated transcript of the interview of Franz Suchomel by Claude Lanzmann for his documentary film 'Shoah'. Held as part of the collections of USHMM. For Suchomel's observations of Christian Wirth, see Appendix XIII.
15 With thanks to the Axis History Forum.
16 The Höfle Telegram states a figure of 71355 for Treblinka, but this is an obvious typing error as the total figures combined reach 1,274,166. This indicates the correct figure to be 713,555 for Treblinka alone until 31 December 1942.
17 Arad, p. 186.
18 Franz Suchomel insists there were only eight gas chambers in this building.
19 Harrison, Muehlenkamp, Myers, Romanov, & Terry, p. 320.
20 *Ibid*, pp. 320-321.
21 The Jerusalem Post, The Changing Face of Memory: Who Defended the Warsaw Ghetto? By Moshe Arens, quoting comments by Jürgen Stroop in 1949.
22 Moczarski, pp. 148-149.

23 Chrostowski, p. 95.
24 Willy Mentz, born in Schönhagen on 30 April 1904, joined the NSDAP in 1932. He was a sawmill worker and milkman before joining a police detachment. In 1940, he was responsible for the cows and pigs at Grafeneck Euthanasia Centre. In 1941, was transferred to the Hadamar gassing facility, where he worked in the food garden until early summer 1942. In July 1942, Mentz was posted to Treblinka extermination camp and served there until it closed in November 1943. He worked at the Lazaret killing station and subsequently at Camp I as an overseer of the agricultural Sonderkommando. At Treblinka, Mentz was subordinate to SS-Unterscharführer August Miete. The Lazaret, a fake infirmary, was surrounded by a barbed-wire fence and was where the sick, old, wounded and troublesome new arrivals were taken directly from the ramp. The Lazaret displayed a Red Cross flag. Mentz wore a white doctor's coat for deceit. His victims were taken behind the barracks to the edge of an open pit where bodies were cremated. They were executed while looking into the inferno. Mentz shot thousands of Jews through the back of the neck and pushed their bodies into the flames. He was known as 'Frankenstein' by the prisoners, and was one of the most feared overseers.

## CHAPTER 15

1 Rieger, p. 74.
2 *Ibid*, p. 80.
3 Testimony of Rosa Benesch, 29 July 1965, held in the Michalsen file, BA Ludwigsburg.
4 Description of Globocnik given to Berndt Rieger in conversation. Rieger, p. 76.
5 BDC, Globocnik SSO file.
6 BDC, Globocnik RuSHA file.
7 *Ibid.*
8 Himmler Dienstkalender 1941–1942, p. 204.
9 BDC, Globocnik SSO file.
10 *Ibid.*
11 *Ibid.*
12 *Ibid.*
13 *Ibid.*
14 Himmler Dienstkalender 1941–1942, p. 545.
15 BDC, Globocnik SSO file.
16 Rickheim letter to Joseph Poprzeczny dated 15 April 1998.
17 BDC, Globocnik SSO file.
18 *Ibid.*
19 *Ibid.*
20 Ottokar Pieschel, Kp. Chef 1./Lw. Bau. Btl. 6/XII; transferred from Luftschutz-Ers.-Abt. 1 to Heimat-Nebel-Kp. 2/XII; 7.8.1943 transferred to LS.-Ers.-Abt. 1 Wurzen; 15.04.1943 Hptm. (d. R. z. V.); March 1944 Hauptmann. Courtesy of Gerhard Raiss. No record of Pieschel could be found in any SS-Dienstaltersliste.
21 BDC, Globocnik SSO file.

## CHAPTER 16

1 Polish underground newspaper, Samo Obrona, July 1943. Referred to in Rieger, p. 136.
2 BDC, Globocnik SSO file.
3 Poprzeczny, pp. 112-113.
4 Summary of a memorandum from Himmler to Globocnik dated 21 July 1941, BDC, Globocnik SSO file.
5 Quote presented in evidence at Nuremberg IMT. USHMM.

6 MA thesis by Karsten Schulz, '*Nationalsozialistische Nachkriegskonzeptionen für die eroberten Gebiete Osteuropas vom Januar 1940 bis zum Januar 1943*', Berlin Technical University Institute for Political Science, 1996.
7 www.opinie.wp.pl.
8 BDC, Wendler SSO file.
9 BDC, Globocnik SSO file.
10 National Archives, Kew. Interrogation of Sporrenberg, WO 208/4673.
11 *Ibid.*
12 *Ibid.*
13 *Ibid.*
14 *Ibid.*
15 *Ibid.*
16 Interrogation of Erich Muhsfeldt, 14 August 1947; Hauptstaatsarchiv Düsseldorf.
17 *Ibid.*

## CHAPTER 17

1 National Archives, Kew. Interrogation of Heinrich Wied, WO 309/521.
2 Nuremberg document NO 2714, Office of Chief Counsel for War Crimes, USA.
3 www.worldcourts.com/imt/eng/decisions/1947.11.03_United_States_v_Pohl.pdf.
4 Rieger, pp. 144-145.
5 *Ibid*, p. 142.
6 Di Gusto and Chiussi, p. 15.
7 BA Ludwigsburg, Michalsen file, testimony of Wilhelmine Trsek provided on 11 June 1964 and 27 April 1965. Reproduced in Rieger, p. 150.
8 Rieger, p. 144.

## CHAPTER 18

1 Poprzeczny, p. 343.
2 *Ibid*, p. 411 note 21.
3 Pucher, p. 133.
4 Testimony of Heinrich Gley at Münster hearing, 28 July 1967, courtesy of Darko Cafuta.
5 Miller, Schulz & McCanliss, pp. 411-412.
6 Di Giusto & Chiussi, p. 42.
7 Details from the report of the Staff Istra Odred partisan unit dated 1 June 1944. Courtesy of Michael Tregenza, Lublin.
8 Testimony of Franz Rum at Münster hearing, 11 July 1967, courtesy of Darko Cafuta.
9 Courtesy of Darko Cafuta, from original transcript of telegraph message. Bruno Coceani was the Police Prefect of Trieste.
10 *Ibid.*
11 Konrad Geng was the usual service driver for Christian Wirth. He was wounded in the partisan attack which succeeded in killing his boss. Following his recovery, Geng remained in Trieste and sometimes drove for Globocnik, escaping with him in 1945. There is evidence that Geng had assisted with the operation of the crematorium at San Sabba. After the war, he worked for the German Foreign Office and was even suggested to identify remains for reburial at Costermano war cemetery. Geng was known to be in Nancy in 1975, but his subsequent fate is unknown.
12 Rieger, p. 156.
13 *Ibid*, p. 157.
14 *Ibid*, p. 159.
15 Testimony of Laurentia Globocnik, 18 August 1964, held in the Michalsen file, BA Ludwigsburg.

16 Di Giusto & Chiussi, pp. 199-203.
17 Rieger, p. 159.
18 According to the interrogation report of Lerch and Michalsen, contained in NA Kew WO 204/13006, Rainer's staff fled from Trieste on 30 April 1945, and the staff of HSSPF Globocnik left the city on 1 May 1945. This is questionable, as Trieste was cut off by Allied forces in the night of 29–30 April 1945. Elements of Tito's troops entered the city after 30 April 1945, following a revolt that day of 3,500 volunteers of the Italian anti-fascist faction of the Comitato di Liberazione Nazionale (CNL) of don Marzari and Fonda Savio.
19 Testimony of Laurentia Globocnik, 18 August 1964, held in the Michalsen file, BA Ludwigsburg.

## CHAPTER 19

1 National Archives, Kew, WO 204/11505.
2 Hugo Herzog (born 26 January 1896) was Gauleiter of Carinthia from 1927 until 1933. He was appointed as *Kreisleiter* of Villach in 1943. He was interned at Wolfsberg until he was sentenced to two years at hard labour and the seizure of his entire assets in 1947. This was reduced on appeal. He died in Klagenfurt on 31 January 1971.
3 National Archives, Kew, WO 170/4622.
4 National Archives, Kew, Statement by Kenneth Hedley dated 4 January 1965, FO 371/179969.
5 Alexander Ramsay was a past Oxford University student and a former member of the London Metropolitan Police. He joined the Parachute Regiment and, in the spring of 1944, was a member of No. 6 Special Force. By May 1945, he was attached to V Corps 8th Army, assisting with the roundup of senior Nazis. Post-war, he became a Public Safety Officer in the British Military Administration in Graz. In 1947, he joined Radio Free Europe as a bureau chief in Hamburg, Brussels and Munich. He married Austrian student Edith Hahnemann in 1946; they had no children. He died on 1 April 1975, aged sixty-three. Peter Quarmby served with the South African Armoured Car Regiment and was on attachment to the 4th Hussars. Guy Wheeler was the adjutant of the 4th Hussars in Paternion, and with the CO on leave, it fell to him to authorise the raiding party. He decided to accompany the group. Edward Birkett was a member of Special Forces on attachment to the 4th Hussars. Kenneth Hedley was the deputy adjutant of the 4th Hussars in Paternion. Also in the arrest party were Provost Sergeant Sowler, Corporal Halstead, Lance-Corporals Lee and Oswald, plus other military policemen.
6 National Archives, Kew, FO 371/179969. Dr Leigh was unable to verify the corpse was that of Odilo Globocnik, but confirms that the prisoner died in his presence.
7 The war diary log lists eight names in Appendix A. Number 2 is 'Gruppenführer *der* SS in TRIESTE GLOVOCNIK [*sic.*]' who was clearly dead and not among them. The eighth prisoner was almost certainly Siegfried Kummerer.
8 National Archives Kew, war diary of the 4th (Queen's Own) Hussars, WO 170/4622; Imperial War Museum.
9 Photocopy of letter written by Brigadier Wheeler on 9 May 1990, a copy of which is in the possession of the author.
10 Williams, Himmler, pp. 150-151.
11 *Ibid*, p. 151.
12 Secretly taped conversation between Rainer and Uiberreither at CSDIC—Combined Services Detailed Interrogation Centre. National Archives, Kew, WO 204/11505 (1 SC/CSDIC/X 3); via Maurice Williams.
13 Independent on Sunday, 19 July 1992, pp. 10-14 (the newspaper replied to an enquiry that images not owned by them are not retained).

## CHAPTER 20

1 Lewi Stone is a Life Sciences professor at Tel Aviv University, and a professor of Biomathematics, RMIT University, Melbourne.
2 Arad, p. 101.
3 Gilbert, p. 402; Memo from Brack to Himmler, 23 July 1942, Nuremberg document NO-205.
4 Poprzeczny, p. 166.
5 Arad, p. 101.
6 *Ibid.*
7 *Ibid*, p. 103.
8 *Ibid*, p. 104.
9 Reinecke was sentenced to life imprisonment at the German High Command Trial in Nuremberg. He was released in 1954 and died on 10 October 1973.
10 Poprzeczny, p. 168.
11 Statement made by Georg Wippern in 1967 during an investigation into his wartime activities. Copy courtesy of Joseph Poprzeczny archive.
12 Poprzeczny archive.
13 Zentrale Stelle der Landesjustizverwaltungen (ZStL) 208 AR-Z 251/59: The Case Against Kurt Bolender et al, Sobibor Case, p. 703. Statement by Werner Dubois, 7 September 1961, Schwelm. In Tregenza, 'The Disappearance of SS-Hauptscharführer Lorenz Hackenholt', 2000.
14 Zentrale Stelle der Landesjustizverwaltungen (ZStL) 208 AR-Z 252/59, Bełżec Case, p190. Letter from the Ludwigsburg Central Office to the Police President of West Berlin, dated 5 November 1959.
15 *Ibid*, p. 193. Archive of the Berlin-Schöneberg Magistrates Court, 72/24 II 1061/53: Official Declaration of Death of Laurenzius Maria Hackenholt, dated 22 August 1953. Copy forwarded to the Ludwigsburg Central Office dated 23 November 1959.
16 ZStL 208 AR-Z 252/59, Bełżec Case, p. 1,370. Search Warrant No. 7 Gs 1116/61, dated 7 July 1961.
17 ZStL 208 AR-Z 74/60, Michalsen case, p. 9,280.
18 Siegfried Graetschus was killed on 14 October 1943 during the Sobibor uprising.
19 ZStL 208 AR-Z 252/59, Bełżec Case, p. 1,421. Statement by Kurt Franz on 14 September 1961 in Dusseldorf.
20 *Ibid,* p1365. Statement by Hans Girtzig on 18 July 1961 in Berlin.
21 *Ibid.*
22 *Ibid*, p. 1,386. Statement by Werner Dubois on 16 September 1961 in Schwelm.
23 *Ibid*, p. 1,512. Statement by Karl Schluch on 11 November 1961 in Kleve.
24 *Ibid*, p. 1,515.
25 *Ibid*, p. 1,511.
26 Landgericht Munich; Case Against Werner Dubois, p. 2,029. Statement by Werner Dubois on 15 September 1971 in Munich.
27 ZStL 208 AR-Z 251/59, Sobibor Case, p. 1,542. Statement by Erwin Lambert on 2 October 1962 in Stuttgart.
28 *Ibid.*
29 OKBL Ds. 1604/45—Zamość, The Death Camp at Bełżec, witness statements.
30 ZStL 208 AR-Z 74/60, Staff of the SS-*und Polizeifuhrer* Lublin, pp. 6,120-6,121.
31 ZStL 208 AR-Z 252/59, Bełżec Case, pp. 1,496-1,497. Statement by Ilse Hackenholt on 31 October 1961 in Sonthofen.
32 *Ibid*, p. 1,527. Statement by Willy Grossmann on 10 November 1961 in Erndtebrück.
33 *Ibid*, p. 1,469. Statement by Robert Juhrs on 11 November 1961 in Frankfurt-am-Main.
34 *Ibid*, p. 1,380. Statement by Karl Schiffner on 19 April 1963 in Salzburg.
35 *Ibid*, 208 AR-Z 251/59, Sobibor Case, p. 2,429. Extracts from the files of the State Prosecutor's Office in Munich, pertaining to the civil action against Ilse Hackenholt by the Social Security Court in Augsburg in 1962.

36 *Ibid*, 208 AR-Z 252/59, Bełżec Case, p. 1,386. Statement by Werner Dubois on 16 September 1961 in Schwelm.

37 *Ibid*, p. 1,527. Statement by Willy Grossmann on 9 November 1961 in Erndtebruck.

38 ZStL 208 AR-Z 251/59, Sobibor Case, and 208 AR-252/59, Bełżec Case. Report to the Senior State Prosecutor at the Regional Court in Munich, dated 16 August 1960. During a house search by police of the Hering's apartment at Sylvaner Weg 2, in Stuttgart-Fellbach, on 18 July 1961, in connection with the Bełżec Case, among other items there were found seven letters to Frau Hering from Heinrich Gley, and two photographs of Gley. The return addresses on the envelopes led to Gley's arrest in Münster. Also, p. 2,440. Helene Schubert (Hering), 2 October 1963, Stuttgart.

39 ZStL 208 AR-Z 251/59, Sobibor Case, p. 2,249. Helene Schubert, 3 August 1962, Waiblingen.

40 Statement by Theo Hackenholt in Gelsenkirchen, 1961. Wording in Tregenza manuscript 'The Disappearance of SS-Hauptscharführer Lorenz Hackenholt'.

41 The complete documented record of the West German police search for Lorenz Hackenholt in 1959–63 is contained in a file with the title: *Sonderakte Fahndung Hackenholt* (Special File on the Search for Hackenholt). According to the records of the Central Office in Ludwigsburg, three copies of this special file exist—at the Central Office, in File No. 208 AR-Z 74/60; at the Office of the State Prosecutor at the Regional Court in Hamburg, in File No. 147 Js 573/60; and in the Office of the State Prosecutor in the Regional Court in Munich I in File No. 110 Ks 3/64. Enquiries by the report author, Michael Tregenza, via the Central Office in Ludwigsburg, for access to these special files, however, produced interesting results. The Ludwigsburg file on Hackenholt was 'missing'; the Office of the State Prosecutor in Hamburg declared that their files are not open to the public, and in any case they have no such 'special file'; and in Munich the file 'could not be found'. Also 'missing' from the Munich archive was a photograph album compiled by the Munich Kriminalpolizei and entered in their Daily Duty Log under Item No. K 5462-202/60, which contained several photographs of Hackenholt. However, a photocopy of this album was later sent to the author from Munich. During research in Germany for his report, the author, Michael Tregenza, was warned by a State Prosecutor familiar with the case, and a police officer, 'not to attempt to look for Lorenz Hackenholt'.

42 Holocaust Education & Archive Research Team. Testimony of Bruno Israel, Chełmno Wachtmeister.

43 Law-Reports of Trials of War Criminals, The United Nations War Crimes Commission, Volume I, London, HMSO, 1947; case no. 4.

44 Yale Law School, the Avalon Project, Nuremberg Trial Proceedings, vol. 12, 23 April 1946. Testimony of Dr Josef Bühler.

45 Wiener Library, GB 1556 WL 526.

46 NA Kew, WO 208/4673, p. 4, Friedl Rau.

47 Website of the Polish Institute of National Remembrance.

## APPENDIX II

1 Jürgen (formerly Josef) Stroop, SSPF Warsaw.

2 Max Jesuiter, personal aide to the SSPF Warsaw.

# BIBLIOGRAPHY

## PUBLISHED SOURCES

Allen, M. T., *The Business of Genocide: The SS, Slave Labor, and the Concentration Camps* (University of North Carolina, 2005)
Aly, G., Chroust, P., and Pross, C., *Cleansing the Fatherland: Nazi Medicine & Racial Hygiene* (Johns Hopkins University Press, 1994)
Arad, Y., *Bełżec, Sobibor, Treblinka: The Operation Reinhard Death Camps* (Indiana University Press, 1987)
Bem, M., *Sobibor Extermination Camp 1942–1943* (Stichting Sobibor, 2015)
Blood, P. W., *Hitler's Bandit Hunters* (Potomac Books, 2008)
Breitman, R., *The Architect of Genocide* (The Bodley Head, 1991)
Browning, C. R., *Ordinary Men: Reserve Police Battalion 101 and the Final Solution in Poland*, revised edition (Harper Perennial, 2017)
Bryant, M. S., *Eyewitness to Genocide: The Operation Reinhard Death Camp Trials, 1955–1966* (University of Tennessee Press, 2014)
Buchheim, H., *Die SS-das Herrschaftinstrument, Befehl und Gerhorsam* (Walter, 1967)
Burleigh, M., *Death & Deliverance: Euthanasia in Germany 1900–1945* (Cambridge University Press, 1994)
Chrostowski, W., *Extermination Camp Treblinka* (Vallentine Mitchell, 2004)
Clay, C., and Leapman, M., *Master Race: the Lebensborn Experiment in Nazi Germany* (Coronet, 1995)
Davidson, E., *The Trial of The Germans* (University of Missouri Press, 1997)
Di Giusto, S., and Chiussi, T., *Globocnik's Men in Italy, 1943–45* (Schiffer, 2017)
Elste, A., *Kärntens braune Elite* (Hermagoras, 1997)
Fricke, D., *Die bürgerlichen Parteien in Deutschland* (Band II, Das Europäische Buch, 1968)
Gilbert, M., *The Holocaust: The Jewish Tragedy* (Collins, 1986); *Holocaust Journey* (Weidenfeld and Nicholson, 1993)
Goebbels, J., *Tagebücher 1924–1945* (Piper, 2003)
Goldhagen, D. J., *Hitler's Willing Executioners. Ordinary Germans & the Holocaust* (Little, Brown & Co., 1996)
Gryn, E., and Murawska-Gryn, Z., *Majdanek* (Panstwowe Muzeum na Majdanku, 1984)
Harvey, E., *Women and the Nazi East* (Yale University Press, 2003)
Hinz-Wessels, A., *Tiergartenstraße 4, Schaltzentrale der nationalsozialistischen Euthanasie-Mord* (Christoph Links Verlag, 2015)
Hohne, H., *Order of the Death's Head* (Coward-McCann, 1970)

Höss, R., *Death Dealer* (Da Capo Press, 1996); *Commandant of Auschwitz* (Pan Books, 1961, reprinted 1974)
Ingrao, C., *The Promise of the East: Nazi Hopes & Genocide* (Polity Press, 2019)
Klee, E., Dressen, W., and Riess, V., *Those Were the Days* (Hamish Hamilton, 1991)
Klee, E., *Euthanasie im NS-Staat* (Fischer, 2004); *Was sie taten—Was sie wurden: Ärzte, Juristen und andere Beteiligte am Kranken- oder Judenmord* (Fischer, 2004)
Longerich, P., *Holocaust: The Nazi Persecution & Murder of the Jews* (Oxford University Press, 2010)
Lukas, R., *Out of the Inferno* (University Press of Kentucky, 1989)
Marszalek, J., *Majdanek, The Concentration Camp in Lublin* (Interpress, 1986)
Mayer, A., *Why Did The Heavens Not Darken?* (Pantheon, 1988)
Medykowski, W. W., *Macht Arbeit Frei? German Economic Policy and Forced Labor of Jews in the General Government, 1939–1943* (Academic Studies Press, 2018)
Miller, M. D., and Schulz, A., *Gauleiter, vol. 1* (R. James Bender Publishing, 2012); *Leaders of the SS & German Police, vol. 2* (R. James Bender Publishing, 2015)
Miller, M. D., Schulz, A., and McCanliss, K., *Leaders of the SS & German Police, vol. 1* (R. James Bender Publishing, 2006)
Moczarski, K., *Conversations With An Executioner* (Prentice-Hall, 1981)
Novitch, M., *Sobibor, Martyrdom and Revolt* (Holocaust Library, 1980)
O'Neil, R., *Bełżec: Stepping Stone to Genocide* (JewishGen Inc., 2008)
Pohl, D., *Von der 'Judenpolitik' zum Judenmord* (Peter Lang, 1993)
Poprzeczny, J., *Odilo Globocnik: Hitler's Man in the East* (McFarland, 2004)
Pucher, S., *Odilo Globocnik: Kämpfer für den Anschluss, Vollstrecker des Holocaust* (Drava, 1997)
Rajca, C., and Wisniewska, A., *Majdanek Concentration Camp* (State Museum Majdanek, 1983)
Rashke, R., *Escape From Sobibor* (Michael Joseph, 1982)
Reitlinger, G., *The Final Solution* (Sphere Library, 1971)
Rieger, B., *Creator of Nazi Death Camps: The Life of Odilo Globocnik* (Vallentine Mitchell, 2007)
Sachslehner, J., *Odilo Globocnik, Hitlers Manager des Todes* (Styria Premium, 2014)
Schellenberg, W., *The Schellenberg Memoirs* (Andre Deutsch, 1956)
Schelvis, J., *Sobibor: A History of a Nazi Death Camp* (Berg, 2007)
Schulte, J. E., *Zwangsarbeit für die SS: Juden in der Ostindustrie GmbH* (Saur, 2000)
Schulz, A., and Wegmann, G., *Die Generale der Waffen-SS und der Polizei, vol. 1* (Biblio Verlag, 2003)
Sereny, G., *Into That Darkness* (Andre Deutsch, 1974)
Weale, A., *The SS: A New History* (Hachette Digital, 2010)
Williams, M., *Heinrich Himmler: A Photo History of the* Reichsführer-*SS* (Fonthill, 2014); *SS Elite: The Senior Leaders of Hitler's SS*, vols 1–3 (Fonthill, 2015–2017); *Heydrich: Dark Shadow of the SS* (Fonthill, 2018)

## OTHER SOURCES

Axis History Forum.
*Bełżec, Sobibor, Treblinka. Holocaust Denial and Operation Reinhard*, by Jonathan Harrison, Roberto Muehlenkamp, Jason Myers, Sergey Romanov, & Nicholas Terry. Holocaust Controversies 2011.
*Der Dienstkalender Heinrich Himmlers 1941-42.* Christians Verlag 1999.
Deutsches Rundfunkarchiv; Recording of Hitler speech before the Reichstag sitting 6 Oct 1939, translation by Kerstin Seemann.
*Die Tagerbücher von Joseph Goebbels.* Volume 1. Saur 2000.
*Documents in Nazi Conspiracy & Aggression.* Yale Law School, The Avalon Project.
*Documents on the Holocaust: Selected Sources on the Destruction of the Jews.* Edited by Yitzhak Arad, Israel Gutman, Abraham Margaliot, Lea Ben Dor, Steven T. Katz, 1999.
*Eichmann Interrogated: Transcript from the Archives of the Israeli Police.* Edited by Jochen von Lang & Claus Sibyll. Farrar, Straus & Giroux 1983.

Haaretz newspaper, Tel Aviv.
*Himmlers Graue Eminenz—Oswald Pohl und das Wirtschafts-Verwaltungshauptamt der SS.* Edited by Peter-Ferdinand Koch, Verlag Facta Oblita 1988.
*In Fear of the Frail: The Treatment of the Disabled at Eichberg Asylum for the Mentally Ill in Nazi Germany.* Thesis submitted by Markus Kreitmair, Simon Fraser University 1995.
Jagiellonian University of Krakow, Institute of History, 2018. Dissertation, Dr Jan Jacek Bruski, *The Ukrainian Central Committee 1940-1945: A Case of Collaboration in Nazi Occupied Poland.*
*Lublin Gazeta Wyborcza*, 27 November 2015. Article by Malgorzata Domagala.
Manuscript, *Christian Wirth—Architect of* Aktion *Reinhard*, by Michael Tregenza.
Manuscript, *Friedrich-Wilhelm Krüger*, by Professor Larry V. Thompson, US Naval Academy; provided by Joseph Poprzeczny.
Manuscript, *From Ostarbeiter to New Australians: A Post-War Western Australian Family—the Poprzecznys of Wyalkatchem, 1950-1970*, by Joseph Poprzeczny.
Manuscript, *Quantifying the Holocaust: Hyperintense kill rates during the Nazi genocide.* A study by Professor Lewi Stone of Tel Aviv University & the RMTI University of Melbourne. Reproduced in Science Advances, 2 January, 2019.
Manuscript, *The Disappearance of SS-Hauptscharführer Lorenz Hackenholt. A Report on the 1959-63 West German Police Search for Lorenz Hackenholt,* by Michael Tregenza.
*Nazi Mass Murder. A Documentary History of the Use of Poison Gas.* Edited by Eugen Kogon, Hermann Langbein & Adalbert Rückerl. Yale University Press 1993.
*Nazi Plunder*. Manuscript by Erwin H. Lerner, 2000.
Polish Information Centre.
Research Article in Science Advances, *Quantifying the Holocaust—Hyperintense Kill Rates During the Nazi Genocide*, by Lewi Stone 2019.
*The Austrian Connection: SS and Police Leader Odilo Globocnik and His Staff in the Lublin District.* Article by Bertrand Perz, Institute of Contemporary History, University of Vienna in Holocaust & Genocide Studies 29, no.3, 2015.
*The Death Camp Treblinka, A Documentary*. Edited by Alexander Donat. Holocaust Library 1979.
*The Speeches of Adolf Hitler, vol. 2.* Edited by Norman H. Baynes, Oxford University Press, 1942.
*Treblinka. Ein NS-Vernichtungslager im Rahmen der* Aktion *Reinhard*. A booklet by Manfred Burba, 1995.
*Typical Nazis. An Unusual Friendship and Sinister Roles.* Translation of original manuscript by Prof. Maurice Williams, 1997.
Wehrmacht Awards Forum.
Wikipedia.org
www.holocausthistoricalsociety.org.uk
www.nizkor.org
www.sobiborinterviews.nl
www.spartacus-educational.com
www.teatrnn.pl

## ARCHIVES

Archives of the 4th (Queen's Own) Hussars, Warwick.
Author's archive.
Bayerisches Staatsarchiv, Munich.
Bayerisches Staatsbibliothek, Munich.
Bundesarchiv, Berlin-Lichterfelde (previously the BDC—Berlin Document Centre, US Mission).
Bundesarchiv, Freiburg (Militärarchiv).
Bundesarchiv, Koblenz.
Bundesarchiv, Ludwigsburg.

Deutsches Rundfunkarchiv, Franfurt am Main.
Imperial War Museum, London and Duxford.
Institut für Zeitgeschichte, Munich.
Joseph Poprzeczny archive.
Michael Tregenza archive.
Osrodek 'Brama Grodska—Teatr NN', Lublin.
Polin Museum, Warsaw.
Politische Archiv, Auswärtiges Amt, Berlin.
Standesamt Paternion.
Stanisław Hantz eV educational institution, Kassel.
State Archives, Lublin.
UK National Archives, Kew (formerly the Public Records Office).
United States Holocaust Memorial Museum, Washington DC.
Wiener Library, London.
Yad Vashem, Jerusalem.
Yivo Institute for Jewish Research, New York.

The Hamburg-Amerika passenger ship *St Louis* anchored off Malecon in Havana.

Via Guilia, Trieste in 1900.

Globocnik's birthplace in Via Guilia as it appeared in 2007.

The Church of San Vivanni Decollato, location of Globocnik's baptism into the Catholic faith on 19 July 1904.

The young baby was baptised before this altar.

Piazza della Caserma in 1909.

Via Guglielmo Marconi 36. In 1913, this building was Via Molin Grande 42.

The Globocnik family lived on the fourth floor.

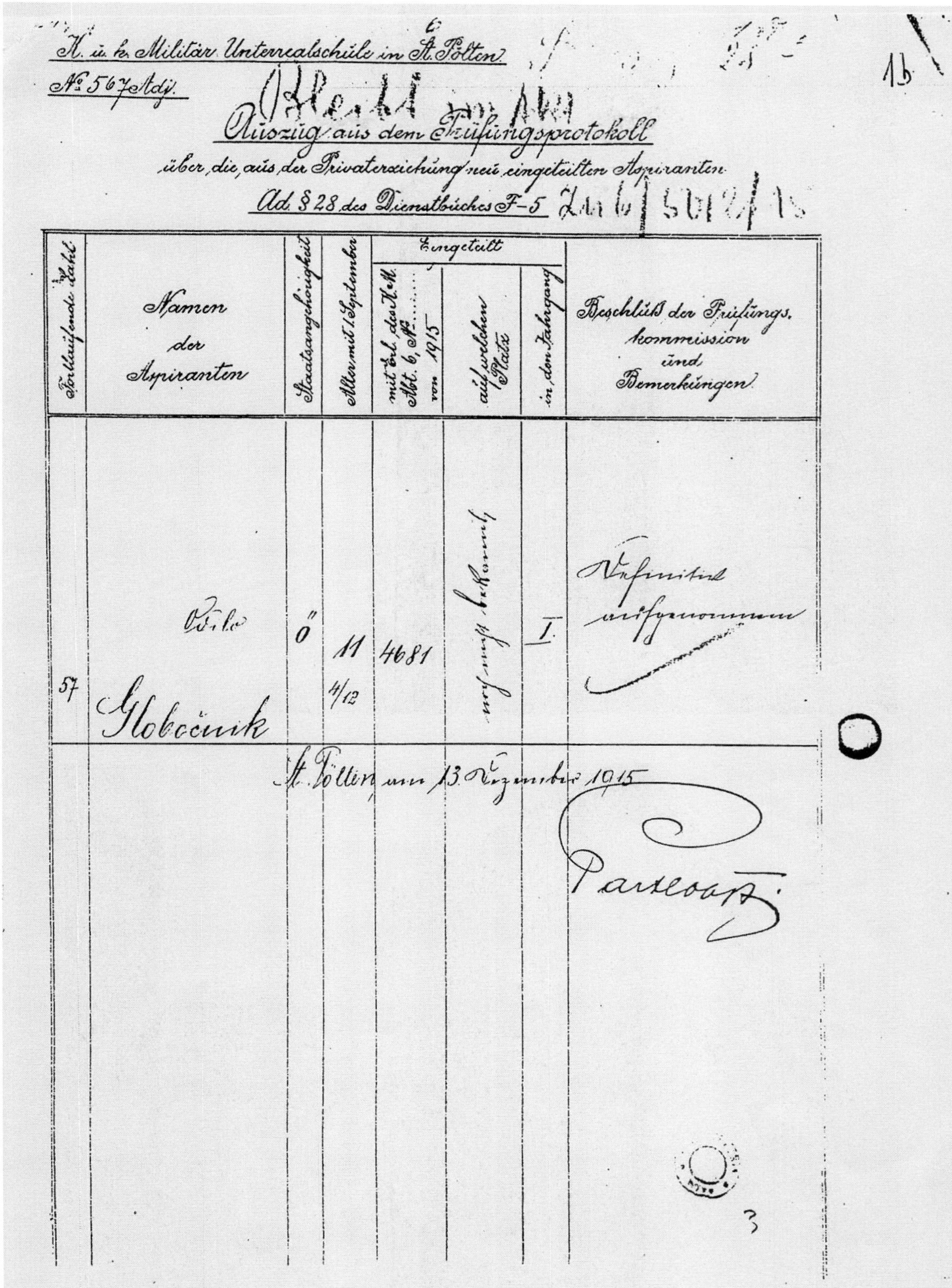

K. u. k. Militär Unterrealschule in St. Pölten

No 567 Adj.

Auszug aus dem Prüfungsprotokoll

über die aus der Privaterziehung neu eingeteilten Aspiranten

Ad. § 28 des Dienstbuches F-5

| Fortlaufende Zahl | Namen der Aspiranten | Staatsangehörigkeit | Alter mit 1. September | Eingeteilt: mit Erl. des K.M. Abt. 6, Nr. ... von 1915 | Eingeteilt: auf welchen Platz | Eingeteilt: in den Jahrgang | Beschluss der Prüfungskommission und Bemerkungen |
|---|---|---|---|---|---|---|---|
| 57 | Odilo Globočnik | Ö | 11 4/12 | 4681 | [illegible] | I. | Definitiv aufgenommen |

St. Pölten, am 13. Dezember 1915

[illegible]

Student Odilo Globocnik's entry in the Military School at St Pölten.

*Left:* The Military Cadet School at St Pölten.

*Below:* Globocnik's first school report at St Pölten. Out of fifty-two students, he attained fifth place. By his third year, he was seventh out of forty-nine students and was considered a very capable student.

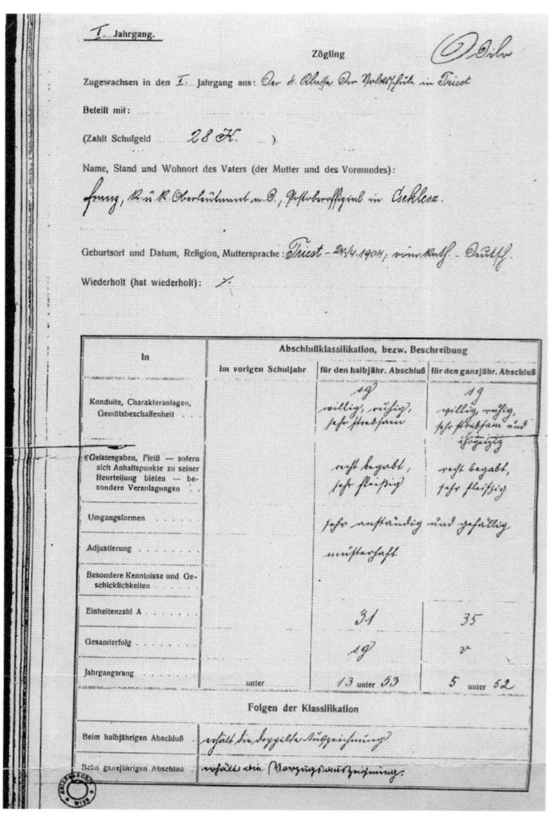

I. Jahrgang.

Zögling Odilo

Zugewachsen in den I. Jahrgang aus: der 4. Klasse der Volksschule in Triest

Beteilt mit:

(Zahlt Schulgeld 28 K.)

Name, Stand und Wohnort des Vaters (der Mutter und des Vormundes):

Franz, k. u. k. Oberleutnant a. D., Postoberoffizial in Csekless.

Geburtsort und Datum, Religion, Muttersprache: Triest – 24/4. 1904; röm.-kath. – deutsch.

Wiederholt (hat wiederholt): /

| In | Abschlußklassifikation, bezw. Beschreibung | | |
|---|---|---|---|
| | im vorigen Schuljahr | für den halbjähr. Abschluß | für den ganzjähr. Abschluß |
| Konduite, Charakteranlagen, Gemütsbeschaffenheit | | [illegible] | [illegible] |
| Geistesgaben, Fleiß — sofern sich Anhaltspunkte zu seiner Beurteilung bieten — besondere Veranlagungen | | [illegible] | [illegible] |
| Umgangsformen | | [illegible] | |
| Adjustierung | | [illegible] | |
| Besondere Kenntnisse und Geschicklichkeiten | | | |
| Einheitenzahl A | | 31 | 35 |
| Gesamterfolg | | [illegible] | [illegible] |
| Jahrgangsrang | unter | 13 unter 53 | 5 unter 52 |

Folgen der Klassifikation

| | |
|---|---|
| Beim halbjährigen Abschluß | [illegible] |
| Beim ganzjährigen Abschluß | [illegible] |

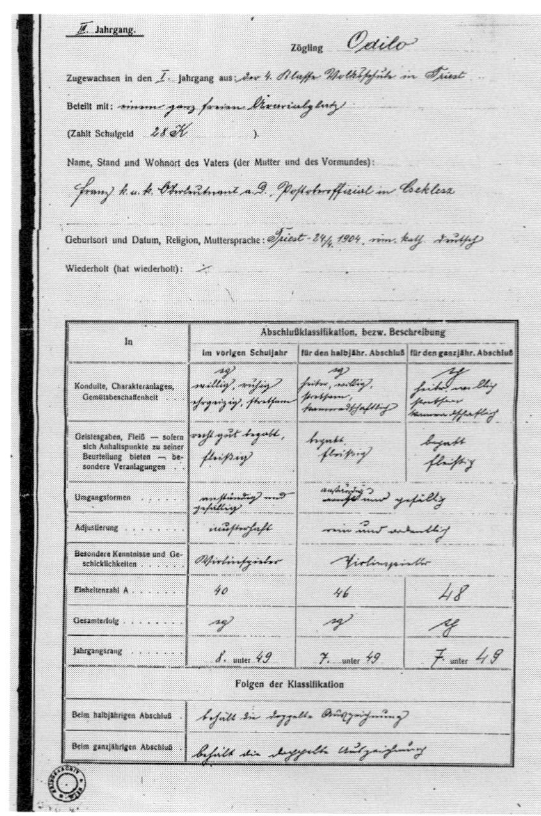

III. Jahrgang.

Zögling Odilo

Zugewachsen in den I. Jahrgang aus: der 4. Klasse der Volksschule in Triest

Beteilt mit: [illegible]

(Zahlt Schulgeld 28 K.)

Name, Stand und Wohnort des Vaters (der Mutter und des Vormundes):

Franz, k. u. k. Oberleutnant a. D., Postoberoffizial in Csekless

Geburtsort und Datum, Religion, Muttersprache: Triest – 24/4. 1904. röm. kath. deutsch

Wiederholt (hat wiederholt): /

| In | Abschlußklassifikation, bezw. Beschreibung | | |
|---|---|---|---|
| | im vorigen Schuljahr | für den halbjähr. Abschluß | für den ganzjähr. Abschluß |
| Konduite, Charakteranlagen, Gemütsbeschaffenheit | [illegible] | [illegible] | [illegible] |
| Geistesgaben, Fleiß — sofern sich Anhaltspunkte zu seiner Beurteilung bieten — besondere Veranlagungen | [illegible] | [illegible] | [illegible] |
| Umgangsformen | [illegible] | [illegible] | |
| Adjustierung | [illegible] | [illegible] | |
| Besondere Kenntnisse und Geschicklichkeiten | [illegible] | [illegible] | |
| Einheitenzahl A | 40 | 46 | 48 |
| Gesamterfolg | [illegible] | [illegible] | [illegible] |
| Jahrgangsrang | 8. unter 49 | 7. unter 49 | 7. unter 49 |

Folgen der Klassifikation

| | |
|---|---|
| Beim halbjährigen Abschluß | [illegible] |
| Beim ganzjährigen Abschluß | [illegible] |

*Right:* Anna Globocnik writes to the Post Direction in Vienna on 15 December 1918. She gives the family address as Getriedegasse 3 in Klagenfurt, Austria.

*Below:* Franz Globocnik addresses a letter to the Post Direction in Vienna on 6 February 1919 detailing his status.

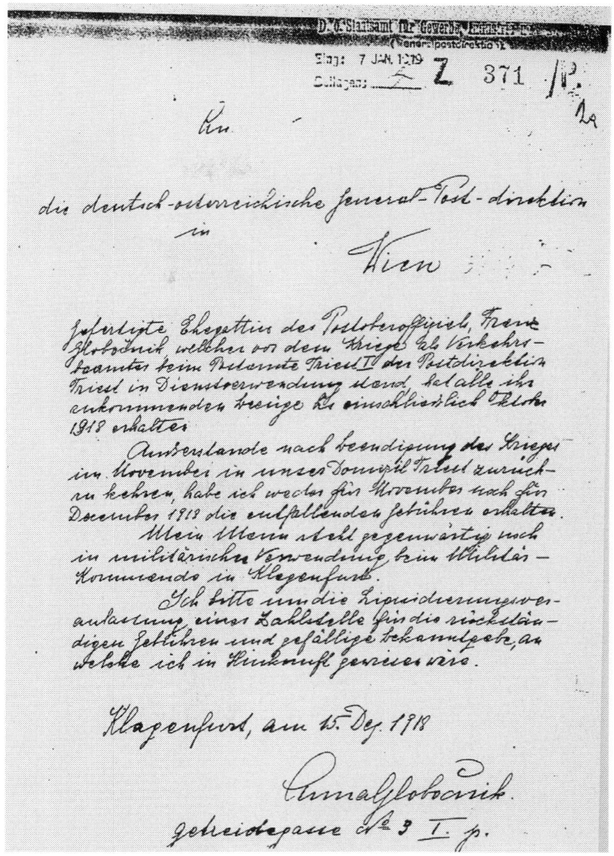

D. ö. Staatsamt für Gewerbe, Industrie ...
(Generalpostdirektion)
Eing: 7 JAN 1919
Beilagen: Z. 371 /P.

2a

An

die deutsch-österreichische General-Post-direktion
in
Wien

Gefertigte Ehegattin des Postoberoffizials Franz Globocnik welcher vor dem Kriege als Verkehrsbeamter beim Postamte Triest II der Postdirektion Triest in Dienstverwendung stand, hat alle ihr zukommenden Bezüge bis einschließlich Oktober 1918 erhalten.

Außerstande nach Beendigung des Krieges im November in unser Domizil Triest zurückzukehren, habe ich weder für November noch für December 1918 die entfallenden Gebühren erhalten.

Mein Mann steht gegenwärtig noch in militärischer Verwendung beim Militär-Kommando in Klagenfurt.

Ich bitte um die Liquidierungsveranlassung einer Zahlstelle für die rückständigen Gebühren und gefällige Bekanntgabe, an welche ich in Hinkunft gewiesen wäre.

Klagenfurt, am 15. Dez. 1918

Anna Globocnik

Getreidegasse No 3 I. p.

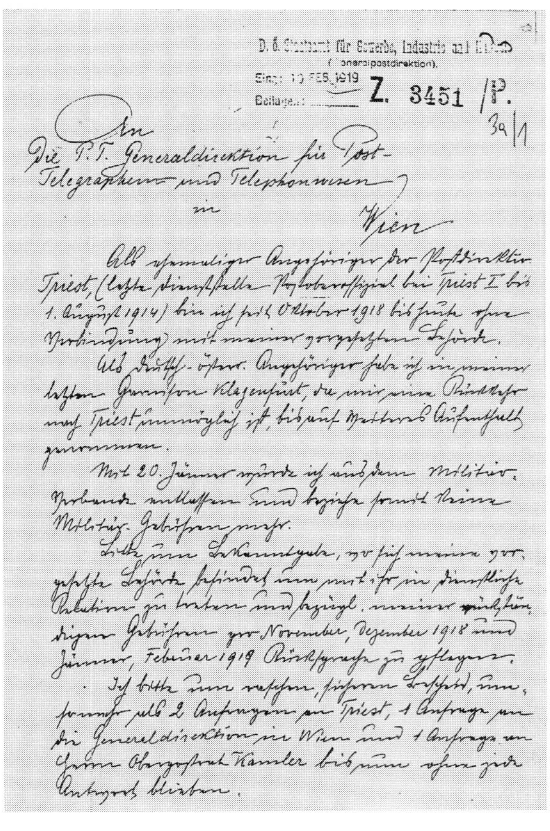

D. ö. Staatsamt für Gewerbe, Industrie und Handel
(Generalpostdirektion).
Eing: 10 FEB 1919
Beilagen: Z. 3451 /P.

39/1

An
Die P.T. Generaldirektion für Post- Telegraphen- und Telephonwesen
in
Wien

Als ehemaliger Angehöriger der Postdirektion Triest, (letzte Dienststelle Postoberoffizial bei Triest I bis 1. August 1914) bin ich seit Oktober 1918 bis heute ohne Verbindung mit meiner vorgesetzten Behörde.

Als deutsch-österr. Angehöriger habe ich in meiner letzten Garnison Klagenfurt, da mir eine Rückkehr nach Triest unmöglich ist, bis auf Weiteres Aufenthalt genommen.

Mit 20. Jänner wurde ich aus dem Militär-Verbande entlassen und beziehe somit keine Militär-Gebühren mehr.

Bitte um Bekanntgabe, wo sich meine vorgesetzte Behörde befindet um mit ihr in dienstliche Relation zu treten und bezügl. meiner rückständigen Gebühren pro November, Dezember 1918 und Jänner, Februar 1919 Rücksprache zu pflegen.

Ich bitte um rasche, sichere Antwort, um, zumal als 2 Anfragen an Triest, 1 Anfrage an die Generaldirektion in Wien und 1 Anfrage an Herrn Oberpostrat Kamler bis nun ohne jede Antwort blieben.

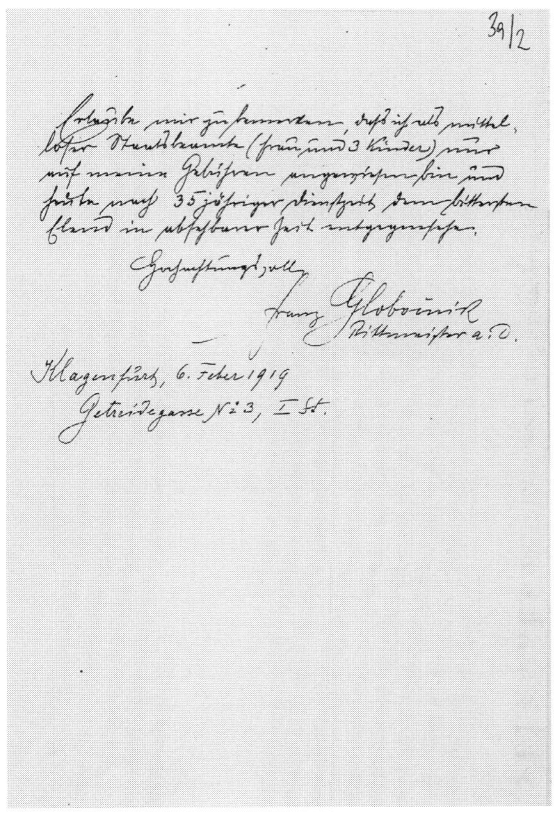

39/2

Erlaube mir zu bemerken, daß ich als mittelloser Staatsbeamter (Frau und 3 Kinder) nur auf meine Gebühren angewiesen bin und heute nach 35jähriger Dienstzeit dem bittersten Elend in absehbarer Zeit entgegensehe.

Hochachtungsvoll

Franz Globocnik
Rittmeister a.D.

Klagenfurt, 6. Feber 1919
Getreidegasse No 3, I St.

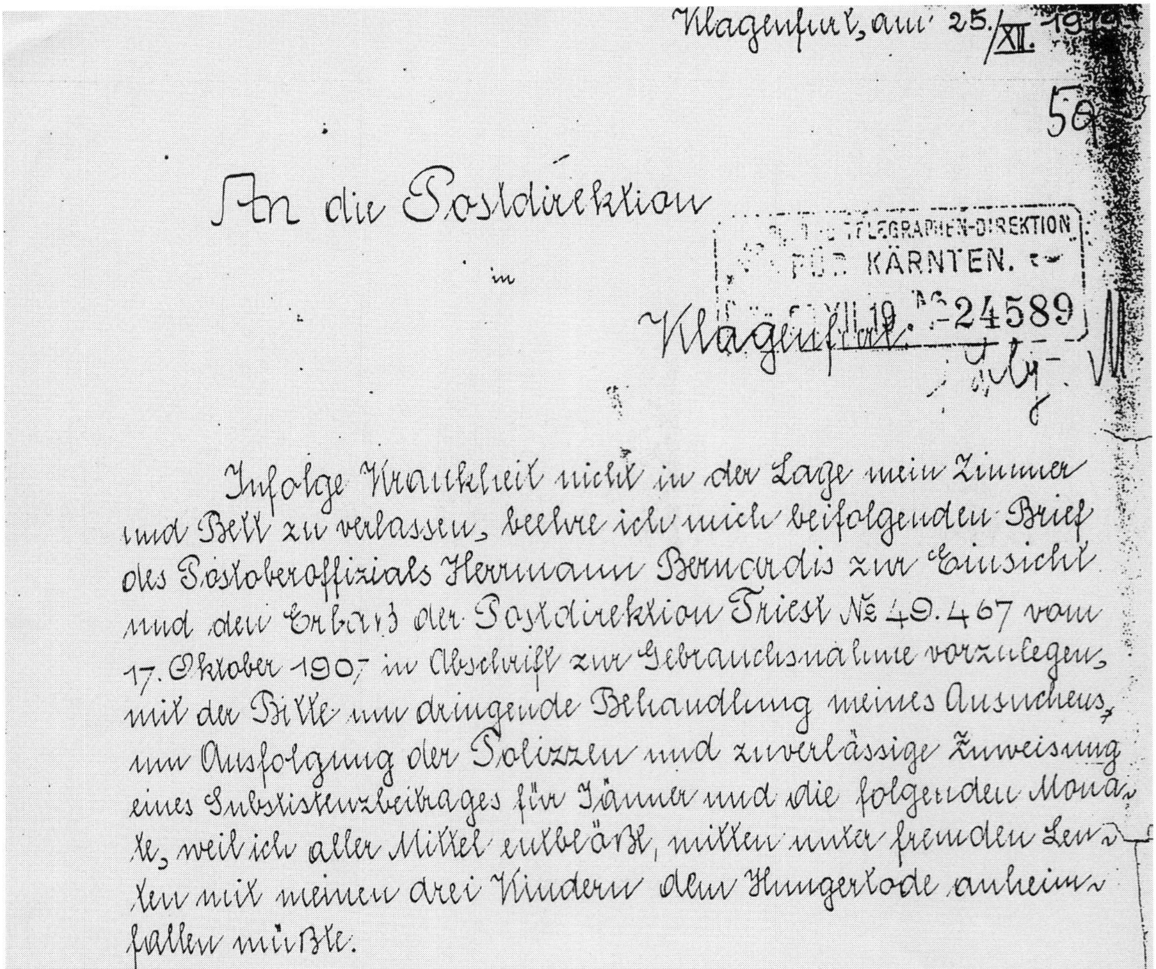

Klagenfurt, am 25./XII. 1919

59

An die Postdirektion

in

Klagenfurt.

TELEGRAPHEN-DIREKTION FÜR KÄRNTEN. XII.19 24589

Infolge Krankheit nicht in der Lage mein Zimmer und Bett zu verlassen, beehre ich mich beifolgenden Brief des Postoberoffizials Hermann Bernardis zur Einsicht und den Erlass der Postdirektion Triest № 49.467 vom 17. Oktober 1907 in Abschrift zur Gebrauchsnahme vorzulegen, mit der Bitte um dringende Behandlung meines Ansuchens, um Ausfolgung der Polizzen und zuverlässige Zuweisung eines Substistenzbeitrages für Jänner und die folgenden Monate, weil ich aller Mittel entbehre, mitten unter fremden Leuten mit meinen drei Kindern dem Hungertode anheimfallen müsste.

Nachdem der Akt № 49.467 für mich ein Wertpapier und die Sicherheit für die bei der Postdirektion in Triest deponierten Polizzen ist, bitte ich vielmals mir eine Empfangsbestätigung zukommen zu lassen.

Hochachtungsvoll

Anna Globočnik

Post-Ober-Officialswitwe

Getreidegasse № 3

Following the death of her husband, Anna Globocnik pleads for financial support from the postal service for her and her three children on Christmas Day 1919.

Getriedegasse 3, Klagenfurt. The Globocniks lived on the first floor.

The entrance to Getriedegasse 3.

The Café Lerch as it appears today.

The Villa Michner in Krumpendorf in the 1920s.

The Technical High School in Klagenfurt.

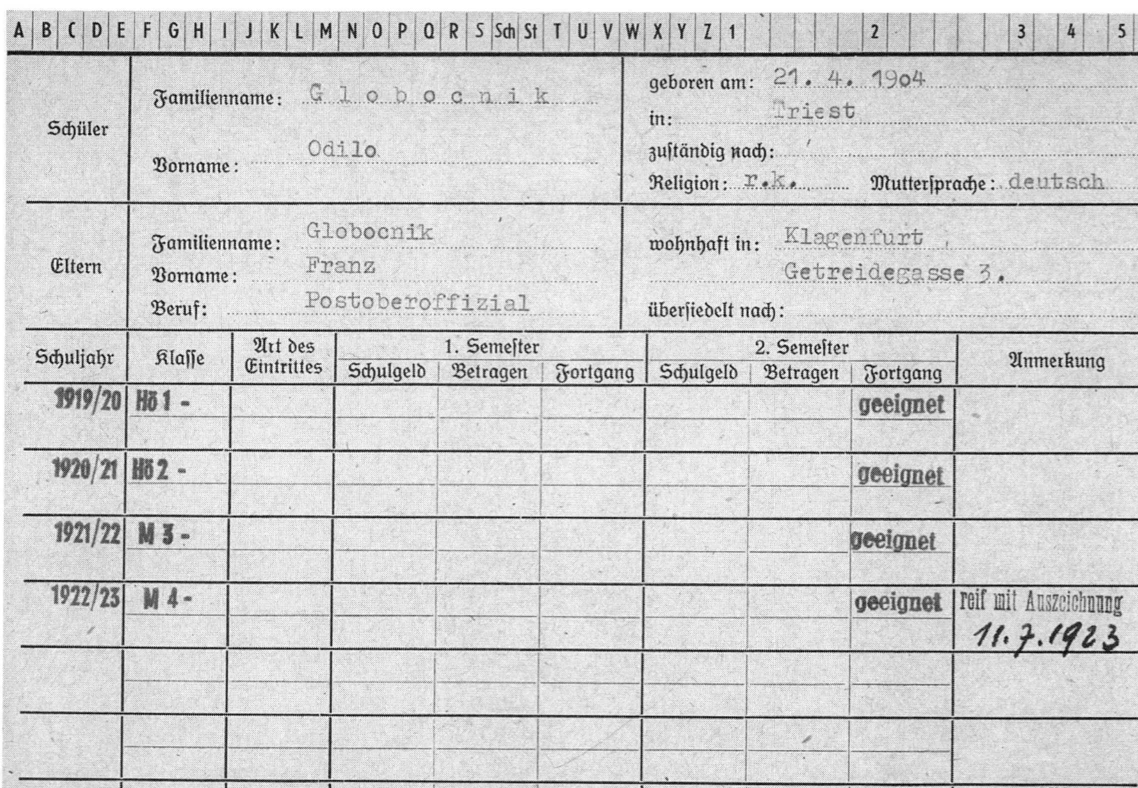

A B C D E F G H I J K L M N O P Q R S Sch St T U V W X Y Z 1 2 3 4 5

**Schüler** — Familienname: Globocnik; Vorname: Odilo
geboren am: 21. 4. 1904; in: Triest; zuständig nach: ; Religion: r.k.; Muttersprache: deutsch

**Eltern** — Familienname: Globocnik; Vorname: Franz; Beruf: Postoberoffizial
wohnhaft in: Klagenfurt, Getreidegasse 3.; übersiedelt nach:

| Schuljahr | Klasse | Art des Eintrittes | 1. Semester | | | 2. Semester | | | Anmerkung |
|---|---|---|---|---|---|---|---|---|---|
| | | | Schulgeld | Betragen | Fortgang | Schulgeld | Betragen | Fortgang | |
| 1919/20 | Hö 1 - | | | | | | | geeignet | |
| 1920/21 | Hö 2 - | | | | | | | geeignet | |
| 1921/22 | M 3 - | | | | | | | geeignet | |
| 1922/23 | M 4 - | | | | | | | geeignet | reif mit Auszeichnung 11.7.1923 |
| | | | | | | | | | |
| | | | | | | | | | |

CPS 3954-46

Technical student Globocnik's report card, indicating his annual suitability to progress to the following semester and his final qualification on 11 July 1923 with distinction.

The central police station in Klagenfurt.

The police file mugshots of Odilo Globocnik.

*Above left:* The young Austrian poet, Ingeborg Teuffenbach. Globocnik was a witness at her marriage to Heinz Capra in 1937.

*Above right:* A young Ernst Lerch.

Another of Globocnik's early associates was Reinhold von Mohrenschildt.

*Clockwise from top left*:

Ebba von Mohrenschildt (married name Natter, then Skreiner).

Hilde von Mohrenschildt (married name Hansemann).

The Carinthian staunch anti-Slovenia and close ally of Globocnik's Austrian-German beliefs, Alois Maier-Kaibitsch, who later held the rank of SS-Standartenführer.

*Above left:* The firm logo of Kärtner Wasserkraftwerke AG, Globocnik's new employer from 1923.

*Above right:* Globocnik's employer, Robert Rapatz.

Globocnik was employed on this 1924 KÄWAG construction at Forstsee, typical of the type of project that occupied the young engineer.

*Above left:* Bishop Adam Hefter, the unwitting courier used by Globocnik to carry explosives to illegal Austrian Nazis.

*Above right:* Villa Oblasser, Krumpendorf in the 1920s. Globocnik used this house as an undercover base.

*Above left:* The interior of Futterweit's jewellery shop following the bomb attack. The bomb exploded outside the premises, shattering the glass door and window, killing Futterweit, seriously injuring a passer-by, and showering the assistant and customer inside with glass fragments.

*Above right:* Futterweit lies dead, killed instantly by the explosion.

*Above left:* Max Grillmayr, Globocnik's co-conspirator.

*Above right:* Globocnik was arrested in late August 1935 in this building on the second floor at Wiedner Hauptstrasse 59, in Vienna.

Globocnik stands at far right, with Friedl Rainer second from left.

Lydia Globocnik, Rainer, and Globocnik watch a garden table tennis game.

Sachslehner identifies the woman on the far left as a Globocnik sister. However, she bears little or no resemblance to Erika Globocnik. It is more likely that this is Greta Michner, Globocnik's ever-present fiancée at this time. Ada Rainer is standing on the bench at the rear. Lydia Globocnik is laughing at the centre of the group, as Friedl Rainer reads something amusing.

Erika Globocnik.

*Left*: Josef Bürckel. *Right*: Hubert Klausner.

Arthur Seyss-Inquart.

*Clockwise from top left:*

Odilo Globocnik worked behind the scenes to bring about the inclusion of Austria in the German Reich under the Nazis.

During the attempted coup in July 1934, former athlete Felix Rinner occupied the government building at the head of a contingent of SS men from Standarte 89.

Franz Hueber, Hitler's choice for Austrian foreign minister.

This photo of Globocnik appeared in the Austrian issue of the *Völkischer Beobachter* on his birthday, 21 April 1938.

Josef Bürckel (right) addresses his cabinet in Vienna. Seated (bottom right) is Friedrich Rainer in SS-Standartenführer uniform. On the left stands SS-Brigadeführer Dr Ernst Kaltenbrunner. Seyss-Inquart and Glaise-Horstenau stand attentively (fourth and fifth from right) in the background.

Nr. 143 Wien, Mittwoch Neues Wiener Tagblatt 25. Mai 1938 3

# Die Gauleiter der Ostmark

August Eigruber, Oberdonau.

Odilo Globotschnigg, Wien.
Aufn.: Ostmark-Bilderdienst, Wien.

Dr. Hugo Jury, Niederdonau.

Franz Hofer, Tirol-Vorarlberg.

Hubert Klausner, Kärnten.

Dr. Friedl Rainer, Salzburg.

Dr. Siegfried Uiberreither, Steiermark.

Alle Aufnahmen: Weltbild, Wien.

A news report of the new Austrian Gauleiter.

Three stills from a film taken at an airfield on the arrival of Josef Bürckel. Globocnik in raincoat. In the first, to his left, appears to be Franz Kutschera.

The new Gauleiter of Vienna, party member Odilo Globocnik. Rewarded at last.

SS-Standartenführer Odilo Globocnik.

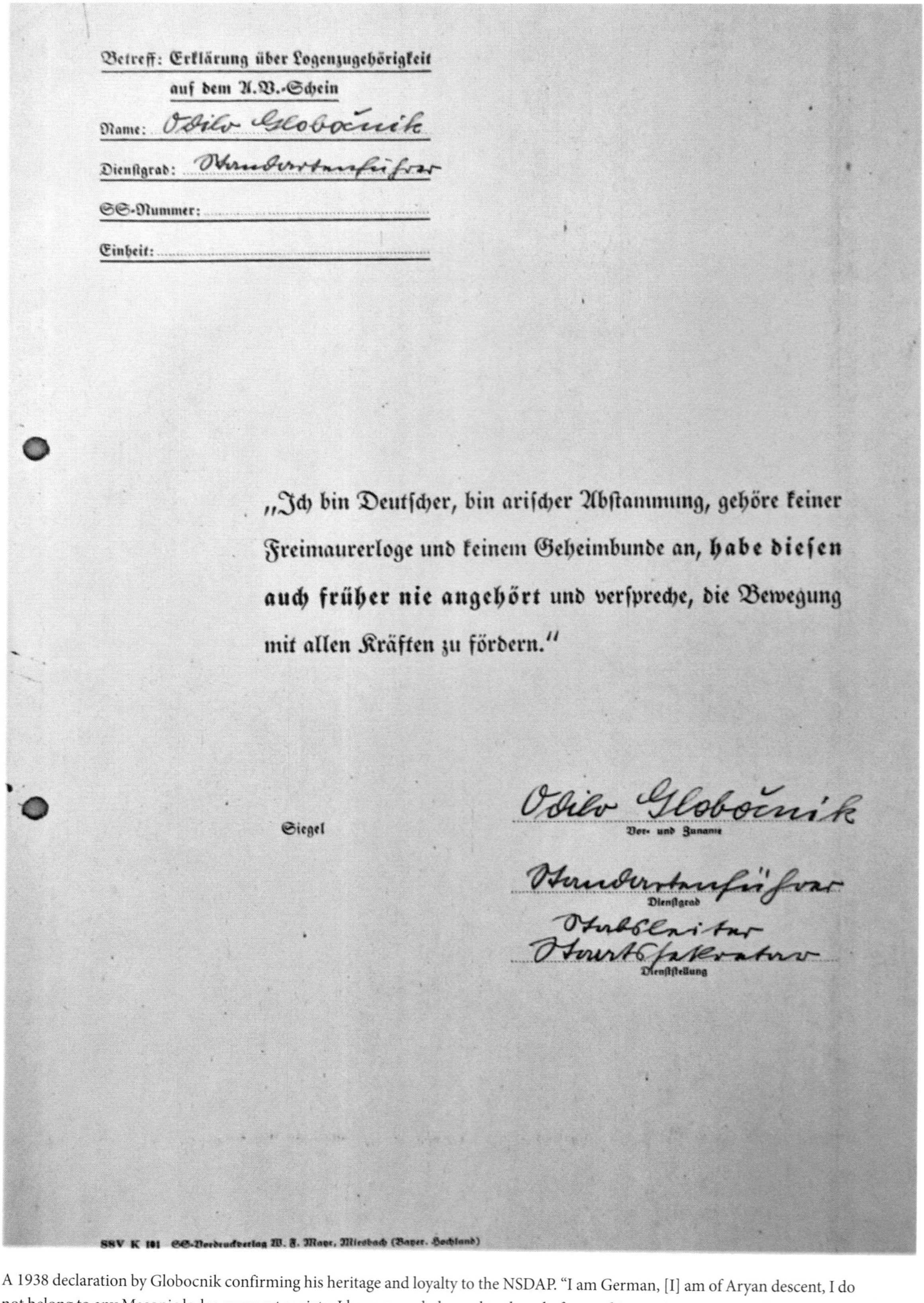

Betreff: Erklärung über Logenzugehörigkeit
auf dem A.V.-Schein

Name: Odilo Globocnik

Dienstgrad: Standartenführer

SS-Nummer:

Einheit:

„Ich bin Deutscher, bin arischer Abstammung, gehöre keiner Freimaurerloge und keinem Geheimbunde an, **habe diesen auch früher nie angehört** und verspreche, die Bewegung mit allen Kräften zu fördern."

Siegel

Odilo Globocnik
Vor- und Zuname

Standartenführer
Dienstgrad

Stabsleiter
Staatssekretär
Dienststellung

SSV K 101 SS-Vordruckverlag W. F. Mayr, Miesbach (Bayer. Hochland)

A 1938 declaration by Globocnik confirming his heritage and loyalty to the NSDAP. "I am German, [I] am of Aryan descent, I do not belong to any Masonic lodge or secret society, I have never belonged to them before and I promise to support the movement with all my might." He signs as a Standartenführer.

The new mayor of Vienna, Hermann Neubacher.

Seyss-Inquart and Gauleiter Globocnik did not see eye-to-eye.

Globocnik looking down at Rudolf Hess and Seyss-Inquart. Behind him is Fridolin Glass.

The Gauleiter (centre) entertains the Reichsführer-SS at a celebration of the martyrs of the July 1934 Putsch.

Gauleiter Globocnik in front of the memorial for the martyrs of the July 1934 Putsch.

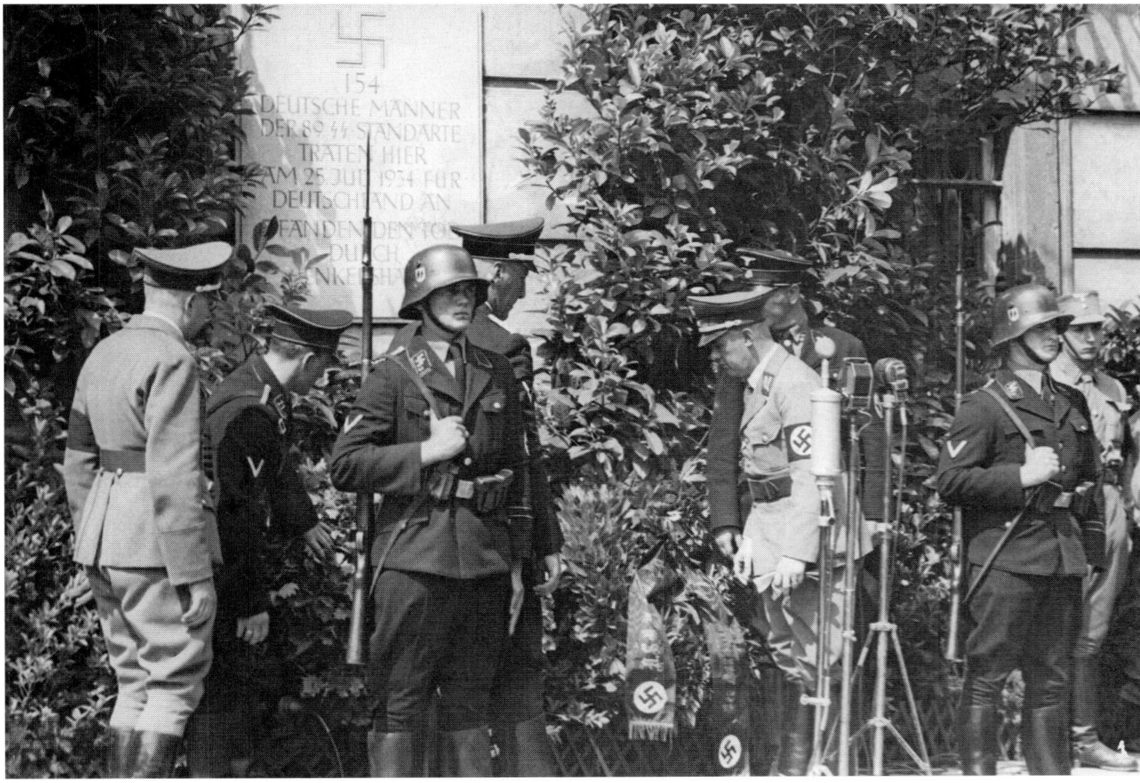


Kaltenbrunner and Globocnik lay wreaths to the men of 89. SS-Standarte executed for their part in the attempted coup.

Seyss-Inquart addresses the crowd. Globocnik stands solemnly at far right.

The memorial ceremony at the location of the execution.

On the fourth anniversary of the July Putsch, Gauleiter Globocnik attends the massive street ceremony held to mark the first celebration under Nazi rule. Seated in the rear of the car is believed to be Paul Gasser. Since the previous month, Gasser was the personal referent and adjutant of Gauleiter Globocnik.

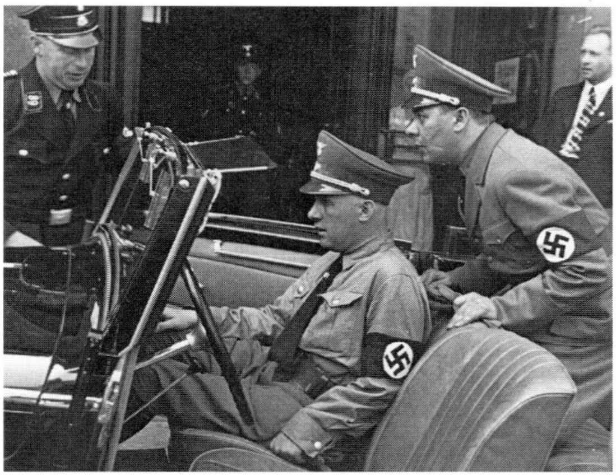

Globocnik in his car.

SS-Oberführer Josef Fitzthum with Globocnik in the background.

Globocnik greets Josef Fitzthum. On the left, in party uniform, is Erwin Rösener.

The Gauleiter salutes the march past from his car. Note the female official photographer crouching to obtain a good shot.

*Above:* Another angle of the same event.

*Right:* The Gauleiter mixes with the marchers.

Globocnik shakes hands with an 'old fighter'.

As the crowd stands around, Globocnik is deep in conversation in the foreground (with left hand raised to his head).

An aerial shot of the Gauleiter in discussion. To the right is the same female photographer.

A distance shot of Globocnik taking the salute from his car. In the background is the Vienna City Hall.

An off-guard moment as the Gauleiter adjusts his trousers.

SS-Standartenführer Globocnik saluting in Vienna. A still frame from a movie.

*Above left:* Globocnik, in Gauleiter uniform, stands between Fridolin Glass and Josef Bürckel. Far left is Josef Fitzthum, next to Herbert Becker.

*Above right:* Globocnik in civilian clothes, with Erich Hilgenfeldt.

Globocnik (left, foreground) with Reinhard Heydrich and Kurt Daluege. Standing is Glaise-Horstenau.

*Above left:* During a visit to Vienna, Rudolf Hess greets onlookers. Following are Globocnik, Klausner, and Bürckel.

*Above right:* Hess salutes Hitler Youth columns. Globocnik is second from left, with Bürckel in his signature light raincoat next to Klausner in black SS-Oberführer uniform.

At an event for Deutschen Arbeitsfront. *Left to right*: Seyss-Inquart, Bürckel, Kaltenbrunner, and Globocnik.

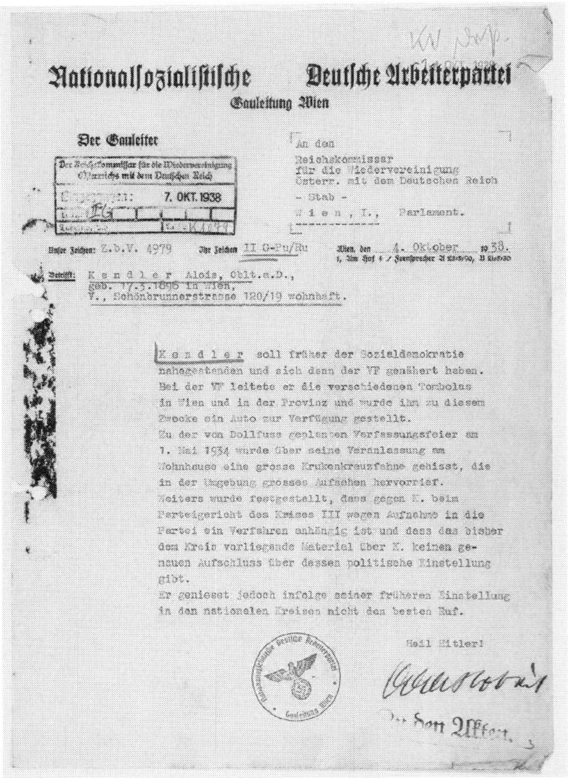

Nationalsozialistische Deutsche Arbeiterpartei
Gauleitung Wien

Der Gauleiter

Der Reichskommissar für die Wiedervereinigung Österreichs mit dem Deutschen Reich
7. OKT. 1938

An den
Reichskommissar
für die Wiedervereinigung
Österr. mit dem Deutschen Reich
- Stab -
W i e n , I., Parlament.

Unser Zeichen: Z.b.V. 4979 Ihr Zeichen II G-Pu/Ru Wien, den 4. Oktober 1938.
I, Am Hof 4 / Fernsprecher

Betrifft: K e n d l e r Alois, Oblt.a.D., geb. 17.3.1896 in Wien, V., Schönbrunnerstrasse 120/19 wohnhaft.

K e n d l e r soll früher der Sozialdemokratie nahegestanden und sich dann der VF genähert haben. Bei der VF leitete er die verschiedenen Tombolas in Wien und in der Provinz und wurde ihm zu diesem Zwecke ein Auto zur Verfügung gestellt.
Zu der von Dollfuss geplanten Verfassungsfeier am 1. Mai 1934 wurde über seine Veranlassung am Wohnhause eine grosse Krukenkreuzfahne gehisst, die in der Umgebung grosses Aufsehen hervorrief.
Weiters wurde festgestellt, dass gegen K. beim Parteigericht des Kreises III wegen Aufnahme in die Partei ein Verfahren anhängig ist und dass das bisher dem Kreis vorliegende Material über K. keinen genauen Aufschluss über dessen politische Einstellung gibt.
Er geniesst jedoch infolge seiner früheren Einstellung in den nationalen Kreisen nicht den besten Ruf.

Heil Hitler!

Globocnik

A letter from Globocnik on Gauleiter-headed stationery.

Globocnik (left) and Fritz Wächtler (right) meeting Reichsleiter Otto Dietrich at Vienna main railway station.

The summer of 1938. Seyss-Inquart and Friedrich Rainer in civilian clothes. Peering over Rainer's left shoulder is Gauleiter Globocnik.

*Left to right*: Hugo Jury, Globocnik, unident., Joachim von Ribbentrop, and Bürckel receive the Reich Foreign Minister at Vienna station.

Gauleiter Globocnik
with an Italian official.

Globocnik entertains Robert and Inge Ley at the Vienna opera. Behind Globocnik is Johannes Blaschke, the later mayor of Vienna.

The Gauleiter was often seen collecting on the streets of his city.

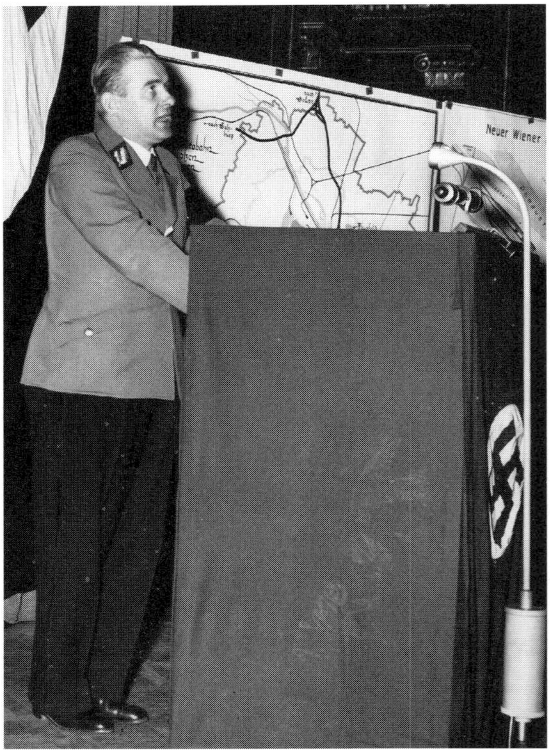

Globocnik was described as an average public speaker. A necessary skill that came with the job.

The Gauleiter examines a new car.

A visit to an exhibition.

Pictured at his desk.

Flanked by Hitler Youth trumpeters, Globocnik delivers a speech.

The Gauleiter speaks.

*Above left:* Yet another turn at the lectern.

*Above right:* Globocnik's fair hair is more obvious in this uniform portrait image.

The Gauleiters visit Munich. *Left to right*: Globocnik, Rainer, Klausner, Kutschera, and, most probably, Seltmann.

Klausner, Rainer, von Schirach, and Globocnik listen as Johannes Blaschke speaks.

Globocnik addresses a meeting of the Auslands Organisation in Vienna.

The senior SS figure in Austria was Dr Ernst Kaltenbrunner, seen here as a SS-Obergruppenführer, later appointed as chief of Security Police and SD for the Reich.

Soon after the Anschluss, Heydrich's SD opened an office in Vienna to handle the registration and expulsion of Jews from the former Austria. The office was set up in the Rothschild Palace.

Adolf Eichmann administered the office 'to assist Jewish emigration'.

Globocnik's old friend and colleague, Friedrich Rainer, was appointed as Gauleiter of Salzburg.

The Rainer family remained close friends of Globocnik until his death in 1945.

Ada and Friedl Rainer obtained a lakeside property at Pörtschach am Wörthersee. The Villa Rainer was visited by Globocnik on numerous occasions, as illustrated by the number of entries in the visitors' book, which now resides in a private collection in the UK. It was also at this house that Globocnik appeared in the last weeks of his life having decamped from Trieste. The Villa Rainer operates to this day as a luxurious hotel.

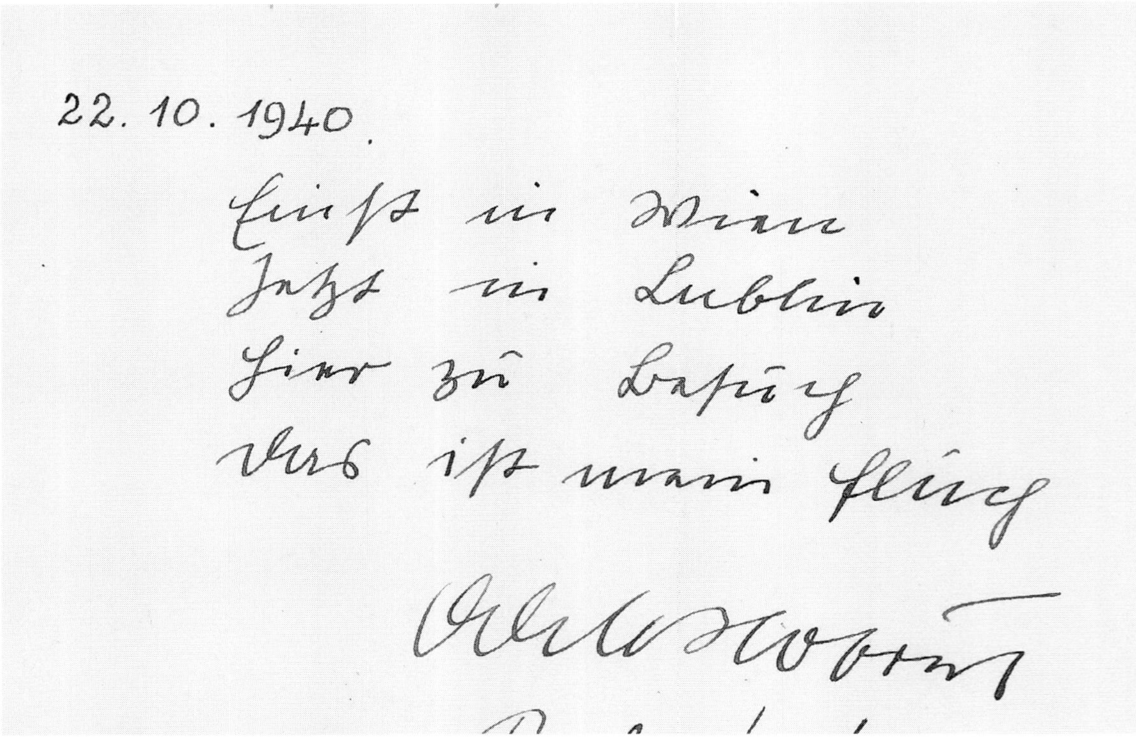
22. 10. 1940.
Einst in Wien
Jetzt in Lublin
Hier zu Besuch
Das ist mein Fluch
Odilo Globocnik

Rainer's visitors' book: '22 October 1940. Once in Vienna, now in Lublin, here to visit, that's my curse! Odilo Globocnik'.

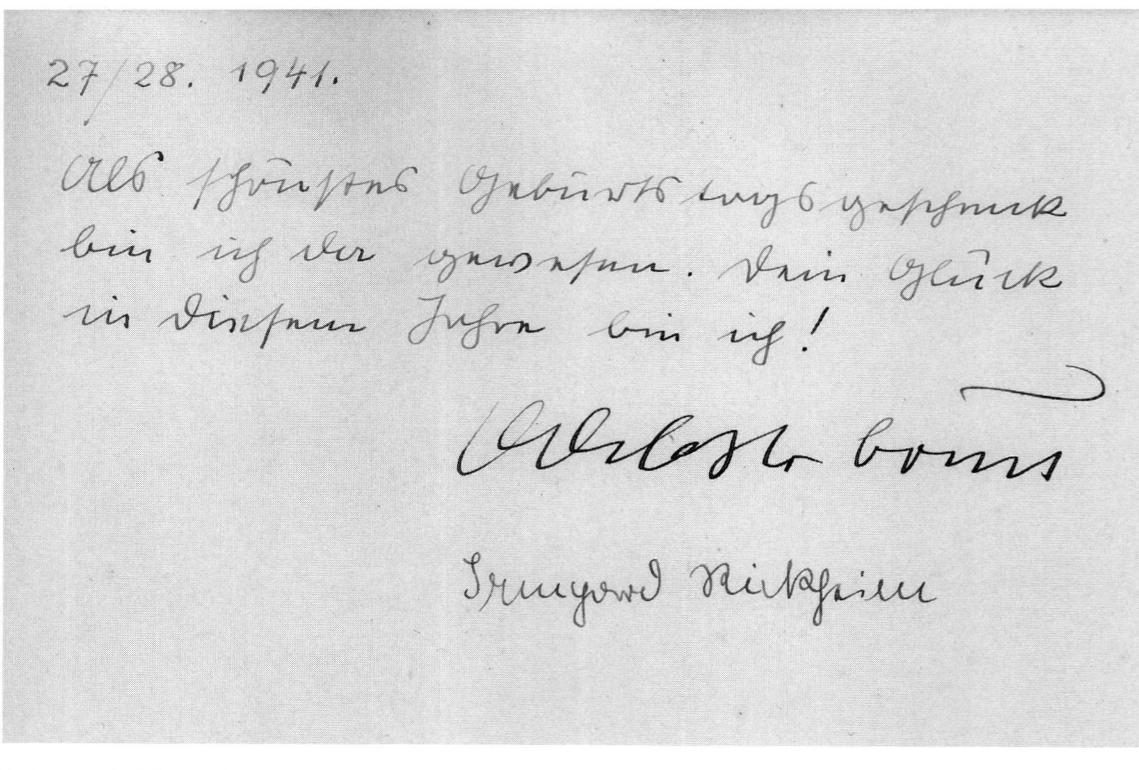
27/28. 1941.
Als schönstes Geburtstagsgeschenk bin ich da gewesen. Dein Glück in diesem Jahre bin ich!
Odilo Globocnik
Irmgard Rickheim

'27/28. 1941. [July]. I was there as your best birthday present. I am your luck for this year! Odilo Globocnik, Irmgard Rickheim'. Dated one week after Himmler's visit to Lublin when he ordered Globocnik to create the new camp at Majdanek and to repopulate the Zamość Land.

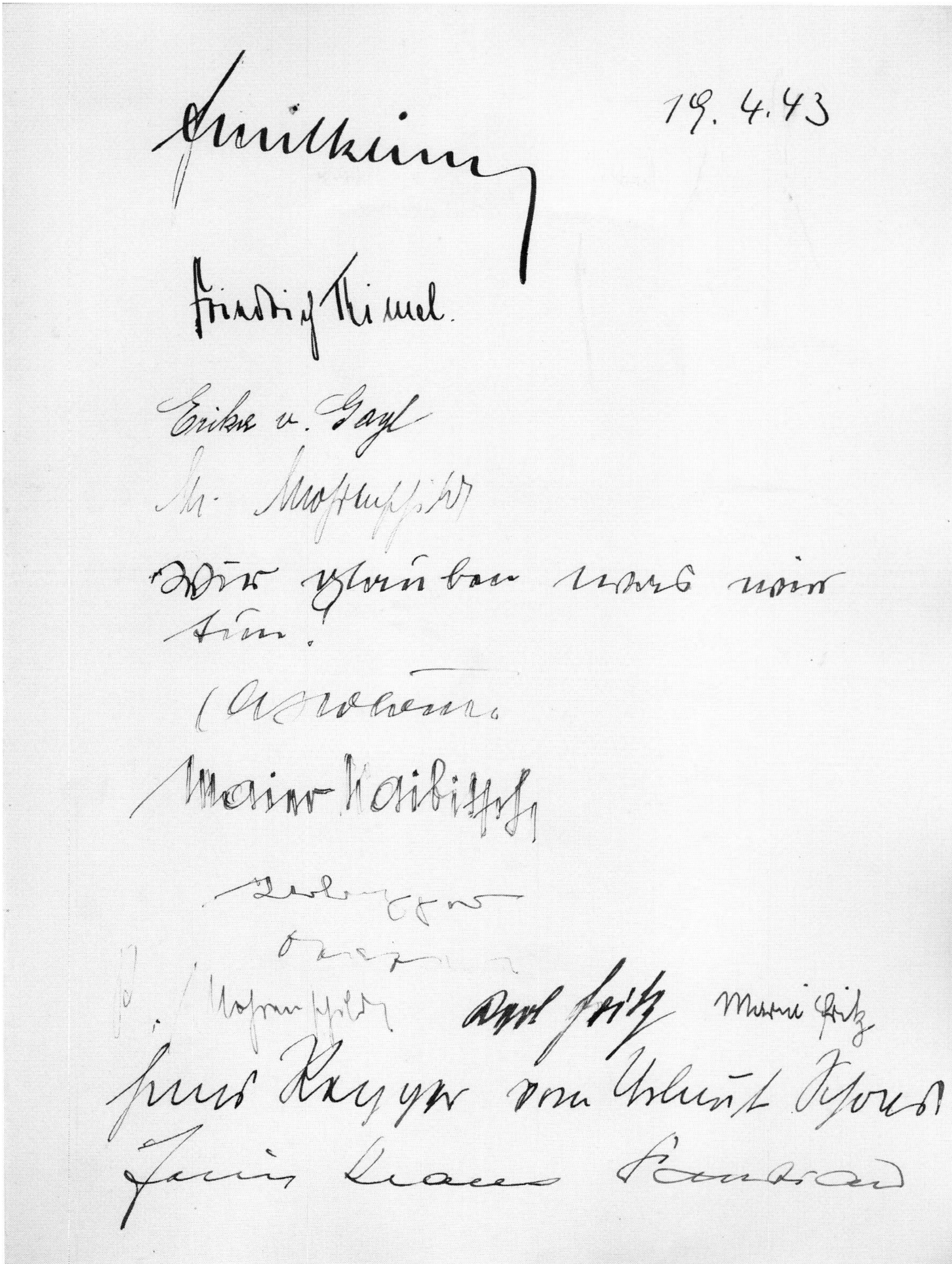


A page from Rainer's guestbook dated 19 April 1943. This is the day that the operation to liquidate the Warsaw Ghetto began and signalled the start of the ghetto uprising. Signatures present include Obergebietsführer Emil Klein, SS-Standartenführer Friedrich Thimel, Erika von Gayl [*Globocnik*], Margarethe von Mohrenschildt, SS-Standartenführer Alois Maier-Kaibitsch, Reinhold von Mohrenschildt, Karl Fritz, and Marni Fritz. Above Globocnik's signature, he has handwritten 'We believe in what we are doing'.

Hotel Kaiserhof in Vienna. Location of Globocnik's temporary home and where he registered his address for the 1938 plebiscite.

The Gauleiter held the SS rank of Standartenführer.

He was promoted to SS-Oberführer on 28 September 1938, with effect from 25 July 1938.

*Left:* Globocnik's cavalier attitude to the finances of the Vienna Gauleitung soon attracted the attention of NSDAP Reich Treasurer Reichsleiter Franz Xaver Schwarz. The Gauleiter's off-hand responses to enquiries by Schwarz's office in Munich, created a powerful enemy in the party.

*Below and next two pages:* A series of newspaper photos, of propaganda value, covering Gauleiter Globocnik's duties.

Reichsminister Dr. Joseph Goebbels wird nach seiner Ankunft in einem Sonderflugzeug auf dem Flugplatz Aspern durch den Gauleiter von Wien Odilo Globocnik herzlich begrüßt

Die neue Holzweber-Siedlung im Kreis V

Rechts: Gauleiter Globocnik gibt den Befehl zum Beginn der Arbeit und nimmt den ersten Spatenstich vor. — Unten: Architekt Laub vom Amt Bürckel erklärt Gauleiter Globocnik den Plan der Holzweber-Siedlung

Bildbeilage des „Ö.B."

## Bilder unseres Kampfes .... aus den Polizeiarchiven!

**Gauleiter von Wien Pg. Odilo Globocnik.**

Er verbüßte insgesamt 65 Wochen für seine nationalsozialistische Überzeugung und seinen nie ruhenden nationalsozialistischen Kampfgeist in Systemkerkern. Diese Aufnahme ist dem Polizeiarchiv Klagenfurt entnommen, wo Globocnik — ein gebürtiger Kärntner — nach dem Parteiverbot im Jahre 1933 zum ersten Male festgenommen und mit Photos und Fingerabdrücken der „politischen Verbrecher"-Kartothek einverleibt wurde. Sein fanatischer Kampfesmut wurde jedoch dadurch niemals gebrochen!

**Aus der Kampfzeit des Nationalsozialismus in Österreich.**

Das Lokal der ersten nationalsozialistischen Versammlung in Rosenau am Sonntagsberg bei Waidhofen, wo Gauleiter Eigruber 1932 trotz wüsten marxistisch-kommunistischen Terrors als nationalsozialistischer Redner auftrat. In der anschließenden Saalschlacht wurde Eigruber schwer verletzt. Die Versammlung aber hatte dennoch stattgefunden!

Gauleiter Globocnik, Polizeivizepräsident Fitzthum, der Gaubeauftragte der DAF. Schneeberger bei einer überraschenden Preiskontrolle in einem Textilwarengeschäft. (Siehe auch Seite 3.)

Aufn.: Schostal, Wien.

Gestern vormittag eröffnete Gauleiter Globocnik die Nach- und Umschulungswerkstätte der Arbeitsgemeinschaft „Eisen und Metall" in der Brigittenau. Gauleiter Globocnik und der Gaubeauftragte der DAF. Schneeberger bei der Besichtigung der Werkstätte. (Siehe auch Seite 8.)

Aufn.: Weltbild, Wien.

Gauleiter Globocnik im Gießraum der Steyrermühl-Druckerei. Von links nach rechts: Hauptschriftleiter Hans Zogelmann, Gaubeauftragter der DAF. Schneeberger, der Gauleiter, Betriebsführer Dr. Winkler, Hauptschriftleiter-Stellvertreter Dr. Hüttig.

Aufn.: Binder, Wien.

***Gauleiter Globocnik eröffnet das Winterhilfswerk im Gau Groß-Wien***

*Das Winterhilfswerk in Wien wurde mit einer Eröffnungskundgebung in der Messehalle auf dem Rotundengelände im Beisein von Vertretern aller öffentlichen Körperschaften eingeleitet. Gauleiter Globocnik hielt die Eröffnungsansprache*

Aufn. Blaha

***Das Deutsche Volkstheater als KdF-Bühne eröffnet***

*Mit einer festlichen Feier, bei der Gauleiter Globocnik eine Begrüßungsansprache hielt, wurde das Deutsche Volkstheater im Zeichen der NS-Gemeinschaft „Kraft durch Freude" als Theater des Volkes seiner Bestimmung übergeben. Als Eröffnungsvorstellung kamen Schillers „Räuber" zur Aufführung*

Aufn. Blaha

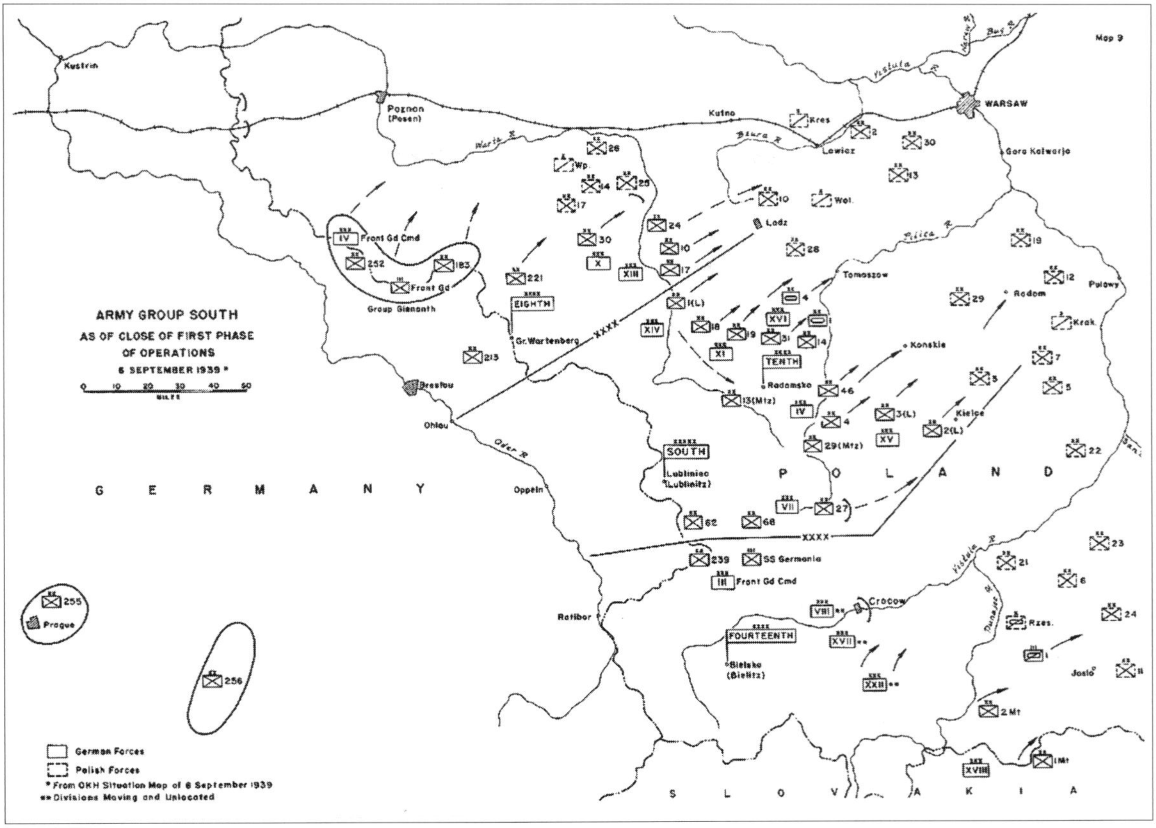


The initial German advance into Poland in early September 1939. Globocnik was attached to SS-Germania, shown here east of Ratibor.

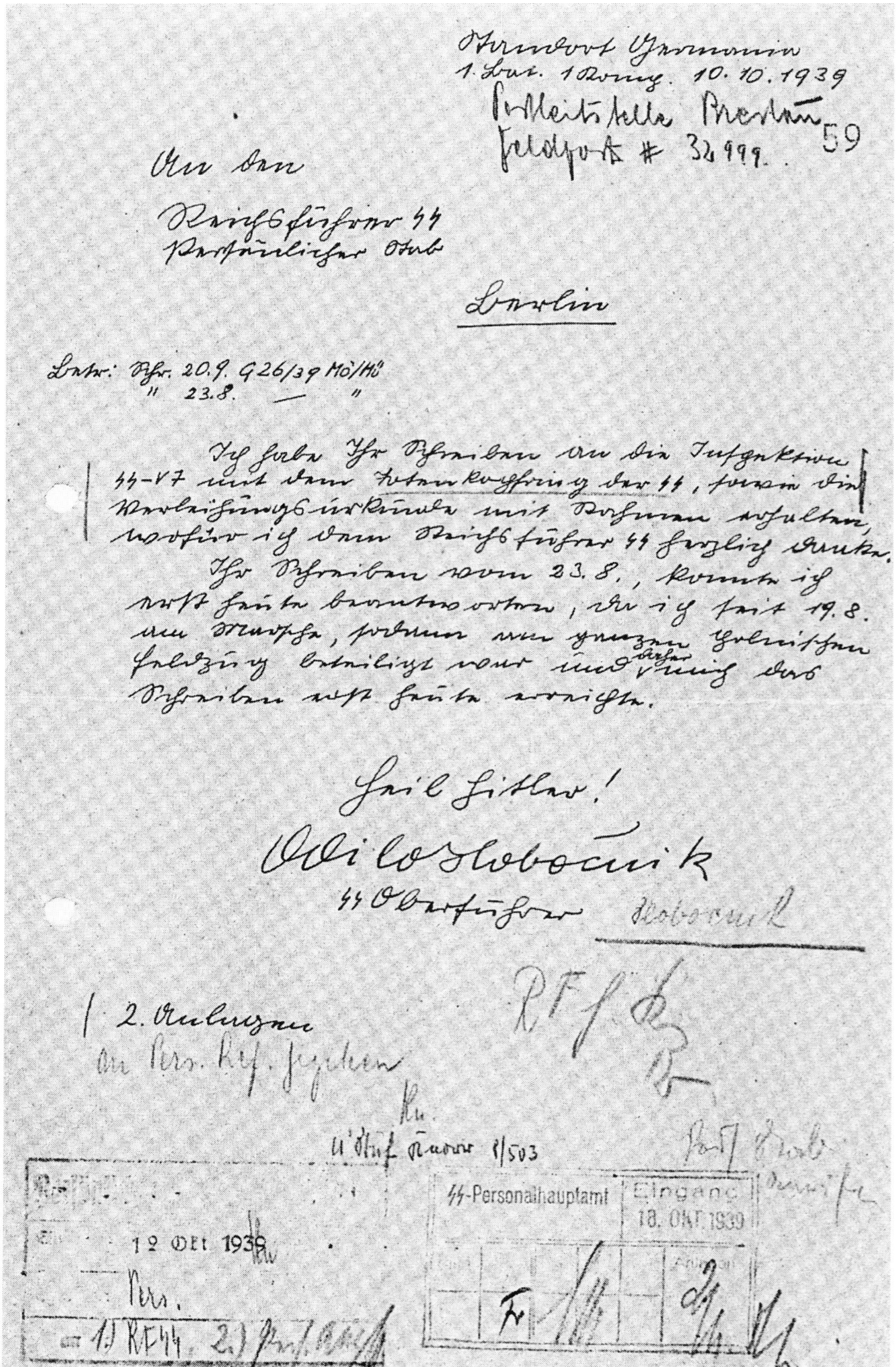

Standort Germania
1. Bat. 1 Komp. 10.10.1939
Postleitstelle Breslau
Feldpost # 32999.

59

An den

Reichsführer SS
Persönlicher Stab

Berlin

Betr.: Ihr. 20.9. G26/39 Mö/Hö
" 23.8. — "

Ich habe Ihr Schreiben an die Inaktiven SS-VT mit dem Totenkopfring der SS, sowie die Verleihungsurkunde mit Freuden erhalten, wofür ich dem Reichsführer SS herzlich danke.

Ihr Schreiben vom 23.8., konnte ich erst heute beantworten, da ich seit 19.8. am Marsche, sodann am ganzen Polnischen Feldzug beteiligt war und daher mich das Schreiben erst heute erreichte.

Heil Hitler!

Odilo Globocnik
SS Oberführer
Globocnik

2. Anlagen

SS-Personalhauptamt Eingang 18. OKT. 1939

12 OKT 1939

SS-Oberführer Globocnik writes to the Reichsführer-SS Personal Staff on 10 October 1939. He apologises for his tardy reply, but his unit has been constantly on the move. Note he provides his address as 'Postleitstelle Breslau, Feldpost No. 32999'. Globocnik had a habit of handwriting his letters to Himmler and his staff, possibly to promote the idea of a personal relationship.

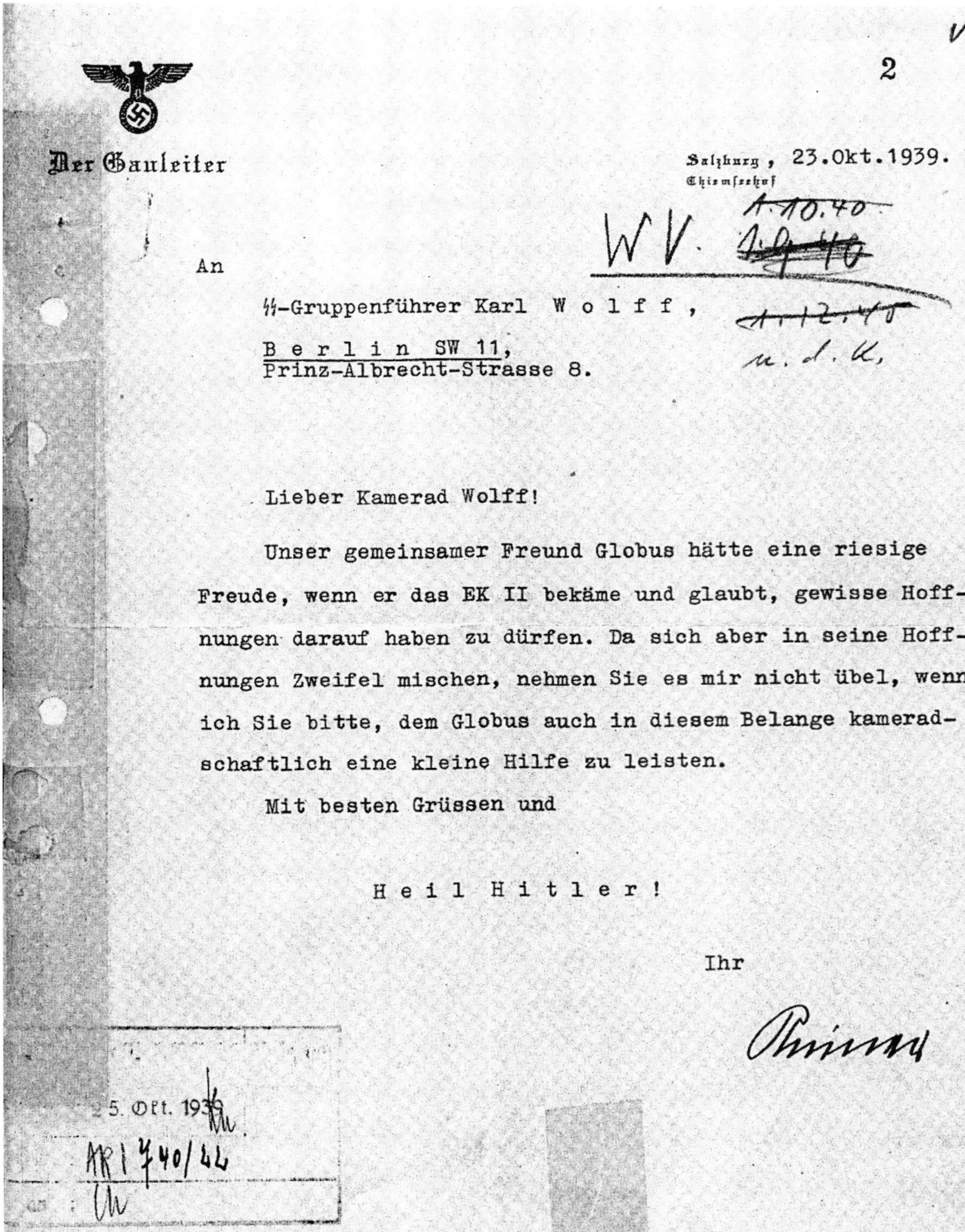

2

**Der Gauleiter**

Salzburg, 23.Okt.1939.
Chiemseehof

WV.

An

SS-Gruppenführer Karl W o l f f ,

B e r l i n SW 11,
Prinz-Albrecht-Strasse 8.

Lieber Kamerad Wolff!

Unser gemeinsamer Freund Globus hätte eine riesige Freude, wenn er das EK II bekäme und glaubt, gewisse Hoffnungen darauf haben zu dürfen. Da sich aber in seine Hoffnungen Zweifel mischen, nehmen Sie es mir nicht übel, wenn ich Sie bitte, dem Globus auch in diesem Belange kameradschaftlich eine kleine Hilfe zu leisten.

Mit besten Grüssen und

H e i l H i t l e r !

Ihr

25. Okt. 1939

AR I 740/42

A perfect illustration of how Friedl Rainer strove to protect and promote his old friend, Globocnik. Here he writes to Karl Wolff, asking for his support. 'Our mutual friend Globus would have great joy if he got the EKII [Iron Cross 2nd Class] and believes that he has some hope for it. But when his hopes are mixed with doubts, I do not mind if I ask you to give Globus a comradely little help in this matter too'.

60

Abschrift                                        Berlin, den 1.November 1939

Der Reichsführer-SS
und Chef der Deutschen Polizei
im Reichsministerium des Innern

O.Kdo.O Nr. 163/39

Betrifft: Stellenbesetzung der SS und Polizei im Generalgouvernement.

1) Als " Höheren SS- und Polizeiführer Ost " habe ich im Einverständnis mit dem Generalgouverneur den SS-Obergruppenführer K r ü g e r , Berlin, eingesetzt. Er untersteht dem Generalgouverneur, Reichsminister Dr. F r a n k , unmittelbar.

2) Dem " Höheren SS- und Polizei-Führer Ost " unterstehen als Befehlshaber der Ordnungspolizei, Generalmajor d. Ordnungspolizei Becker, als Befehlshaber der Sicherheitspolizei und des SD. SS-Brigadeführer Streckenbach, als Führer der SS und des Selbstschutzes der SS-Oberführer Hintze.

3) Zu Kommandeuren der Polizei bei den Distriktschefs ernenne ich:

für den Distrikt Warschau: den SS-Gruppenführer M o d e r ,Bln.
" " " Lublin: den SS-Brigadeführer Globocnik, Berlin
" " " Radom: den SS-Oberführer Katzmann, Breslau
" " " Krakau: den SS-Gruppenführer Zech, Berlin

Dienststellung und Dienstbefugnisse sind durch Sondererlaß geregelt.

An
a) den Herrn Generalgouverneur in Polen Reichsminister Dr. F r a n k, L o d z - nebst 4 Abdr. für 4 Distriktchefs -

b) den Höheren SS- und Polizeiführer SS-Obergruppenführer K r ü g e r, L o d z -mit je 1 Abdr. für die Befehlshaber der Ordn. Polizei, Sicherheitspol. und SD, undden Führer der SS und des Selbstschutzes.

c) den SS - Gruppenführer M o d e r , Berlin
d) den SS - Oberführer K a t z m a n n , Breslau, Kleinburgerstr. 17
e) den SS - Gruppenführer Z e c h , Krakau

F.d.R.d.A.
[illegible]

gez. H. H i m m l e r

Himmler's order posting Globocnik as SS and Police Leader in Lublin. Note that on this order, dated 1 November 1939, Himmler refers to Globocnik as SS-Brigadeführer, a rank he did not acquire until almost three weeks later. This is probably because Hitler had to personally approve promotions to Brigadeführer and above. Himmler lays out the basic command arrangements for the role of SS and Police in the general government.

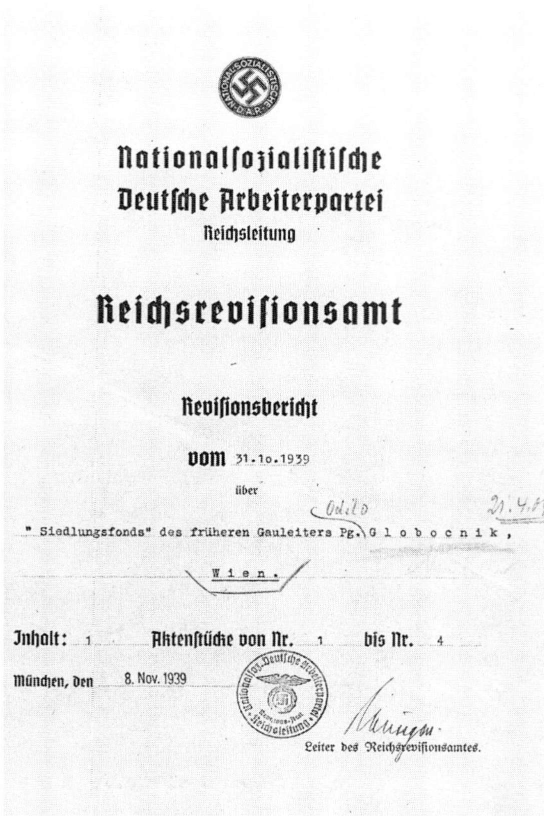

Nationalsozialistische
Deutsche Arbeiterpartei
Reichsleitung

**Reichsrevisionsamt**

**Revisionsbericht**

vom 31.10.1939

über

" Siedlungsfonds" des früheren Gauleiters Pg. G l o b o c n i k ,

W i e n .

Inhalt: 1 Aktenstücke von Nr. 1 bis Nr. 4

München, den 8. Nov. 1939

Leiter des Reichsrevisionsamtes.

*Clockwise from top left:*

Globocnik's problems with Schwarz soon began. This is the cover of the audit settlement report for Globocnik's financial accounts as Gauleiter of Vienna.

Governor General Dr Hans Frank.

Globocnik's immediate boss, SS-Obergruppenführer Friedrich-Wilhelm Krüger, HSSPF Ost, based in Krakow.

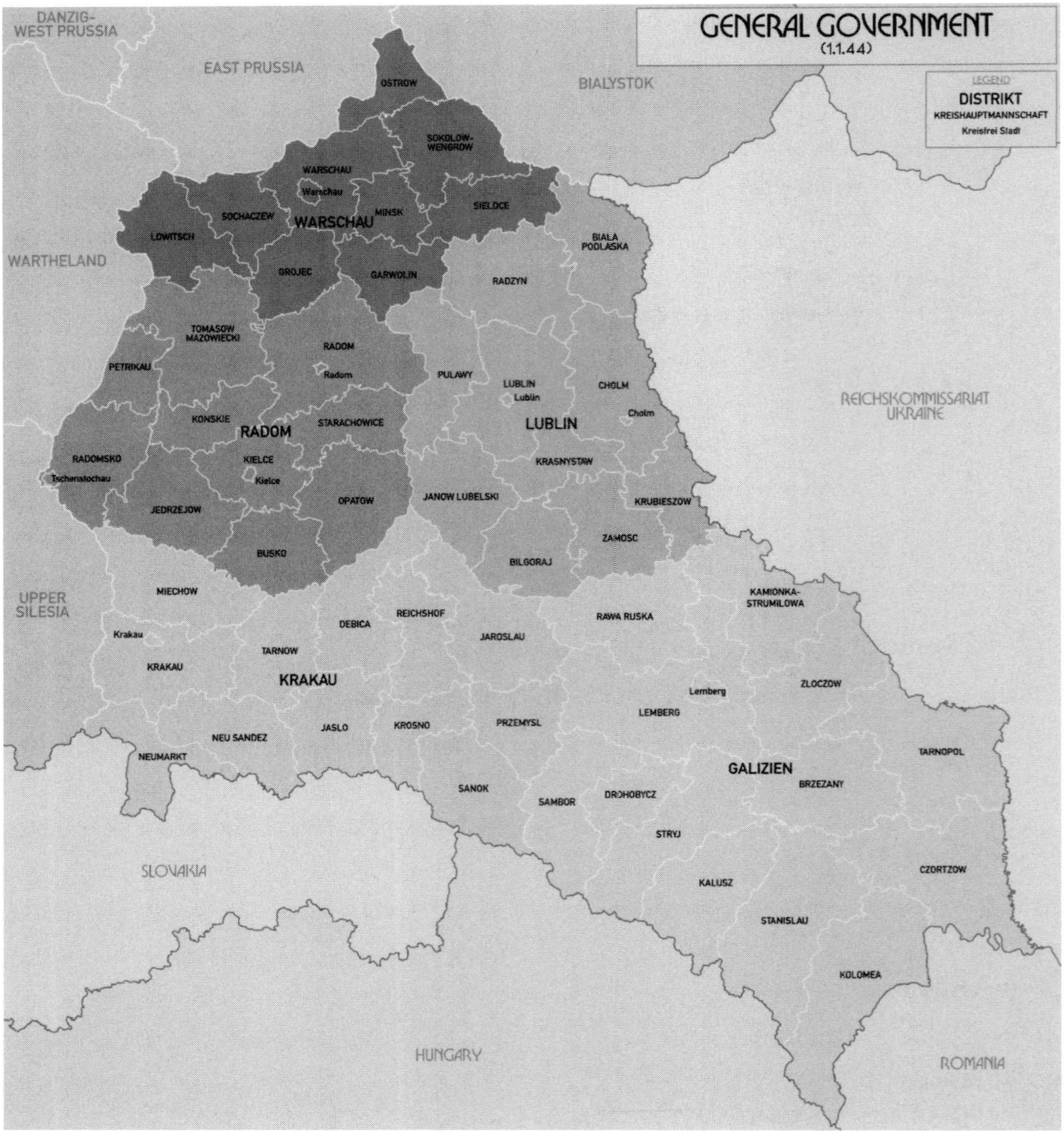


The districts of the General Government after the inclusion of Galicia.

It is unclear where the new SSPF stayed on his arrival in Lublin, but given his penchant for luxurious hotels, it is more than likely he stayed initially at the premier hotel in the city, the Grand Hotel, which had easy access to his new office nearby.

The site of the Haberlau house prior to construction.

Left stands Gustaw Haberlau. Centre is his daughter, Irena Lobarzewski, and on the right is her husband, Witold Lobarzewski. These three were the original occupants and owners of the future Globocnik villa in Lublin.

A contemporary image of the house.

Another contemporary image, with an unidentified woman standing on the raised terrace.

The house from the garden, with SS orderly.

*Above left:* A contemporary shot of the house from the street. Note the security fencing.

*Above right:* Globocnik's small living room, complete with Hitler portrait on the wall.

The interior today. The wooden radiator surround and Greek-style marquetry over the doors was installed by Globocnik, and still survives.

The bedroom of the SSPF. Globocnik's recessed bed space with marquetry above and original wooden panelling.

*Above left:* The paved area of garden and the outside of the bowling alley, now demolished.

*Above right:* The interior of the bowling alley at the Globocnik villa. Globocnik, in uniform with back to camera, has just hurled his bowl along the alley. He particularly enjoyed bowling, a popular game at the time.

The site of the SS casino and bowling alley for the use of SS personnel in 2014. The entire complex has since been demolished to make way for 'modern progress'.

Lubomelska in 1938. The driveway to the future Globocnik villa is in the foreground at left.

The same location during the time of Globocnik's occupation. Note the German sentry post opposite the entrance to Globocnik's driveway.

A nearby guesthouse used by Globocnik for special guests. Photo 2014.

He was joined in Lublin by Reinhold von Mohrenschildt.

The von Mohrenschildt couple.

*Left:* Erika von Gayl (Globocnik) found a teaching position in Lublin and moved there with her mother.

*Top right:* A newspaper photo of the new SS and Police commander of Lublin.

*Above right:* A rare photo of Josef 'Sepp' Nemec.

*Clockwise from top left:*

Dr Frank during a visit to a sugar refinery in Lublin. On the left is SS-Brigadeführer Friedrich Schmidt, the first governor of Lublin.

Walter Gunst, the first commander of the infamous Lubliner Selbstschutz. Gunst was dismissed for corruption.

A member of Globocnik's Sonderdienst Lublin.

Ludolf Jakob von Alvensleben (far left), the successor of Walter Gunst. The others are Eric Spaarmann (in the background), Hans Kölzow (centre), and Christian Schnug (right).

Lublin Governor Ernst Zörner with men of the Sonderdienst.

The SS and Police Leader in Lublin, SS-Brigadeführer Odilo Globocnik.

*Above left:* Dr Karl Hofbauer was appointed by Globocnik as the Special Representative for the Resettlement of Jews.

*Above right:* Kurt Claasen (previously Kurt Kutschera), a resettlement officer on Globocnik's staff in Lublin.

Globocnik visiting a labour camp.

*Above left:* Dr Marek Alten of the Lublin Judenrat. He was shot in the ghetto at Majdan Tatarski during the liquidation of the ghetto on 9 November 1942.

*Above right and below:* Forced labour in the Lublin District.

Horse show at Lipowa Street sports ground in the summer of 1939. This photo shows inside the main gate and should be compared with the photo of Himmler arriving in his car at the Lipowa Street camp. At this opening ceremony are Jerzy de Tramecourt (centre), Brigadier General Piotr Skuratowicz (far right), Brigadier General Wladyslaw Anders (second right), Brigadier Bronislaw Regulski (over Tramecourt's left shoulder), and Brigadier General Mieczyslaw Smorawinski (saluting, left). Tramecourt was shot by the Germans in November 1939; Smorawinski and Skuratowice were both murdered at Katyn in 1940; Anders was arrested and tortured by the NKVD, but was subsequently released; and Regulski became the military attaché in London for the Polish Government-in-Exile.

The guests of honour spectate from the shaded canopy on the grounds of the later labour camp. In the background are the stables at the rear of the residential buildings in Marii Curie-Sklodowskiej, which still exist today. Many of the stables were converted into barracks for the prisoners and were demolished post-war to make way for a modern shopping centre.

A rare photograph of the interior of the stables.

Himmler alighting from his car at the gatehouse of the Lipowa Street labour camp. Globocnik and Krüger are seated in the car, which displays a SS1 number plate and the personal standard of the Reichsführer-SS. Compare with earlier photo of Polish generals at the horse show opening ceremony.

Himmler with his lieutenants surrounding him on the grounds of the new Lipowa Street labour camp. In the background are the rear of the buildings in Marii Curie-Sklodowskiej. The timber watch tower appears to be still under construction, and the stables and garages are visible in the background. Included in the group are Krüger, Fegelein, Wolff, Dolp, Hofmann, and Nemec.

A later image, showing the same timber watch tower, now complete, and some new erected barracks. The camp fencing also appears to have been erected. The former stables and garages are on the right, parallel with the buildings in Marii Curie-Sklodowskiej.

Himmler photographed during a visit to Lipowa Street camp. *Left to right*: Krüger, Globocnik, Himmler, Kammler, unident., Wolff, and Peiper.

Globocnik, Hermann Dolp, and Himmler. Dolp was the first nominated commandant of Lipowa Street.

The relationship between Dr Frank and Globocnik suffered over clashes of authority and perceived insubordination.

The entrance to the civilian governor of Lublin's office.

The NSDAP headquarters building in Lublin was the 'Adolf Hitler Haus'.

The military headquarters were situated in a former Jewish building. Note the Hebrew inscription over the main portico.

SS-Obergruppenführer August Heissmeyer pays Globocnik a visit in Lublin.

Another visitor was Karl-Maria Demelhuber. Hermann Fegelein stands next to Globocnik.

*Above left*: Dr Frank (second from left) visits the frontier with the Russian occupied zone. Governor Ernst Zörner is third from right.

*Above right*: The two leading figures in the policy of resettlement, Alfred Rosenberg and Heinrich Himmler.

Ulrich Greifelt. Far left is Dr Konrad Meyer-Hetling.

Dr Frank addresses the crowd at a function. Behind him stands Kurt Daluege and behind him is Adolf Hühnlein. In helmet and white lapels is Friedrich-Wilhelm Krüger, with Herbert Becker partly obscured behind him. To his left are Globocnik, Hans Jüttner, and Fritz Katzmann.

*Left to right*: Paul Riege, Hermann Höfle, Kurt Daluege, Adolf Hühnlein, Herbert Becker, and Globocnik.

Globocnik and Katzmann behind Krüger and Dr Frank.

The guests leave the dias. Dr Frank and Hühnlein lead the party, with Daluege, Jüttner, and Globocnik following behind. At the rear, Katzmann's head is visible and Becker can be seen in profile.

During a visit by Himmler. Globocnik in conversation with Becker, and Seyss-Inquart discusses something with Wolff.

Globocnik and Krüger centre. On the right is Ernst Lerch.

Globocnik and Krüger.

In this image, the tall man second from right is often mistaken for Globocnik, who is actually standing at far right.

**Der SS und Polizeiführer**
**im Distrikt Lublin**

Lublin, den 28. Januar 1941

Persönlicher Stab Reichsführer-SS
Schriftgutverwaltung
Akt. Nr. Geh. / 115

Gl./Hi.

Persönlibh !

An

SS-Gruppenführer Karl Wolff,
Chef des Persönlichen Stabes
beim Reichsführer SS,
Berlin SW.11
Prinz-Albrechtstr. 8

Wolff
R.

Lieber Gruppenführer Wolff !

Ich habe von Friedl Rainer folgendes Schreiben erhalten:

"Ich habe Michner am 18.1.41 folgendes geschrieben:

"Pg.Globocnik hat sich mir gegenüber sofort bereit erklärt, in einem angemessenen Rahmen zu Ihrer finanziellen Entlastung beizutragen. Es stünde ihm dafür ein schon einmal erwähnter Betrag von RM 10 000.-- sogleich zur Verfügung.

8000 M

an Globus

Die von Ihnen angegebenen Summen übersteigen diesen Betrag beträchtlich, doch kann ich nicht annehmen, dass Sie diese Beträge als Forderungen aufzustellen beabsichtigen, da ein Zusammenhang doch nicht gegeben erscheint.

Um den Fall glatt und endgültig abzuschliessen, bitte ich um Mitteilung, ob Sie den Betrag von RM 10 000.-- als ausreichend ansehen würden oder welche Erhöhung Ihnen vorschwebt, damit die Schadloshaltung Ihres Fräulein Tochter durchgeführt ist."

17.III.

Darauf habe ich nachstehende Antwort erhalten:

"Bestätige den Empfang Ihres gesch. Schreibens vom 18.d.Mts. und teile mit, dass der Betrag von RM 15 000.-- demnach ca. die Hälfte der am Besitze lastenden Verbindlichkeiten mir angemessen erscheint. Beiliegend einige Erlagscheine auf unser Postsparkassenkonto." "

Die RM 15 000.-- habe ich gerade noch gehabt und sie sofort erlegt. Ich bitte, Gruppenführer, dies zur Kenntnis zu nehmen und hoffe, dass damit die Angelegenheit endgültig bereinigt ist, und dass auf Grund dieses ganzen Abschlusses der Reichsführer die Überzeugung bekommen wird, dass mein Handeln richtig war und mir kein Vorwurf von Unanständigkeit mehr gemacht werden kann.

Mit herzlichem Gruss
und
Heil Hitler ! Globocnik

Globocnik could not shake off the dispute with Herr Michner over the broken engagement with his daughter. As late as January 1941, Globocnik pleads his case with Himmler, who agrees to forward 8,000 RM to his protégé, Globus, in March 1941.

Globocnik explains his plans during a visit by Dr Frank to the southern border region. Left, with binoculars, is Hermann Dolp.

Dr Frank listens to Globocnik. Also present are Ernst Zörner (fourth from left) and Josef 'Sepp' Nemec (far right).

Globocnik and Dr Frank lead the party along the earth embankment. Behind them are Nemec and Dolp.

Krüger, Dr Frank, and Globocnik are an attentive audience in Krakow. Behind Krüger, in the second row, sits Hermann Senkowsky.

The audience salutes.

Globocnik attends a funeral in Lublin. To his left is 'Sepp' Nemec.

Reichsleiter Dr Ley and Dr Frank at Krakow. In the background, in political uniform, is Globocnik.

Globocnik salutes at far right.

Globocnik at far left, next to Ludwig Fischer. Otto Wächter is second from right.

Himmler in Lublin. Far left is Lothar von Seltmann.

A newspaper photo showing Globocnik with Lothar von Seltmann (left) in Hitler Youth uniform.

Lothar von Seltmann in Lublin.

*Far left:* Dr Franz Stanglica.

*Near left:* Gustav Hanelt.

*Above left:* Waltraut Hanelt moved to Lublin with her husband. She was employed at the SS-Mannschaftshaus, working for Stanglica and her husband.

*Above right:* Adolf Bareuther. Globocnik's operational deputy for the cleansing of the Zamość region. Declared missing in Trieste 1945.

The barracks of Police Regiment 25 in Lublin. Stanglica and Hanelt operated from their offices on the top floor. Today, the building is part of the Lublin University of Natural Science.

August Heissmeyer is shown around a resettled farmstead by Globocnik.

Heissmeyer takes time to chat to a resettled Volksdeutsche farmer.

Heissmeyer and Globocnik leaving a Volksdeutsche house. Note the swastika flag on the interior wall.

Himmler during a visit to a resettled Volksdeutsche community. Right is Werner Lorenz; Globocnik far left; and Krüger in leather SS greatcoat.

Globocnik alights from his car.

At a meeting in Krakow, Globocnik sits opposite Dr Frank.

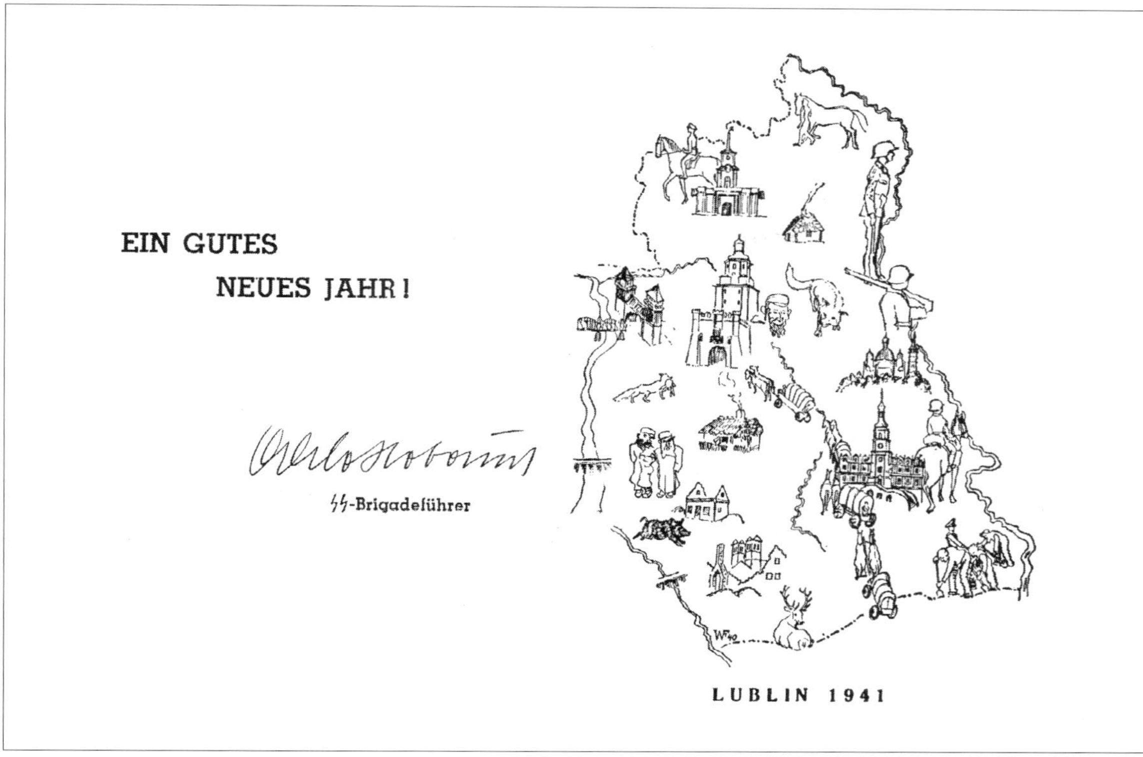


A New Year greetings card sent by Globocnik 1941. The sketches depict Lublin, Zamość, Jews, SS and Police Strongpoints, the construction of the defence ditches, and resettled Volksdeutsche.

Georg Michalczyk, an early member of SS-Standarte 23.

Michalczyk changed his name to the more Aryan-sounding Michalsen.

Michalsen played a major role in Aktion Reinhardt and the resettlement policy of Globocnik. He remained loyal to his boss and was captured with him in May 1945.

*Above:* Hans Maubach in his Hitler Youth uniform.

*Left:* Hans Maubach. He had a love for fine clothes and French cigarettes.

The handsome Maubach was popular with the ladies.

Charlotte Maubach. At first, Maubach occupied quarters opposite the Globocnik villa in Lublin, but he was soon joined by his wife. Rumours persisted that her ancestry was not entirely Aryan, and this may be the reason that Maubach left Lublin.

Hermann Höfle. The administrator of Aktion Reinhardt.

Himmler is received by Globocnik's staff at Lublin airfield. *Left to right*: Nemec (obscured), Maubach, Höfle, Lerch, unident.

Himmler and Krüger climb into Himmler's transport. Note the RFSS personal car pennant.

The party arrive at Globocnik's villa in Lublin. *Left to right*: Globocnik, Katzmann, Himmler, Krüger, Maubach, and Globocnik's dog.

Hanelt salutes the Reichsführer-SS on the side path of Globocnik's villa. Beside Himmler is Globocnik, followed by Nemec, Wolff, and Krüger. In the background is Katzmann.

Wolff, Krüger, Himmler and Globocnik, during the RFSS visit.

The beautiful town square in Zamość, also known as Himmlerstadt (2014 photo).

Himmler and Krüger. Globocnik's immediate superiors and the architects of Aktion Reinhardt.

Globocnik escorts Himmler around one of his camps.

Karl Otto Koch was selected for the post of commandant of the new Lublin concentration camp.

An aerial shot of Lublin. The destruction of parts of the city is evident.

Lublin railway station.

The Jewish market in Lublin. Note the Star of David insignia worn on the armbands.

Occupants of the Jewish ghetto in Lublin.

*Above:* Globocnik's kingdom. The streets of Lublin, seen from a building used as a barracks by the SS.

*Right:* SS troops marching in Lublin.

A former school building used as a SS barracks. This photo is dated 23 February 1942 and the barracks are identified as the Bernhardiner-Kaserne.

A building used by the SS.

The rear entrance of the office of the SS and Police Leader of Lublin.

The old Lublin castle, used as a prison by the Gestapo. The structures in the foreground are just inside the southern perimeter of the ghetto district.

These SS troops are taking part in a training exercise on the outskirts of the city on 8 July 1941.

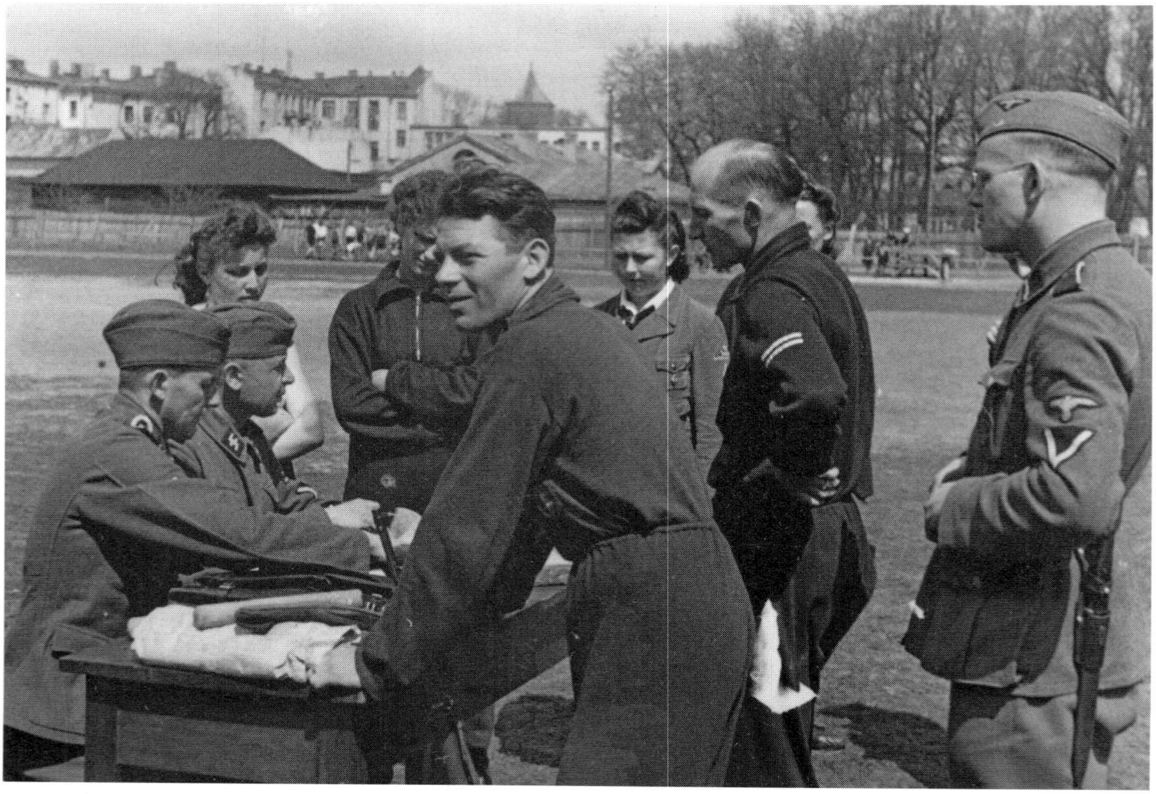

German personnel during a sports day in Lublin on 22 June 1942.

SS at the Lublin shooting range. The officer is SS-Obersturmführer Offermann.

Gustav Hanelt practices his shooting skills.

*Previous page, above:* SS and Police personnel at the Lublin firing range.

*Previous page, below:* SS and Police relax for the camera. These troops were used for guarding prisoners, ghetto liquidation and special operations such as 'Harvest Festival'.

Having fun on a motorcycle.

A SS officer with his Mauser pistol watches as his female companion pets a dog at the firing range. Note the 'broom handle' extension for accuracy.

Another way for the SS to relax was the bathing lido situated a few hundred metres from Globocnik's villa inside the restricted German zone. Here, SS men could relax with girlfriends and secretarial staff.

The SS guard contingent at the Lipowa Street camp.

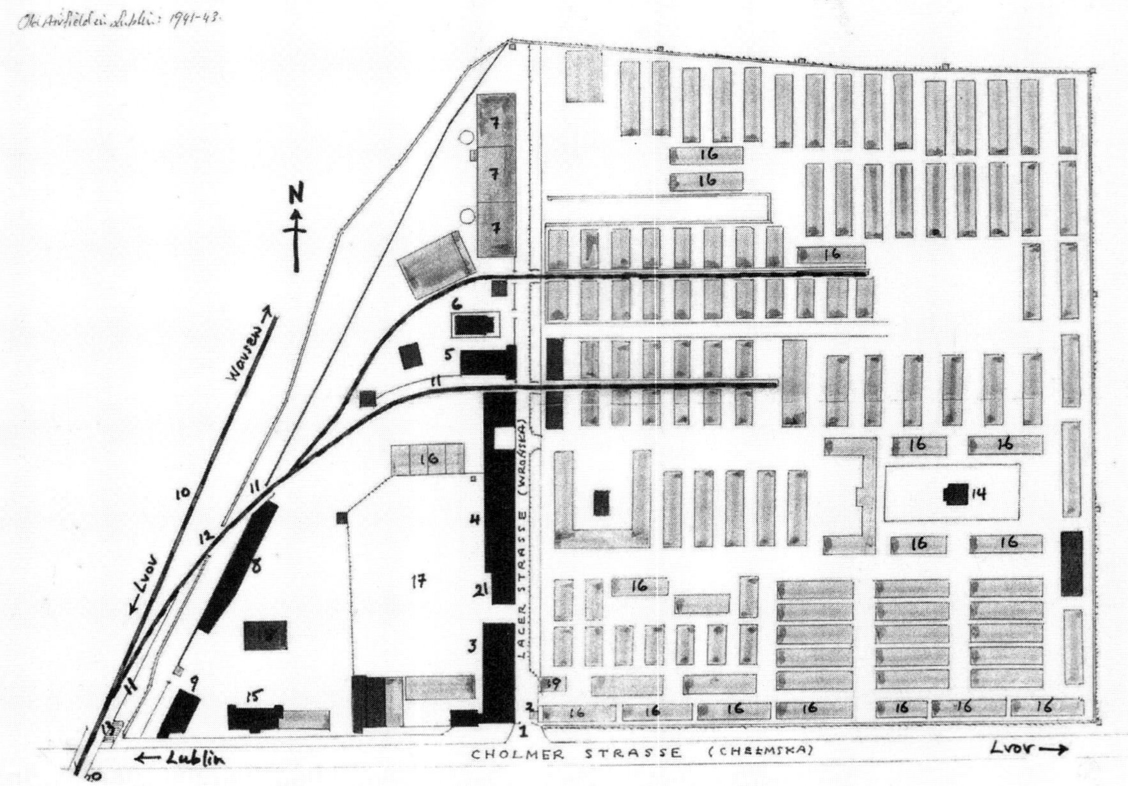


Map of the Old Airfield Camp by Michael Tregenza.

1. Main entrance (Wirth hanged prisoners from gate crossbar).
2. Guard.

3. and 7. Aircraft hangars where clothes, footwear, and luggage searched for valuables and sorted.

4. DAW workshops.

[5–6 should be transposed (original Polish plan was wrong)].

5. SS casino.
6. Disinfection/gas chamber*.
8. Roofing tar paper workshop;
9. Wirth's Aktion Reinhardt Inspectorate office. [SS restaurant on first floor.]
10. Main railway line.
11. Unloading ramps for incoming loot/prisoners selected for work.
12. Rail spur.
13. Rail control box.
14. Disinfection/gas chamber*.
15. SS barracks.
16. Warehouses for sorted/cleaned clothing.
17. Storage area for clothes and footwear waiting to be sorted.
18. Unidentified building.
19. Guard hut at entrance to camp barracks area.
20. Railway bridge over Cholmer Strasse.
21. Holding centre for selection of work brigades.

*6. and 14. originally used only for disinfection of clothing; after arrival of Aktion Reihardt staff (Hackenholt especially), used also for gassing prisoners; Hackenholt commented, 'It's a waste of time and effort sending them to KZ-Majdanek'.

Blown up aerial photo of Wirth's office and SS dining room (right) with SS barracks top left. (9 and 15 on map. Modern image.)

Former sorting sheds of the Airfield Camp at the junction of ul. Chełmska (Cholmer Strasse) and ul. Wronska (Lager Strasse); number 3 on the map. Since this photograph was taken, the sheds have been demolished.

The buildings at the Old Airfield Camp were used to stable horses of 2. SS Cavalry Regiment. This photograph is possibly located at the site of the camp.

Prisoners being marched under guard between the Old Airfield camp and Lipowa Street camp. Sorting warehouses of the airfield camp can be seen in the background.

The same location, but these prisoners appear to be Polish soldiers.

Polish army prisoners under SS guard.

Jewish prisoners, under SS guard, sorting out useable bricks from a pile of rubble from destroyed Lublin buildings.

SS guards in Lublin and what appears to be two Jewish labourers. Note the flexible cosh held by the SS NCO.

Prisoners under SS guard gather at a break for food, judging by the cans in some of their hands.

Two SS men with a police armourer in Lublin.

*Left column from top:*

SS drivers in Lublin.

Koch's replacement at Majdanek was Max Koegel. Under his stewardship, gas chambers were installed in the camp.

Hermann Florstedt succeeded Koegel as commandant of Majdanek. He is photographed here with his wife, Charlotte, in 1929. She killed herself in 1949.

*Right column:*

Martin Weiss. New Majdanek commandant at the time of the 'Harvest Festival' massacre, although officially appointed the day after.

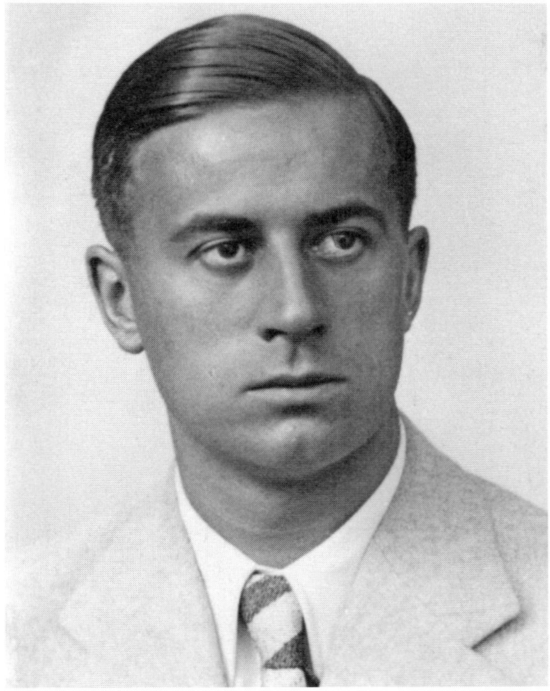

*Above left:* Artur Liebehenschel, the last commandant at Majdanek. He was also the replacement for Höss at Auschwitz.

*Above right:* Dr Karl Brandt, Hitler's personal escort physician, tasked to investigate the case of Gerhard Kretschmar, the severely disabled child.

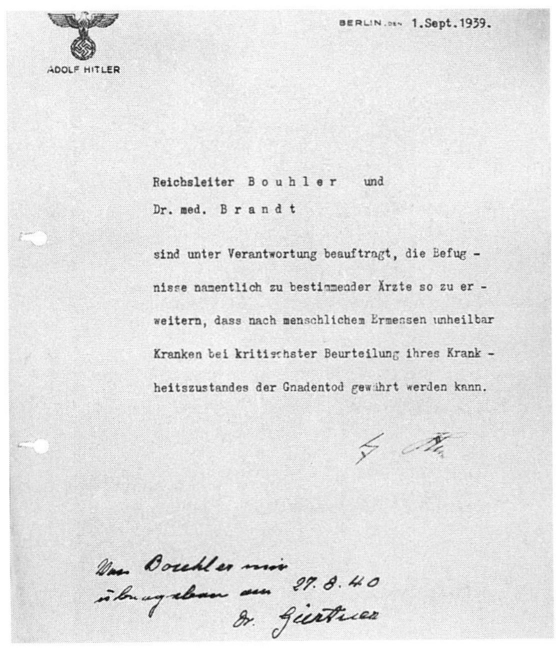

ADOLF HITLER

BERLIN, DEN 1.Sept.1939.

Reichsleiter B o u h l e r und

Dr. med. B r a n d t

sind unter Verantwortung beauftragt, die Befug - nisse namentlich zu bestimmender Ärzte so zu er - weitern, dass nach menschlichem Ermessen unheilbar Kranken bei kritischster Beurteilung ihres Krank - heitszustandes der Gnadentod gewährt werden kann.

Von Bouhler mir übergeben am 27.8.40 Dr. Gürtner

*Left:* Reichsleiter Philipp Bouhler. Titular head of the euthanasia programme.

*Above:* Dated retrospectively to coincide with the beginning of hostilities, Hitler's signature on the memo authorising the euthanasia programme.

A rare photograph of Frau Viktor Brack being introduced to Hitler. Brack is left and Bouhler is seated to Hitler's right.

The only known photograph of Tiergartenstrasse 4 in Berlin.

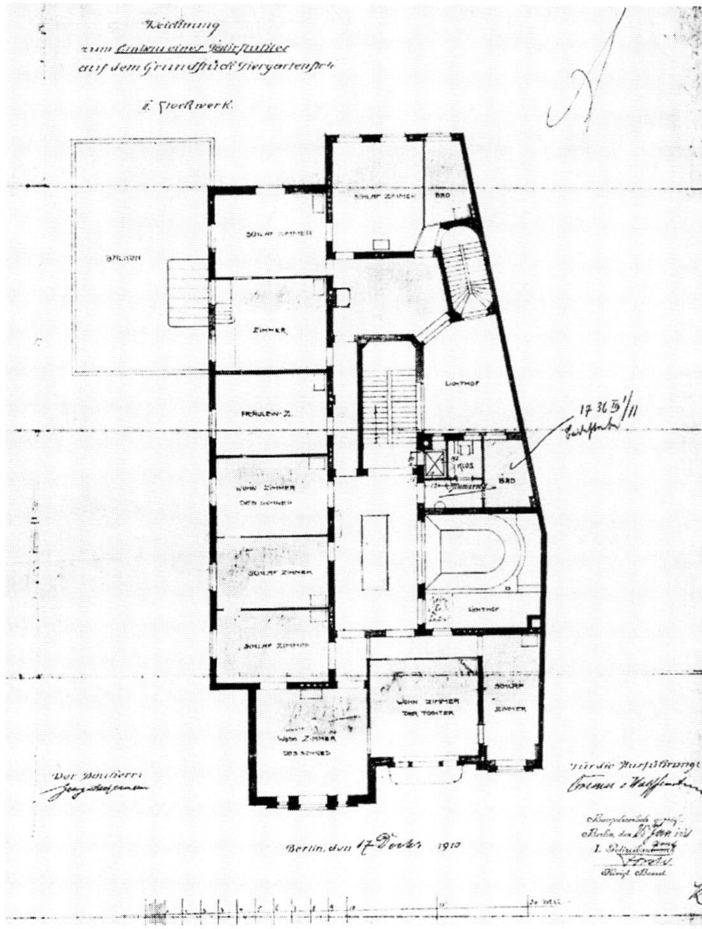


Floorplan of Tiergartenstrasse 4 dated 1910.

**SA der NSDAP**

**Der Führer der Obergruppe III**

Berlin W 35, den 4. Juli 1934.
Tiergartenstraße 4/4a
Fernruf: A 1 Jäger 0036

Briefb. Nr.: 15/34
Betr.:
Bezug:
Beilagen:

Herrn
General der Landespolizei
Daluege.

1934 letter heading of SA-Obergruppe III at Tiergartenstrasse 4/4a.

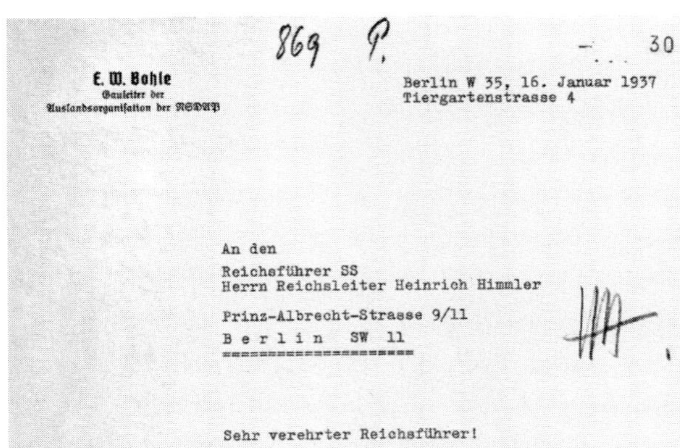

869 P. 30

**E. W. Bohle**
Gauleiter der
Auslandsorganisation der NSDAP

Berlin W 35, 16. Januar 1937
Tiergartenstrasse 4

An den
Reichsführer SS
Herrn Reichsleiter Heinrich Himmler
Prinz-Albrecht-Strasse 9/11
B e r l i n SW 11

Sehr verehrter Reichsführer!

Letter heading in 1937 of Ernst Bohle, the head of the NSDAP Auslandsorganisation, at Tiergartenstrasse 4. Note the pencilled initials of Himmler.

Viktor Brack.

Werner Blankenburg.

Brack, in SS-Standartenführer uniform, seated at his desk in the Berlin Reich Chancellery.

*This and following page:* The ornate interior of Tiergartenstrasse 4, prior to alterations.

Two interior rooms at the time they were used by Paul Graupe.

*Near right:*
Erwin Lambert was a bricklayer employed on the structural alterations to Tiergartenstrasse 4.

*Far right:* Professor Werner Heyde.

*Above left:* Professor Paul Nitsche.

*Above right:* Dr Carl-Heinz Rodenberg, whose own son suffered from encephalitis, promoted the use of sterilisation for mentally ill and disabled patients.

Personal-Ausweis

Eigenhändige Unterschrift des Inhabers.

Es wird hiermit bescheinigt, daß der Buchinhaber die durch obenstehendes Mitglied dargestellte Person und Mitglied der Nat.-soz. Deutschen Arbeiter-Partei ist, sowie die darunter befindliche Unterschrift eigenhändig vollzogen hat.

Innsbruck, den 9. XII. 32.

Die Bezirksleitung (Unterschrift und Stempel)

9
2*

*Above left:* Dr Albert Widmann, the chemist expert on poison gas.

*Above right:* Of all the doctors used in the T4 programme, Dr Irmfried Eberl was the only one to command a death camp.

*Left to right*: Erich Bauer, Rudolf Lonauer, Viktor Ratka, Friedrich Mennecke, Paul Nitsche, and Gerhard Wischer.

*Left to right*: Valentin Faltlhauser, secretaries Ilse Haus and Lieselotte P., Frau Eva Mennecke, and Otto Hebold.

Female nursing staff at Hadamar.

The kitchen staff at Hartheim. Far left is none other than Kurt Franz, and next to him is Paul Bredow.

*Above*: Two of the T4 Gekrat bus drivers, including Franz Mayrhuber, with 'burners' Josef Vallaster and Vincenzo Nohel.

*Left:* One of the grey buses used to transport patients to their place of murder.

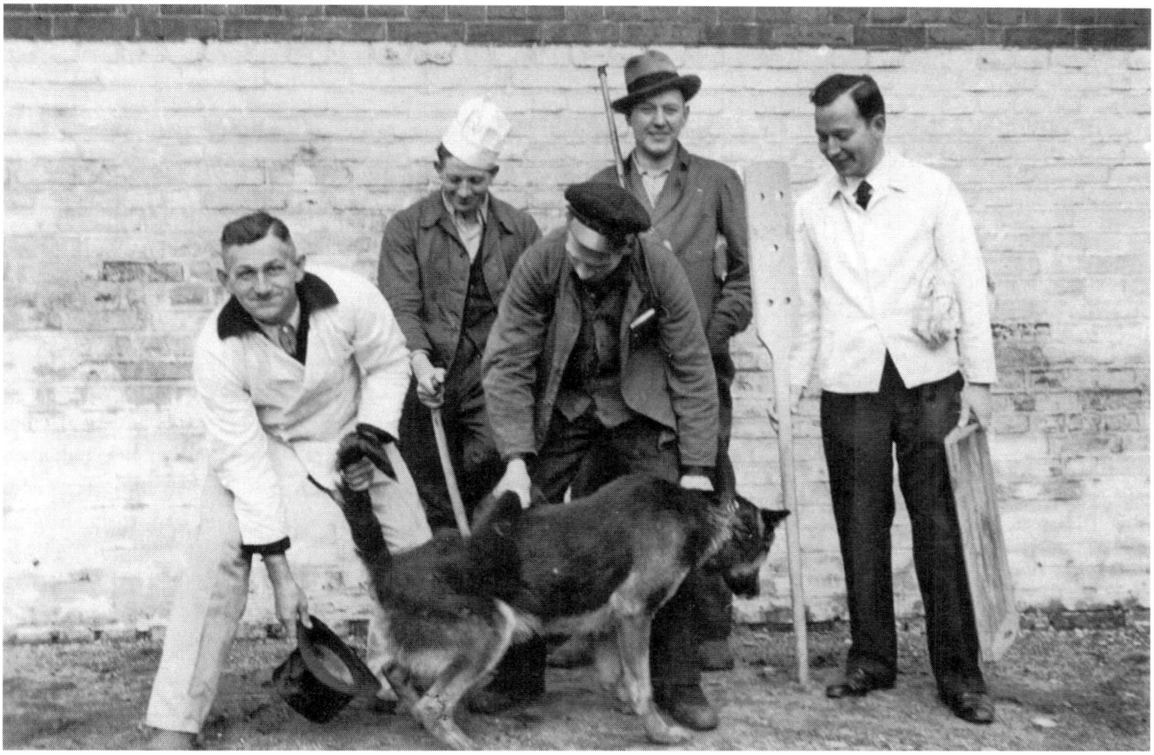

A snapshot taken at Brandenburg. Fooling around for the camera are Johann Niemann in chef's hat, Kurt Bolender in trilby, and August Hengst far right. The other two are not identified.

*Above left:* Johann Niemann (*left*) and Gottfried Schwarz (*right*), photographed near the T4 facility at Bernburg.

*Above right:* Executive head of the T4 office, Friedrich Tillmann.

*Above left:* T4 accountant Alfred Ittner. Later served at Sobibor and was responsible there for the receipt of valuables from those destined for the gas chamber.

*Above right:* Gerhard Bohne. Legal head of the T4 camouflage company, Reich Association of Sanatoriums and Care Institutions, and therefore the co-organiser of Aktion T4.

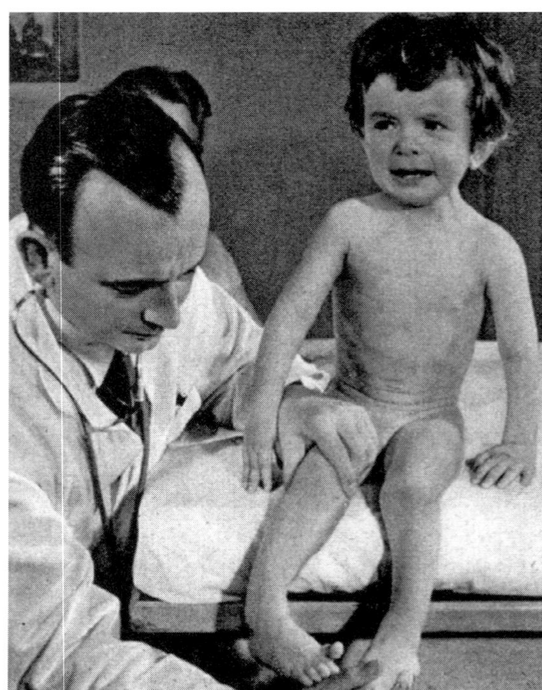

*Above left:* Dr Hans Hefelmann, one of the main organisers and implementers of the euthanasia programme.

*Above right:* Dr Ernst Wentzler, one of the paediatric reviewers and an expert on rickets.

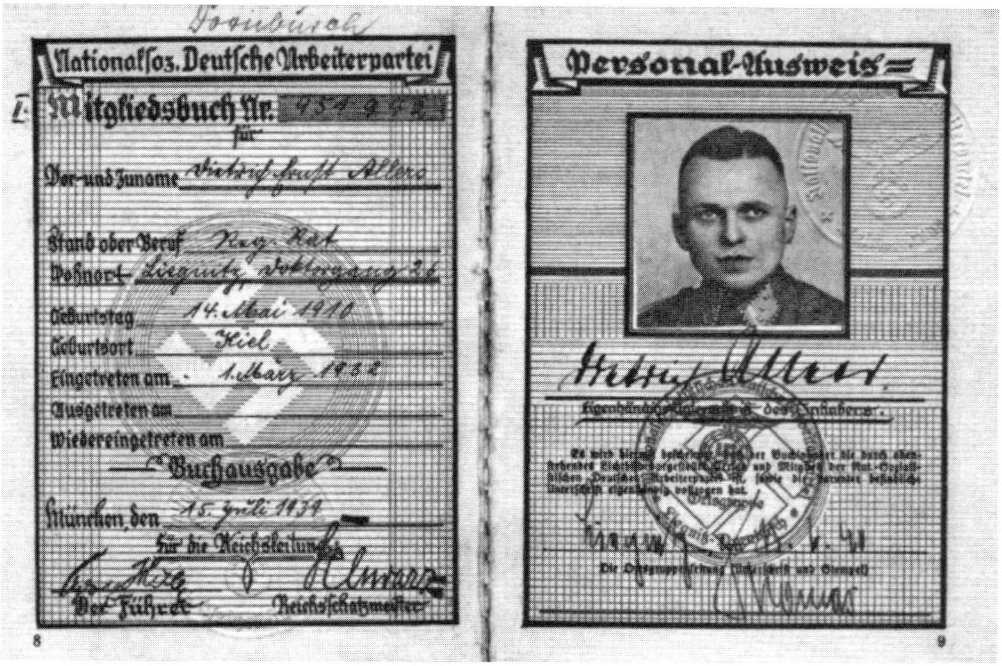
Nationalsoz. Deutsche Arbeiterpartei

Mitgliedsbuch Nr.

für

Vor- und Zuname Dietrich Ernst Allers

Stand oder Beruf Reg. Rat

Wohnort Liegnitz

Geburtstag 14. Mai 1910

Geburtsort Kiel

Eingetreten am 1. März 1932

Ausgetreten am

Wiedereingetreten am

Buchausgabe

München, den 15. Juli 1934

Für die Reichsleitung

Der Führer Reichsschatzmeister

8

Personal-Ausweis

Eigenhändige Unterschrift des Inhabers

Es wird hiermit bescheinigt, daß der Buchinhaber die durch obenstehendes Lichtbild vorgestellte Person und Mitglied der Nat.-Sozialistischen Deutschen Arbeiterpartei ist, sowie die darunter befindliche Unterschrift eigenhändig vollzogen hat.

Die Ortsgruppenleitung (Unterschrift und Stempel)

9

The NSDAP membership book of Dietrich Allers.

Professor Max de Crinis.

Dr Bodo Gorgass.

Dr Georg Renno.

Sonnenstein Castle.

Hadamar euthanasia centre.

The crematorium in use at Hadamar.

The Brandenburg facility in 1937. It was here that the first experimental gassing took place.

Hartheim Castle in Austria.

*Above left:* The crematorium furnace at Hartheim belching smoke.

*Above right:* The killing centre at Grafeneck. The elevated facility still operates as a mental health sanatorium.

*Above:* A modern photo of the facility at Bernburg.

*Right:* A view inside the former gas chamber at Bernburg.

Haus Schoberstein at the Attersee. Used as a recreation facility for the staff of T4, the headquarters moved here later in the war.

T4 staff taking a rest and recuperation break at the Attersee. In this group are Karl Ludwig (second left), Willi Mentz (third right), and Max Beulich (far right).

Partying staff at Hartheim.

Nursing staff from Hadamar on trial post-war. Front left is Dr Adolf Wahlmann.

*Above left:* State Secretary in the General Government and Dr Frank's deputy was Josef Bühler. He represented Frank at the Wannsee Conference, chaired by Heydrich, in January 1942.

*Above right:* Along with Odilo Globocnik, the man credited with killing large numbers of Polish Jews is Fritz Katzmann. He escaped justice after the war and lived under the assumed name 'Bruno Albrecht', revealing his true identity on his deathbed in Darmstadt in 1957.

*Left:* The Lublin warehouse at Chopin Street 27.

*Above:* Inside, the rooms and corridors had shelves stuffed with all manner of property seized from evacuees.

The Aktion Reinhardt headquarters were established at the Julius Schreck SS barracks. Hermann Höfle moved into small rooms behind the circular window in the loft space under the roof. Note the sentry box at the gate in this wartime image (*left*). Below is modern photograph of the side aspect of the building.

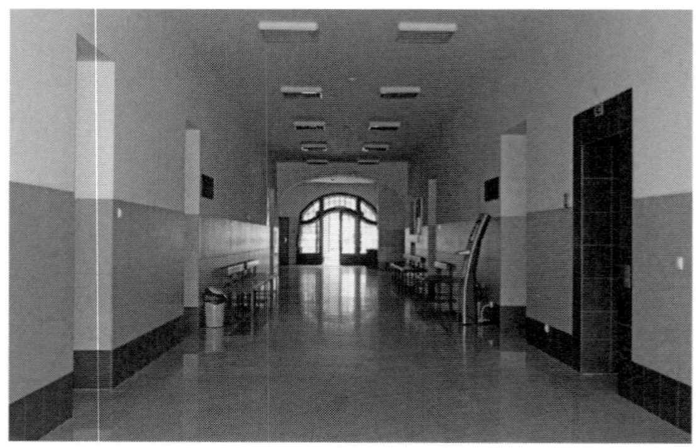

*Above and middle right:* The interior ground floor as it appears today.

*Above:* One of the upper floors.

The real power behind the Aktion Reinhardt throne. Senior staff of the SS-Wirtschaftsverwaltung Hauptamt. *Left to right*: Richard Glücks, August Frank, Oswald Pohl, Hans Lörner, and Hans Kammler.

State Secretary in the Finance Ministry, Fritz Reinhardt.

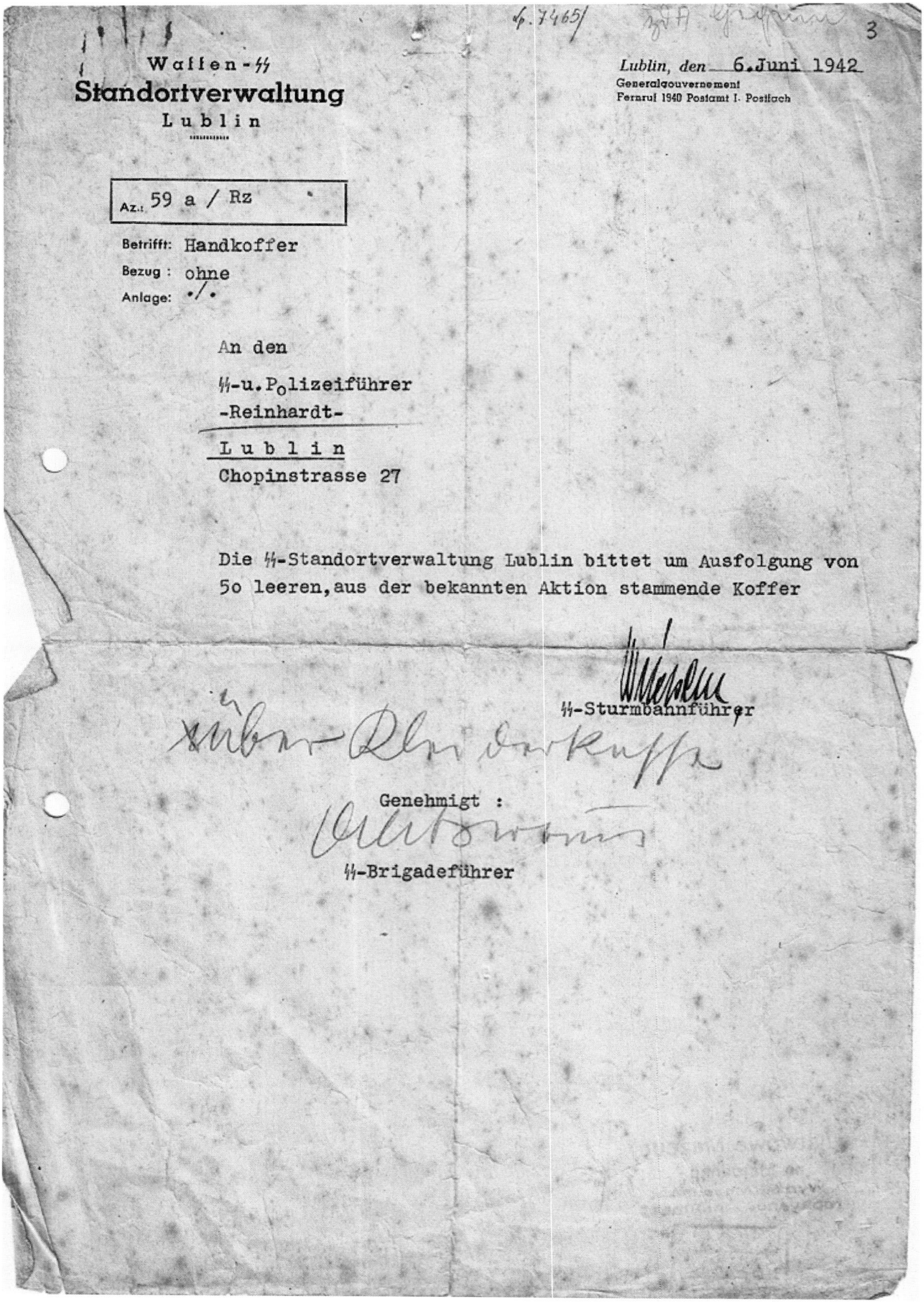

Waffen-SS
Standortverwaltung
Lublin

*Lublin, den* 6.Juni 1942
Generalgouvernement
Fernruf 1940 Postamt I. Postfach

Az.: 59 a / Rz

Betrifft: Handkoffer
Bezug : ohne
Anlage: ./.

An den
SS-u. Polizeiführer
-Reinhardt-
Lublin
Chopinstrasse 27

Die SS-Standortverwaltung Lublin bittet um Ausfolgung von 5o leeren, aus der bekannten Aktion stammende Koffer

SS-Sturmbannführer

Genehmigt :

SS-Brigadeführer

The first document discovered bearing the name of Aktion Reinhardt. It is dated 6 June 1942 and is signed by Georg Wippern. Globocnik has added a note and his signature in blue crayon pencil.

The inspector of Aktion Reinhardt, Christian Wirth.

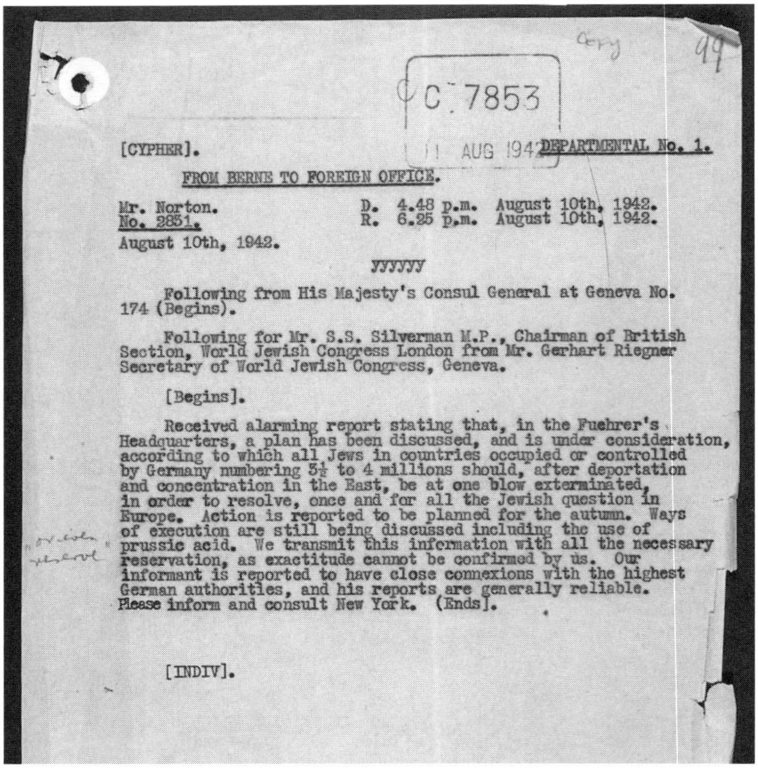

C. 7853

11 AUG 1942

[CYPHER]. DEPARTMENTAL No. 1.

FROM BERNE TO FOREIGN OFFICE.

Mr. Norton. D. 4.48 p.m. August 10th, 1942.
No. 2831. R. 6.25 p.m. August 10th, 1942.
August 10th, 1942.

yyyyyy

Following from His Majesty's Consul General at Geneva No. 174 (Begins).

Following for Mr. S.S. Silverman M.P., Chairman of British Section, World Jewish Congress London from Mr. Gerhart Riegner Secretary of World Jewish Congress, Geneva.

[Begins].

Received alarming report stating that, in the Fuehrer's Headquarters, a plan has been discussed, and is under consideration, according to which all Jews in countries occupied or controlled by Germany numbering 3½ to 4 millions should, after deportation and concentration in the East, be at one blow exterminated, in order to resolve, once and for all the Jewish question in Europe. Action is reported to be planned for the autumn. Ways of execution are still being discussed including the use of prussic acid. We transmit this information with all the necessary reservation, as exactitude cannot be confirmed by us. Our informant is reported to have close connexions with the highest German authorities, and his reports are generally reliable. Please inform and consult New York. (Ends).

[INDIV].

By the time of this telegraphed message, Aktion Reinhardt was well underway.

*Above left:* Richard Thomalla was given the job of building the death camps.

*Above right:* Hermann Höfle. As administrative head of Aktion Reinhardt, Höfle was one of the few Lublin SS officers who had full access to the plans for the destruction of the Polish Jews.

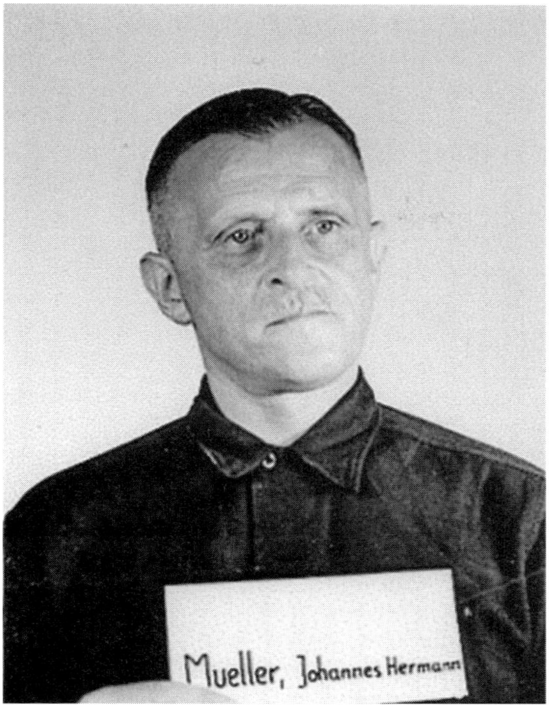

*Above left:* Johannes Hermann Müller, head of Sipo and SD in Lublin.

*Above right:* Dr Friedrich Suhr. Legal head in Eichmann's office, dealing with Jewish evacuation matters and 'atonement' payments. He subsequently commanded two commandos of Einsatzgruppe C, and committed suicide in 1946.

*Above left:* Hermann Krumey, SD evacuation expert.

*Above right:* Dieter Wisliceny, another Jewish evacuation expert on Eichmann's staff.

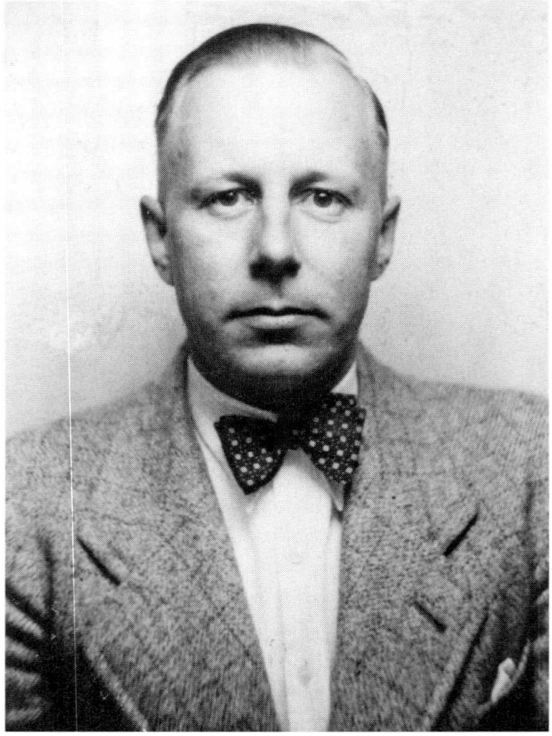

*Above left:* An old collaborator of Globocnik from pre-Anschluss days in Austria, Franz Novak, was employed in Eichmann's department as a transport expert.

*Above right:* Walter Rauff, helped design the gas van.

The interior of a gas van.

The excavated site of the manor house at Chełmno with the church in the background.

'Nobody liked doing this job … I more or less feared that we belonged to a doomed group'—Hans-Heinz Schütt, SS-Oberscharführer in T4 and Aktion Reinhardt, was acquitted post-war.

*Above and top right:* Wirth was joined in Lublin by his loyal adjutant, Josef Oberhauser.

*Right:* Gottfried Schwarz had been employed as a crematorium 'burner' in T4. He joined Wirth and Oberhauser in Poland, and was appointed as Wirth's deputy commandant at Belzec. Transferred to the Adriatic Coastland Operational Zone as a member of Abteilung 'R', he was killed by partisans on 19 June 1944 and lies buried at Costermano in Italy.

A man who would become a major participant in the death camps of Aktion Reinhardt was Lorenz Hackenholt. He is circled here in his local SS unit in Gelsenkirchen.

*Above left*: A large number of the personnel required for Aktion Reinhardt received training at the Trawniki camp and were a mixture of Ukrainians, Byelorussians, and citizens of Baltic States. Here Himmler inspects Trawniki men during his visit on 19 July 1942. The figure third from left is Hermann Höfle.

*Above right:* Amon Göth was an early member of Aktion Reinhardt and was later immortalised by the film *Schindler's List*.

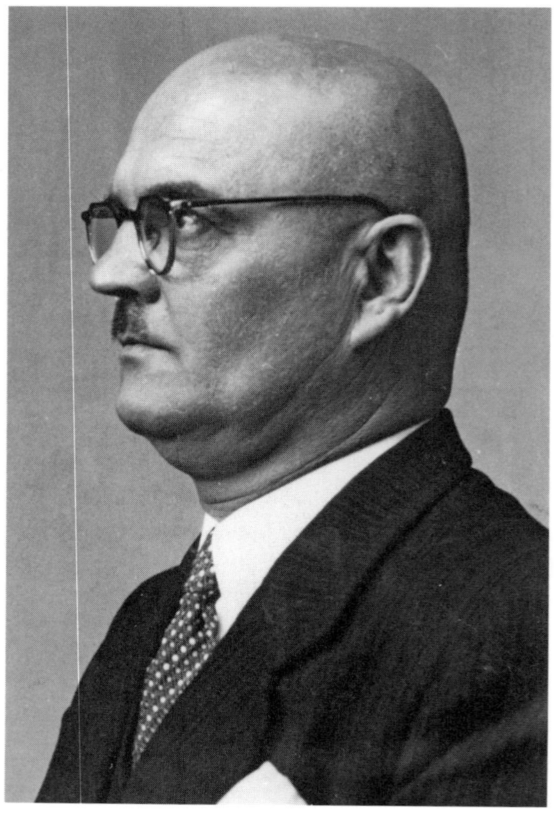

The man selected by Globocnik to command the first death camp at Belzec was Stuttgart police detective Christian Wirth. As such, and as the subsequent Inspector of Aktion Reinhardt camps, the efficient Wirth epitomised everyone's idea of a brutal and emotionless administrator, generating fear in both the prisoners & his own staff.

During the entire time Wirth was in Poland, he wore the green police uniform. He took to wearing SS uniform on his transfer to OZAK, where he was entitled to wear the SD sleeve diamond as a result of his criminal police background and by the nature of his secretive duties. Left is Wirth with Franz Reichleitner in the background. This photo was taken in September 1940 after Josef Vallaster's marriage to Hartheim nurse, Elisabeth Gust. The happy couple are in the middle with an unidentified woman at far right. Probably taken at Hartheim Castle.

*Above left:* The happy Vallaster couple, Elisabeth and Josef. During the Sobibor uprising, Vallaster was killed by prisoners while he was ordering a new pair of slippers for his wife.

*Above right:* Wirth's Ukrainian driver.

Opposite the office of the SSPF in Lublin stands this small building. For a time, it was occupied by Christian Wirth as his quarters.

Jews were ordered to congregate in Lublin in preparation for evacuation.

They were assembled at the former Marhaszala Synagogue below castle hill for 'evacuation to the East'.

From the assembly point, the Jews were marched along ul. Kalinowszczyzna towards the Umschlagplatz (dispersal point).

The Lublin Umschlagplatz was selected for its location and rail link. From here, it was a short rail journey by freight car to Belzec and oblivion.

Rudolf Goeckel, the station master at Belzec.

Early prisoners at Belzec, probably employed at sorting the belongings of arrivals. The sorting sheds are behind them.

Rudi Kamm. The same sorting barracks on the right and the perimeter fence in the left background.

The camp administration office at Belzec.

Belzec camp guards.

*Near right:* A member of the camp staff.

*Far right:* Two Ukrainian camp guards at Belzec.

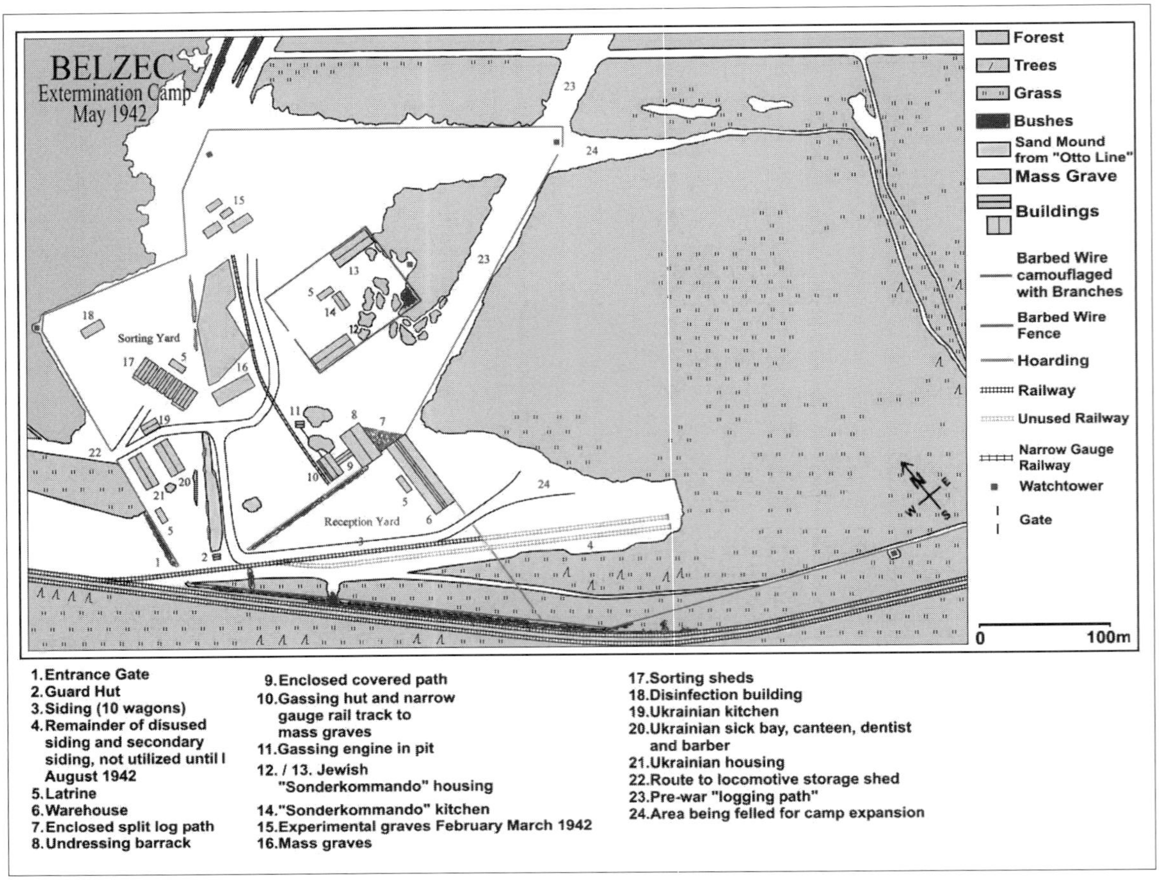


Belzec first phase.

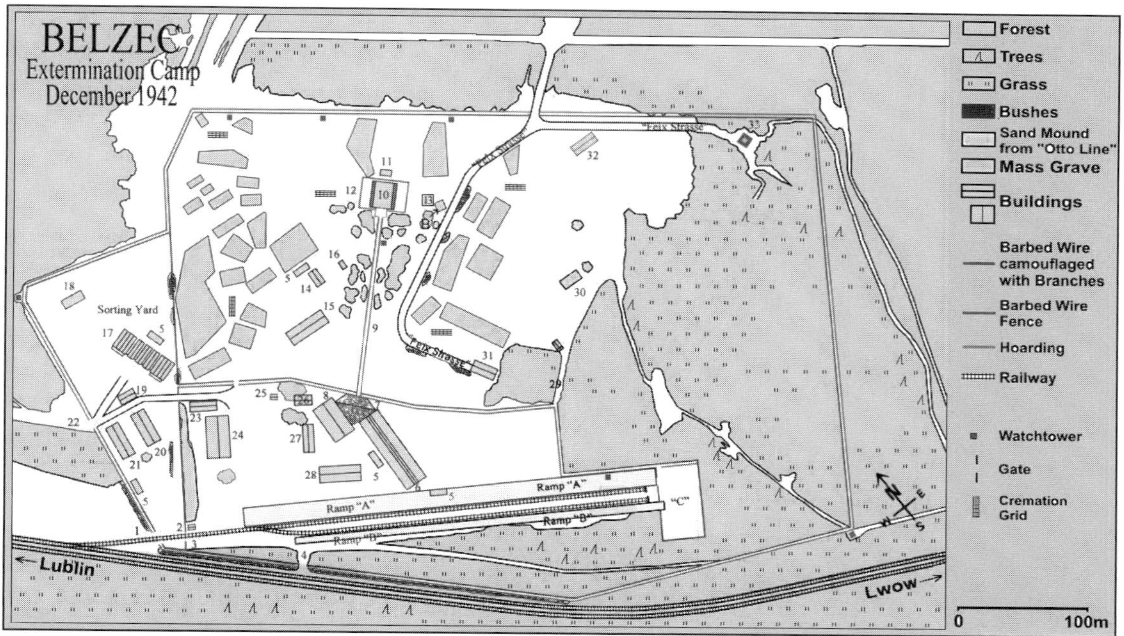


"A" Ramp A (20 wagons)
"B" Ramp B (20 wagons)
"C" Holding "pen" for ramp "B" - transport and detention area for the elderly, infirm, or "difficult" deportees
1. Entrance gate
2. Guard hut
3. Gate for "handing over the transport"
4. 2nd entrance gate
5. Latrines
6. Warehouse
7. Enclosed split log path
8. Undressing and "Barbers" barrack for women
9. "Die Schleuse" (The Sluice) - Camouflaged barbed wire path to gas chambers
10. "Stiftung Hackenholt" (The Hackenholt Foundation) - Gas chamber building
11. Gassing engine hut
12. Camouflaged netting raised on poles covering the gas chambers
13. Bone crushing machine on platform
14. "Sonderkommando" kitchen
15. "Sonderkommando" housing
16. Gallows
17. Sorting sheds
18. Disinfection building
19. Ukrainian kitchen
20. Ukrainian sick bay, canteen, dentist and barber
21. Ukrainian housing
22. Route to locomotive storage shed
23. Tailors / shoemakers workshop
24. SS Garage
25. Electric generator
26. Jewish "skilled workers" kitchen
27. Laundry, sewing, stitching workshop and women's housing
28. "Skilled workers" barrack
29. Route from holding pen to "Lazarett"
30. "Lazarett" pit used for shooting victims
31. Dispensary
32. Ukrainian nightshift housing
33. High watchtower erected on bunker overlooking the camp
B Bonemill pit

Belzec second phase.

SS staff at Belzec, standing behind the Kommandantur. Wirth used this building as his office and his lodgings. *Left to right (in uniform)*: Friedrich Tauscher, Karl Schluch, unident., unident., Karl Gringers, Ernst Zierke, Lorenz Hackenholt, Artur Dachsel, and Heinrich Barbl. Today, the building still exists as a residential house on the main road about 300 metres west of the camp area. In 2014, it was unoccupied.

Early in 1942, Trawniki men demonstrate their firepower in the yard of the Belzec Kommandantur. Centre, in SS uniform, stands Johann Niemann.

Austrian Jews being deported to Belzec.

Another deportation train being loaded.

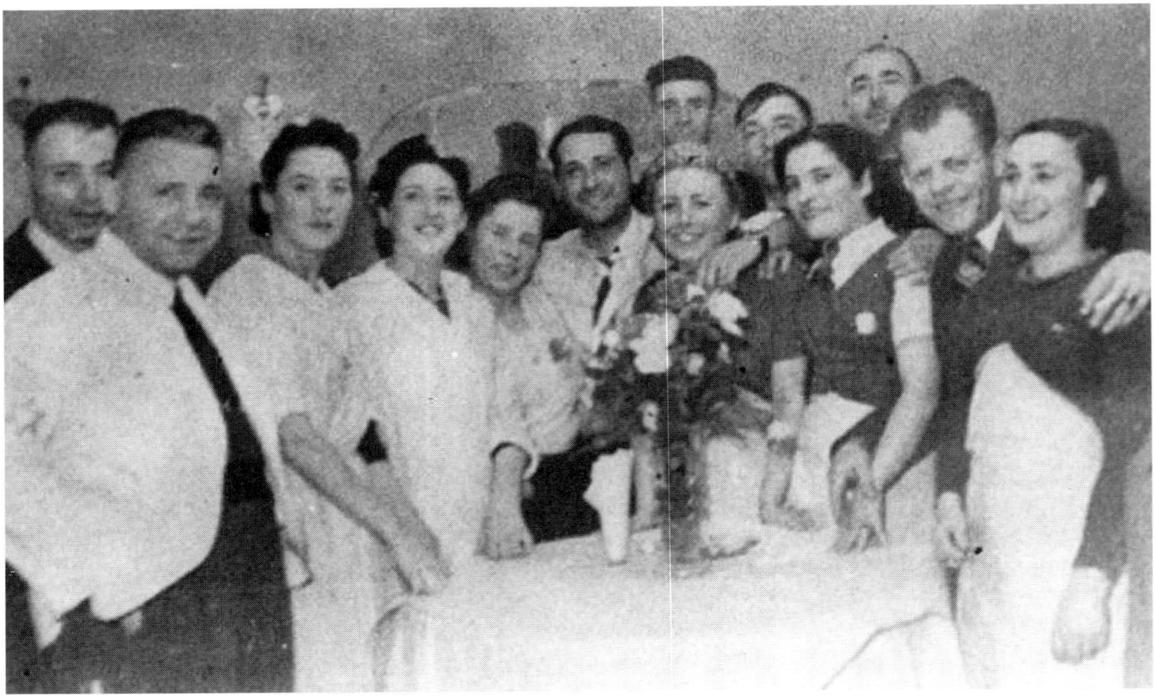

A Jewish informant used by Globocnik lived and ran a popular restaurant within the Lublin Ghetto perimeter at ul. Lubartowska 15. Known as 'the Ghetto King', Szama Grajer is pictured (centre) with his staff. When the ghetto was liquidated, Globocnik could not afford to let Grajer survive as he knew too much. Hermann Worthoff shot Grajer on Globocnik's orders.

Comrades in arms at Belzec. *Left to right*: Oberhauser, Jirmann, and Franz.

Wirth's replacement as Belzec commandant was Gottlieb Hering. After Belzec closed, Hering was appointed as commandant of Poniatowa and oversaw the massacre of 'Harvest Festival' in November 1943. He transferred to Trieste with Globocnik and died on 9 October 1945.

Hering (right) enjoying a beer with his Belzec comrade Heinrich Gley.

Kurt Franz.

Dr Kurt Gerstein.

Professor Wilhelm Pfannenstiel.

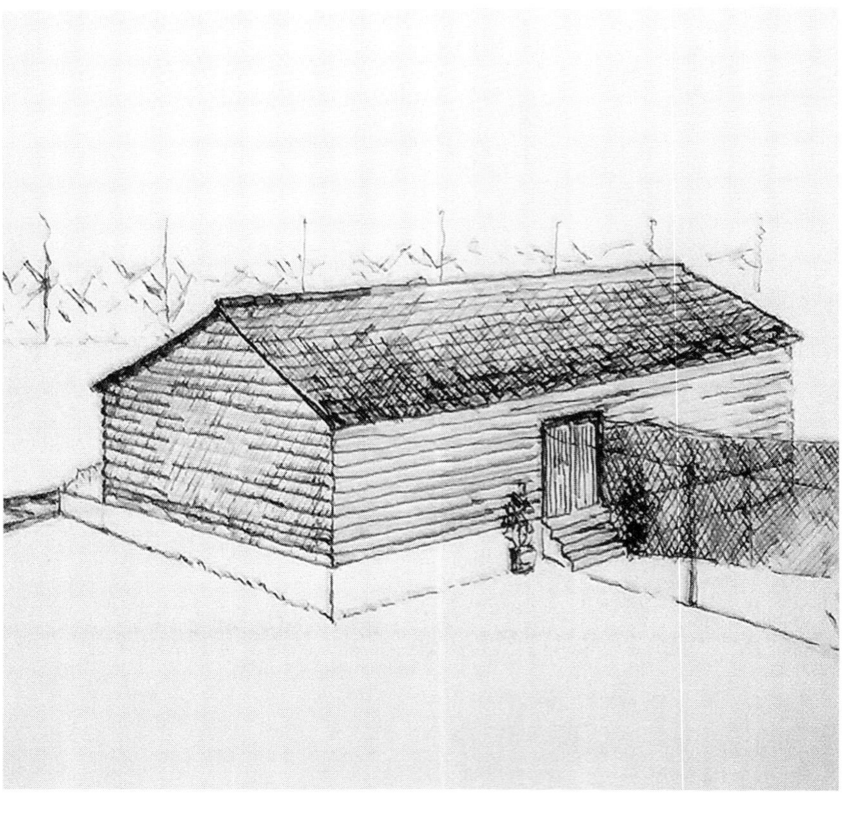

An artist's impression of what the first gassing hut at Belzec may have looked like, based on witness descriptions. (*Sketch by Carol Amis*)

The second phase gassing facility at Belzec. Drawing by the late William Rutherford.

The area of the former Belzec camp in 1945. The camp stood on the sandy soil to the right. The main railway line is on the left, with the camp spur in the centre foreground.

Post-war excavations of the camp buildings.

*Above and top of next page:* The modern camp memorial ground as it appeared in 2014.

A rusting gas/shower pipe dug up at the site and now on display in the Belzec memorial museum.

The west side façade of Georg Wippern's SS-Standortverwaltung building as it appeared during the war.

*Above left:* The south facing front of the building during the war.

*Above right:* A wartime image. This was the location of Wippern's strong room, built in the basement to hold the valuables, cash, and precious stones and metals plundered from the victims of Aktion Reinhardt. Note the face at the window, bottom left.

The southern front façade and the east side of the former SS-Standortverwaltung building as it appears today.

The west and southern facades today. The building, once a school for domestic science, is now used as an ophthalmic clinic.

The rear of the building with the modern car park which was once an elegant garden and overlooked trees. This is believed to be the garden location described by Franz Stangl for his initial meeting with Globocnik.

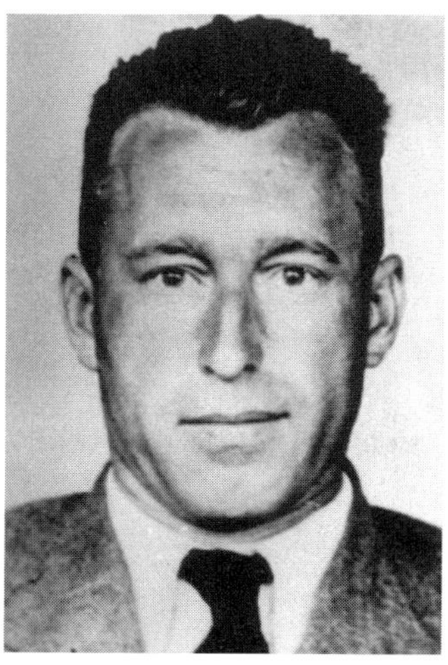

*From top to bottom:*

At the rear of the building, overlooking the former garden, stood these buildings. The lower structures were described by witnesses as 'barracks' and housed the smelting oven used to melt down precious metals. The rear of the main building is away to the right.

Globocnik in conversation with August Frank, the author of the memo instruction which regulated the handling of goods seized by the SS.

Globocnik selected the Austrian policeman and T4 staffer Franz Paul Stangl as the commandant of the new gassing facility at Sobibor.

Kurt Bolender. Stangl was aware of Bolender's efficiency from the T4 programme. He selected Bolender as an ideal deputy at Sobibor.

As with Belzec, Sobibor was planned in the same locality as an existing labour camp. This photo was almost certainly taken during a visit by Globocnik to the Sobibor site prior to the operation of the death camp. The station buildings are in the background. Second from left is Ernst Lerch, and the officer far left resembles Lothar von Seltmann.

The same location in 2014.

Karl Frenzel.

Staff at Sobibor enjoying their off-duty time. Commonly identified as left to right: Paul Groth, unident., Werner Dubois, Siegfried Graetschus, Kurt Bolender, and Ernst Zierke. (These are subject to discussion.)

*From top to bottom:*

Stangl (in SS uniform, fifth from right) hosts a 'get-together' for some of his staff in his house opposite Sobibor station. *Left to right*: Gerhard Borner, Karl Frenzel, unident., Franz Stangl, Erich Bauer, Gustav Wagner, unident., and Hubert Gomersky.

Stangl's house at Sobibor as it appeared in 2014. This building, outside the camp perimeter, is not to be confused with the 'Swallow's Nest' within the camp which was also used as accommodation for officers.

The Sobibor camp entrance in early 1943. This gate was used mainly by camp staff. Those destined for the gas chamber and the few held as prisoners, arrived almost exclusively by train via the rail spur to the right of this gate.

A view of the Vorlager from the south-east. The camp gate is visible in the left foreground. The buildings in the foreground from the left to right are the "Swallow's Nest" (accommodation for camp staff), the camp magazine, the guardhouse and the combined dentist & Trawniki arrest cell on the right foreground. The fire watchtower can be seen right of centre. The entrance to the 'tube' is hidden to the right of the watchtower, with Camp III beyond the trees to the right. A section of the camp ramp can just be seen in the bottom right corner.

This photo was taken in early summer 1943, from a guard watchtower on the southern perimeter, looking east across Camp I. The camp gate is at the far end of the outer fence line. The commandant's house lies out of camera shot to the right of the camp gate. The rail spur and ramp are behind the buildings in the background.

Photo taken from the Vorlager looking north-east. The tall forestry fire watchtower is prominent in the centre, with a guard tower to the right, behind which lies the 'tube' and the direction of Camp III.

*Left to right*: Rudolf Kamm, Willi Wendland, Heinrich Unverhau, Fritz Konrad and Johann Klier. They are standing in front of the new Kasino (a type of dining/relaxing room) in early summer 1943. Note the carefully manicured grass and flower beds, with trellising against the wall. The buildings are obviously constructed of sturdier materials than timber.

Johann Niemann (left) before his promotion to SS-Untersturmführer. Niemann was killed during the prisoner uprising on 14 October 1943. On the right is Franz Hödl.

Winter 1942/1943. In front of the old Sobibor Kasino. On horseback are Niemann (left) and Beckmann (right). Standing (left to right) are Frenzel, Bauer and unident.

Enjoying the sunshine on the new Kasino terrace in summer 1943 are Niemann in his white summer tunic, having been promoted to SS-Untersturmführer, and Gustav Wagner (right).

Rarely seen in photographs, camp commandant Franz Reichleitner (far left) on the Kasino terrace. In the centre, with his arm around a female employee in the Kasino, is the Sobibor 'Gasmeister', Erich Bauer. Extreme right is Niemann and Schulze is in the background.

The woman is almost certainly one of the local Polish women employed in the camp Kasino. She embraces Franz Reichleitner, while Eric Bauer smiles for the camera.

Left to right: Arthur Dachsel, Johann Niemann, Franz Reichleitner and Erich Bauer. Dachsel was the oldest man employed on Aktion Reinhardt. Note the SD diamond on Reichleitner's sleeve.

Willi Wendland (left) and Rudi Kamm (right) in front of the goose coop in Camp II at Sobibor. Camp survivor, Mordechai Goldfarb, testified that the geese were stirred up for each action so that their honking would cover the sound of any screams from the victims in the gas chamber.

Trawniki men photographed on the parade ground in front of Camp III at Sobibor in 1943. In the centre foreground is Ivan Demjanjuk. Camp III is hidden behind the line of trees in the background. On the extreme left, the roof of the building in which the women had their hair cut off prior to gassing is just visible. Slightly right of it, part of the gas chamber roof emerges above the treeline. This is the only known existing image of the Sobibor gas chamber building.

*Above left:* Erich Bauer, the 'Gasmeister' at Sobibor.

*Above right:* Erwin Lambert. His bricklaying expertise and his experience with the T4 programme resulted in his use in the construction of the Aktion Reinhardt gas chambers.

Karl Frenzel (left) and Erich Bauer (right) photographed after their transfer to OZAK.

In July 1943, personnel from Aktion Reinhardt visited Berlin. On the grounds of the Old Lublin Airfield camp, Trawniki men load their luggage onto the bus. Looking directly at the camera is guard, Alexander Kaiser. Aktion Reinhardt storage buildings can be seen left and in the background.

During the visit to Berlin. *Left to right*: Arnold Oels, the director of personnel for Aktion Reinhardt in the Führer Chancellery, Dietrich Allers with his arm in a sling, Johann Niemann, Werner Blankenburg, and guard Bienemann.

An aerial view of the Sobibor terrain dated 28 May 1944. The railway line running north to south bisects the image. The former camp area is comprised of the three light shaded areas to the left of the railway line. The former camp commandant's house is the small building just visible to the south of the camp. Some original buildings in the former Vorlager still exist. The former Camp III area, containing the gas chambers and burial pits, is the most northern light shaded area.

On 14 October 1943, the prisoners in Sobibor rebelled, killing a number of camp personnel. Among them was the acting commandant, Johann Niemann. He was struck with an axe in the camp tailor shop. His corpse is on the right in this photograph.

The funeral ceremony for the Sobibor fallen. SS-Obersturmführer Gottlieb Hering (right) addresses the mourners. To his right stand Dietrich Allers and Werner Blankenburg. Also visible are Willi Wendland, Alexander Kaiser, Ernst Zierke and Franz Wolf, whose brother Josef Wolf had been killed. The tall bespectacled SS officer is often mistakenly identified as Ernst Lerch, but it is not him as his rank and decorations do not fit Lerch at this date. His identity remains a mystery.

The mourners salute the fallen.

The former camp commandant's house in relation to the earlier camp area which lies to the left of the road in the trees (2014).

The abandoned Sobibor railway station in 2014. The building is original.

The view from the station towards the camp area in 2014.

The original buffer at the end of the camp rail spur (2014).

Just after this photograph was taken in 2014, the camp memorial area was closed for excavations. Remains of the brick foundations of the gas chambers were uncovered in the tarmac area to the right of the memorials.

The foundations of the original gas chambers were excavated in 2014.

An artist impression of a gas chamber at Sobibor (copied from an original drawn by the late William Rutherford).

**P r o g r a m m**

**zum Besuch des RF-SS am 18. und 19.Juli 1942**

**Sonnabend, den 18.7.42:**

| | |
|---|---|
| 12.oo bis 14.30 Uhr | Mittagessen und Kaffee im Haus des SS- und Polizeiführers, |
| | anschliessend Fahrt über Parkstrasse, Sachsenstrasse, Warschauerstrasse, Mannschaftshaus, |
| 15.00 bis 17.00 Uhr | Besichtigung des SS-Mannschaftshauses, |
| | Rückfahrt Warschauerstrasse, Distriktstrasse zur Julius-Schreck-Kaserne |
| 17.00 bis 18.00 Uhr | Besichtigung der volkspolitischen Dienststellen beim SS- und Polizeiführer |
| 18.00 bis 19.00 Uhr | Besuch der Chopinstrasse 27 und SS-Standortverwaltung |
| 19.30 bis 20.30 Uhr | Abendessen beim SS- und Polizeiführer mit anschliessenden Besprechungen |

**Sonntag, den 19.7.42:**

| | |
|---|---|
| 7.30 Uhr | Frühstück im Haus des SS- und Polizeiführers |
| 8.30 Uhr | Abfahrt nach Trawniki |
| 9.oo Uhr | Ankunft und 30 Min. Besichtigung des Lagers Trawniki |
| 10.15 Uhr | Ankunft im Cholm, 1 Std.Besichtigung der 2.SS-R-Reiter-Schwadron mit kleinem Imbiss |
| 11.30 Uhr | Abfahrt vom Bahnhof Cholm nach Sobibor, Fahrt und Besichtigung 1 Std.45 Min. |
| 13.15 Uhr | Ankunft im Cholm |
| 13.30 bis 14,15 Uhr | Mittagessen bei der 2.SS-Reiter-Schwadron |
| 14.15 bis 15.00 Uhr | Besichtigung des Flüchtlingslagers im Cholm |
| 15.oo Uhr | Abfahrt nach Wysokie |
| 16,15 Uhr | Ankunft in Wysokie |
| 17.15 Uhr | Abfahrt nach Lublin |
| 18.3o Uhr | Ankunft in Lublin, Besichtigung des KGL und der Bekleidungswerke, 1 Std. |
| 20.00 Uhr | Abendessen im Haus des SS- und Polizeiführers. |

**Gäste:**

Reichsführer-SS
SS-Obergruppenführer Pohl
SS-Obergruppenführer Krüger
SS-Oberführer Kassel
SS-Standartenführer Prof.Dr.Wüst
SS-Hauptsturmführer Grothmann
SS-Hauptsturmführer Schnittker
Biermeier

Proof that Himmler visited Sobibor on 19 July 1942. The programme for his visit to Lublin on 18–19 July 1942, including an inspection of the Chopin Street warehouse.

*Above left:* Josef Vallaster was previously employed as a 'burner' at Hartheim. He transferred to Sobibor in 1942 where he was a supervisor of the gas chambers. He was killed in the prisoners' revolt in October 1943.

*Above right:* Sobibor railway station 2014.

The exact same location during the war.

This photograph was used to identify Paul Groth (centre) as a stoker in the Hartheim facility. In April 1942, he was transferred to Sobibor to supervise the sorting of clothes. At the end of 1942 he was assigned to Belzec, where he would be in charge of the train which brought Jews from Belzec to Sobibor for execution in the early summer of 1943. On the right is Paul Bredow.

Plan of Treblinka II.

Aerial view of Treblinka memorial site.

The first commandant of Treblinka II, Dr Irmfried Eberl.

Eberl photographed in Poland.

Eberl was replaced by Stangl as a result of his inability to cope with the large numbers of transports. Stangl, seen here in white tunic in conversation with Kurt Franz at Treblinka, immediately set about improving the efficiency of the killing process and the disposal of corpses.

*Left:* Kurt Franz, known as 'the Doll' by the prisoners due to his boyish good looks, was the final commandant of Treblinka II. He oversaw the last murders and the dismantling of the camp.

*Above:* Left to right: Paul Bredow, Willi Mentz, Max Möller, and Josef Hirtreiter. A photo reportedly taken at the camp zoo.

*Above left:* Franz Suchomel was employed as a photographer at Hadamar. At Treblinka, he was responsible for the confiscation of valuables from incoming transports. He also performed duty at Sobibor in October 1943. He was interviewed by Claude Lanzmann for his ground-breaking documentary *Shoah* when he repeated a song prisoners at Treblinka were forced to learn—'We know only the word of our Commander. We know only obedience and duty. We want to serve, to go on serving until little luck ends it all. Hurrah!'

*Above right:* August Miete, the 'Angel of Death' at Treblinka, carried out thousands of murders at the camp Lazaret, assisted by Willi Mentz.

*Above left:* Karl Pötzinger. Employed at both the Brandenburg and Bernburg euthanasia centres, Pötzinger was transferred to Treblinka II where he supervised the gas chambers before taking charge of the exhumation and cremation operation. He was transferred to Italy where he was seriously wounded in an air raid, finally dying of his wounds on 22 December 1944. He is buried at Costermano.

*Above right:* Jewish deportees being loaded onto a freight train at Siedlce on 22 August 1942. Their destination was the gas chamber at Treblinka.

The point at which the deportee trains left the line between Malkinia and Siedlce, and headed towards Treblinka II. The branch line is no longer in use and the tracks have been removed, but the route of the rail line remains as a dirt track and can be seen clearly from the air like a scar across the countryside. Nearly all victims of the gas chambers at Treblinka travelled this route.

The camp memorial site in 2014. The stone sleepers and the raised platform mark the location of the former camp ramp where thousands of deportees arrived at Treblinka. Within hours, the vast majority were dead. The hundreds of large stones litter the memorial site and signify towns and villages from where evacuations began.

The view from the ramp towards the massive monument. Behind the monument is the site of the former gas chambers and the cremation and burial area. The reception compound and the so-called 'tube' were to the left, between the ramp and the monument.

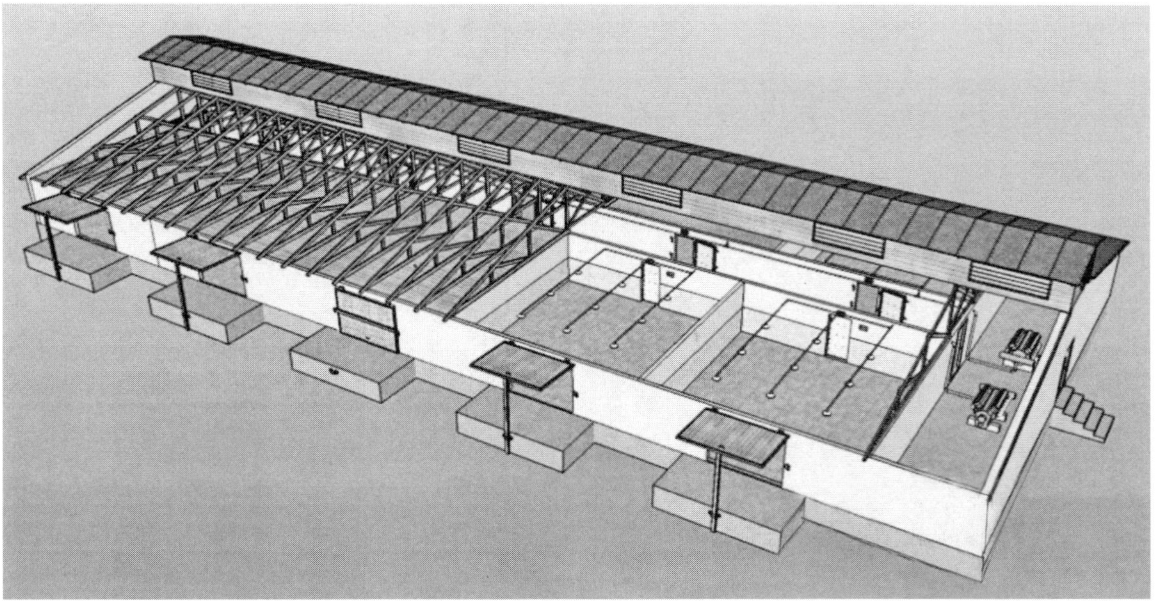

Artist's impression of the large second gas chamber building at Treblinka II. (*Artist copied from a computerised drawing by Peter Laponder on ARC website*)

Impression of the new gas chamber building at Treblinka. The 'tube' is on the right and prisoners entered the structure via a doorway opposite the 'tube'. The steps on the left provided access to the engine rooms. (*Image from the ARC website, credited to ARC & BBC co-operation*)

A mechanical grab used at Treblinka. The original first gas chamber building is just visible in the bottom left, directly under the grab. This image was discovered in the Kurt Franz photo album entitled *Schöne Zeiten* (lovely times).

Two camp guards 'joy riding' on the mechanical grab. This digger was reportedly also used at Belzec.

The grab in use at Treblinka.

*Above left:* In locations throughout occupied territories, the Germans attempted to cover up their crimes by disinterring the thousands of bodies buried at various murder sites in order to cremate them. SS-Standartenführer Paul Blobel was placed in command of this operation.

*Above right:* SS guard jogging at Treblinka. He has been identified as Pinnemann.

*Above left:* The majority of guards at the death camps of Aktion Reinhardt were men who had undergone training at Trawniki. These guards are photographed with their SS supervisor at Trawniki.

*Above right:* The face of Aktion Reinhardt. The majority of SS personnel were NCOs.

Lorenz Hackenholt had a hand in the design and operation of the gas chambers at Belzec, Sobibor and Treblinka. He continued his murderous work at the Old Airfield camp in Lublin and subsequently in the OZAK region where he also participated in anti-partisan operations. Considered one of the more culpable of Aktion Reinhardt, he disappeared at the end of the war and escaped justice.

The liquidation of the Warsaw Ghetto started on 16 May 1943. The SS man with the SD sleeve diamond is Josef Blosche.

High-level strategy meeting. Stroop is obstructed and has his hands on his hips.

Stroop (in profile) with Askari troops during the operation.

Askari troops look at women who appear to be dead during the Warsaw Ghetto operation.

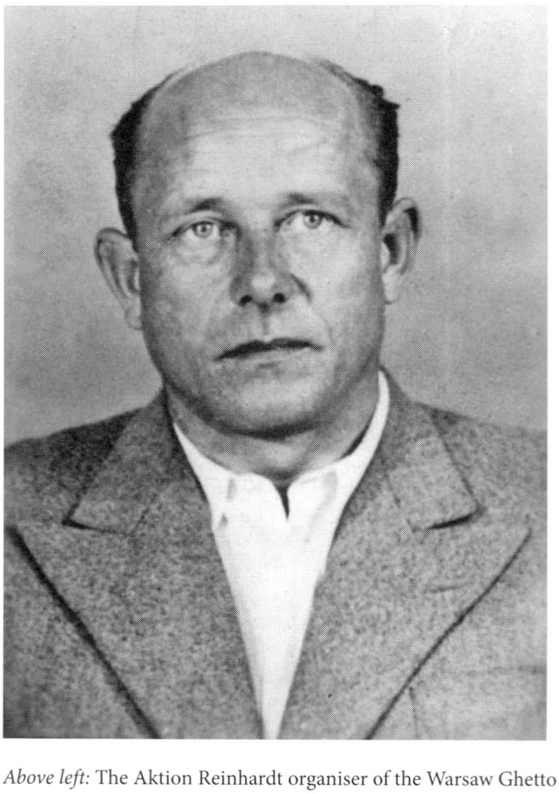

*Above left:* The Aktion Reinhardt organiser of the Warsaw Ghetto liquidation, Hermann Höfle.

*Above right:* The man chosen by Himmler to sort out the catastrophe at the Warsaw Ghetto liquidation, Jürgen Stroop.

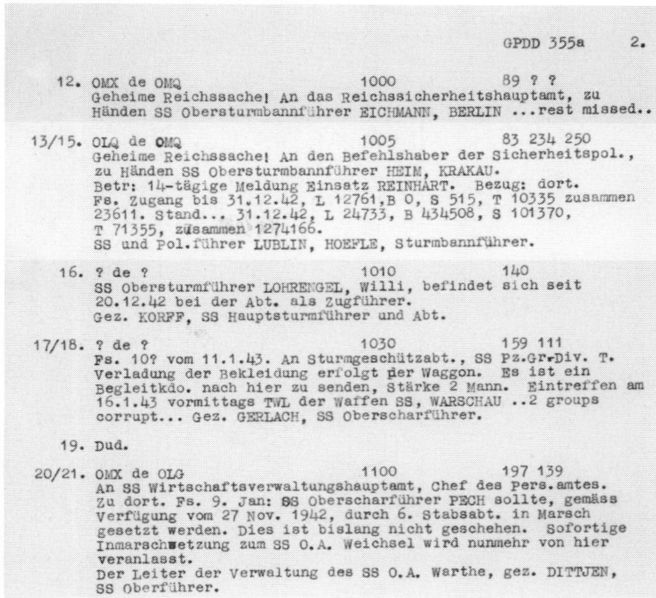

GPDD 355a 2.

12. OMX de OMQ 1000 89 ? ?
Geheime Reichssache! An das Reichssicherheitshauptamt, zu Händen SS Obersturmbannführer EICHMANN, BERLIN ...rest missed..

13/15. OLQ de OMQ 1005 83 234 250
Geheime Reichssache! An den Befehlshaber der Sicherheitspol., zu Händen SS Obersturmbannführer HEIM, KRAKAU.
Betr: 14-tägige Meldung Einsatz REINHART. Bezug: dort.
Fs. Zugang bis 31.12.42, L 12761, B 0, S 515, T 10335 zusammen 23611. Stand... 31.12.42, L 24733, B 434508, S 101370, T 71355, zusammen 1274166.
SS und Pol.führer LUBLIN, HOEFLE, Sturmbannführer.

16. ? de ? 1010 140
SS Obersturmführer LOHRENGEL, Willi, befindet sich seit 20.12.42 bei der Abt. als Zugführer.
Gez. KORFF, SS Hauptsturmführer und Abt.

17/18. ? de ? 1030 159 111
Fs. 10? vom 11.1.43. An Sturmgeschützabt., SS Pz.Gr.Div. T. Verladung der Bekleidung erfolgt per Waggon. Es ist ein Begleitkdo. nach hier zu senden, Stärke 2 Mann. Eintreffen am 16.1.43 vormittags TWL der Waffen SS, WARSCHAU ..2 groups corrupt... Gez. GERLACH, SS Oberscharführer.

19. Dud.

20/21. OMX de OLG 1100 197 139
An SS Wirtschaftsverwaltungshauptamt, Chef des Pers.amtes.
Zu dort. Fs. 9. Jan: SS Oberscharführer PECH sollte, gemäss Verfügung vom 27 Nov. 1942, durch 6. Stabsabt. in Marsch gesetzt werden. Dies ist bislang nicht geschehen. Sofortige Inmarschsetzung zum SS O.A. Weichsel wird nunmehr von hier veranlasst.
Der Leiter der Verwaltung des SS O.A. Warthe, gez. DITTJEN, SS Oberführer.

*Clockwise from top left:*
Max von Herff visited Warsaw during the ghetto action. As head of SS personnel, he also reported on Globocnik and declared his opinion that Globocnik should marry.

The Höfle telegram transcript discovered at the National Archives, Kew.

Ernst Lerch at a party given by Globocnik in his villa in Lublin.

During one particular party, Globocnik's eye fell upon one of the young pretty secretaries, Irmgard Rickheim.

121

**Der SS- und Polizeiführer im Distrikt Lublin**

Lublin, den 5. Juli 1941

P e r s ö n l i c h !

An den
Reichsführer-SS
und Chef der Deutschen Polizei
H e i n r i c h H i m m l e r
B e r l i n

Prinz-Albrecht-Strasse 7

Reichsführer!

Ich habe mich mit Fräulein Irmgard R i c k h e i m verlobt und bitte Sie, Reichsführer, mir zu diesem Schritt die Genehmigung zu erteilen.

H e i l H i t l e r !

SS-Brigadeführer

Globocnik's short letter to Himmler, informing him of his relationship with Irmgard.

Der Reichsführer-SS

128

Führer-Hauptquartier 14. 7.1941

Persönlicher Stab Reichsführer-SS
Schriftgutverwaltung
Akt.Nr. Geh. / 175

Lieber Globus !

An und für sich freue ich mich, daß Sie sich endlich verlobt haben. Seien Sie bitte nicht böse, wenn ich nicht weiß, wer Fräulein Rickheim ist. Solche Kenntnis kann ich mir nur verschaffen, wenn Sie mir das ordnungsgemäße Heiratsgesuch einreichen, was im Krieg ja ohnedies nicht schwer ist, da das Verfahren sehr stark abgekürzt ist. Ich sehe diesem Gesuch mit Freude entgegen und hoffe zuversichtlich, dann Ihr Heiratsgesuch genehmigen zu können.

Heil Hitler !

2.) an den
Gauleiter und Reichstatthalter
SS-Gruppenführer Rainer,
Salzburg
Kapitelplatz 2

durchschriftlich mit der Bitte um Kenntnisnahme.

i.A.

SS-Sturmbannführer

Himmler's reply. Addressed to Globus, Himmler states he does not know who Miss Rickheim is and asks Globocnik to submit his official application for marriage to the SS Race Office.

Himmler's idea of a suitable partner for Globocnik was Gisela Mauermayer, the German discus gold medallist at the Berlin Olympics in 1936.

Irmgard was popular with Globocnik's close circle. Here she is having fun during a Globocnik party, with Hermann Höfle.

Irmgard (left) with an unidentified woman.

Irmgard with Gerda Fuhrmann, 1942.

*Clockwise from top left:*

The couple enjoyed horse-riding together. Globocnik was obviously very taken by the younger Rickheim and his feelings grew into love.

Irmgard loved animals, and although Globocnik's feelings for her were not reciprocated on the same level, she realised that her attachment to the powerful SSPF would provide a desirable lifestyle.

The young, fun loving Irmgard was affectionate to Globocnik, and the couple enjoyed an extremely active sex life.

Globocnik and Irmgard leaving the villa in Lublin.

Irmgard petting a local dog during her stay in Zakopane.

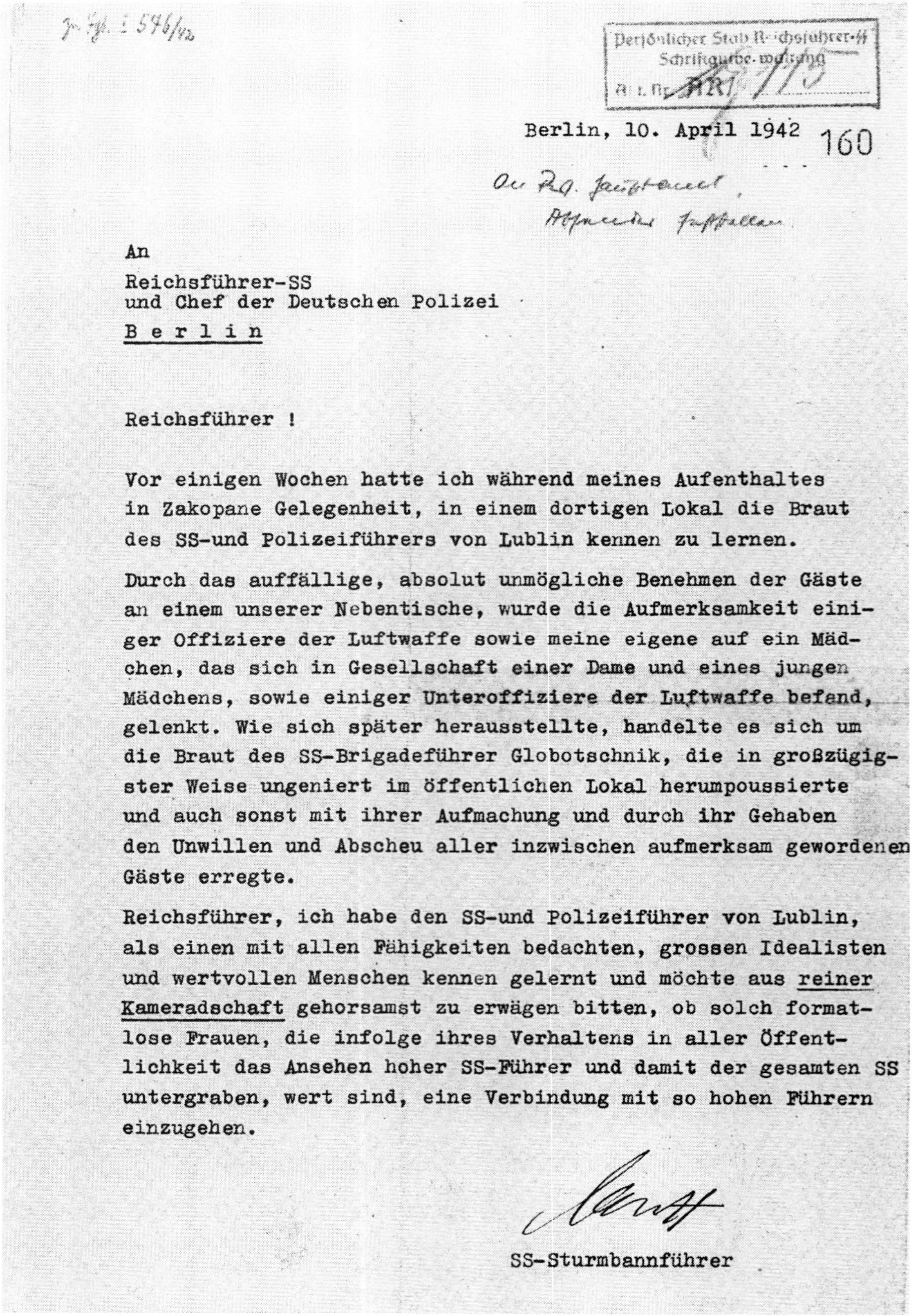

Persönlicher Stab Reichsführer-SS
Schriftgutverwaltung
Akt. Nr.

Berlin, 10. April 1942 160

An

Reichsführer-SS
und Chef der Deutschen Polizei
B e r l i n

Reichsführer !

Vor einigen Wochen hatte ich während meines Aufenthaltes in Zakopane Gelegenheit, in einem dortigen Lokal die Braut des SS-und Polizeiführers von Lublin kennen zu lernen.

Durch das auffällige, absolut unmögliche Benehmen der Gäste an einem unserer Nebentische, wurde die Aufmerksamkeit einiger Offiziere der Luftwaffe sowie meine eigene auf ein Mädchen, das sich in Gesellschaft einer Dame und eines jungen Mädchens, sowie einiger Unteroffiziere der Luftwaffe befand, gelenkt. Wie sich später herausstellte, handelte es sich um die Braut des SS-Brigadeführer Globotschnik, die in großzügigster Weise ungeniert im öffentlichen Lokal herumpoussierte und auch sonst mit ihrer Aufmachung und durch ihr Gehaben den Unwillen und Abscheu aller inzwischen aufmerksam gewordenen Gäste erregte.

Reichsführer, ich habe den SS-und Polizeiführer von Lublin, als einen mit allen Fähigkeiten bedachten, grossen Idealisten und wertvollen Menschen kennen gelernt und möchte aus reiner Kameradschaft gehorsamst zu erwägen bitten, ob solch formatlose Frauen, die infolge ihres Verhaltens in aller Öffentlichkeit das Ansehen hoher SS-Führer und damit der gesamten SS untergraben, wert sind, eine Verbindung mit so hohen Führern einzugehen.

SS-Sturmbannführer

The damaging letter addressed to Himmler, complaining of Irmgard's behaviour.

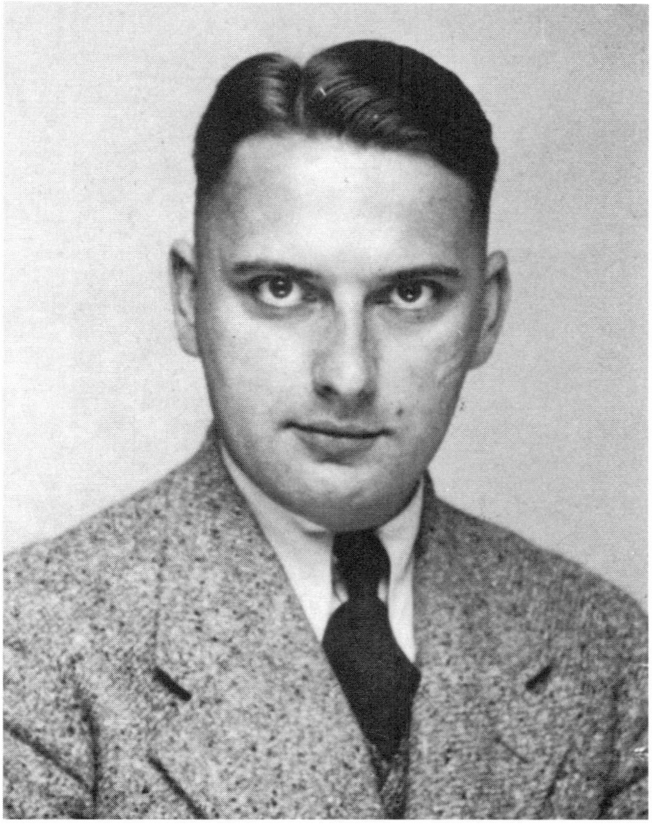

Dr Rudolf Brandt, Himmler's personal advisor.

The two influences in Globocnik's life, Rainer and Himmler.

SS-Brigadeführer Odilo Globocnik, SS and Police Leader in Lublin.

The abandoned Kickich Palce at Sobieszyn where Irmgard was exiled (modern photo).

Irmgard Lakin (Rickheim) in later life. She died in 2015.

Wilhelmine Trsek in later life.

Globocnik during a visit to Trawniki in the winter of 1942–43.

A contingent of guards at Trawniki around the time of Globocnik's visit. Note the camp buildings in the background.

An inspection visit to Trawniki. The officer in the foreground is Max Cichotzski, Globocnik's personal adjutant.

The same visit. Cichotzski is in the centre.

Globocnik in conversation with an unidentified SS-Hauptsturmführer from Trawniki. The structures visible over Globocnik's right shoulder appear to be rabbit hutches. Rabbits were bred at several concentration camps for their fur coats.

At a farm in Zamość.

Sonderdienst men used in the Zamość action.

Sonderdienst and SS together in the Zamość lands. An excellent shot of the Sonderdienst uniform being worn by Sonderdienststreifenführer Müller.

This image from the Zamość resettlement action is captioned 'Hauptmann Eder und Fräulein Buhsler'.

The Rotunda at Zamość, scene of numerous executions.

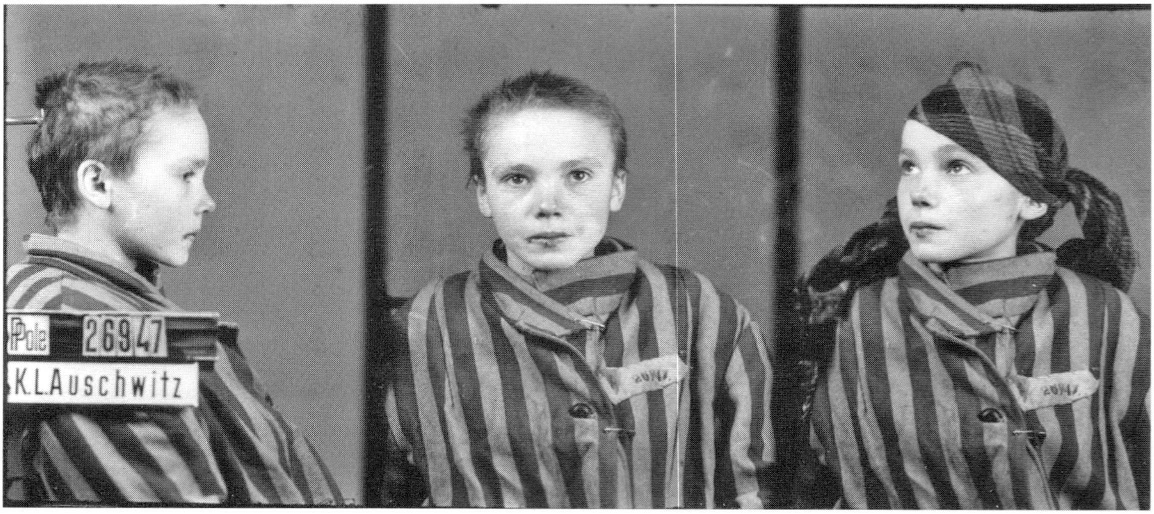


Just one of the Zamość children deported to Auschwitz.

Cremation smoke arising from Majdanek during the Operation Harvest Festival massacre.

Globocnik's replacement as SSPF Lublin, Jakob Sporrenberg.

Richard Wendler was not unhappy to see the back of Globocnik.

**Der SS - und Polizeiführer im Distrikt Lublin** 1

**SS - Gruppenführer Odilo G L O B O C N I K.**

**1940 bis Juli 1943**

| | |
|---|---|
| **1. Engerer Stab:** | |
| Adjutant: | HJ.-Gefolgsch.-F. Max C I C H O T Z K I |
| Stabsführer: | SS-Stubaf. Sepp N E M E T Z |
| | SS- " Hermann H Ö F L E |
| | SS- " Ernst L E R C H |
| Persönlicher Referent: | SS- " Hans M A U B A C H |
| Personalabteilung: | SS-H.Stuf. Herbert U L B R I C H |
| Arbeitseinsatz: | SS- " Georg M I C H A L S E N |
| | SS- " Kurt C L A A S E N |
| | SS-U.Stuf. G Ö T H |
| Verwaltung: ) | SS- " Willi S C H E P E R |
| SS-Führerheim: ) | SS-H.Scharf. L E I S T I K O |
| Lebensmittelkarten-) ausgabestelle: ) | SS-O.Scharf. Sepp S L A N Y |
| 2. Deutsche Ausrüstungswerke Lublin, einschl. Sägewerk Pulawy: | SS-U.Stuf. Horst R I E D E L<br>SS-O.Stuf. Wolfgang M O H W I N K E L |
| 3. Ost-Industrie G.m.b.H. Lublin: | SS-H.Stuf. Dr. Max H O R N |
| 4. SS-Standortverwaltung: | SS-Stubaf. Georg W I P P E R N |
| Unterabteilungen: | |
| a) SS - Kleiderkasse | SS-O.Scha. Z i m m e r m a n n |
| b) SS - Gut R U R Y | mehrere Unterführer (Namen unbekannt) |
| c) SS- Ausbildungslager T r a w n i k i : | SS-Stubaf. Karl S T R E I B E L |
| d) Arbeitslager Trawniki: | SS-O.Scharf. Franz B A R T E T Z K O |
| e) " Poniatowa: | SS-O.Stuf. Name unbekannt |
| f) " Budzyn: (Flugzeugwerke Heinkel) | SS-O.Stuf. Willi F R A N Z |
| g) Bekleidungslager Lublin ( alter Flughafen) | SS-H.Stuf. O B E R M E Y E R |
| 5. SS-Standortkommandantur: ( örtliche Aufsicht ) | SS-Stubaf. E I M A N N<br>SS- " L A N G E |
| 6) Truppenwirtschaftslager der Waffen-SS, Lublin: | SS-Stubaf. S C H R A U F S T E T T E R<br>SS-H.Stuf. M E I S T E R<br>SS- " von P I S T O R<br>SS-O.Stuf. K U L L M A N N<br>SS- " B R U C H M A N N |



*Above and next page:* A list of the staff under SSPF Globocnik in Lublin.

| | |
|---|---|
| 7. Forschungsstelle für Ostunterkünfte: | SS-H.Stuf. Gustav H A N E L T<br>SS- " Werner S C H R I E V E R |
| 8. SS-Mannschaftshaus: | SS- " " " |
| 9. Reichskommissar f.d. Festigung deutschen Volkstums in Lublin: | SS-U.Stuf. Hartmut P F E I F F E R |
| in Zamosc: | SS-O.Stuf. B A R E U T H E R<br>SS- " W E R N E R |
| 10. Volksdeutsche Mittelstelle: | HJ.-Gefolgsch.F..von S E L T M A N N<br>SS-Stubaf. K L E M E N S |
| 11. Der Führer im Rasse - u. Siedlungswesen: | SS-Stubaf. D I E H L<br>SS-H.Stuf. R I E T Z |
| 12. Zentral-Krankenrevier mit Teil-Lazarett, Entbindungsheim, Apotheke, optischen u.orthopäd.-Werkstätten: | SS-Stubaf. Dr.Kurt S I C K E L<br>SS- " Dr.Heinz P O E T S C H L A C K |
| SS-Zahnstation: | SS-O.Stuf. Dr.Dieter M A H L E R |
| 13. SS-Zentralbauleitung Lublin: | SS-H.Stuf. N A U M A N N<br>SS-U.Stuf. G R O T H E |
| in Z A M O S C : | SS-H.Stuf. Richard T H O M A L L A |
| 14. Betriebsgruppe Wirtschaft ( SS-Güter ) | SS-Stubaf. D U N K E L |
| 15. SS-Sonderkommando Dirlewanger, Lublin: | SS-Stubaf.Dr.Oskar D I R L E W A N G E R |
| 16. SWG Siedlerwirtschaftsgemeinschaft Zamosc: | Aufsichtsrat:<br>SS-Gruppenführer G L O B O C N I K<br>Kaufmann Herbert N A U M A N N<br>SS-Stubaf.Dr. C L A U S<br>Leiter der Abt.Ernährung u.Landwirtschaft<br>Dr. B E C K E R<br>Leiter der Abt. Wirtschaft<br>beim Chef des Distrikts Lublin. |

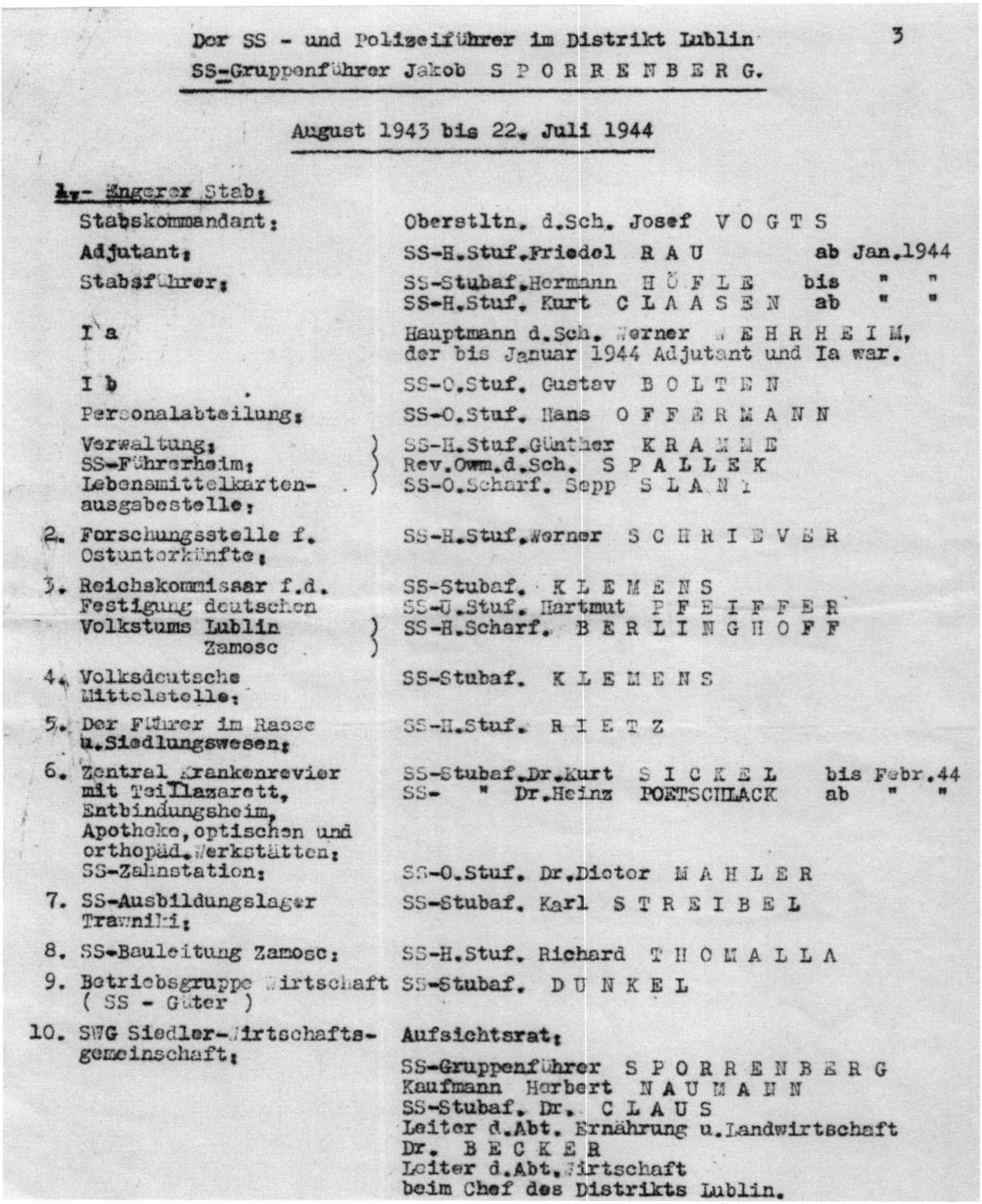

Der SS - und Polizeiführer im Distrikt Lublin 3

SS-Gruppenführer Jakob S P O R R E N B E R G.

August 1943 bis 22. Juli 1944

1.- Engerer Stab:

| | |
|---|---|
| Stabskommandant: | Oberstltn. d.Sch. Josef V O G T S |
| Adjutant: | SS-H.Stuf.Friedel R A U ab Jan.1944 |
| Stabsführer: | SS-Stubaf.Hermann H Ö F L E bis " "<br>SS-H.Stuf. Kurt C L A A S E N ab " " |
| I a | Hauptmann d.Sch. Werner W E H R H E I M, der bis Januar 1944 Adjutant und Ia war. |
| I b | SS-O.Stuf. Gustav B O L T E N |
| Personalabteilung: | SS-O.Stuf. Hans O F F E R M A N N |
| Verwaltung:<br>SS-Führerheim:<br>Lebensmittelkarten-ausgabestelle: | SS-H.Stuf.Günther K R A M M E<br>Rev.Owm.d.Sch. S P A L L E K<br>SS-O.Scharf. Sepp S L A N Y |
| 2. Forschungsstelle f. Ostunterkünfte: | SS-H.Stuf.Werner S C H R I E V E R |
| 3. Reichskommissar f.d. Festigung deutschen Volkstums Lublin<br>Zamosc | SS-Stubaf. K L E M E N S<br>SS-U.Stuf. Hartmut P F E I F F E R<br>SS-H.Scharf. B E R L I N G H O F F |
| 4. Volksdeutsche Mittelstelle: | SS-Stubaf. K L E M E N S |
| 5. Der Führer im Rasse u.Siedlungswesen: | SS-H.Stuf. R I E T Z |
| 6. Zentral Krankenrevier mit Teillazarett, Entbindungsheim, Apotheke, optischen und orthopäd. Werkstätten; | SS-Stubaf.Dr.Kurt S I C K E L bis Febr.44<br>SS- " Dr.Heinz POETSCHLACK ab " " |
| SS-Zahnstation: | SS-O.Stuf. Dr.Dictor M A H L E R |
| 7. SS-Ausbildungslager Trawniki: | SS-Stubaf. Karl S T R E I B E L |
| 8. SS-Bauleitung Zamosc: | SS-H.Stuf. Richard T H O M A L L A |
| 9. Betriebsgruppe Wirtschaft ( SS - Güter ) | SS-Stubaf. D U N K E L |
| 10. SWG Siedler-Wirtschafts-gemeinschaft: | Aufsichtsrat:<br>SS-Gruppenführer S P O R R E N B E R G<br>Kaufmann Herbert N A U M A N N<br>SS-Stubaf. Dr. C L A U S<br>Leiter d.Abt. Ernährung u.Landwirtschaft<br>Dr. B E C K E R<br>Leiter d.Abt. Wirtschaft<br>beim Chef des Distrikts Lublin. |

A list of staff under SSPF Sporrenberg in Lublin.

213

Der Reichsführer-SS
Persönlicher Stab
Tgb.Nr. 39/153/43 g
Ra/Bn

Feld-Kommandostelle, den 9. Juli 1943.

Persönlicher Stab Reichsführer-SS
Schriftgutverwaltung
Akt. Nr. Geh.

An den
Chef des SS-Personalhauptamtes
SS-Gruppenführer von H e r f f
**B e r l i n**

Lieber Gruppenführer !

Ich unterrichte Sie vorsorglich von der Absicht des Reichsführer-SS, den SS-Gruppenführer G l o b o c n i k als Höhere SS- und Polizeiführer Russland-Mitte einzusetzen und an die Stelle des SS-Gruppenführers Globocnik den SS-Gruppenführer S p o r r e n - b e r g zum SS- und Polizeiführer in Lublin zu berufen. Die endgültige Entscheidung gebe ich Ihnen dann kurz fernschriftlich durch.

H e i l H i t l e r !

SS-Obersturmbannführer.

Himmler originally intended to transfer Globocnik to Minsk as Higher SS and Police Leader Russland-Mitte, but he altered his plans and Globus went to Trieste instead. In this memo, Brandt informed von Herff of Himmler's original idea.

zum Akt Nr. 9/1738

Der Reichsführer-SS
und
Chef der Deutschen Polizei
I 1995/43 Ad

Feld-Kommandostelle, den 13. Sept. 1943.

SS-Personalhauptamt
23. SEP. 1943

1.) An
SS-Gruppenführer und
Generalleutnant der Polizei G l o b o c n i k

\- - - -

Ich ernenne Sie zum

Höheren SS- und Polizeiführer
in der Operationszone Adriatisches Küstenland.

Sie sind dem Obersten Kommissar für die Operationszone Adriatisches Küstenland, Gauleiter R a i n e r sowie dem Höchsten SS- und Polizeiführer im Gebiet der Heeresgruppe B, SS-Obergruppenführer und General der Waffen-SS W o l f f , unterstellt.

gez. H. H i m m l e r .

2.) An das SS-Personalhauptamt
B e r l i n

durchschriftlich mit der Bitte um Kenntnisnahme und Unterrichtung aller in Frage kommenden SS-Hauptämter und SS-Dienststellen übersandt.

i.A.

Brandt

SS-Obersturmbannführer.

Globocnik's posting to Trieste as Higher SS and Police Leader of the Operational Zone of the Adriatic Coast.

Upon his arrival in Trieste, Globocnik lodged initially at via Nizza 21 (today, via Coroneo 21).

He found a more permanent residence at the Villa Ara (top right in this 1917 photograph). As in Lublin, Globocnik preferred to work from home, and in practice he used the villa as his office in addition to his lodgings.

Photos of the Villa Ara are extremely rare. The building stood above wartime tunnels. Although the villa has been demolished, the tunnels still exist and are open to the public. One such tunnel provided underground access to the Tribune building which housed offices of the Gauleiter and the HSSPF OZAK. The tunnel complex is known as 'Kleine Berlin'.

The Tribune building. The Villa Ara can just be seen centre left, indicating its close proximity.

The Trieste SS headquarters (right) in Piazza Oberdan in 2007.

Himmler's representative in Trieste. In effect, the duties of SS and Police Leader in Trieste were carried out by Erasmus Freiherr von Malsen-Ponickau, prior to his transfer to Pola in 1944.

The Risiera Di San Sabba. This image of the former rice mill was taken immediately post-war. It shows the original entrance gate and the Kommandantur left foreground.

The Kommandantur contained the office and the living quarters of the commandant. The building on the left and the original gate have both been demolished, but the Kommandantur still stands today.

The Kommandantur in 2007.

Inside the main courtyard 2007.

The main cell block 2007.

The interior of the cell block 2007.

The ruin of the crematorium building immediately post-war, showing the destruction caused by the SS explosives.

The old rice mill today. The outline of the former crematorium building is clearly visible, with the memorial area roped off.

Gottlieb Hering in SS uniform.

Christian Wirth in SS uniform.

The new Higher SS and Police Leader for the Operational Zone of the Adriatic Coastland, SS-Gruppenführer und Generalleutnant der Polizei Odilo Globocnik.

*Clockwise from right:*

Globocnik inspecting the guard of honour at the Tribune building (also known as the Palace of Justice) in Trieste. The occasion was the celebration for Hitler's birthday on 20 April 1944.

The HSSPF addresses the crowd. Behind him is Bernhard Griese.

In this image, the SS officer in spectacles behind Globocnik is Ernst Lerch. The SA officer looking down is Werner Blankenburg.

*Clockwise from left:*

The guests salute.

A newspaper report photograph.

On the steps of the Tribune.

His speech over, Globocnik salutes. A good view of his Golden Party Badge.

The honour guard salutes the boss.

Honoured guests at the quayside in Trieste on 20 April 1944. Left to right: Globocnik, Rainer, General Ludwig Kübler, and Generalleutnant Harry Hoppe.

For some inexplicable reason, Globocnik and Kübler have swapped positions. The SS-Brigadeführer behind Hoppe's right shoulder is Malsen-Ponickau.

Kübler does not look happy.

Another view of the parade. Far right is Malsen-Ponickau, next to Hoppe.

The guests disperse. Left is Globocnik and centre is SS-Standartenführer Walter Bestmann, the commander of the SS-Junkerschule Klagenfurt.

A very rare photograph showing Werner Blankenburg (centre in spectacles). Behind him stands Dieter Allers (over his left shoulder). The man standing to Blankenburg's right in Hitler Youth uniform is almost certainly Max Cichotzski, Globocnik's personal adjutant.

Viktor Brack pictured during his military service with SS-Division 'Prinz Eugen'.

Two private snapshots of SS-Standartenführer Viktor Brack.

T4 and Aktion Reinhardt men in Globocnik's office in Trieste on 19 April 1944. Now known as Abteilung 'R'. *Left to right*: Gottlieb Hering, unidentified (probably not a former T4 man), Franz Stangl, Josef Oberhauser, Gottfried Schwarz, and Lorenz Hackenholt. They are about to receive decorations from Globocnik.

Globocnik decorates Lorenz Hackenholt with the Iron Cross 2nd Class. Gottfried Schwarz in the background.

Hackenholt's comrades celebrate his award with a drink in the Café Locanda 'Venezia Giulia' opposite the Risiera Di San Sabba. *Left to right*: Lambert, Löffler, Schiffner, Plikat, Girtzig, Hackenholt, Dubois, Bredow, and Schneider.

Christian Wirth (centre) with Schwarzenbacher on the left. The officer on the right is understood to be Jürgen Lassmann.

A photo taken at the Risiera Di San Sabba. *Left to right*: Hackenholt, Hering, Wirth, Stangl, unidentified Polizei officer.

A strategy meeting during Unternehmen 'Braunschweig', somewhere on the Karststrasse. Identified are Globocnik, Wirth, Oberhauser, and possibly Michalsen and Hering. This is the only known photo of Globocnik and Wirth together.

Wirth (left) and Hering with men of Abteilung 'R' in the courtyard of the Risiera Di San Sabba.

In front of the Basa Restaurant in Marcossina. *Left to right*: Oberhauser, Wirth, and Kretschmer.

*Above left:* Kretschmer, Oberhauser, and Wirth at the same location.

*Above right:* Franz Reichleitner was killed by partisans on 3 January 1944. His funeral took place soon after at the Opicina military cemetery. Wirth (centre) speaks at the funeral ceremony. Reichleitner's remains were subsequently moved to Costermano.

*Right:* Reichleitner's final resting place at Costermano.

Globocnik inspecting an Italian volunteer unit.

The HSSPF OZAK is entertained by a SS unit. The Untersturmführer is unidentified.

On 26 May 1944, Christian Wirth's car was ambushed by partisans at this stretch of the Karststrasse. He was killed at the scene.

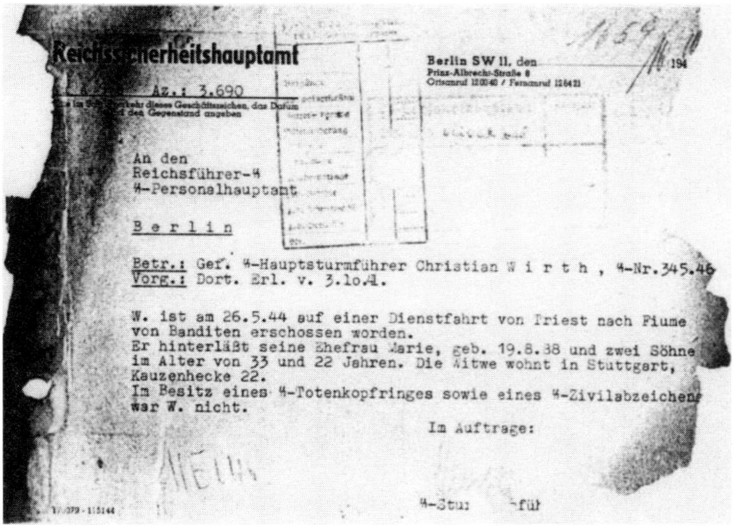

Reichssicherheitshauptamt

Berlin SW 11, den 194
Prinz-Albrecht-Straße 8
Ortsruf 120040 / Fernruf 126421

Az.: 3.690

An den
Reichsführer-SS
SS-Personalhauptamt

Berlin

Betr.: Gef. SS-Hauptsturmführer Christian W i r t h , SS-Nr.345.46
Vorg.: Dort. Erl. v. 3.10.41.

W. ist am 26.5.44 auf einer Dienstfahrt von Triest nach Fiume von Banditen erschossen worden.
Er hinterläßt seine Ehefrau Marie, geb. 19.8.88 und zwei Söhne im Alter von 33 und 22 Jahren. Die Witwe wohnt in Stuttgart, Kauzenhecke 22.
Im Besitz eines SS-Totenkopfringes sowie eines SS-Zivilabzeichens war W. nicht.

Im Auftrage:

SS-Stur[illegible]führer

The Sipo report of his death.

Wirth's replacement was Dieter Allers.

Christian Wirth was buried in the military cemetery at Opicina. His funeral was a grand military send off, attended by Globocnik (third from right), Blankenburg (fourth from right), Malsen-Ponickau (seventh from right), and Dieter Allers (far left in SA uniform).

Dieter Allers looks towards the camera.

Shots are fired in salute at the graveside.

Blankenburg and Globocnik centre. The head of Allers is just visible over a steel helmet left of centre. Note the Italian volunteers wearing berets in the left foreground.

Senior mourners salute.

Werner Blankenburg pays his respects at the coffin, which was draped in a SS flag.

Blankenburg salutes the coffin of the man who ensured that Aktion Reinhardt ran efficiently.

*Above left:* The grave marker for Christian Wirth at Costermano.

*Above right:* Gottfried Schwarz was killed on 19 June 1944 and was buried initially at Opicina, but now lies in Costermano.

*Above left:* OZAK was under the operational command of the HöSSPF Northern Italy, Karl Wolff. Globocnik and Wolff were on friendly terms.

*Above right:* Wolff pays a visit on Globocnik.

Wolff and Globocnik have their backs to the camera. The officer in spectacles is Ernst Lerch.

*Above left:* The civil authority in OZAK was held by Friedrich Rainer.

*Above right:* The Carinthian pair's friendship endured. A newspaper photograph.

At the barracks of the Karstwehr Battalion during the change of command. *Left to right, front row*: Rainer, Brand, and Globocnik. *Second row, left to right*: Luftwaffe Hauptmann Dr Bischetsrieder, Bestmann, Berschneider, and Weiland.

Globocnik making his way to the burial of a Carinthian Hitler Youth leader who had been killed in action. The man on Globocnik's right is possibly his adjutant, Max Cichotzski, as he appears similar to the HJ leader next to Blankenburg in an earlier image.

The mourners at the same funeral around the grave. The Brigadeführer on Globocnik's right is Karl Hermann.

Strategic discussion about defensive positions in OZAK. Rainer points at the map. Globocnik is just visible over his shoulder, and Albert Kesselring wears the Afrika cuffband. Left is General Kübler.

Kesselring and Globocnik share an amusing moment. Rainer is second left.

Kesselring's outstretched arm obscures Globocnik.

Globocnik strikes a Naploeonic pose as Rainer (centre) holds everyone's attention. Kesselring is in lightweight summer dress.

*Above left:* Globocnik in Montespino (now Dornberk). On his right is Werner Mundhenke.

*Above right:* Globocnik beside an armoured car in Carie (now Harije).

A newspaper photograph. The troops in the background appear to be Italians.

An artist's sketch of the HSSPF OZAK. From *Adria*, newsletter for the German forces in the Operations Zone Adriatic Coastland, issue no. 3, September 1944.

Globocnik maintained his links with Klagenfurt. When visiting the town, he stayed at Schloss Emmersdorf.

The palatial interior of the castle today.

*Above left:* Having lost the support of his mentor, Heinrich Himmler, Globocnik sought a suitable bride who would please the Reichsführer-SS. He had been acquainted with Lore Peterschinegg, a local Carinthian BDM leader since pre-Anschluss days. She was flattered by his proposal and duly accepted.

*Top right:* Lore Peterschinegg.

*Above right:* A newspaper photo of Globocnik in lightweight summer dress at the time of his courtship of Lore Peterschinegg.

The couple were married in Klagenfurt on 22 October 1944. Friedl Rainer acted as the witness. Note that Rainer wears SS-Obergruppenführer uniform.

Even at this stage of the war, Globocnik and his new wife took a short break as a honeymoon. They stayed at the Burghof Kyffhäuser near Roßla in the Harz Mountains. This postcard image shows how the lodge would have looked at the time of the Globocniks' visit.

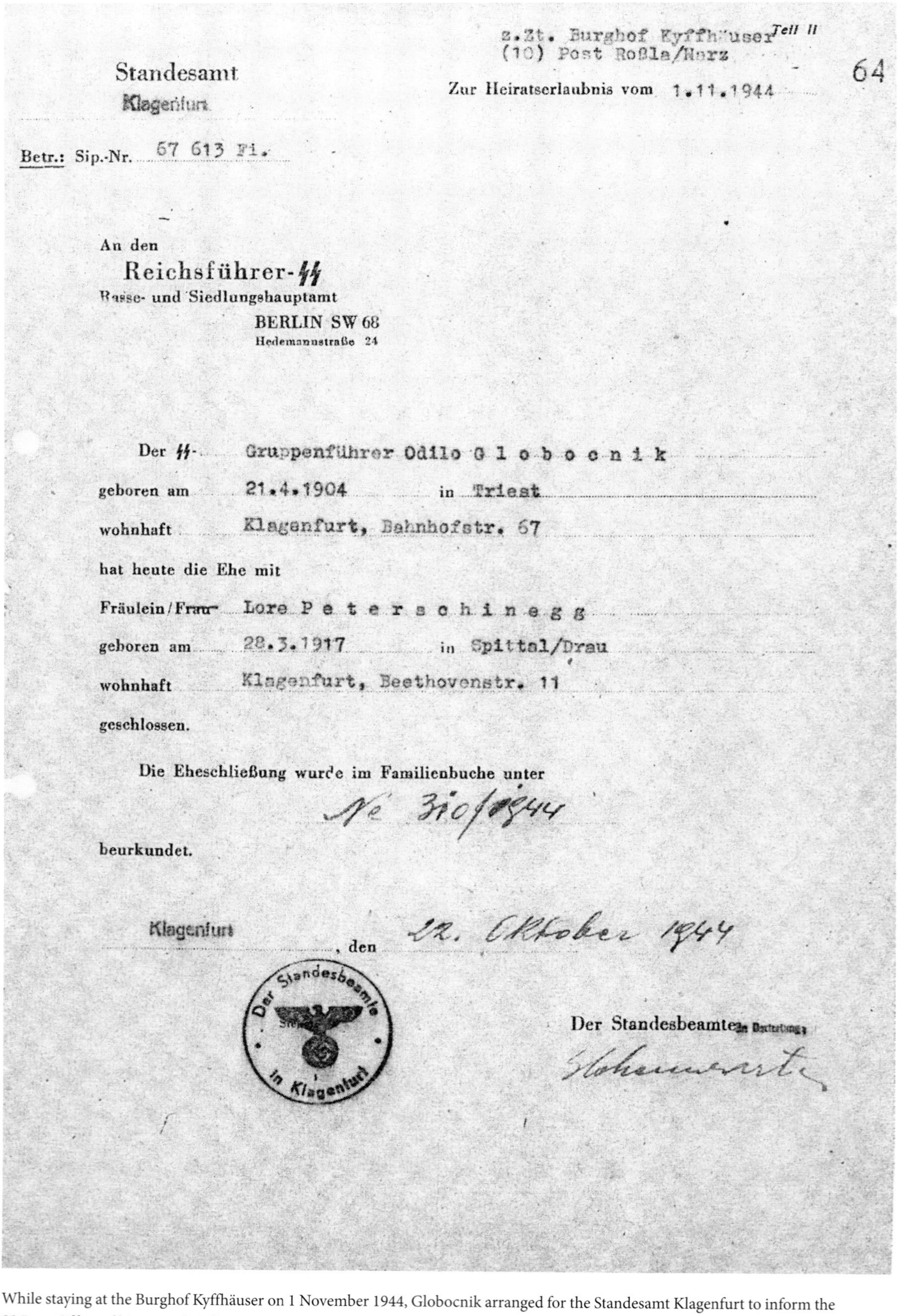

z.Zt. Burghof Kyffhäuser *Teil II*
(10) Post Roßla/Harz

64

Standesamt
Klagenfurt

Zur Heiratserlaubnis vom 1.11.1944

Betr.: Sip.-Nr. 67 613 Fi.

An den
Reichsführer-SS
Rasse- und Siedlungshauptamt
BERLIN SW 68
Hedemannstraße 24

Der SS- Gruppenführer Odilo G l o b o c n i k
geboren am 21.4.1904 in Triest
wohnhaft Klagenfurt, Bahnhofstr. 67
hat heute die Ehe mit
Fräulein/~~Frau~~ Lore P e t e r s c h i n e g g
geboren am 28.3.1917 in Spittal/Drau
wohnhaft Klagenfurt, Beethovenstr. 11
geschlossen.

Die Eheschließung wurde im Familienbuche unter
Nr 310/1944
beurkundet.

Klagenfurt, den 22. Oktober 1944

Der Standesbeamte
in Klagenfurt

Der Standesbeamte in Vertretung
Hohenwarter

While staying at the Burghof Kyffhäuser on 1 November 1944, Globocnik arranged for the Standesamt Klagenfurt to inform the SS Race Office of his nuptials. The marriage was entered under reference 310/1944 in the Klagenfurt marriage book.

*Above and right:* Globocnik meeting Austro-Hungarian veterans, 1945.

Globocnik is wearing both the German Cross in Gold and in Silver.

SS-Gruppenführer Globocnik poses for the camera.

*Above left:* A late informal photograph, possibly taken at Schloss Emmersdorf.

*Above right:* Louise Guyon-Witzschel in Allied custody. She is often erroneously quoted as Globocnik's secretary in Trieste, but this has no basis. In fact, she worked for SS-Hauptsturmführer Adalbert Schindlmayer in Tolmezzo in the SS Liaison Office for White Russian volunteers.

Ernst Lerch far left, and third from right is Lorenz Hackenholt.

Ernst Lerch in sunglasses.

Lerch (centre) discussing tactics with a Serbian Chetnik (left) and a young unidentified SS-Hauptsturmführer in the Vipacco River valley in the spring of 1945.

Men of Abteilung 'R' in the OZAK region. *Left to right*: Gomerski, Bredow, Pötzinger, Oberhauser, and Seidel.

A photo taken in Lipa on the day of the massacre, 30 April 1944, when around 300 villagers were murdered. Clearly visible is Josef Oberhauser, on the left, appearing to take a photograph.

The two helmeted Abteilung 'R' soldiers are (left) Gustav Münzberger, and (right) Josef Hirtreiter. Münzberger operated the gas chambers at Treblinka, while Hirtreiter served at Treblinka and Sobibor.

A section of the defensive ditch being excavated on the orders of Globocnik.

Hotel Enzian at Neusach on the Weißensee. Globocnik intended to establish a HQ at Neusach, but it did not materialise. The remnants of Globocnik's staff lodged here prior to climbing to their hideout at the Moßlacher Alm. They discarded their weapons in the lake.

The east end of the Weissensee with the area of the Mößlacher Alm indicated.

A watercolour painting of the Mößlacher Alm as it appeared in 1945. Since then, it has gone through extensive alterations with the first floor extended.

The west façade of the structure, showing the exterior staircase to the level of the first floor.

As the building appears today. The left side of the original building had two floors. Globocnik and Rainer occupied the then single storey on the right side. The first floor on the right half has since been added.

The dilapidated wooden hut on the right is original and can be seen in the contemporary watercolour painting. The hut on the left did not exist in 1945. Note the timber supply lift for a cable connection to the farm below which is also a post-war addition.

The interior room believed occupied by Globocnik and Rainer.

Schloss Paternion main entrance.

Paternion village. The castle is in the centre, and the lock-up building used by the British is just visible to the right of the church spire, in an elevated position. It was demolished post-war and this is the only known photograph.

The interior of the castle courtyard. This is what Globocnik would have seen as he paced in the courtyard.

The section of the castle used as temporary HQ by the 4th Hussars.

Alexander Ramsay went inside and called Globocnik by name from a balcony overlooking the courtyard. It is believed to be the balcony on the right which can also be seen in the previous image.

Having given himself away by a slight movement of the head, Globocnik was escorted to the lock-up via this arched gateway. View from under the arch, looking back into the courtyard.

The lock-up was an old storage building, located about 150 yards up this track and it stood at the top of the incline on the left.

The view of the castle from the site of the former lock-up building. The archway through which Globocnik was escorted can be seen at the end of the track.

Upon reaching the lock-up, Globocnik bit on a concealed glass ampoule in his mouth and collapsed on the track. All efforts to save him failed and he quickly succumbed to the cyanide. In this initial photograph, the body lies where it fell. The wall of the lock-up is on the right, with the castle situated behind the British officers.

The British pose with the body of Globocnik. This photograph is taken from a different angle, with the lock-up on the left.

The other prisoners arrested with Globocnik were brought out to identify the body. Standing against the wall on the left is Kenneth Hedley. Far right is Ernst Lerch, with Friedrich Rainer centre and Hermann Höfle between him and Hedley. Behind them are Karl Hellesberger (left) and Georg Michalsen.

Globocnik's body has been moved to the side of the track and part-covered with a blanket. Hermann Höfle is in the foreground, with Georg Michalsen and Karl Hellesberger behind. The British officer with the dark beret has been identified as Lieutenant Birkett.

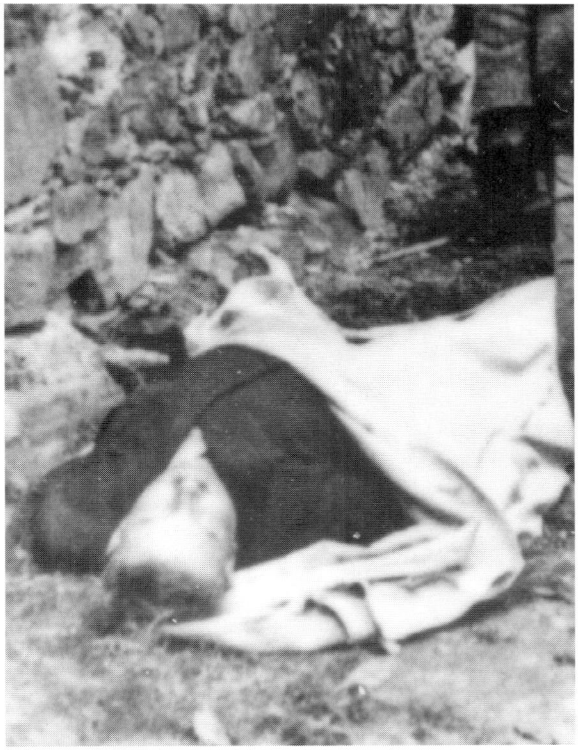

Globocnik's body dressed in a dark double-breasted jacket.

The same location today.

Globocnik's final resting place in an unmarked grave.

After the war, Friedrich Rainer was tried and executed in Ljubljana, then Yugoslavia.

The Rainer family grave. The date of Rainer's death on the headstone is incorrect. Evidence suggests that he provided information for the Yugoslav authorities and was not executed until November 1950.

*Above left:* Jakob Sporrenberg was captured in Norway. He was interrogated by the British at the London Cage and was subsequently handed over to Polish authorities in 1946. After further interrogations in Poland, he was tried in Warsaw for war crimes and hanged on 6 December 1952.

*Above right:* Dr Karl Brandt died on the scaffold at Landsberg on 2 June 1948.

*Above left:* Brack was hanged at Landsberg on 2 June 1948. His T4 partner, Werner Blankenburg, avoided justice and died under the false name of Werner Bieleke in Stuttgart-Wangen on 28 November 1957.

*Above right:* Dr Rudolf Brandt, throughout the war Himmler's personal advisor (often incorrectly referred to as his secretary) also paid with his life at Landsberg on 2 June 1948.

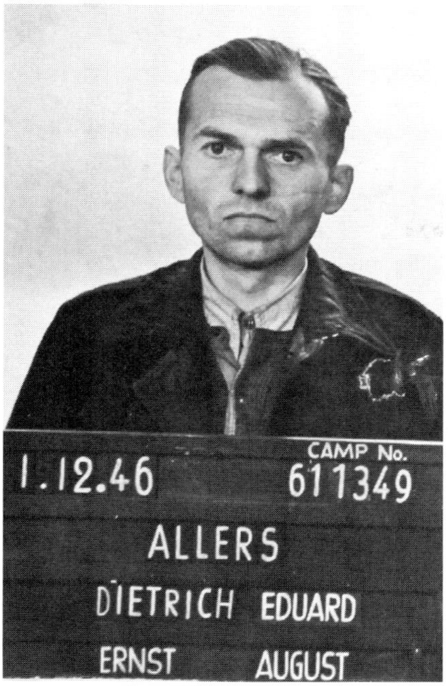

*Above left:* Dietrich Allers in Allied captivity.

*Above right:* Ludolf Jakob von Alvensleben in Russian captivity.

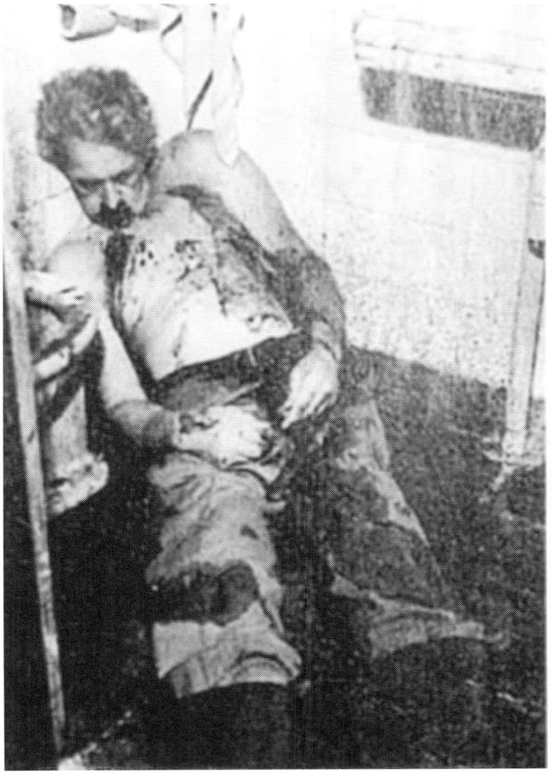

*Above left:* Hermann Höfle hanged himself in Vienna on 21 August 1962.

*Above right:* Gustav Wagner was found dead in Sao Paulo in October 1980. Despite a knife protruding from his chest, his lawyer insisted it was suicide.

Josef Oberhauser at one of his post-war hearings in West Germany during the 1960s. He died a free man on 20 November 1979 in Munich.

The defendants in the Sobibor process in Hagen, 1965.

*Clockwise from top left:*

Ernst Lerch escaped justice. The Café Lerch in Klagenfurt became a well-known music venue and its owner played host to many famous musicians. Apparently, he died in 1997 never having answered the allegations against him. He also refused all contact with Globocnik's son, Peter.

Franz Stangl was finally tracked down and arrested in Brazil in 1967. He was extradited by West Germany and tried for his crimes. Found guilty, he was sentenced to life in prison. He died of a heart attack in Düsseldorf Prison on 28 June 1971.

Kurt Franz served twenty-eight years in prison. He was released in 1993 on grounds of ill health. He lived another five years and died a free man in Wuppertal on 4 July 1998.

John Demjanjuk. He died in Bad Feinbach, Germany, on 17 March 2012 aged ninety-one.

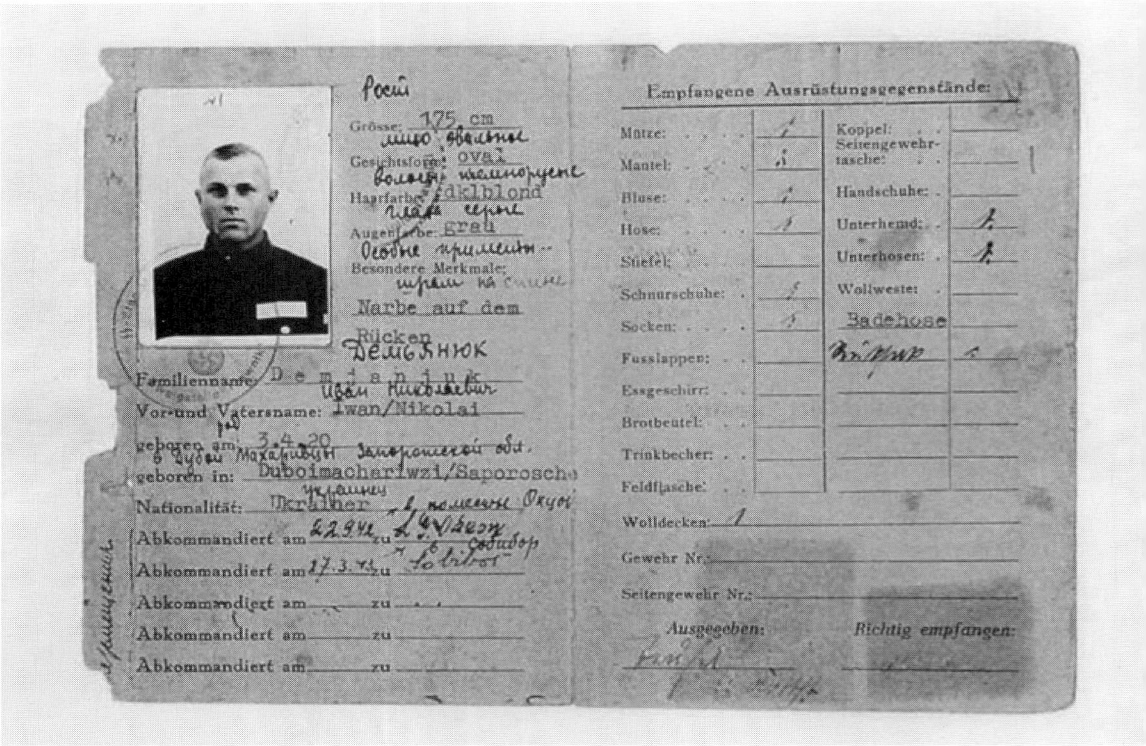

Grösse: 175 cm
Gesichtsform: oval
Haarfarbe: dklblond
Augenfarbe: grau
Besondere Merkmale: Narbe auf dem Rücken
Familienname: Demjanjuk
Vor- und Vatersname: Iwan/Nikolai
geboren am: 3.4.20
geboren in: Duboimacharwzi/Saporosche
Nationalität: Ukrainer
Abkommandiert am 22.9.42 zu L.G. Okzew
Abkommandiert am 27.3.43 zu Sobibor
Abkommandiert am zu
Abkommandiert am zu
Abkommandiert am zu

Empfangene Ausrüstungsgegenstände:

| | | | |
|---|---|---|---|
| Mütze: | 1 | Koppel: | |
| Mantel: | 1 | Seitengewehrtasche: | |
| Bluse: | 1 | Handschuhe: | |
| Hose: | 1 | Unterhemd: | 1 |
| Stiefel: | | Unterhosen: | 1 |
| Schnurschuhe: | 1 | Wollweste: | |
| Socken: | 1 | Badehose | |
| Fusslappen: | | | |
| Essgeschirr: | | | |
| Brotbeutel: | | | |
| Trinkbecher: | | | |
| Feldflasche: | | | |

Wolldecken: 1
Gewehr Nr.:
Seitengewehr Nr.:
Ausgegeben: Richtig empfangen:

The questionable Ausweis provided by Russian authorities and used as evidence in the trial of Demjanjuk.

*Above left:* Johann Schwarzenbacher.

*Above right:* Believed to be the family of Trawniki commandant Karl Streibel.